T0350749

Multimodal Human Computer Interaction and Pervasive Services

Patrizia Grifoni
Istituto di Ricerche sulla Popolazione e le Politiche Sociali
Consiglio Nazionale delle Ricerche, Italy

INFORMATION SCIENCE REFERENCE

Hershey · New York

Director of Editorial Content:	Kristin Klinger
Senior Managing Editor:	Jamie Snavely
Managing Editor:	Jeff Ash
Assistant Managing Editor:	Carole Coulson
Typesetter:	Carole Coulson
Cover Design:	Lisa Tosheff
Printed at:	Yurchak Printing Inc.

Published in the United States of America by
Information Science Reference (an imprint of IGI Global)
701 E. Chocolate Avenue,
Hershey PA 17033
Tel: 717-533-8845
Fax: 717-533-8661
E-mail: cust@igi-global.com
Web site: http://www.igi-global.com/reference

and in the United Kingdom by
Information Science Reference (an imprint of IGI Global)
3 Henrietta Street
Covent Garden
London WC2E 8LU
Tel: 44 20 7240 0856
Fax: 44 20 7379 0609
Web site: http://www.eurospanbookstore.com

Library of Congress Cataloging-in-Publication Data

Multimodal human computer interaction and pervasive services / Patrizia
Grifoni, editor.
     p. cm.
  Includes bibliographical references and index.
  Summary: "This book provides concepts, methodologies, and applications used to design and develop multimodal systems"--Provided by publisher. ISBN 978-1-60566-386-9 (hardcover) -- ISBN 978-1-60566-387-6 (ebook) 1. Human-computer interaction. 2. Interactive multimedia. 3. Ubiquitous computing. I. Grifoni, Patrizia, 1959-
  QA76.9.H85M853 2009
  004.01'9--dc22
                                                    2008055308
British Cataloguing in Publication Data
A Cataloguing in Publication record for this book is available from the British Library.

All work contributed to this book is new, previously-unpublished material. The views expressed in this book are those of the authors, but not necessarily of the publisher.

Table of Contents

Section I
Multimodality: Basic Concepts

Section II
From Unimodal to Multimodal Interaction: Applications and Services

Section III
Multimodal Interaction in Mobile Environment

Section IV
Standards, Guidelines, and Evaluation of Multimodal Systems

Detailed Table of Contents

Section I
Multimodality: Basic Concepts

The first section introduces some of the basic concepts and describes the main theoretical and practical problems and features of multimodal interaction, with a particular focus on mobile devices. Starting from a study on people acceptance and adoption of technologies and models, with a particular focus on mobile devices in the first chapter, this section has been highlighted how naturalness of multimodal interaction facilitates its acceptance and its wide use diffusion by a large part of people. From Chapter II to Chapter IX the basic concepts, theories, and technologies involved in the study of multimodal interaction and multimodal systems are provided.

This chapter, investigating into mobile phone adoption by elderly people, highlights how acceptance is a preliminary step respect to the technology adoption. In particular, the authors propose and describe the novel senior technology acceptance and adoption model (STAM), which incorporates acceptance factors into the adoption process.

This chapter gives some definitions and basic concepts on multimodality, and describes the different approaches used in the multimodal interaction. In particular, approaches that use new semantic technologies and technologies connected with the Semantic Web fields are discussed.

This chapter describes the different approaches that the literature proposes to combine different input for multimodal systems (fusion process), their features, advantages, and di-advantages.

This chapter deals with presenting an approach to multimodal input fusion based on powerful combinational categorical grammar. The proposed approach was validated through users' experiments demonstrating its usefulness for mobile context according to its low computational costs.

Chapter V

This chapter, starting form considering that more natural the interaction is more ambiguous can be its interpretation, describes the different approaches proposed by the literature in the interpretation process of multimodal input. Moreover, this chapter provides a classification of multimodal ambiguities. Finally, methods used for solving the different classes of ambiguities are presented.

This chapter deals with the information output arrangement and organization (multimodal fission). Considering information structure as the basic concept, the chapter provides some basic notions and describes the most relevant approaches discussed in the literature for designing outputs using different kinds of modality and synchronizing them.

This chapter discusses the importance and features of intelligent interaction stimulated by the wide use of mobile devices for providing new services. In particular, the chapter deals with modeling for enhancing flexibility and adaptability of multimodal systems. In particular, the described machine learning approach proposes an initial static user model based on stereotypes; then, the model is revised/adjusted by considering the user interaction with the device/context.

Chapter VIII

This chapter, starting from the assumption that designing and implementing interaction is a critical issue, proposes a model-based user interface design process (MBUID), in which a multimodal interface can be defined by means of a high abstraction level. The proposed approach permits to generate prototypes that can be evaluated in the intermediate phases of the system development.

Chapter IX

This chapter addresses the concrete aspect of the temporal and spatial organization of human pointing actions for multimodal human computer interaction. Indeed, the organisation of the human pointing gestures in time and space is an essential aspect when using hand-free interaction techniques. The authors provide readers with a substantial knowledge about the temporal and spatial organization of the pointing gesture.

Section II
From Unimodal to Multimodal Interaction: Applications and Services

The second section of this book presents chapters describing problems faced when designing, implementing, and using multimodal systems. These problems and their solutions are discussed considering specific modal and multimodal applications. An example of solution for ambiguities is provided combining auditive and visual modalities; the problem of accessing objects and services supplied by multimodal mobile applications is faced by multimodal systems in different scenarios using ontologies permitting interoperability between different environments and semantic interoperability for cooperation. The collaborativeness in designing interactive systems is discussed as a relevant issue to handle specific problems and face them on the field. Finally, the importance to make information and services accessible is highlighted, and one adopted solution for visually impaired people is described.

Chapter X

Emiliano Castellina, Politecnico di Torino, Italy
Fulvio Corno, Politecnico di Torino, Italy
Paolo Pellegrino, Politecnico di Torino, Italy

This chapter discusses the eye tracking and speech recognition technologies and describes a multimodal system that integrates the two involved input channels. It describes how the combined use of speech and gaze permits to achieve mutual disambiguation.

Chapter XI

Fabio Pittarello, Università Ca' Foscari Venezia, Italy
Augusto Cementano, Università Ca' Foscari Venezia, Italy

This chapter, starting from the critic aspect of accessing objects and services in a complex environment by users, introduces a methodology to design a system usable and able to help a user to access these objects and services. In particular, this methodology is based on the identification of the user-oriented features of the environment and on their mapping onto a virtual world.

Chapter XII

Domenico M. Pisanelli, CNR-ISTC, Italy
Claudio De Lazzari, CNR IFC, Italy
Emilio Bugli Innocenti, Netxcalibur, Italy
Norma Zanetti, Netxcalibur, Italy

This chapter discusses the importance of ontologies for multimodality describing an on-board vehicle multimodal interaction system. It introduces a modular ontology that, enabling semantic interoperability devoted to allow cooperation between the road infrastructure and drivers, supports the on-board vehicle multimodal interaction.

Chapter XIII

Barbara R. Barricelli, Università degli Studi di Milano, Italy

Andrea Marcante, Università degli Studi di Milano, Italy

Piero Mussio, Università degli Studi di Milano, Italy

Loredana Parasiliti Provenza, Università degli Studi di Milano, Italy

Marco Padula, Istituto per le Tecnologie della Costruzione – Consiglio Nazionale
*   delle Ricerche, Italy*

Paolo L. Scala, Istituto per le Tecnologie della Costruzione – Consiglio Nazionale
*   delle Ricerche, Italy*

This chapter presents a methodology for collaborative and evolutionary design of interactive systems. This methodology is derived from empirical real case experiences. The described software environment is discussed emphasising the pervasiveness and usability features connected with multimodality of interaction and portability of the system, and permitting to coordinate desktop and mobile devices use.

Chapter XIV

Simone Bacellar Leal Ferriera, Universidade Federal do Estado do Rio de Janeiro, Brazil

Denis Silva da Silveira, Programa de Engenharia de Produção - COPPE/UFRJ, Brazil

Marcos Gurgel do Amaral Leal Ferreira, Holden Comunicação Ltda, Brazil

Ricardo Rodrigues Nunes, Universidade Federal do Estado do Rio de Janeiro, Brazil

This chapter deals with providing usability and accessibility features according to the W3C directives focusing on interaction between visually impaired people and Internet. Moreover, it is presented a study on the field carried out in Brazil, with the purpose to verify and integrate the knowledge acquired by the literature about the different types of impositions and limits that these users can have.

Chapter XV

Marcus Specht, Open University of the Netherlands, The Netherlands

This chapter describes the experiences of designing mobile and pervasive learning carried out in the European project RAFT. A flexible and powerful approach provided by a widget based design for the user interface is presented; this approach enables the use of mobile phones, PDAs, tablet PCs, desktop computers, as well as electronic whiteboard.

Section III
Multimodal Interaction in Mobile Environment

The third section of this book discusses of multimodal interaction in mobile environment, according to the devices limitations and the different contexts where people can use them. Some architectural solutions, adaptation methods, and uses to the different contexts are presented. A particular attention was devoted to multimodal interfaces for mobile GIS, due the implicit nature of their spatial and temporal information, the involvement of visual channel, and their tendency to be used in different context by different users. Finally, another emerging scenario discussed by chapters contained in this section deals with the use of multimodal mobile systems for social applications such as e-learning; in particular, specific methods to make adaptable a mobile-learning system and addressing how mobile multimodal interaction is changing many individual and social activities are described.

Chapter XVI

Giovanni Frattini, Engineering IT, Italy
Fabio Corvino, Engineering IT, Italy
Francesco Gaudino, Engineering IT, Italy
Pierpaolo Petriccione, Engineering IT, Italy
Vladimiro Scotto di Carlo, Engineering IT, Italy
Gianluca Supino, Engineering IT, Italy

This chapter describes an architecture for mobile multimodal applications used to conveniently manage inputs and outputs in order to make the dialog natural, intuitive, and user centred, according to the needs of ubiquitous and context aware applications. The advantages in using a prevalent speech driven interaction, mainly in mobile contexts, when hands or other body parts of users can be busy are underlined.

Chapter XVII

Stefania Pierno, Engineering IT, Italy
Vladimiro Scotto di Carlo, Engineering IT, Italy
Massimo Magaldi, Engineering IT, Italy
Roberto Russo, Engineering IT, Italy
Gian Luca Supino, Engineering IT, Italy
Luigi Romano, Engineering IT, Italy
Luca Bevilacqua, Engineering IT, Italy

This chapter describes a platform, based on a grid approach, used to develop multichannel, multimodal, and mobile context aware applications. It describes problems and solutions using a scenario about emergencies and crisis management. The platform, however, has a general validity and allows to supply services by a multimodal user interface; the GRID approach enables to optimise the computing load due to the multiple input channels processing.

Chapter XVIII

Julie Doyle, University College Dublin, Ireland
Michela Bertolotto, University College Dublin, Ireland
David Wilson, University of North Carolina at Charlotte, USA

This chapter, starting from the assumption that the user's interface is a critical aspect of interaction systems, discusses how to design and develop multimodal interfaces for mobile GIS. It describes in particular the multimodal mobile GIS CoMPASS, which enables users to interact by speech and gestures.

This chapter faces one of the most relevant challenges arising with the wide use of Web and mobile devices: making contents accessible personalizing interfaces for highly mobile individuals, for people with limited devices, for people with disabilities, and so on. A personalized multimodal user interface for browsing XML content types is presented as an example of adaptive and natural interaction.

This chapter describes the multimodal mobile virtual blackboard system, a mobile learning system allowing consultation among students and professors. The focus of the description is on the multimodal solution of the user's interface for the context aware learning system. The chapter, describing the system, suggests good practices to follow in designing and implementing mobile multimodal interfaces.

This chapter describes cause-effect connections between changes that mobile devices, such as mobile phones, PDAs, iPods and smart phones have on improving and modifying the learning process, and how this improvement is modifying the learning tools and the environment in which learning takes place.

Section IV
Standards, Guidelines, and Evaluation of Multimodal Systems

This section presents the emerging standards and guidelines for mobile multimodal applications design and usability evaluation. Standards for multimodal interaction provided by W3C are described and a visual interaction design process for mobile multimodal systems is sketched. Finally, a selection of "classical" methods and some new developed methods for testing usability in the area of multimodal interfaces are given.

This chapter presents current and emerging standards supporting multimodal applications with a particular focus on voice and GUI interaction. Among the major standards, are described the W3C multimodal architecture, VoiceXML, SCXML, EMMA, and speech grammar standard. Finally, the chapter highlights how standards can represent a basis for the future of multimodal applications.

This chapter, presenting a framework for designing visual representations for mobile multimodal systems, traces some guidelines. The chapter is focused on the output modalities. The proposed guidelines are grouped in "two sets: (i) a set of high-level design requirements for visual representations of interactions on mobile multimodal systems; and (ii) a set of ten specific design requirements for the visual elements and displays for representing interactions on mobile multimodal systems."

This chapter, concluding the book, faces one of the most relevant aspects when designing, implementing, and using an interface: its usability. Usability is a focal point for the wide diffusion of each kind of systems. Multimodality, jointly with mobile devices, is an element that can contribute to reach this goal. However, a mobile device with a multimodal interface is not necessarily usable. For this reason this chapter presents a selection of "classical" methods, and introduces some new developed methods for testing usability in the area of multimodal interfaces.

Preface

This book provides a contribution on the theories, techniques, and methods on multimodality and mobile devices for pervasive services. It consists of 24 chapters that provide an in-depth investigation of new approaches, methods, and trends.

Humans communicate using their five senses in a synergistic manner expressing key-concepts involving different modalities and/or two or more modalities simultaneously. Indeed, human-human communication involves, in a synergistic manner, several communication channels; it can use gesture, sketch drawing, handwriting, facial expressions, gaze, and speech or their combination.

Multimodal interaction systems can combine visual, auditory, and other kinds of information in a flexible and powerful dialogue manner, enabling users to choose one or more interaction modalities. The use of multimodality combined with mobile devices allows a simple and intuitive communication approach everywhere and every time. The synergistic approach in using more than one modality to interact with computers—or more generally with other devices such as mobile devices–makes dialogue and communication flexible, natural, and robust also for its closeness with the human-human one.

Effectiveness and naturalness of communication is particularly relevant for services. The great diffusion of mobile devices, along with the development of multimodal interaction, presents a new challenge for telecommunication companies and all organizations that can be involved in providing new services using mobile devices. One requirement for these services is that they and their information have to be accessible to every mobile situation.

Even if in the last years several efforts have been carried out to provide computer and mobile devices interfaces with a similar flexibility, naturalness, and robustness, a lot of theoretical and technological problems need to be faced when designing and implementing very natural, flexible, and robust multimodal human computer interaction approaches.

Naturalness, flexibility, and robustness of interaction approaches are key elements to produce new and pervasive services for people. In developing multimodal pervasive services, it is essential to consider perceptual speech, audio, and video quality for the optimum communication system design, the effective transmission planning, and management respect to the customer requirements.

BOOK OBJECTIVE

The book aim is to provide theoretical and practical scenarios, concepts, methodologies, standards, definitions, and applications used to design and develop multimodal systems, focusing on mobile devices and pervasive services. It gives an overview of the existing works in this sector, discussing the different strategies adopted for the fusion input process, optimization processes on mobile devices, ambiguity and error handling related to one or more modalities, the fission process, the personalization and adaptation of multimodal mobile services, and the accessibility and usability criteria. Moreover, the book contains some significant examples of pervasive multimodal mobile applications; it discusses as acceptance is the basic condition for a wide use of each service, and it analyses transformations produced in some sectors, such as, for example, e-learning, using both multimodal interaction and mobile devices.

AUDIENCE

Academics, researchers, technicians, students in computer science, and all experts involved in designing multimodal and mobile pervasive services will find this book a valuable contribution to their knowledge and they will find it a stimulus for new scientific activities on the important topics involved.

ORGANIZATION

The book contains 24 chapters organized in four sections. The first section introduces some of the basic concepts and describes the main theoretical and practical problems and features of multimodal interaction.

The second section describes how some particular multimodal applications overcome design problems connected with combining different modalities and how ontologies can be useful to improve interoperability of different environments and naturalness of multimodal interaction. Chapters contained in the third section consider methods and problems of multimodal interaction focusing on mobile devices and considering their adaptability and usability features. This section introduces a discussion on changes on the communication and services fruition produced by using mobile devices in the particular scenario of e-learning. Finally, the fourth section of this book contains chapters that describe standards, some guidelines, and evaluation methods for multimodal systems.

The first section is opened by a study on people acceptance and adoption of mobile devices proposed by Judy van Biljon and Karen Renaud in the first chapter. Acceptance is the first step for the wide adoption and diffusion of a new technology. In particular, the chapter investigates the "mobile phone adoption by older users" proposing the novel senior technology acceptance and adoption model (STAM), which incorporates acceptance factors into the adoption process.

From Chapter II to Chapter IX the basic concepts, theories, and technologies about multimodal interaction and multimodal systems are provided; these chapters give an overview of the lifecycle of information and data characterizing multimodal interaction.

In particular, in Chapter II Ferri and Paolozzi give an overview of the main problems, definitions, and concepts related to multimodality, describing the "different approaches used in the multimodal interaction," mainly addressing those approaches that use the new semantic technologies as well as the Semantic Web ones.

Naturalness of multimodal interaction depends on its feature of involving all five human senses simultaneously. D'Ulizia, in Chapter III, provides an overview of the different approaches of the literature to combine and integrate different input modalities (fusion process).

Based on state of art review on multimodal input fusion approaches, Chen and Sun in Chapter IV present a novel approach to multimodal input fusion based on speech and gesture, or speech and eye tracking, using a combinational categorical grammar. This approach has been validated for mobile context.

"Naturalness and flexibility of the dialogue" can produce a very complex interpretation process and the presence of ambiguities can be a relevant problem to face. Caschera, in Chapter V analyses approaches that have to cope issues connected to the interpretation process. She provides a classification of ambiguities into recognition, segmentation, and target ambiguities, and describes methods for solving different classes of ambiguities.

Naturalness of the multimodal interaction implies a symmetric communication between humans and machines (computers, mobile devices, and so on). For this reason when a user interacts with a multimodal system, s/he produces a multimodal input that is fused and interpreted. The multimodal system usually reacts and produces an output, which requires to be interpreted by the user. The output arrangement and organization (multimodal fission) is a focal point that is faced by Grifoni in Chapter VI. This chapter provides some basic concepts involved in the fission process design and describes some of the most relevant approaches discussed in the literature, with a particular attention on the mobile devices use.

The problem of flexibility and capability to adapt functionalities on mobile devices to the users is faced in Chapter VII by Esposito, Basile, Di Mauro, and Ferilli. The chapter presents a two-phase construction of the user model: an initial static user model, and revised/adjusted model by considering the information collected by the user interaction with the device/context.

Designing and developing human machine interfaces is a critical task due to the fact that it is a time consuming and expensive task. This fact is particularly evident for multimodal environments. Coninx, De Boeck, Raymaekers, and Vanacken with Chapter VIII propose a model-based user interface design process (MBUID), in which the interface is defined by means of high level of abstraction, which gives the opportunity for creating intermediate prototypes and user evaluation, ultimately resulting in better and cheaper virtual environment interfaces.

This first section ends with Chapter IX addressing the concrete aspect of the temporal and spatial organization of human pointing actions for multimodal human computer interaction, faced by Müller-Tomfelde and Chen. The role of pointing gestures combined with other modalities is presented and developers are provided "with substantial knowledge about the temporal-spatial organization of the pointing gesture."

The second section of this book collects specific methodologies for designing and implementing multimodal systems. In Chapter X, Castellina, Corno, and Pellegrino describe a multimodal system integrating speech-based and gaze-based inputs for interaction with a real desktop environment. The proposed approach shows how the combined use of auditive and visual clues permits mutual disambiguation in the interaction with a real desktop environment.

Pittarello and Celentano, in their chapter titled "*Multimodality and Environment Semantics,*" provide a methodology devoted to identify the user-oriented features of the environment describing the physical environment at different levels of granularity, functionally, and geometrically. A scene-independent ontology permits a level of interoperability between different environments. The chapter ends presenting a case study about the creation of a guided tour through the indoors and outdoors of the town of Venice using a multimodal web browser.

The importance in using an ontology for multimodal systems in different use cases has a further evidence in Chapter XII, "*An Ontology Supporting an On-Board Vehicle Multimodal Interaction System,*" by Pisanelli, Lazzari, Innocenti, and Zanetti. In that chapter, they introduce ontologies (Vehicle Security, Road and Traffic Security, Meteorological, Users' Profiles and Travel) supporting an on-board vehicle multimodal interaction system, which enables semantic interoperability for cooperation between the road infrastructure and assisting the driver.

Barricelli, Marcante, Mussio, Parasiliti, Provenza, Padula, and Scala, in Chapter XIII, propose a methodology supporting a collaborative and evolutionary design of an interactive system. The proposed approach uses the metaphor of the "workshop of an artisan." It starts from empirical experience to handle problems faced on the field, considering the need to interact everywhere and every time with mobile devices.

An important aspect that multimodality can face is connected with the possibility that it has to improve the information and services accessibility, and the possibility of any person to make use of them. Bacellar, Leal Ferriera, Silva da Silveira, Gurgel do' Amaral, Leal Ferriera, and Rodrigues Nunes, in Chapter XIV titled, "*Making the Web Accessible to the Visually Impaired,*" face the problem of making accessible information to blind persons. A study aimed at identifying and defining usability guidance compliant with accessibility W3C directives to facilitate the interaction between visually impaired people, and their access to Web information and services, has been presented.

The potentiality to improve the access of people having different physical, psychological, and cognitive attitudes to different information and services is one of the features of multimodal interaction that makes it very attractive for e-learning, and in particular for mobile learning. Spetch, in Chapter XV depicts the experience carried out in the European project RAFT. A widget based approach design for the user interface enables to build clients for a variety of hardware and devices in the learning environment, from mobile phones, PDAs, and tablet PCs.

Section III discusses and details problems, features, and applications of multimodal interaction focusing the attention in the case of mobile devices.

In chapter XVI, Frattini, Corvino, Gaudino, Petriccione, Scotto di Carlo, and Supino discuss how a speech driven interaction between user and service delivery systems may be the ideal solution for the development of ubiquitous and context aware applications; indeed, even if people have eyes and hands busy because they are making other activities too, they are usually able to interact using speech. The authors propose in their chapter an architecture for building mobile multimodal applications describing their experiences.

"A GRID approach to providing multimodal context-sensitive mobile social service" is presented in Chapter XVII by Pierno, Scotto di Carlo, Magaldi, Russo, Supino, Romano, and Bevilacqua. When designing a mobile information system, it is not only important input-output channels management and information presentation, but also context-awareness. The authors have described a platform that supports the development of multichannel, multimodal, mobile context aware applications, and its use in an emergency management scenario.

In Chapter XIII, Doyle, Bertolotto, and Wilson depict an application providing mapping services and discuss the importance of opportunely identifying the visualization and interaction modes. Multimodal interfaces for mobile GIS represent a challenge according to the need to use them in different context and by different users, simplifying the inherent complexity of the majority of GIS interfaces. The chapter describes the multimodal mobile GIS CoMPASS, which uses a combination of speech and gesture input.

Using multimodal systems on mobile devices to access information and services can require to generate the user interface on-the-fly according to the different contents, devices, and user's needs. Chapter XIX, by Encelle, Baptiste-Jessel, and Sèdes, presents an "*Adapted Multimodal End-User Interfaces for XML-Content.*" This system is characterized by a user interfaces for browsing particular XML content types that can be personalized; it is described in particular its use for visual impaired people.

The usability of mobile devices with their small screen is faced by Davcev, Trajkovik, and Gligorovska in Chapter XX, which describes a "*Multimodal Mobile Virtual Blackboard*" system. The system faces the addressed problem of adapting the application features to the specific user's preferences and to the current use of the system. Adaptability is obtained by using XML agents and fuzzy logic.

The wide diffusion of cell phones, smart phones, personal digital assistants, and other mobile devices, and the possibility to design and to implement a very natural multimodal interaction is changing the approach to many individual and social activities. D'Andrea, Ferri, Fortunati, and Guzzo in their chapter,

"Mobile *Devices to Support Advanced Forms of E-Learning,*" describe that these transformation are producing a deep change in e-learning tools and in the environment in which e-learning takes place.

The fourth section of this book discusses standards for multimodal applications, some guidelines to follow, in particular for visual representation of interaction for mobile multimodal systems. Finally, usability evaluation methods for multimodal applications on mobile devices are discussed.

Dahl, in Chapter XXII describes standards for multimodal interaction focusing the presentation on standards for voice and GUI interaction (W3C Multimodal Architecture, VoiceXML, SCXML, EMMA, and speech grammar standards).

Focusing on *"Visual Representation of Interaction for Mobile Multimodal Systems,"* Deray and Simoff, in Chapter XXIII, present a framework for designing visual representations for mobile multimodal systems, suggesting moreover a set of design guidelines.

The final chapter of the book describes the relevant problem of usability evaluation for multimodal interfaces mainly for mobile applications and services. In this chapter, Bernhaupt depicts a selection of "classical" methods for usability evaluation and introduces some new emerging methods for testing usability of multimodal interfaces with a particular focus on mobile devices.

Patrizia Grifoni
Istituto di Ricerche sulla Popolazione e le Politiche Sociali
Consiglio Nazionale delle Ricerche, Italy

Acknowledgment

The editor would like to acknowledge the help of all involved in the collation and review process of the book, without whose support the project could not have been satisfactorily completed.

Most of the authors of chapters included in this book also served as referees for chapters written by other authors. Thanks go to all those who provided constructive and comprehensive reviews.

Special thanks go to all the staff at IGI Global, and in particular to Rebecca Beistline and Christine Bufton, for their continuous and professional support.

In closing, I wish to thank all of the authors for their insights and excellent contributions to this book.

Patrizia Grifoni
Istituto di Ricerche sulla Popolazione e le Politiche Sociali
Consiglio Nazionale delle Ricerche, Italy

Section I
Multimodality:
Basic Concepts

The first section introduces some of the basic concepts and describes the main theoretical and practical problems and features of multimodal interaction, with a particular focus on mobile devices. Starting from a study on people acceptance and adoption of technologies and models, with a particular focus on mobile devices in the first chapter, it has been highlighted how naturalness of multimodal interaction facilitates its acceptance and its wide use diffusion by a large part of people. From chapter two to chapter nine the basic concepts, theories and technologies involved in the study of multimodal interaction and multimodal systems are provided.

Chapter I
A Qualitative Study of the Applicability of Technology Acceptance Models to Senior Mobile Phone Users

Judy van Biljon
University of South Africa, South Africa

Karen Renaud
University of Glasgow, UK

ABSTRACT

We report on an investigation into mobile phone adoption by older users. Technology adoption is a process from ignorance to considering it a necessity. Moreover, acceptance is an essential precursor of adoption. Many models consider either acceptance or adoption, but in fact these are interrelated. Furthermore, most theoretical models are based on responses from students or economically active adults. This begs the question: Do existing models incorporate the phases and the factors that lead to mobile phone adoption and acceptance by older adults? We thus studied the needs, uses, and limitations of older users and then gathered information about experiences and opinions of these users. We then mapped the verified acceptance factors against adoption processes in a two-dimensional matrix. This led to the proposal for the novel senior technology acceptance and adoption model (STAM), which incorporates acceptance factors into the adoption process, thereby consolidating the research in both these areas.

INTRODUCTION

This chapter addresses technology acceptance and use in the context of the senior mobile phone user. These users are an oft neglected group in product development and marketing, yet in most developed societies they are the only growing age group (Mallenius *et al.*, 2007). The uptake of new technologies has been studied from two perspectives: acceptance factors and adoption process.

Several models of technology acceptance have been proposed and tested (Lee, 2007; Venkatesh *et al.*, 2003). In the field of Management Information Systems (MIS), a number of *technology acceptance models* have been proposed, which focus on *factors* influencing acceptance without considering the process (Renaud & Van Biljon, 2008). Sociological studies take a meta-view by considering the adoption *process,* including technology's acceptance, rejection and use (Haddon, 2003). Lee (2007) suggests that different approaches be merged in order to benefit from all their strengths. In this chapter we will be merging acceptance and adoption approaches since this enhances our understanding of *factors* influencing progression through the different *adoption phases*. It is important to consider acceptance and adoption together since adoption will not occur without a person having accepted the technology – the person may own the technology, but without accepting it he or she is unlikely to adopt it. Non-adoption means that it is unlikely to be utilised effectively or upgraded. In effect, significant non-adoption by any sector of society will lead to fewer sales and therefore market research is especially interested in acceptance.

In predicting adoption, knowledge of the end users is as important as the functionality of a device (Holzinger *et al.*, 2008). Current acceptance models have been quantitatively verified, using students or economically active adults as participants (Lee, 2007). This begs the question: *Do existing models incorporate the phases and the factors that lead to mobile phone adoption and use by older adults?* A literature study of the needs, limitations and expectations of the older adult mobile phone user made it clear that they demand added value in the form of a more social, active, meaningful and independent life (Mallenius et al., 2007). In terms of simple economics, the value of the phone can be expressed as *value = f(usefulness, ease of use).* How each factor is rated depends on each person's individual needs (perceived usefulness) and abilities (perceived

ease of use) and it is difficult to come up with a definitive way of measuring these. However, knowing which factors *mediate* ease of use and usefulness provides an insight into perceived value. The obvious matter for investigation is whether current mobile phones generally deliver this value to elderly users. We address this by verifying, *qualitatively*, the factors mentioned in the quantitatively derived models, and assessing their influence in the adoption process.

Firstly, we need to identify a set of factors relevant to mobile phone acceptance. We constructed five scenarios related to senior mobile phone usage and presented these scenarios to participants in semi-structured interviews. The participants' responses were used to validate or deny the identified factors. Furthermore we interviewed older users, asking about use of their mobile phones with a specific focus on ease of use. Our findings are presented in an *acceptance matrix* which maps the validated *factors* against the domestication technology *adoption progression*. This helps us to understand the factors that play a part in leading users down the road towards wholehearted adoption of a particular technology.

The next two sections present the theoretical groundwork by presenting an overview of technology acceptance and adoption research. The following section examines the context of the elderly mobile phone user. Next we outline the qualitative study and present our results. The final section proposes the adoption matrix and presents the Senior Technology Adoption and Acceptance Model (STAM) and contextualises the findings.

TECHNOLOGY ADOPTION PROCESSES

There are two primary technology adoption process models: : Rogers' innovation diffusion model (Rogers, 2003) and the domestication approach (Silverstone & Haddon, 1996). Rogers'

Table 1. Four dimensions of domestication adoption process (Lee, 2007) :66

Dimension	Description	Examples of potential themes relevant in user experience research
Appropriation	Process of possession or ownership of the artifact.	Motivation to buy a product Route to acquire information about a product Experience when purchasing a product
Objectification	Process of determining roles product will play	Meaning of a technology What function will be used in users' life? Where is it placed? How is it carried?
Incorporation	Process of interacting with a product	Difficulties in using a product (usability problems) Learning process (use of instructional manual)
Conversion	Process of converting technology to intended feature use or interaction	Unintended use of product features Unintended way of user interaction Wish lists for future products

innovation diffusion model focuses on marketing and sales processes proposing various levels of progression from not having used the technology to full adoption. Rogers (2003) proposes the following five stage process of product adoption: the knowledge phase where the person gets to know about the product; the persuasion phase where he or she becomes persuaded of a need for the product; the decision phase which leads to a purchase; the implementation phase where the item is used and the confirmation phase where the individual seeks to confirm that he or she made the right decision in purchasing the product.

Silverstone and Haddon (1996) proposed the domestication approach to deal with a more global analysis of acceptances *ex post facto*. They proposed the *domestication of technology* as a concept used to describe and analyze the processes of acceptance, rejection and use as described in Table 1 (Silverstone and Haddon, 1996). Users are seen as social entities and the model aims to provide a framework for understanding how technology innovations change, and are changed, by their social contexts. Clearly there are similarities between the two models. We selected the domestication theory adoption process for our purposes in charting acceptance factors since it is focuses on the *ex post facto* adoption process more than the decision to buy or not.

TECHNOLOGY ACCEPTANCE MODELS

Examples of technology acceptance models are the Technology Acceptance Model (TAM) (Davis, 1989) and the Unified Theory of Acceptance and Use of Technology Model (UTAUT) (Venkatesh et al., 2003) each of which focus on technology acceptance within organisations (Ling, 2001). Here we present details of the different technology acceptance models and finally we consider technology acceptance models tailored specially to acceptance of mobile phones. From these we extract a set of factors relevant to mobile phone acceptance by senior users.

Technology Acceptance: Factors

The Technology Acceptance Model (TAM) proposes a number of factors that are essential in determining user attitude towards accepting a new technology, as shown in Figure 1. (Davis, 1989; Malhotra & Galletta,1999). TAM incorporates six distinct factors (Davis, 1989; Pedersen, 2005):

- *External variables* (EV), such as demographic variables, influence perceived usefulness (PU) and perceived ease of use (PEU).

Figure 1. Technology Acceptance Model (Davis, 1989)

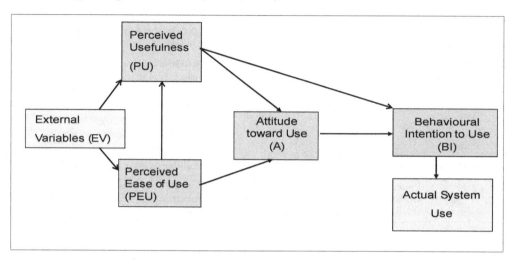

- *Perceived usefulness* (PU) is defined as 'the extent to which a person believes that using the system will enhance his or her job performance' (Venkatesh et al., 2003).
- *Perceived ease of use* (PEU) is 'the extent to which a person believes that using the system will be free of effort' (Venkatesh et al., 2003) .
- *Attitudes towards use* (A) is defined as 'the user's desirability of his or her using the system'(Malhotra & Galletta, 1999). Perceived usefulness (PU) and perceived ease of use (PEU) are the sole determinants of attitude towards the technology system.
- *Behavioural intention* (BI) is predicted by attitude towards use (A) combined with perceived usefulness (PU
- *Actual use* (AU) is predicted by behavioural intention (BI).

Venkatesh et al. (2003) extended TAM and developed the Unified Theory of Acceptance and Use of Technology (UTAUT), which attempts to explain user intentions to use an information system and subsequent usage behaviour. An important contribution of UTAUT is to distinguish between factors *determining* use behaviour namely the constructs of performance expectancy,

effort expectancy, social influence and facilitating conditions and then factors *mediating* the impact of these constructs. The mediating factors are gender, age, experience, and voluntariness (i.e. the degree to which use of the innovation is perceived as being of free will). Both TAM and UTAUT can be applied to any technology type but there is some value in specialising the models for particular technologies. The following section discusses the application of models in the mobile technology area.

Specific Models for Mobile Technology Acceptance

Kwon and Chidambaram (2000) propose a model for mobile phone acceptance and use which includes the following components: demographic factors, socio-economic factors, ease of use, apprehensiveness, extrinsic motivation (perceived usefulness), intrinsic motivation (enjoyment, fun) social pressure and extent of use. They found that perceived ease of use significantly affected users' extrinsic and intrinsic motivation, while apprehensiveness about cellular technology had a negative effect on intrinsic motivation (Kwon & Chidambaram, 2000). The limitation of this model is that it does not include infrastructural

Figure 2. Diagrammatic representation of MOPTAM(Van Biljon, 2007)

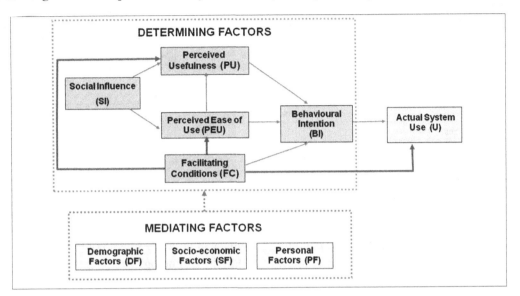

factors, which are essential in considering mobile technology. The Mobile Phone Technology Adoption Model (MOPTAM) (Van Biljon, 2007), depicted in Figure 2, integrates TAM with the determining and mediating factors from UTAUT and then adapts the result to model the personal mobile phone use of university students.

Based on exploratory research, Sarker and Wells (2003) propose a framework that relates *exploration* and *experimentation* to the *assessment of experience* that determines *acceptance outcome*. The mediating factors distinguished are: context, technology characteristics, modality of mobility, communication/task characteristics and individual characteristics.

Research on technology adoption of the elderly was done by Holzinger *et al.*(2008) and also by (Lee, 2007) but none of these studies proposed a new technology adoption model. Table 2 summarises the most fundamental factors incorporated into the models listing the following factors: Social influence (SI), Perceived Ease of Use(PEU), Perceived Usefulness (PU), Facilitating Conditions (FC), Behavioural Intention (BI), Demographic Factors (DF), Socio-Economic Factors(SE) and Personal Factors(PF). Note that

perceived ease of use is the common factor across all the models.

CONTEXT OF THE SENIOR ADULT

The mobile phone needs of the elderly centre around critical services such as emergency and health support that enhance safety and those services that make everyday life and tasks easier (Lee, 2007; Mallenius et al., 2007). The elderly position mobile phone use in terms of *value*, which is mostly based on communication, safety aspects and the support of independence (Holzinger *et al.*, 2008, Lee, 2007, Van Biljon, 2007). Regarding perceived usefulness (PU) it can thus be said that senior mobile users use mobile phones in the following areas:

• **Safety and security:** Kurniawan (2007) claims a security-related focus drives the mobile phone market for older users. She says that older people use phones to make them feel less vulnerable when alone at home and more confident going out alone. They used their mobile phones mostly in emergencies or to contact family members.

Table 2. Factors influencing mobile phone acceptance

Factors	Models and theories				
	TAM	UTAUT	Kwon & Chidambaram	Sarker & Wells	MOPTAM
SI	No	Yes	Yes	Yes	Yes
PEU	Yes	Yes	Yes	Yes	Yes
PU	Yes	No	No	Yes	Yes
FC	No	Yes	No	Yes	Yes
BI	Yes	Yes	Yes	No	Yes
DF	External variables	No	Yes	Yes	Yes
SE	External variables	No	Yes	Yes	Yes
PF	No	No	No	Yes	Yes

- **Communication:** The importance of communication and the social influence is noted (Lee, 2007; Mallenius et al., 2007) but described in more detail under the social context.

- **Organisation:** The mobile phone offers the potential for organising and synchronising activities in new and cost effective ways. This organisation can be of a personal nature, such as using the reminders to compensate for memory failure, or the phone book to store telephone numbers.

- **Information:** The number of seniors surfing the Internet is steadily increasing (Ziefle & Bay, 2004), evidence of their need for, and readiness to use, the Internet to get information they require. The use of a mobile phone to access the Internet is an obvious next step for all users, and the elderly are no exception.

In the mobile context, the user and the equipment can be mobile and the surroundings may therefore change constantly. This opens up fundamental differences in the context of use between the traditional computing environments and information appliances such as mobile phones (Iacucci, 2001). Four different aspects of the mobile phone context have been noted (Jones & Marsden, 2005; Kiljander, 2004) in past research:

physical context, social context, mental context and the technological context as discussed in the following sections.

Physical Context

The physical context denotes the physical constraints of the usage environment (Jones & Marsden, 2005; Kiljander, 2004). We need to consider both the physical limitations of the device as well as the limitations of the surrounding physical context. Screen size, memory, storage space, input and output facilities are more limited in mobile devices such as mobile phones (Brewster, 2002; Young, 2003), while sound output quality is often poor with restricted voice recognition on input (Dunlop & Brewster, 2002).

The undeniable potential of the 'gray' market is hampered by the physical and cognitive limitations of aging. Elderly mobile phone users make use of fewer mobile phone features than younger users (Lee, 2007). Ziefle and Bay (2004) suggest that elderly mobile phone users do not have a mental model of the ubiquitous hierarchical menu system used by mobile phones. They struggle to find the features they want to use and therefore do not use them. This is confirmed by a study carried out by Osman *et al.* (2003) who interviewed 17 elderly users and asked them to name the most important features of a mobile phone. 'Easy menus' was mentioned most often, followed by large screen. The latter is unsurprising since many elderly users have impaired vision. Another factor mentioned is that they require large buttons, due to the inevitable decrease in manual dexterity experienced by many elderly users (Lee, 2007). It follows that the effects of aging, such as impaired hearing, vision and loss of manual dexterity impact negatively on the ease of use of mobile phones. However, it would be a mistake to classify users strictly according to age. Mallenius *et al.* (2007) argue for using functional capacity (consisting of the physical, psychological and social aspects), rather than age as a facilitating condition.

Social Context

Social context concerns the social interaction involved and enabled by using the mobile device (Jones & Marsden, 2005; Kiljander, 2004). Phillips and Sternthal (1977) found that with increasing age comes reduced involvement with other people, as confirmed by Abascal and Civit (2001). The reasons are argued by experts, but the net effect is unarguable: reduced access to information that is readily available to younger people. Elderly people make extensive use of the television to give them the information they no longer get from other people (Phillips & Sternthal, 1977). The social contact they *do* have is primarily with their extended family and this group appears to provide them with the advice and support they need. Friends and relatives, especially the opinion of children and grand-children impact the behaviour of the elderly mobile phone user (Lee, 2007; Mallenius et al., 2007), therefore social influence as proposed in most of the technology acceptance model in Table 2, is an important factor in the mobile phone acceptance of older people.

Mental Context

The mental context relates to aspects of the user's understanding of the mobile handset usage model (Kiljander, 2004). Mobile phones are acquired by a widespread population of users who will probably not have any formal training in operating them and consider them as devices to be used rather than computers to be maintained (Dunlop & Brewster, 2002). Furthermore, device vendors consolidate multiple functions into a single device. The mobile user has to handle interleaving of multiple activities and multiple public faces, previously unknown when only a landline or a stationary computer was used (Preece *et al.*, 2002). Cognitive demands are exacerbated due to physical constraints on size, bandwidth and processing power, which restricts the communication bandwidth and places extra demands on the user's attention (Hyyppä *et al.*, 2000). The mental strain described above is amplified for the elderly mobile phone user, most of whom did not grow up with computers (Holzinger *et al.*, 2008). People perform more slowly and with less precision as they age, elderly users appear to have difficulty learning how to use a new mobile phone (Botwinick, 1967) and use fewer of the available features (Van Biljon, 2007). The *ability* to learn is not impaired but the *rate* of learning *is* reduced (Baldi, 1997; Salthouse, 1985). Burke and Mackay (1997) mention that the formation of new memory connections is impaired with age. Therefore it is beneficial to allow elderly people to regulate their own rate of information processing. They struggle to filter out irrelevant stimuli so it takes them longer to process the relevant information in order to learn to use the device (Phillips & Sternthal, 1977). This is because they have reduced visual processing speed (Jackson & Owsley, 2003) and working through mobile phone menus is likely to be more difficult for them, purely because of this.

Technological Context

The technological context refers to the mobile infrastructure including the networks available, services provided, costing and features of the mobile device (Jones & Marsden, 2005). Findings indicate that the elderly consider spending very carefully and the price of a device or service is a differentiator for use (Mallenius et al., 2007; Van Biljon, 2007). The mobile context poses unique challenges and opportunities in terms of mobility, portability and personalisation (Yuan & Zhang, 2003), and yet there is an overlap between the factors influencing mobile phone adoption and technology adoption in general (Kwon & Chidambaram, 2000). Therefore we will now consider factors from models for technology adoption as the basis for proposing a model for mobile phone adoption.

THE QUALITATIVE STUDY

Thirty four elderly people participated in our study (10 male and 24 female). The participants per age distribution were: 60-70 years: 13, 70-80 years: 16 and 80-90 years: 5. Considering mobile phone use, 19 of the participants had contracts and 15 used pre-pay. They obtained the phones by buying them (16), having the phone bought by someone else (3) or getting the phone as a gift (15). The majority who bought the phones themselves were in the 60-70 age group, i.e. the younger participants in our group.

Scenarios

Five scenarios seniors typically encountered in their everyday lives were presented to the participants and they were requested to comment. The participants responded actively, providing the following information:

- **Scenario 1** (obtaining information about mobile phones): Relating to information gathering, the responses fell into three groups: 9 said that people would ask their children; two said that they should ask people of their own age(not their children); while

23 reckoned that people would go to mobile phone vendors for information.

- **Scenario 2** (accepting a cast-off phone): Relating to the impact of decreased ability to learn versus other motivations, three main groups of responses arose: 11 answered yes, citing the economical 'You can sell the old one'; the philosophical 'You should take the challenge'; and the pragmatic: 'The old phone may be getting out of date' as reasons. Seventeen answered no, stating memory loss and difficulty in learning as reasons. A third group of 6 reasoned that it depended on the person and the circumstances.
- **Scenario 3** (emergencies such as having a stroke): Relating to safety and ease of use, 21 participants said that a mobile phone could be useful in emergencies, 12 felt that the older person would be 'too scared and confused', or 'unable to find spectacles'. The rest felt that theoretically it was a good idea, but not practical since older people find phones difficult to use, even more so when stressed.
- **Scenario 4** (accessory in helping to remember): Relating to the need for organisation, 28 reckoned that people could set a reminder, of these five had reservations about whether older people would manage to do that, whilst one was unsure that a mobile phone would be of any help.
- **Scenario 5** (safety aid in travelling): Relating to safety and usefulness the majority(27) agreed that it could be useful, they gave different reasons such as the traveller contacting (phone or SMS) the family or vice versa, while some believed it could be used by a third party in the event of an emergency.

Interviews on Use

It is clear that *ease of use* cannot really be self-reported. It is far more enlightening to observe users making use of a product. We therefore asked participants to name the three features they used most often, and to show us how their phone performed the features.

We intended to count the button presses in the second part of this process in order to gauge effort expended and consequent ease of use. We had to discontinue this since it became obvious that the participants had difficulty finding their most-used features. Some participants asked the experimenter for assistance in finding the feature, others tried various routes down the menu structure before triumphantly locating the desired feature. We felt that the button press count was so inaccurate as to be useless and therefore discontinued counting. Since the type of mobile possessed by the participants was diverse the unavoidable conclusion is that most phones have serious ease of use issues whatever make they are, as least as far as our participants were concerned.

DISCUSSION

Sarker and Wells (2003) suggested an exploration and experimentation module, and certainly we had the sense that many of our participants had experimented with their phones soon after coming into possession of them. Some communicated a sense of frustration, verbalised as follows:

I just can't use that predictive text, even though my daughter has tried to show me how.

I am sure there is a way to get the phone to remind you about things, but I can't find it. Please could you help me find my phone numbers – I have tried but I can't find them.

If the participants did indeed engage in an exploration phase, the obvious outcome of that phase would be the usage of features they had discovered and could use. Table 3 lists the features our participants told us they used regularly (see question 8 in Appendix A) and therefore depicts the outcome of their experimentation with, and exploration of, the phone. We confirmed that a general intention to use the phone plus their sense that the phone could be useful, when they first got it, resulted in a period of experimentation. However, their current use appeared to include only a minimal subset of features – mostly related to communicating as they would use traditional phones.

Table 4 relates the acceptance factors identified during the interviews to the domestication dimensions to form a two-dimensional adoption matrix. Note that no evidence of *conversion phase* activities was uncovered while social influence is prevalent in all of the first three stages. For this group, perceived usefulness (PU) and perceived ease of use (PEU) are often not considered in the appropriation phase since many of the elderly do not select their own phones. This gap may provide an explanation for the observed lack of acceptance. Usefulness and ease of use are considered in the

Table 3. Feature use frequency (N=32)

Feature	Sum	Associated factor
Phone book	24	user context – memory limitations
SMS	14	user context – economic limitations
Phone using number	11	user context – need for social contact
Alarm	9	perceived usefulness
Check Missed calls	4	social influence
Camera	4	social influence

objectification phase and incorporation phases where some concerns about usefulness, and serious concerns about ease of use, were identified.

It became clear that participants fell into two distinct groups: those who had mastered the beast and those who were bemused by it. The former were more adventurous in their use of the phone, using more than just the minimal communication facilities. The latter appeared to own the phone merely because it had been given to them. They clearly saw that the phone could be useful, especially in emergencies, but they did not enjoy ownership the way the former group did. It appeared that for the latter group full adoption had not occurred—they had not *converted* to the technology—and this is likely to be due to a less than wholehearted acceptance of the technology. Our findings suggested that all users had explored the mobile phone but some of them found a number of features too difficult to locate and reverted to using it merely as a mechanism for phoning people when not at home – using a fraction of the functionality of the phone.

As demonstrated, the two-dimensional adoption matrix that relates the technology *acceptance factors* that have emerged from quantitative research to the *adoption phases* identified through quantitative research can be useful in identifying and even predicting gaps in the technology adoption process. The challenges that face each generation or user group are different, but the influence of acceptance factors on adoption phases, as presented by the adoption matrix, will remain relevant. In the next section we discuss a model for modelling the context of the elderly mobile phone user based on this adoption matrix.

PROPOSING STAM

Based on the integration of the three main activities in our research approach: a literature study on technology adoption models, an investigation into the context of the senior user and the findings from our interviews, we proposed the Senior Technology Acceptance & Adoption Model (STAM) (Renaud & Van Biljon, 2008) as depicted in Figure 3. STAM consists of the following components, defined as:

- *User Context* such as demographic variables, social influence and personal factors such as age and functional ability, for example. Social influence is the prevalent external variable and therefore depicted as a module within the user context. Social influence aligns with Rogers' observability innovation attribute.

- *Perceived usefulness* is defined as 'the extent to which a person believes that using the system will enhance his or her job performance' (Venkatesh et al., 2003). This

Table 4. Adoption matrix: Relating domestication progression to factors

	Factors			
Dimension	SI	PU	PEU	BI
Appropriation (Scenarios: 1,2)	Yes	No	No	No
Objectification (Scenarios 2,3,4)	Yes	Yes	Yes	Yes
Incorporation Identified in observation	Yes	Yes	Yes	Yes
Conversion	No evidence in observation or interviews			

aligns with Rogers compatibility and relative advantage innovation attribute (Rogers, 2003).

- *Intention to Use* is influenced by perceived usefulness and also by user context.
- *Facilitating conditions* refer to the mobile phone infrastructure and cost. This includes variables such as system service, system quality, cost of the handset and cost of the service as determined by the business model of the service providers.
- *Experimentation and Exploration,* which is the module where the user first starts using the technology and forms first impressions of the ease of use. Note that the experience obtained here will feed back into confirmed usefulness. The importance of this module confirms findings by Arning and Ziefle (2007) that performance was the main predictor of ease of use. It also aligns with Rogers' (2003) trialiability innovation attribute.
- *Ease of learning & use* results from the perceived ease of use ie. 'the extent to which a person believes that using the system will be free of effort' (Venkatesh et al., 2003), and the final conclusion about ease of use is directly influenced by the experimentation and exploration stage. This aligns with Rogers' (2003) complexity innovation attribute. Finally, whereas other models do not incorporate the ease of learning aspect, the senior model needs to, since difficulty in learning to use a device is a determining factor for the elderly (Ziefle & Bay, 2004) as is the fear of failure (Arning & Ziefle, 2007).
- *Confirmed usefulness* is the usefulness of the person's phone to him or her – composed of the features he or she is able to learn to use.
- *Actual use* is indirectly predicted by the outcome of the experimentation, which leads to ease of learning & use. Facilitat-

ing conditions and the consequent ease of learning & use predict actual use.

Finally, *acceptance* or *rejection* is predicted by ease of learning and use and actual use, with the former more strongly influencing acceptance. STAM, like UTAUT and MOPTAM does *not* include attitude as a determining factor. Van Biljon (2007) found no significant correlation between attitude towards use and any of the other determinants. This is supported by our observation that most people between the ages of 10 and 70 use mobile phones and indeed all our participants intended to use their phones. Dissatisfaction with the ease of use of the phone did not deter people from intending to use the phone – the social influences were far too strong to be offset by a phone that was difficult to use. What *was* affected by ease of use was actual use of the phone, and eventual acceptance.

Figure 3 depicts the Senior Technology Acceptance and Adoption Model (STAM) which models both acceptance factors and adoption phases from first ownership towards actual acceptance or rejection. STAM captures the context of the elderly mobile phone user in an improved way since it incorporates technology acceptance factors into the adoption phases. For elderly people the appropriation phase (see Table 1) is often skipped. They seldom make the decision to buy as their first phone is often given to them or bought for them (note that fewer than 50% of our participants bought their current phone themselves). Several researchers have tested the applicability of TAM to specific groups. For example, technology adoption by physicians (Chismar & Wiley-Patton, 2003). Aggelidis and Chatzoglou (2008) worked on technology acceptance in hospitals while Fife and Pereira studied the adoption levels of mobile data services between and within national markets (Fife & Pereira, 2005). However, the elderly user is different from other users in one very important way.

Most technology adoption models incorporate a phase which represents the stage where the person makes the decision to purchase the new innovation. Rogers (2003) categorises people in terms of how long, after the product is launched, it takes for them to purchase the product. Hence, mobile phones are a special case because many of our participants did *not* purchase their mobile phones. Some were given the phones by children, others by friends.

For this group it seems that Rogers'(2003) first three stages are skipped and the elderly user is often catapulted directly into the 4th stage: implementation, or the second stage of the domestication process, *objectification*, without being able to purchase the particular product that best suits his/her needs. It appears that intention to use is influenced primarily by external factors such as filial affection and safety and security concerns. From our observations it is clear that ease of use does not mediate intention to use – but it *does* influence actual use of the mobile phone. Many of our participants had phones, and pronounced themselves mobile phone users, but did not actually use the phone because of usability issues.

In the objectification phase (see Table 1) determining the role the technology will play

manifests in the behavioural intention which is influenced by *social factors* and *perceived usefulness*. The incorporation phase describes the interaction with the technology as represented by the *experimentation and exploration* module. It is well known that the elderly consider spending very carefully and the price of a device or service is a differentiator for use (Mallenius et al., 2007; Van Biljon, 2007). This is depicted in the *facilitating conditions* module. Facilitating conditions, *perceived usefulness* and *ease of learning* and use all influence *actual use*. Acceptance implies that the user has progressed through all the phases without being derailed by the various mediating and determining factors. Rejection would result from a poor experimentation experience and a resulting perception that the device is too difficult to learn or to use. Whereas most other models imply eventual acceptance by all users, our experience suggests otherwise, and our model reflects this. STAM is not the first attempt at modelling technology acceptance by the elderly adult user. Arning and Ziefle (2007) studied the influence of TAM factors on performance and found a significant correlation between performance and ease of use. That correlation was even stronger for the elderly age group. This study's findings thus

Figure 3. Senior Technology Acceptance & Adoption Model (STAM)

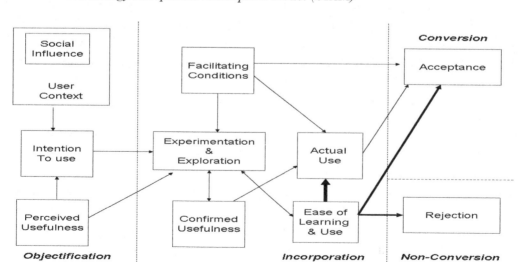

confirm theirs about the dominant influence of ease of use in full-adoption. Phang *et al.* (2006) presented a model for representing the factors that influence intention to use, where perceived ease of use as well as perceived usefulness was found to be highly significant in determining intention to use. However, they found that age was not significant in determining *intention to use*. This, too, is consistent with our findings that the elderly clearly intend to use a mobile phone. However, *actual* use is clearly hampered by poor ease of use. While confirming the importance of perceived usefulness and ease of use as fundamental factors determining technology acceptance for this age group, there are also significant differences between these models because they focus on different components of the adoption process. In contrast STAM depicts the transition from usage to acceptance and conversion (adoption) – a step that some users will never take, since their progress is inhibited by poor ease of use and consequent less than optimal *confirmed* usefulness. Elderly people have the added complication of often skipping the appropriation phase and this provides a plausible explanation for the fact that some elderly mobile phone users never progress to acceptance and conversion.

Towards contextualising this research it should be noted that existing technology acceptance models only partially model the factors that influence the acceptance and adoption of the mobile phone by the elderly. *Value = f(usefulness, ease of use),* and each of these aspects plays a vital role in contributing towards the value of the phone. Moreover, ease of use clearly prevents our users from utilising available functionality. Thus elderly users are getting far less than the optimal value out of their mobile phones. Another problem with existing technology acceptance models is that they model mainly the appropriation phase without due consideration of the other phases in the adoption process. This study provides evidence that intention to use does not necessarily lead to actual use and acceptance. Therefore adoption models should

incorporate acceptance, especially when they aim to support an understanding of technology adoption by groups with special needs.

CONCLUSION

This study investigated mobile phone acceptance by the elderly adult user. We considered existing technology acceptance models and extracted a set of factors that could influence mobile phone acceptance. These factors were filtered by considering the context of the elderly and then validated by means of semi-structured interviews that included the presentation scenarios. The main contribution of this study is the technology adoption matrix which was used as the basis for proposing STAM, a model for the adoption process as driven by the factors that influence mobile phone acceptance in the context of the elderly mobile phone user. By relating acceptance factors to adoption phases STAM provides an explanation why many elderly adults never reach the final adoption phase and never fully accept the technology. The adoption matrix can also be useful in modelling technology acceptance of other demographic groups and other technologies.

ACKNOWLEDGMENT

We acknowledge the National Research Foundation of South Africa for financially supporting this project.

REFERENCES

Abascal, J., & Civit, A. (2001). Universal access to mobile telephony as a way to enhance the autonomy of elderly people. *WUAUC 2001.* Alcacer so Sal. Portugal.

Aggelidis, V.P., & Chatzoglou, P.D. (2008). Using a modified technology acceptance model in hospitals. *International Journal of Medical Informatics*,.doi:10.1016/j.ijmedinf.2008.06.006

Arning, K., & Ziefle, M. (2007). Understanding age differences in pda acceptance and performance. *Computers in Human Behaviour, 23*, 2904-2927.

Baldi, R.A. (1997). Training older adults to use the computer. Issues related to the workplace, attitudes, and training. *Educational Gerontology, 23*, 453-465.

Botwinick, J. (1967). *Cognitive processes in maturity and old age*. Springer.

Brewster, S. (2002). Overcoming the lack of screen space on mobile computers. *Personal and Ubiquitous Computing, 6*(3), 188-205.

Burke, D.M., & Mackay, D.G. (1997). Memory, language, and ageing. *Philosophical Transactions of the Royal Society B: Biological Sciences, 352*(1363), 1845-1856.

Chismar, W.G., & Wiley-Patton, S. (2003). Does the extended technology acceptance model apply to physicians? In *Proceedings of the 36ᵗʰ Annual Hawaii International Conference on System Sciences*, doi 10.1109/HICSS.2003.1174354.

Davis, F.D. (1989). Perceived usefulness, perceived ease of use, and user acceptance of information technology. *MIS Quarterly, 13*(3), 319-340.

Dunlop, M., & Brewster, S. (2002). The challenge of mobile devices for human computer interaction. *Personal and Ubiquitous Computing, 6*(4), 235–236.

Fife, E., & Pereira, F. (2005, June 2-3). Global acceptance of technology (gat) and demand for mobile data services. *Hong Kong Mobility Roundtable*.

Haddon, L. (2003). Domestication and mobile telephony. In *Machines that become us: The social context of personal communication technology* (pp. 43-56). New Brunswick, NJ: Transaction Publishers.

Holzinger, A., Searle, G., Kleinberger, T., Seffah, A., & Javahery, H. (2008). Investigating usability metrics for the design and development of applications for the elderly. *ICCHP 2008, LNCS, 5105*, 98-105.

Hyyppä, K., Tamminen, S., Hautala, I., & Repokari, L. (2000, October 23-25). *The effect of mental model guiding user's action in mobile phone answering situations*. Paper presented at the Electronical Proceedings from the 1ˢᵗ Nordic Conference on Computer Human Interaction, Stockholm, Sweden.

Iacucci, G. (2001). Bridging observation and design in concept development for mobile services. In *Third international symposium on human computer interaction with mobile devices, ihmhci*. Lille, France.

Jackson, G.R., & Owsley, C. (2003). Visual dysfunction, neurodegenerative diseases, and aging. *Neurology and Clinical Neurophysiology, 21*(3), 709-728.

Jones, M., & Marsden, G. (2005). *Mobile interaction design*. Hoboken, NJ: John Wiley and Sons.

Kiljander, H. (2004). *Evolution and usability of mobile phone interaction styles*. Unpublished doctoral dissertation, Helsinki University of Technology, Helsinki.

Kurniawan, A. (2007). Interactions. *Mobile Phone Design for Older Persons, July & Aug*, 24-25.

Kwon, H.S., & Chidambaram, L. (2000). A test of the technology acceptance model: The case of cellular telephone adoption. In *Proceedings of the 33ʳᵈ Hawaii International Conference on System Sciences*, Hawaii (Vol. 1). IEEE Computer Society.

Lee, Y.S. (2007). *Older adults' user experiences with mobile phone: Identification of user clusters and user requirements.* VA: Virginia Polytechnic Institute and State University.

Ling, R. (2001). *The diffusion of mobile telephony among Norwegian teens: A report from after the revolution.* Paper presented at ICUST, Paris. Telenor R&D.

Malhotra, Y., & Galletta, D.F. (1999). Extending the technology acceptance model to account for social influence: Theoretical bases and empirical validation. In *Proceedings of the 32nd Annual Hawaii International Conference on System Sciences* (Vol. 1). IEEE.

Mallenius, S., Rossi, M., & Tuunainen, V.K. (2007). Factors affecting the adoption and use of mobile devices and services by elderly people – results from a pilot study. *6th Annual Mobile Round Table.* Los Angeles, CA.

Osman, Z., Maguir, M., & Tarkiainen, M. (2003). Older users' requirements for location based services and mobile phones. *LNCS, 2795,* 352-357.

Pedersen, E. (2005). Adoption of mobile internet services: An exploratory study of mobile commerce early adopters. *Journal of Organizational Computing and Electronic Commerce, 15*(3), 203-222.

Phang, C.W.J., Sutano, A., Kankanhalli, L., Yan, B.C.Y., & Teo, H.H. (2006). Senior citizens' acceptance of information systems: A study in the context of e-government services. *IEEE Transactions on Engineering Management.*

Phillips, L., & Sternthal, B. (1977). Age differences in information processing: A perspective on the aged consumer. *Journal of Marketing Research, 14*(2), 444-457.

Preece, J., Sharp, H., & Rogers, Y. (2002). *Interaction design--beyond human-computer interaction.* New York: John Wiley & Sons, Inc.

Renaud, K., & Van Biljon, K. (2008). Predicting technology acceptance by the elderly: A qualitative study. In C. Cilliers, L. Barnard, & R. Botha (Eds.), *Proceedings of SAICSIT 2008* (Vol. 1, 210-219). Wildernis, South Africa: ACM Conference Proceedings.

Rogers, E.M. (2003). *Diffusion of innovations* (5th ed.). New York: The Free Press.

Salthouse, T.A. (1985). Speed of behavior and its implications for cognition. In J.E. Birren, & K.W. Schaie (Eds.), *Handbook of the psychology of aging* (2nd ed.). New York: Van Nostrand Reinhold.

Sarker, S., & Wells, J.D. (2003). Understanding mobile handheld device use and adoption. *Communications of the ACM, 46*(12), 35-40.

Silverstone, R., & Haddon, L. (1996). Design and the domestication of information and communication technologies: Technical change and everyday life. In *Communication by design: The politics of information and communication technologies* (pp. 44-74). Oxford, UK: Oxford University.

Van Biljon, J.A. (2007). *A model for representing the motivational and cultural factors that influence mobile phone usage variety.* (Doctoral dissertation, University of South Africa, Pretoria). Retrieved from http://etd.unisa.ac.za/ETD-db/theses/available/etd-09062007-131207/unrestricted/thesis.pdf

Venkatesh, V., Morris, M.G., Davis, G.B., & Davis, F.D. (2003). User acceptance of information technology: Toward a unified view. *MIS Quarterly, 27*(3), 425-478.

Young, T. (2003). Software interface design for small devices. Retrieved on October 12, 2006, from http://www.cs.ubc.ca/~trevor/writings/SmallScreenDesign.pdf

Yuan, Y., & Zhang, J.J. (2003). Towards an appropriate business model for m-commerce. *Mobile Communications, 1*(1-2), 35-56.

Ziefle, M., & Bay, S. (2004). Mental models of a cellular phone menu. Comparing older and younger novice users. In *Lecture Notes in Computer Science: Mobile Human-Computer Interaction (MobileHCI 2004),* (LNCS 3160/2004, pp. 25-37).

ENDNOTE

[1] We use the terms senior, elderly and older adult to refer to people over the age of 60.

APPENDIX A: QUESTIONNAIRE

1. What is your mother-tongue (first language that you learned to speak)? ....

2. Are you?

[a]	Male	[b]	Female

3. How old are you?

[a]	60- 69	[b]	70- 79	[c]	80 or older

4. How would you describe your general level of computer experience?

[a]	None - I have never used a computer	
[b]	Low - I have used a computer belonging to someone else	
[d]	Medium - I own a computer	
[e]	High - I am comfortable using a computer	

5. Is your phone?

[a]	Contract	[b]	Pay as you Go

6. Did you?

[a]	Buy your phone	[b]	It was bought for me
[c]	It was passed on by someone else		

7. Scenarios presented in questionnaire:

1) Jim lives alone. One of his children has emigrated. He is 75 years old and needs to keep in touch. He has decided to get a mobile phone so he can receive pictures and messages. Who should he get advice from before he goes to buy a phone?

2) Leslie is a 75 year old with a mobile phone, which was given to him by his daughter, and he has been using it for 2 years. He now feels confident using it. She has now renewed her contract and wants to give him her old Cell Phone. Do you think he will take it?

3) Pam has had a stroke. She is worried that it will happen again. Do you think she could use her mobile phone in some way to make her feel less vulnerable?

4) Peter, aged 85, needs to take his medication every day at 12 noon and he keeps forgetting. Can his mobile phone help him?

5) Tim likes to travel alone now that he has retired. His family is concerned about him. He says they shouldn't worry because he has his mobile phone with him. Is he right? What should he do to allay their fears?

APPENDIX A: QUESTIONNAIRE

8. Tick features that the participant uses and record keys pressed to do so:	
Alarm	Games
Calculator	Torch
Calendar	Phone with Phone Book (save numbers)
Camera	Phone typing in number
Check missed calls	Photo album/gallery
SMS	Picture messaging
SMS with predictive text	Personalised ringtones
E-mail	Profiles(change volume etc.)
Transfer Money	Set reminders on calendar
FM radio	Stopwatch
Other? Features you would like to use but don't know how to: ...	

Chapter II
Analyzing Multimodal Interaction

Fernando Ferri
Istituto di Ricerche sulla Popolazione e le Politiche Sociali
Consiglio Nazionale delle Ricerche, Italy

Stefano Paolozzi
Istituto di Ricerche sulla Popolazione e le Politiche Sociali
Consiglio Nazionale delle Ricerche, Italy

ABSTRACT

Human-to-human conversation remains such a significant part of our working activities because of its naturalness. Multimodal interaction systems combine visual information with voice, gestures, and other modalities to provide flexible and powerful dialogue approaches. The use of integrated multiple input modes enables users to benefit from the natural approach used in human communication. In this paper, after introducing some definitions and concepts related to multimodal environment, we describe the different approaches used in the multimodal interaction fields showing both theoretical research and multimodal systems implementation. In particular, we will address those approaches that use the new semantic technologies as well as the ones related to the Semantic Web fields.

INTRODUCTION AND BACKGROUND

There is a great potential for combining speech and gestures and other "modalities" to improve human-computer interaction because this kind of communication resembles more and more the natural communication humans use every day with each other.

Nowadays, there is an increasing demand for a human-centred system architecture with which humans can naturally interact so that they do no longer have to adapt to the computers, but vice versa. Therefore, it is important that the user can interact with the system in the same way as with other humans, via different modalities such as speech, sketch, gestures, etc. This kind of multi-modal human-machine interaction facilitates the communication for the user of course, whereas it is quite challenging from the system's point of view.

For example, we have to cope with spontaneous speech and gestures, bad acoustical and visual conditions, different dialects and different light conditions in a room and even ungrammatical or elliptical utterances which still have to be understood correctly by the system. Therefore, we need a multimodal interaction where missing or wrongly recognized information could be resolved by adding information from other knowledge sources.

The advantages of multimodal interaction are evident if we consider practical examples. A typical example for multimodal man machine interaction which involve speech and gestures is the "Put That There" from Bolt (Bolt, 1980). Since that time, lots of research has been done in the area of speech recognition and dialogue management so that we are now in the position to integrate continuous speech and to have a more natural interaction. Although the technology was much worse in these times, the vision was very similar: to build an integrated multimodal architecture which fulfils the human needs. The two modalities can complement each other easily so that ambiguities can be resolved by sensor fusion. This complementarity has already been evaluated by different researchers and the results showed that users are able to work with a multimodal system in a more robust and stable way than with a unimodal one. The analysis of the input of each modality could therefore serve for mutual disambiguation. For example, gestures can easily complement to the pure speech input for anaphora resolution.

Another reason for multimodal interaction is the fact that in some cases the verbal description of a specific concept is too long or too complicated compared to the corresponding gesture (or even a sketch) and in these cases humans tend to prefer deictic gestures (or simple sketches) than spoken words. On the other hand, considering for example the interaction of speech and gesture modalities, there are some cases, where, for example deictic gestures are not used because the object in question is too small, it is too far away from the user, it belongs to a group of objects, etc.; here, also the principles of Gestalt theory have to be taken into account which determine whether somebody pointed to a single object or to a group of objects.

Moreover, there it has been also empirically demonstrated that the user performance is better in multimodal systems than in unimodal ones, as explained in several works (Oviatt, 1999; Cohen et al., 1997; Oviatt et al., 2004). Of course, it is clear that the importance to have a multimodal system than a unimodal one strictly depends on the type of action being performed by the user. For instance as mentioned by Oviatt (Oviatt, 1999), gesture-based inputs are advantageous, whenever spatial tasks have to be done. Although there are no actual spatial tasks in our case, there are some situations where the verbal description is much more difficult than a gesture and in these cases, users may prefer gestures.

As shown by several studies, speech seems to be the more important modality which is supported by gestures as in natural human-human communication (Corradini et al., 2002) This means that the spoken language guides the interpretation of the gesture; for example, the use of demonstrative pronouns indicates the possible appearance of a gesture. Therefore, several studies have been proved that speech and gestures modalities are co-expressive (Quek et al., 2002; McNeill & Duncan, 2000) which means that they present the same semantic concept, although different modalities are used. This observation can be extended also to other modalities that may interact with speech modality.

The advantage of using multimodal systems instead of adopting unimodal ones relies not only in the fact that there are more efficient, but also the number of critical errors can be reduced. In other words, the multimodal systems are more flexible and less error-prone and most of the users prefer them compared to unimodal ones. Furthermore, as we have been proved by several studies, the combination of both modalities strictly depends on the semantics (Oviatt, 1999).

The importance of multimodal systems is also related to the analysis of the interaction between the human user and the system itself.

Multimodal interaction can be seen as a *multimodal dialogue* between humans and computers. In this view a semantic empowered structure, is needed to manage the different aspects of the interaction. The new generation Web, the "Semantic Web" can be a solution for solving this problem. General purpose ontologies and domain ontologies make up the infrastructure of the Semantic Web, which allow for accurate data representations with relations, and data inferences. Therefore we can assert that the needed semantic infrastructure can be an ontological infrastructure.

In this paper we describe the different approaches used in the multimodal interaction fields showing both theoretical research and multimodal systems implementation. In particular we will address those approaches that use the new semantic technologies, such as ontologies from the Semantic Web field, and describe how these approaches can aid the interpretation of the multimodal dialogue between human and machines.

HUMAN INPUT MODALITIES AND LEVELS OF INTERACTION

A human-computer interaction can be described in several layers, taking the user from a specific goal, formulating a task and/or subtasks, carrying out these actions whereas receiving feedback on the physical level, and evaluating the result.

An action is usually started in order to achieve some specific goal in the user's intention, this objective which has to be prepared, and finally presented and articulated through physical actions and utterances. The presentation and feedback

by the computer passes through several stages as well, before it can be displayed to the user, possibly in various modalities including speech, haptic, etc., in order to be successfully perceived by the user.

In literature, we can discern three levels of human-computer interaction that involves different modalities, they are namely: semantic, syntactic, and lexical (Dix et al., 1993). However for more specific cases more levels can be described, for example Nielsen in his virtual protocol model (Nielsen, 1986), specified a task and a goal level above the semantic level, and an alphabetical and physical level below the lexical level. The Layered Protocol is another example of a more complex model (Taylor, 1988) used to describe the "multimodal dialogue" using the speech modality, but also applied to general user interface issues. When more modalities are included in the interaction, models have to be refined in order to be effective. Applying the Layered Protocol in the interaction, defines the concept of E-Feedback which has to do with expectations of the system of the user, and the I-Feedback which communicates the lower level interpretations of the user's actions by the system (Engel et al., 1994).

The human-computer interaction can be based on addressing all possible and available modalities, including visual, sound and speech related ones. Through these modalities, it is possible to involve all the five senses (seeing, hearing, smelling, tasting and feeling) in the interaction. For example our sense of touch, the tactual sense, has three sources: the signals from the receptors in the skin (that regulate the cutaneous sensitivity) informing our tactile sense, the receptors in the muscles and joints that regulate our awareness of the location, orientation and movement of body parts, and the signal that occurs when a person is actively moving by sending signals from the brain to the muscles. On another side haptic perception involves all three channels, which is usually the case when a person manipulates an object or interacts with systems through a physical interface (Loomis & Leederman, 1986).

21

In order to better analyse the interaction between humans and systems, it is necessary to study the different senses involved by each modalities; the majority of these studies have been done in the field of psychology of human perception. However, the majority of this research is based on stimulus-response paradigms in pre-fixed laboratory conditions.

In the context of HCI research, we also need to take into account the whole interaction cycle, and preferably study the distinct modalities in more complex situations. Indeed, in real life, perception and action are closely linked. Therefore the work of Gibson is useful in the study of human-computer interaction, because of his characterization of "active perception" and the role of the context that represents an important part of the whole interaction (Gibson, 1979). Gibson proposed to "consider the senses as perceptual systems", subdivided them in five categories (one for each sense) of systems, namely: Basic Orientation, Auditory, Haptic, Taste/Smell, and Visual. He also emphasised the activity in each system, such as listening, looking and touching rather than hearing, seeing and feeling.

Finally, interactions can be performed in several "modes" (that are different from modalities), for instance a text modality or a manipulation modality. Moreover, human actions can also be unconscious actions and in some cases also involuntary. The description of modes is primarily based on the human output modalities with which it influences its environment and communicates with other people (possibly through the use of convenient technologies). The modes that have been studied in literature are namely: symbolic (e.g., text, speech, etc.), iconic, non-verbal, (e.g. accompanying symbolic mode), involuntary (or unconscious) and even subconscious. It is important to observe that these modes are often influenced by the different contexts: for example when typing on a keyboard the movements of the fingers (gestures), may have a different meaning than, tapping on a PDA or inputting a particular device.

MULTIMODAL SYSTEM ARCHITECTURE

In this section we present a general multimodal input architecture that can be useful to understand some issues related to the analysis of interaction in human-computer multimodal systems. The architecture we describe, attempts to be modular and domain independent and is based on the works of the University of Cambridge and the MIT. Most notably, dialog management components are neglected to focus on completing the system and handling multimodal inputs; the incorporation of a dialogue manager and knowledge base into this framework is straightforward. A figure of sample architecture is presented. In Fig. 1 the overall design of a multimodal system is presented at logical level, showing the interaction between components. As we can see in the figure the multimodal system takes multimodal inputs that derive from the fusion of different modalities (e.g. speech, sketch, gesture, etc.). Each modality is characterized by a different grammar that describe the features of the particular modality and that must be implemented by the system developer.

This framework presents three kinds of component:

- A modality recogniser (for each modality) that translates user input according to the proper grammar (e.g. for speech recognizer this represent a module that translates the user's spoken words in chunk of input information)
- A multimodal input fuser that takes input from various recognisers (for each modality recognisers) and fuses their results into a complete semantic frame for the application.
- An application that accepts semantic frames and provides user feedback through multimodal output.

Figure 1. Multimodal System Architecture

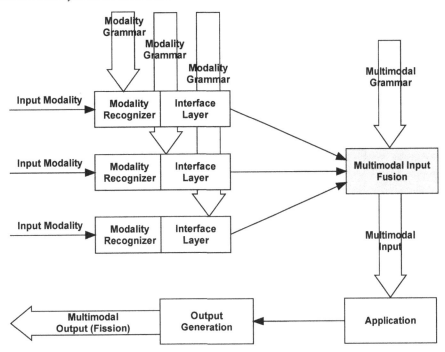

This configuration defines communication between components and isolation of the multimodal input fuser from specific recogniser technology and the application itself. Thus, the best recogniser technologies from different sources can be used and/or implemented in the overall system. In the general case, recognisers can be added to the multimodal system by writing an interface layer that converts the recogniser's output to a convenient input that conforms to those accepted by the Multimodal Input Fusion module. To apply it to the specific application, only grammars need to be written to specify the allowable modality commands and the correspondent multimodal commands that are accepted.

SEMANTIC-BASED MULTIMODAL INTERACTION PATTERNS

A number of researches have improved multimodal interaction techniques so that they appear "natural", in a human sense. Each of them has used different kinds of procedures in order to enhance the best performance of their applications. Multimodal interaction patterns refer to the possible relationships between the inputs representing a multimodal production, for example in the temporal, spatial or semantic domain. Temporal relationships, in particular, are crucial for correctly interpreting multimodal interaction, in both human-to-human and human-to-computer communication. Multimodal input fusion systems rely on such knowledge to validate or refuse possible fusion of inputs. Most of the past implemented systems have employed artificially or arbitrary defined values, even though some methods using syntactic or semantic combinations based on machine learning have been developed (Gupta & Anastasakos, 2004). The qualitative and quantitative aspects of the temporal relationships have been analyzed in several researches in order to provide a better design of multimodal input fusion modules, but also to progress the fundamental understanding of human communication.

Figure 2. Sequential and simultaneous interaction

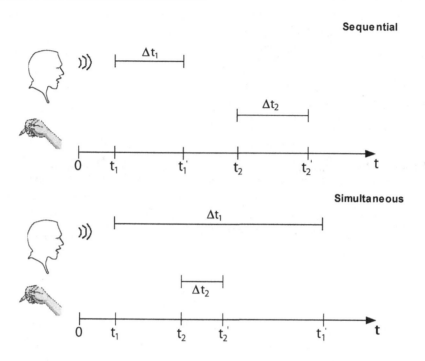

An interesting analysis of the preferred integration patterns when using pen and speech was defined in the QUICKSET system (Oviatt et al., 2004); on the basis of these researches a number of experiments were performed involving speech and handwriting. These experiments helped distinguish two groups of multimodal integrators, namely: (i) sequential and (ii) simultaneous.

The first group produced multimodal inputs sequentially, one modality at a time, in other words each time interval is characterized by only one modality. The second group considers overlapped modalities, at least partially, in the time dimension, in other words each time interval can be characterized by one or more modalities. An example of the two groups is showed in Fig. 1 (for the sake of simplicity we show only speech and sketch modalities interaction).

It is also important to state that both overlapping and non-overlapping interactions can also be divided in other six types of cooperation between modalities, namely Complementarity, Concur-

rency, Equivalence, Redundancy, Specialization and Transfer (Martin, 1997).

The authors also show that machine learning techniques could be used to quickly classify the user's temporal pattern as soon as they begin to interact (Oviatt et al., 1997; Huang et al., 2006).

Moreover, beside of the simple temporal analysis, their study also determined the types of tasks more likely to induce multimodal interaction, as opposed to unimodal interaction. It was found that spatial location commands (e.g. modify, move) represented about the 86% of all multimodal inputs, against the percentage decreases to 11% for selection commands (e.g. zoom, label), and 3% for function commands (e.g. print, scroll).

Finally, the study also shown that the order of semantic constituents in multimodal interactions from their corpus was different from the order in spoken English, but mainly due to the position of the locative constituents at the beginning in multimodal, and at the end in corresponding spoken inputs (Oviatt et al., 1997).

The study of multimodal interaction patterns has been less prominent for other modality combinations, especially when input recognition is a major concern. Typical examples are the systems involving the gesture modality.

In "Put that There" project, a sensor based on electromagnetic field variations has been used. That sensor is employed to obtain the position and orientation of the hand from a fixed transmitter. The "Put That There" device is a small cube, and requires a chord, hence is fairly cumbersome and obtrusive while only limited information can be obtained (Bolt, 1980). Data gloves that were employed later, allowed a more complex gesture inputs due to finger position sensing but as a hindrance they can prevent correct movements.

Vision-based hand tracking and shape recognition became a reality a few years later, involving a range of algorithms and devices (e.g., single or stereo cameras). However, despite of the large amount of studies and the improvements in the devices creation, vision-based recognition rates are not yet satisfactory. Due to this fact, the possibility to successfully combining such inputs with other modalities is currently seen as the most promising path to success.

Multimodal interaction patterns studies were also made in gesture and speech systems. A relevant example is the Hauptmann's framework (Hauptmann, 1989). In this framework a set of methodologies and techniques to formalise and quantify speech and gesture interaction, with a view to automation, were defined. This work is based on the study of user preferences and intuitive behaviours when using speech and hand gesture to move a 3D virtual object. As a result of this study a set of very detailed statistics were reported on the usage of words, lexicon, syntactic structure, hand and finger gestures. These statistics highlights the type of multimodal interaction preferred by users and when it occurs. However, the results appear as an unstructured set of percentages, which are difficult to implement in a generic way and lack to represent a useful way for underlining a multimodal interaction system.

Finally, a psychological approach has been used to provide a formal framework for the study of speech and gesture interaction. For example, an interesting study has underlined the existence of low level relationships between gesture, gaze and speech, suggesting cross-modal segmentation based on specific features of those modalities (Quek et al., 2000). More recently, a Hidden Markov Model-based implementation was used to improve disambiguation of speech with gestures (Kettebekov, 2004).

MULTIMODAL INTERACTION IN THE SEMANTIC WEB

The development of a context-aware, multimodal interface to the Semantic Web (Fensel et al. 2003), in other words, ontologies and semantic Web services, is a very interesting task since it combines many state-of-the-art technologies such as ontology definition, ontology management, advanced dialog systems, interface descriptions such as EMMA (Baggia et al., 2007), OWL-S (Martin et al., 2004), WSDL (Christensen et al., 2001), RDF (Beckett, 2004), SSML (Burnett et al., 2004) and composition of Web services.

A lot of interest has been shown in studying methodologies and techniques for augmenting Semantic Web applications with multimodal interfaces.

In this scenario mobile devices may serve as an easy-to-use user interaction device which can be queried by natural language speech or handwriting, and which can understand human hand gestures (for example through a mobile device camera). The main task of these researches is to develop a multimodal dialog interface providing a "natural" interaction for human users in the Human-Computer interaction paradigm (Pantic et al., 2006). Many challenging tasks, such as interaction design for mobile devices with restricted computing power, have to be addressed; practically the user should be able to use the mobile device as a question-answering system, using (as an example) speech and gestures to ask for information stored in form of ontologies, or other information like weather forecast accessible through Web services, Semantic Web pages (Web pages enriched with semantic annotation or wrapped by semantic agents), or the Internet.

In last years, several researches have been made to incorporate semantic information in some way or another with multimodal environments. We can identify two lines of researches in this context: the first one focuses on system integration while the second other focuses on interaction.

One interesting approach was developed by Irawati et al. (Irawati et al., 2005), (Irawati et al., 2006). They proposed a semantic virtual environment in which information can be classified into domain dependent and domain independent information. This information is represented through the use of convenient ontologies. The authors present their framework (MultiModal Manipulation for 3D Interaction framework, M3I) in which interaction devices such as keyboard, mouse, joystick, tracker, can be combined with speech modality to give a command to the system. They also define an object ontology based, on the authors' idea, on the common sense knowledge which defines relationships between virtual objects. Taking into account the available user context and the pre-defined object ontology, semantic integration component integrates the interpretation result from input manager, and then sends the result to the interaction manager. Therefore, this result will be used and mapped into a proper object manipulation module. In this way the system can understand the user intention and assist him achieving his objective avoiding nonsensical manipulations.

The authors state that in their solution domain dependent information is specific to the application while their domain independent information remains static. The exact coupling of the semantic information with the multimodal manipulation framework is not extensively discussed, but we suppose it to be strictly coupled with the domain independent information.

An interesting work that is based on the incorporation of semantic information in a multi-user system was proposed, always in the context of virtual systems (Otto, 2005). In this work the authors introduced a framework which combines the W3C Resource Description Framework (RDF), with his world model which has a similar structure as VRML or x3D. The above two solutions have as drawback that their semantic information is strictly connected to the system, so it is difficult to interface with other systems.

A first attempt at semantic interaction is the work of Kallman in which the framework, designed for simplicity, was created for Smart Objects. (Kallmann & Thalmann, 1999). This framework is developed in such a way that the virtual object aids the user to accomplish a pre-programmed possible interaction. Such objects are called Smart Objects, in the sense that they know how the user can interact with them, giving clues to aid the interaction. These objects have pre-defines interaction behaviours and are self-aware of how and where (the context) the user could interact with them.

The work of Abacy et al. integrates action semantics, expressed by the use of proper rules, such that these actions can be used for action planning purposes by intelligent agents trying to achieve a particular objective or task (Abacy et al., 2005).

Another interesting but slightly different approach has been proposed by Conti et al. They created a semi-automatic tool through which it is possible to understand the speech input of the user along with other modality of input (Conti et al., 2006). During the coding process of the application, it is possible to add extra semantic tags to the code which are, during the whole compilation, processed such that they can be used by the framework for understanding the input user, mapping his/her intention. This approach is very useful for speech input but it is hard to use these semantic tags for other goals.

Another reference resolution approach, that is interesting to remark, is based on the incorporation of several parameters such as a spatial references, features, common ground, naming and which are very similar to semantic information represented in ontologies (Pfeiffer & Latoschik, 2004).

Reference resolution approach was also been addressed in the VIENA system (Wachsmuth et al., 1995; Wachsmuth et al., 1997). In this system objects and places could be referenced both by writing and by word speech input accompanied by mouse clicks. The system, as stated by the authors, can distinguish three different frames of reference during the whole analysis process. Namely they are: i) *egocentric*, that is based on the user's view, that can be considered static during the interaction process, ii) *intrinsic*, that is based on particular object features (e.g., a selected front area of a desk, etc.), iii) *extrinsic*, that is based on a communication partner's view.

Martinez proposed an extension of existing open file formats (such as VRML and X3D) (Martinez, 2004). In this extension the file definition is enriched with metadata describing each object that is characterized by unique identifiers. Using this approach, Martinez proposes to use them as semantic information that can be combined with fuzzy logic for reference resolution, the resolving of the referent, which can be effectively used during interaction. The main problem of fuzzy logic, in this context, is that the system has to contain correct fuzzy sets that can be seen as a limit.

An important concept to be explored is the Semantic reflection (Latoschik & Frolich, 2007). The current approach refers to an extensible, module-based architectures that must be able to separate specific application content from the internals component of the framework. This is a challenging task due to the close data and control flow coupling but distinct data representations between the various modules. For this problem, semantic reflection can represent a possible solution. It is an extension to the pre-existent reflection paradigm from object-oriented programming

languages. Their approach is mainly oriented to permit independent model to be easily integrated (e.g. physics, graphics and haptics). This approach grants a bi-directional communication between the implemented models.

Gutiérrez et al. have presented (Gutiérrez et al., 2005) a system along with a conveniently implemented tool which allows, as stated by the authors, for real-time configuration of multimodal virtual environments. Both devices and interaction itself are presented using an xml-based formalism. Each different modality is then joined using their tool to define which particular device modality is activated by which interaction modality.

SmartWEB represents another system that studies the multimodal interaction through the use of Ontological Knowledge Bases (Engel & Sonntag, 2007; Sonntag et al., 2007). The system prototype is based on a Personal Digital Assistant (PDA). The PDA serves as an easy-to-use user interaction device which can be queried by natural language speech or handwriting, and which can understand particular signs (e.g. hand gestures) on the PDA touch-screen. It is also possible to analyze head movements that can be perceived by the PDA camera. This approach shows the strength of Semantic Web technology for information gathering during multimodal interaction, especially the integration of multiple dialog components, and show how knowledge retrieval from ontologies and Web services can be combined with advanced interaction features based on multimodal dialogue. The ontological infrastructure of SmartWEB, the SWIntO (SmartWEB Integrated Ontology), is based on an upper model ontology realized by merging well chosen concepts from two established foundational ontologies, namely DOLCE (Gangemi et al., 2002) and SUMO (Niles & Pease, 2001). These two ontologies are merged in a unique one: the SmartWEB foundational ontology SMARTSUMO (Cimiano et al., 2004).

From the analysis of these studies an important observation can be done: a key element in understanding multimodal interaction in particular for those semantic-based approaches is the reference resolution. As briefly introduced in the first part of this section, reference resolution is a process that finds the "most proper referents to referring expressions". The term referring expression is a phrase that is given by a specific user during his/her inputs (that can be typical for speech input, but it is valid also for other modalities) to refer to a specific entity (or entities). A referent is an entity (e.g. a specific object) to which the user wants to refer to.

CONCLUSION

Multimodal interaction provides the user with multiple modalities of interfacing with a system beyond the traditional input/output devices (keyboard, mouse, etc.). The user typically provides input in one or more modalities, and receives output in one or more modalities. Inputs are obviously subject to input processing. For instance, speech input may be input to a speech recognition engine, including, for instance, semantic interpretation in order to extract meaningful information.

Analyzing multimodal interaction it is important because the real interaction between humans and systems may be conflicting, in particular in that the interpretations of the input may not be consistent (e.g. the user says "yes" but clicks on "no"). Semantic information attached to the interaction session can be useful to help the interpretation of the user's will. In this paper we address the most interesting Semantic Web approaches used to give an added value to multimodal interaction systems.

REFERENCES

Abacy, T., Cyger, J., & Thalmann, D. (2005). Action semantics in smart objects. In *Workshop Towards SVE* (pp. 1-7).

Baggia, P., Burnett, D.C., Carter, J., Dahl, D.A., McCobb, G., & Raggett, D. (2007). EMMA: Extensible multimodal annotation markup language, W3C recommendation. Retrieved from http://www.w3.org/TR/emma/

Beckett, D. (Ed.). (2004). RDF/XML syntax specification (rev.), W3C recommendation. Retrieved from http://www.w3.org/TR/rdf-syntax-grammar/

Bolt, R.A. (2004). Put-that-there: Voice and gesture at the graphics interface. In *7th Annual Conference on Computer Graphics and Interactive Techniques*, Seattle, WA (pp. 262-270). New York: ACM Press.

Burnett, D.C., Walker, M.R., & Hunt, A. (Ed.). (2004). Speech synthesis markup language (SSML), version 1.0, W3C recommendation. Retrieved from http://www.w3.org/TR/speech-synthesis/

Cimiano, P., Eberhart, A., Hitzler, P., Oberle, D., Staab, S., & Studer, R. (2004). *The smartweb foundational ontology* (Tech. Rep. AIFB). University of Karlsruhe, Germany, SmartWeb Project.

Cohen, P., Johnston, M., McGee, D., Oviatt, S., Pittman, J., Smith, I., Chen, L., & Clow, J. (1997, November 9-13). QuickSet: Multimodal interaction for distributed applications. In *Proceedings of the 5th ACM International Conference on Multimedia*, Seattle, WA (pp. 31-40).

Conti, G., Ucelli, G., & De Amicis, R. (2006). "Verba volant scripta manent" a false axiom within virtual environments. A semiautomatic tool for retrieval of semantics understanding for speech-enabled vr applications. *Computers & Graphics, 30*(4), 619-628.

Corradini, A., Wesson, R., Cohen, P. (2002, October 14-16). A map-based system using speech and 3D gestures for pervasive computing. In *Proceedings of the 4th IEEE International Conference on Multimodal Interfaces (ICMI'02)*, Pittsburgh, PA (pp. 191-196).

Christensen, E., Curbera, F., Meredith, G., & Weerawarana, S. (2001). Web services description language (WSDL) 1.1, W3C note. Retrieved from http://www.w3.org/TR/wsdl

Dix, A., Finlay, J., Abowd, G., & Beale, R. (1993). *Human-computer interaction*. Englewoods Cliffs: Prentice Hall.

Engel, F.L., Goossens, P., & Haakma, R. (1994). Improved efficiency through I- and E-feedback: A trackball with contextual force feedback. *International Journal Man- Machine Studies, 41*, 949-974.

Engel, R., & Sonntag, D. (2007). Text generation in the smartWeb multimodal dialogue system. In *KI 2007* (pp. 448-451).

Fensel, D., Hendler, J.A., Lieberman, H., & Wahlster, W. (Eds.). (2003). Spinning the Semantic Web: Bringing the World Wide Web to its full potential. In D. Fensel, J.A. Hendler, H. Lieberman, & W. Wahlster (Eds.) *Spinning the Semantic Web*. MIT Press.

Gangemi, A., Guarino, N., Masolo, C., Oltramari, A., & Schcneider, L. (2002). Sweetening ontologies with DOLCE. In *13th International Conference on Knowledge Engineering and Knowledge Management (EKAW02),* Spain (LNCS 2473, p. 166).

Gibson, J.J. (1979). *The ecological approach to visual perception*. Boston: Houghton Mifflin.

Gutiérrez, M., Thalmann, D., & Vexo, F. (2005). Semantic virtual environments with adaptive multimodal interfaces. In *Proceedings of the 11th International Multimedia Modeling Conference 2005* (pp. 277-283).

Gupta, A.K., & Anastasakos, T. (2004, October 4-8). Dynamic time windows for multimodal input fusion. In *Proceedings of the 8th International Conference on Spoken Language Processing (INTERSPEECH 2004 - ICSLP)*, Jeju, Korea (pp. 1009-1012).

Kallmann, M., & Thalmann, D. (1999). Direct 3D interaction with smart objects. In *Proceedings of the ACM symposium VRST* (pp. 124-130).

Kettebekov, S. (2004, October 13-15). Exploiting prosodic structuring of coverbal gesticulation. In *Proceedings of the 6th International Conference on Multimodal Interfaces (ICMI 2004)*, State College, PA (pp. 105-112). New York: ACM Press.

Hauptmann, A.G. (1989). Speech and gestures for graphic image manipulation. In *SIGCHI Conference on Human Factors in Computing Systems: Wings for the Mind*, (pp. 241-245). New York: ACM Press.

Huang, X., Oviatt, S., & Lunsford, R. (2006). Combining user modeling and machine learning to predict users' multimodal integration patterns. In S. Renals, S. Bengio, & J.G. Fiscus (Eds.), *MLMI 2006* (LNCS 4299, pp. 50-62). Heidelberg: Springer.

Irawati, S., Calder'on, D., & Ko., H. (2005). Semantic 3D object manipulation using object ontology in multimodal interaction framework. In *Proceedings of ICAT'05* (pp. 35-39).

Irawati, S., Calder'on, D., & Ko., H. (2006). Spatial ontology for semantic integration in 3D multimodal interaction framework. In *ACM International Conference on VRCIA* (pp. 129-135).

Latoschik, M.E., & Frolich, C. (1986). Semantic reflection for intelligent virtual environments. In *Virtual Reality Conference, 2007 (VR '07)* (pp. 305-306). IEEE.

Loomis, J.M., & Leederman, S.J. (1986). Tactual perception. In *Handbook of Perception and Human Pperformance* (p. 31).

Martin, D., Burstein, M., Hobbs, J., Lassila, O., McDermott, D., McIlraith, S., Narayanan, S., Paolucci, M., Parsia, B., Payne, T., Sirin, E., Srinivasan, N., & Sycara, K. (2004). OWL-S: Semantic markup for Web services, W3C member submission. Retrieved from http://www.w3.org/Submission/OWL-S/

Martin, J.C. (1997). Toward intelligent cooperation between modalities: The example of a system enabling multimodal interaction with a map. In *Proceedings of the International Conference on Artificial Intelligence (IJCAI'97) Workshop on Intelligent Multimodal Systems*, Nagoya, Japan.

Martınez, J. I. (2004). *An intelligent guide for virtual environments with fuzzy queries and flexible management of stories.* Unpublished doctoral dissertation, Universidad de Murcia.

McNeill, D., & Duncan, S. (2000). Growth points in thinking-for speaking. In D. McNeill (Ed.), *Language and Gesture.* Cambridge, MA: Cambridge University Press.

Nielsen, J. (1986). A virtual protocol model for computer-human interaction. *International Journal Man-Machine Studies, 24*, 301-312.

Niles, I., & Pease, A. (2001, October). Towards a standard upper ontology. In C. Welty, & B. Smith (Eds.), *Proceedings of the 2nd International Conference on Formal Ontology in Information Systems (FOIS-2001)*, Ogunquit, ME.

Otto, K. A. (2005). The semantics of multiuser virtual environments. In *Workshop towards SVE* (pp. 35-39).

Oviatt, S. (1999). Mutual disambiguation of recognition errors in a multimodal architecture. In *Proceedings of the Conference on Human Factors in Computing Systems (CHI'99)* (pp. 576-583). New York: ACM Press.

Oviatt, S. (1999, November). Ten myths of multimodal interaction. In *Communications of the ACM, 42*(11), 74-81.

Oviatt, S., Coulston, R., & Lunsford, R. (2004, October 13-15). When do we interact multimodally? Cognitive load and multimodal communication pattern. In *the 6th International Conference on Multimodal Interfaces (ICMI 2004)*, State College, PA (pp. 129-136). New York: ACM Press.

Oviatt, S., Coulston, R., Tomko, S., Xiao, B., Lunsford, R., Wesson, M., & Carmichael, L. (2003, November 5-7). Toward a theory of organized multimodal integration patterns during human-computer interaction. In *the 5th International Conference on Multimodal Interfaces (ICMI 2003)*, Vancouver, Canada (pp. 44-51). New York: ACM Press.

Oviatt, S., DeAngeli, A., & Kuhn, K. (1997, March 22-27). Integration and synchronization of input modes during multimodal human-computer interaction. In *SIGCHI Conference on Human Factors in Computing Systems*, Atlanta, GA (pp. 415-422).

Pfeiffer, T., & Latoschik, E. (2004). Resolving object references in multimodal dialogues for immersive virtual environments. In *Proceedings of the IEEE VR2004*, Chicago, IL (pp. 35-42).

Pantic, M., Pentland, A., Nijholt, A., & Huang, T. (2006). Human computing and machine understanding of human behavior: A survey. In *Proceedings of the 8th International conference on Multimodal Interfaces (ICMI '06)*, New York, NY (pp. 239-248). ACM Press.

Quek, F., McNeill, D., Bryll, R., Kirbas, C., Arlsan, H., McCullough, K.E., Furuyama, N., & Gesture, A.R. (2000, June 13-15). Speech and gaze cues for discourse segmentation. In *IEEE Conference on computer Vision and Pattern Recognition (CVPR 2000)*, Hilton Head Island, SC (pp. 247-254).

Quek, F., McNeill, D., Bryll, B., Duncan, S., Ma, X., Kirbas, C., McCullough, K.-E., & Ansari, R. (2002, September). Multimodal human discourse: Gesture and speech. *ACM Transactions on Computer-Human Interaction (TOCHI), 9*(3).

Sonntag, D., Engel, R., Herzog, G., Pfalzgraf, A., Pfleger, N., Romanelli, M., & Reithinger, N. (2007). SmartWeb handheld - multimodal interaction with ontological knowledge bases and Semantic Web services. *Artifical Intelligence for Human Computing 2007*, 272-295.

Taylor, M.M. (1988). Layered protocol for computer-human dialogue. *International Journal Man-Machine Studies, 28*, 175-218.

Wachsmuth, I., Lenzmann, B., & Cao, Y. (1995). *VIENA: A Multiagent Interface to a Virtual Environment (ICMAS 1995)* (p. 465).

Wachsmuth, I., Lenzmann, B., Jörding, T., Jung, B., Latoschik, M.E., & Fröhlich, M. (1997). A virtual interface agent and its agency. *Agents 1997*, 516-517.

KEY TERMS AND DEFINITIONS

Gestalt Theory: Gestalt psychology (also Gestalt of the Berlin School) is a theory of mind and brain that proposes that the operational principle of the brain is holistic, parallel, and analog, with self-organizing tendencies; or, that the whole is different than the sum of its parts. The classic Gestalt example is a soap bubble, whose spherical shape is not defined by a rigid template, or a mathematical formula, but rather it emerges spontaneously by the parallel action of surface tension acting at all points in the surface simultaneously. This is in contrast to the "atomistic" principle of operation of the digital computer, where every computation is broken down into a sequence of simple steps, each of which is computed independently of the problem as a whole. The Gestalt effect refers to the form-forming capability of our senses, particularly with respect to the visual recognition of figures and whole forms instead of just a collection of simple lines and curves.

Modality: The term is used to describe the distinct method of operation within a computer system, in which the same user input can produce different results depending of the state of the computer. It also defines the mode of communication according to human senses or type of computer input devices. In terms of human senses the categories are sight, touch, hearing, smell, and taste. In terms of computer input devices we have modalities that are equivalent to human senses: cameras (sight), haptic sensors (touch), microphones (hearing), olfactory (smell), and even taste. In addition, however, there are input devices that do not map directly to human senses: keyboard, mouse, writing tablet, motion input (e.g., the device itself is moved for interaction), and many others.

Multimodality: By definition, "multimodal" should refer to using more than one modality, regardless of the nature of the modalities. However, many researchers use the term "multimodal" referring specifically to modalities that are commonly used in communication between people, such as speech, gestures, handwriting, and gaze. Multimodality seamlessly combines graphics, text and audio output with speech, text, and touch input to deliver a dramatically enhanced end user experience. When compared to a single-mode of interface in which the user can only use either voice/ audio or visual modes, multimodal applications gives them multiple options for inputting and receiving information.

Multimodal Fusion: A strong argument for multimodal input processing is what is generally referred to as multimodal fusion. By combining information coming from different modalities it is possible to improve recognition quality and/or confidence. However, multimodal fusion relies fundamentally on different modalities containing redundant information. It is important to distinguish between fusion at the signal level and fusion at the semantic level. In the case of lip movements and speech, fusion is theoretically possible at the signal level, while in the famous "put that there" example of deictic dereferencing, fusion is possible (and necessary) only at the semantic level. For semantic fusion to operate, both modalities need to have their own independent level of accuracy and confidence.

Multimodal System: In the general sense, a multimodal system is defined as the particular system which supports communication with the user through different modalities such as voice, handwriting, gesture, emotions, etc. Literally, the term "multi" refers to "more than one" and the term "modal" may cover the notion of "modality" as well as that of "mode". Modality refers to the type of communication channel used to acquire information. It also covers the way an idea is expressed or perceived, or the manner an action is performed. Mode refers to a state that determines the way information is interpreted to extract or convey meaning. In an interaction process, whether it is between humans or between human users and a computer system, both the modality and the mode come into play. The modality defines the type of data exchanged whereas the mode determines the context in which the data is interpreted. Therefore, if we consider a more system-centered view, multimodality can be seen as the capacity of the system to communicate with a user by means of different types of communication channels and to extract and convey meaning automatically. It is possible to state that both multimedia and multimodal systems use multiple communication channels. But in addition, a multimodal system is able to automatically model the content of the information at a higher level of abstraction

NLP: The term is the acronym of Natural Language Processing (NLP). NLP is a range of computational techniques for analyzing and representing naturally occurring text (free text) at one or more levels of linguistic analysis (e.g., morphological, syntactic, semantic, pragmatic) for the purpose of achieving human-like language processing for knowledge-intensive applications. NLP includes:

- *Speech synthesis:* Although this may not at first sight appear very 'intelligent', the synthesis of natural-sounding speech is technically complex and almost certainly requires some understanding of what is being spoken to ensure, for example, correct intonation;

- *Speech recognition:* Basically the reduction of continuous sound waves to discrete words.

- *Natural language understanding:* Here treated as moving from isolated words to "meaning"; Natural language generation: generating appropriate natural language responses to unpredictable inputs.

- *Machine translation:* Translating one natural language into another.

Resource Description Framework (RDF): RDF is the standard for encoding metadata and other knowledge on the Semantic Web. In the Semantic Web, computer applications make use of structured information spread in a distributed and decentralized way throughout the current Web. RDF is an abstract model, a way to break down knowledge into discrete pieces, and while it is most popularly known for its RDF/XML syntax, RDF can be stored in a variety of formats. This article discusses the abstract RDF model, two concrete serialization formats, how RDF is used and how it differs from plain XML, higher-level RDF semantics, best practices for deployment, and querying RDF data sources.

Semantic Web: The Semantic Web is an evolving extension of the World Wide Web in which the semantics of information and services on the Web is defined, making it possible for the Web to understand and satisfy the requests of people and machines to use the Web content. It derives from Tim Berners-Lee's vision of the Web as a universal medium for data, information, and knowledge exchange. The Semantic Web core comprises a set of design principles, collaborative working groups, and a variety of enabling technologies. Some elements of the Semantic Web are expressed as prospective future possibilities that have yet to be implemented or realized.

Usability: The term identifies that quality of a system that makes it easy to learn, easy to use and encourages the user to regard the system as a positive help in getting the job done. Usability is defined by five quality components. Learnability that defines how easy it is for users to accomplish basic tasks the first time they encounter the design. Efficiency that defines users' quickness in performing tasks. Memorability, that is important when users return to the design after a period of not using it, in order to define how easily they can re-establish proficiency. Errors, that defines how many errors users make, how severe are these errors, and how easily they can recover from errors. Satisfaction: that defines the satisfaction of the users using the systems.

User: A person, organization, or other entity, that employs the services provided by an information processing system, for transfer of information. A user functions as a source or final destination of user information. An end user is any individual who runs an application program or system.

User-Centered Design: The term identifies a design process in which the needs, wants, and limitations of the end user of an interface or an application play an important and extensive role. User-centered design can be characterized as a multi-stage problem solving process that not only requires designers to analyze and foresee how users are likely to use an interface, but to test the validity of their assumptions with regards to user behaviour in real world tests with actual users. This kind of testing is necessary as it is often very difficult for the designers and the developers of an interface to understand intuitively what a first-time user of their design experiences, and what each user's learning curve may look like.

Virtual Environments Systems: Virtual environments systems are interactive, highly-intuitive computer systems that give users the illusion of displacement to another location. Generally the restrictive approaches define virtual environments as three-dimensional, real time, immersive, multi-sensorial and interactive simulations of a space that can be experienced by users via three-dimensional input and output devices and through different I/O modalities (such as speech, sketch, gesture, handwriting, etc.). Virtual environments technology will better accommodate the unique characteristics of human users. Indeed, we can define virtual environments as interactive, virtual displays enhanced by special processing and by non-visual modalities (such as speech and haptic as an example), to convince users that they are immersed in a "virtual" space.

Chapter III
Exploring Multimodal Input Fusion Strategies

Arianna D'Ulizia

Istituto di Ricerche sulla Popolazione e le Politiche Sociali
Consiglio Nazionale delle Ricerche, Italy

ABSTRACT

Human-computer interaction is a discipline that aims at enabling the interaction between humans and computational machines. In the last years, several efforts have been made to make this interaction more intuitive and natural. In this direction, multimodal interaction has emerged as the future paradigm of human-computer interaction. In order to enable a natural dialogue between users and computer systems, in multimodal systems the two main challenges to face are: to combine and integrate information from different input modalities (fusion process) and to generate appropriate output information (fission process). Our specific concern in this chapter is with the fusion of multiple input modalities.

INTRODUCTION

In recent years, people are increasingly surrounded by objects in the everyday environment that are equipped with embedded software and wireless communication facilities and which they need to interact with. For instance, mobile phones, PDAs and portable PCs are used by an increasing amount of people to develop everyday activities. This phenomenon produces the need to simplify the access to these technological devices by rendering human-computer interaction more similar to human-human communication. As a consequence, the "universal accessibility" concept is acquiring an important role in the research area of human-computer interaction (HCI). This discipline deals with the design, development and implementation of computational systems devoted to enable the interaction with human beings. Three of the main emerging research directions of the HCI, in line with the universal accessibility concept, are: (i) to make this interaction more intuitive, natural and efficient by integrating multiple input-output modalities, (ii) to enable a broader spectrum of users, with different ages and skill levels as well as users with disabilities, to access technological devices, and (iii) to increase the level of freedom offered to users. In particular, multimodal interaction, which refers to the simultaneous or alternative use of several modalities, has emerged as the future paradigm of human-computer interaction that advances the implementation of universal accessibility.

This enhancement is also demonstrated by the studies of Oviatt et al. (Oviatt et al., 1997; Oviatt and Cohen, 2000; Oviatt et al., 2000) that emphasize the benefits of multimodal systems in terms of usability, accessibility, flexibility and efficiency compared to unimodal ones. In particular, a multimodal interaction improves usability, as it provides users with the means to choose among different available modalities. Secondly, multimodality improves accessibility to the device by encompassing a broader spectrum of users, enabling those of different ages and skill levels as well as users with disabilities. Finally, it offers improved flexibility and interaction efficiency.

Several aspects characterize multimodal interaction compared to usual interaction through graphical user interfaces (GUIs). Firstly, a GUI requires atomic and unambiguous inputs (such as the selection of an element by mouse or the insertion of a character by keyboard), whereas a multimodal interaction involves several simultaneous inputs that have to be recognized and opportunely combined by managing the uncertainty of inputs through probabilistic techniques. The process of integrating information from various input modalities and combining them into a complete command is called *multimodal fusion*. Secondly, in a multimodal interaction temporal constraints of inputs have to be taken into account and consequently it requires a time-sensitive architecture and the recording of time intervals of each

modalities. Finally, in a GUI the output messages are conveyed to the user through a single medium (the graphical display), whereas in a multimodal system a way of disaggregating outputs through the various channels has to be found in order to provide the user with consistent feedback. This process is called *multimodal fission*, in contrast with multimodal fusion.

Consequently, in the design and development of a multimodal system the two main challenges to face concern the multimodal fusion and fission processes. Our specific concern in this chapter is with the fusion of multiple input modalities. In particular, we intend to give a comprehensive analysis of current fusion approaches, considering two main classifications, namely according to the data fusion level (e.g. the fusion process takes places in the dialogue management system, as well as at grammar level) and the mathematical method (e.g. based on statistical or artificial intelligence techniques).

The remainder of the chapter is organized as follows. After a brief introduction about basic terms and concepts of human-computer interaction theory, we investigate current multimodal fusion mechanisms, classifying them according to the data fusion level and the applied mathematical method. Final conclusions are given at the end of the chapter.

BACKGROUND

In this section we review some basic terms and concepts of human-computer interaction theory.

The success of the human-computer communication depends on the reaching of a common ground by exchanging information through the communication modalities. Such a communication modality refers to the medium or channel of communication that conveys information (Coutaz and Caelen, 1991). Multimodality refers to the quality of a system to allow more than one communication modality to be used during human-computer interaction.

A general model of multimodal human-computer communication is shown in Figure 1. Four different kinds of input/output communication modalities can be identified, according to the study of Schomaker et al. (Schomaker, 1995):

- The *human output modalities*, that are devoted to control and manipulate computational systems by achieving a high level of interactivity and naturalness of the multimodal interface. The speech is the dominant modality that carries most of the information content of a multimodal dialogue. However, gesture and gaze modalities are extensively studied in literature as efficient input modalities that are better suited to represent spatio-temporal information and are usually complementary modalities of the speech input;

- The *human input channels*, that are devoted to perceive and acquire information coming from the feedback channels of computational systems. The most frequently used perception channels are eyes, ears and touch, among which the first is the dominant input modality that receives the most information flow, followed by the auditive and tactile channels;

- The *computer input channels*, through which the computer gets information from the human output modalities. Some examples of computer input channels are microphone, camera, keyboard, mouse. Once acquired, the inputs need to be brought together and interpreted in order to give a coherent meaning to the multimodal act of the user;

- The *computer output modalities*, that are devoted to give feedback to the user, as, for instance, visual feedback, speech synthesizer, haptic feedback and so on.

In order to allow that the multimodal human-computer communication process takes place successfully, the actions that the user expresses through the human output modalities have to be acquired by the system through the computer input modalities, and the human input channels of the user have to be able to perceive and understand feedback from the computer output channels.

The informational flow that involves the human output and computer input modalities is named *input flow*, whereas the flow that involves the human input and computer output channels is named *feedback flow*. The multimodal fusion takes place during the input flow, therefore in this chapter we focus the discussion on this. In

Figure 1. The multimodal human-computer communication process

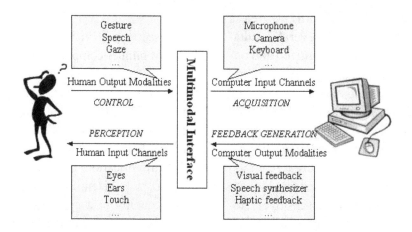

particular, the acquisition and integration, by the side of the system, of the multimodal inputs that the user expresses through the human output modalities will be our specific topic.

Concerning the human output modalities, six different types of cooperation between these modalities can be identified, as described in the typology proposed by Martin et al. (2001):

- **Equivalence:** Several modalities cooperate by equivalence if the same information may be processed as an alternative by either of them;
- **Specialization:** Modalities cooperate by specialization if a specific kind of information is always processed by the same modality;
- **Redundancy:** Modalities cooperate by redundancy if the same information is processed by these modalities;
- **Complementarity:** Several modalities cooperate by complementarity if different information are processed by each modality but have to be merged;
- **Transfer:** Modalities cooperate by transfer if information produced by a modality is used by another modality;
- **Concurrency:** Several modalities cooperate by concurrency if different information are processed by several modalities at the same time but must not be merged.

In multimodal systems, fusion techniques are mostly applied to complementary and redundant modalities in order to integrate the information provided by them. In particular, complementary modalities provide the system with non-redundant information that have to be merged in order to get a complete and meaningful message. In the same way, redundant modalities require a fusion process that avoids non-meaningful information, increasing, at the same time, the accuracy of the fused message by using one modality to disambiguate information in the other ones.

Having looked at conceptual aspects of multimodal communication, we now turn to architectural features of a multimodal system. A common architecture of a multimodal system (Oviatt, 2002), that involves speech, sketch and handwriting modalities, is depicted in Figure 2. During the acquisition phase, the input that the user expresses through these human output modalities is acquired through the appropriate computer input channels (touch-pad for sketch and handwriting, and microphone for speech) and processed by the related recognition modules (sketch and handwriting recognition and Natural Language Processing (NLP), respectively) in the subsequent recognition phase. Afterwards, the multimodal fusion system carries out the integration of the recognized inputs, by removing possible redundancy, merging complementary information from each modality and synchronizing the information in order to produce a meaningful and correct input. At this point, the dialogue management system aims at processing the integrated multimodal message/command by activating appropriate applications and service in order to retrieve the output to be returned to the user (decision phase).

The mapping between the input message expressed by the user and the corresponding output returned by the system is defined *input interpretation*. Thus the interpretation process involves, generally, four phases, corresponding to the main architectural levels of a multimodal system, from the top to the bottom (see Figure 2): the acquisition, recognition, integration and decision phases (levels). Although the acquisition, recognition and decision are consecutive phases, the same doesn't occur for the integration phase (where the fusion process takes place), because in some systems the integration phase is prior to the recognition or decision phases, whereas in other systems it's just the opposite.

Multimodal systems have been largely studied since the 1980's when the first original system "put-that-there" was developed by Bolt (1980). This system used speech and the location of a

Figure 2. A common architecture of a multimodal system

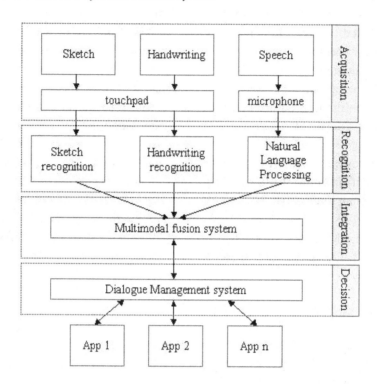

cursor on a touchpad display to allow simple deictic reference, as for example "create a blue square here". Note that a deictic is a word (e.g., "this", "that", "here", "there", etc.) that specifies identity or spatial or temporal location from the perspective of a speaker in the context in which the communication occurs. Deictic expressions are commonly used in multimodal interaction.

As well as the "put-that-there" system, several attempts to overcome common graphical user interface have been made since the 1990's until now (Neal and Shapiro, 1991; Nigay and Coutaz, 1995; Cohen et al. 1997; Vo, 1998; Wahlster et al. 2001). CUBRICON (Neal and Shapiro, 1991) used typed and spoken sentences and deictic mouse clicks as input in order to interact with a two-dimensional map. MATIS (Multimodal Airline Travel Information System) (Nigay and Coutaz, 1995) allows the user to ask for information about the departure/arrival time of air flights by using

speech and pen-based gesture modalities, along with mouse clicks and keyboarding. QuickSet (Cohen et al. 1997) was developed with the aim of training Californian military troops and used speech and pen-based gestures to interact with a geo-referenced map. QuickTour (Vo, 1998) is a multimodal system that enables a spoken and pen-based interaction to navigate geographical maps. The Smartkom (Wahlster et al. 2001) is another multimodal dialogue system that merges gesture, speech and facial expressions for both input and output via an anthropomorphic and affective user interface.

In the next sections we illustrate some of the main characteristics of multimodal fusion, namely the data fusion level (e.g. the fusion process takes places in the dialogue management system, as well as at grammar level) and the adopted mathematical method (e.g. based on statistical or artificial intelligence techniques). We also provide several examples of fusion approaches corresponding to the illustrated characteristics.

DATA FUSION LEVELS IN MULTIMODAL FUSION

The input signals, expressed by the user through the human output modalities and acquired by the system through the computer input modalities, can be combined at several different levels (Sharma et al. 1998). As introduced in the previous section, a multimodal system is composed of four main architectural levels (acquisition, recognition, integration and decision). The integration level, in which the fusion of the input signals is performed, may be placed: (i) immediately after the acquisition level and we refer to the *fusion at the acquisition*, or signal, *level*; (ii) immediately after the recognition level and in this case we refer to the *fusion at the recognition*, or feature, *level*; (iii) during the decision level and we refer to the *fusion at the decision*, or conceptual, *level*.

The *fusion at the acquisition level* (see Figure 3.a) consists in mixing two or more, generally electrical, signals. As this kind of fusion may be performed if the signals are synchronized and of the same nature (two speech inputs, two sketch inputs, etc.) it cannot be applied to multimodal inputs, which may be of different nature. Consequently, we don't take into account this level of fusion hereafter.

The *fusion at the recognition level* (named also *early fusion* or *recognition/feature-based fusion*) consists in merging the outcomes of each recognizer by using integration mechanisms, such as, for example, statistical integration techniques, agent theory, hidden Markov models, artificial neural networks, etc. The integrated sentence is therefore processed by the decision manager that provides the most probable interpretation of the sentence (see Figure 3.b). Thus a unimodal recognition stage and an integrated decision stage characterize the interpretation process of the

early fusion. This strategy is generally preferred for closely and synchronized inputs that convey the same information (redundant modalities), as for example speech and lip movements for speech recognition or voice and video features for emotion recognition. The main drawbacks of the early fusion are the necessity of a large amount of data for the training, and the high computational costs.

The *fusion at the decision level* (named also *late fusion* or *decision/conceptual-based fusion*) means merging neither the signals nor the features of each recognized input, but directly the semantic information that are extracted from the specific decision managers (see Figure 3.c). In fact, in this kind of fusion the outcomes of each recognizer are separately interpreted by the decision managers and the extracted semantic meanings are integrated by using specific dialogue-driven fusion procedures to yield the complete interpretation. Late fusion is mostly suitable for modalities that differ both in their nature and in the time scale. This implies that a tight synchrony among the various communicative modalities is essential to deliver the correct information at the right time. As each input modality is separately recognized and interpreted, the main advantages of this kind of fusion rely on the use of standard and well-tested recognizers and interpreters for each modality, as well as the greater simplicity of the fusion algorithms.

In addition to these three levels of multimodal fusion, a fourth level, named *hybrid multi-level fusion*, can be identified (as described also in (Vo, 1998)). In this kind of fusion the integration of input signals is distributed among the acquisition, the recognition and decision levels. In particular, the interdependence among modalities, that allows predicting subsequent symbols knowing previous symbols in the input data flow, is exploited to improve accuracy of the interpretation process. This implies that a joint multimodal language model, which relies on the symbols acquired during the acquisition phase and is governed by their semantic meanings extracted during the decision phase, is the basis of the hybrid multi-level fusion strategy.

To sum up, depending on the data fusion level at which the input signals are combined multi-modal fusion strategies can be broadly classified as: recognition-based, decision-based and hybrid multi-level.

Recognition-Based Fusion Strategies

To achieve the integration of input signals at recognition level, multimodal systems have to rely on appropriate structures to represent these signals. In particular, three main representations

Figure 3. Possible levels of multimodal data fusion: a) fusion at signal level; b) fusion at recognition level; c) fusion at decision level

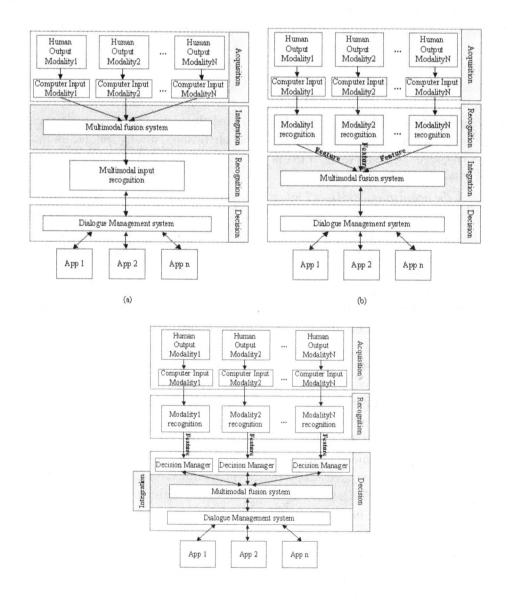

can be found in literature, namely: action frame (Vo, 1998), input vectors (Pavlovic et al., 1997) and slots (Andre et al., 1998).

In the approach based on *action frame*, proposed by Vo (1998), the multimodal input is regarded as a set of parallel information streams. Each stream represents one unimodal input coming from a computer input modality (e.g. a sequence of words and phrases in spoken modality, shapes in gestures, etc.) and consists of elements associated to a set of parameters. The integration of unimodal inputs consists in producing a sequence of input segments, named parameter slot, which separately contributes to the multimodal input interpretation, that is called action frame. Such an action frame specifies the action that has to be performed in response to the multimodal input. Each parameter slot specifies one action parameter and should contain enough information to determine the value of the corresponding parameter. The integration of the information streams is carried out through the training of a Multi-State Mutual Information Network (MS-MIN). More in detail, this network allows to find an input segmentation and a corresponding parameter slot assignment in order to extract the actual action parameters from the multimodal input. To achieve that the *a posteriori* probability of the parameter slot assignment conditional on the input segmentation is introduced. This probability is estimated by output activations in the MS-MIN network and can be interpreted as the score of a path that goes through the segmented parameter slots. An example of path over two multidimensional inputs (the spoken words "How far is it from here to there" and the drawing of an arrow between two points) is shown in Figure 4.

Therefore, a path score maximization algorithm is applied to find the input segmentation and the corresponding parameter slot assignment. This algorithm creates an extra layer on top of the network. In particular, each output unit of the MS-MIN is an output state and the top layer of the network produces the best sequence of states that fits the input, according to the path score maximization algorithm. The main advantage of this approach relies on the use of the MS-MIN network that allows the incremental and automatic learning of the mapping from input messages to output actions and the consequent improvement of the interpretation accuracy during the real use.

The *input vectors* proposed by Pavlovic et al. (1997) are used to store the outputs of the visual and auditory interpretation modules. More in detail, the visual module firstly tracks the features of the video data by using skin color region segmentation and motion-based region tracking algorithms and the time series of the tracked features is stored into an input vector. Secondly, these features are dynamically classified by using Probabilistic Independence Networks (PINs) and Hidden Markov Models (HMMs). Therefore, the output of this module consists in a set of higher level features ranged from gestural movement elements, called visemes (e.g. "left movement"), to full gestural words (e.g. symbol for "rotate about x-axis"). The auditory module has the same architecture and functioning of the visual module applied to audio data. A HMM PIN allows to classify the auditory features into auditory elements, called phones, and full spoken words. The integration of the two interaction modalities is carried out through a set of HMM PIN structures (see Figure 5), each corresponding to a predefined audio/visual command. The state of each HMM is defined according to the input vectors containing the high level features coming from the auditory and visual modules. As the multimodal integration occurs after a two-stage recognition process (for audio and visual data, distinctly) and before the interpretation of the joint features has been performed, the fusion approach of Pavlovic et al., similarly to the action frame approach, can be classified as a recognition-based fusion strategy.

In the strategy based on *slots* (Andre et al., 1998), the information inputted by the user is stored into a slot buffer, which allows back referencing of past lexical units (e.g.: "it" can be used

Figure 4. The output path of the MS-MIN of Vo (1998)

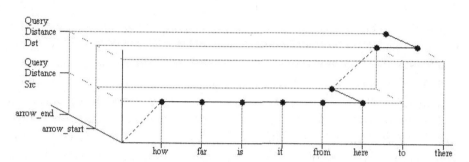

Figure 5. The multimodal integration approach of Pavlovic et al. (1997)

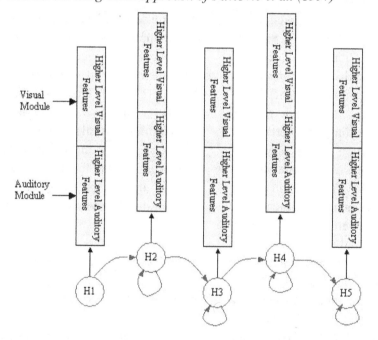

to reference the previously selected object). The command language of the application is encoded in semantic units called frames. The command frames are composed of slots, i.e. lexical units provided by the multimodal input. For instance, considering the "move frame" two slots can be identified: "object" (to specify the object) and "where" (to specify the final position). The frames are predefined (computed off line) and are application-dependent. The parser extracts the lexical units from different input modalities and fills the appropriate slots in the slot buffer. The slot buffer is continuously monitored checking for filled frames. Once a frame is filled (enough information to generate a command), the fusion agent sends it to be executed in the current application. The main advantage of this architecture is the uniform access of the input modes.

In all the three fusion strategies, described above, the input signals are merged after recognizers have transformed them into a more appropriate representation (action frames, input vectors, and slots) but before any interpretation has been assigned to the unimodal input. This has led us to classify them as recognition-based fusion strategies.

The main advantage of these strategies relies on the great coherence with the human-human communication paradigm in which the dialogue is considered as a unique and multimodal communication act. Analogously, the recognition-based fusion strategies merge the recognized inputs into a unique multimodal sentence that has to be opportunely interpreted. Moreover, they allow an easier inter-modality disambiguation. The main drawbacks of the recognition-based fusion strategies consist in the significant computational load and the high dependency on time measures. This dependency implies as well a large amount of real data to train the network (both the MS-MIN and the PIN HMM).

Decision-Based Fusion Strategies

In the decision-based approach, the outcomes of each recognizer are separately interpreted by specific decision managers and then sent to the dialogue management system that performs their integration by using specific dialogue-driven fusion procedures to yield the complete interpretation. To represent the partial interpretations coming from the decision managers and achieve the integration of input signals at decision level, past and actual multimodal systems employ several kinds of structures, namely: *typed feature structures* (Cohen et al., 1997; Johnston, 1998), *melting pots* (Nigay and Coutaz, 1995; Bouchet et al., 2004), *semantic frames* (Vo and Wood, 1996; Russ et al., 2005), and *time-stamped lattices* (Corradini et al., 2003).

The *typed feature structures*, originally proposed by Carpenter (1992), are used by Cohen et al. (1997) to represent the semantic contributions of the different input modalities. In particular, this data structure consists of a two main elements: the type that specifies the class which the input

to be represented belongs to, and a collection of feature-value pairs, in which the values can be atoms or another feature structure. An example of typed feature structure representing the syntactic features of a proper noun is shown in Figure 6.a. Feature structures and atoms are assigned to hierarchically ordered types. The authors achieve the integration of spoken and gestural inputs through a unification operation over these typed feature structures. Such operation requires pairs of feature structures or pairs of atoms that are compatible in type and the result of the unification is the more specific feature structure or atom in the type hierarchy. Figure 6.c shows the unification of the two feature structures represented in Figures 6.a and 6.b., that is the syntactic features of the word "dog". To select the best unified interpretation among the alternative solutions probabilities are associated with each unimodal input. This decision-based fusion strategy is implemented in QuickSet, a multimodal system briefly described in the background section.

Johnston (1998) carries on the study of Cohen et al. (1997) introducing a grammar representation in which spoken phrases and pen gestures are the terminal elements of the grammar, referred to as lexical edges. Each lexical edge is assigned grammatical representations in the form of typed feature structures. For instance, to represent the spoken word 'helicopter' the feature structure in Figure 7 is created, where the *cat* feature indicates the basic category of the element, the *content* feature specifies the semantic content, and the remaining features represent the modality, temporal interval and the probability associated with the edge. Multimodal grammar rules are encoded as feature structure rule schemata that can be hierarchically ordered allowing the inheritance of basic constraints from general rule schemata. The application of these rules enables the unification of two candidate edges and the consequent fusion of the corresponding multimodal elements.

Although these two approaches, based on typed feature structures, provide a generally applicable

Figure 6. An example of typed feature structures unification

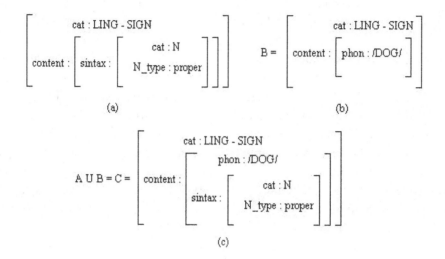

representation for the different modalities and the exploitation of well-known grammar-based techniques extensively explored in natural language processing, they show significant limitations on the expressivity and complexity.

The fusion strategy based on *melting pots*, proposed by Nigay and Coutaz (1995), was originally implemented within the MATIS multimodal system, briefly introduced in the background section. As shown in Figure 8, a melting pot is a 2-D structure, in which the vertical axis contains the "structural parts", i.e. the task objects generated by the input actions of the user, and the horizontal axis is the time. The fusion is performed within the dialogue manager by using a technique based on agents (PAC-Amodeus agents). Three criteria are used to trigger the fusion of melting pots. The first criterion, referred to as microtemporal fusion, is used to combine information that is produced either in parallel or over overlapping time intervals. The second criterion, called macrotemporal fusion, takes care of either sequential inputs or time intervals that do not overlap but belong to the same temporal window. A further criterion, referred to as contextual fusion, serves to combine input according to contextual constraints without attention to temporal constraints.

A refinement of the approach of Nigay and Coutaz (1995) has been carried out by Bouchet et al. (2004) and implemented in the ICARE (Interaction CARE - Complementarity Assignment, Redundancy and Equivalence) framework. Such framework considers both pure modalities, described through elementary components, and combined modalities, specified through composition components. Two kinds of elementary components are defined: the device components that abstract the captured input signals into recognized inputs, and the interaction language components that abstract the recognized inputs coming from the device components into commands. Finally, the composition components describe the fusion criteria of data provided by the elementary components, in line with the criteria defined in (Nigay and Coutaz, 1995). The main advantage of the ICARE approach relies on the component-based structure that allows to reduce production costs ensuring a high reusability and maintainability.

In the approach based on *semantic frames,* proposed by Vo and Wood (1996), input from each modality is parsed and transformed into a semantic frame containing slots that specify command parameters. The information in these partial

Figure 7. An example of representation of a spoken word by typed feature structure

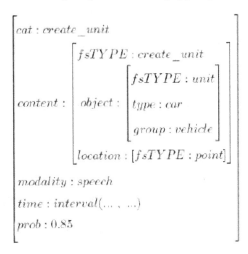

Figure 8. The structure of a melting pot (Nigay and Coutaz, 1995)

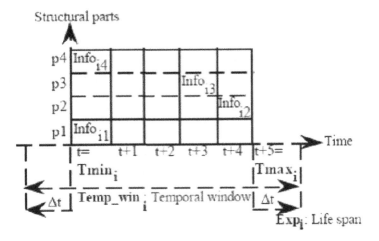

frames may be incomplete or ambiguous if not all elements of the command were expressed in a single modality. A domain independent frame-merging algorithm combines the partial frames into a complete frame by selecting slot values from the partial frames to maximize a combined score. This approach is quite similar to the melting-pot strategy described above.

The use of semantic frames with slots is followed also by Russ et al. (2005). As opposed to the previous fusion mechanism, in the approach of Russ et al. each slot (called main slot) contains also the connections to a semantic network, as well as the attributes associated to each recognized input (contained into the attribute slots), as shown in Figure 9. A node in the network consists of a term and an activation value. If a connected node of the semantic network is activated, the slots of the frames are filled with the attributes as well as the activation values of the nodes. Therefore, the overall activation of a frame corresponds to the probability that the user input correlates with the frame. As each input can have multiple interpretations, this probability is taken into account to evaluate the best candidate interpretation. The main advantage of this approach is the uselessness of knowing a predetermined language or specific commands.

In the approach based on *time-stamped lattices*, proposed by Corradini et al. (2003), each recognizer produces a set of interpretation hypotheses where each hypothesis stands for an independent and diverse interpretation of the input signal. These hypotheses are encoded by means of word lattices where several paths through the word lattice reflect the individual interpretations or n-best lists. The fusion engine combines the time-stamped lattices received from the recognizers, selects its multimodal interpretation, and passes it on to the dialogue manager. The selection of the most probable interpretation is carried out by the dialogue manager that rules out inconsistent information by both binding the semantic attributes of different modalities and using environment content to disambiguate information from the single modalities.

All the approaches introduced above occur at decision level, since individual input coming from the specific recognizers are partially interpreted before their integration.

The main advantage of these strategies is the multi-tasking, as different multimodal channels, recognizers and interpreters are arranged for carrying out independent unimodal input processing at the same time. This implies also the possibility

to use standard and well-tested recognizers and interpreters for each modality. On the other hand, decision-based fusion strategies are characterized by a high complexity of the inter-modality disambiguation, particularly when dealing with more complex modalities that need not only pairs item-time but full lattices from each channel to disambiguate the multimodal input.

Hybrid Multi-Level Fusion Strategies

In the hybrid multi-level approach, the integration of input signals is distributed among the acquisition, the recognition and decision levels. To parse multiple input streams and to combine their content into a single semantic representation three main methodologies have been applied in literature: *finite-state transducers* (Johnston and Bangalore, 2000), *multimodal grammars* (Sun et al., 2006; D'Ulizia et al., 2007) and *dialogue moves* (Perez et al., 2005).

The approach based on *finite-state transducers* was proposed by Johnston et al. (2000). The authors perform multimodal parsing and understanding by using weighted finite-state transducers (FSTs) running on three tapes, in which the first tape represents the speech stream (words), the second the gesture stream (gesture symbols), and the third their combined meaning (meaning symbols). The transitions of the FST, which consist

Figure 9. The structure of the semantic frame of Russ et al. (2005)

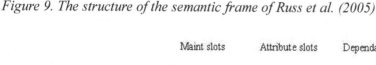
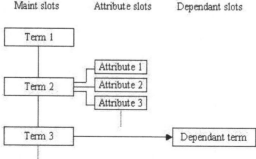

of an input and output symbol, are traversed if the input symbol matches the current recognized symbol and generates the corresponding output symbol. Figure 10 shows an example of transducer relating the spoken command "Email this person and that organization" and the gesture with the pen on the appropriate person and organization on the screen. Modality integration is carried out by merging and encoding into a FST both semantic and syntactic content from multiple streams. In this way, the structure and the interpretation of multimodal utterances by using FST is roughly equivalent to a context-free multimodal grammar that parses the inputs and yields the output tape providing semantic information.

The FST approach is very versatile and provides a high degree of flexibility, allowing a huge spectrum of multimodal commands to be implemented. On the other hand, this approach does not support mutual disambiguation, i.e., using information from a recognized input to enable the processing of any other modality. Moreover, a huge amount of data is required to train the FST limiting portability.

In the approach based on *multimodal grammars*, the outcomes of each recognizer are considered as terminal symbols of a formal grammar and consequently they are recognized by the parser as a unique multimodal sentence. Therefore, in the interpretation phase the parser uses the grammar specification (production rules) to interpret the sentence. This fusion strategy has been implemented in the MUMIF system (Sun et al., 2006). The fusion module of MUMIF applies a multimodal grammar to unify the recognized unimodal inputs into a unique multimodal input that is represented by using the TFS (Typed Feature Structures) structure proposed by Carpenter (1992). The MUMIF multimodal grammar is composed of two kinds of rules: lexical rules that are used to specify the TFS representation and grammar rules that constrain the unification of input.

The use of multimodal grammars is followed also by D'Ulizia et al. (2007). As opposed to the previous fusion mechanism, in the approach of D'Ulizia et al. a hybrid multimodal grammar is used, which encodes a Constraints Multiset Grammar (CMG, i.e. a kind of multi-dimensional grammar well-suited to specify the syntax of multimodal input) into Linear Logic in order to represent also semantic aspects. Once the set of terminal and non-terminal symbols, corresponding to the unimodal inputs coming from the recognizers, and the production rules are defined, the multimodal parsing process is carried out according to the production rules. The approach of D'Ulizia et al. allows the reasoning about multimodal languages providing a prerequisite for being able to resolve ambiguities and for integrating parsing with semantic theories. The main drawback relies on the high complexity.

The *dialogue moves* are used by Perez et al. (2005) to represent multimodal user inputs coming from the lexical-syntactical analyzer. This structure, originally proposed by Quesada et al. (2000), is based on the DTAC, consisting of a feature-value structure with four main features, which are DMOVE, TYPE, ARG and CONT. An example of DTAC for the command "Turn on the kitchen light" is shown in Figure 11. The DTAC is quite similar to the typed feature structure of Carpenter (1992). This approach is implemented in the Delfos system, consisting of Multimodal input pool, a Natural Language Understanding (NLU) module and a collaborative dialogue manager. The multimodal input pool receives and stores all inputs (each one considered as an independent dialogue move) including information such as time and modality. The NLU module parses the input and adds further features in the DTAC structure, such as the modality of the event, the time at which the event started and ended. The dialogue manager checks the input pool regularly to retrieve the corresponding input. It operates by means of update unification rules, that define under what conditions the integration of DTAC

Figure 10. A finite-state transducer in the approach of Johnston et al. (2000)

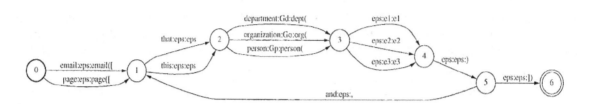

will happen. If more than one input is received during a certain time frame, further analysis is performed in order to determine whether those independent multimodal inputs are truly related or not.

The main advantage of the hybrid multi-level fusion strategies relies on the similarity with the paradigm used in the human-human communication, in which the dialogue is considered as a unique linguistic phenomenon. On the other hand, they are characterized by a high complexity of the inter-modality disambiguation.

MATHEMATICAL METHODS IN MULTIMODAL FUSION

In this chapter we will investigate existing fusion approaches based on the mathematical method applied to perform the integration of the input signals.

In the decision stage of the fusion process, statistical methodologies are often applied in order to take a decision on the interpretation of the multimodal sentence according to the knowledge of the acquired input signals. Classical statistical models applied in the literature are bayesian network, hidden markov models, and fuzzy logic.

An alternative to statistical methodologies is represented by artificial intelligence-based techniques, such as neural networks and agent theory. These techniques, similarly to statistical ones, are well-suited for classification and recognition tasks in the multimodal fusion domain.

Therefore, depending on the mathematical method applied to perform the integration of the input signals, multimodal fusion strategies can be broadly classified as: statistical and artificial intelligence-based.

Statistical Fusion Strategies

The nature of the input signals, expressed by the user through the human output modalities and acquired by the system through the computer input modalities, can be characterized by a certain degree of uncertainty associated with the imperfection of data, frequently hard to recognize. To deal with this uncertainty statistical models, which consider previously observed data with respect to current data to derive the probability of an input, have been extensively used in the literature. In fact, most of multimodal systems, especially those that perform the fusion at recognition level, rely on statistical fusion strategies that use models of probability theory to combine information coming from different unimodal inputs. In particular, three main statistical methods can be applied in the fusion process: *bayesian network* (Toyama and Horvitz, 2000; Chu et al., 2004, Garg et al., 2003), *hidden markov models* (Zhihong et al., 2006; Gaitanis et al, 2007), and *fuzzy logic* (Lau et al., 2004).

A large number of fusion techniques are based on *bayesian network* theory. In particular, Bayes' theory is well suited to solve the decision problem of classifying an input into one class among several closed-set possibilities. This decision usually relies

Figure 11. An example of dialogue move in the approach of Perez et al. (2005)

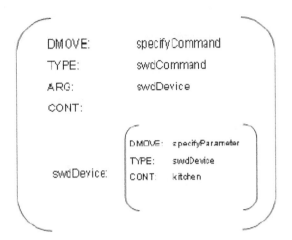

on a maximum a-posteriori probability, assuming to know the a-priori and conditional probabilities of the input data set. A general formula for the evaluation of the a-posteriori probability is given in equation (1), where the a-posteriori probability *Pr(Y|X)* represents the belief of hypothesis Y given the information X . This probability is obtained by multiplying *Pr(Y)*, the prior probability of the hypothesis Y, by *Pr(X|Y)*, the probability of receiving X, given that Y is true. The estimation of this last function occurs through an approximation process, usually referred to as the likelihood function. The accuracy of this function depends on the quality of the model of the class.

$$\Pr(Y \mid X) = \frac{\Pr(X \mid Y)\Pr(Y)}{\Pr(X)}, \qquad (1)$$

Toyama et al. (2000) employ a bayesian modality fusion to integrate the outputs of multiple visual tracking algorithms for a head tracking system. The Bayesian network model is instantiated with a set of observations including the modality report and the status of a set of context-sensitive indicators. An example of bayesian network model for fusing two modalities over time is depicted in Figure 12. The parameters of the network, that are the conditional probabilities of input events,

are learned through an offline training procedure that is able to convert the training data into a sets of probabilities representing the respective conditional contexts. The training of the network influence the fusion process, particularly the sparsity of the training data set causes inaccuracy and difficulties in the use of the model.

Chu et al. (2004) use a hybrid multi-level fusion technique relied on a modified Bayesian classifier by adjusting the importance of the individual classifiers using exponential weights. Fusion is performed both at the feature and the decision level, thus enabling separability of the classes using minimum number of features. However, the product-combination technique suggested in their method is susceptible to noise.

In addition to head tracking and speech-audio recognition systems, Bayesian networks have also been applied to the multimodal speaker detection task. In particular, Garg et al. (2003) developed a speech-based command and control interface for a Smart Kiosk. The input signals, coming from the camera and microphone of the kiosk, are captured by a set of five "off-the-shelf" visual and audio sensors: a neural network-based face detector, a gaussian skin color detector, a face texture detector, a mouth motion detector, and an audio

Figure 12. An example of bayesian network model for fusing two modalities in the approach of Tomaya et al. (2000)

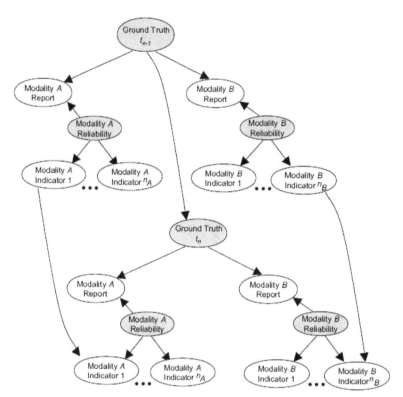

silence detector. The integration of these sensors is performed through a comprehensive bayesian network, which is composed of:

- A visual network, which fuses the outputs of the skin color, texture and face detector sensors in order to estimate whether a user is visible in front of the kiosk and if his/her mouth is moving;
- An audio network, which combines the outputs of the mouth motion and silence detector sensors in order to infer whether speech production is occurring;
- An integrated audiovisual network that combines the visual and audio sub-networks to the contextual information, as shown in Figure 13.

Bayesian network models have the attractive feature of combining an intuitive graphical representation with efficient algorithms for inference. However, the need of learning algorithms to model the standard parameters of the network can lead to non-optimal decisions in classification tasks.

Hidden Markov Models (HMMs), either in their standard form or in their hierarchical variants, are another probabilistic graphical model, well suited for fusing different unimodal inputs. These models are a particular kind of dynamic bayesian network, which encodes dependencies among sets of random variables evolving in time. Gaitanis et al. (2007) apply these models to perform modality fusion at decision level. In particular, they defined a probabilistic multi-agent hidden markov model (M-AHMEM) in which each modality is modeled as an agent and the

Figure 13. The integrated audiovisual network of Garg et al. (2003)

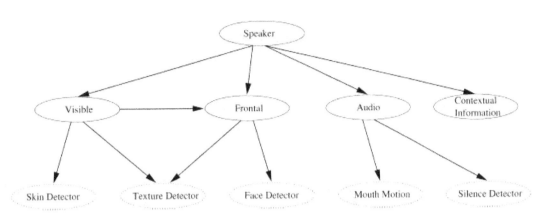

silence detector. The integration of these sensors is performed through a comprehensive bayesian network, which is composed of:

- A visual network, which fuses the outputs of the skin color, texture and face detector sensors in order to estimate whether a user is visible in front of the kiosk and if his/her mouth is moving;
- An audio network, which combines the outputs of the mouth motion and silence detector sensors in order to infer whether speech production is occurring;
- An integrated audiovisual network that combines the visual and audio sub-networks to the contextual information, as shown in Figure 13.

Bayesian network models have the attractive feature of combining an intuitive graphical representation with efficient algorithms for inference. However, the need of learning algorithms to model the standard parameters of the network can lead to non-optimal decisions in classification tasks.

Hidden Markov Models (HMMs), either in their standard form or in their hierarchical variants, are another probabilistic graphical model, well suited for fusing different unimodal inputs.

These models are a particular kind of dynamic bayesian network, which encodes dependencies among sets of random variables evolving in time. Gaitanis et al. (2007) apply these models to perform modality fusion at decision level. In particular, they defined a probabilistic multi-agent hidden markov model (M-AHMEM) in which each modality is modeled as an agent and the modality fusion is regarded as a cooperation that takes part inside the team formed by these agents. The M-AHMEM model represents the behaviours (policies) at different levels of abstraction and for different actors inside a team. Each policy, like a contingent plan, specifies the order of actions at all applicable states to achieve the goal. An example of representation of the action "Copy_object_O" through the M-AHMEM model is shown in Figure 14, where two agents are modeled, for gesture and voice, and a team that combines data from the two agents is defined.

HMMs are also used by Pavlovic et al. (1997) to dynamically classify the visual and auditory features of video-audio data. A description of the functioning of their HMM-based approach has been given in section "Recognition-based fusion strategies" (see Figure 5).

Fuzzy logic is another statistical method, used in the decision phase of the fusion process, that

Figure 14. The representation of the action "Copy_object_O" through the M-AHMEM model of Gaitanis et al. (2007)

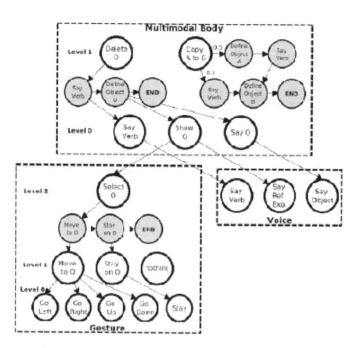

allows to incorporate effects of external conditions affecting the performance of the decision task. This statistical methodology has been applied by Lau et al. (2004) in a multimodal biometric system in order to verify the user's identity through his/her facial features, voice and fingerprints. In order to process imprecise information due to adverse lighting conditions for face identification, mismatches in conditions under which the fingerprint identification is performed, or noise for the speech identification, six input fuzzy variables are used, each one having a fuzzy set that defines the favored external conditions of the variable. These conditions are formulated by three groups of fuzzy IF-THEN rules. Each group controls the output variable for the face, speech and fingerprint, respectively. An example of fuzzy rule for the face identification is:

IF (*FaceFindingConf* is *high*) and (*Illuminance* is *medium*) THEN (w_{face} is *high*).

Fuzzy logic generalizes probability and therefore is able to deal with approximate reasoning to draw (imprecise) conclusions from imprecise premises.

Statistical fusion strategies have the main advantage that well-known algorithms exist for the estimation of the model parameters (EM algorithms, Maximum likelihood criteria, Maximum-a-posteriori techniques,...) and for the search of the best model (Viterbi decoding, beam search,...). On the other hand, statistical fusion strategies are characterized by a lot of adjustments due to problems occurring in real contexts of use, such as the insufficiency of the training data, inaccuracy of the model, etc.

Artificial Intelligence-Based Fusion Strategies

Similarly to statistical methods, artificial intelligence techniques have been extensively applied by lots of multimodal systems to perform the fusion of input signals at recognition and decision levels. In particular, the most of the artificial intelligence-based fusion strategies use the *agent theory* Nigay and Coutaz, 1995) and *neural networks* (Meier et al., 2000; Lewis and Powers, 2002).

The *agent theory* is applied by Nigay et al. (1995) in the MATIS system. As introduced in section "Decision-based fusion strategies", this system adopts the PAC-Amodeus agents to perform the fusion at decision level. These cooperative agents are modelled as a three facet structures, where the control facet is the most important for the fusion as it manages the relationships with other agents. Every PAC agent has access to a fusion engine through its control facet. When calling the engine, a PAC agent provides a melting pot as an input and receives a list of melting pots as output parameter. The fusion of information is performed by exchanging melting pots across the hierarchy of agents. As one hierarchy per task exists, each hierarchy handles the melting pots that are related to the task it models. The root agent of the hierarchy maintains information about melting pots and the PAC agents interested by these melting pots.

The use of the agent theory in the fusion process enables an automatic adaptivity to the input quality, taking into account eventual changes of the accuracy of inputs.

Neural networks are used by Meier et al. (2000) in a speech recognition system that integrate auditory and visual (lip movements) signals. They adopted a particular kind of neural network, named Multiple State-Time Delayed Neural Network (MS-TDNN), which is composed of an acoustic and a visual TDNN. These two sub-nets are trained separately and their outputs are combined by the phonetic layer, as shown in Figure 15. The combined activation of this layer for a given phoneme is expressed as a weighted summation of the acoustic network activation and the corresponding visual unit.

Another approach based on neural networks and devoted to the integration of auditory and visual inputs for speech recognition has been proposed by Lewis et al. (2002). In particular, they adopted three neural networks, namely visual, acoustic and late integration networks. The fusion of auditory and visual signals requires the following phases: the first phase consists in the training of the acoustic and visual subnets; successively, the training data is passed through these two networks and two outputs (Aoutput and Voutput in Figure 16) are produced; finally, the outputs of the sub-networks are concatenated and this new data is used to train the late integration network. As a high amount of errors can exist in these three networks, two more networks are applied to predict errors of each sub-networks. The general architecture of the system proposed by Lewis et al. is shown in Figure 16.

The main advantages of neural networks rely on their generalisability, the unnecessarity of assumptions about the underlying data and poor susceptibility to noise. However, this methodology is characterized by a slow trainability and variance due to rate.

CONCLUSION

In this chapter we have analyzed some fundamental features of multimodal fusion systems. A first important characteristic is the level at which the input signals are combined. In this respect we have shown that multimodal fusion strategies can be broadly classified as: (i) recognition-based, characterized by a unimodal recognition stage and an integrated decision stage; (ii) decision-based, where a unimodal recognition and interpretation phases are carried out before performing the integration of the extracted semantic meaning; (iii) hybrid multi-level, based on a distributed integration of input signals among the acquisition, recognition and decision levels. Secondly, we have briefly analysed the main mathematical methods

Figure 15. The MS-TDNN network of Meier et al. (2000)

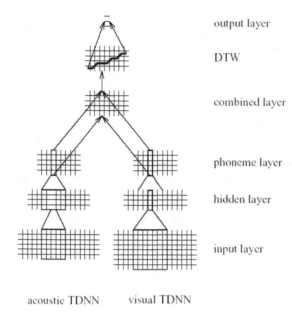

Figure 16. The fusion approach proposed by Lewis et al. (2002)

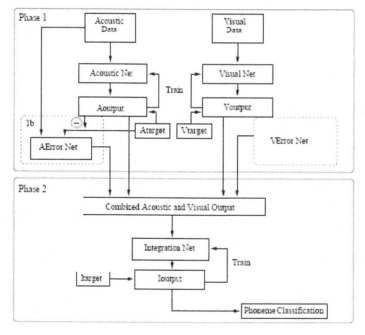

applied to perform the integration of multimodal inputs, with a specific focus on statistical and artificial intelligence techniques.

REFERENCES

Andre, M., Popescu, V.G., Shaikh, A., Medl, A., Marsic, I., Kulikowski, C., & Flanagan J.L. (1998, January). Integration of speech and gesture for multimodal human-computer interaction. In *Second International Conference on Cooperative Multimodal Communication*, Tilburg, The Netherlands (pp. 28-30).

Bolt, R. (1980). Put-that-there: Voice and gesture at the graphics interface. *Computer Graphics, 14*(3), 262-270.

Bouchet, J., Nigay, L., & Ganille, T. (2004). Icare software components for rapidly developing multimodal interfaces. In *Proceedings of the 6th International Conference on Multimodal Interfaces (ICMI '04),* New York, NY (pp. 251-258). ACM.

Carpenter, B. (1992). *The logic of typed feature structures*. UK: Cambridge University Press.

Chu, S.M., Libal, V., Marcheret, E., Neti, C., & Potamianos, G. (2004, June 27-30). Multistage information fusion for audio-visual speech recognition. In *Proceedings of the (IEEE) International Conference on Multimedia and Expo 2004, (ICME '04)*, New York, NY (Vol. 3, pp.1651-1654).

Cohen, P.R., Johnston, M., McGee, D., Oviatt, S.L., Pittman, J., Smith, I.A., Chen, L., & Clow, J. (1997). Quickset: Multimodal interaction for distributed applications. *ACM Multimedia*, 31-40.

Corradini, A., Mehta, M., Bernsen, N.O., & Martin, J.-C. (2003). Multimodal input fusion in human-computer interaction on the example of the ongoing NICE project. In *Proceedings of the NATO-ASI Conference on Data Fusion for Situ-ation Monitoring, Incident Detection, Alert, and Response Management*, Yerevan, Armenia.

Coutaz, J., & Caelen, J. (1991, November). A taxonomy for multimedia and multimodal user interfaces. In *Proceedings of the 1st ERCIM Workshop on Multimedia HCI*, Lisbon.

D'Ulizia, A., Ferri, F., & Grifoni, P. (2007, November 25-30). A hybrid grammar-based approach to multimodal languages specification. In *OTM 2007 Workshop Proceedings*, Vilamoura, Portugal (LNCS 4805, pp. 367-376). Springer-Verlag.

Gaitanis K., Vybornova, M.O., Gemo, M., & Macq, B. (2007). Multimodal high level fusion of input commands as a semantic goal-oriented cooperative process. *12th International Conference "Speech and Computer" (SPECOM 2007)*.

Garg, A., Pavlovic, V., & Rehg, J.M. (2003). Boosted learning in dynamic bayesian networks for multimodal speaker detection. In *Proceedings IEEE* (No. 9, pp.1355-1369).

Johnston, M. (1998, August 10-14). Unification-based multimodal parsing. In *Proceedings of the 36th Annual Meeting of the Association for Computational Linguistics and 17th International Conference on Computational Linguistics (COLING-ACL '98)*, Montreal, Canada (pp. 624-630).

Johnston, M., & Bangalore, S. (2000). Finite-state multimodal parsing and understanding. In *Proceedings of the International Conference on Computational Linguistics*, Saarbruecken, Germany.

Lau, C.W., Ma, B., Meng, H.M., Moon, Y.S., & Yam, Y. (2004). Fuzzy logic decision fusion in a multimodal biometric system. In *Proceedings of the 8th International Conference on Spoken Language Processing (ICSLP)*, Korea.

Lewis, T.W., & Powers, D.M.W. (2002). Audio-visual speech recognition using red exclusion and neural networks. In *Proceedings of the 25th*

Australasian Conference on Computer Science. Australian Computer Society, Inc., Melbourne, Australia (pp. 149-156).

Martin, J.C., Grimard, S., & Alexandri, K. (2001). On the annotation of the multimodal behavior and computation of cooperation between modalities. In *Proceedings of the Workshop on Representing, Annotating, and Evaluating Non-Verbal and Verbal Communicative Acts to Achieve Contextual Embodied Agents*, Montreal, Canada (pp. 1-7).

Meier, U., Stiefelhagen, R., Yang, J., & Waibel, A. (2000). Towards unrestricted lip reading. *International Journal of Pattern Recognition and Artificial Intelligence, 14*(5), 571-585.

Neal, J.G., & Shapiro, S.C. (1991). Intelligent multimedia interface technology. In J. Sullivan, & S. Tyler (Eds.), *Intelligent user interfaces* (pp. 11-43). New York: ACM Press.

Nigay, L., & Coutaz, J. (1995). A generic platform for addressing the multimodal challenge. In *Proceedings of the Conference on Human Factors in Computing Systems*. ACM Press.

Oviatt, S.L. (2002). Multimodal interfaces. In J. Jacko, & A. Sears (Eds.), *Handbook of human-computer interaction*. New Jersey: Lawrence Erlbaum.

Oviatt, S., & Cohen, P. (2000). Multimodal interfaces that process what comes naturally. *Communications of the ACM, 43*(3), 45-53.

Oviatt, S., Cohen, P., Wu, L., Vergo, J., Duncan, L., Suhm, B., Bers, J., Holzman, T., Winograd, T., Landay, J., Larson, J., & Ferro, D. (2000). Designing the user interface for multimodal speech and gesture applications: State-of-the-art systems and research directions for 2000 and beyond.

Oviatt, S., De Angeli, A., & Kuhn, K. (1997). Integration and synchronization of input modes during multimodal human-computer interaction. In *Proceedings of the Conference on Human Factors in Computing Systems (CHI'97)*, New York, NY (pp. 415-422). ACM Press.

Pavlovic, V.I., Berry, G.A., & Huang, T.S. (1997). Integration of audio/visual information for use in human-computer intelligent interaction. In *Proceedings of the 1997 International Conference on Image Processing (ICIP '97)*, (Vol. 1, pp. 121-124).

Pérez, G., Amores, G., & Manchón, P. (2005). Two strategies for multimodal fusion. In *Proceedings of Multimodal Interaction for the Visualization and Exploration of Scientific Data*, Trento, Italy (pp. 26-32).

Quesada, J. F., Torre, D., & Amores, G. (2000). Design of a natural command language dialogue system. Deliverable 3.2, Siridus Project.

Russ, G., Sallans, B., & Hareter, H. (2005, June 20-23). Semantic based information fusion in a multimodal interface. *International Conference on Human-Computer Interaction (HCI'05)*, Las Vegas, NV (pp. 94-100).

Schomaker, L., Nijtmans, A.J., Camurri, F. Lavagetto, P., Morasso, C., Benoit, T., et al. (1995). A taxonomy of multimodal interaction in the human information processing system. *Multimodal Integration for Advanced Multimedia Interfaces (MIAMI). ESPRIT III, Basic Research Project 8579.*

Sharma, R., Pavlovic, V.I., & Huang, T.S. (1998). Toward multimodal human-computer interface. In *Proceedings of the IEEE, Special Issue on Multimedia Signal Processing, 86*(5), 853-869.

Sun, Y., Chen, F., Shi, Y.D., & Chung, V. (2006). A novel method for multisensory data fusion in multimodal human computer interaction. In *Proceedings of the 20th Conference of the Computer-Human Interaction Special Interest Group (CHISIG) of Australia on Computer-Human Interaction: Design, Activities, Artefacts, and Environments*, Sydney, Australia (pp. 401-404).

Toyama, K., & Horvitz, E. (2000). Bayesian modality fusion: Probabilistic integration of multiple vision algorithms for head tracking. In *Proceedings of the Fourth Asian Conference on Computer Vision*, Tapei, Taiwan.

Vo, M.T. (1998). *A framework and toolkit for the construction of multimodal learning interfaces.* Unpublished doctoral dissertation, Carnegie Mellon University, Pittsburgh, PA.

Vo, M.T., & Wood, C. (1996, May 7-10). Building an application framework for speech and pen input integration in multimodal learning interfaces. In *Proceedings of the Acoustics, Speech, and Signal Processing (ICASSP '96), IEEE Computer Society* (Vol. 6, pp. 3545-3548).

Wahlster, W., Reithinger, N., & Blocher, A. (2001). SmartKom: Multimodal communication with a life-like character. In *Proceedings of Eurospeech*, Aalborg, Denmark.

Zhihong, Z., Yuxiao, H., Ming, L., Yun, F., & Huang, T.S. (2006). Training combination strategy of multistream fused hidden Markov model for audio-visual affect recognition. In *Proceedings of the 14th Annual ACM International Conference on Multimedia*, Santa Barbara, CA (pp. 65-68).

KEY TERMS AND DEFINITIONS

Communication Modality: The medium or channel of communication that conveys information.

Human-Computer Interaction (HCI): Discipline concerned with the design, evaluation and implementation of interactive computing systems for human use and with the study of major phenomena surrounding them.

Multimodal Fission: The process of disaggregating outputs through the various channels in order to provide the user with consistent feedback.

Multimodal Fusion: The process of integrating information from various input modalities and combining them into a complete command.

Multimodal Interface: System that allows input and/or output to be conveyed over multiple channels such as speech, graphics, and gesture.

Multimodal Interaction: Interaction with the virtual and physical environment through natural modes of communication.

Multimodality: Quality of a system to allow more than one communication modality to be used during human-computer interaction.

Chapter IV
An Efficient Unification–Based Multimodal Language Processor for Multimodal Input Fusion

Fang Chen
National ICT Australia, Australia & University of Sydney, Australia

Yong Sun
National ICT Australia, Australia & University of Sydney, Australia

ABSTRACT

Multimodal user interaction technology aims at building natural and intuitive interfaces allowing a user to interact with computers in a way similar to human-to-human communication, for example, through speech and gestures. As a critical component in a multimodal user interface, multimodal input fusion explores ways to effectively derive the combined semantic interpretation of user inputs through multiple modalities. Based on state–of-the-art review on multimodal input fusion approaches, this chapter presents a novel approach to multimodal input fusion based on speech and gesture; or speech and eye tracking. It can also be applied for other input modalities and extended to more than two modalities. It is the first time that a powerful combinational categorical grammar is adopted in multimodal input fusion. The effectiveness of the approach has been validated through user experiments, which indicated a low polynomial computational complexity while parsing versatile multimodal input patterns. It is very useful for mobile context. Future trends in multimodal input fusion will be discussed at the end of this chapter.

INTRODUCTION TO MULTIMODAL INPUT FUSION

Multimodal interaction systems allow a user to interact with them by using his/her own natural communication modalities such as pen gesture, text and spoken language, graphical marks etc. After speech and pen gesture were used as input modalities in some researches, other modalities, such as hand gesture and eye gaze, have been addressed as well. To understand a user's meaning conveyed through his/her use of multiple modalities, Multimodal Input Fusion (MMIF) integrates users' input from different modalities and derives a semantic interpretation from them for a system to act upon. It is an area that deals with various input modalities and finds users' meaning in a particular instance, application or task. With the development of multimodal interface on mobile devices, multimodal input fusion has to deal with computational complexity, besides the existing issues.

The aim of MMIF is to:

a. Identify the combination of input modalities and multimodal input patterns; and
b. Interpret both unimodal input and multimodal inputs; and
c. Cope with modality alternation for one multimodal utterance and support modality combination (complementary) for one utterance.

There is an important distinction between the aims of MMIF:

- Combining complementary inputs from different modalities, for example, a user touching an object to be deleted on a touch screen and saying 'delete'.
- Improving the robustness of signal recognition, for example audio-visual speech recognition, or combined gaze and speech input (Zhang, Imamiya, Go & Mao 2004).

The pre-request for successful MMIF includes:

- Fine grained time-stamping of user's multimodal input (beginning and end); and
- Parallel recognizers for a modality. Based on probabilistic methods, the recognition results from parallel recognizers can be used to produce n-best list; and
- Unified representation schema for output of all recognizers; and

- Time sensitive recognition process.

On the other hand, a successful MMIF should be able to

- Handle input signals that may or may not be temporally overlapped; and
- Disambiguate inputs among different modalities; and
- Deal with simultaneous and/or sequential multimodal inputs; and
- Distribute to allow more computational power.

In a mobile device with a multimodal application, speech can be used as the primary modality because traditional user interface peripherals may not be available or appropriate. The most common instance of such interfaces combines a visual modality (e.g. a display, keyboard, and mouse) with a voice modality (speech). Other modalities such as pen-based input may be used, as well. In the more recent mobile devices, modalities can involve global positioning systems (GPS), and mapping technologies, digital imaging, barcode scanning, radio frequency identification (RFID) and other newer, intelligent technologies. In this kind of applications, users have more options to express their meaning, and tend frequently to switch between interaction modalities owing to a number of external factors such as background noise. Because multiple modalities can be used together to express a meaning, multimodal inputs tend to be more concise and meaningful. For example, "from the corner of Edi Ave. and George Street" can be concisely expressed as "from 🖝" with speech and a point gesture.

Types of MMIF

As shown in Figure 1, in general, multimodal input fusion can occur at two levels:

- Feature level (also known as "early fusion"), integration at the signal/feature extraction level; and
- Semantic level (also known as "late fusion") integration at the recognized symbol level

Early Fusion

Early fusion integrates multimodal inputs after the feature extraction of each input mode. It belongs to signal processing domain which often looks at recognition of combined features. Feature level fusion is most common between modalities that are closely related together and can be correlated fairly closely. For example, in audio-visual speech recognition, speech input can be fused with corresponding lip movements on video input at the recognition stage. Feature level fusion can also be performed between unrelated modalities for one-off multimodal inputs, for example, identifying a person based on his voice and face. This kind of fusion can be summarized as following:

- It is usually based on multiple Hidden Markov models or temporal neural networks;
- It is ideal for closely coupled and synchronized input modalities, where both input channels provide corresponding information to one another;

- The recognition of one modality channel can affect the recognition process in the corresponding modality;
- Associated problems with early fusion are modeling complexity, computational load and the large amount of training data required to build such a system. Till now, there are no freely available multimodal training corpora to use on such components.

Late Fusion

In one multimodal turn, all multimodal inputs compose of a multimodal utterance which can express a certain meaning. The goal of late fusion is to find the meaning. Late fusion (semantic fusion) integrates symbols recognized from multimodal input signals. Being applied after best interpretation for each input mode is determined; it is adopted more in the computer science/human computer interaction domain for heterogeneous input modes. It integrates related (but complementary) inputs that occur sequentially or simultaneously. A good example is pen and speech input. The summarization of late fusion can be:

- It is for input modes that differ in type of content or processing time;

Figure 1. Two possibilities for MMIF

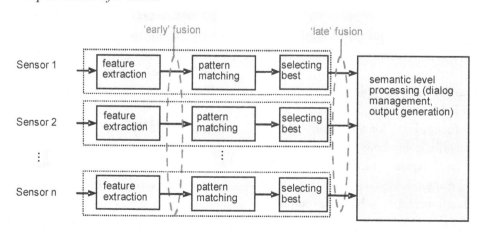

- It involves individual recognizers for each modality and the results of the recognition are integrated complementarily;
- It is easy to scale up and adopt different modalities.

Both early fusion and late fusion can produce an *n*-best list of possibilities, from most confident to least confident at the feature or semantic level interpretations. We will focus on 'late' fusion or semantic fusion in this chapter.

MMIF Related Steps

MMIF discussed in this chapter focuses on late fusion whose inputs are recognized signals. As shown in Figure 2, to derive a MMIF result, the following steps are needed, collecting captured signals, controlling and registering input devices, recognizing them, segmenting them to multimodal utterances and fusing out the semantic interpretation of the utterances.

Collecting captured signals is done by input devices, which could be microphones, touch screen, keyboard, video or any environmental sensors. Registered input devices send out captured signals as soon as they are received.

The "Controlling and registering input devices" module receives real time input from each of the input devices. Each input is time-stamped with the time when it is recorded by the input device. It is important that this is done at the input device and NOT when it is received. This is because latency may switch the order in which the user provided each of the inputs and any information that may be gleaned about the time intersection between input streams is lost. All inputs are then translated to a format understood by the recognizers. This module also handles dynamic registration and deregistration of input devices, keeps track of their capabilities and assigns identifications. There may be more than one input device of the same type and this module may decide whether to consider all inputs or only selected inputs.

The recognizing task is undertaken by *recognizers*. In a "Members-Teams-Committee" inspired design, two or more recognizers may be able to "team-up" and produce a combined n-best list of results in cases where the modalities are closely coupled in time such as lip-movement recognition and speech recognition. The teams that may be formed between recognizers are known a-priori. There may also be more than one recognizers for each type of input modality,

Figure 2. Steps to derive the semantic interpretation of a multimodal utterance

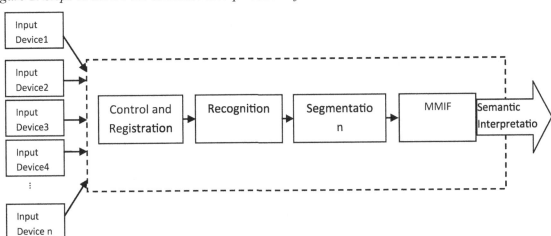

each able to output a set of n-best results. The 'best' single and combined results are sent to the segmentation module. Recognizing results are discrete symbols.

Because there is no punctuations in symbols recognized by recognizers, the multimodal input streams have to be segmented to multimodal utterances for follow-up process. That is the task of segmentation function. The function of segmentation is to determine the borders of a multimodal utterance in multimodal input stream. Temporal relationship among multimodal inputs are utilized in multimodal input segmentation. Some systems use a static time window; a temporal gap in multimodal input bigger than the time window is regarded as a border between multimodal utterances. To produce a more accurate result, others make use of other information in multimodal input as well. More accurate the multimodal utterance is segmented; more natural interaction can be achieved.

An MMIF module combines recognized symbols from different modalities to present a coherent piece of semantic information for a system to act upon. It synchronizes input from multiple modalities, resolves cross-modal references and rank multiple interpretations. The output of an MMIF module is the semantic interpretations of a multimodal utterance.

Although different steps related of MMIF have been introduced conceptually, some steps are merged together, others are simplified/ignored due to specific environments in practice. Most signal recognizers recognize signals from one modality, and generate uncertain recognition results, therefore, an MMIF module should be able to deal with uncertain data and generate its conclusion.

Utilizing the Fusion Results

Without being utilized, fusion results will be useless. As illustrated in Figure 3, after the possible semantic interpretations of a multimodal utterance are derived, they are sent to Dialog Management module. With the context information, a Dialog management module selects the most suitable one to control the Application Background. Conventionally, the semantic interpretation is the truth or satisfaction conditions of multimodal inputs, ignoring those aspects that are influenced by the context of its use. Dialog Management takes care about everything to do with the context, and to a large extent it is used to sweep up all the difficult aspects that are not considered in MMIF.

The Dialog Management module may also access to a set of knowledge bases that include information about the user, their input history, the tasks that can be accomplished by the application etc.

Two Challenges to MMIF

Though a multimodal user interaction system brings some advantages in usability, the MMIF is more complex than the unimodal input processing, such as the natural language processing. It deals with more challenges than those in unimodal processing.

The first is about the *linear order* in temporal domain. The words of a sentence follow a fixed linear order. An atomic input unit from a

Figure 3. A conceptual framework to utilize MMIF results

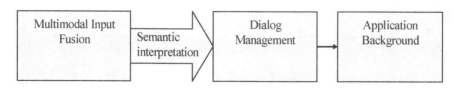

recognizer to the MMIF is referred as a symbol. A complete set of symbols recognized from multimodal input signals is termed as a multimodal utterance which is usually bounded by the user's silence. In a multimodal utterance, the linear order of symbols from multiple modalities is variable, but the linear order of symbols from one modality is invariable. For example, when a traffic controller wants to divert traffic on a road, he/she issues a multimodal command "divert traffic on this road to this street" while pointing to a road and a street in a map with the cursor of his/her hand on a screen. The gestures may be issued before, in-between, or after speech input, but the street pointing gesture is always after the road pointing gesture. This problem definition is different from Rudzicz (2006a) and Johnston (1998), which presume multimodal inputs are permutable, no matter whether they are from one or multiple modalities.

The second is about the *semantic contribution*. The word string of a sentence determines the semantic interpretation of the sentence in a grammar. In a multimodal utterance, the symbol string from one modality contributes partially to the utterance's syntactic structure and semantic interpretation. The notation of a multimodal utterance is a speech symbol string followed by a colon and a gesture symbol string. For example, when a traffic controller wants to block traffic on a part of a road in front of a digital map displayed on a large screen, he/she issues a multimodal command by saying "block traffic on this road between this street and that street" and pointing the corresponding entities on the map "Campbell_ Road", "Musgrave_Street" and "Loftus_Street"; the multimodal utterance representation is "block traffic on this road between this street and that street : Campbell_Road Musgrave_Street Loftus_Street". In this example, we can only find the multimodal utterance is a verbal phrase with incomplete semantic interpretation "block traffic on a road between two streets" from speech input. A complete semantic interpretation can

be derived from neither speech input nor gesture input. They can only be integrated from inputs from both modalities.

Approaches to Semantic MMIF

To achieve MMIF, various approaches have been proposed. Some are based on finite-state machine. Others base on unification operation. At the beginning, unification-based fusion was proposed in Johnston et al. (1997) to process versatile multimodal utterance patterns. Later, a finite-state based approach (Johnston and Bangalore, 2000) emerged to overcome the computational complexity issue of unification-based approaches. Based on these two tracks, different approaches have been proposed to meet different requirements in applications and environments.

Unification-Based MMIF

In the unification-based MMIF approach, the fusion module applies a unification operation on multimodal utterances according to a multimodal grammar.

During unification operation, when two terms are unified, they are compared;

- If one is a variable, another is a constant; the variable will be bound to the other one.
- When both of them are constants, if they are equal then unification succeeds, otherwise unification fails.

In this kind of approaches, multimodal utterances, intermediate results and fusion results are represented in *Typed Feature Structures* (TFS) (Carpenter, 1992). A TFS consists of two pieces of information. The first is a type. Every feature structure must have a type drawn from the inheritance hierarchy. The other kind of information specified by a feature structure is a finite, possibly empty, collection of feature/ value pairs. A feature value pair consists of a

Figure 4. Feature structure for "M1A1 platoon"

$$create_unit\begin{bmatrix} object: \begin{bmatrix} type: m1a1 \\ echelon: platoon \end{bmatrix} unit \\ location: [\ ]point \end{bmatrix}$$

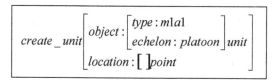

Figure 5. Interpretation of a point gesture

$$command\begin{bmatrix} location: \begin{bmatrix} xcoord: 95305 \\ ycoord: 94365 \end{bmatrix} point \end{bmatrix}$$

Figure 6. Multimodal interpretation of a utterance

$$create_unit\begin{bmatrix} object: \begin{bmatrix} type: m1a1 \\ echelon: platoon \end{bmatrix} unit \\ location: \begin{bmatrix} xcoord: 95305 \\ ycoord: 94365 \end{bmatrix} point \end{bmatrix}$$

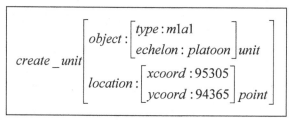

feature and a value, where the value is an atom or a feature structure. Unification of TFSs is an operation that determines the consistency of two structures according to a multimodal grammar. Consistent structures are combined to a single TFS. It can be found in many published works such as Johnston et al. (1997), Johnston (1998) and Holzapfel, Nickel & Stiefelhagen (2004). Considering a unification example from Johnston et al. (1997), a user says, "M1A1 platoon", and gestures on a point on the screen. The speech and gesture inputs are assigned the feature structures in Figure 4 and Figure 5. And they are unified to the feature structure in Figure 6.

In Kaiser et al. (2003) and Kaiser et al. (2004), the unification-base MMIF was as following. As shown in Figure 7, there are a Natural Language Parser (NLP) and a Multimodal Integrator (MI) to undertake the multimodal fusion task. The NLP maps each parsable speech string into a TFS. Once a gesture is received, its gesture hypotheses are converted into a TFS. MI unifies speech TFSs and gesture TFSs with an internal chart parser. This process generates single object TFSs of the type specified for the speech/gesture combination, which are subsequently enrolled in the chart. Whenever the chart's agenda empties, the complete edges present on the chart become the multimodal n-best list, and the top member of this list is regarded as the multimodal fusion result.

This kind of approaches can handle a versatile multimodal utterance styles because all symbols in an utterance are supposed to be permutable. For example, for the utterance "pick up it" as speech and a pointing gesture to specify the object, they will try not only the order "pick up it ☞" but also all other orders, such as "up pick it ☞" and "it pick up ☞" to find the semantic interpretation of it. However, it suffers from significant computational complexity (Johnston & Bangalore, 2000). Some unification-based approaches adapt Earley's chart parser (Earley, 1970) to multimodal processing, but that shows a prohibitive exponential computational complexity. Most of these approaches assume there is

Figure 7. A Multimodal Interaction Architecture (Based on Kaiser et al., 2003)

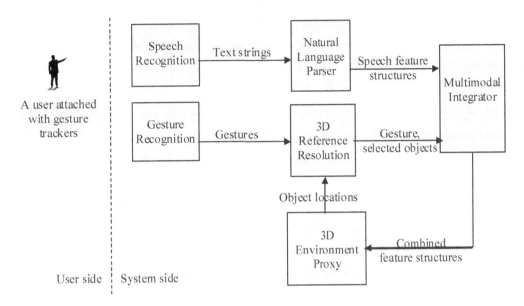

not a linear order in a multimodal utterance. The temporal order of multimodal inputs is ensured by temporal constrains in parsing process. But it does not provide a natural framework for combining probabilities of speech and gesture events (Johnston & Bangalore, 2000). Development of the multimodal grammar rules is a laborious process and requires significant understanding of integration technique.

Unification-based approach has been enhanced in different aspects. A unification-based approach in mutual disambiguation of speech and pen-based gesture which supports combinations of speech with a single gesture is discussed in Oviatt (1999). In Portillo, Garcia & Carredano (2006), a unification-based approach with probabilistic parsing is presented. However, it is not clear the computational complexity of the approach.

Finite-State Based Multimodal Input Fusion

Finite-state based approach was adopted in Johnston & Bangalore (2000). In this approach, a finite state device is used to encode multimodal

integration patterns, the syntax of speech phrase, gesture unit and the semantic interpretation of these multimodal utterances. Johnston & Bangalore (2000) uses a multimodal context-free grammar to describe the inputs from speech and gesture. The terminals in the grammar consist of literals of the form **W:G:M** where **W** is the words from speech input, **G** is the input from gesture represented as atomic symbols, and **M** is their multimodal interpretation. The multimodal grammar specification is compiled into a finite-state device running on three information flow tapes. A tape represents either an input stream (**W** stream or **G** stream) or an output stream (**M** stream). There are two input streams for speech (**W** stream) and gesture (**G** stream) modalities respectively. The third one is the output stream (**M** stream) for the multimodal interpretation. The finite state device consists of states and transitions. A transition from one state to another is labeled with multimodal grammar denoting the inputs required in speech and/or gesture to perform the transition. Multimodal fusion is achieved by parsing spoken and gesture inputs using the finite state machine. During parsing, the transition from one state to another outputs the meaning **M** associated with that grammar fragment. The finite-state device receives **W** stream and **G** stream in the form of words and gesture symbols respectively and outputs their meaning according to the pre-defined multimodal grammar. The collection from the **M** stream for a parse through the multimodal inputs represents the multimodal interpretation of the multimodal utterance.

Considering a fragment of the multimodal grammar shown in Figure 8, it allows a user to issue commands such as "email this person and that organization" and gesture on appropriate person and organization. In the grammar, the non-terminals in the multimodal grammar are atomic symbols. The multimodal aspects of the grammar become apparent in the terminals. Each terminal contains three components **W:G:M** corresponding to the 3 tapes, where **W** is for the spoken language stream, **G** is the gesture stream, and **M** is the combined meaning. The epsilon symbol is used to indicate when one of these is empty in a given terminal. The symbols in **W** are words from the speech stream. The symbols in **G** are of two types. Symbols like *Go* indicate the presence of a particular kind of gesture in the gesture stream, while those like *e1* are used as references to entities referred to by the gesture. Simple deictic pointing gestures are assigned

semantic types based on the entities they are references to. *Go* represents a gesture reference to an organization on the display, *Gp* to a person, and *Gd* to a department. Figure 9 shows the three tape finite state device that is compiled based on the grammar. The above input is parsed to generate *email([person(id1), org(id2)])* where *id1* and *id2* are the specific entities that are generated by the gesture.

By assuming that a multimodal utterance has a certain order, this approach achieves efficient multimodal parsing. For example, for the utterance "pick up it" as speech and a pointing gesture to specify the object, the input order should be "pick up it ☞". However, this kind of approaches does not support the permutation in inputs. The same utterance in a different order, like "pick it up ☞", needs to be licensed by another rule in the context-free grammar. That will cause considerable categorial ambiguity when providing adequate coverage by the grammar. More importantly, there is no systematic relationship predicated between the multiple categories despite the fact that they prescribe the same meaning with alternative temporal orders.

While three-tape finite state devices are feasible in principle (Rosenberg, 1964); current techniques only support two information flow tapes finite-state machine. Thus, the implementation of

Figure 8. A Multimodal Grammar (Based on Johnston and Bangalore, 2000)

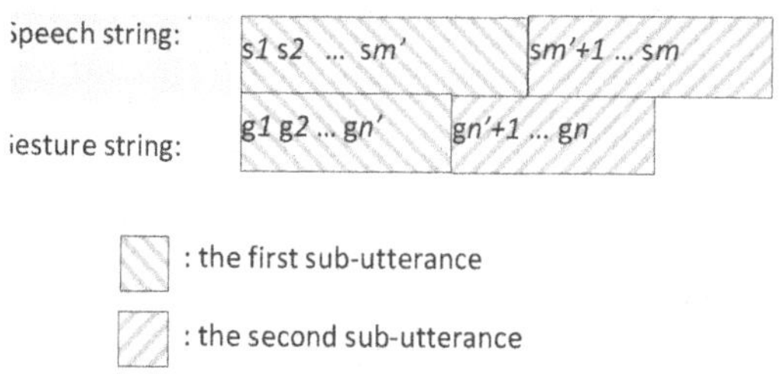

this approach requires converting three tapes finite state machine to two tapes finite state machine. This can be a significant issue when scaling to complex applications and/or more than two modalities. So, it is a light-weighted implementation which is suitable for small applications. Recently, in Latoschik (2005), a similar approach, which uses a modified temporal augmented transition network to integrate speech, gesture and context information in parallel, was reported. This kind of semantic fusion approach makes it possible to tightly couple multimodal fusion with speech and gesture recognition.

BACKGROUND AND PRELIMINARY NOTIONS

Combinatory Categorial Grammar (CCG) (Steedman, 2000) grammar is adapted to define the multimodal utterances in the MMIF approach introduced in next section. It is a form of lexicalized grammar in which the application of syntactic rules is entirely conditioned on the syntactic type (category).

Categories identify constituents as either atomic categories or functions. Atomic categories, such as N, NP, S and so on, may be further distinguished by features, such as number, case etc. Functions (such as verbs) bear categories identifying the type of their results (such as verbal phrase) and that of their argument(s)/complement(s). Functions also define the order in which the arguments must combine, and whether they must occur to the right or the left of the function. Therefore CCG is mildly context-sensitive. It can describe multimodal utterances more sophisticatedly than a context-free grammar which is used in most of other unification-based MMIF approaches. Lexical entries are specified by pairing symbols with

Figure 9. A Finite state device for multimodal parsing (Based on Johnston and Bangalore, 2000)

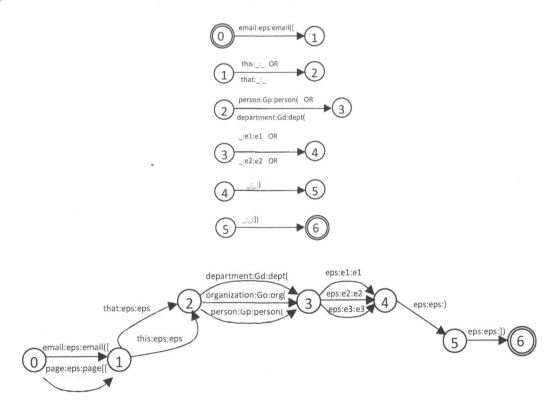

categories and their semantic interpretations. For example, the CCG lexicon in Figure 10 defines that "select" should follow a noun phrase (np) and precede an np, the final result is a sentence (s) after these arguments are ful-filled. It also defines "np/n" as the category of "the" and "n" as the category of "Macgregor_Street".

CCG also defines a set of rules to combine two categories and type-raise a category to another one, such as application rules, composition rules, crossing composition rules and type-raising rules (see Figure 11).

The CCG parsing process of "select the Macgregor_Street" is illustrated in Figure 12. Firstly, three words are assigned categories defined in lexicon, respectively. Then, "the" is combined with "Macgregor_Street" to an "np" according to forward application rule. Finally, "select" is combined with "the Macgregor_Street" to "s\np" which is typically a verbal phrase which follows an np to form a sentence (s). Because of CCG's semantic transparency, the semantic interpretation for an utterance is built compositionally and in parallel to the syntactic derivation. CYK (Younger, 1967) algorithm is used to apply the rules in CCG to multimodal utterances. The parsing algorithm

proposed later borrows the notion of CYK algorithm. We will focus on syntactic derivation of a multimodal utterance firstly and address the semantic interpretation later in next sections.

POLYNOMIAL UNIFICATION-BASED MULTIMODAL PARSING PROCESSOR

Multimodal input fusion on a mobile device requires less computational complexity. To achieve a low polynomial computational complexity while parsing multimodal inputs in versatile styles, a fusion approach termed as Polynomial Unification-based Multimodal Parsing Processor (PUMPP) (Sun, Shi, Chen & Chung, 2007b) was proposed recently. Different from other fusion approaches, it adopts CCG to define multimodal utterances and specify their syntactic structures and semantic interpretations. CCG provides a mildly context sensitivity while the grammars in other approaches are context-free. CCG also has more generative power than a context-free grammar. The permutation of multimodal inputs can be specified in the grammar rather than supposed by parsing algorithms. The multimodal grammar developers pay less attention to implementation in this approach than in previous unification-based approaches. An algorithm is designed to process parallel multimodal inputs while keeping a low computational complexity. With the principle in the algorithm, it can be easily extended to handle

Figure 10. A CCG lexicon example

```
select :- s\np/np

the :- np/n
Macgregor_Street :- n
```

Figure 11. CCG rules

```
Forward Application (>):      X/Y Y => X

Backward Application (<):     Y X\Y => X

Forward Composition (>B):     X/Y Y/Z => X/Z

Backward Composition (<B):    Y\Z X\Y => X\Z

Forward Type-raising (>T):    X => T/(T\X)
```

Figure 12. A CCG parsing example

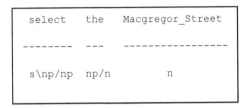

Figure 13. A multimodal utterance and its sub-utterances

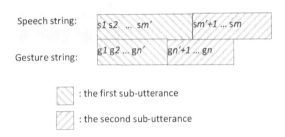

inputs from more than two modalities. With the semantically complementary relationship, it can also disambiguate recognized multimodal inputs. It has been successfully applied in applications with speech; hand gesture and eye gaze as input modalities.

The main novelties of the approach over traditional unification-based approach lie in these aspects:

- The parsing algorithm can handle two parallel input strings while maintaining the low polynomial computational complexity.
- CCG grammar is adapted to define multimodal utterances and specify their syntactic structures and semantic interpretations. That provides a mildly context sensitivity, and the grammars in most of other unification-based approaches are context-free.
- The multimodal inputs are parsed symbol by symbol rather than phrase by phrase as in other unification-based MMIF approaches.

Basic Principle in PUMPP

The parsing result of a multimodal utterance is the sequential composition of parsing results of its sub-utterances. In Figure 13, a multimodal utterance "s*1* s*2* … s*m* : g*1* g*2* … g*n*" composes of two sub-utterances. The first one covers speech symbols from s*1* to s*m'* and gesture symbols from g*1* to g*n'*. The second one covers speech symbols from s*m'+1* to s*m* and gesture symbols from g*n'+1* to g*n*. The parsing result of the utterance is the sequential composition of parsing results of these two.

With this principle, PUMPP will never try to combine "s*3* : g*2*" with "s*1* : g*3*", because the speech inputs are not in temporal order. Therefore, PUMPP supposes the temporal order between symbols from one modality in a multimodal utterance is fixed.

Architecture of the PUMPP

The architecture of the PUMPP is illustrated in Figure 14. It is made up of two elements. The

Figure 14. The architecture of the PUMPP

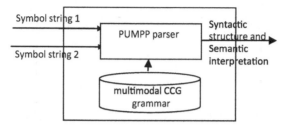

multimodal CCG grammar defines multimodal utterance styles and semantic interpretation. The PUMPP parser applies the CCG rules to categories of symbols of a multimodal utterance. The symbol strings are received and processed by the PUMPP parser symbol by symbol. This processing style enables incremental parsing between symbols from different modalities. The output of the parser is all possible syntactic structures and the semantic interpretations of the multimodal utterance which can be used for pragmatic processing in a specific application.

For PUMPP, speech input is represented as a string of words, which are referred as speech symbols. However, the representation of gesture inputs needs some discussions. We classify gesture input of the processor into two categories, expressive gesture and deictic gesture.

An expressive gesture can indicate a specific meaning independent of the context information. For example, a user holds his/her fist to mean "mark somewhere as an accident site". An expressive gesture can be represented with a symbol which is assigned the meaning of it.

On the other hand, deictic gestures can only be understood in a context within which it is issued. For example, when a user points to an entity in a context, what he/she wants to refer to is the entity rather than the coordinate of his/her hand cursor. Therefore, there is a task to recognize the entities referred to by deictic gestures from their coordinates within a specific context. If the task is accomplished right after gesture recognition, the efficiency of the multimodal system can be

improved in a certain degree. For PUMPP, the recognized symbol for a deictic gesture represents the entity it referred to. For example, a pointing gesture pointing to "River Terrace" is represented with symbol "River_Terrace".

Algorithm in the PUMPP

The algorithm in PUMPP is based on CYK algorithm designed for natural language processing, a kind of unimodal processing. CYK algorithm uses a simple two-dimensional matrix to record the constituents in parsing process. Based on its principle, we designed the matrix to record constituents and the loops to calculate the constituents in parsing parallel symbol strings.

Matrix to Record Parsing Constituents

For a sentence of length n, the CYK algorithm works with the upper-triangular portion of an $n \times n$ matrix. To accommodate the parsing constituents of two parallel input symbol strings, the two-dimensional matrix in original CYK algorithm is replaced by a four-dimensional matrix. For a multimodal utterance "A B C : x y", the matrix to record parsing constituents is illustrated in Figure 15. The first pair of index of a cell marks the speech span of the sub-utterance and the second marks the gesture span of the sub-utterance. The cell(1,3;0,2) records the parsing results for the sub-utterance (BC:xy) spanning from 1 to 3 for speech symbols (BC) and from 0 to 2 for gesture symbols (xy). The first row of the matrix contains

Figure 15. The matrix for the multimodal utterance "A B C : x y " in PUMPP

A multimodal utterance bounded by integers:

0 A 1 B 2 C 3 : 0 x 1 y 2

Extended Matrix:

(speech span) 0,0	0,1	1,2	0,2	2,3	1,3	0,3
0,0	A (0,1;0,0)	B (1,2;0,0)	AB (0,2;0,0)	C (2,3;0,0)	BC (1,3;0,0)	ABC (0,3;0,0)
0,1 (gesture span) x (0,0;0,1)						
1,2 y (0,0;1,2)		B:y (1,2,1,2)				
0,2 xy (0,0:0,2)					BC:xy (1,3;0,2)	ABC:xy (0,3;0,2)

Figure 16. Flow-chart to calculate the constituents in a cell for a multimodal sub-utterance in the algorithm of PUMPP

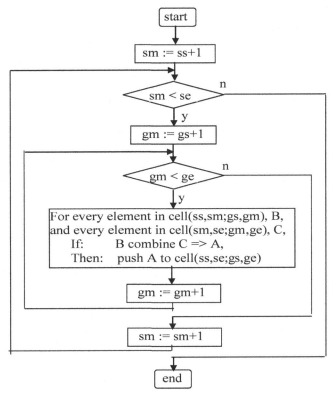

the parsing results of sub-utterances which do not have gesture symbol strings (gesture spans from 0 to 0). The first column of the matrix contains the parsing results for gesture only sub-utterances. The parsing results for the whole utterance are kept in the bottom-right cell (0,3;0,2). In practice, a function is used to map an index pair to an integer. The two pairs of integer indices of a cell are converted to two integer indices. Therefore, the four-dimensional matrix is flattened to a two-dimensional matrix.

Calculating the Constituents in a Cell of the Matrix

In the CYK algorithm, the constituents for a sub-sentence spanning i to j are calculated from all sub-sentence pairs which can concatenate to the sub-sentence. In the PUMPP parsing algorithm, the constituents for a sub-utterance spanning *ss* to *se* in speech and *gs* to *ge* in gesture are calculated from all sub-utterance pairs whose speech concatenations cover from *ss* to *se* and gesture concatenations cover from *gs* to *ge* (see Figure 16).

Extending the PUMPP Algorithm to Handle More Than 2 Modalities

This algorithm can be easily extended to handle *n* modalities with the following principles while keeping polynomial computational complexity:

- Using n-dimensional matrix to record parsing constituents;
- Making the cell for a sub-utterance spanning modality x from $m_x s$ to $m_x e$ (x ranges from *1* to *n*) as cell($m_1 s$, $m_1 e$; $m_2 s$, $m_2 e$; … ; $m_n s$, $m_n e$);
- Adding 3 nested loops for each modality; two for looping through the cells in the matrix, one for calculating the content in a cell.

Discussion About the Algorithm

The PUMPP algorithm can parse two parallel input symbol strings which are speech and gesture in the experiment. The basic insight behind this algorithm is that analyses of shorter sub-utterances can be recorded in the matrix and reused for the analyses of increasingly larger sub-utterances, which leads to polynomial recognition times instead of exponential in the length of a multimodal utterance. Flattening a four-dimensional matrix to a two-dimensional facilitates the algorithm to be understood and implemented. The CYK algorithm has worst-case computational complexity n^3 for recognizing a sentence with n words in the context-free case. Its worst-case computational complexity is n^6 for Vijay-Shanker and Weir (1990) generalization to CCG with a complex structure-sharing technique for categories. The proposed algorithm adds three more nested loops due to the second modality, and its computational complexity is still polynomial. Although no experiment with the proposed parser has been done on a real set of multimodal utterances, the experiments by Komagata (Komagata, 1997; Komagate, 1999) with a CYK parser for hand-build CCG grammar fragments of English and Japanese for real texts from a constrained medical domain suggest that average-case parsing complexity for practical CCG-based grammars can be quite reasonable in practice. This improvement overcomes the drawback of unification-based MMIF approaches in computational complexity claimed in (Johnston & Bangalore, 2005).

Disambiguating Speech Recognition Results with PUMPP

With the complementary relationship between the speech symbol string and the gesture symbol string of an utterance, PUMPP can disambiguate speech recognition results. Due to ambient noises, speaker variations and many other mismatches, some ASR systems provide several possible recognition symbol strings rather than a certain one. If the most possible one is what a user wants to say, speech recognition by ASR is regarded as successful. In practice, limited deictic gesture and a few types of expressive gestures result in virtually errorless gesture recognitions. PUMPP sequentially tries to integrate possible speech symbol strings with the recognized gesture symbol string until a parsing result can be derived. If the possible speech symbol string PUMPP stops at is not the most possible speech symbol string, but it is what a user wants to say; PUMPP successfully disambiguates speech recognition results.

Implementation of PUMPP

The implementation of PUMPP is based on openCCG (Baldridge, Kruijff & White, 2003) which is designed to parse sentences with CCG grammars. One of the most straightforward extensions is to add a multimodal parsing package opennlp.ccg.mparse based on package opennlp. ccg.parse. The CYK parsing algorithm was replaced by the PUMPP algorithm. The matrix was changed from a square whose size is the length of a sentence with a rectangular whose

width and depth are determined by the lengths of speech symbols and gesture symbols. The implementation of category structure, CCG rules, semantic structure and grammar loading facility in openCCG are kept.

Understanding the PUMPP Results with a Dialog Management Module

Without being utilized, PUMPP result will be useless. It is useful to discuss how to understand PUMPP result in a system. With the semantic interpretation and the discourse information, a Dialog management module can control an application background. Here, we use a multimodal presentation system, Multimodal Presentation Markup Language 3D (MPML3D) player, as an example to explain the mechanism.

As shown in Figure 17, The MPML3D player acts as a combination of multimodal input pre-processing module, dialog management module and application background. It accepts the multimodal presentation content from the content generation module; and delivers the specified multimodal presentation to a user. During the presentation, it also listens to the signals captured by an eye

Figure 17. The structure of a multimodal presentation system

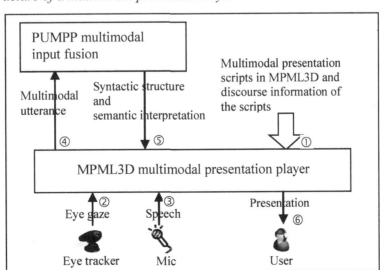

Figure 18. The input and output of THE HINGE

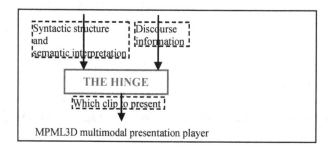

Figure 19. Three feature structures

$$\left[Agreement \quad \left[Person \quad 3rd \right] \right] \qquad (1)$$

$$\left[Agreement \quad \left[Number \quad single \right] \right] \qquad (2)$$

$$\left[Agreement \quad \begin{bmatrix} Person & 3rd \\ Number & single \end{bmatrix} \right] \qquad (3)$$

tracker and a Mic. The captured eye fixations are interpreted to the entities being fixated on. A speech recognizer attached to the MPML3D player recognizes the captured speech signal to speech strings. The MPML3D player constructs a multimodal utterance with these information, and passes it to the PUMPP multimodal input fusion module which returns all possible syntactic structures and semantic interpretations of the utterance as the fusion result. With the semantic interpretation and the discourse information, THE HINGE, which is the component in MPML3D player to utilize MMIF results, decides the content to deliver to a user in the next step.

Figure 18 highlights the input and output of THE HINGE. Specifically, they are the PUMPP result and the presenting decision. In the discourse information, each presentation clip is assigned a *triggering condition*. Syntactic structure, one part of PUMPP result, is represented in feature structure, and another part of PUMPP result, semantic interpretation, is represented in hybrid logic. For a dialog management module, semantic

interpretation of a multimodal utterance is more important than its syntactic structure.

Subsumption in Hybrid Logic

Feature Structures and Subsumption

Feature structures were used in some of previous researches to represent semantic interpretation. They are simply sets of attribute-value pairs, where attributes are atomic symbols, and values are either atomic symbols or feature structures themselves. In Figure 19, feature structure (1) has an attribute *"Agreement"* whose value is another feature structure, which has an attribute *"Person"* and value *"3rd"*.

As introduced in previous section "Unification-based MMIF", when two feature structures are unified, they are compared with every attribute in anyone of them. (1) If one's value is a variable or not specified, another's value is a constant; the variable will be bound to the other one. (2) When both of them have constant values; if their values are equal then unification succeeds, otherwise unification fails. The result of unification is two identical feature structures or fail. In Figure 19, the unification result of (1) and (2) is (3). Intuitively, unifying two feature structures produces a new one which is more specific (having more attributes) than, or is identical to, either of the input feature structures. We say a more general feature structure **subsumes** an equally or more specific one. In Figure 19, both (1) and (2) subsume (3). If feature structure A subsumes B, B satisfies all constraints outlined by A. Although feature structures can be used to represent semantic interpretation, hybrid logic is more suitable to capture meaning. More information about feature structure and unification operation can be found at Jurafsky & Martin (2008).

Hybrid Logic and Feature Structures

A hybrid logic (Baldridge & Kruijff, 2002) formula can be viewed as a flat conjunction of the heads and dependents inside it. Hybrid logic provides an internal means to refer to propositions. A hybrid logic formula can be formulized as:

head
dependent1
dependent2…

A dependent can be one of the following:

- Nominal: Proposition
- Nominal: <Mod>Proposition
- Nominal: <Mod>Nominal2

✶ Nominal2 is another nominal which refers other dependents.

For example, the formula in Figure 20 is a hybrid logic formula. Its head is *m1*. The dependents specify the value of the head and its properties. "*<HasProp>s1:proposition*" specifies that the *m1* has an attribute "*HasProp*" whose value is a nominal *s1*.

Although feature structures are essentially a two-dimensional notation for hybrid logic (Blackburn 2000), by making use of *nominals*, hybrid logic allows adjuncts to insert their semantic import into the meaning of the head. This flexibility makes it amenable to represent a wide variety of semantic phenomena in a propositional setting, and it can furthermore be used to formulate a discourse theory (Baldridge & Kruijff, 2002). The track from grammar to discourse can be covered with a single meaning formalism. That is one of the reasons why we chose hybrid logic to represent semantic interpretation of multimodal utterances and discourse information.

Hinging Semantic Interpretation of Multimodal Utterances and Multimodal Presentations

To determine the clip in corresponding with a multimodal utterance, every clip is assigned a *triggering condition* in discourse information, which is the loosest semantic interpretation to select this clip. For example, for the clip "*Flash memory is the memory medium of this EasyMP-*

Figure 20. A hybrid logic formula

```
@m1 (@s1:proposition(storage) ^
     @m1:phys-obj(medium) ^
     @m1:phys-obj(<num>sg) ^
     @m1:phys-obj(<HasProp>s1:proposition))
```

Figure 21. A triggering condition in hybrid logic.

```
@q (@q:quantification(what) ^
    @q:quantification(<Body>e:state) ^
    @e:state(be) ^
    @e:state(<Arg>x:phys-obj) ^
    @x:phys-obj(medium) ^
    @x:phys-obj(<Modifier>m) ^
    @m(<Ref>y:appliance) ^
    @y:appliance(EasyMP3Pod))
```

Figure 22. The Flowchart for "subsume(Head of Tdep, Head of Sutterance)".

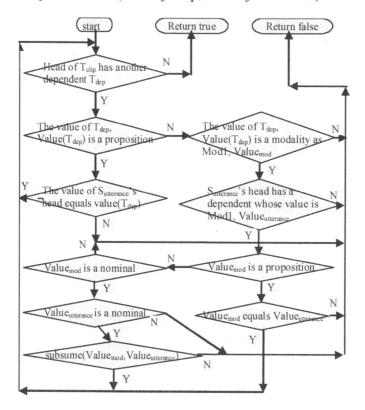

3Pod", the *triggering condition* in Figure 21 is defined. It subsumes the semantic interpretation of multimodal utterances such as "*what is the storage medium of this easy one*" while fixating on "*EasyMP3Pod*", "*what is the memory medium of this easy one*" while fixating on "*EasyMP3Pod*", and so on. To verify if the semantic interpretation of a multimodal utterance ($S_{utterance}$) satisfies the *triggering condition* of a clip (T_{clip}), THE HINGE

checks if T_{clip} subsumes $S_{utterance}$ with the process described in Figure 22.

EXPERIMENTS

In this section, we will describe several experiments conducted to verify different aspects of PUMPP.

Table 1. Summarization of the multimodal utterances in the experiment

Item									Total
speech length <=5	√	√	√						
speech length >5				√	√	√	√	√	
deictic gesture length = 1		√	√		√	√			
deictic gesture length = 2							√		
deictic gesture length = 3								√	
with expressive gesture	√		√	√	√				
Number of multimodal utterances	6	29	1	5	1	1	3	3	49
% to whole multimodal utterance set	12.24	59.18	2.04	10.20	2.04	2.04	6.12	6.12	100.00

Table 2. Summarization of multimodal utterances and their parsing results

Category	Number of parsing results per utterance	Number of multimodal utterances	%
1	0	2	4.08
2	1	38	77.55
3	2	4	8.16
4	3	1	2.04
5	10	1	2.04
6	11	3	6.12
Total		49	100.00

Parsing Two Parallel Symbol Strings with PUMPP

This experiment was designed and conducted to verify:

1. If the PUMPP can handle two parallel input symbol strings; and
2. The number of parsing results generated by the PUMPP for a multimodal utterance.

Multimodal Utterance Set

Multimodal utterances in the experiment were collected and selected from previous user study (Chen et al., 2005; Ruiz, Taib & Chen, 2006) about map-based traffic incident management, such as "zoom in" with a gesture point to the top-left quadrant of a map and "the interaction of State_Circle and Brisbane_Avenue" with a hand shape gesture to indicate "mark ... as an incident site".

Table 1 is a summarization of the multimodal utterances in this experiment. In the multimodal utterance set, there were 49 multimodal utterances with 91 words for speech and 50 symbols for gesture. Symbol length of an utterance ranged from 3 to 14. Five types of expressive gesture were included in the lexicon.

Preliminary Results and Analysis

Because multimodal utterances used in the experiment are more tool-oriented, most of the expected parsing results are verbal phrases which are imperative.

From Table 2, we can see the following:

1. The proposed processor can parse most utterances, except 2 multimodal utterances (Category 1, 4.08%);
2. Most utterances (Category 2, 77.55%) derive a unique parsing result;
3. About 10% (Category 3&4) utterances have slight parsing ambiguity in parsing results; and
4. About 8% (Category 5&6) utterances result in significant parsing ambiguity.

According to our analysis, there are mainly three reasons causing parsing ambiguities. They are (1) the permutation between multimodal inputs from different modalities; (2) unnecessary type-raising and (3) multiple prepositional phrases decorating a noun.

One of the multimodal utterances which has ambiguity in parsing results is "Pitt_Street and Market_Street : accident". Three of its parsing results are shown in Figure 23. In parsing result 1 of Figure 23, "accident :- n/n" is combined with "Market_Street :- n" to n. In parsing result 2 of Figure 23, "accident :- n/n" is combined with "Pitt_Street :- n" to n. In parsing result 3 of Figure 23, "accident :- s\none_np/np" combines with "Pitt_Street and Market_Street :- np" to s\none_np. This observation demonstrates the PUMPP algorithm tries different combination possibilities while keeping the order of symbols in one modality. It also demonstrates that the variable linear order of multimodal symbols from different modalities is a cause of parsing ambiguity although the input from one modality may screen out inappropriate symbols from the other modality.

Applying type-raising rule to generate a new category from an existing category facilitates com-

Figure 23. Three parsing results of an ambiguous multimodal utterance due to modality permutation

```
#  | Parsing Result
---+----------------------------------------------------
1  | Pitt_Street  and    accident Market_Street
   | -----------  ---    -------- -------------
   |      n      np\n/n     n/n          n
   |                     ----------------------->
   |                                n
   |                ----------------------------<
   |                         np\n
   | ------------------------------------------->
   |                      np
---+----------------------------------------------------
2  | accident Pitt_Street  and   Market_Street
   | -------- -----------  ---   -------------
   |    n/n          n       np\n/n        n
   | -------------------->
   |         n
   |                          ------------------>
   |                                   np\n
   | ----------------------------------------<
   |                      np
---+----------------------------------------------------
3  |   accident  Pitt_Street  and  Market_Street
   |   --------  -----------  ---  -------------
   | s\none_np/np       n       np\n/n        n
   |                            ------------------>
   |                                   np\n
   |                ------------------------------<
   |                            np
   |   ------------------------------------------->
   |                      s\none_np
```

position of categories, and it also over-generates categories when there is no further composition. For example, in Figure 24, after speech phrase "the corner of Bell_Avenue and River_Terrace" derives an "np" as parsing result 1, it is applied forward and backward type-raising in parsing result 2 and parsing result 3 in Figure 24. Another two more parsing results are derived.

When there are two prepositional phrases decorating a noun, the PUMPP generates all possible results without any common sense. For example, in Figure 25, "between White_River and South_Split" decorates "Lytton_Road" in parsing result 1, then "on Lytton_Road between White_River and South_Split" decorates "directions". In parsing result 2 of Figure 25, first, "on Lytton_Road" decorates "directions"; second,

"between White_River and South_Split" decorates "directions on Lytton_Road".

To clarify parsing ambiguities, parsing results can be chosen by the dialog management module based on the context information, and probabilistic parsing can be introduced into parsing algorithm as well.

The computational complexity of PUMPP has been discussed previously. In this experiment, the parsing time ranges from 0ms to 271ms. The utterance with the longest parsing time has 12 symbols from speech, 2 symbols from gesture and 10 parsing results. That means the multimodal parsing has very little impact on the system reaction time, especially in an interactive process in which the parsing process is triggered as soon as a multimodal symbol is received.

Figure 24. Three parsing results of an ambiguous multimodal utterance due to type-raising

#	Parsing Result
1	the corner of Bell_Avenue and River_Terrace --- np
2	---------------------------------------<T s$1\@i(s$1/@inp)
3	--------------------------------------->T s/@i(s\@inp)

Figure 25. Two parsing results of a noun with two decorative prepositional phrases

```
 #   Parsing Result
     directions on Lytton_Road between White_River and South_Split
     --------   ---  ----------  -----------------------------------
       n        n\n/n    n                              n\n
 1                       --------------------------------------------<
                                        n
                         -------------------------------------------->
                                               n\n
     ----------------------------------------------------------------<
                         n

     directions on Lytton_Road between White_River and South_Split
     ---------  -------------  -----------------------------------
       n            n\n              n\n
 2   ------------------------<
              n
     ------------------------------------------------------------<
                         n
```

Disambiguating Speech Recognition Results with Gesture Recognition Results

To verify the ability of PUMPP to disambiguate speech recognition results, an experiment is conducted.

Experiment Setup

In the experiment, there were 10 subjects, 8 males and 2 females, aging from 20 to 40. All of them are native English speakers. The multimodal CCG (MCCG) grammar and multimodal utterances were same as those in experiment "Parsing two Parallel Strings with PUMPP". Forty-nine speech phrases which are legitimate to the MCCG were pre-scripted for subjects to read. Their voice was recorded by Microsoft Sound Recorder with a general Mic. In case of unexpected mistakes, the subjects were required to read the phrases twice, but only one voice track was used.

For a public multimodal command-control interface, it is cumbersome to calibrate an ASR with every user to improve speech recognition accuracy. Therefore, a neural network speaker-independent ASR (Fonix VoiceIn 4.0, www. fonix.com) was used in this experiment. All possible phrases were defined in Fonix Grammar nodes. As illustrated in Figure 26, the Mic of PC2 captures speech signals replayed by PC1. The speaker-independent ASR running on PC2 recognizes speech signals to a 4-Best list. Gesture inputs to PUMPP are pre-computed to simulate errorless gesture recognition. PUMPP is running

on PC2 to accept the 4-Best list. Both the 4-Best lists and PUMPP results were logged. The pre-scripted speech phrases were regarded as what a user wants to say.

Experiment Result and Analysis

Let N_{ASR} be the number of successful speech recognition by ASR, N_{PUMPP} be the number of speech recognition successfully disambiguated by PUMPP, and then $N_{ASR,PUMPP}$ is defined as N_{ASR} plus N_{PUMPP}. Table 3 summarizes the experiment result. We use the N_{ASR} and $N_{ASR,PUMPP}$ as two groups of data for a paired t test.

The test result is t(9)=2.262, p<0.05. The number of N_{ASR} and $N_{ASR,PUMPP}$ in Table 3 are statistically different significantly. Therefore, PUMPP can disambiguate speech recognition results.

There was still a gap between the Number of $N_{ASR,PUMPP}$ and the total number of speech phrase, 49. One cause is the pre-scripted phrase is not in the 4-best list. Speaker independent ASRs are obviously less accurate than speaker dependent ones. Voice of subjects was recorded, replayed and captured by a general microphone and a speaker which is not sophisticate for audio signal. However, that condition resembles the practical environment and provides more room for PUMPP disambiguation. The other cause is that PUMPP did not correctly disambiguate speech symbol string, although it is semantically complementary with the pre-computed gesture symbol string. In this case, the MCCG can be re-fined to improve PUMPP's disambiguation ability.

Figure 26. Experiment setup 1

Table 3. Experiment result

Subject #	N_{ASR}	ASR sentence accuracy	N_{PUMPP}	$N_{ASR,PUMPP}$	ASR,PUMPP sentence accuracy
1	36	73.47%	2	38	77.55%
2	28	57.14%	0	28	57.14%
3	30	61.22%	0	30	61.22%
4	32	65.31%	0	32	65.31%
5	39	79.59%	3	42	85.71%
6	35	71.43%	4	39	79.59%
7	39	79.59%	1	40	81.63%
8	33	67.35%	2	35	71.43%
9	36	73.47%	0	36	73.47%
10	38	77.55%	3	41	83.67%
Average		70.61%			73.67%

Experiment of Utilizing PUMPP Results

To analyze the performance of utilizing PUMPP results in a multimodal system, another experiment was conducted.

Setup and Scenario

In the experiment, there was a virtual sales scenario where a team of two 3D animated agents present MP3 players (EasyMP3Pod and MP3Advance) to a human user. Each of the two agents (female and male) can perform body and facial gestures (emotional expressions). A user is seated in front of the monitor screen, as shown in Figure 27. Agents and environment are controlled by the MPML3D player attached with eye tracking and speech recognition function.

After an interactive presentation between the two agents, a user can ask some questions based on the presentation with his/her speech and eye gaze. The system would present a corresponding clip as a response to the question. Sample multimodal utterances asked by users are listed in Table 4.

Early Observations and Analysis

More than half multimodal utterances triggered corresponding responses. Others fell into the following categories. (1) Incorrect Responses Observed. When a user asked "How big is its storage for pictures" while fixating on *"EasyMP-3Pod"*, the system answered the whole storage size of the EasyMP3Pod rather than the size for pictures. Because the *triggering condition* of EasyMP3PodStorageClip ($T_{EasyMP3PodStorage}$) is more general than that of EasyMP3PodPicStorageClip ($T_{EasyMP3PodPicStorage}$), and $T_{EasyMP3PodStorage}$ firstly subsumed the semantic interpretation of the utterance. That implies that *triggering conditions* should not be compatible (one can subsume another one) with others. Or, if multiple *triggering conditions* can subsume the semantic interpretation of an utterance, a confirmation from the user should be pursued. (2) No Reply. There are several causes. Firstly, it is due to the instability of eye gaze fixation and eye tracking. After an intentional fixation, a user's eye gaze may lie on or be recognized as laying on another entity in the screen. Therefore, an incorrect multimodal utterance was constructed for multimodal input fusion. Secondly, a user uses words which are out of the vocabulary of the presentation. That implies speech recognition and/or multimodal input fusion should be able to at least skip/ignore them. During multimodal content generation, the key words should be used repeatedly; therefore, a user will prefer to use them in his/her multimodal questions.

FUTURE TRENDS OF MMIF

Being an essential component, the progress and challenges of MMIF will align with the progress of a multimodal system.

Firstly, MMIF should concisely support more modalities. Because there are limited findings on how different communication modalities or combined modes are organized during human-computer interaction and no empirical results are publicly available; one of the major challenges is the development of cognitive hypothesis in human-computer interaction, which suggests people's interaction style in different stress level. In natural communication, to relief their cognitive stress, people tend to select the most efficient/ convenient modalities to convey their meaning. That implies that the number of modalities in human-computer interaction will increase, but each modality will be used shortly and concisely. Therefore, MMIF will deal with more versatile and concise multimodal utterances. It is also very common that people omit a lot in natural communication by relying on information of a certain situation/environment that they are in. That indicates multimodal utterances will be very context sensitive. And MMIF should have intimate relationship with dialog management.

Secondly, techniques to support disambiguation between signals at different levels will spring up. There are two reasons for ambiguities in multimodal systems. One is there are noises in multimodal signal or some defects in signal recognition. This can be resolved by improving signal recognition technique and making the most use of multimodal signal. The other one is that a multimodal utterance can have multimodal interpretations. This kind of confusion can be clarified with context information, or further interaction between a system and a user. MMIF can disambiguate multimodal symbol strings

Figure 27. Experiment setup 2

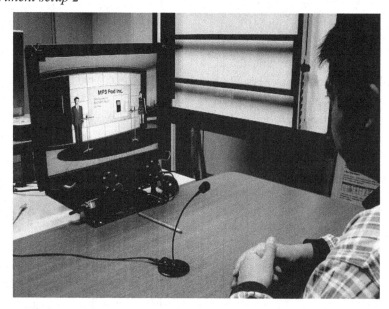

Table 4. Sample multimodal utterances with speech and eye gaze as input modalities in the experiment

#	Speech Input	Eye gaze fixation
1	How big is its storage	EasyMP3Pod
2	How many songs can it hold	MP3Advance
3	How many songs can this powerful one hold	MP3Advance
4	Does this simple one have FM tuner	MP3Advance
5	What functions does this big one come with	EasyMP3Pod
6	What is the storage medium of this easy one	EasyMP3Pod
7	What is the storage medium of this simple one	MP3Advance
8	Does this lovely one have a screen	EasyMP3Pod
9	How many buttons does it have	EasyMP3Pod

with complementary relationship between them; therefore, it may be able to make significant contributions in multimodal disambiguation in a multimodal system.

In the future, the MMIF related standards will emerge. Now, it is an exhausting task to develop an MMIF module for an application. And the fusion module is hard to be reused due to the lack of standards such as standards for multimodal input, standards for recognized inputs, standards for semantic interpretation and how to define a multimodal grammar. Public standards for MMIF are critical for a universal and open MMIF module.

To design and/or evaluate different MMIF approaches, public corpora are essential. As the proliferation of research in multimodal interactions, this kind of corpora will be published definitely.

New technology results in new languages. In applications on mobile devices, new multimodal utterances, which are incomplete to those in human-to-human communication but logically correct in the application, will emerge. This trend requires a multimodal grammar to be flexible enough to license versatile combinations of multimodal symbols.

As far as we can see, multimodal utterances will emphasis on expressive power and efficiency by means of more modalities. Therefore, MMIF needs to support more alternative modalities.

CONCLUSIONS AND FUTURE WORKS

With the proliferation of mobile devices, the interest and necessity for using multimodal interfaces on these devices are increasing. MMIF is an indispensable and most essential component of a multimodal system. PUMPP, the work presented in this chapter, perform with simplicity and low computational cost. It is ideal for mobile devices. Its novelties lie in (1) It can handle multimodal utterances that are from more than 2 modalities; (2) it is the first time to adopt CCG grammar in MMIF and flexibly describe multimodal utterances; (3) It adopts a single formalism—hybrid logic to represent semantic interpretation of multimodal utterances and discourse information so that the relationship between them can be described directly.

Among multimodal fusion approaches, early fusion is only useful for pairs of inputs that are closely coupled. Hence, a late fusion component is needed to handle the diverse input modalities in a multimodal system. PUMPP, a multimodal language processor which integrates symbol strings recognized by signal recognizers from multiple modalities, is proposed to meet this requirement. It targets applications in which complementary multimodal inputs can be recognized to symbols and occur sequentially or simultaneously.

By sophisticatedly disclosing the peculiarities of multimodal utterances from our point of view, we established the prerequisite of PUMPP. In a multimodal utterance, the linear order of inputs from multiple modalities is variable; however, the linear order from one modality is invariable. To tackle issues about exponential computational complexity in multimodal parsing, PUMPP algorithm is designed to parse two parallel input stings from multiple modalities in multimodal user interaction and generate the semantic interpretation compositionally in parallel to the syntactic derivation. Its computational complexity is polynomial.

Although PUMPP can integrate most multimodal utterances in the experiment, there are also some parsing ambiguities in parsing results which can be further clarified through applying other methods such as probabilistic parsing and context sensitizing.

Although PUMPP supposes the symbols from one modality in a multimodal utterance are linearly ordered by default, it can treat the permutation of the symbols from one modality as a special case. PUMPP can function to disambiguate speech symbols with gesture symbols. Statistical analysis of the experiment result about its disambiguation ability indicates the improvement to speech recognition is significant.

We also found that the more detailed the MCCG is defined; the more helpful PUMPP is to disambiguate speech symbols. Even if the correct speech recognition is found, PUMPP

may not derive a unique parsing result because one multimodal utterance can have several semantic interpretations. In future work, we plan to introduce probabilistic parsing to mitigate the ambiguity in parsing results.

To utilize the PUMPP result, we propose a concept, subsumption on hybrid logic, to hinge multimodal input fusion and output generation in an agent-based multimodal presentation system. In it, the subsumption on feature structure is adapted to hybrid logic to check the generalization of one hybrid logic formula over another one. That enables a system to respond to multimodal utterances flexibly. The preliminary experiment result supports its flexibility on the system performance. We also observed the overall performance of the system is closely related to other modules in the system.

There are a couple of directions that can be explored in the future. The first is to research how to cooperate with speech and gesture recognizer to achieve a practical result. PUMPP can accept input lattice to couple multimodal parsing with signal recognition. Second, probabilistic parsing can be introduced to mitigate the ambiguity in parsing results. Third, research on semantic representation to cooperate with the dialog management can also be a pending topic. Fourth, the compatibility between hybrid logic formulas (the *triggering conditions*) should be further investigated. Another one, but not the last one, is the research on communication between fusion results and discourse information.

REFERENCES

Baldridge, J., Kruijff, G., & White, M. (2003). *OpenCCG*. Retrieved from http://openccg.source-forge.net

Baldridge, J., & Kruijff, G. M. (2002, July 6-12). Coupling CCG and hybrid logic dependency semantics. In *Proceedings of ACL 2002*, Philadelphia, PA. ACL.

Bangalore, S., & Johnston, M. (2000, October 16-20). Integrating multimodal language processing with speech recognition. In *Proceedings of ICSLP 2000*, Beijing, China. ISCA.

Blackburn, P. (2000). Representation, reasoning, relational structures: A hybrid logic manifesto. *Journal of the Interest Group in Pure Logic, 8*(3), 339-365.

Carpenter, B. (1992). *The logic of typed feature structures*. Cambridge University Press.

Chen, F., Choi, E., Epps, J., Lichman, S., Ruiz, N., Shi, Y., et al. (2005, October 4-6). A study of manual gesture-based selection for the PEMMI multimodal transport management interface. In *Proceedings of ICMI2005*, Trento, Italy.

Earley, J. (1970) An efficient context-free parsing algorithm. *Communication of ACM 13, 2*, 94-102. New York.

Holzapfel, H., Nickel, K., & Stiefelhagen, R. (2004, October 13-15). Implementation and evaluation of a constraint-based multimodal fusion system for speech and 3D pointing gestures. In *Proceedings of ICMI 2004*, State College, PA.

Johnston, M., Cohen, P.R., McGee, D., Oviatt, S.L., Pittman, J.A., & Smith, I. (1997, July 7-12). Unification-based multimodal integration. In *Proceedings of the 35th Annual Meeting of the Association for Computational Linguistics and 8th Conference of the European Chapter of the Association for Computational Linguistics*, Madrid, Spain (pp. 281-288). ACL.

Johnston, M. (1998) Unification-based multimodal parsing. In *Proceedings of COLING-ACL'98*, Montreal, Canada (pp. 624-630). ACL.

Johnston, M., & Bangalore, S. (2000, July 31-August 4) Finite-state multimodal parsing and understanding. In *Proceedings of COLIN2000*, Saarbrücken, Germany.

Johnston, M., & Bangalore, S. (2005) Finite-state multimodal integration and understanding.

Journal of Natural Language Engineering 11.2. Cambridge: Cambridge University Press.

Jurafsky, D., & Martin, J.H. (2008) *Speech and language processing: An introduction to natural language processing, computational linguistics, and speech recognition, second ed.* Pearson: Prentice Hall.

Kaiser, E., Olwal, A., McGee, D., Benko, H., Corradini, A., Li, X., Cohen, P., et al. (2003, November 5-7). Mutual disambiguation of 3D multimodal interaction in augmented and virtual reality. In *Proceedings of the 5th International Conference on Multimodal Interfaces*, Vancouver, Canada. ACM.

Kaiser, E., Demirdjian, D., Gruenstein, A., Li, X., Niekrasz J., Wesson, M., et al. (2004, October 13-15). Demo: A multimodal learning interface for sketch, speak, and point creation of a schedule chart. In *Proceedings of ICMI 2004*, State College, PA.

Komagata, N. (1997). Efficient parsing for CCGs with generalized type-raised categories. In *Proceedings of the 5th International Workshop on Parsing Technologies*, Boston, MA (pp. 135-146). ACL/SIGPARSE.

Komagata, N. (1999). *Information structure in texts: A computational analysis of contextual appropriateness in English and Japanese.* Unpublished doctoral dissertation, University of Pennsylvania, PA.

Latoschik, M.E. (2005, October 4-6). A user interface framework for multimodal VR interactions. In *Proceedings of ICMI'05*, Trento, Italy (pp. 76-83). ACM.

Oviatt, S. (1999, May 15-20). Mutual disambiguation of recognition errors in a multimodal architecture. In *Proceedings of the SIGCHI Conference on Human Factors in Computing Systems: The CHI is the Limit*, Pittsburgh, PA (pp. 576-583). ACM.

Portillo, P.M., Garcia G.P., & Carredano, G.A. (2006). Multimodal fusion: A new hybrid strategy for dialogue systems. In *Proceedings of ICMI'06*, Banff, Canada. ACM.

Rosenberg, A.L. (1964). On n-tape finite state acceptors. *FOCS*, 76-81.

Rudzicz, F. (2006, July). Clavius: Bi-directional parsing for generic multimodal interaction, In *Proceedings of COLING/ACL 2006*, Sydney, Australia.

Ruiz, N., Taib R., & Chen, F. (2006, November 20-24). Examining redundancy in multimodal input. In *Proceedings of OZCHI 2006*, Sydney, Australia.

Steedman, M. (2000). *The syntactic process.* Cambridge, MA: The MIT Press.

Sun, Y., Shi, Y., Chen, F., & Chung, V. (2007, November 28-30) An efficient unification-based multimodal language processor in multimodal input fusion. In *Proceedings of OZCHI2007*, Adelaide, Australia. ACM.

Tan A.H. (1995). Adaptive resonance associative map. *Neural Networks Archive, 8*(3), 437-446. Vijay-Shanker, K., & Weir, D. (1990). Polynomial time parsing of combinatory categorical grammars. In *Proceedings of ACL'90*, Pittsburgh, PA. ACL.

Younger, D.H. (1967). Recognition and parsing of context-free languages in time $O(n^3)$. *Information and Control, 10*, 189-208.

Zhang, Q., Imamiya, A., Go, K., & Mao, X. (2004). Resolving ambiguities of a gaze and speech interface. In *Proceedings of the 2004 Symposium on Eye Tracking Research & Applications*, San Antonio, TX (pp. 85-92). ACM.

KEY TERMS AND DEFINITIONS

Deictic Gesture: In multimodal human-computer interaction, a deictic gesture is a gesture whose meaning relies absolutely on context.

Expressive Gesture: In multimodal user interaction, an expressive gesture is a gesture that conveys a specific meaning independent of the context information.

Gesture Unit: A gesture unit is the unit of visible bodily action giving meaning or part-meaning.

Multimodal Turn: In multimodal human-computer interaction, a multimodal turn refers to an opportunity or segment that comes successively to a user to express his/her meaning to a system.

Multimodal Utterance: In multimodal human-computer interaction, a multimodal utterance refers to a complete set of symbols recognized from multimodal input signals in one multimodal turn.

Phrase: A phrase is a group of words that construct a single syntactic structure.

Pragmatics Processing: In human-computer interaction, pragmatic processing applies the semantic interpretation of an utterance to matters with regard to their practical requirementsor consequences.

Semantic Interpretation: Semantic interpretation is the truth or satisfaction conditions of a multimodal utterance, ignoring those aspects that are influenced by the context of its use.

Symbol: In a multimodal user interface, a symbol is an atomic input unit from a recognizer to the multimodal input fusion module.

Syntax: In linguistics, syntax is the rules of a language that show how the words of that language are to be arranged to make a sentence of that language.

Chapter V
Interpretation Methods and Ambiguity Management in Multimodal Systems

Maria Chiara Caschera
Istituto di Ricerche sulla Popolazione e le Politiche Sociali-Consiglio Nazionale delle Ricerche, Italy

ABSTRACT

Naturalness and flexibility of the dialogue between users and multimodal systems can produce more than one interpretation and consequently ambiguities. This chapter deals the problem to correctly recognize user input for enabling a natural interaction. In particular, it analyses approaches that have to cope with issues connected to the interpretation process, dividing them into recognition-based, decision-based, and hybrid multilevel fusion strategies, and providing descriptions of some example of these methods. Moreover, this chapter provides classifications of ambiguities classifying them at a more general level in recognition, segmentation, and target ambiguities, and dividing them in a more detailed way in lexical, syntactical, and pragmatic ambiguities. Considering these classifications, this chapter analyses how interpretation methods support the correct recognition of ambiguities. Finally, this chapter presents methods applied after the interpretation process and that integrate it for solving different class of ambiguities using the dialogue between the user and the system.

INTRODUCTION

A multimodal system allows to receive, to interpret, and to process input, and to generate as output two or more interactive modalities in an integrated and coordinated way. This fact is connected to the purpose to make the system's communication characteristics more similar to the human approach that is often multimodal and it is obtained combining different modalities.

In fact, multimodal systems combine visual information (involving images, text, sketches and so on) with voice, gestures and other modalities (see Figure 1) providing natural dialog approaches using intelligent and personalized approaches.

In particular, user communication with a multimodal system involves sending and receipting of a multimodal representation (message) between the two, and this message can be modal or multimodal.

The Figure 2 underlines that during multimodal dialog, the user's actions or commands produces a message, which has to be interpreted by the system, and vice-versa materialization produced by the system has to be interpreted by the user (Caschera et al., 2007c).

In particular, input digital channels acquire user input's information that is transformed by different process activities and this sequential transformation of input defines the interpretation function. Considering the output direction this information is manipulated in order to be made perceivable by the user, and this sequence

of transformation defines the rendering function (Coutaz et al., 1993).

However, the naturalness and flexibility of the dialogue provided by the use of different modalities of interaction can produce more than one interpretation of the user input and consequently one ambiguity. In fact, the identification of one and only one meaning of multimodal input is a crucial aspect in order to provide a flexible and powerful dialog between the user and the system.

Therefore, the focus of this chapter is to deal ambiguities connected to the interpretation process. In this scenario, the role of interpretation methods is very important because they have the purpose to identify the meaning of the user input and it finds the most proper association to the user intention.

In multimodal systems, the combination of different modalities generates the cohabitation of ambiguities connected to the single modality in a multimodal system. Ambiguities can be due to the incorrect interpretation of one modality and moreover they can appear when each modality

Figure 1. Example of modalities involved during multimodal interaction

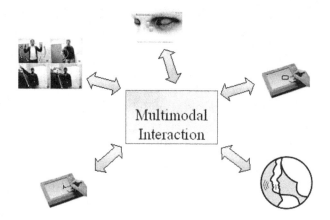

Figure 2. User-system multimodal dialog

is correctly interpreted, but the combination of information generated by each modality is not coherent at the semantic level. In fact, information coming from each separate input modality can be correctly and univocally interpreted by the multimodal system, while the interpretation can become ambiguous considering information opportunely combined.

Therefore, during the multimodal interaction ambiguities can be produced by: the propagation at multimodal level of a modal input ambiguity; and combining un-ambiguous modal information containing contrasting concepts in multimodal dialogue.

In particular, let us suppose that the system allows the user to interact using voice and sketch input. In this case the system combines speech and sketch modalities and it can be affected both to speech and sketch ambiguities. Multimodal ambiguities can be caused by both the interpretation process of each modality and the interpretation process of the combined multimodal input.

Until now several tools have been developed to correctly interpret multimodal input combining inputs generated by different interaction modalities.

The interpretation approaches are mainly defined in order to specify the meaning of the multimodal input of the user and they consequently are correlated to the management of ambiguities that can appear during the interpretation process. In particular ambiguities are due to the possibility to interpret user input in more than one way.

Starting from the notion that ambiguity is closely connected to the possibility to interpret multimodal input in different ways, it is necessary to analyse methods for interpreting multimodal input in order to define an overview of treatment of ambiguities in modal and multimodal systems. This consideration springs from the fact that the interpretation of multimodal input depends on the formal method used to define multimodal input. So in order to detect and solve multimodal ambiguities it is necessary to analyse methods for defining multimodal input considering the different classes of ambiguities.

This chapter will analyse the interpretation process of modal and multimodal input. In order to give a complete view of the process, the first section will provide an analysis of selected methods for interpreting multimodal input. This treatment is not exhaustive because it is out of the focus of this chapter but it is necessary for introducing problems connected to the interpretation process. An exhaustive treatment of methods for defining multimodal input is given in a further chapter [chapter titled: Exploring Multimodal Input Fusion Strategies].

Starting from techniques for interpreting modal and multimodal input, this chapter will focus on ambiguity connected to the interpretation process. Modal and multimodal ambiguities will be dealt and therefore this chapter will provide main classifications of ambiguities presented in Literature. Starting from these classifications the chapter will analyse how ambiguities are repre-

Figure 3. Modal and multimodal ambiguities

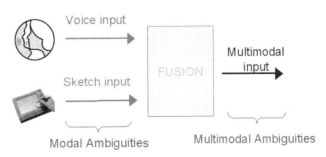

sented and how they are managed by methods for solving them.

MEANINGFUL FEATURES OF INTERPRETATION METHODS

The interpretation process is one important unit for building multimodal systems. The interpretation of user input is strictly connected to different features, such as available interaction modalities, conversation focus, and context of interaction. A correct interpretation can be reached by simultaneously considering semantic, temporal and contextual constraints.

For example in multimodal system based on video and audio input (Harper and Shriberg, 2004) the interpretation defines a multimodal corpus of digital and temporally synchronized video and audio recordings of human monologues and dialogues.

Literature provides different methods to interpret multimodal input. An exhaustive treatment of methods for fusing and interpreting multimodal input has been developed in the chapter [chapter titled: Exploring Multimodal Input Fusion Strategies]. This classification divides multimodal input fusion strategies taking into account the level where the fusion has been executed: at the acquisition level; at the interpretation level; and at the decision level.

The focus of this chapter is to provide an analysis of ambiguities connected to the interpretation process in multimodal system underlining how methods provided in Literature manage them. Therefore, starting from the fusion strategies provided in a further chapter [chapter titled: Exploring Multimodal Input Fusion Strategies], this section deals with a selection of Mathematical methods for interpreting multimodal and modal input using recognition-based fusion strategies, decision-based fusion strategies and hybrid multilevel fusion strategies.

In particular, considering recognition-based strategies the following section will analyse how HMMs (Rabiner, 1989) can be used to interpret user input. This chapter provides Attributed Relational Graphs method (Chai et al., 2004) as example of decision-based strategies. Finally, taking into account hybrid multilevel strategies examples of this class of methods will be provided.

Recognition-Based Approaches

Meaningful recognition-based approaches are the Hidden Markov Models that are stochastic models that allow supporting the interpretation of the user input. These methods have been used for modelling speech input (Resch, http://www.igi.tugraz.at/lehre/CI) different sketching styles (Sezgin and Davis, 2005), handwriting (Hu et al., 1994) and gesture (Eickeler et al., 1998).

In detail, for defining the interpretation of the input, this method uses a sequence of vectors of features extracted from modalities used during the interaction process. This sequence is compared with a set of hidden states that can represent the speech word, the letter of the handwritten word or the drawing by the sketch modality according to the definition of the parameters of the model and the modalities to be interpreted. The purpose of this method is to identify the model that has the highest probability to generate the observed output, given the parameters of the model.

In detail, the set of the parameters that characterise the Hidden Markov model are:

- The set of the state
- The prior probabilities that define the probability that a specific state is the first state
- The emission probabilities that define the probability of a specific observation in a specific state
- The observation sequence.

In this model an important parameter to define is the number of HMM states. In fact, in the case that this number is short thence the discrimination power of the model is reduced because more than one pattern should be modelled on one state. In the other hand whether this number is excessive thence the number of training samples is not sufficient compared to the number of the model parameters. Therefore in literature two different approaches have been developed to determine the number of the HMM states. The first one uses a fixed number of states training each category of samples with the same number of states. The second approach uses a variable number of states dividing each component in sub-components according to a specific criterion and associating each sub-component by an HMM state.

Decision-Based Approaches

The interpretation process can be applied also at the decision level. Therefore this section provides an analysis considering how an example of decision-based approach, the referent resolution approach, can be used to correctly interpret information coming from multiple modalities such as sketch, speech, gesture and handwriting.

In particular, when we have different type of interaction modalities, it is not easy to identify all objects, which a user refers during his/her input, and to correctly interpret the combination of the modal input. Users can make precise, complex or ambiguous references. Consequently the Literature has proposed a process that finds the most proper referents to objects, which a user refers during the input. This process is known in literature as referent resolution (Chai et al., 2006). In detail this method aims to find the most proper meaning for the expression defining the user input as a referring expression, and the specific entity or entities to which she/he refers as referents.

The referent resolution problem implies the dealing of different types of references. This problem has been coped with probabilistic approaches, for example using a graph-matching algorithm (Chai et al., 2004). This approach represents in-

formation belonging to different modalities and contest by attributed relational graphs (Tsai and Fu, 1979), and the referent resolution problem is solved as a probabilistic graph-matching problem. In detail, information concerning each modality is represented by an attributed relational graph, and the referent resolution problem are dealt using information about properties of referring expressions and referents and inter-relations among nodes of the same graph. Each node of the graph represents an entity and it contains semantic and temporal information about the entity. An edge defines relation between two entities and it includes: temporal relation that represents the temporal order between the two entities during the interaction process; and semantic type relation between the two entities that expresses if the two entities express the same semantic type.

In (Chai et al., 2004) three attributed relational graphs (AGRs) are defined: the first contains information about the speech input; the second is connected to the gesture input; and the last refers to the conversation context defining an history AGR that includes information about objects referred during the last interaction.

Hybrid Multilevel Approaches

The last section of this paragraph describes examples of hybrid multilevel approaches; those interpret multimodal input at different levels: acquisition, recognition and decision levels.

An example of this class of methods is finite-state mechanisms (Johnston and Bangalore, 2005) based on weighted finite-state automaton with multimodal grammar. This method parses, understands and integrates speech and gesture inputs by a single finite-state devices defining three-tape finite state automaton that represent speech input, gesture input and their combined interpretation. The speech and gesture streams are combined considering their content into a single semantic representation. The interpretation of the multimodal command is defined using a multimodal context-free grammar where each terminal symbol contains three components: the spoken language stream, the gesture stream and the combined meaning. However this approach is limited because the multimodal grammar is not able to recognize any string that is not accepted by the grammar. To overcome this issue a corpus-driven stochastic language model has been defined (Johnston and Bangalore, 2005 a). In this approach the finite-state-based interpreter is combined with an edit-based transducer for lattice inputs defined by speech and gesture modalities. This edit machine allows integrating stochastic speech recognition with handcrafted multimodal grammars.

Furthermore Literature provides to interpret user input using parse tree (Collins, 1997) with semantic grammars (Gavalda and Waibel, 1998) considering semantic information associated with the interpretation of the sentence and converting the parse tree into a set of typed feature structures (Carpenter, 1992), where feature structures represent objects in the domain and relationships between objects.

A further hybrid approach for correctly interpret multimodal input is proposed in (Caschera et al., 2007a) that analyses the structure of multimodal sentences and connections between elements that compose them using the attribute-based structure of the Constraint Multiset Grammar (Chok and Marriott, 1995) and the concept of recourses provided by the Linear Logic (Girard, 1987). This approach defines user's input as composed of a set of terminal elements of the grammar that contain information about: the input modality that expresses each element; the representation of each element in the specific modality; the temporal interval connected to each element; the semantic of each element considering its representation in the modality; the syntactic role that each element plays in user input. While non-terminal elements of the grammar are decomposed in terminal elements by Linear Logic and, in particular, by: the production rules of the grammar; the context

rules that consider the domain knowledge and the discourse context knowledge; and temporal rules that combine terminal elements considering the fact that their temporal intervals are temporally closed or not.

AMBIGUITIES CONNECTED TO THE INTERPRETATION PROCESS

Methods introduced in the previous section aim to define a correct and unique interpretation of the user's input, but the naturalness of the multimodal interaction defines richness of the language that can produce difficulties during the interpretation process, such as ambiguities.

In detail, an ambiguity is due to the fact that the interpretation function associates a multimodal input with more than one description. One of the reasons for ambiguities is that a single space is used to represent different kinds of information. Another reason is that the user gives his/her own semantics to the information, but sometimes his/her actions do not represent his/her intentions, producing an ambiguous or incorrect interpretation by the system. Moreover ambiguities can be produced by the inaccuracy of the user input.

The system can also represent information in different ways, one of which must be chosen. So ambiguities are found at different levels: the user's action and interpretation and the system's interpretation and materialization.

Ambiguities can be also due to noise that is introduced by the users' interaction behaviours and by tools and sensors. Therefore, during the interaction process errors can be caused by users or by the system.

In particular, approaches described in the previous section have to cope with ambiguities connected to the interpretation process of the system.

The Literature has widely treated ambiguities providing classifications of them. Therefore, this section will present the main proposed classifications of ambiguities and the following section will analyse how they are dealt during the interpretation process.

Ambiguities can be classified at different levels, in fact they can be analysed considering them connected to the inaccuracy of the user input or they can be analysed considering properties of the language dividing them into lexical, syntactical and pragmatic ambiguities.

Ambiguities due to the inaccuracy of the user input can be classified in three main classes: the recognition ambiguity that appears when the recogniser returns more than one interpretation of the user input; the segmentation ambiguity that appears when is not clear how to group user inputs; and target ambiguity that is connected to the focus of the user input that is not clear (Mankoff et al., 2000). In particular, segmentation ambiguity appears when a portion of an element is considered as an element itself. Moreover this kind of ambiguities can appears when the elements to interpret have complex structures and they are composed of different elements. In this case a subpart of an element can be considered as an element itself.

A more detailed classification divides ambiguities in lexical, syntactical and pragmatic ambiguities according to the linguistic properties of the language (Berry et al., 2001).

In particular, lexical ambiguities are connected to issues related to the semantic meaning of the user input. In (Caschera et al., 2007b) lexical ambiguities are divided in: lexical ambiguities that appear when one element of the language has more than one accepted meaning and so it can have different interpretations; lexical relationship ambiguities appear if a relationship between two elements of the language has different meanings; and scope ambiguities that arise when the user input provides different scooping relations. In detail, an example of ambiguities connected to the semantics of the elements of the language arises when the same element can be differently interpreted in different contexts. In fact, considering the element *"bank"*,

it can be interpreted by the multimodal system as a shore of the river and as a financial institution according to the contexts (Buvac, 1996).

A further example of ambiguities (scope ambiguity) appears when the user asks to the system information about a restaurant selecting two different restaurants. In this case the system is not able to identify which one of the restaurant is the focus of the user.

Considering syntactical ambiguities, they appear when alternative structures can be generated for the user input during the interpretation process. These ambiguities are connected to roles of elements of the languages and they appear when they have more than one role during the interpretation process and they include: analytic, gap, attachment and occlusion ambiguities.

In particular analytic ambiguity appears if the categorization of the element is not clear. An example of analytic ambiguity in given by Hirst in (Hirst, 1987). The author describes more than one pattern for the sentence *"The Tibetan history teacher"*. In particular this sentence can be interpreted as: *the teacher of the Tibetan history* or the *Tibetan teacher of history*.

Also gaps ambiguities are connected to issues about the structure of the user input and they arise when one element of the user input is omitted producing a gap.

Moreover, attachment ambiguity is a further kind of syntactical ambiguities and it arises when elements of the user input can be legally attached to different parts of the input defining different meanings. An example of attachment ambiguity appears when the user says the sentence *"he wrote a letter to the woman with the pen"* using the speech modality while using gesture she indicates a man. This ambiguity is due to the fact that the system is not able to decide between these cases: 1) in the first interpretation *"with the pen"* is attached to the verb *"wrote"*; 2) in the second interpretation *"with the pen"* is attached to the element *"woman"*. These two interpretations define different meaning for the sentence because in the first case, the man is using a pen to write a letter; while in the second, the woman has the pen.

A further type of analytic ambiguities is the occlusion (Futrelle, 1999) that arises when different elements of the language are overlapped. In this case the interpretation can be not univocally defined because it is difficult to understand if these elements are separately used or they are components of the same element.

Finally, pragmatic ambiguity appears when user input has several interpretations in the context in which it is expressed. While the meaning of semantic ambiguities is independent from the context, the meaning of pragmatic ambiguities is context-dependent. In particular, a pragmatic ambiguity appears when is not clear which element of the language a pronoun or deictic refers to (Caschera et al., 2007a).

The previous classification are widely analysed in interaction systems that mainly use natural language-based input. However this classification can be applied also to visual languages (D'Ulizia et al., 2007).

The following section analyses these classifications of ambiguities using the interpretation methods that are previously described, and introducing a further classes of methods that are able to integrate the interpretation methods by the dialogue with users.

HOW METHODS DEAL CLASSES OF AMBIGUITIES

Starting from the classifications provided in the previous section, this chapter provides example of previously presented methods analysing how they can support the recognition of classes of ambiguities.

In particular, methods for solving ambiguities due to the inaccuracy of the user input can be dealt using recognition-based approach. In particular, examples of these approaches are presented showing how statistical approaches can be used to deal the inaccuracy of the user input. In addi-

tion, this chapter provides how hybrid multilevel approaches deal syntactical ambiguities. Then, this section describes how decision-based and hybrid multilevel approaches allow to cope with lexical ambiguities. Finally, this chapter presents methods that are applied after the interpretation process and integrate it for solving different class of ambiguities. These methods are based on the dialogue between the user and the system and they are classified as a-posterior methods because they are applied after the fusion process and they allow user to repeat his/her input (Caschera et al., 2007a).

How Recognition-Based Approaches Solve Ambiguities Due to the Inaccuracy

Ambiguities due to the inaccuracy of the user input can be mainly managed using recognition-based approaches. In particular statistical approaches can be used: Thresholding and Historical Statistics.

The Thresholding method (MacKenzie and Chang, 1999) expresses the correctness of the user input using a probability and it compares it to a threshold. In detail, the recogniser returns a confidence score measuring the probability that a user input was correctly recognized. In the case that this confidence measure is below a pre-defined threshold then the system discards the interpretation.

The Historical Statistics method provides probabilities of correctness of the user input by performing a statistical analysis of historical data about ambiguities. It can be used if the confidence score is not available and it usually provides a default probability of correctness for a given interpretation. This approach is based on a confusion matrix, which is the matrix whose values give the estimation of the number of times that the recogniser confused the user input.

These statistical approaches are based on statistical theories such as: Hidden Markov Models, fuzzy logic, and Bayesian networks.

The adaptivity of the Hidden Markov Models provides that they can be applied to several pattern recognition applications.

For example, in speech recognition, isolated word can be recognized using HMMs assuming that each word is modelled by distinct HMMs (Rabiner, 1989). Furthermore this approach assumes that there is a training set of occurrences for each word, and each occurrence constitutes an observation sequence, which is the appropriate representation of the characteristics of the word.

Considering the sketch interaction, sketches are often compositional and incremental therefore observation symbols of the HMM respond to the encoding of input strokes in terms of lines of different orientations (Sezgin and Davis, 2005). In particular the incremental property of the strokes implies to consider the structure of a current stroke taking account of the previous and the next stroke. Therefore this sequence is modelled using a left-to-right HMM (Jiang and Sun, 2005) in adaptive way because the number of states in multi-strokes sketch recognition is dynamically determined by the structural decomposition of the target pattern. The model is defined by a training stage and the recogniser provides the probabilities and the recognition results in the sequence of probabilities from high to low using the trained HMM.

The problem of correct handwriting recognition has been treated using different approaches: using words models, using models based on letters, and using sub-character models. The second one of these approaches has been dealt by an HMM based on strokes (Hu et al., 1994). This approach considers letters as a concatenation of strokes and each stroke is modelled by one-state HMM.

Finally, considering the gesture recognition, to recognize dynamic gesture HMMs classify human's movements over a sequence of image (Eickeler et al., 1998). This system divides images in meshes and counts the number of pixels that represent the person for each mesh. The system composes a feature vectors that are classified based on discrete HMMs.

For solving issues connected to the inaccuracy of the user input fuzzy logic is widely used due to its ability to describe the classification of uncertainty. This method is based on the concept of fuzzy set (Zadeh, 1978) that provides a general representation of uncertainty considering different degrees of membership values. In particular, elements of a fuzzy set belong to the set with different graduations and the degree for each one of the elements gives the degree of certainty that the element belongs to the set. Therefore, fuzzy logic defines the appropriate fuzzy set via membership functions to be associated to each user input in order to solve the vagueness and the ambiguities of the interaction behaviours connected to imprecision and noises.

Uncertainties and so ambiguities in user input are also dealt in Literature using Bayesian networks.

These approaches model the set of interpretations by an acyclic direct graph and a set of probabilistic distribution. In the graph each node represents one interpreted element and each arc gives the relationship between the two connected nodes. Different interpretations are related to different probabilities that can be influenced by factors such as the context.

How Decision-Based and Hybrid Multilevel Approaches Solve Lexical Ambiguities

In this section examples of methods for dealing lexical ambiguities are presented. Here both examples of decision-based and hybrid multilevel approaches are provided.

How Decision-Based Approaches Solve Lexical Ambiguities

Starting from the description of lexical ambiguities provided in the previous section, this paragraph would underline how decision-based approaches have been used in order to detect and solve lexical ambiguities.

In particular we analyse how the methods proposed in the previous section based on attributed relational graphs (Chai et al., 2004) is used to solve this kind of ambiguities.

In this approach the speech graph is considered as the referring graph, while gesture graph and the history graph are combined in the referent graph adding new edges to connect every gesture nodes to all history nodes.

This approach aims to find the most probable association among referents and referring expression taking into account semantic, temporal and contextual constraints. Therefore, the referent resolution problem is solved finding the best mach between the referring graph and the referent graph and satisfying temporal, semantic and contextual constraints.

The referent resolution problem has been also handled to solve deictic and anaphoric expressions (Huls et al., 1995).

Modal input can be inaccurate and in particular when user uses gesture modality displayed objects can be too small for human finger so she/he can selects more than one object using only one gesture input generating an ambiguity. To deal this ambiguity [C20] proposes the definition of a history graph that is composed of a list of elements that are in focus during the last interaction of the user. The ambiguities problems are solved as a graph-matching problem that aims to define the best match between the history graph and graphs generated by modal input optimising the satisfaction of temporal, semantic and contextual constraints.

How Hybrid Multilevel Approaches Solve Lexical Ambiguities

This section will underline how hybrid multilevel approaches have been used in order to detect and solve lexical ambiguities.

This kind of ambiguities has been taken into account by finite-state mechanisms (Johnston and Bangalore, 2005) based on weighted finite-state automaton with multimodal grammar described in the previous section. This method provides lattice representations for gesture and speech input. If the input is ambiguous then the input stream is represented by a lattice, which indicates all its possible interpretations. In order to solve ambiguities this method provides a transducer that represents the relationship between gesture and speech, and in particular, it represents the relationships between a particular gesture input stream and all the possible word sequences that could co-occur with the specific input stream. This transducer is composed with gesture interpretations providing a mutual compensation among the input modalities.

A further method for dealing lexical ambiguities is provided in (Buvac, 1996) and it is based on a Formal Theory of Context. This approach uses the logic of context representing fact about the context and reasoning with context. This method uses first order structures to describe what is true in the context. These structures describe two types of context: knowledge base context that refers to possible states in the context; and discourse context that refers to particular states in the discourse. In particular, discourse states consist of: states that refer to facts defined in the discourse or that are known in the discourse; and interpretations of predicate symbols in the discourse context considering them according to predicate symbols in knowledge base context. In the case that a predicate symbol is interpreted differently in different discourse contexts, so ambiguities appear. Therefore ambiguities are related to interpretations of predicate symbols in the discourse context. For solving ambiguities this approach uses common sense knowledge or it directly asks users what is the particular meaning of his/her input.

Moreover, the management of lexical ambiguities can be dealt using the approach described in the section concerning interpretation methods (Caschera et al., 2007a) that expresses multimodal input by Constraint Multiset Grammar and Linear Logic. In (Caschera et al., 2007a) user input is structured as a parse tree and each leaf of the tree is a terminal element of the grammar. For example, let us suppose that the user interacts with the system using sketch and speech and she/he says by the speech modality:

)))"Show this in Rome"

While the user simultaneously draws the sketch in Figure 4.

The Figure 4 can be interpreted both as a river and a street, because they are both elements of the domain. So the meaning of the user's input is not clearly identified and the identified elements of the user input are shown in Figure 5.

In this example the parse tree connected to the user input is shown in Figure 6.

This approach identifies multimodal ambiguities applying rules in Linear Logic to the leaves of the parse tree of the input. In particular, a lexical ambiguity is identified when two elements (E^i, E^j) that have the same parent have two different meanings. Therefore, the rule that allows identifying this ambiguity is the following:

$$(E^i_{concept} \neq E^j_{concept}) \otimes (E^i_{repr} \equiv E^j_{repr}) \otimes (E^i_{mod} \equiv E^j_{mod}) \otimes (E^i_{role} \equiv E^j_{role}).$$

In particular the alignment of the element E^2 and the element E^5 provides a lexical ambiguity because the element E^5 has two different meanings (river and street). So the rule that allows identifying this ambiguity is the following:

$$(E^5_{concept} \neq E^{5'}_{concept}) \otimes (E^5_{repr} \equiv E^{5'}_{repr}) \otimes (E^5_{mod} \equiv E^{5'}_{mod}) \otimes (E^5_{role} \equiv E^{5'}_{role})$$

How Hybrid Multilevel Approaches Deal Syntactical Ambiguities

This section will focus on how hybrid multilevel approaches allow detecting and solving syntactical ambiguities.

This kind of ambiguities is connected to the structural properties of the user input and in particular, they are mainly detected analysing the structure of possible parse trees of the user input (Collins, 1997).

Syntactic ambiguities are dealt integrating a semantic construction process into a parser analysing the structural properties of the user input and mapping parse trees to different logical representations (Harper, 1994). This process produces a number of parse trees connected to the possible interpretations of the user input; therefore a problem of this approach is the quite great number of parse trees to represent. To overcome this

Figure 4. User input by sketch modality

Figure 5. Elements in the multimodal input

E select	E this	E in	E' Rome

	E river		
	E street		

97

Figure 6. Parse of the multimodal input

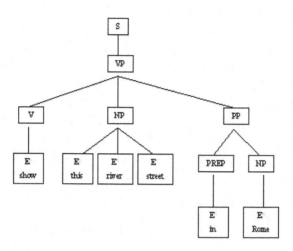

problem Literature provides a method based on highest preference choice (Alshawi and Crouch, 1992) that selects the most likely parse that cannot necessarily be the correct parse.

To avoid the issue connected to the great number of possible parse trees the Description Theory has been proposed (Hirst, 1987). This approach does not provide a whole description of the trees but a partial one representing only those relations that are common to all consistent trees. However this approach is only syntactical and it has to be combined with a semantic interpreter that recognizes if inputs, which have the same structure, are different at the semantic level.

Moreover to overcome problems connected to the great number of structural representations of the user input the shared-packed parse forest approach has been proposed (Harper, 1994). This method stores all parses of user input in a compact form using a data structure that is defined by terminal and non-terminal nodes. These nodes contain lists of node numbers of the children that build a parse of that constituent and, in particular, nodes, which participate in multiple parses, have multiple arcs that enter in the node. This structure allows detecting ambiguities by traversing the forest of trees analysing the paths in the structure.

How A-Posterior Resolution Methods Integrate the Interpretation Methods

The a-posterior methods integrate the interpretation methods providing a dialogue with the user providing the repetition of the user input and allowing user to directly select among a list of possible interpretations. Therefore these methods are defined as mediation techniques (Mankoff et al., 2000a) because they imply the user's action in the disambiguation process. These methods are particularly useful for the resolution of ambiguities caused by imprecision and noise that can produce all the classes of ambiguities defined in the previous section.

The first method consists of the repetition of the user input in order to avoid more than one interpretation. In this case user can repeat some or all of his/her input. In multimodal system the repetition can be made by a different modality. For example, if a user has drawn a figure that can be interpreted both as a river and a street, she/he can repeat the input using the speech modality saying the word "river". Therefore the system can disambiguate the input adding redundant information and it is able to correctly interpret the input. It is possible to gather that the repetition using a different modality can be more effective because using the same modality the user can provide the same ambiguities.

The repetition of the user input can be also applied not on the whole input, but only locally to solve an ambiguity. In (Avola et al., 2006) it is applied to a sketch-based interface for solving ambiguities due to the inaccuracy of the user's input.

In this case the user draws a rectangle and he/she does not close the shape (Figure 7) and the system is not able to interpret the drawing. Therefore, the user partially repeats his/her drawing completing the drawing of the boundary of the rectangle (Figure 8). In this case the correction is related only to a component part of the sketched object to be interpreted.

The second mediation approach is the choice that allows user directly selecting the interpretation that best fit his/her intention among a set of possible candidates. In fact during the dialogue, the system returns the set of possible interpretations of the user input and the user directly select the interpretation. In order to show this approach we can consider the example provided in (Avola et al., 2006) where the user draws a rectangle without closing the shape (Figure 9a). In this case

the system shows to the user two interpretations: i) a rectangle (Figure 9a$_1$), ii) a polyline (Figure 9a$_2$). The user selects one of these two interpretations according to his/her intention.

One of the problems of the choice technique is that it allows only to choice among a fix set of choices. In order to overcome this problem (Mankoff et al., 2000a) proposes to extend the n-best list allowing dynamic filtering, allowing to specify parameters, such as the length of the word and individual characters.

CONCLUSION

This chapter has dealt the problem to correctly recognize user input in order to enable a natural interaction between the user and the system. Therefore it has analysed interpretation methods, ambiguities connected to the interpretation process and how interpretation methods and a-posterior resolution ones deal ambiguities in multimodal and modal interfaces.

In particular, considering interpretation methods, it has dealt recognition-based fusion strategies, decision-based fusion strategies and hybrid multilevel fusion strategies providing descriptions of some example of these methods.

Figure 7. User input before repetition

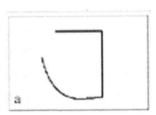

Figure 8. User input after repetition

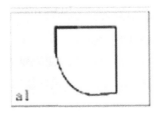

Figure 9. Ambiguity solved by choice method

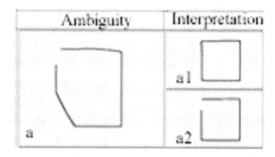

After then, classifications of ambiguities have been provided and, in particular, two different classifications have been presented. The first one classifies ambiguities at a more general level in: the recognition ambiguity that appears when the recogniser returns more than one interpretation of the user input; the segmentation ambiguity that appears when is not clear how to group user input; and target ambiguity that is connected to the focus of the user input that is not clear. The second one has provided a more detailed classification dividing ambiguities in lexical, syntactical and pragmatic ambiguities. In particular, in the lexical ambiguities' class is divided in: lexical ambiguities, lexical relationship ambiguities, and scope ambiguities. Finally syntactical ambiguities have been analysed considering: analytic ambiguity, gap ambiguity, attachment ambiguity, and occlusion.

Considering these classifications and the interpretation strategies this chapter has analysed how these methods support the recognition of ambiguities. In detail, methods for solving ambiguities due to the inaccuracy of the user input has been treated using recognition-based approach, such as statistical approaches. Moreover, this chapter has provided how hybrid multilevel approaches deal syntactical ambiguities. Furthermore, lexical ambiguities have been dealt using decision-based and hybrid multilevel approaches. Finally, this chapter has described methods that integrate the

interpretation process for solving different class of ambiguities. These methods are classified as a-posterior methods because they are applied after the fusion process and they allow user to repeat his/her input producing a dialogue.

REFERENCES

Alshawi, H., & Crouch, R. (1992). Monotonic semantic interpretation. In *the Proceedings of the 30th Annual Meeting of the Association for Computational Linguistics.*

Avola D., Caschera, M.C., & Grifoni, P. (2006). Solving ambiguities for sketch-based interaction in mobile enviroments. *Workshop on Mobile and Networking Technologies for social applications (MONET 06), Springer-Verlag,* (LNCS 4278, pp. 904-915).

Berry, D.M., Kamsties, E., Kay, D.G., & Krieger, M.M. (2001). *From contract drafting to software specification: Linguistic sources of ambiguity* (Tech. Rep.). Canada: University of Waterloo.

Buvac, S. (1996). Resolving lexical ambiguity using a formal theory of context. In K. Van Deemter, & S. Peters (Eds.), *Semantic ambiguity and underspecification.* CSLI Publications.

Carpenter, B. (1992). *The logic of typed feature structures.* Cambridge University Press.

Caschera, M.C., Ferri, F., & Grifoni, P. (2007a). An approach for managing ambiguities in multimodal interaction. *OTM Workshops*, (1), 387-397.

Caschera, M.C., Ferri, F., & Grifoni, P. (2007b). *Management of ambiguities. Visual languages for interactive computing: Definitions and formalizations*. Hershey, PA: IGI Publishing.

Caschera, M.C., Ferri, F., & Grifoni, P. (2007c). Multimodal interaction systems: Information and time features. *International Journal of Web and Grid Services, 3*(1), 82-99.

Chai, J.Y., Hong, P., & Zhou, M.X. (2004). A probabilistic approach to reference resolution in multimodal user interfaces. In *Proceedings of 9th International Conference on Intelligent User Interfaces (IUI)* (pp. 70-77).

Chai, J.Y., Prasov, Z., & Qu, S. (2006). Cognitive principles in robust multimodal interpretation. *Journal of Artificial Intelligence Research, 27*, 55-83.

Chok, S.S., & Marriott, K. (1995). Automatic construction of user interfaces from constraint multiset grammars. In *11th International IEEE Symposium on Visual Languages* (pp. 242-245.

Collins, M. (1997). Three generative, lexicalised models for statistical parsing. In *Proceedings of the 35th Meeting of the Association for Computational Linguistics and the 7th Conference of the European Chapter of the ACL* (pp. 16-23).

D'Ulizia, A., Grifoni, P., & Rafanelli, M. (2007). Classification of ambiguities. In *Visual languages for interactive computing: Definitions and formalizations*. Hershey, PA: IGI Publishing.

Eickeler, S., Kosmala, A., & Rigoll, G. (1998). Hidden Markov model based continuous online gesture recognition. In *Proceedings of International Conference on Pattern Recognition, 2*, 1206-1208.

Futrelle, R.P. (1999). Ambiguity in visual language theory and its role in diagram parsing. *IEEE Symposium on Visual Languages, IEEE Computer Society*, Tokyo (pp. 172-175).

Gavalda, M., & Waibel, A. (1998). Growing semantic grammars. In *Proceedings of ACL/Coling 1998*, Montreal, Canada.

Girard, J.-Y. (1987). Linear logic. *Theoretical Computer Science, 50*, 1-102.

Harper, M.P. (1994). Storing logical form in a shared-packed forest. *Computational Linguistics, 20(4)*, 649-660.

Harper, M.P., & Shriberg, E. (2004). Multimodal model integration for sentence unit detection. *ICMI 2004* (pp. 121-128).

Hirst, G. (1987). Semantic interpretation and the resolution of ambiguity. Cambridge, UK: Cambridge University Press.

Hu, J., Brown, M.K., & Turin, W. (1994). Handwriting recognition with hidden Markov models and grammatical constraints. *Fourth International Workshop on Frontiers of Handwriting Recognition*, Taipei, Taiwan.

Huls, C., Claassen, W., & Bos, E. (1995). Automatic referent resolution of deictic and anaphoric expressions. *Computational Linguistics, 21*(1), 59–79.

Jiang, W., Sun, Z. (2005, August 18-21). Hmm-based online multistroke sketch recognition. In *Proceedings of the Fourth International Conference on Machine Learning and Cybernetics*, Guangzhou (pp. 4564-4570).

Coutaz, J., Nigay, L., & Salber, D. (1993). The MSM framework: A design space for multisensori-motor systems. In L. Bass, J. Gornostaev, C. Unger (Eds.), *Human computer interaction*. In *3rd International Conference EWHCI'93, East/West Human Computer Interaction*, Moscow (LNCS 753). Springer Verlag.

Johnston, M., & Bangalore, S. (2005a). Finite-state multimodal integration and understanding. *Journal of Natural Language Engineering 11.2*, 159-187.

Johnston, M., & Bangalore, S. (2005b). Combining stochastic and grammar-based language processing with finite-state edit machines. In *Proceedings of IEEE Automatic Speech Recognition and Understanding Workshop.*

MacKenzie, I.S., & Chang, L. (1999). A performance comparison of two handwriting recognisers. *Interacting with Computers, 11*, 283-297.

Mankoff, J., Hudson, S.E., & Abowd, G.D. (2000a). Providing integrated toolkit-level support for ambiguity in recognition-based interfaces. *CHI 2000*, 368-375.

Mankoff, J., Hudson, S.E., & Abowd, G.D. (2000b). Interaction techniques for ambiguity resolution in recognition-based interfaces. *UIST 2000*, 11-20.

Rabiner, L.R. (1989). A tutorial on hidden Markov models and selected applications in speech recognition. In *Proceedings of the IEEE, 77*, 257-285.

Resch, B. Hidden Markov models-a tutorial for the courses computational intelligence. Retrieved from http://www.igi.tugraz.at/lehre/CI

Sezgin, T.M., & Davis, R. (2005). HMM-based efficient sketch recognition. In *Proceedings of the 10th International Conference on Intelligent User Interfaces (IUI 05)* (pp. 281-283). ACM Press.

Tsai, W.H., & Fu, K.S. (1979). Error-correcting isomorphism of attributed relational graphs for pattern analysis. *IEEE Transactions on Systems, Man, and Cybernetics, 9*, 757-768.

Zadeh, L. (1978). Fuzzy sets as a basis for a theory of possibility. *Fuzzy Sets and Systems, 1,*3-28.

KEY TERMS AND DEFINITIONS

A-Posterior Methods: Process that provides a dialogue with the user by the repetition of the user input and allowing user to directly select among a list of possible interpretations.

Ambiguities: Identification of more than one meaning of multimodal input.

Input Fusion: Process that combines visual information (involving images, text, sketches and so on) with voice, gestures and other modalities.

Interpretation: Process that associates user's actions to his/her intentions during the interaction process.

Interpretation of Multimodal Input: Process that identifies the meaning of the user input.

Multimodal System: A system that supports different modalities of interaction such as sketches, speech, gaze, gestures, handwriting and other modalities.

Resolution Methods: Methods for solving modal and multimodal ambiguities that find the most proper association to the user intention.

Chapter VI
Multimodal Fission

Patrizia Grifoni
Istituto di Ricerche sulla Popolazione e le Politiche Sociali
Consiglio Nazionale delle Ricerche, Italy

ABSTRACT

An important issue for communication processes in general, and for multimodal interaction in particular, is the information output arrangement and organization (multimodal fission). Considering information structure, intonation, and emphasis for the output by speech, considering moreover spatio-temporal coordination of pieces of information for visual (video, graphics, images, and texts) outputs, designing outputs for each kind of modality, and synchronizing the different outputs modalities is one of the most relevant challenges of the multimodal interaction design process; it is called fission. This challenge is becoming more and more important with the use of a lot of different interaction devices from laptop to mobile and smart-phones, in different contexts. This chapter provides some basic concepts involved in the fission processes design and describes some of the most relevant approaches discussed in the literature.

INTRODUCTION

Designing how to combine different outputs from modal channels for different pieces of information is a very important and critical issue in multimodal interaction systems. It consists of a process that considers these pieces of information and how to present and structure them; it is the *fission* process. Foster, (2002) defines fission as *"the process of realising an abstract message through output on some combination of the available channels"*.

This process can be conceived (Foster, 2002) as consisting of three main steps: (1) *content selection and structuring,* (2) *modality selection* (3) *output coordination.* The first step consists in selecting and organizing the content to be included in the presentation, the second step consists of specifying modalities that can be associated with the different contents of the previous step and finally the third step consists of coordinating the outputs on each channel in order to form a coherent presentation.

The fission process, and more generally, the information presentation activities are closely connected with the *information structure,* independently from the different modalities. It was introduced by Halliday (1967) and was initially used to structure a sentence into parts such as *focus, background, topics,* and so on. Focus identifies "information that is new or at least expressed in a new way" (Steedman 2000). Background, expresses old or given information. Lambrecht (1994) defines the information structure as "a component of GRAMMAR, more specifically of SENTENCE GRAMMAR" (Lambrecht, 1994).

Starting from Natural Language the information structure notion has been extensively used for the different interaction approaches and visual information too, independently from the used channel that could be referred to both, written texts as well as speech. Elements such as *syntactic structures, word order, intonation* and *prosody* in speech, *layout presentation* in visual communication, are all elements that contribute to identify the information structure. Considering informativeness of phrases composing sentences or visual elements that compose an image, the *focus* and *background* concepts (or others similar that will be specified below) have been introduced.

Indeed, structuring visual information (images, graphics, video, texts) requires spatial and temporal coordination of the different pieces of information. The spatial level usually organizes the information layout while the temporal one (considered for movies only) involves organization for the different pieces of information on the time.

The use of focus and background notion can be extended to information structure associated with multimodal utterance. Indeed, usually when two or more than two modalities are jointly used, some of them provide the new information and some others give the information context. The modality that usually is involved in expressing the focus is the prevalent modality, i.e. the modality that can significatively express the information content. It will be convenient to choose the prevalent modality according to the different users and contexts. For example it is not a good idea to choose a prevalent output modality that uses visual channel for systems used by visually impaired people, or speech when the environment presents sounds noises.

The literature proposes a lot of definitions for context and in particular for *interaction context.* Anind Dey et al. (2001) define the interaction context as "*any information that can be used to characterize the situation of an entity. An entity is a person or object that is considered relevant to the interaction between a user and an application, including the user and application themselves".*

Therefore, users and interaction tools are part of the context. This chapter is focused on fission process for multimodal systems. In particular, fission process needs to consider *what* information has to be presented according to the interaction context and, *how* this information can be presented in term of information structure, the chosen modalities for the output and their coordination/synchronization. The next section details the notions of information structure and in particular of discourse structure and its connections with intonation. According to the notion of information structure the design process for the output of visual information is provided.

Finally the chapter discusses the main features of the multimodal interaction design, detailing the multimodal fission design process.

FROM DISCOURSE STRUCTURE TO INTONATION

Grosz, and Sidner, (1986), defined the discourse structure as a complex notion consisting of: (i) a linguistic structure, which characterizes the language contained in the text/speech itself;(ii) an attentional structure, including information about the relative salience of objects, properties, relations, and intentions at any point in the discourse; and (iii) an intentional structure, connecting the discourse segment goals.

Halliday (1967) introduced the notion of Information Structure (IS), and the connected theory was developed by Steedman (1990; 1991; 2000). This theory proposes the dependence of intonational structure by the meaning. In particular, sentences (for natural language) could be partitioned, as previously said, into categories such as *focus/background* and *topic/comment*.

The Focus is the informative/new part of the discourse, while the background is the uninformative/unknown part. Usually, accented and, hence, salient parts are the most informative and new; consequently they identify the focus. The remaining part is the background. *"Focus marks what is new or unexpected in a sentence"* (Buring, 2007). Chomsky (1971) defined the focus as *"the phrase containing the intonation center"*. The focus can contain one word, one phrase or the whole sentence.

Therefore, the notion of information structure can be associated to the previously introduced concepts of focus and background, or *theme* and *rheme,* or *topic* vs. *comment/focus,* which are all notions used to bipartite sentences. In particular, *theme* and *rheme* respectively correspond to *topic* and *comment*: they indicate what a phrase is about and what is said about the topic.

One method to separate a sentence focus from its background is to consider the former as the answer to a question. As more than one question can be usually formulated for the same answer, more than one possible focus can be identified.

That is, in order to correctly identify focus, it can be necessary to consider the right question that can be associated with a given answer.

Let us consider the following example:

The sentence *Mary studied mathematics* can be the answer to more than one question. In particular, as showed by Q1 and Q2, it can be the answer to two questions:

Q1: What did Mary study at the university?
A: Mary studied MATHEMATICS

Q2: What did Mary do?
A: MARY STUDIED MATHEMATICS

In the first case (query Q1) the answer focuses on the discipline studied by Mary, while in the second one (Q2) the focus is represented by the action Mary is doing.

In Figure 1 you find the example described by Steedman (2000), to explain focus, background theme and rheme concepts using the query approach.

Steedman distinguishes the shared topic as the *theme* and the new information as the *rheme*. The theme is what is being talked about, and the rheme is what is being said about. Theme and rheme can next be divided into focus and background.

In (Hirschberg, et al.. 1987) the authors discussed the correspondences between some intonational characteristics and the discourse structure highlighting the relationship between pitch range and discourse structure, the way phrasing and accent to indicate cue phrase usage, and the information tune to convey about speaker intentions. Moreover, Steedman, & Kruijff-Korbayová (2001), and Steedman (2003) showed that assigning theme and rheme and generating intonation structure implies considering pitch accents. In order to represent accents, considering intonation and prosody, L and H are respectively used to represent a high tone and a low tone, while * represent a tone aligned with a stressed syllable (Pierrehumbert, Hirschberg, 1990).

Figure 1. Focus, background, theme, rheme

Q: I know that Mary likes the man who wrote the musical.

       But who does she ADMIRE ?

A: Mary   ADMIRES   the women who   DIRECTED   the show
       Background   Focus   Background   Focus   Background

                     Theme   Rheme

Table 1. Pitch Accent Patterns

	Agree	Disagree
Theme	L+H*	L*+H
Rheme	H* or (H*+L)	L* or (H+L*)

Steedman showed that accent can vary according to the agreement between participants and these different alignment are showed in Table 1).

Information structure identifiable using intonation can be extended to visual information too and its features and fission for visual information is discussed in the next section.

VISUAL INFORMATION AND FISSION

This section discusses the fission process for visual information, where they are all information that humans can perceive using eyes.

The greatest part of studies about Information structure had been deeply influenced by the cultural experiences of the 20th century and in particular by the Gestalt theory. This theory was introduced for the visual perception, but it influenced the philosophy and the culture during all the 20th century. It was based on the holistic view according to a whole is more than the sum of units that compose it. Information structure concept and perceptual theories converge in some principles. An important principle is the *Figure/ground principle*, which shows the human perceptual *tendency to separate figures from their backgrounds*; figures correspond to the focus, while the ground is the environment or background surrounding the figure. In Figure 2 an example of this partition is showed.

Gestalt theory has deeply influenced the cultural scenario during the 20th century and linguistic too, producing a dichotomy between the most important part and a secondary one for sentences, analogously with visual representation, extending it to other modalities. The first part is the most relevant in terms of informativeness, while the secondary one is the less informative. This dichotomy corresponds with the figure and its background for visual information. According to this theory the output has to present the content following a psychological structure.

In general people communicate using text, tables, images, videos etc. that can be combined in order to edit a document, a message, a web page, a system interface, and so on. The user's interpretation process is a crucial aspect for communication in different sectors such as in scientific areas, in social and economic field as well as in other sectors. Graphs, drawings, charts, dot maps, tables, formulas, text, etc. can be chosen by users

Figure 2. Focus and background in Gestalt theory

according to their different information goals, different contexts and devices used for accessing this information.

The central questions to face when defining a document, a web page or a system interface are:(i) identify information to be presented, (ii) choose the manner to use, combine and arrange information to be presented, (iii) define their relationships.

Once identified information to be presented, it is necessary to choose modalities. Text can be used both, alone and jointly with other visual modalities providing a comment or an explanation of other visual and graphical information. Information presented using a text, or text jointly with other kinds of visual information, or any their arrangement could be differently perceived by a user according to their different spatial organization.

Let us suppose to consider documents or systems interfaces or web pages involving visual information given by text, graphics, tables, sketches, images and so on. The shape of information (information layout) implicitly gives context and information nature, the manner and environment of its use, and also something about authors. For example a document can shape information according to a hierarchy suggesting its importance; i.e. the title is the shortest summary of a document; it should highlight the whole content, and

is intended to give concise global information. Authors, therefore, should put the title in an immediately visible position. In this section some principles and guidelines to establish how to visually arrange a document or a visual interface are given. Some suggestions are provided about when using a table is better than using a graphics, using an image can be clearer than a text, or they can be combined. Indeed, some of the layout guidelines and Gestalt laws (which can be useful for arranging visual information) are suggested.

That is, combining text and graphic information can be considered as a kind of multimodal information output.

The steps that need to be carried out are: (i) identify the most relevant information, (ii) decide what kind of visual presentation can be more opportune to be used, (iii) what visual features can be used to adequately represent the chosen information (i.e. lines, colors, positions…), (iv) how information has to be spatially arranged on the screen (layout).

Once the most relevant information to be presented has been identified, it is necessary to consider the opportunity to use such kind of presentation instead of another one (text, graphs, charts and so on). In order to carry out this step it is possible to answer some questions:

When Is it Better to Use Text?

The use of text is a very important aspect of communication among humans. Indeed, the human communication history gives and underlines the importance of using texts as a means of communication that objectifies information to be exchanged, as specified in (Goody, J. and Watt, I. 1968), transmitting it over space and preserving it over time. There are some areas, such as legal, administrative and similar one that require the use of text. The use of text in these different sectors is usually highly codified in its structure; for this reason it is easier to reduce any ambiguity in their interpretation and to transmit their content over space and time. Textual information can be moreover used to express, and save oral information in as writing, minimizing the information loss respect to the oral expression.

When Is it Better to Use Tables?

Tables have to be preferred to present exact quantitative information (single different values) according to their descriptive variables. Indeed, as suggested in (APA, 1994) quantitative data are preferably presented using tables because the easily allow user to access each value even if a great amount of data has to be showed.

When Is it Better to Use Graphs, Charts or Dot Maps?

Graphs, charts and dot maps are useful to represent data emphasizing their relations, their values, percentages and trends; for this reason they are particularly effective and synthetic to describe and represent phenomena.

When Is it Better to Use an Image?

All information that deeply involve spatial concepts, statically or dynamically, can be conveniently presented using an image or a sequence of images. Figures can shortly describe a situation, an abstract concept or idea. Visual information contained in a picture captures a real scene at a time instant, a video provides scenes sequences, while drawing a shape by hand can help humans to represent their ideas even if they are not completely defined. The use of visual information can be very useful when codified; indeed, in this case its meaning is fastly and univocally perceived and interpreted by people. This is the situation of using the road signs, or the icons used in visual interfaces for HCI. Differently, it is very frequent the situation in which the provided visual information is incomplete or imprecise to univocally associate to it a meaning. This can be due to the different people cultures, their physical and psychological abilities and perceptive capabilities, to the context situation, such as environmental features.

However, even if ambiguous, visual information can be used in order to fastly express sketched ideas during working meetings or in the starting steps of the designing processes, in order to discuss and refine them.

Combining the different kinds of visual representation can be the best solution to enhance advantages and to overcome the different disadvantages previously considered. Indeed, information incompleteness using graphs, charts, dot maps or images can be filled up by their combined use with text. Each one of us can see that tables, charts, and so one, are always integrated by captions and textual comment that explain their content. Textual information can be complementary, as they add information to the visual one, or can be redundant, as they describe what is visually represented. This approach, which uses visual and textual representation of information in a redundant manner, is usually recommended by web pages design and implementation guidelines.

Moreover, when a visual output has to be arranged, it is necessary to select relevant information, to establish the visual features to be used in order to adequately represent them (i.e. lines, colours, positions, and so on), and it is necessary to define how information has to be spatially arranged on the screen (layout). The layout structure provides how different information chunks are spatially arranged; it can depend on the different topics (i.e. laws, poems, and so on) and on the different people culture. Visually well organized and presented information allows people to unambiguously interpret them due to the clarity in communication purpose.

Combining visual information by figures, tables, graphs, charts or dot maps and text has to follow the following principles:

- When using figures, tables, graphs, charts or dot maps in the output production it is necessary to consider the idea they have to represent and what kind of figure is better to reach the goal,
- The figures, tables, graphs, charts or dot maps have to provide more information respect to the text it are connected with, or they have to convey it in a more synthetic way,
- The figures, tables, graphs, charts or dot maps have to be easy to read and understand and, it has not to contain unnecessary visual elements because they could distract the user attention,
- All figures, tables or pieces of text diagrammatically arranged, need to follow a unique, consistent style.

A general criterion to arrange the different pieces of information (independently from the community the user belongs to, and the context) is that the information chunks have to be characterized by the same visual features such as fonts, size, and so on, for text belonging to a table. Both, paper documents as well as e-documents can composed by different types of information chunks (images, tables, movies, videos, sounds, titles, paragraphs, and so on), whose combination improves the communication effectiveness.

Sizing, spacing and placing visual chunks of information within a window or a page define the information layout, i.e. the visual information structure. Defining the layout consists of identifying:

- **Focus:** That is visual information users have to firstly notice,
- **Flow:** A path along the presented visual elements needs to be easily captured by people according to the logical sequence that can be involved in a communication process (this is particularly useful for visual interfaces),
- **Grouping:** Visual information are spatially grouped according to their functions so that their relations can be easily perceived,
- **Emphasis:** Visual information chunks need to be emphasized according to their importance,
- **Alignment:** It gives the coherent placement of information (for example left alignment can be normally used for pieces of text in a generic document, for text contained into a column, while a right alignment can be opportunely suggested for columns numeric data. Some more guidelines can be found in (http://msdn.microsoft.com/en-us/library/aa511279.aspx), in which some more indications are provided.

In particular the layout, when considering the different classes of interaction devices (laptops, desktops, smart-phones, mobile devices), needs to be *device independent* for the same class of devices. Indeed, resolution of different monitors cannot influence the visual layout. Moreover the layout has to allow users to *easily scan* the content they are looking for with a first glance. The layout needs to be adapted according to the different surfaces in its *size* and in distributing the content (*balance*). The visual layout needs to be more *simple* that is possible in order to limit the users' cognitive overhead; according to this goal pages and interfaces need to be consistent, i.e. they have to preserve their layout or similar ones (*consistency*).

Even if the device independence is an important concept to consider, changing the communication device class (i.e. changing from personal computers to smart-phones) requires taking into account of the device feature. Indeed, the advanced visualization techniques used on desktop computers need to be revised. The large diffusion of mobile devices such as smart-phones, and the interest on services they can provide anywhere and anytime is highlighting the importance of considering the problem of mobile devices output visualization.

In (Chittaro, L. 2006), six elements had been suggested for designing the visual output on using mobile devices: *Mapping, Selection, Presentation, Interactivity, Human factors, Evaluation*. They are described as follows:

- **Mapping.** A visualization contains numbers, strings, and other data into graphics that can be represented by several visual features such as lines, colors, lengths, positions, curvatures, animations, and so on. A good design for visual representation requires a precise mapping between data objects and relations and visual objects and relations must be defined and consistently applied throughout the application. It must make conceptually important aspects perceptively important.

- **Selection.** Among available data, what is relevant to the considered task? On one hand, visualizing insufficient data will lead users to make sub-optimal or plainly wrong decisions; on the other hand, burdening users with unnecessary data will make it more difficult to reason about a given problem. Although selection is an important aspect of any visualization, it is critical in mobile device visualizations because the limited space restricts how much information the screen can display.

- **Presentation.** How is the visualization laid out on the available screen space? Even if the designer has identified a clear, intuitive visual mapping and selected data the user really needs, the application can still be ineffective if the display is too little to show everything. A convenient way to present the visualization on the available screen is essential.

- **Interactivity.** A high level of interactivity is important to increase user engagement of observed data and enhance exploration abilities.

- **Human factors.** Does the interface take into account human perceptual and cognitive capabilities? Users must be able to quickly recognize and easily interpret visualization. General information about visual perception is readily accessible in textbooks, and research results targeted at mobile visualizations are increasingly available—for example, to determine what a limited number of pixels can communicate.

- **Evaluation.** Has the visualization's effectiveness been tested on users? Rigorous user evaluation procedures are common practice in the field of human-computer interaction (HCI). For example, Catherine Plaisant recently surveyed the unique challenges of information visualization evaluation. Mobile device interfaces require additional consideration—for example, use of phone emulators can lead to unreliable results, and complex variables such as distraction should be measured".

Mapping, selection and presentation when using mobile devices require to consider that displays are very limited due to the small size, low resolution, few colors, and other factors characterizing them; moreover, graphic representations for mobile systems (due to the hardware features) need to adopt a lower and limited level respect to the desktop one.

Designing output for mobile devices requires considering environmental factors such as light conditions, the presence of other visual information sources that could distract the human attention.

Even if visual presentation of information enables a very natural communication, the effectiveness in communication process is highly improved if conveyed information is multimodally arranged. The problem of designing multimodal output is discussed in the next section.

FROM MULTIMODAL INTERACTION TO MULTIMODAL FISSION

Naturalness, robustness and flexibility of multimodal interaction are features deriving on one side by the multimodal nature of human-human communication, and on the other side by robustness and flexibility of a well designed multimodal interfaces.

In (Reeves et al., 2004) guidelines to design multimodal interfaces were presented. The authors identified six main elements to be taken into account in designing multimodal interfaces: the *requirements specification*, the *multimodal input* and *output specification, adaptivity, consistency, feedback* and finally *error prevention/handling.* Following guidelines has to permit a very natural interaction approach and to improve the system robustness by redundant or complementary information. Below the focal aspects of these guidelines (Reeves, 2004) are described.

Considering Users' Requirements is a central aspect for interaction naturalness. Indeed, user's psychological characteristics, her/his cognitive abilities, motivation, level of experience, domain and task characteristics, cultural background, and physical abilities need to be considered in order to potentially involve a "broadest range of users and contexts of use" with the goal to make possible the system use for all people and for each use, involving the different modalities opportunely combined.

The interface has to permit *privacy and security maintenance*, enabling modalities warranting these features. For example "non-speech alternatives should also be provided when users enter personal identification numbers, passwords".

In order to improve the quality of multimodal interaction and the use of *Multimodal Input and Output* some principles can be used. In particular, the design of an effective multimodal interaction has to *Maximize human cognitive and physical abilities.* To achieve this goal it is fundamental to consider human aspects such as attention, or working memory, to reduce the user's cognitive load according to the involved people physical abilities. For this purpose the design has to avoid using more modalities if un-necessary, and has to "Maximize the advantages of each modality to reduce user's memory load in certain tasks and situations". The input and output modalities can be opportunely combined so that:

- Spatial information and parallel processing can be managed considering System visual presentation coupled with user manual input,
- State information, serial processing, attention alerting, or issuing commands can use a System auditory presentation coupled with user speech input,
- Modalities have to be added if and only if they improve the users' satisfaction and efficiency in the interaction in a given context,
- Output and input styles need to be coherent and output has to match to acceptable users' input style.

Considering guidelines provided in (Reeves et al., 2004), according to the general tendency to consider *speech* as the prevalent modality, the *modalities integration* during the design activity has to use "multimodal cues to improve collaborative speech"; moreover the output modalities need to be temporally well synchronized; it is necessary to share system interaction state across modalities in order to support: the user's alternative interaction modalities choice, the management of multi-device and distributed interaction and the users' interaction history capturing.

A very natural and flexible interaction needs to adapt itself to the different users and contexts. In particular, it can be important to adapt the interface with the user's age, preferences, skill, sensory or motor impairment and to the noisy environments; moreover some context constraints, such as bandwidth constraints, can be overcome and the information presentation can be adapted to the user's features and display device. Adaptivity cannot produce different results in the interaction process. Indeed, presentation and prompts features have to be shared enabling a *consistent* interaction, where consistency is obtained designing the multimodal interaction as follows:

- Systems output has to be independent from the different input modalities, and it has to produce the same results;
- It has to permit a consistent interaction combining modalities across applications (for example consistent shortcuts have to be designed);
- System-initiated or user-initiated state switching is effectively detected and the system after the user's input interpretations appropriately provides feedback when it initiates a modality change.

The interaction design has to foresee the system *feedback* after the user's input interpretations of modalities with a holistic approach as a whole. Designing exits from a task, a modality, or from the system, and designing an undo function can minimize user's errors and can improve error handling.

The literature proposes different approaches to the problem of users' requirements specification and designing systems, proposing lifecycle models such as: *waterfall model, V model, incremental model, spiral model, Unified Process model, Unified Modeling Language*, and so on.

In traditional waterfall model all the requirements are directly specified at the beginning of the process. But, due to the complexity of the multimodal system, some requirements can change over the software life cycle. The *V model* (also said VEE) is a process that represents the sequence of steps in a project life cycle development. It gives a graphical representation of the activities and results that have to be produced during software design. The left side of *V* gives the decomposition of requirements, and creation of system specifications, while the right side of the *V* relies on integration of parts and their verification. Using the *incremental model* it is possible to reduce the starting charge and overcome difficulties connected with the impossibility to have all necessary information for a good output design at the beginning of the process; indeed, incremental model creates a partial system, which will be extended later. In order to face the problem of continuous emerging of new requirements during the software lifecycle, the *Spiral model* conceives a system using successive prototypes.

The importance of managing and designing the output is increasing according to the diffusion of mobile devices, which are presenting new kinds of problems connected with the "situation" in which the output is produced. Different output for the same or different modalities can deeply influence the information structure for multimodal communication. However designing, choosing and opportunely managing outputs for multimodal systems is a complex activity, due to the richness of environments, systems and user's features. The output presentation in multimodal systems, after selecting content to be presented and considering their structure, has to consider the modalities to be used and their coordination in the fission process.

A lot of information influencing the most opportune output can vary according to parameters connected with the context, the user and all choices carried out need to be validated to avoid a bad output implementation.

The conceptual model WWHT (What-Which-How-Then) for multimodal presentation of information and the design of the multimodal systems output is described in (Rousseau et al., 2006).

This model, as described by the acronym is based on the concepts "What", "Which", "How" and "Then", and in particular:

- *What* is the information to present?
- *Which* modality or modalities combination should we use to present this information?
- *How* to present the information using the chosen modalities?
- and *Then*, how to handle the evolution of the resulting presentation?

Independently from the lifecycle model adopted in the software design and development process, the multimodal fission process, as specified in the introduction of this chapter, consists of some general steps. According to the approach adopted in COMIC they mainly consist of: *content selection and structuring, modality selection* and *output coordination* (this chapter refers to it as *Modalities coordination*).

Content Selection and Structuring

Selecting content and its structure is a crucial aspect for discourse comprehension. As specified in previous sections *Information structure* consists of two parts: the part that connects an utterance to the rest of the discourse (the *theme* or *background*), and the part that gives new information on that theme (the *rheme or focus*); moreover it is necessary to produce a coherent content and consequently its structure too coordinating what a speaker is producing with things a hearer is or can be attending to.

The *Rethorical structure* notion is also very relevant in computational linguistics as it provides the relations between adjacent discourse elements.

Foster (2002) in her studies summarizes and underlines the growing consensus among researchers in computational linguistics about the identification of "at least three types of structure" in discourse computational models: the *Intentional structure*, the *Informational structure* and the *Attentional structure*.

Intentional structure attains roles that utterances play in the speaker's discourse purpose; indeed, discourses participants could have more than one communication goal, but only one is identified as the primary one. It is the reason of the discourse existence.

Informational structure gives the semantic relationships between the information conveyed by discourse utterances. *Attentional structure* contains information about the objects, properties, relations, and discourse intentions that are most salient at any given point in the discourse.

The content selection and structuring generally needs to consider these characteristics of the discourse structure; in particular following the McKeown (1985) approaches proposed for *Text Generation*, a schema based approach or a plan-based approach can be adopted.

For example the schema-based approach enables to encode standard patterns of discourse using rhetorical predicates such as *analogy* (comparison with a known object), *constituency* (describing parts of the described object), and *attributive* (describing properties associated with an object). Defining these schemata it is possible to select contents according to the communication goal.

The schema-based approach cannot take into account of the intentional aspect of information and their connection with the information structure in an opportune manner. For this reason the plan-based approach can be more adequate. It is based on the Mann & Thompson (1987) Rhetorical

Structure Theory, and in particular on the concept of Rhetorical relation. A Rhetorical relation links two or more utterances into a unit and indicates the constraints between the utterances, the constraints on their combination, and the effects the users' communication intentions.

Modality Selection

As previously specified selecting one modality instead of another for generating the output for text or visual information in all its different forms of presentation can depend on the information features, the users' characteristics and their information goals, their perceptive abilities, the available output modalities and by constraints connected with different factors of context. Different modalities can convey different types of information.

Indeed, as just specified before, and as specified in (Reeves et al., 2004) in order to "Maximize the advantages of each modality to reduce user's memory load in certain tasks and situations" for example a graphical presentation can be opportune for spatial information, the use of natural language can be useful for descriptions, while haptic modality can be suitable for presenting movement, while audio channel can be more opportune when temporal information are involved. Moreover, some modalities can complement each other, and when used together. For example, vision and touch are naturally jointly used when things are under use, manipulation or exploration and speech is often annotated with gestures. That is, in (Lemmela, 2008) inputs and outputs modalities are divided into groups of visual, audio and haptic modalities as presented below.

These modality classes include a set of input and output modalities. For example auditory outputs include speech, auditory icons, earcons, sonification, audification and music, while inputs include speech, voice and non-speech audio.

The step of the modality selection has to consider some principles proposed starting from

some experimental studies for the *output design* introduced by Stéphanie Buisine and Jean-Claude Martin in their (Buisine and Martin, 2003) and from guidelines introduced in (Reeves et al., 2004) for the multimodal interfaces design. These principles are the *input-output symmetry* principle, the *output appropriateness* principle, the *user's appropriateness* principle and the *modality turning* principle.

- **Input-output symmetry:** A general principle to follow is the symmetry in designing the interaction in order to avoid the users disorientation. When users interact by speech, gesture, and sometimes facial expressions or body posture, this symmetry has to concern the interaction modalities (i.e. the same modalities have to be used for input and output), the characteristics of communication and the observed cooperation between different modalities discussed in the next section;

- **Output appropriateness:** It is important to use an appropriate output. Indeed, appropriate outputs may induce a multimodal input behavior, which is easier to process.

- **User's appropriateness:** Multimodal interaction requires even more attention to users' profile respect to designing other kinds of interaction because of their physical, psychological, cognitive and perceptive capabilities and preferences.

- **Modality turning:** Use multimodal cues both in input and output to improve speech turns when the user interacts with an agent (Cassell & Vilhjalmsson, 1999), (Gustafson, 2002), the system has to capture when its feedback is expected; for this reason it requires also to be adapted to input. (Thórisson, 1999).

Modalities Coordination

When using two or more than two modalities the user can perceive, and consequently s/he can differently interpret them according to the different manner information is arranged on the different modalities. That is, in a similar manner to visual information that can be differently structured considering layout guidelines and Gestalt laws, the different modalities can be opportunely co-ordinated to organize the output.

The design process has to decide how to combine and to coordinate modalities. It is important to consider that the modalities coordination plays a relevant role too as users' perceptive abilities and other characteristic can deeply change according to different modalities coordination for the same chunks of information. The multimodal fission besides associating the most appropriate modality to each chunk of information has to define the best combination of different modalities. Multimodal outputs can be combined according to the different modalities cooperation rules defined in (Martin, 1999):

- *Equivalence* involves the option of choosing between several modalities that can all equally well convey a particular chunk of information.
- *Specialization* implies that specific kinds of information are always conveyed by the same modality.
- *Redundancy* indicates that the same chunk of information is conveyed by more than one modality.
- *Complementarity* denotes several modalities that convey complementary chunks of information.
- *Transfer* implies that a chunk of information processed by one modality is then treated by another modality.
- *Concurrency* describes the case of several modalities conveying independent information in parallel.

When designing the coordination among different modalities, it is necessary to consider that they can change according to the different involved users and the different contexts in which the output is produced. These different aspects are more evident when using mobile devices.

Multimodal Fission for Mobile Devices

Defining the multimodal output for mobile devices requires to take into account of the differences between users and context due to the fact that each user, everywhere and every time can interact with the mobile multimodal system. That is, the user generally uses mobile devices in different situations. For this reason the output design requires taking into account of some aspects connected with users and contexts (Obrenovic, Abascal, Starcevic, 2007). Indeed, for example, using speech or a visual output can be convenient or not according to the user's privacy needs, her/his perception abilities and the light and acoustic features of the context where s/he is situated when s/he is waiting for the output. Indeed, an adequate use of modalities in different situations can improve the quality of human perception, attention and understanding. That is, it could be better to avoid speech output in noisy environments or when privacy requires some information will be maintained reserved, as well as for users with auditory impairments. There exist different criteria to establish what is the opportune manner to choose the best output modality or the best manner to combine some of them. A general principle that can be used for designing the output modalities is the principle of *adaptability to the cooperation between modalities*. Limiting to the output the principle defined by Stéphanie Buisine and Jean-Claude Martin, which suggests to adapt the recognition system restricting it for the output design, the new principle establishes that if modalities involved by the output for particular classes of message (for example a car alarm message for the driver) usually adopts always the same cooperation class, then the output has to be produced according this cooperation class. Choosing the same coopera-

Figure 3. First level of the modality ontology

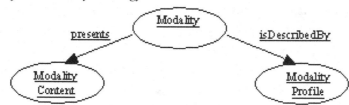

Figure 4. Information presentation level of the modalities ontology

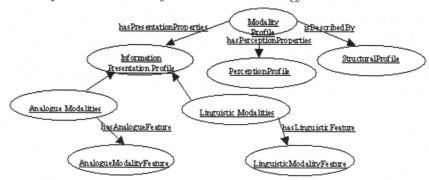

tion class means to choose the same information structure; indeed it corresponds to define the information layout when considering visual information. Information needs to be arranged towards the different modalities; sometimes this arrangement can need to be flexible enough to adapt itself to the users preferences.

More detailed constraints are proposed in Obrenovic et al. (Obrenovic, Abascal, Starcevic, 2007), which contains an approach classifying the interaction constraints into external and user's constraints. External constraints are the social, environmental and device constraints, while user's constrains include the user's features such as for example her/his physical and psychological abilities and dis-abilities, emotional and cognitive context and user preferences.

Bachvarova, van Dijk and Nijholt (2007) proposed a unified knowledge-based approach to the process of choosing the most appropriate modality or combining them, which is based on a Modality Ontology (MO). In particular, the proposed ontology models each modality feature

and relationships among the different modalities; its knowledge has to model *"the capacity of each modality to represent different types of information, knowledge about the cognitive and perception related aspects of each modality's nature, and knowledge about the structural dependencies that exist between the different modalities and that determine the syntax of a given modality combination"*.

The ontology consists of three main levels. The first level is mainly used for the modality allocation; the second and the third level are used for combining modalities.

In the proposed ontology the Modality presents *ModalityContent,* according to the MPEG-7 ontology content representation, and it is described by *ModalityProfile.* (Figure 3)

The *ModalityProfile* contains the *information presentation*, the *perception*, and the *structural profile.*

The *information presentation* level expresses knowledge about the advantages and dis-advantages in using different modalities for different information. The ontology structures the information presentation classifying modalities into *linguistic* and *analogue modalities*.

Linguistic modality is referred to the existing syntactic semantic-pragmatic systems of meaning for text and speech, to represent abstract concepts and relationships. Linguistic modality may not adequately represent visual information, sound, feel, smell or taste. Indeed they can be adequately represented using analogue modalities. That is, an *Analogue modality* is particularly useful to provide visual/spatial information. It is generally characterized by similarity between the representation and what it represents (Bernsen, 1994), (Stockl, 2004). Images, Graphs, Maps and Diagrams are considered as analogue modalities.

Analogue and linguistic representations can be usefully combined in multimodal fission process.

In designing the multimodal output and the modality profile, the human perceptual-sensory system and how it perceives the modality is a very relevant factor.

In particular, the proposed ontology distinguishes among visual, auditory and haptic modalities, according to the visual, hearing and touch sensory. Moreover the ontology presents static and a dynamic modality perception. Finally, the *structural profile* expresses the structural dependencies among the different modalities involved in the multimodal output.

Lemmela (2008) in her studies identified characteristics and advantages in using different modalities. Discussing about three main classes of output modalities - that are *Visual, Auditory* and *Haptic* one - she presents types of modalities belonging to each class, their features and indication about when it could be better to use each one of them.

Auditory output modalities involve speech and sound, while subclasses of haptic modalities are Tactile and kinaesthetic. Discussing on visual information Lemmela (2008) considered text and graphic information without involving temporal features. This chapter, extending her point of view, considers visual information as referring to movies too. For this reason the Visual modalities class is characterized by the fact that it can involve only spatial, or spatio-temporal dimensions for movies; moreover the output has to involve eyesight only. Auditory output information features consider temporal dimension only and involve hearing human sensory. Haptic output considers both, the spatial and temporal dimensions at the

Table 2. Uses and features of output modalities

Output	Visual	Auditory	Haptic
Types	Text, graphic information, Movies	Speech, sound	Tactile, kinaesthetic
Features	Involves mainly Spatial dimension (only movie involve temporal dimension). It involves eyesight.	Involves Temporal dimension only. It involves hearing.	Both, spatial and temporal dimensions need to be considered. This output involves touch.
When use it	When privacy is necessary and the user can focus her/his attention on the screen. When environmental noises represent a problem in using other modality classes.	When the user cannot use the screen (because s/he cannot put her/his attention on it having another focus, or it is partially or completely occluded to her/his vision).	It can be used mainly when the output needs to stimulate all human senses different from eyesight and hearing, and the output can directly act on the environment
When avoiding to use it	When the user cannot use the screen (because s/he cannot put her/his attention on it having another focus, or the screen is partially or completely occluded to her/his vision).	When privacy is necessary. When environmental noises represent a problem in using this modality class.	When information cannot be opportunely conveyed.

same time and involve the touch human sensory. Table 2 summarizes features of the three classes of output modalities and provides synthetic suggestions about when it can be opportune to use modalities of the different classes, and when it is better to avoid to use them.

CONCLUSION

The presentation of information plays a primary role in the communication process; it involves the selection of the most relevant information to be presented and its structure. The importance of arranging outputs has been demonstrated by a lot of studies and among them by studies on speech and features characterizing speech for communication processes and, by studies on the importance of layout for visual information and its perception. The diffusion of multimodal systems has produced scientific discussion and studies on theories and techniques concepts used for arranging multimodal outputs in order to produce their adequate users' perception and interpretation.

Selecting and structuring a multimodal presentation can follow the same principles usually adopted for text and discourse structures. The notion of information structure is a basic notion for the production of output using natural language, in visual communication as well as in the multimodal information fission process. Following this common notion the chapter has provided some elements that can be used to design outputs from modal to multimodal ones.

REFERENCES

American Psychological Association. (1994). *Publication manual of the American Psychological Association (4th ed.).* Washington, DC.

Bachvarova, Y.S., van Dijk, E.M.A.G., & Nijholt, A. (2007, January 25-26). Towards a unified knowledge-based approach to modality choice. In *Proceedings Workshop on Multimodal Output Generation (MOG 2007)*, Aberdeen, Scotland (pp. 5-15).

Buring, D. (2007). Intonation, semantics, and information structure. In G. Ramchand, & C. Reiss (Eds.), *The Oxford handbook of linguistic interfaces.*

Buisine, S., & Martin, J. (2003). Design principles for cooperation between modalities in bidirectional multimodal interfaces. In *CHI'2003 Workshop on Principles for Multimodal User Interface Design*, Florida (pp. 5-10).

Cassell, J., Vilhjalmsson, H. (1999). Fully embodied conversational avatars: Making communicative behaviors autonomous. *Autonomous Agents and Multiagent Systems, 2*, 45-64.

Chittaro, L. (2006). Visualizing information on mobile devices. *IEEE Computer, 39*(3), 40-45.

Chomsky, N. (1971). Deep structure, surface structure, and semantic interpretation. In D.D. Steinberg, & L.A. Jakobovits (Eds.), *Semantics. An interdisciplinary reader in philosophy, linguistics, and psychology* (pp. 183-216). MA: Cambridge University Press.

Dey, A.K., Salber, D., & Abowd, G.D. (2001). A conceptual framework and a toolkit for supporting the rapid prototyping of context-aware applications. In T.P. Moran, & P. Dourish (Eds.), *Human-Computer Interaction, 16*(2-4), 97-166.

Foster, M.E. (2002). State of the art review: Multimodal fission. Public deliverable 6.1, COMIC project.

Goody, J., & Watt, I. (1968). *The consequences of literacy, in literacy in traditional societies.* Cambridge University Press, Goody Ed.

Grosz, B., & Sidner, C. (1986). Attention, intentions, and the structure of discourse. *Computational Linguistics 12*(3), 175-204.

Gustafson, J. (2002). Developing multimodal spoken dialogue systems. Empirical studies of spoken human-computer interaction. Doctoral dissertation.

Halliday, M.A.K. (1967). Notes on transitivity and theme in English, part II. *Journal of Linguistics, 3*, 199-244.

Hirschberg, J., Litman, D., Pierrehumbert, J., & Ward, G. (1987). Intonation and the intentional discourse structure. In *Proceedings of the Tenth International Joint Conference on Artificial Intelligence*, Milan, Italy (pp. 636-639).

Joshi, A.K., Marcus, M.P., Steedman, M., & Webber, B.L. (1991). Natural language research. In *Proceedings of HLT*.

Lambrecht, K. (1994). *Information structure and sentence form*. London: CUP.

Lemmelä, S. (2008). Selecting optimal modalities for multimodal interaction in mobile and pervasive environments. *IMUx (Improved Mobile User Experience) Workshop, Pervasive 2008 (Sixth International Conference on Pervasive Computing)*, Sydney, Australia.

Mann, W.C., & Thompson, S.A. (1987). *Rhetorical structure theory: A theory of text organization*. USC/Information Sciences Institute (Tech. Rep. No. RS-87-190). Marina del Rey, CA.

Martin, J.C. (1999). Six primitive types of cooperation for observing, evaluating, and specifying cooperations. In *Proceedings of AAAI*.

McKeown, M.G. (1985). The acquisition of word meaning from context by children of high and low ability. *Reading Research Quarterly, 20*, 482-496.

Obrenovic, Z., Abascal, J., & Starcevic, D. (2007). Universal accessibility as a multimodal design issue. *Communications of the ACM, 50*, 83-88. New York: ACM.

Pierrehumbert, J., & Hirschberg, J. (1990). The meaning of intonational contours in the interpretation of discourse. In P. Cohen, J. Morgan, & M. Pollarck (Eds.), *Intentions in communication* (pp. 271-311). Cambridge, MA: MIT Press.

Reeves, L.M., Lai, J., Larson, J.A., Oviatt, S., Balaji, T.S., Buisine, S., et al. (2004). Guidelines for multimodal user interface design. *Communications of the ACM, 47*, 57-59. New York: ACM.

Rousseau, C., Bellik, Y., Vernier, F., & Bazalgette, D. (2006). A framework for the intelligent multimodal presentation of information. *Signal Processing, 86*(12), 3696-3713.

Steedman, M. (1990). Structure and intonation in spoken language undestanding. *ACL 1990*, 9-16.

Steedman, M. (2000). Information structure and the syntax-phonology interface. *Linguistic Inquiry, 31*, 649-689.

Steedman, M. (2003). Information-structural semantics for English intonation. *LSA Summer Institute Workshop on Topic and Focus*, Santa Barbara.

Steedman, M., & Kruijff-Korbayová, I. (2001). Introduction two dimensions of information structure in relation to discourse structure and discourse semantics. In I. Kruijff- Korbayová & Steedman (Eds.), *Proceedings of the ESSLLI 2001 Workshop on Information Structure*.

Thórisson, K.R. (1999). A mind model for multimodal communicative creatures and humanoids. *International Journal of Applied Artificial Intelligence, 13*(4-5), 449-486.

KEY TERMS AND DEFINITIONS

Gestalt Theory: The Gestalt theory is a theory proposed by a group of psychologists around the 1920's in Germany to systematcially study human perceptual organisation.

Human-Computer Interaction (HCI): Discipline concerned with the design, evaluation and implementation of interactive computing systems for human use and with the study of major phenomena surrounding them.

Modality: It is the medium that conveys information, in particular the human sense that can receive the machine output (visually, auditory, tactile) and the sensor that can receive the input from human, considering inputs by different modes (i.e. text, speech, gesture, and so on) .

Multimodal Fission: The process of organising and sinchronising a multimodal system outputs through the different channels in order to provide the user and/or the environment with consistent feedback.

Multimodal Interaction: It is the interaction approach adopted by users to communicate in a natural manner with machine, virtual and physical environment using multiple modes involving several communication channels of communication.

Multimodal System: It is a system that allows user's input and/or output to be conveyed over multiple channels such as speech, gesture and so on.

Chapter VII
Machine Learning Enhancing Adaptivity of Multimodal Mobile Systems

Floriana Esposito
Università di Bari, Italy

Teresa M. A. Basile
Università di Bari, Italy

Nicola Di Mauro
Università di Bari, Italy

Stefano Ferilli
Università di Bari, Italy

ABSTRACT

One of the most important features of a mobile device concerns its flexibility and capability to adapt the functionality it provides to the users. However, the main problems of the systems present in literature are their incapability to identify user needs and, more importantly, the insufficient mappings of those needs to available resources/services. In this paper, we present a two-phase construction of the user model: firstly, an initial static user model is built for the user connecting to the system the first time. Then, the model is revised/adjusted by considering the information collected in the logs of the user interaction with the device/context in order to make the model more adequate to the evolving user's interests/ preferences/behaviour. The initial model is built by exploiting the stereotype concept, its adjustment is performed exploiting machine learning techniques and particularly, sequence mining and pattern discovery strategies.

MOTIVATION

The mobile device area is increasing as shown by the variety of the products and services available. Indeed, the user needs require a device able to interact more intelligently. To this concern, one of the most important features of a mobile device concerns its flexibility and capability to adapt the functionality it provides to the users. In particular, an adaptive system might be able to adapt its functionality according to the users' objectives, tasks and interests. However, "Not all humans reason, behave and expect the same when interacting with a device; the interfaces are the same for all users, but not all users are the same" (Jacobs, 2004). Thus, a key process to make a system adaptive is personalization of the access to the information by means of user and context models.

A user model is a representation of a person's attitude, behaviour, preferences and regularities when exploiting some kind of device or moving in a given context. It can describe the user at different levels of granularity and complexity, depending on the amount of resources available and on the specific task it is intended for. Furthermore, a model can represent a whole group of users rather than a single individual: indeed, it is often the case that, independently on their specific preferences and taste, users playing a same role in a system are likely to share common needs and ways of interaction.

The exploitation of user models might be very useful in improving the interaction between the user and the system itself, in order for the latter to adapt more easily and straightforwardly the functionalities it implements to the former. More formally, "A user model is an explicit representation of information regarding a single user or a group of users. This information should be useful for enhancing the interaction between the environment and this user or this group of users. The representation should preferably allow the

user model to be interpreted by devices as well as by humans." (Jacobs, 2004).

When building a user model four aspects must be taken into account: description language (that has to be primarily machine-readable, but as an additional desirable feature should be easily interpretable by humans as well), techniques for actually building the models and then exploiting them to relate the (static) information they contain to the specific user and working session at hand (dynamic), and last but not least ways for assessing the actual correctness and suitability of the model itself.

Building user models, however, is a very difficult task, because very often a person's behaviour and preferences vary in time and according to the different environments, situations and objectives (Kaplan et al., 1993; Souchon et al., 2002). Furthermore, the task is made harder when contextual parameters are to be taken into account. For these reasons, automatically learning user models is a hot research topic and many different approaches and techniques have been proposed to accomplish this task (Si et al.,2005; Siewiorek et al.,2003; Randell and Muller, 2000; Liao et al., 2007).

Nevertheless, learning user models is a hard task due to its intrinsic complexity but also to a number of needs to be fulfilled. Even when they are to be learned automatically, the explicitly available knowledge should be easily integrated in the model. Often the model cannot be built before the user exploitation of the system, but must be developed during it by mining the user's interaction log files. Even more difficult, the user can change his/her behavior, causing the model to change in time (a problem known as 'concept drift'). Some environments involve very complex components and features, asking for a more powerful representation language such as first-order logic, that also has the advantage of being easily understood by humans. Finally, the user behavior emerges very often from sequences of actions, rather than a single event, and hence time has to be taken into account as well.

In this work we propose the exploitation of Machine Learning techniques to build user models. Specifically, a *full* user model should take into account three aspects: the static profile, the behavioural one and the content-based profile. The first aspect concerns a general description of the user. The second regards the user habits in a predefined context during the interaction with the device. Finally, the content-based aspect concerns the topics the user is interested in. In this chapter, the aspects we are interested in are the static and, in particular, behavioural profile.

Static profile contains the user features that are not modifiable during the interaction. To collect this kind of information, a registration phase is required. In this phase, the user is asked to compile a questionnaire. The information gathered in this process is used by an expert system that builds the static profile. This process is based on the idea of stereotype (Rich, 1979; Rich, 1989; Rich, 1998; Kobsa, 1990; Kay, 1994) already exploited in the personalization tasks (Ardissono et al., 2004).

The behavioural profile describes the user behavioral characteristics such as requiring more frequently the audio files than the visual ones, slow or fast interaction with the device. This component of the model can be automatically learned by the logs of user interaction with the device along with a description of the context the user is in. It is worth noting that in order to be able to learn such profile, a first-order knowledge representation formalism may be crucial due to the more structured and complex features and relations involved in environment/user descriptions. The approach proposed in this chapter allows to tackle complex scenarios in which a situation and the actors involved in it evolve in both time and space. Indeed, starting from information about user/context, we should think to profile, for example, a user entering a room (home, office, museum, etc.) by describing contextual information (such as position in the room) and temporal information

with the aim for the device to provide dynamic and adaptive functionality in the environments according to the user habits.

To perform such tasks we propose Inductive Logic Programming (Muggleton and De Raedt, 1994) algorithms for discovering *logical* patterns, i.e. user behavioral profiles, in relational sequences describing both the context and the user involved in it.

RELATED WORK

In order for a system to be defined adaptive, it must adapt the services it provides to the users, i.e. it should provide users with optimized service/access according to particular needs of individual users or user groups. The main problem of the systems is their inability to support different needs of individual users due to their incapability to identify those needs, and, more importantly, to the insufficient mappings of those needs to available resources/services. A key issue to reach this kind of adaptivity is personalization. A lot of works have been done on this topic in different environments, with different applications and taking into account different parameters. In particular, we focus our attention on strategies that use the concept of stereotype to model and categorize a user in order to provide the most suitable service (Finin, 1989; Brajnik and Tasso, 1992; Paiva and Self, 1994; Orwant, 1995; Kobsa and Pohl, 1995) and on those that exploit machine learning techniques to model the user interests and behaviour (Brusilovsky et al., 2007; Cook, 2006; Augusto and Nugent, 2006; Rao and Cook, 2004; Heierman III and Cook, 2003; Dolog et al., 2003).

Specifically, in the following we present some shell systems for user modeling that provide functionalities for the definition of stereotypes and the modality of reasoning on them. The GUMS system (Finin, 1989) allows the definition of a stereotype hierarchy. Each stereotype is made up of definite facts that have to be all fulfilled in order for the stereotype to be applied to the user. If one of these facts is contradicted by new information about the user, the stereotype is abandoned and replaced by the most specific direct or indirect superordinate stereotype that does not contain the contradictory fact. The initial stereotype to assign to a user must be selected by either the user model developer or the application system, and only a single stereotype may apply to the user at a time.

In UMT (Brajnik and Tasso, 1992) the user model developer can define hierarchies of user stereotypes that are made up of user subgroups characteristics in the form of attribute-value pairs. To activate and apply a stereotype to the current user, a set of conditions are to be proven by means of a rule interpreter that allows the user model developer to define user modeling inference rules.

A different way to represent the assumptions about the user is employed in TAGUS (Paiva and Self, 1994) that expresses them using first-order formulas, with meta-level operators that denote different attitudes of the user towards these formulas such as belief, goal, capability of reasoning. It is a shell system for user modeling in interactive application systems, as well as for student modeling in intelligent tutoring systems and interactive learning environments.

In general, the above shell systems for user modeling receive information about the user from the application and supply it with assumptions about the user. In contrast, user model servers, such as DOPPELGANGER (Orwant, 1995), are centralized user modeling components for all users and all applications on a network. Thus, the applications employ DOPPELGANGER's assumptions for tailoring their behaviour to users, and users can connect to the server directly to view or edit their user models. Importantly, the membership of the extracted user model in a stereotype is probabilistic and the transparent file access across the network allows one to use an adaptive application on any computer on the

network, with only a single user model for each application.

Finally, BGP-MS (Kobsa and Pohl, 1995) allows the representation of more than one type of assumption about the user at the same time, and supports both user interviews and inferences that are based on the user's actions and can be carried out concurrently with the operation of the application system.

All these systems perform a match between the stereotypes initially defined by the user model developer and the facts about the user collected during his/her interaction with the system. A step forward in order to make the systems completely autonomous in adapting themselves to different user needs is the exploitation of machine learning techniques in the steps of user model construction and user categorization for two reasons: the person's behavior and preferences vary not only in time but also according to different environments, situations and objectives (Kaplan et al., 1993; Souchon et al., 2002); furtermore a lot of contextual parameters have to be considered. For example, planning a museum visit cannot be the same for all users. Indeed, it should reflect interests as diverse as history, architecture, pictorial technique and style, authors, etc.. Furthermore, this same information should be provided at different levels, e.g. teacher or academic scholar, young or old visitor, expert or not, etc., and in a range of languages. Additional factors which affect planning could be the item disposition in the museum rooms and the duration of the visit. For these reasons, machine learning approaches have been exploited to accomplish this task (Si et al., 2005; Randell and Muller, 2000; Liao et al., 2007; Cheverst et al., 2000).

In (Si et al., 2005), the Synapse system is presented. It learns user habits exploiting a chronological order of the contexts in order to predict and provide the more relevant functionalities in a given context and in different modes. In particular, the Hidden Markov Model (HMM) (Rabiner, 1990) is used to build the stochastic model that is made up of continuous cycles of learning phase and executing phase. In this system, the HMM components are the hidden states, corresponding to a service to indicate the situation in which the service is used, and the observations of states are represented by a vector of sensor events extracted from sensor data. During the learning phase, Synapse learns the relationships between sensor events and services by exploiting recorded histories of them. Successively, in the executing phase, Synapse exploits the learned models and the current state of the sensors to predict the most likely services to provide to the user by computing the occurrence probability of each service through a filtering algorithm and sorting them. If a probability is higher than a threshold, the corresponding service will start. The personalization is achieved by treating the user ID as a sensor event.

In (Randell and Muller, 2000) a Neural Network is trained with information provided by the sensors concerning the speed of moving of the user and the environment in which the user is, in order to learn models for an intelligent tourists' guide that, for example, is quiet when the user runs, presents a graphical interface when the user is still or is sitting. The Neural Network was trained on a collection of ground-truth of ten people performing various activities: walking, running, sitting, walking upstairs, downstairs, and standing. Then, using such models, a GPS based Tourist Guide wearable Computer application was modified in order to include a multimedia presentation which provides the information using different media according to the user's activity as well as location. The modification consisted in formulating a set of rules that are fired according to the current state of the user obtained by performing a matching between the models learned by the neural network and the information provided by the sensors. Similarly, in (Liao et al., 2007) an intelligent guide of a museum is modelled on the user interests and context behaviours exploiting Hierarchical Markov Models.

The GUIDE project (Cheverst et al., 2000) investigated the provision of context-sensitive mobile multimedia computing support for city visitors by developing systems and application-level support for hand-portable multimedia end-systems which provide information to visitors as they navigate an appropriately networked city. The end-systems are context-sensitive, they have knowledge of their users and of their environment including their physical location. This information is used to tailor the system's behaviour in order to provide users with an intelligent visitor guide.

The systems above presented use the stereotypes or machine learning techniques to model the user. A previous work exploiting the stereotype combined with machine learning techniques in the personalization tasks is presented in (Ardissono et al., 2004). In this work, the user model is exploited in the Personal Program Guide system (PPG) to personalize the preference lists for TV programs. The User Modeling Component of the PPG is made up of three modules: the Explicit Preferences Expert, the Stereotypical UM Expert and the Dynamic UM Expert consisting in a bayesian network trained with evidence about the user's selections of TV programs.

Each component manages a private user model: The Explicit Preferences Expert stores the information elicited from the user; the Stereotypical User Model stores the prediction on the user's preferences inferred from prior information about TV viewer categories; the Dynamic User Model stores the estimates on the user's preferences inferred by observing the user viewing behavior. Finally, the predictions provided by the three Experts are combined by means of a formula to estimate the user's preferences employed to personalize the recommendation of TV programs.

Even in this case, the adopted strategies work on low level informations and are not able to deal with more structured scenarios. In our proposal we exploit information on both the user and the context in which he/she is in order to discover relational/behavioural user profiles. Furthermore, differently from the method above reported that exploits various strategies and combines the single results by means of a formula to estimate the user's preferences, in our approach the strategies cooperate: an initial user profile is generated by means of stereotypes and successively it is adjusted automatically by means of machine learning techniques.

BUILDING THE STATIC PROFILE

Static profile contains the user characteristics acquired by means of a preliminary registration phase in which the user is asked to compile a questionnaire. The information gathered in this process may be improved by means of a psycho-attitudinal test submitted by an expert system that successively builds the static profile.

This process is based on the idea of stereotype (Rich, 1979; Rich, 1989; Rich, 1998; Kobsa, 1990; Kay, 1994). A stereotype is made up of a body and a trigger or prediction component. The body represents the preferences shared by all the users belonging to a stereotype and provides the information necessary to assign a given user to a stereotype. A user can be assigned to one or more stereotypes, while a stereotype can be assigned to none or to a group of users (possibly made up of a single user). The case of a stereotype with no assignment is due to particular case of stereotyped classes that contain particular and rare features not frequently present in the users. The trigger describes the features and the preferences of a typical user belonging to a stereotyped class. Each modelled feature (or group of features) is part of one or more stereotypes thus allowing for the hierarchical construction of the stereotypes tree which root is the most general stereotype any_person.

The static profile is obtained by means of a matching process between the initial user features (age, sex, work, education, handicap, etc.) and a set of stereotypes describing the main user classes. Specifically, the matching is performed by means of a set of activation rules codified by an expert that will activate the association of a stereotype for one or more users and of a user to one or more stereotypes. Each activation rule will fire only a stereotype while a stereotype could be fired by more than one of such rules. Matching is performed exploiting probabilistic models and is used to predict the user preferences and the interaction way. In particular, after the user login:

- If the user enters name/surname only, the probablity of the relative modelled features will be set to 0.5;
- If the user fills the complete questionaire with the provided user features (age, sex, work, education, handicap, etc.), then the probability of the features of the static profile will be assigned according to a knowledge base containing a set of expert codified rules;
- If the user fills the complete questionaire and performs the psycho-attitudinal test in order to improve the user profile, then the probablity value of the features will be established by the expert system;
- If the user is not new to the system, then the probablity value of the features could be automatically modified by means of user logs collected in the previous user interactions.

INDUCING THE BEHAVIORAL PROFILE

The induction of behavioural user profiles shows an inherent propension to be modelled by means of sequences of events/objects related to each other. Sequences are the simplest form of structured patterns and different methodologies have been proposed in the data mining research area to face the problem of sequential pattern mining, firstly introduced by (Agrawal and Srikant, 1995), with the aim of capturing the existing maximal frequent sequences in a given database.

However, the classical existing approaches, that look for patterns in a single dimension, seem inadequate for inducing behavioural user profiles. Indeed, the user profiling domain, and more specifically the user modelling task, requires an intelligent framework that should take into account not only a person's attitude and preferences but also its behaviour and regularities when moving in a prespecified context, in order for the framework to adapt more easily and straightforwardly the functionality that it implements to the former.

This has led to the exploitation of a more powerful knowledge representation formalism as first-order logic with the aim of looking for patterns that involve multiple relations. Some works facing the problem of knowledge discovery in multi-relational data mining research area are present in literature (Moyle and Muggleton, 1997; Popelnsky, 1998; Dehaspe and Toivonen, 1999; Rodríguez et al., 2000; Malerba and Lisi, 2001). On the other hand, behavioural user profiles might concern, besides multirelational data, also data on multiple dimensions and, hence, the mining of sequential patterns from multi-dimensional information turns out to be very important. An attempt to propose a (two-dimensional) knowledge representation formalism to represent spatio-temporal information based on multi-dimensional modal logics is proposed in (Bennett et al., 2002), while the first work presenting algorithms to mine multi-dimensional patterns has been presented in 2001 by Pinto et al. (Pinto et al., 2001). However, all the works in multi-dimensional data mining have been restricted to the propositional case, not involving a first-order representation formalism, i.e. they consider flat descriptions of events, entities and objects not involving relations between them. To our knowledge, there exists no contribution presenting a framework to manage the general case of multi relational data in which multi-dimensional (for example, spatial and temporal) information may co-exist.

For these reasons, we developed an inductive logic programming (Muggleton and De Raedt,

1994) framework allowing the system to represent and reason about multi-dimensional relational descriptions with the aim of discovering maximal frequent patterns representing the user profiles.

The first-order logic representation gives us the possibility to encode temporal, spatial and other dimensional features without requiring to discriminate between them. Furthermore, it is possible to represent any other domain relation and let them co-exist with other dimensional ones. Finally, a first-order knowledge representation formalism is crucial to take into account more structured and complex features and relations involved in context and user descriptions. A logical formalism for mining temporal patterns in a task of user modelling has already been proposed in (Jacobs, 2004) in which the user behaviour is described according to the temporal sequences of his/her actions. On the other hand, the approach we propose allows to tackle many complex scenarios such as context modelling, in which a situation and the actors involved in it evolve both in time and space.

Background

We use Datalog (Ullman, 1988) as a representation language for the domain knowledge and patterns, that here is briefly reviewed. For a more comprehensive introduction to logic programming and inductive logic programming we refer the reader to (Bratko, 2001; Muggleton and De Raedt, 1994; Lavrac and Dzeroski, 1994).

The representation formalism is based on the notion of first-order language. It consists in a set of formulæ, that are defined on a hierarchy of symbolic structures: terms, atoms, literals which make up the clauses and then, by collecting these into sets, represent logic programs. Specifically we are interested in terms and atoms as described in the following: A term is a variable (User1, User2, ...), or a constant (user1, user2, user3, ...), or, also, a function symbol (f, g, ...) applied to one of the previous, or to another term. The terms represent the arguments of the atoms, like in age(User1,20) age is a predicate symbol (age,name, p, q ...).

As previously reported, sequences are the most natural form to represent the user's behaviour and, consequently, patterns (subsequences) are the most suitable way to encode the user's profile model. Formally,

- A sequence in our framework is defined as an ordered list of Datalog atoms separated by the operator $<$, $l_1 < l_2 < ... < l_m$;
- Given a sequence $\sigma = (e_1, e_2, ... e_m)$ of m elements, a sequence $\sigma' = (e'_1, e'_2, ... e'_k)$ of length k $<$ m is a subsequence (or pattern) of σ if for a given h $<$ m-k holds $e_{h+i} < e_{i+1}$, $1 \leq i \leq k$. The frequency of a subsequence in a sequence is the number of all the possible values of h such that the condition just reported holds;
- A pattern σ' of a sequence σ is maximal if there is no pattern σ'' of σ more frequent than σ' and such that σ' is a subsequence of σ''.

Representing the User's Behaviour and the User Profile Models

Sequences to Describe the User's Behaviour and Patterns to Represent the Learned User Profile Models

In the following we give some technical details on both the multi-dimensional relational sequences and the patterns exploited to represent respectively the user's behaviour and interaction with the system/environment and the learned user profiles.

The simplest way to represent the user's behaviour is a sequence of literals each representing a step performed by the user in one dimension, for example the time dimension. Thus the following sequence: `move(user1,room5)<location(user1,room5)<talk(room5,user1,machine _ learning _ course)< move(user1,room4)` represents a

1-dimensional relational sequence. In general, for this kind of sequences, referring to one dimension only, the operator $<$ may be omitted as follows

```
move(user1,room5)location(user1,room5)
talk(room5,user1,machine _ learning _ course)
move(user1,room4)
```

where it is implicit, for instance, that the atom `move(user1,room4)` follows the atom `talk(room5,user1,machine _ learning _ course)`.

However, in order to make the proposed framework more general and able to deal with more complex and structured data, we adopt the concept of fluents introduced by J. McCarthy (McCarthy and Hayes, 1969) in which: "after having defined a situation, st, as the complete state of the universe at an instant of time t, a fluent is defined as a function whose domain is the space of situations. In particular, a propositional fluent ranges in (true,false), thus, for example, raining(x, st) is true if and only if it is raining at the place x in the situation st ."

The concept of fluent allows to use a fluent with the aim of indicating that an atom is true for a given event by considering a sequence as an ordered succession of events for each dimension. Thus, in our description language, we have: dimensional atoms, referring to dimensional relations between events involved in the sequence, and non-dimensional atoms that may be fluent atoms, explicitly referring to a given event (i.e., one of whose argument denotes an event), or non-fluent atoms, denoting relations between objects (with arity greater than 1), or characterizing an object (with arity 1) involved in the sequence.

The choice to add the event as an argument of the predicates is necessary for the general case of n-dimensional sequences with $n > 1$. In this case, indeed, the operator $<$ is not sufficient to express multi-dimensional relations and we must use its

Example 1. The following set of Datalog atoms

```
move(entering1,user1,room5)(entering1<entering2)
move(entering2,user1,room4) near(room5,room4)
```

denotes a 1-dimensional relational sequence with three non-dimensional atoms (move(entering1,user1,room5) move(entering2,user1,room4) near(room5,room4)) and one dimensional atom (entering1 < entering2).

Specifically, move(entering1,user1,room5) denotes the fluent move(user1,room5) at the event "entering1", move(entering2,user1, room4) denotes the fluent move(user1, room4) at the event "entering2", (entering1 < entering2) indicates that the event entering2 is the direct successor of entering1 and near(room5,room4) represents a generic relation between the objects room5 and room4.

Another way to read the previous example is the following: "move(user1,room5) is true in the event "entering1", the event "entering1" gives rise to the event "entering2" where move(user1,room4) is true, and there is a relation near between room5 and room4."

general version $<_i$, $1 \leq i \leq n$. Specifically, $(e_1 <_i e_2)$ denotes that the event e_1 gives rise to the event e_2 in the dimension i. Hence, in our framework a multi-dimensional representation is supposed to be a set of events, and a sequence of events corresponds to each dimension.

So far, we introduced the general case of one-dimensional sequence. However, in order to deal with relational data in more than one dimension we have to define what is our intention of multi-dimensional sequence, describing the user's behaviour and context, and what are the operators allowing the multi-dimensions to co-exist in the (multi-dimensional) patterns, describing the user profile learned model. In our framework a multi-dimensional relational sequence is a set of Datalog atoms, involving k events and concerning n dimensions, in which there are non-dimensional atoms (fluents and non-fluents) and each event may be related to another event by means of the operators $<_i$, $1 \leq i \leq n$.

Thus, given a set $\mathcal{D}$ of dimensions, we define:

- NEXT_I(X,Y) - $<_i$: *next step on dimension* $i, \forall i \in \mathcal{D}$. This operator indicates the direct successor on the dimension i. For instance, $(entering <_{time} sitting)$ denotes that the event *sitting* is the direct successor of the event *entering* on the dimension *time*;
- follows_i(X,Y) - $\lhd_i$: *after some steps on dimension* $i, \forall i \in \mathcal{D}$. This operator

encodes the transitive closure of $<_i$. For example, $(entering \lhd_{spatialx} sitting)$ states that the event *sitting* occurs somewhere after the event *entering* the dimension *spatialx*;

- follows_at_i(N,X,Y) - O^n_i operator: *exactly after N steps on dimension* $i, \forall i \in \mathcal{D}$. This operator calculates the nth direct successor. For instance, $(entering\ O^n_{spatialz}\ sitting)$ states that the event *sitting* is the nth direct successor of the event *entering* on the dimension *spatialz*.

Note that the $<_i$ will describe the dimensional characteristics in the sequences, while all the three dimensional operators $<_i$, $\lhd_i$ O^n_i, will be used to represent the discovered patterns, i.e. the user models. In particular, the following set of rules will be used to discover, and add them in the learned multi-dimensional pattern, the *high order* operators, follows_at_i follows_i, a given multi-dimensional sequence made up of next_i operator only.

```
follows _ at _ i(1,X,Y)  ←  !.
follows _ at _ i(K,X,Y)  ←  next _ i(X,Z),K1
is K - 1,     follows _ at _ i(K1,Z,Y).


follows _ i(X,Y) ← next _ i(X,Y).
follows _ i(X,Y)  ←  next _ i(X,Z),
follows _ i(Z,Y).
```

In this way, a *multi-dimensional relational pattern* is a set of Datalog atoms, involving k

Example 2. With the previously defined dimensional operators, an example of a simple temporal sequence could be

```
move(entering1,user1,room5) activity(talking,user1,room5)
move(leaving,user1,room5)
(entering1 <time leaving) (entering1 <time talking) (entering1 <spatial entering2)
move(entering2,user1,room4)
(talking < time leaving) (talking < time entering2)
near(room5,room4)
activity(coffee_break,user1,room4)
(leaving < spatial entering2) (entering2< spatial coffee_break)
```

and the corresponding temporal patterns that may be true when applied to it are

```
move(entering1,user1,room5)(entering1 <time talking) activity(talking,user1,room5)

move(entering1,user1,room5) (entering1 ◁time leaving) move(leaving,user1,room5)

move(entering1,user1,room5) (entering1 O²time entering2) move(entering2 user1 ,room4) [if
we consider 2 as hours].
```

events and regarding n dimensions, in which there are non-dimensional atoms and each event may be related to another event by means of the $<_i$, $\triangleleft_i$ and O^n_i, $1 \leq i \leq n$. In particular the model to be learned will be the maximal frequent pattern with a high frequency in long sequences.

Learning the User Profile Models

After having defined the formalism for representing sequences and patterns, here we describe the algorithm for frequent multi-dimensional relational pattern mining based on the same idea as the generic level-wise search method, known in data mining from the APRIORI (Agrawal et al., 1996). The level-wise algorithm makes a breadth-first search in the lattice of patterns ordered by a specialization relation $\preccurlyeq$. The search starts from the most general patterns, and at each level of the lattice the algorithm generates candidates by using the lattice structure and then evaluates the frequency of the candidates. In the generation phase, some patterns are taken out using the monotonicity of pattern frequency, i.e. if a pattern is not frequent then none of its specializations is frequent.

The mining method is outlined in Algorithm 1. The generation of the frequent patterns is based on a top-down approach: The algorithm starts with the most general patterns of length 1, generated by adding to the empty pattern a non-dimensional atom.

Successively, at each step it tries to specialize, by adding atoms to the pattern, all the potential frequent patterns, discarding the non-frequent patterns and storing those whose length is equal to a defined threshold *maxsize*. Note that the length of a pattern is defined as the number of non-dimensional atoms.

Specifically, given the set $\mathcal{D}$ of dimensions, the set $\mathcal{F}$ of fluent atoms, the set $\mathcal{P}$ of non-fluent atoms, the specialization of the patterns is obtained as follows:

- **Adding a non-dimensional atom**
  - The pattern S is specialized by adding a non-dimensional atom $F \in \mathcal{F}$ (a fluent) referring to an event already introduced in S;
  - The pattern S is specialized by adding a non-dimensional atom $P \in \mathcal{P}$:

- **Adding a dimensional atom**
  - The pattern S is specialized by adding the dimensional atom $(x <_i y)$ $i \in \mathcal{D}$, relating the events x and y, iff $\exists$ a fluent $F \in \mathcal{F}$ in S whose event argument is x and there not exist atoms $(x \triangleleft_i y)$ and $(x\, O^n_i\, y)$ in S;
  - The pattern S is specialized by adding the dimensional atom $(x \triangleleft_i y)$ $i \in \mathcal{D}$, relating the events x and y, iff $\exists$ a fluent $F \in \mathcal{F}$ in S whose event argument is x and there not exist atoms $(x <_i y)$ and $(x\, O^n_i\, y)$ in S;
  - The pattern S is specialized by adding the dimensional atom $(x\, O^n_{i1}\, y)$ $i \in \mathcal{D}$, relating the events x and y, iff $\exists$ a fluent $F \in \mathcal{F}$ in S whose event argument is x and there not exist atoms $(x <_i y)$ and $(x \triangleleft_i y)$ in S.

A dimensional atom is added iff there exists a fluent atom referring to its starting event. This is to avoid useless chains of dimensional predicates like this $p(e_1,a)$ $(e_1 <_i e_2)$ $(e_2 <_i e_3)$ $(e_3 <_i e_4)$, that is obviously a subset semantically equivalent to $p(e_1,a)$ $(e_1\, O^3_i\, e_4)$.

The algorithm uses a background knowledge $\mathcal{B}$ containing the multi-dimensional sequence and a set of constraints that must be satisfied by the generated patterns. In particular $\mathcal{B}$ contains:

- *Maxsize(M)*: Maximal pattern length;
- *Minfreq(m)*: Indicates that the frequency of the patterns must be larger than m;
- *Dimension(next_i)*: Indicates that the sequence contains events on the dimension i. One can have more that one of such atoms, each of which denoting a different dimension. In particular, the number of these atoms represents the number of the dimensions.
- *Type(p)*: denotes the type of the predicate's arguments p. 'e' indicates that the argument is an event;
- *Negconstraint([$p_1,p_2,...p_n$])*: Specifies a constraint that the generated patterns must not fulfill;

Algorithm 1: MDLS

REQUIRE: $\Sigma = \mathcal{B} \cup \mathcal{U}$, where $\mathcal{B}$ is the background knowledge and $\mathcal{U}$ is the set of ground atoms in the sequence S.

Ensure: P_{max}: the set of maximal frequent patterns

$P \leftarrow$ { initial patterns }

$P_{max} \leftarrow \varnothing$

WHILE $(P \neq \varnothing)$ DO

 $P_s \leftarrow \varnothing$

 FOR (ALL $p \in P$) DO

  /* generation step */

  $P_s \leftarrow P_s \cup$ {all the specializations of p that satisfy all the constraints posconstraints, negconstraints or atmostone}

$P \leftarrow \varnothing$

for (all $p \in P_s$) **do**

 /* evaluation step */}

 if (freq(p) $\geq$ minfreq) **then**

  if (length(p) = maxsize) **then**

   $P_{max} \leftarrow P_{max} \cup$ {p}

  else

   $P \leftarrow P \cup$ {p}

- *Posconstraint([p₁,p₂,...pₙ])*: Specifies the constraint that the generated patterns must fulfill;

- *Atmostone([p₁,p₂,...pₙ])*: This constraint discards all the generated patterns that make true more than one predicate among $p_1,p_2,...$ p_n. For instance, *atmostone([red(X), blue(X), green(X)])* indicates that each constant in the pattern can assume at most one of *red, blue* or *green* value;

The `dimension(next_i)` predicate, specifying the number of dimensions the sequence is based on, allows to the corresponding definitions of the predicates `follows_at_i follows_i` (previously introduced) to be automatically generated and added to the background knowledge $\mathcal{B}$.

The type declaration specifies a language bias indicating what predicates can be used in the patterns and allowing to formulate constraints on the variable bindings. The solution space is further pruned by using some positive and negative constraints specified by the `negconstraint posconstraint` literals. The last pruning choice is defined by the `atmostone` literals. This last constraint is able to describe that some predicates are of the same type.

Since each pattern must start with a non-dimensional predicate, the frequency of a multi-dimensional relational pattern $P = (p_1, p_2, ..., p_n)$ in a multi-dimensional relational sequence S is equal to the number of different ground literals used to instantiate (to different terms correspond different objects) and make true the literal p_1 in Σ (see Example 3).

A Case Study

The analysis of the use of Unix command shell represents one of the classic applications in the domain of adaptive user interfaces and user modelling. Greenberg (Greenberg, 1988) collected logs from 168 users of the unix csh, divided into 4 target groups: 55 novice programmers, 36 experienced programmers, 52 computer scientists and 25 non-programmers.

Each Greenberg's log file corresponding to a user is divided into login sessions denoted by a starting and an ending time record. Each command entered in each session has been annotated with the current working directory, alias substitution, history use and error status. Furthermore, each command name may be followed by some options and some parameters. For instance the command `ls -a *.c` has name `ls`, option `-a` and parameter `*.c`.

As pointed out in (Jacobs and Blockeel, 2001), this is a relational problem, since commands are

Example 3. Given the following sequence

$S \equiv p(e_1,a)\ q(a,t)\ q(a,s)\ (e_1 < e_2)\ p(e_2,b)\ q(b,a)$

and the pattern

$P \equiv p(E,X)\ q(X,Y)$

there are 3 way to instantiate P from Σ in such a way that to different terms correspond different objects, i.e.

$\theta_1 = \{ E/e_1, X/a, Y/t \},$
$\theta_2 = \{ E/e_1, X/a, Y/s \},$
$\theta_3 = \{ E/e_2, X/b, Y/a \}.$

However, since θ_1 and θ_2 map the same constants to the variables of p(E,X) (the first literal of the pattern), the frequency of P on S is equal to 2.

---

interrelated by their execution order (or time), and each command can be possibly related to one or more parameters. A shell log may be viewed as a 2-dimensional sequence, since each command is followed by another command (first dimension) and each command line is composed by an ordered sequence of tokens (i.e., command name, options and parameters). Each shell log has been represented as a set of logical ground atoms to form a sequence as follows.

command(e) is the predicate used to indicate that e is a command. The command name has been used as a predicate symbol applied to e;

parameter(e,p) has been used to indicate that p is the parameter of e. The parameter name has been used as a predicate symbol applied to p;

current directory(c,d) indicates that d is the current directory of command c;

next c(c1,c2) ($<_c$) indicates that command c2 is the direct command successor of c1;

next p(p1,p2) ($<_p$) indicates that parameter p2 is the direct parameter successor of p1.

For instance the following shell log

```
cp paper.tex newpaper.tex
latex newpaper
xdvi newpaper
```

should be translated as

```
command(c1), '$cp'(c1),
    next_p(c1,c1p1), parameter(c1p1,'paper.
                                    tex'),
    next_p(c1p1,c1p2),
    parameter(c1p2,'newpaper.tex'),
next_c(c1,c2), '$latex'(c2),
    next_p(c2,c2p1),
            parameter(c2p1,'newpaper'),
    next_c(c2,c3), '$xdvi'(c3),
next_p(c3,c3p1),parameter(c3p1,'newpaper')
```

In this way it is possible to discover patterns such as

```
command(L), '$latex'(L),
```

```
    next_p(L,LP), parameter(LP,P),
next_c(L,X), '$xdvi'(X),
    next_p(X,XP), parameter(XP,P)
```

Figure 1 reports statistics on MDLS performance on the Greenberg dataset. The first four columns denote, respectively, the user name, the number of literals of the sequence, the number of sessions for each user log file and the total number of commands in the log file. For each user some experiments have been made. The kind of experiment carried out is denoted in the fifth column that reports the operators used in the experiment. For instance $<_c$ and $<_p$ indicate that only these two operators have been used in the experiment. We see that, as the number of commands and dimensional operators grows, runtime increases. Note that each session represents a sequence and a log file is a collection of sequences. There is no correlation between two sessions in a log file.

DISCUSSION AND CONCLUSION

One of the most important features of a mobile device concerns its flexibility and capability to adapt the functionalities it provides to the users. However, the main problem of the systems present in literature is their inability to support different needs of individual users due to their incapability to identify those needs, and, more importantly, to the insufficient mappings of those needs to available resources/services. The approaches we considered in this paper concern the use of the concept of stereotype to model and categorize a user in order to provide the most suitable service and the use of machine learning techniques to model the user interests and behaviour.

In general, the former approaches perform a match between the stereotypes initially defined by the user model developer and the facts about the user collected during his/her interaction with the system. The latter ones exploit low level informations coming from sensors to build a user profile and hence are not able to deal with complex scenarios involving relationships betwen objects or making temporal and spatial information co-exist in the descriprion of the context.

In our proposal, we presented strategies to build an initial user profile based on the concept of stereotypes and then automatically and inductively adjust some features of such initial model by means of logs of user interaction with the device/context. The approach we proposed is a two phase construction of the user model: firstly, an initial static user model is built for the user connecting to the system the first time. Successively, the model is revised/adjusted by considering the information collected in the logs of the user interaction with the device/context in order to make the model more adequate to the evolving user's interests/preferences/behaviour. The initial model is built by exploiting the stereotype concept, its adjustment is performed exploiting machine learning techniques and particularly, sequence mining and pattern discovery strategies.

The representation language and the approach proposed in this chapter allows one to tackle complex scenarios. Indeed, starting from information about user/context, it is possible to profile, for example, a user accessing to a museum by describing contextual information (such as position in the room, brightness, noise), temporal information (how many time the user spent on an item), device characteristics, user behaviour in such a context (such as requiring more frequently the audio files than the visual ones, requiring a detailed description of the item just after visualizing it, slow or fast interaction with the device). In this way, we are able to provide the system with useful information in order to give dynamic and adaptive functionality in the environments according to the automatically learned user model.

Figure 1 MDLS performances (time in secs.). |S|: n. of literals in the sequence; |Ses|: n. of sessions for user log file; |C|: total number of commands in the log file; Op: dimensional operators used; L: max length of the patterns; F: min freq of the patterns; |MP|: n. of found maximal patterns; Sp: required specializations.

User	|S|	|Ses|	|C|	Op	L	F	Time	|MP|	Sp
n9	2654	73	357	$<_C$	5	5	1.17	45	3597
				$<_C<_P$	5	5	2.68	45	9513
				$<_C \bigcirc_C^n$	5	5	2.58	91	8495
				$<_C \lhd_C \bigcirc_C^n$	5	5	28.94	149	29081
				$<_{C,P} \lhd_{C,P} \bigcirc_{C,P}^n$	5	5	99.06	218	76299
n17	5366	61	848	$<_C$	5	10	2.36	38	4512
				$<_C<_P$	5	10	3.58	18	6434
				$<_C \bigcirc_C^n$	5	10	7.95	47	10808
				$<_C \lhd_C \bigcirc_C^n$	5	10	37.06	39	19198
				$<_{C,P} \lhd_{C,P} \bigcirc_{C,P}^n$	5	10	144.38	25	25142
n7	12355	80	1231	$<_C$	5	15	6.10	64	7716
				$<_C<_P$	5	15	19.33	77	24046
				$<_C \bigcirc_C^n$	5	15	16.30	139	20744
				$<_C \lhd_C \bigcirc_C^n$	5	15	138.06	162	51363
				$<_C$	5	80	1.78	9	953
				$<_C<_P$	5	80	4.06	11	2493
				$<_C \bigcirc_C^n$	5	80	4.14	16	2479
				$<_C \lhd_C \bigcirc_C^n$	5	80	42.55	29	6745
				$<_{C,P} \lhd_{C,P} \bigcirc_{C,P}^n$	5	80	164.99	49	17505

REFERENCES

Agrawal, R., Manilla, H., Srikant, R., Toivonen, H., & Verkamo, A. (1996). Fast discovery of association rules. In U. Fayyad, G. Piatetsky-Shapiro, P. Smyth, & R. Uthurusamy (Eds.), *Advances in knowledge discovery and data mining* (pp. 307-328). AAAI Press.

Agrawal, R., & Srikant, R. (1995). Mining sequential patterns. In *Proceedings of the International Conference on Data Engineering (ICDE95)* (pp. 3-14).

Ardissono, L., Gena, C., Torasso, P., Bellifemmine, F., Difino, A., & Negro, B. (2004). *Personalized digital television –targeting programs to individual viewers* (Vol. 6, pp. 3-26). Springer.

Augusto, J.C., & Nugent, C.D. (Eds.) (2006). *Designing smart homes, the role of artificial intelligence* (LNCS 4008). Springer.

Bennett, B., Cohn, A.G., Wolter, F., & Zakharyaschev, M. (2002). Multi-dimensional modal logic as a framework for spatio-temporal reasoning. *Applied Intelligence, 17*(3), 239-251.

Brajnik, G., & Tasso, C. (1992). A flexible tool for developing user modeling applications with nonmonotonic reasoning capabilities. In *Proceedings of the Third International Workshop on User Modeling*, Dagstuhl, Germany (pp. 42-66).

Bratko, I. (2001). *Prolog programming for artificial intelligence, 3rd ed.* Boston: Addison-Wesley Longman Publishing Co., Inc.

Brusilovsky, P., Kobsa, A., & Nejdl, W. (Eds.) (2007). *The adaptive web: Methods and strategies of Web personalization* (LNCS). Berlin: Springer.

Cheverst, K., Davies, N., Mitchell, K., Friday, A., & Efstratiou, C. (2000). Developing a context-aware electronic tourist guide: Some issues and experiences. In *CHI'00: Proceedings of the SIGCHI conference on Human factors in computing systems*, New York (pp. 17-24). ACM.

Cook, D.J. (2006). Health monitoring and assistance to support aging in place. *The Journal of Universal Computer Science, 12*(1),15-29.

Dehaspe, L., & Toivonen, H. (1999). Discovery of frequent datalog patterns. *Data Mining and Knowledge Discovery, 3*(1), 7-36.

Dolog, P., Henze, N., Nejdl, W., & Sintek, M. (Eds.) (2003). Towards the adaptive Semantic Web. *First Workshop on Principles and Practice of Semantic Web Reasoning.*

Finin, T.W. (1989). Gums: A general user modeling shell. In A. Kobsa, & W. Wahlster (Eds.), *User models in dialog systems* (pp. 411-430).

Greenberg, S. (1988). *Using unix: Collected traces of 168 users* (Res. Rep. No. 88/333/45). Alberta, Canada: University of Calgary, Department of Computer Science.

Heierman III, E.O., & Cook, D.J. (2003, December 19-22). Improving home automation by discovering regularly occurring device usage patterns. In *Proceedings of the 3rd IEEE International Conference on Data Mining (ICDM 2003)*, Melbourne, FL (pp. 537-540). IEEE Computer Society.

Jacobs, N., & Blockeel, H. (2001). From shell logs to shell scripts. In C. Rouveirol, & M. Sebag (Eds.), *Proceedings of the 11th International Conference on Inductive Logic Programming* (Vol. 2157, pp. 80-90). Springer.

Jacobs, N. (2004). *Relational sequence learning and user modelling.* Unpublished doctoral dissertation, K.U. Leuven, Leuven, Belgium.

Kaplan, C., Fenwick, J., & Chen, J. (1993). Adaptive hypertext navigation based on user goals and context. *User Modeling and User-Adapted Interaction, 3*(3), 193-220.

Kay, J. (1994). Lies, damned lies, and stereotypes: Pragmatic approximations of users. In A. Kobsa,

& D. Litman (Eds.), *Proceedings of the 4ᵗʰ International Conference on User Modeling UM94* (pp. 175-184). MITRE, UM Inc.

Kobsa, A. (1990). Modeling the user's conceptual knowledge in BGP-MS, a user modeling shell system. *Computational Intelligence, 6*(4), 193-208.

Kobsa, A., & Pohl, W. (1995). The user modeling shell system bgp-ms. *User Modeling and User-Adapted Interaction, 4*(2), 59-106.

Lavrac, N., & Dzeroski, S. (1994). *Inductive logic programming: Techniques and applications.* New York: Ellis Horwood.

Liao, L., Patterson, D., Fox, D., & Kautz, H.A. (2007). Learning and inferring transportation routines. *Artificial Intelligence, 171*(5-6), 311-331.

Malerba, D., & Lisi, F. (2001). Discovering associations between spatial objects: An ilp application. In *Proceedings of the 11ᵗʰ International Conference on Inductive Logic Programming* (LNCS 2157, pp. 156-166). Springer.

McCarthy, J., & Hayes, P. (1969). Some philosophical problems from the standpoint of artificial intelligence. In B. Meltzer, & D. Michie (Eds.), *Machine Intelligence 4* (pp. 463-502). Edinburgh University Press.

Moyle, S., & Muggleton, S. (1997). Learning programs in the event calculus. In *Proceedings of the 7ᵗʰ International Workshop on Inductive Logic Programming* (pp. 205-212). Springer.

Muggleton, S., & De Raedt, L. (1994). Inductive logic programming: Theory and methods. *Journal of Logic Programming, 19/20*, 629-679.

Orwant, J. (1995). Heterogeneous learning in the doppelgänger user modeling system. *User Modeling and User-Adapted Interaction, 4*(2), 107-130.

Paiva, A., & Self, J. (1994). Tagus: A user and learner modeling system. In *Proceedings of the Fourth International Conference on User Modeling*, Hyannis, MA (pp. 43-49).

Pinto, H., Han, J., Pei, J., Wang, K., Chen, Q., & Dayal, U. (2001). Multi-dimensional sequential pattern mining. In *CIKM '01: Proceedings of the Tenth International Conference on Information and Knowledge Management*, New York (pp. 81-88). ACM Press.

Popelínsky, L. (1998). Knowledge discovery in spatial data by means of ILP. In *Proceedings of the Second European Symposium on Principles of Data Mining and Knowledge Discovery* (pp. 185-193). Springer.

Rabiner, L. (1990). A tutorial on hidden Markov models and selected applications in speech recognition (pp. 267-296).

Randell, C., & Muller, H. (2000). Context awareness by analysing accelerometer data. In B. MacIntyre, & B. Iannucci (Eds.), *Proccedings of the 4ᵗʰ International Symposium on Wearable Computers* (pp. 175-176). IEEE Computer Society.

Rao, S.P., & Cook, D.J. (2004). Predicting inhabitant action using action and task models with application to smart homes. *International Journal on Artificial Intelligence Tools, 13*(1), 81-99.

Rich, E. (1979). *Building and exploiting user models.* Unpublished doctoral dissertation, Pittsburgh, PA.

Rich, E. (1989). Stereotypes and user modeling. In A. Kobsa, & W. Wahlster (Eds.), *User models in dialog systems* (pp. 35-51). Berlin, Heidelberg: Springer.

Rich, E. (1998). User modeling via stereotypes. In *Readings in intelligent user interfaces* (pp. 329-342). San Francisco: Morgan Kaufmann Publishers Inc.

Rodríguez, J., Alonso, C., & Böstrom, H. (2000). Learning first order logic time series classifiers. In J. Cussens, & A. Frisch (Eds.), *Proceedings of the 10ᵗʰ International Workshop on Inductive Logic Programming* (pp. 260-275). Springer.

Si, H., Kawahara, Y., Morikawa, H., & Aoyama, T. (2005). A stochastic approach for creating context-aware services based on context histories in smart home. In *ECHISE2005, Pervasive 2005 Proceeding* (pp. 37-41).

Siewiorek, D., Smailagic, A., Furukawa, J., Krause, A., Moraveji, N., Reiger, K., Shaffer, J., & Wong, F.L. (2003). Sensay: A context-aware mobile phone. In *Proceedings of the 7th IEEE International Symposium on Wearable Computers (ISWC'03)*, Los Alamitos, CA (p. 248). IEEE Computer Society.

Souchon, N., Limbourg, Q., & Vanderdonckt, J. (2002). Task modelling in multiple contexts of use. In *DSV-IS '02: Proceedings of the 9th International Workshop on Interactive Systems. Design, Specification, and Verification*, London (pp. 59-73). Springer-Verlag.

Ullman, J. (1988). *Principles of database and knowledge-base systems, vol. I*. Computer Science Press.

KEY TERMS AND DEFINITIONS

Apriori Algorithm: In computer science and data mining, Apriori is a classic algorithm for learning association rules. Apriori is designed to operate on databases containing transactions (for example, collections of items bought by customers, or details of a website frequentation). As is common in association rule mining, given a set of itemsets (for instance, sets of retail transactions, each listing individual items purchased), the algorithm attempts to find subsets which are common to at least a minimum number C (the cutoff, or confidence threshold) of the itemsets. Apriori uses a "bottom up" approach, where frequent subsets are extended one item at a time (a step known as candidate generation), and groups of candidates are tested against the data. The algorithm terminates when no further successful extensions are found.

First-Order Logic (FOL): A formal deductive system used in mathematics, philosophy, linguistics, and computer science. FOL uses a wholly unambiguous formal language interpreted by mathematical structures. FOL is a system of deduction that extends propositional logic by allowing quantification over individuals of a given domain of discourse. While propositional logic deals with simple declarative propositions, first-order logic additionally covers predicates and quantification. A first-order theory consists of a set of axioms (usually finite or recursively enumerable) and the statements deducible from them given the underlying deducibility relation. Usually what is meant by 'first-order theory' is some set of axioms together with those of a complete (and sound) axiomatization of first-order logic, closed under the rules of FOL. A first-order language has sufficient expressive power to formalize two important mathematical theories: ZFC set theory and Peano arithmetic. A first-order language cannot, however, categorically express the notion of countability even though it is expressible in the first-order theory ZFC under the intended interpretation of the symbolism of ZFC. Such ideas can be expressed categorically with second-order logic.

Inductive Logic Programming (ILP): Is a subfield of machine learning which uses logic programming as a uniform representation for examples, background knowledge and hypotheses. Given an encoding of the known background knowledge and a set of examples represented as a logical database of facts, an ILP system will derive a hypothesised logic program which entails all the positive and none of the negative examples. A unifying theory of Inductive Logic Programming is being built up around lattice-based concepts such as refinement, least general generalisation, inverse resolution and most specific corrections.

Machine Learning (ML): The study of computer algorithms that improve automatically through experience. As a broad subfield of artificial intelligence, machine learning is concerned with the design and development of algorithms and techniques that allow computers to "learn". At a general level, there are two types of learning: inductive, and deductive. Inductive machine learning methods extract rules and patterns out of massive data sets. The major focus of machine learning research is to extract information from data automatically, by computational and statistical methods.

Pattern Mining: Is the task of finding existing patterns in data. In this context patterns often means association rules. The original motivation for searching association rules came from the need to analyze supermarket transaction data, that is, to examine customer behaviour in terms of the purchased products. For example, an association rule "beer => chips (80%)" states that four out of five customers that bought beer also bought chips.

Stereotype: A stereotype is a simplified and/or standardized conception or image with specific meaning, often held in common by people about another group. A stereotype can be a conventional and oversimplified conception, opinion, or image,

based on the assumption that there are attributes that members of the other group hold in common. Stereotypes are sometimes formed by a previous illusory correlation, a false association between two variables that are loosely if at all correlated. Stereotypes may be positive or negative in tone. They are typically generalizations based on minimal or limited knowledge about a group to which the person doing the stereotyping does not belong. Persons may be grouped based on racial group, ethnicity, religion, sexual orientation, age or any number of other categories.

User Modeling: Is a cross-disciplinary research field that attempts to construct models of human behavior within a specific computer environment. Contrary to traditional artificial intelligence research, the goal is not to imitate human behavior as such, but to make the machine able to understand what the expectations, goals, information needs, desires (etc.) of a user are in terms of a specific computing environment. Furthermore, the goal is to utilize this understanding to assist the user in performing computing tasks. The computer representation of the user's goals (etc.) is called a user model and systems that construct and utilize such models are called user modeling systems.

Chapter VIII
Model–Based Design for Multimodal Interaction in a VE

Karin Coninx
Hasselt University, Belgium

Joan De Boeck
Hasselt University, Belgium

Chris Raymaekers
Hasselt University, Belgium

Lode Vanacken
Hasselt University, Belgium

ABSTRACT

The creation of virtual environments is often a lengthy and expensive process. Especially defining the interaction dialog between the user and the environment is a difficult task, as the communication is often multimodal by nature. In this chapter, we elaborate on an approach which facilitates the development of this kind of user interfaces. In particular, we propose a model-based user interface design process (MBUID), in which the interface is defined by means of high level notations, rather than by writing low level programming code. The approach lifts the design to a higher level of abstraction, resulting in a shortened development cycle leaving the opportunity for creating intermediate prototypes and user evaluation, ultimately resulting in better and cheaper virtual environment interfaces.

INTRODUCTION

Much attention has been paid lately to the use of virtual environments (VEs). Applications range from computer games to scientific simulations. For this purpose, several frameworks, such as VR Juggler [Bierbaum et al., 2001] and XVR [Carrozzino et al., 2005] have been created. However, little attention has been paid to development tools, which allow the designer of a virtual environment to abstract away from the code level. Existing tools, such as Virtools [Virtools inc, 2008], support the design of VE applications by using a graphical notation. Although, this provides a first necessary step, it is important to take advantage of further abstractions, where the design of a virtual environment is refined from a conceptual phase to the actual implementation using a tool-supported process. This allows domain specialists, designers and developers to concentrate on their part in the creation of a VE application, while still being able to discuss design decisions with each other.

On the other hand, over the last years, the design of form-based and multi-device user interfaces using high-level specifications has been investigated extensively. Often, a Model-Based User Interface Design (MBUID) process is employed. In such an approach several models are used to describe the different aspects of user interaction. Those models may describe the tasks performed by the application, the dialog with the user and the presentation of the User Interface elements. Based on these models, the final application can be created using a (semi-)automatic process.

The advantages that are provided by using a MBUID process can also benefit the creation of virtual environments. However, due to the highly-dynamic nature of the interaction in VEs, the requirements for the design process are more complex. VEs try to provide an interface to the user which is as intuitive as possible. Therefore, the user interaction is not restricted to a limited set of possibilities, but is based on direct manipulation and multimodal interaction such as speech, the sight, the hearing and touch as we know from the real world. This obviously complicates the design of the user interface in such a VE.

Applying multimodal interaction often requires the use of specialised hardware, such as stereo projection, 3D trackers and haptic devices. As each device has to be handled in a specific way,

a design process should also be able to abstract away from those specific technical details, while still allowing to use all the functionality (e.g. haptic feedback).

To achieve an intuitive interface, metaphors are often used in order to transfer knowledge a user already has from previous experiences or from within the real world. Examples include the ray casting technique [Liang and Green, 1994] for object selection, where an object is selected by simulating pointing at it with a flashlight; another example is the flying vehicle metaphor [Ware and Osborne, 1990] for navigation, where the virtual camera is moved as if it is mounted on a flying vehicle.

Metaphors have the benefit to transfer earlier knowledge from the user to the new situation, however, it is difficult to predict in advance whether or not a solution will succeed in this aim. Therefore, newly proposed metaphors have to be extensively tested and adjusted. A process that facilitates the creation of an interactive virtual environment should hence provide an easy manner to realise such interaction techniques.

Finally, the interaction techniques do not stand on their own. They act upon the object available in the 3D world. Users should for instance be able to open a door by pushing it open. Walls on the other hand should not move if they are pushed against. It is therefore necessary to take this kind of semantic information into account when designing the interaction.

MBUID may be a promising solution in order to simplify the creation of virtual environments, by abstracting from the programming code, and lifting the design process to a higher level. However, the difficulties and special requirements of virtual environments pose a challenge to model-based design of the interaction. In this chapter, we give a comprehensive overview of the benefits, problems and possible solutions when bringing a MBUID process into the domain of virtual environments.

MODEL-BASED USER INTERFACE DESIGN

Model-based User Interface Design intends to design the user interface from a much higher level than by drawing an interface and writing programming code. By using high-level models, the final user interface is incrementally derived, which should facilitate the development cycle of the interface.

Over the last years, the principles of Model-based User Interface Design (MBUID) already have been largely investigated, mainly applied for traditional form-based desktop user interfaces [Vanderdonckt, 2005]. The recent need for flexible development of contemporary interactive applications even has raised the attention for this approach. Indeed, mobile applications [Mori et al., 2002], context-sensitive multi-device user interfaces [Calvary et al., 2003] and distributed and migratable user interfaces [Clerckx et al., 2004] require easier ways to develop a user interface than by writing programming code. The increased attention and research effort causes MBUID currently finding its way from the academic research to practical applications in industrial projects, not only for designing the final interactive application, but also for rapid prototyping and even for reverse engineering, e.g. by using the UsiXML approach [Vanderdonckt et al., 2004]).

Most model-based processes have several properties in common (e.g. [Calvary et al., 2003, Clerckx et al., 2004, Luyten et al., 2003, Mori et al., 2004]) show that they have several properties in common. Nearly all processes start with some kind of a task model and evolve towards the final user interface using an incremental approach. During each increment, one model is converted into the next by means of an automatic transformation (through mapping rules) or by a manual adaptation by the user.

Multimodality, including speech input, voice output and pen-based interaction, is a central topic in many research projects. However, most of the contemporary research activities in the area of MBUID still concentrate on 2D applications, in

Figure 1. Schematic Overview of the MBUID Process

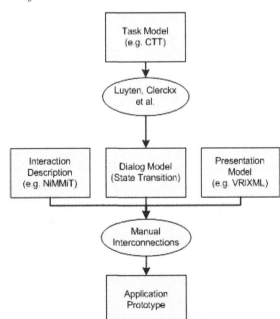

which interaction is done in two dimensions with traditional or pen-based input, even when working with 3D scenes or data. In the next section, we describe how MBUID can be applied to the design of an interactive virtual environment.

MODEL-BASED DESIGN OF A VIRTUAL ENVIRONMENT

Only recently, the application of MBUID approaches has been broadened in its scope, and research initiatives in this area pay increased attention to the design of highly-interactive applications, such as virtual environments and mixed reality applications [Dubois et al., 2004]. Although MBUID has proven its value in dialog and web-based interface generation, none of the existing approaches seems directly and entirely usable for the design of an IVEs. They all lack the possibility to describe direct manipulation techniques (directly interacting with the virtual world instead of clicking buttons and menus) and metaphors using a single rich modality of interaction or multiple modalities. Some approaches such as ICO [Navarre et al., 2005] specifically focus on the interaction techniques, but do not describe an entire process. A good MBUID process should therefore consider the task model, the user interface widgets (such as dialogs and menus) as well as the description of possible interaction techniques for direct manipulation supporting multimodal input and output (such as speech, gestures and haptics).

In this chapter, we demonstrate how a process, based on common MBUID principles, and using a task model, a dialog model and a presentation model, can be extended with an interaction description model in order to suit the needs for a model-based development approach for a multimodal interactive VE application. The proposed approach is shown in figure 6.1. The process is known as the VR-DeMo process (according to the IWT projects name VR-DeMo, IWT 030248).

For a detailed description of this project, we refer the interested reader to [Raymaekers et al., 14], [Coninx et al., 2006b], [De Boeck et al., 2006] and [Bille et al., 2004].

After explaining the main steps of this process in the following paragraphs, we will discuss the advantages of a tool supporting the model-based development approach in the last section of this chapter.

Task Model

The process may start from a task model, describing the possible tasks and their mutual relations. We prefer describing these models using Concur-TaskTrees [Paterno, 2000], as this model allows a comprehensive decomposition of all possible tasks (user, computer and interactive tasks) of the application, together with their mutual relationships. Based on temporal relationships between the tasks, a dialog model is derived from this task model using the algorithm of Clerckx et al. [Clerckx et al., 2004]. The result of this transformation is a collection of Enabled Task Sets (ETS) [Paterno, 2000], where an ETS groups all tasks that can be executed at a particular moment in time. These different ETSs then correspond to the states in the dialog model, as will be described below.

In the proposed approach, the task model is optional, which means that alternatively the designer directly can start modelling the application by creating a dialog model.

Dialog Model

The dialog model plays a central role in the presented approach. Either directly created by the user, or imported from a task model, the dialog model is implemented as a state transition diagram with each state implicitly containing the tasks that can be performed in a given situation (expressed in a certain ETS). For instance, when the user has chosen to manipulate a given object (and thus is in a given 'state' of the application), he can only move or rotate an object, and is for instance unable to create a new object. Some tasks explicitly perform a state transition to another state, enabling other tasks.

Interactive virtual environments strongly rely on the user input, which obviously means that we have to define how the user may interact with the system. This means that most tasks are initiated by the user by operating one or more of the available input devices, such as a (3D) mouse, tracker, haptic device or a microphone. All input generates events, triggering the task to be executed (if that task is enabled in the current 'state').

Presentation Model

To support menu-based and form-based interaction with the VE in addition to direct manipulation, the dialog model is annotated with a presentation model, describing the UI widgets (menus, dialogs, etc). As in many MBUID approaches, the presentation model describes an abstract user interface, which means that it does not define how the interface will exactly look like, but only what functionality is provided by what kind of widgets (menus, buttons, dials, ...). For the final user interface, we use hybrid 2D/3D user interface elements such as 2D menus or dialogs positioned in 3D according to the findings in [Coninx et al., 1997] and [Raymaekers and Coninx, 2001]. The presentation model is described using VRIXML, an XML-based User Interface Description Language (UIDL), suitable for 2D/3D hybrid menus [Cuppens et al., 2004].

Interaction Description

From the point of view of interaction, the interaction description model as shown in the process overview Figure 1 is a central artefact in order to enhance an MBUID approach for use in the context of virtual environments. The interaction model, which is in fact an annotation of the dialog model, describes the direct manipulation and multimodal

interaction from the user with the virtual objects. As explained later, most traditional MBUID approaches lack the support for direct manipulation and multimodal interaction. Therefore we developed NiMMiT, Notation For MultiModal Interaction Techniques. NiMMiT is developed to describe interaction techniques at a higher level than by writing code. An interaction technique can be seen as a complex ensemble of multimodal information that is merged and applied in order to execute a compound task which consists of several sub-tasks. A good example may be 'touching an object to push it away'. NiMMiT is a graphical notation, inheriting the formalism of a state-chart in order to describe the (multimodal) interaction within the virtual environment. Furthermore, it also supports dataflow which is important in the user interaction, as well. We will elaborate in more detail on NiMMiT later in this chapter.

Application Generation

The interconnection of the presentation model and the interaction description with the dialog model is a manual process, in which the designer has to indicate which events, directly coming from a device or (indirectly) produced by a UI element, correspond to a given task. A task then can be a simple atomic task, as described in the task model, or it can be a more complex action described using NiMMiT.

After annotating the dialog model, an application prototype is generated, which can be executed immediately. The prototype also contains the application code and some metadata containing the contents of the models. If necessary, a programming specialist can still tweak the code. The last step can be considered as an iterative process, which means that the interaction description model, the presentation model, and the final annotation of the dialog model, can be altered, while possible changes in the programming code are preserved.

NIMMIT, NOTATION FOR MULTIMODAL INTERACTION TECHNIQUES

As explained before, in particular the lack of support for multimodal interaction and direct manipulation prevents most traditional MBUID approaches of being applicable in the context of virtual environments. Neither the task model, the dialog model or the presentation model supports the expressive power which is necessary to describe actions such as 'When the cursor hits an object, the object sticks to the cursor and keeps there until the user speaks the words -release object-'. Moreover, at the end of the process, we would like to generate an application (or prototype) that can directly execute these desired interaction paradigms. In the remainder of this section, we list the requirements of a notation to describe interaction in virtual environments, and we explain how our notation NiMMiT accomplishes these requirements.

Requirements for Describing User Interaction

In our opinion, high-level design of an interaction technique supporting automatic execution of the created diagrams obliges a candidate notation to support the following requirements. The notation must be:

- Event driven,
- State driven,
- Sata driven,
- And must support encapsulation for hierarchical reuse.

One by one, we will provide a motivation for these requirements.

Event Driven

Interaction techniques are inherently driven by user-initiated actions, which we define as events. Since human interaction is multimodal by nature, it can be interpreted as a combination of unimodal events [Bernsen, 1994] (e.g. pointer movement, click, speech command, gesture, etc.). An event has the following properties:

- A source, indicating the modality and/or abstract device that caused it (speech, pointing device, gesture, etc.),
- An identification, defining the kind of the event itself (button click, speech command, etc.),
- Parameters, giving additional information about the event (e.g. the pointer position). Events can be seen as the 'initiators' of different parts of the interaction.

State Driven

An interactive system does not always have to respond to all available events when a user is interacting with the virtual world. Most of the time, specific events must have occurred before other events are enabled. For instance, the user first needs to click the pointer's button for selecting an object, before being able to drag an object. Therefore, at this stage in describing our approach, we basically consider an interaction technique to be expressed in a finite state machine, in which each state defines to which set of events the system will respond. The occurrence of an event or combination of events initiates a state transition to another state in which other events are available.

Data Driven

Restricting an interaction technique to a description by means of a 'finite state machine' triggered by 'events' is not realistic and prevents practical application. It may be clear that indispensable data flow occurs throughout the execution of an interaction technique. For instance, a user may be required to first select an object before moving that object around. Obviously, certain data, such as the selected object, must be transferred between the different tasks of the interaction technique. Therefore, a notation to describe interaction techniques should support data flow.

Encapsulation for Hierarchical Reuse

Because facilitating the development process of virtual environments and improving the efficiency of the development are overall goals in this research, we must consider that some subtasks of interaction techniques recur rather frequently. Selecting objects is an example of a very common component. When modelling a new interaction technique, the designer should be able to reuse descriptions that were created earlier. That way, recurring components do not have to be modelled repeatedly. In other words, the notation should support encapsulation of

entire diagrams. This allows existing diagrams to be reused as a subtask of a new description. Development efficiency increases significantly through the possible reuse of such basic building blocks for interaction tasks.

NiMMiT Primitives

Trying to find a notation, that meets the aforementioned requirements, we encountered notations in several categories. The following notations with rather general purposes can roughly be divided in two families: state driven and data driven methods. State driven notations, such as State Charts [Harel, 1987] and Petri-nets [Petri, 1962] are based on the formal mechanisms of finite state machines. Data driven notations, such as Labview [National Instruments, 2006] (a graphical programming language) or UML [Ambler, 2004] focus specifically on the data-or object flow.

In the domain of user interaction, we find some notations, mostly based upon the aforementioned general solution, but optimised for a specific pur pose. For instance, Interaction Object Graphs [Carr, 1997] and ICO [Navarre et al., 2005, Palanque and Bastide, 1994], are mainly state driven

Figure 2. An example of a NiMMiT diagram

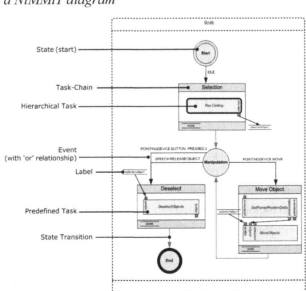

notations, while InTml [Figueroa et al., 2002] and ICon [Dragicevic and Fekete, 2004, Huot et al., 2004], are two very similar notations, using a data flow architecture.

A detailed comparison of the existing solutions is beyond the scope of this chapter. We refer the interested reader to [De Boeck et al., 2007b] and [De Boeck et al., 2007a]. However, none of the aforementioned notations entirely fulfills the above listed requirements, while being easy to learn and ultimately supporting automatic execution of the diagram. Therefore, we introduce NiMMiT, a graphical Notation for MultiModal Interaction Techniques, inheriting the formalism of a state-chart. Figure 2 shows an example of a simple NiMMiT diagram, describing an interaction task that allows the user to select an object using 'Ray Casting' [Liang and Green, 1994] after which the object can be moved around. Referring to the figure showing the NiMMiT notation for this example, we explain the basic building blocks of NiMMiT and provide some additional comments related to the diagram.

States and events. Since the NiMMiT notation is state driven and event driven, a diagram can basically be considered a state chart. An interaction technique is always initiated in the starting state (double-bordered circle), and terminates in the end state (bold circle). A state responds to a limited set of events, such as speech recognition, a pointer movement, a button click, etc. The recognition of an event causes a list of tasks (task chain) to be executed.

To support multimodality, events can be related to each other with 'and' or 'or' relations. Figure 2 shows an 'or'-relation between a button-press event and a speech event, which both can be used to release the selected object. As events coming from the user will never occur at exactly the same time, Nigay's Melting Pot principle is used to resolve the synchronisation problem [Nigay and Coutaz, 1995].

Task chain and tasks. A task chain is a strictly linear succession of tasks. The rectangles labelled

'Selection', 'Move Object' and 'Deselect' represent the task chains in our example, the smaller yellow rectangles inside the task chain represent the individual tasks. The next task in the chain is executed if and only if the previous task has successfully been completed without an error. When a task chain is interrupted, either 'rolling back to the previous state' or performing an 'error state transition' will take place, depending on the concrete situation and tasks in the task chain.

The set of possible tasks obviously depends on the application domain; in each particular case, the most common tasks should be predefined and directly accessible by the designer. Clearly, it is impossible to predefine every conceivable task. Therefore, the designer can add custom tasks, which can be implemented by means of a scripting language (LUA) or a programming language (C++).

Data flow, data types and labels. In a task chain, data is passed from one task to another. Therefore, each task provides input and output ports. The port's colour (as well as a small letter inside) indicates its data type; obviously only ports of the same type can be linked to each other.

An output port of a preceding task is typically connected to an input port of a next task. These input ports are either required or optional, indicated by the shape of the input port (a square means 'Required', a circle means 'Optional'). To share data between tasks in different task chains, or to store data for later reuse, we provide high-level variables in the form of labels. The content of a label is maintained as long as the NiMMiT diagram is operational, and its scope is the entire diagram.

State transition and conditional state transition. After a task chain has successfully been executed, a state transition takes place. The interaction technique moves either to a new state or back to the current state (in a loop). In a new state, the interaction technique may respond to another set of events. A task chain can have a conditional state transition associated with it; the value of the chain's label indicates which transition is to be executed (not shown in Figure 2).

Encapsulation for hierarchical use. An interaction technique can hierarchically be reused as a task in a task chain since the interfaces of atomic tasks in a task chain and of interaction techniques as a whole are similar. When such a task is activated, the execution of the current interaction technique is temporarily suspended waiting for the inner interaction technique to finish.

Referring to Figure 2, we recognise most NiMMiT primitives. The diagram starts in the 'start'-state, waiting for an 'idle'-event, which by definition occurs as soon as no other events are fired. We can hence assume that after starting the NiMMiT diagram, the first task chain (Selection) is executed immediately. This task chain contains a hierarchical task that suspends the current diagram in order to perform a ray casting selection technique, described in another NiMMiT diagram. After the selection has been completed successfully, the result (obviously the selected object) is stored in the label 'SelectedObject'. Thereafter we move on to the 'Manipulation' state, where three events are available. When the pointer device moves, the 'Move Object' task chain is executed, getting the current position of the pointer and moving the selected object. When either a button is pressed, or the speech command to release the object is recognised, the 'Deselect' task chain is executed, deselecting the selected object. After this has successfully been done, the 'end'-state is activated, closing the current interaction technique.

Primitives for User Evaluation

In the previous paragraphs, we have explained the basic building blocks of NiMMiT and we have shown how these can be used to describe interaction techniques. NiMMiT allows a designer to quickly create an interaction technique at a higher level, but without being too restrictive, as developers still can extend the set of predefined tasks according to their own needs. As a consequence of the simplified way of creating an interaction technique, this approach stimulates a designer to quickly try different alternative interaction techniques. Comparing the proposed alternatives usually implies a lot of ad-hoc programming to collect data for the evaluation process. The NiMMiT 'Interaction description model' however, contains some primitives in order to support automatic data collection in a usability test.

Clearly, adding automation to usability evaluation will have many potential benefits, such as time efficiency and cost reduction [Ivory and Hearst, 2001]. In this paragraph, we will shortly explain how the collection of user data can be achieved using three primitives: probes, filters and listeners. The description of an example user experiment conducted using NiMMiT can be found in [Coninx et al., 2006a].

Probes

A probe can be seen as a measurement tool that is connected at a certain place in a NiMMiT diagram, like an electrician placing a voltmeter on an electric circuit. Probes can be placed at different places in the diagram: attached to a state, a task chain, a task or at an input/output port of a task. An example is given in Figure 3(a), in which a probe is connected to the 'Start'-state. The probe returns relevant data about the place where it is connected to, in a structured way:

- State probes contain all events that occur while the state is active.
- Task Chain probes contain the activation event(s) of the task chain, its status (executed, interrupted or failed), and the value of the label indicating the correct state transition.
- Task probes indicate whether or not the execution of the task succeeded.
- Port probes contain the value of the port to which they are connected.

Each event-loop, the data of all probes of the diagram is evaluated and returned. If a probe is connected to a place which was not active in the current phase of the interaction, it returns empty. In this way, NiMMiT's probes are a useful tool to debug an interaction technique. For instance, by placing a probe on all states of a diagram, one can verify the correct order of the states or check for the events that are recognised. By placing a probe on an output port of a task, the output of that task can be verified. This can lead to a significant reduction of the time necessary to find logical errors in a diagram, so that the probe is not only useful in the context of usability evaluation.

Filters

In order to collect data for a formal evaluation of an interaction technique, the output of a probe is not always directly suitable. Therefore, NiMMiT defines the concept of filters. A filter can be seen as a meta-probe: a probe which listens to the values of one or more probes. As filters are probes themselves, filters can be connected to other filters as well. A filter can rearrange or summarise the data from the probes it is connected to, but it can also just wait until legal data arrives for the first time, and then start, stop or pause an internal timer. The latter approach is a good example of how probe data can be used for measuring the time spent between two states of an interaction.

Although the output necessary for a user experiment can be versatile, very often the same patterns return, such as summarising a distance, counting the elapsed time or logging success or not. For these patterns, NiMMiT contains a standard set of commonly used filters such as, but not restricted to, (conditional) counting, distance measuring and time measuring. Of course, experienced users can still develop custom filters according to their special needs. As filters can be connected to several probes, even across diagrams, they are depicted in a separate diagram as shown in Figure 3(b). This figure shows a TimingFilter that starts counting when the first probe returns valid input, and stops counting as soon as the second probe returns its first valid input.

Listeners

Filters and probes do not provide any output; they only collect and structure data. By connecting a listener to a probe or a filter, the output can be redirected to the desired output medium. By default, there are listeners that can write data directly to a file, to a text window, or even send it onto the network to an external computer which can be dedicated to handle, store or visualise the collected data. Experienced developers can write their own listeners, if necessary. Figure 3(b) shows a file-listener that writes the data coming from the TimingFilter to a file.

Figure 3. NiMMiT Primitives For User Evaluation

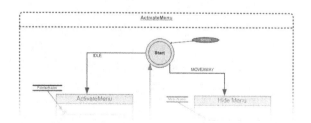

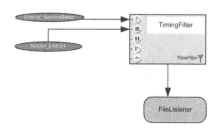

(a) A Probe connected to a State

(b) Two Probes connected to a Timing filter and a File Listener

Advanced Features

Support for Multimodal Interaction

NiMMiT is designed to support multimodal interaction. Based on the idea that a multimodal interaction is caused by several unimodal events [Bernsen, 1994], the notation supports different kinds of multimodality as identified by several taxonomies: sequentially multimodal and simultaneously multimodal inter action [Sturm et al., 2002], but also the CARE properties [Coutaz et al., 1995]. Remark that considering the CARE properties, two complementary unimodal events can either be sequential or simultaneous. In the following list, we explain how both taxonomies are fully supported by NiMMiT.

- Sequential multimodality (or some cases of assignments and complementarities) can be implemented by defining subsequent states that respond to events coming from different sources as shown in Figure 4(a).

For instance, an object can be moved via a gesture in one state; in the subsequent state, it is then deselected by speech.

  o Simultaneous multimodality (or some other cases of complementary modalities), as well as redundancy is supported by using the AND-operator between the affecting

  o **Events:** The object is moved by a movement of the virtual pointer, together with a speech command. In this case both events are depicted on the same event-arrow. An example in NiMMiT is given in Figure 4(b).

- Strictly spoken, according to the taxonomy of Sturm et al. [Sturm et al., 2002], Equivalent modalities are no example of multimodal interaction, since only one of both equivalent modalities is present at a given time. In NiMMiT, this pattern is carried out using the OR-operator. Figure 4(c) shows an example of two equivalent modalities.

Figure 4. Examples of multimodal support of NiMMiT

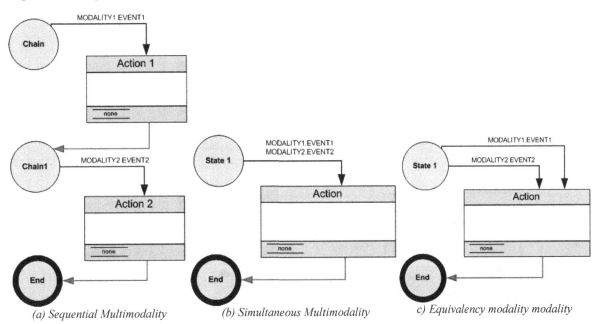

(a) Sequential Multimodality   *(b) Simultaneous Multimodality*   *c) Equivalency modality modality*

Other situations in which different modalities control different parts of the interaction simultaneously, are supported by running two or more NiMMiT diagrams in parallel. For instance, one part of an interaction technique, such as grabbing and holding an object can be controlled by the movements of the user's non-dominant hand in one diagram, while a second diagram controls the editing of the object by the dominant hand. Synchronisation between the active diagrams is achieved by their input and output ports.

Automatic Execution of a Diagram

One of the key requirements of the process we describe in this chapter is that the application, resulting from the definition of and iteration over the different models, can be executed directly. This implies that a NiMMiT diagram, defining the interaction description model, also must be executable. We have chosen to achieve this goal by means of a NiMMiT interpreter.

The execution process is depicted in Figure 5. A NiMMiT diagram, created using a NiMMiT edi-

tor, is saved in an XML-based syntax, describing all the primitives such as events, states and tasks, and their mutual dependencies. The NiMMiT interpreter then loads one or more diagrams and follows the flow of these diagrams. The runtime, supporting the framework and generated model serializations, is required to capture the user input and deliver them to the interpreter as an event. Triggered by these events, the interpreter selects the appropriate task to execute.

CONTEXTUAL AND SEMANTIC INFORMATION

Designing an application from a high-level point of view, allows the designer to think in terms of high-level entities and relations. Therefore, a MBUID process may benefit from features such as the applications context of use or semantic knowledge about the environment. In the remainder of this section we will illustrate how exploiting contextual or semantic information may facilitate the design of the user interface.

Figure 5. The NiMMiT Interpreter

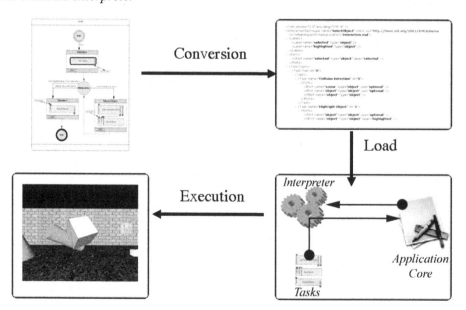

Exploiting Contextual Information

In the scope of this chapter we define contextual information as the information related to the application's context of use. In general, this may refer to the location where the application is used, but also to the devices or modalities that are available in certain circumstances. In the domain of form-based interfaces, the use of contextual data at the level of the task-model or the dialog-model has been described by several authors. Clerckx et al. [Clerckx et al., 2004] for instance realize this by extending the task model with a 'decision' task. The 'decision' task denotes a junction in the task model where each subtree of the 'decision' task describes the subtasks according to the status of the current context. In short, exactly one subtree of the decision task can be active at runtime. In [Clerckx et al., 2007], a way to link constraints to the leaf tasks in the task model is introduced, to specify which modalities are the most desirable in order to perform the corresponding task. This approach provides a runtime selection of a suitable modality with respect to the available interaction techniques surrounding the user at a certain moment in time.

There are reasons to believe that the use of contextual information can be an aid for the designer of a virtual environment, as well. Indeed, a VE application can be used in a variety of setups, all supporting different modalities dependent on the context, for instance the same application can be used in a desktop setup, or in an immersive setup using a head mounted display. However, there are also situations where a context may be switched dynamically at runtime: for instance when a user is in a setup where a different set of devices can be chosen at runtime offering more suitable properties for a given task, or in a collaborative environment, where the context changes when a new user joins the environment.

Imagine a user interacting in a 3D environment and standing in front of a large (stereo-enabled) projection screen. Interaction with the world can be done either using a 3D mouse and a Phantom haptic device, but an alternative is present using two pinch-gloves. The first alternative offers the user the experience of having force feedback, but in a very limited workspace. The second solution offers an intuitive two-handed interaction paradigm with a much larger workspace, but without any force feedback. Obviously, the first alternative will be used when the user is seated at a table, while the second solution is more convenient while standing. Changing from either seated to standing or vice versa, can be considered as a context switch, enabling and disabling the appropriate devices.

Strictly spoken, without dedicated primitives in the interaction description model, adding 'context awareness' to this level should result in a different interaction diagram per context (or even per combination of contexts, as different contexts may be orthogonal to each other). This obviously may result in an explosion of the number of similarly-looking interaction description diagrams.

Consider the example in Figure 6(a), where in the 'Start' state two different events (e.g. by two different modalities) could trigger the execution of 'Taskchain1'. In the context-supported approach, we would like to be able to associate a different context with both events. This means that 'event1' should only be available in context X, while 'event2' is only available in context Y. Adding this contextual knowledge to events transforms the view of the diagram depending on which context of the diagram we are viewing. If we are watching a certain context, the arrows belonging to that context will become visible, but when viewing no particular context, context arrows are used to indicate that context dependent events are present as can be seen in Figure 6(b). Additional details and a more elaborate example on this approach, where the I/O device depends on the context, can be found in [Vanacken et al., 2007a].

Exploiting Semantic Information

In this section we propose two ways of exploiting semantic information in the context of interaction with the virtual environment. First, we will elaborate on the use of semantic information for automatically generating a speech grammar to interact with the virtual environment. Then, we will present the use of semantic information from within the interaction diagram. Very often, the meaning of what an object actually is defines how the object is interacted with. Keeping this in mind, it might be useful for a designer to explicitly use this semantic information while designing the interaction with the environment. Indeed, applying the knowledge of 'what' an object is, or the family it belongs to, may avoid the writing of a lot of ad-hoc code. In this section we explain how such semantic data can be applied directly from within the interaction diagram, allowing the user only to do a certain operation on a given family of objects.

A first example of using semantic information during conceptual modelling is to automatically generate a speech grammar. In current approaches, when a speech input modality is desired, the developer has to define the speech grammar in advance, taking into account all synonyms and alternative wordings. When changing the application or the definition of the world, the grammar has to be adapted accordingly. The other way around occurs very often, namely a change in the grammar has its consequences to the programming code, as well. When semantic information of the environment is available, the scene, the interaction and the speech grammar can be coupled.

The generation process of the grammar consists of several steps, shown in Figure 7.

In a first step, the virtual scene is conceptually modelled [Bille et al., 2004]. During this phase, semantic data must be generated in addition to the regular scene data (usually stored in X3D). The semantic data can be represented as an ontology e.g. in OWL format [OWL Web Ontology

Figure 6. The use of context primitives in NiMMiT

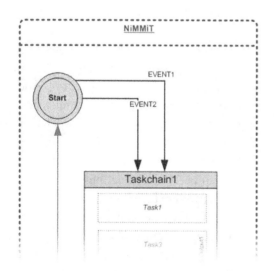 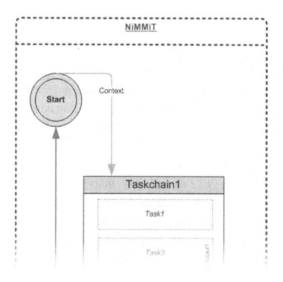

(a) Example of two events mutually excluded by the current context arrow

(b) Events can be combined in a context arrow

Figure 7. Automatic Speech Grammar Generation

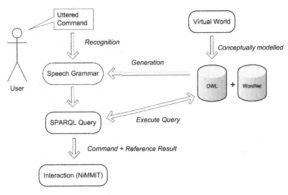

Figure 8. A Simple Ontology

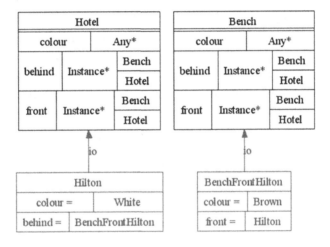

Language, 2008], in Figure 8 a simple excerpt is illustrated.

The semantic data is used to automatically generate a speech grammar. The structure of the grammar is based on an <action><object> structure [Sharma et al., 2000], a complete overview of the structure can be found in [Vanacken et al., 2007b].

Finally, this speech grammar is further annotated with synonyms using a lexical database for English: WordNet [WordNet, 2008].

At runtime, when an utterance is captured, the following flow is followed in order to generate the final 'speech command' that is used in the NiMMiT diagram.

- First, when spoken, the utterance is translated to a query. Using OWL ontologies, this can be expressed using SPARQL [SPARQL Query Language for RDF, 2008]).

- The query is then resolved by the semantic data represented by the ontology.

- Next, the resulting information consists of the names of those virtual objects that satisfy the query. These can consequently be passed on as input, represented by a speech event, for an interaction in the virtual environment such as selecting an object. This speech event can be used in the NiMMiT interaction model.

We have concluded from a case study that users mainly used words contained by the speech grammar during interaction with the application. For a more detailed description of this process of the automatic generation of a speech grammar, the interested reader can refer to [Vanacken et al., 2007b].

Adding Semantic information To NiMMiT

A problem, that frequently arises when designing an interaction diagram, is the fact that part of the interaction depends on the generated virtual world, say the scene. For instance, the designer wants the user to manipulate only certain objects in the world, while features such as the floor or the wall must remain fixed. Typically, using a graphical notation such as NiMMiT, this would result in a lot of ad-hoc code (in the form of custom tasks) that have to check whether or not the current object is of a certain type. Obviously, the use of custom code is not recommended in a high level design process. Moreover it may be clear that this custom code is less reusable among different applications, or even in a worst case scenario has to be written specifically for a given scene.

The use of semantic information, in the form of an OWL ontology can be applied, so that only items of a certain concept may participate to a particular interaction technique. In order to be able to represent semantic information we introduce the NiMMiT datatype: 'Concept'. A concept is directly mapped to a concept of the ontology (class).

The application of the knowledge of a concept is practically implemented using some specific predefined tasks in NiMMiT. Note however, that it is still possible to define a custom task to use the semantic information in another way.

Usually semantic information will be used at runtime in order to check if a certain object has a special feature for the given interaction (e.g. haptic snapping of chairs under a table). In this context, the following tasks are indispensable: 'GetObjects' and 'IsOfConcept', (Figure 9). The 'GetObjects' task outputs objects of certain concepts in the 'objects' output port. It has a required input port 'concepts' which represents all concepts which are valid and an optional input port 'objects'. When this port contains no input data the task will search for all objects of the given concept(s), otherwise it will select the right objects from the input objects for the given concept(s). In order to check if an object belongs to the concept(s), the semantic world is queried for the concepts of the objects. Similar as in Figure 7, a SPARQL query is sent to the OWL file which represents the virtual world and its concepts. 'IsOfConcept' has a similar purpose; this task checks if objects are of certain concepts and returns the result in the Boolean output port: 'bool'.

In the context of using ontologies within the interaction description model, we would also

Figure 9. Predefined tasks for applying concepts

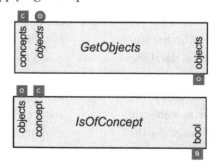

like to remark that the tree-structure of an ontology offers a very high flexibility. Imagine an ontology hierarchy as follows: Thing-Residence-Hotel-Hotel Chain. It is now possible to apply an interaction technique to e.g. all residences by selecting the parent concept 'Residence'. Similarly, it is also possible to define only a certain type of residence, for example 'Hotel'. The granularity of the possible selections depends on the definition of the ontology.

This approach for integrating semantic information has been tested in two case studies. In a first case study we incorporated the usage of semantic information in a selection technique, this allowed to only select objects from a certain semantic type, the interactive objects. Thus, if a designer wanted that the user was only able to select interactive objects (e.g. furniture) he could indicate this in the input port of the selection technique. A second case study was a driving simulator in which a force feedback steering wheel was integrated. We needed to know which surface we were driving on such that realistic force feedback could be given through the steering wheel.

In both case studies we have shown that we prevent hard-coded semantic information into the interaction through the usage of the new concept datatype. In the first case study we provided solutions which use the newly introduced predefined tasks, while in the second case study it seemed better to add the semantic information to the custom tasks which were present. A discussion on when to opt for predefined or custom tasks and some problems with regard to both options are presented more thoroughly in [Vanacken et al., 2007c]

TOOL SUPPORT

As any other development methodology, model-based development of a virtual environment will be most useful and productive if it is well supported by development tools. More concretely,

there is a need for several kinds of tools, amongst which graphical diagram editors, that also ensure that all generated diagrams are syntactically and semantically correct. Furthermore, there is a need for tools to annotate the diagrams, for tools converting one model into another model and for generating the (XML-based) meta-files that are the result of the design process.

It obviously falls out of the scope of this chapter to give a detailed description of a range of tools that match the variety of MBUID processes, or to elaborate in detail on the tool set that suits the VR-DeMo process presented above. Instead we briefly illustrate how the aforementioned process is supported by CoGenIVE (Code Generation for Interactive Virtual Environments). We emphasize how the tool is used throughout the process for the different models (task model, dialog model, presentation model and interaction model). The part of the VR-DeMo process that is supported by CoGenIVE is marked in Figure 10.

Task Model and Dialog Model

It has been highlighted that a task-model may be the start of the development process. Because the task model is optional and because several good tools for creating ConcurTaskTrees (CTT) exist (see e.g.[Mori et al., 2002]), CoGenIVE does not contain an editor for creating CTTs, see also Figure 10. Instead a task tree may be imported, in which case it is directly converted into a dialog model.

The dialog model may be a result of a CTT conversion, or the designer may have chosen to design the dialog model from scratch, by dragging the states onto the canvas (top window pane of Figure 11).

Interactive virtual environments strongly rely on the user's input. As a consequence we have to define how the user can interact with the system. In Figure 11, the window pane in the lower left reflects the events that are available. The list is populated as a result of the selected devices as well as the UI elements that are defined in the

Figure 10. Schematic Overview of the MBUID Process

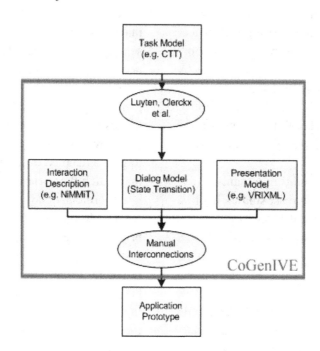

presentation model. The events may be connected with the tasks (in the right bottom pane) for a given state of the application (selected from the top window pane). Selectable tasks are either predefined tasks or NiMMiT models describing previously defined custom interaction techniques. Examples of predefined tasks are common tasks for the application domain such as selecting or deleting an object. In the bottom pane in Figure 11, the manual interconnections depicted in Figure 1 are defined.

Presentation Model

The presentation model describes menus and dialog boxes and so on. For these common widgets, it is easy for the user to be able to design these user interface elements in a familiar way. To design these widgets, CoGenIVE supports 'drag and drop' while filling out the requested properties. Typically, each UI element and each item must have a name, defining the final event that will be

fired when activated. The presentation model in CoGenIVE is represented using an abstract visualization, because the appearance of menus and dialog boxes may be slightly different dependent on the rendering engine and/or the platform.

Interaction Description

As described before, a NiMMiT diagram is basically a state chart, with each state representing the set of events to which the interaction responds at a given point in time. The editor, which is basically a Microsoft Visio control, allows the basic building blocks to be dragged onto the canvas. The tasks, forming a task-chain, are picked from a list in the bottom right window pane. For each element, the properties can be altered: for instance the name of a state, or the event associated with a call of a task chain. At its turn each NiMMiT diagram is considered a new task, and hence appears in the bottom right pane for hierarchical (or even recursive) reuse.

Figure 11. Designing the Dialog Model

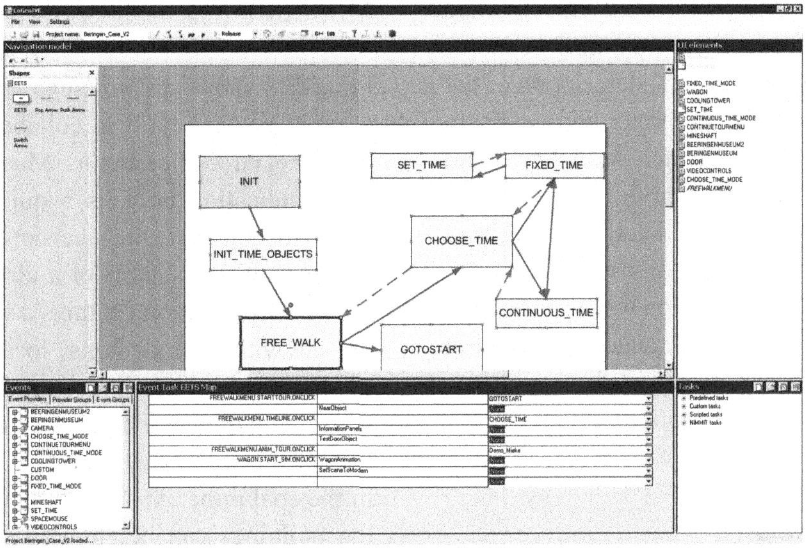

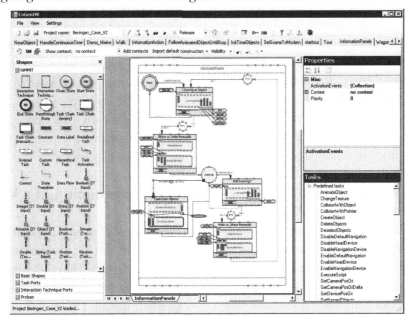

Figure 12. Designing the Interaction Model using the NiMMiT notation

The NiMMiT] editor ensures that the created diagrams are semantically and syntactically correct. For instance, it ensures that each state transition arrow ends in a new state, and that labels of a correct type are connected to the input ports of a task. This results in semantically correct meta-files that can be executed directly by the NiMMiT interpreter.

Application Prototype

An application prototype can be generated when all models (dialog model, presentation model and interaction model) are created and mutual interconnected. This prototype contains some automatically generated programming code, together with the (XML-based) description of the models, the NiMMiT interpreter and the main application framework (which in theory could be any arbitrary VR framework). The application prototype is compiled immediately resulting in an executable prototype. When desired, the code can be tweaked before compilation when specialized features need to be added. Changed code (within the designated areas) is preserved when a new iteration of the process is done.

CASE STUDIES

Given the fact that the VR-DeMo process is supported by the CoGenIVE tool, we have been able to realize several case studies in order to validate our process and the supporting tool. In this section, we briefly describe some applications that have been created by the model-based approach described in this chapter. This must give the reader an impression of the variety of virtual environments that can be created. Rather complex applications require the integration of third party software or require a lot of application-specific code. Other interactive prototypes can be realized completely or to a large extent with the CoGenIVE tool once the 3D scene is designed. During the realization of the case studies, the involved team members logged their effort. Providing a detailed overview of the findings is beyond the scope of this paper. Overall, the experiences with the model-based VR-DeMo process and the supporting CoGenIVE tool have been positive. Briefly formulated, one can say that the higher the degree of interactivity of the developed prototype, the higher the perceived (and registered) gain in development time. The basis for comparison is the developers' experience with other development processes and tools, and relative comparison of the registered development times for the three cases explained below.

Cultural Heritage: Virtual Coal Mine Museum

Figure 13 shows an birds-eye view of a Virtual Coal Mine Site, built in collaboration with the 'Provinciaal Galloromeins Museum (PGRM)'. The application built, is a quick prototype in order to convince the decision makers of the museum of the benefits of a virtual tour on the site. The application contains a virtual tour onto the site with several 'stops', locations where the user can 'ask' some questions about the current features on the site. The demo also contains some video billboards, playing a movie about the life in the coal mine. At some places, the interior of the buildings can be shown using QuickTime VR movies. Finally, using a dialog, the user can control 'the current time', giving an impression of the evolution of the site throughout the ages. The virtual mine museum is a case study that demonstrates the value of the VR-DeMo process and CoGenIVE tool for fast prototyping of interactive virtual environments. Apart from some special features, the complete virtual environment has been automatically generated. It is a fully functional, navigatable environment that the user can interactively explore.

Tele-Conferencing in a Virtual Room

This case study has been built in collaboration with ANDROME, a company that is developing a video conferencing API. The model-based approach applied during the creation of this application was extremely useful. This prototype application was intended to experiment with possible interaction metaphors in a 3D virtual environment hosting a video conferencing (Figure 14(a)). Several interaction metaphors and several setups were developed and evaluated. The final application contains three modes: a general discussion mode, in which all participants are visible sitting on a table; a presenter mode in which the presenter is visible together with a slide-show, and finally a

Figure 13. Virtual Coal Mine

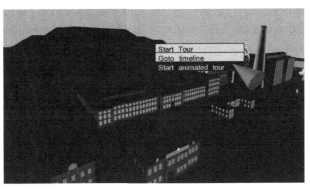

Figure 14. Tele-Conferencing System and Car Simulation

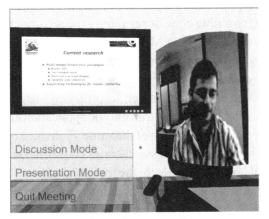

(a) Teleconferencing System

(b) Car Simulation

presentation mode where all participants are visible but the presenter is standing behind a desk. There are interaction metaphors to assign users to chairs, to switch chairs and to switch speakers. One of the challenges in this case study was the integration of the 3rd party video conferencing API (Intellivic). This case demonstrates the use of the VR-DeMo process for the realization of an environment that combines a significant interactive part and a coupling to a pre-existing back-end application. The model-based approach and the CoGenIVE tool have stimulated exploring several interaction metaphors and discussing these with the company representative. The structured approach of NiMMiT is beneficial to link to the conferencing API.

Driving Simulator

The last case study is built in cooperation with LMS, a company that creates applications for the physical simulation of all kinds of vibrations. One of their applications is a 'virtual car sound' (VCS) modeler, simulating the acoustics of the interior of a car, complete with engine, road and wind noise. The aim of this project is to build a driving simulator that communicates with the VCS module, offering an interactive (and multimodal) interface to the engineer who is evaluating the car's sound (Figure 14(b)). It is obvious that the network communication and the physical car model are separate modules that are to be integrated into the application by means of customly created code. Comparable to the previous case study, this driving simulator demonstrates the use of the VR-DeMo process for the realization of an environment that combines an interactive part and a coupling to pre-existing back-end code. However, in this case, the interaction is less dominant than in the previous case, which resulted in somewhat less gain in efficiency of the development. Still, the structured approach of NiMMiT is beneficial to link to the VCS module, and CoGenIVE allowed to efficiently build a visual, interactive 3D front-end to the simulation software. In this case study, we have applied the semantic information from the world in order to provide adequate force feedback when the driver is driving on different surfaces (on-road, off-road, grass, asphalt,...)

DISCUSSION AND FUTURE DIRECTIONS

In this chapter, we proposed Model-Based User Interface design as a solution in order to facilitate the design process of interactive virtual environments. As MBUID allows designing applications in a more high-level manner, less effort has to be spent writing programming code. However, especially in the domain of virtual environments, it is currently unclear up to what level a MBUID process is usable by designers that have little to no programming experience. It may turn out that some parts in the process could be carried out by designers while other parts still have to be performed by developers. For example, designers could create a task model and the presentation model (menus and dialogs). They could also make a first draft of the interaction model without specific tasks and/or detailed data flow. While the task model is automatically converted into a dialog model, the custom parts of the interaction model and the finishing of the dataflow up to the lowest level can then be implemented by a developer. The designer then can define the interconnection

between the different models, finishing the process to the generation of the prototype application.

It may be clear that keeping the example in mind, there is still an intense cooperation needed between the designer and a programming specialist, although that the contribution of the latter is significantly less than using the classical approach. A possible solution to establish this contribution may be the adoption of an 'Extreme Programming' approach in which a designer and developer work closely together in a cooperation where the designer creates the models and the developer checking the feasibility of the designs, as well as adding the necessary low level details for which programming code or scripting is necessary. An advantage is that a MBUID process lends itself very well for rapidly creating prototypes. However, the creation of a complete application requires more effort. In this chapter, we proposed MBUID as a solution to create a prototype application and convince stakeholders of the value. From here on, as the MBUID process generates code, this code could be used a basis for the final application. On the other hand, it is hard to judge how useful this code base is, and how easy it can be extended to finish the application. In the example described in this chapter, another problem is the fact that all NiMMiT code is stored in an XML based format and interpreted at runtime. Hence, it can only be adapted using the provided tool support, which means that the MBUID process has to be kept operational up until the final application, while it is still unknown that this is desired.

After all, Model-Based User Interface Design is currently finding its way from academic research to commercial applications. This evolution is mainly driven by the need to easily create multi-device interfaces that work on the contemporary variety of mobile and desktop devices. In the domain of Virtual Environments however, the model-based approach is relatively new. Hence, as can be understood from this paragraph, several open issues still have to be overcome. It may be expected that in the next upcoming years, more fundamental research is needed before bringing these processes in practice. From our own experience in our research lab, however, we found that the model-based approach turns out to be very promising for the generation of an interactive virtual environment, giving the opportunity to easily create prototypes in a very iterative way with close interaction between the designer on one side and the customer or the user on the other side.

CONCLUSION

Current approaches for developing interaction for virtual environments have not been very efficient, as a lot of functionality have to be implemented using low-level programming code. On the other hand, Model-Based User Interface Design has shown much potential for designing interactive applications [Stolze et al., 2007, Heinrich et al., 2007]. This approach offers several benefits, as it lifts the design of a user interface to a much higher level of abstraction. Unfortunately, current MBUID processes are mostly limited to 2D interfaces applied in form-based applications, mobile devices or multi-device interfaces, which makes that they are not directly applicable to interactive VEs.

We illustrated how MBUID can be brought to the domain of interactive VEs, by adding an interaction description model, the model that describes the multimodal interaction with the user in a high level. As an example we discussed the VR-DeMo process in detail. NiMMiT is a graphical notation that can be used to describe the user interaction, both at a high level (for easy reasoning by the designer) as well as at a lower level (for the automatic execution).

A common drawback of high-level approaches is that while lifting up the process to a higher level, it reduces the number of features and limits the flexibility of a low-level approach. As NiMMiT task chains may contain predefined tasks, selected from a list, the high level requirement is fulfilled as a designer does not have to worry about the low level issues of for instance collision detection. On the other hand, the reduction of features is avoided by the fact that new tasks can be created either using a scripting language, or by implementing new features in the form of new custom tasks. In the case studies, we have illustrated this approach by implementing a physical car model, by establishing a network communication protocol, and by integrating third party APIs.

REFERENCES

Ambler, S. (2004). *Object primer, the agile model-driven development with UML 2.0.* Cambridge University Press.

Arens, Y., & Hovy, E. (1990). How to describe what? Towards a theory of modality utilization. In *Proceedings of the 12th Conference of the Cognitive Science Society* (pp. 18-26).

Bernsen, N.O. (1994). Foundations of multimodal representations: A taxonomy of representational modalities. *Interacting With Computers, 6*(4).

Bierbaum, A., Just, C., Hartling, P., Meinert, K., Baker, A., & Cruz-Neira, C. (2001). Vr juggler: A virtual platform for virtual reality application development. In *Proceedings of Virtual Reality 2001 Conference*, Yokohama, Japan (pp. 89-96).

Bille, W., Pellens, B., Kleinermann, F., & De Troyer, O. (2004). Intelligent modelling of virtual worlds using domain ontologies. In *Proceedings of the Workshop of Intelligent Computing (WIC), held in conjunction with the MICAI 2004 Conference*, Mexico City, Mexico (pp. 272-279).

Calvary, G., Coutaz, J., Thevenin, D., Limbourg, Q., Bouillon, L., & Vanderdonckt, J. (2003). A unifying reference framework for multi-target user interfaces. *Interaction with Computers, 15*(3), 289-308.

Carr, D. (1997). Interaction object graphs: An executable graphical notation for specifying user interfaces. In *Formal methods for computer-human interaction* (pp. 141-156). Springer-Verlag.

Carrozzino, M., Tecchia, F., Bacinelli, S., Cappelletti, C., & Bergamasco, M. (2005). Lowering the development time of multimodal interactive application: The real-life experience of the xvr project. In *Proceedings of the International Conference on Advances in Computer Entertainment Technology*, Valencia, Spain (pp. 270-273).

Clerckx, T., Luyten, K., & Coninx, K. (2004). Dynamo-AID: A design process and a runtime architecture for dynamic model-based user interface development. In *9th IFIP Working Conference on Engineering for Human-Computer Interaction jointly with 11th International Workshop on Design, Specification, and Verification of Interactive Systems EHCI-DSVIS 2004*, Hamburg, Germany (pp. 77-95). Springer-Verlag.

Clerckx, T., Vandervelpen, C., & Coninx, K. (2007). Task-based design and runtime support for multimodal user interface distribution. In *Engineering Interactive Systems 2007; EHCI/HCSE/DSVIS*, Salamanca, Spain.

Coninx, K., Cuppens, E., De Boeck, J., & Raymaekers, C. (2006). Integrating support for usability evaluation into high level interaction descriptions with NiMMiT. In *Proceedings of 13th International Workshop on Design, Specification and Verification of Interactive Systems (DS-VIS'06)*, Dublin, Ireland (Vol. 4385).

Coninx, K., De Troyer, O., Raymaekers, C., & Kleinermann, F. (2006). VR-DeMo: A tool-supported approach facilitating flexible development of virtual environments using conceptual modelling. In *Virtual Concept 2006 (VC 06)*, Cancun, Mexico.

Coninx, K., Van Reeth, F., & Flerackers, E. (1997). A hybrid 2D/3D user interface for immersive object modeling. In *Proceedings of Computer Graphics International '97*, Hasselt and Diepenbeek, BE (pp. 47-55).

Coutaz, J., Nigay, L., Salber, D., Blandford, A., May, J., & Young, R.M. (1995). Four easy pieces for assessing the usability of multimodal interaction: The CARE properties. In *Proceedings of INTERACT95*, Lillehammer (pp. 115-120).

Cuppens, E., Raymaekers, C., & Coninx, K. (2004). VRIXML: A user interface description language for virtual environments. In *Developing user interfaces with XML: Advances on user interface description languages* (pp. 111-117). Gallipoli, Italy.

De Boeck, J., Gonzalez Calleros, J.M., Coninx, K., & Vanderdonckt, J. (2006). Open issues for the development of 3D multimodal applications from an MDE perspective. In *MDDAUI Workshop 2006*, Genova, Italy.

De Boeck, J., Raymaekers, C., & Coninx, K. (2007). Comparing NiMMiT and data-driven notations for describing multimodal interaction. In *Proceedings of TAMODIA 2006* (LNCS, pp. 217-229).

De Boeck, J., Vanacken, D., Raymaekers, C., & Coninx, K. (2007). High-level modeling of multimodal interaction techniques using nimmit. *Journal of Virtual Reality and Broadcasting, 4*(2).

Dragicevic, P., & Fekete, J.-D. (2004). Support for input adaptability in the ICON toolkit. In *Proceedings of the 6th International Conference on Multimodal Interfaces (ICMI04)*, State College, PA (pp. 212-219).

Dubois, E., Gray, P., Trevisan, D., & Vanderdonckt, J. (2004). Exploring the design and engineering of mixed reality systems. In *Proceedings of International Conference on Intelligent User Interfaces* Funchal, Madeira (pp. 374-375).

Figueroa, P., Green, M., & Hoover, H.J. (2002). InTml: A description language for VR applications. In *Proceedings of Web3D'02*, AZ (pp. 53-58).

Harel, D. (1987). Statecharts: A visual formalism for complex systems. *Science of Computer Programming, 8*, 321-274.

Heinrich, M., Winkler, M., Steidelmuller, H., Zabelt, M., Behring, A., Neumerkel, R., & Strunk, A. (2007). Mda applied: A tas-model driven tool chain for multimodal applications. *Task Models and Diagrams for User Interface Design (TAMODIA'07)* (pp. 15-27).

Huot, S., Dumas, C., Dragicevic, P., Fekete, J.-D., & Hegron, G. (2004). The magglite post-wimp toolkit: Draw it, connect it, and run it. In *Proceedings of the 17th ACM Symposium on User Interface Software and Technologies (UIST 2004)*, Santa Fe, NM (pp. 257-266).

Ivory, M.Y., & Hearst, M.A. (2001). The state of the art in automating usability evaluation of user interfaces. *ACM Computing Surveys, 33*(4), 470-516.

Liang, J., & Green, M. (1994). JDCAD: A highly interactive 3D modeling system. *Computer and Graphics, 18*(4), 499-506.

Luyten, K., Clerckx, T., Coninx, K., & Vanderdonckt, J. (2003). Derivation of a dialog model from a task model by activity chain extraction. In *Proceedings of 10th International Conference on Design, Specification, and Verification of Interactive Systems DSVIS 2003*, Madeira (LNCS 2844, pp. 203-217). Berlin: Springer–Verlag.

Mori, G., Patern`o, F., & Santoro, C. (2002). CTTE: Support for developing and analyzing task models for interactive system design. *IEEE Transactions on Software Engineering, 28*(8), 797-813.

Mori, G., Patern`o, F., & Santoro, C. (2004). Design and development of multidevice user interfaces through multiple logical descriptions. *IEEE Transactions On Software Engineering, 30*(8), 1- 14.

National Instruments. (2006, June). National instruments lab view. Retrieved from http://www.ni.com/

Navarre, D., Palanque, P., Bastide, R., Schyn, A., Winckler, M., Nedel, L., & Freitas, C. (2005). A formal description of multimodal interaction techniques for immersive virtual reality applications. In *Proceedings of Tenth IFIP TC13 International Conference on Human-Computer Interaction*, Rome, Italy.

Nigay, L., & Coutaz, J. (1995). A generic platform for addressing the multimodal challenge. In *Proceedings of ACM CHI'95 Conference on Human factors in Computing Systems*, Denver, CO.

OWL Web Ontology Language. (2008, January). OWL. Retrieved from http://www.w3.org/TR/owl-features/

Palanque, P., & Bastide, R. (1994). Petri net based design of user-driven interfaces using the interactive cooperative objects formalism. In *Interactive systems: Design, specification, and verification* (pp. 383-400). Springer-Verlag.

Paterno, F. (2000). *Model-based design and evaluation of interactive applications*. Springer-Verlag.

Petri, C.A. (1962). Fundamentals of a theory of asynchronous information flow. In *IFIP Congress* (pp. 386-390).

Raymaekers, C., & Coninx, K. (2001). Menu interactions in a desktop haptic environment. In *Proceedings of Eurohaptics 2001*, Birmingham, UK (pp. 49-53).

Raymaekers, C., Coninx, K., Boeck, J.D., Cuppens, E., & Flerackers, E. (May 12-14). High-level interaction modelling to facilitate the development of virtual environments. In *Proceedings of Virtual Reality International Conference*, Laval, France.

Sharma, R., Zeller, M., Pavlovic, V.I., Huang, T.S., Lo, Z., Chu, S., Zhao, Y., Phillips, J.C., & Schulten, K. (2000). Speech/gesture interface to a visual-computing environment. *IEEE Computer Graphics and Applications, 20*(2), 29-37.

SPARQL Query Language for RDF. (2008, January). SPARQL. Retrieved from http://www.w3.org/TR/rdf-sparqlquery/

Stolze, M., Riand, P., Wallace, M., & Heath, T. (2007). Agile development of workflow applications with interpreted task models. *Task Models and Diagrams for User Interface Design (TAMODIA'07)* (pp. 8-14).

Sturm, J., Bakx, I., Cranen, B., Terken, J., & Wang, F. (2002). The effect of prolonged use on multimodal interaction. In *Proceedings of ISCA Workshop on Multimodal Interaction in Mobile Environments*, Kloster Irsee, Germany.

Vanacken, L., Cuppens, E., Clerckx, T., & Coninx, K. (2007). Extending a dialog model with contextual knowledge. In M. Winckler, H. Johnson, & P.A. Palanque (Eds.), *TAMODIA* (LNCS 4849, pp. 28-41). Springer.

Vanacken, L., Raymaekers, C., & Coninx, K. (2007a). Automatic speech grammar generation during conceptual modelling of virtual environments. In *Intuition 2007*, Athens, Greece.

Vanacken, L., Raymaekers, C., & Coninx, K. (2007b). Introducing semantic information during conceptual modelling of interaction for virtual environments. In *WMISI '07: Proceedings of the 2007 Workshop on Multimodal Interfaces in Semantic Interaction* (pp. 17-24).

Vanderdonckt, J. (2005). A MDA compliant environment for developing user interfaces of information systems. In *Proceedings of 17ʰ Conference on Advanced Information Systems Engineering CAiSE'05*, Porto, Portugal (pp. 16-31).

Vanderdonckt, J., Limbourg, Q., Michotte, B., Bouillon, L., Trevisan, D., & Florins, M. (2004). Usixml: A user interface description language for specifying multimodal user interfaces. In *Proceedings of W3C Workshop on Multimodal Interaction WMI'2004*, Sophia Antipolis (pp. 35-42).

Virtools Inc. (2008, April). Virtools Dev. Retrieved from http://www.virtools.com

Ware, C., & Osborne, S. (1990). Exploration and virtual camera control in virtual three dimentional environments. *Computer Graphics, 24*.

WordNet. (2008, January). Retrieved from http://wordnet.princeton.edu/

KEY TERMS AND DEFINITIONS

Context-Awareness: Different contexts, may require alternative interaction techniques. In the scope of this chapter a context refers to a different physical setup of the environment: different devices, different poses of the user (such as seated or standing), etc.

Interaction Technique: An interaction technique can be seen as a complex ensemble of (multimodal) information initiated by the user, which is merged and applied in order to execute a compound task in a computer environment.

Model-Based User Interface Design: MBUID is an approach in which a user interface is described by means of high-level models instead of low-level programming code. The advantage of this approach is that it lifts the design of a user interface to a higher level of abstraction.

Multimodal Fusion and Fission: Interaction in a virtual environment is often multimodal by nature. A modality is defined as a single mechanism in order to express information [Arens and Hovy, 1990].

Semantic Information: Semantic information, in this context, refers to the meta-knowledge known in a virtual environment by the nature of objects. The information may include knowledge about the kind of objects (building, furniture,. . .) and relations between objects (lays on, next to,...)

User Evaluation: This refers to the process of (formally) evaluating a newly proposed interface. User evaluation is typically performed by measuring the performance of a real user interacting with the interface.

Virtual Environment: A computer generated environment or virtual world mostly visualised in 3 dimensions. Virtual environments provide the user with a rich and intuitive user interface often mimicking interaction paradigms from the real world.

Chapter IX
Temporal and Spatial Aspects of Pointing Gestures

Christian Müller-Tomfelde
CSIRO ICT-Centre, Australia

Fang Chen
National ICT Australia, Australia

ABSTRACT

The detailed and profound understanding of the temporal and spatial organisation of human pointing actions is key to enable developers to build applications that successfully incorporate multimodal human computer interaction. Rather than discussing an ideal detection method for manual pointing we will discuss crucial aspects of pointing actions in time and space to develop the right solution for a particular application. One core element of pointing in the temporal domain is the so called dwell-time, the time span that people remain nearly motionless during pointing at objects to express their intention. We also discuss important findings about the spatial characteristics of the target representation for the pointing gesture. The findings foster better understanding of the role of pointing gestures in combination with other modalities and inform developer with substantial knowledge about the temporal-spatial organisation of the pointing gesture.

INTRODUCTION

Some of humans' intentions can be anticipated and identified in real life situations from their actions and the context in which they are performed. An important and frequent gesture is the manual pointing action that allows humans to refer naturally and intuitively to distant objects in the environment. In a more general definition, pointing by a human at an object is understood as "how one organism manipulates the visual attention of another to some distant entity" (Leavens, 2004).

With respect to gesture research in the context of language and semiotic, the pointing gesture or deictic gesture is named as one of four types of gestures that accompany utterances (co-verbal) (McNeill, 1992). Unlike iconic and metaphoric gestures, the deictic gesture does not convey an image of an object but rather establishes a link between what is uttered and the current spatial context. Manual or free-hand pointing can be considered as a "referential act" and therefore, represents a basic means to communicate with others aside speech. This embodiment of communication makes use of implicit references, whereby movements of the body bind objects in the world to cognitive programs (Ballard et al., 1997). A single human can easily coordinate and execute actions and it requires little effort for another human to predict the actions and recognise the intention merely by watching the movements. Therefore, pointing represents a basic and ubiquitous device to communicate with others (Kita, 2003) and is often used in communicative situation to establish a common ground over the course of the conversation (Clark & Wilkes-Gibbs, 1986). Consequently, this has also implications for ways humans interact with computers. It is important to understand what "behavior" or what kind of "reaction" has to be exhibited by the computer in order to meet the expectation of the user, especially when a computer should operate like a dialogue partner or accept more intuitive input signals from humans. It is also important to understand how humans perform manual pointing to select the best method to detect the act of pointing and the referenced object in a particular use context or application. This chapter provides an overview about the temporal and spatial aspects of human pointing in order to implement accurate and effective pointing gesture recognition and to successfully develop in multimodal applications.

BACKGROUND: POINTING IN THE CONTEXT OF MULTIMODAL HCI

In the typical situation of human computer interaction the user moves a physical device such as a mouse so that a screen cursor is placed over an element of the two-dimensional graphical user interface. With respect to the prior definition of pointing, the user's referential act raises the "attention" of the computer as a dialogue partner (Maybury & Wahlster, 1998; Schomaker et al., 1995) for the object located under the screen cursor. After placing the cursor on the target, the user usually clicks on a mouse button and therefore explicitly signalling the intention to execute the function or the command that is associated with that interface element. This overall interaction is known as "point and click". Furthermore, an interaction technique referred to as hovering is used in situations in which a mouse-click is not applicable or available for the user, e.g., during "drag and drop" or in pen-based interfaces. Nevertheless, to select a function, the user must hold the pointing device motionless for a certain period of time, to trigger a hover event by temporal discrimination. This provides information about the object in the focus of the attention. The "act" of hovering replaces the explicit click and allows for the selection of the target object.

In non-WIMP (Windows Icons Menus Pointing devices) based computer systems the free-hand gesture as a mode of input is still a relatively new phenomenon in the fields of multimodal user interface and human-computer interaction (HCI) research. Despite insightful studies into their uses in command and control interfaces, e.g., (Schapira & Sharma, 2001), there is a need for improved understanding of how they can best be applied to practical interfaces. The explicit act of clicking becomes substituted in non-WIMP interfaces either by an event of another modality or by an event created by temporal and spatial segmentation. On the one hand, tool-based interfaces, e.g., using pen-based gestures are inherently robust, offering clearly defined pen-up/pen-down events and exhibiting fewer tracking artefacts, due to the physical contact of the pen with the drawing surface. On the other hand, computer vision-based manual gestures provide the advantages of free-hand interaction that is more appropriate and intuitive for some applications relying on the notion of a three-dimensional environment. Here, the free-hand pointing gesture provides an intuitive access to distant objects using a laser pointer metaphor (Bolt, 1980; Bowman & Hodges, 1997). Furthermore, in multimodal research, information of multiple modalities becomes fused to model the interaction at a higher level of abstraction (Nigay & Coutaz, 1993). Nevertheless we assume, as stated in (Schapira & Sharma, 2001) that a deictic referential act based only on the temporal and spatial segmentation hand movements ("point and wait"), i.e., without other modalities such as speech, is the user preference and highly applicable in most applications.

COMPONENTS OF THE POINTING GESTURE

In order to clarify what part of the pointing gesture is addressed, we provide a detailed description a pointing gesture. The pointing gesture is a process that consists of three major elements or sections. Firstly, a person has to position and orient his/her pointing tools towards the object at which they intend to point. Secondly, the person's hand remains motionless for a certain period of time while holding the pointing device towards the target. This period of time is called the *dwell-time period* and is important to allow others to recognise the pointing gesture. A pointing gesture can only be recognised when the clear separation between this and the prior period is possible for an observer. We assume that during the dwell period the pointing person maintains a certain constant distance to the target. This allows the spatial discrimination of the gesture which is another prerequisite for successful detection of pointing gestures (Chen et al., 2005). The observer combines the information about the object the person is pointing at with the "act" of dwelling and recognises the selection of the target object. Thirdly, the person starts to move the pointing device away from the focused target (see Figure 1).

Similar phases of the pointing gesture are proposed in the literature, e.g., the phases of the moving towards and away from the target are called strokes and frame the central hold or dwell period (Kettebekov & Sharma, 2000). In Figure 1 the second phase of the pointing gesture can be further decomposed if one considers an explicit feedback to acknowledge the detection of a gesture. In this case the dwell time (DT) is divided into the period before the feedback stimulus (S) and after. The first period is named the feedback

Figure 1. The temporal structure of a human pointing gesture with confirmation feedback. The dwell-time (DT) is the sum of the feedback delay time (FT) and the exit time (ET) after the feedback stimulus (S).

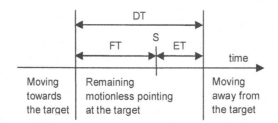

delay time (FT), it lasts until the feedback stimulus is presented. The user reacts to this stimulus to move on. The latter period of time is called exit time (ET) and is comparable to a stimulus reaction time. The elements that form the spatial aspect of a pointing action can be defined as follows: There is the boundary of the object that a person is pointing at. We assume a generic target on a two-dimensional plane with a circular shape and a particular size, the *object radius*. The *selection radius* is equal or larger than the object radius and defines the area in which a person has to dwell pointing with the finger or a tool at the object to select it (see Figure 2).

Since we are focussing on the interaction with computers with standard displays, we assume that targets are lying in a two-dimensional display plane in space and that the shapes of the targets are basic, such as circles and rectangles. However, the pointing actions are performed in the three-dimensional space. The idealistic temporal and spatial structure of a pointing gesture, as depicted in Figure 1 and 2, is a simplified model of real life situations and consequences have to be considered. For instance, the transition between the first and second temporal phase (see Figure 1) can happen multiple times when the person adjusts the orientation of the pointing tool. In that case, the tool does not remain motionless during the second phase. Another ambiguous situation can occur when the person aimlessly dwells in a resting position of the hand or when the pointing person is less close to the target object during the dwell period

than while approaching the target. Therefore, the definition of motionless and proximity is relative and depends on the perspective of the observer and the context of the action. The physical velocity of the pointing tool and its position are good candidates to derive parameters for temporal and spatial discrimination. As experiments have shown also the distance to the centre of the target might be larger during the dwell period than during the time moving toward the target (Chen et al., 2005). Therefore, using merely the spatial distance is not sufficient and only knowledge about the interplay between temporal and spatial characteristics leads to successful detection of a pointing gesture.

POINTING IN MULTIMODAL HCI APPLICATIONS

With the emergence of the notion of disappearing computer and intelligent environments, pointing interaction is now a popular choice for interaction. Most applications that are using pointing interactions address issues of novel forms of interaction in information enriched environments or with large computer displays. An early example of an interactive system that involves pointing in combination with other modalities, such as speech, is Richard Bolt's "Put-that-there" system from 1980 (Bolt, 1980). Several applications can be found in the literature in which the time the user remains motionless pointing at an object is used

Figure 2. Spatial elements or areas for the pointing gesture. The selection radius marks the areas the user has to place the distant cursor in order to select the object confined by the object radius.

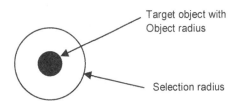

to control an application. The research problem of detecting a pointing gesture is usually tackled using the spatial as well as the temporal information of the interaction.

Techniques for vision-based gesture tracking and recognition have proliferated in recent years, e.g., (Jojic et al., 2000; Nickel & Stiefelhagen, 2003; Schapira & Sharma, 2001; Wilson & Shafer, 2003). Although fewer researchers have experimented with the usability issues surrounding their applications as an input mode. One previous study on vision-based gesture selection strategies (Schapira & Sharma, 2001) compared 'point and wait' (i.e. hold hand for a pre-determined fixed time to select current cursor position), 'point and speak' (i.e. speak to select current cursor position) and 'point and shake' (i.e. shake hand to select current cursor position) selection strategies. They found that users preferred the 'point and wait' strategy, which also gave the lowest error rate for the task tested despite requiring a slightly longer time-to-completion than other strategies. Their experiments also suggested that target position and size were two important factors in the design of vision-based gesture input, but did not give a figure for the minimum effective target size (Schapira & Sharma, 2001).

In other literature we reviewed, the time the user's hand must remain motionless to allow the system to detect an act of selection varies. The range of the dwell-time begins with 300 ms (Bohan et al., 1997; Parker et al., 2005; Schapira & Sharma, 2001), continues with 500 ms (Chen et al., 2005; Müller-Tomfelde & Paris, 2006), 1 second (Malerczyk, 2004; Parker et al., 2005; Špakov & Miniotas, 2004) and stops at values of about 2 second (Nickel & Stiefelhagen, 2003). The adjustment of the dwell-time is usually based on ad hoc experiences of the developer. Formal evaluations have been done only in applications that use eye movements to control a cursor (Hansen et al., 2003; Špakov & Miniotas, 2004). Manual pointing interactions are used, for instance, to control home entertainment components, such as

CD players, televisions, amplifiers etc. (Wilson & Shafer, 2003). In this, the core interaction technique is based on pointing with a dedicated tool or wand towards the component the user wants to control. The user points at the target and holds the device motionless for a moment or presses a button to select the target. In an experimental setup, participants received an audio feedback when the pointing device was held motionless for "a brief period (less than one second)". Aspects of wall-based laser pointer interaction are examined and reported in (Peck, 2001). In that study participants were asked to aim at a target with the laser pointing device. A feedback time of about one second was proposed to acquire the target. However, the selection of this feedback time was basically motivated by the accuracy constraint of the underlying technology and was not based on user preferences.

In other approaches for multimodal interaction in virtual environments, the accuracy of the pointing gesture detection increases by fusing hand and head orientation detection (Nickel & Stiefelhagen, 2003). The authors presented work on real time tracking for 3D pointing interaction using video cameras. They stated that the average length of the pointing gesture of 10 participants of an evaluation was 1.8 s. The motionless phase revealed the highest duration variance (from 100 ms to 2.5 s). In (Müller-Tomfelde & Paris, 2006) dwell-based interaction is used in combination with a force feedback device in the context of the training of motor skills. A dwell-time of 500 ms is used here to discriminate gestures using a hierarchical network of software motion sensors operating on the real-time stream of raw user interaction data. (Malerczyk, 2004) describes another interactive application with large displays that rely only on the manual pointing gesture of the user. The author suggests a dwell-time on the target of approximately one second to transform the "act" of dwelling into a "button-selected" event. However, the author did not give any further background information about this choice for the time period.

In a study about interaction on tabletop computer displays with objects on the far side of a table, a dwell of the input cursor was also used to indicate a selection (Parker et al., 2005). The dwell-time there was set to 300 ms but wasn't studied further, since the authors primarily addressed issues of Fitts' law. A comparison of the performance of the selection by mouse-click and by mouse-dwelling was a subject of the study presented in (Hansen et al., 2003). The authors conducted a study with 25 participants comparing object selection by mouse click and by mouse dwell. They stated that the interaction techniques based on a mouse-click was on average about 150 ms faster than the selection by dwelling. The dwell-time activation introduced more errors and was therefore less efficient. The majority of participants reported that the fixed dwell-time of 500 ms was too short. Therefore, the authors recommended a dwell-time of 750 ms for novices and proposed an adaptation of the dwell-time for individual users but a formal evaluation was not reported.

ASPECTS OF POINTING ACTIONS

Temporal Aspects of Pointing

The prevailing approach in the context of temporal aspects of human actions is the hierarchical organisation of human behaviour in time scales (Ballard et al., 1997; Newell, 1990). The scales start at the neuron activity level where it takes about 1 millisecond to generate an electrical signal to communicate with another neuron. The scale ends at the cognitive level with period of 2-3 s (Ballard et al., 1997; Pöppel, 1997). The interesting interval for the work and experiments presented in this chapter is assumed to be in the range of a couple of hundreds of milliseconds to about one second, since most of the previously described approaches can be found here. We now present results of related work which concentrates in particular on the perception of the delay between an intentional action and its effect in the environment.

In (Haggard et al., 2002) the authors report on an experiment that was addressing the issue of intentional binding between voluntary actions and their effects. The participants' task was to press a key and to receive a delayed auditory feedback. Afterwards, they were asked to judge the onset times of their actions and the perceived feedback. In general, the onset time of pressing the key was judged to happen later while the onset time of the feedback was judged to be earlier. At delay times between the key press and the auditory feedback of about 250 ms, the participant perceived the time gap between both events to be relatively shorter than for a delay time of about 650 ms. In other words, with a decreasing delay time between the key press action and the auditory feedback, the "perceptual attraction" or binding effect became increased. The authors argued that this phenomenon helps humans coherently experience their own actions and provides a sense of controlling events in the outside world.

In another recent study about the action-effect relationship (Sato & Yasuda, 2005), participants were asked to which extent they felt that an effect was a consequence of their own action or of the action of the experimenter. Different temporal delays of up to 600 ms were introduced between the action and an auditory feedback. The experiment revealed that the feeling of being the author of the effect decreased with increased temporal delay. In the context of pointing and selecting of objects, it is assumed that a short or zero delay for a feedback causes a strong feeling of being author of the selection, while a longer delay suggests that the selection might be done by someone or something else.

Based on the idea of the hierarchical organisation of human behaviour suggested by Newell (1990), Ballard *et al.* (1997) argue for a time scale that defines a special level of abstraction. The level is called "Embodiment Level" because the constraints of basic physical acts influence the nature of cognitive operations at a time period of about a third of a second. It is at this level that primitives, such as movements of the eyes or taps on a key of the keyboard happen (Card et al., 1983). These primitives are distinguished from those of the next higher cognitive level, such as typing a word or dialling a number (Ballard et al., 1997). We assume that a pointing action is more than basic movement primitive since it includes also cognitive aspects. An appropriate temporal scale of these referential primitives is expected to be greater than the Embodiment Level (300 ms), while it should be less than the temporal scale of action of a higher cognitive level (2-3 s).

In the research area of hypertext presentation and exploration, Meyer *et al.* (1999) presented a study about the relationship of system response delay and the time the user is watching a hypertext page before moving onto a new page. The experiment revealed interesting effects under the condition of different delay times between the click on a hyperlink and the appearance of the corresponding new page. The time the participants remained on the page was correlated with the time they waited for the page until a response delay of 3 s. Furthermore, the emotional workload increased above this temporal threshold. The results underpin the existence of a universal constant of segmentation for the temporal integration of successive events into perceptual units of about 2 to 3 s duration (Pöppel, 1997). Schleidt *et al.* (1987) presented a study about the temporal integration of successive events and short term movements. Videotapes of behaviour scenes of different cultures were analysed. The result of the study supported the assumption that both the human perception and the "overt behaviour is characterised by a similar time constant". This refers also to a temporal window of 2 to 3 s, in which the "short term movement episodes" with obvious segmentations happen. The question that arises from the latter two studies is whether or not

the motionless time period while pointing has a similar constant character.

In brief, the literature we studied strongly indicates a time period of about 500-1000 ms for an appropriate feedback delay time for dwell-based pointing actions. At this delay the intentional binding between action and effect still supports the users' experience of controlling the environment. The suggested time span is confined by particular time scales of human information processing and the majority of existing HCI approaches use delayed feedback below 1 s. Assuming a standard reaction time to a visual stimulus of about 300 ms (exit time, see Figure 1) a resulting natural dwell-time is expected to be about 800-1300 ms.

SPATIAL ASPECTS OF POINTING

Two-dimensional pointing is important with our normal desktop user interactions. Three-dimensional interaction with spatial pointing is very useful for applications with large screen or in the environment with various embedded devices. Pointing has been treated as an important aspect in collaborative environments. Kirstein & Müller (1998) had used laser pointers as tools for interaction in shared displays and demonstrated how to acquire laser projections for display interaction based on camera. Previous studies in experimental psychology tell us that the spatial interaction, such as pointing, is strongly influenced by the visual feedback that is provided to participants (Bridgeman et al., 1997). People believe that pointing becomes unreliable without proper visual feedback in display environments, especially when there are multiple potential targets cross multiple displays.

Formal predictive models adopted by human machine interaction research such as Fitts' Law (Fitts, 1954) have provided an understanding of the spatial factors that limit users' abilities to perform spatial interactions in a variety of situations. It is clear that the impact of visual feedback on spatial interaction is a complex research issue. Past studies have also proved that there is a strong connection between the perceptual structure of visual information in an interactive display environment and the control structures of the input methods that used in the interaction (Wang et al., 1998).

An important standard to test interfaces comes is described in the International Organization for Standardization (ISO) Standard 9241-9: Requirements for non-keyboard input devices (ISO, 1998). Six circular targets are configured in a ring formation as shown in Figure 3 and test persons are instructed to select them in a fixed sequence, as described in (Chen et al., 2005). This configuration reflects the influence of the size of a target object on the performance of the selection process. However, since multiple targets are displayed also the spacing of the target object has an influence on the selection process.

As depicted in Figure 2 the selection radius can be larger than the object radius and ambiguous configuration can occur when the spacing of objects is not sufficient enough and result in the intersection of selection radii of adjacent target. In (ISO, 1998) the ISO Standard 9241-9 is used to investigate the differences of selection strategies for vision based interfaces. Selection time and error rates were the measures to compare different strategies. Learning and fatigue effect can influence the performance over time. Furthermore, the selection radius is confining a hypothetical area

and is depending on the subjects' preferences as well as on the particular characteristics of the setup in which the pointing in performed. Here, the distance to the display area where the target objects are presented plays has an important influence on the selection performance.

THE ORGANISATION OF POINTING

In this section we describe the basic findings that constitute the pointing gesture in time and space. Rather than reporting about specific values for an ideal detection we present results that reveal fundamental relationships that are useful when developing interactive multimodal applications. It is up to an iterative approach in the particular application to find optimal values for the various parameters. This approach also guarantees that not system constraints such as latency and computational power control of the quality of the interaction. It is the average human performance that should inform the development of the interface. This user-centred approach is more likely to be successful and accepted by end users.

Dwell-Time

Two exploratory studies in an interactive environment had been conducted to gain further knowledge about temporal aspects of dwelling on targets during pointing actions (Müller-Tomfelde, 2007). Here, the basic communication process

Figure 3. Target configuration and definition of the spatial organization

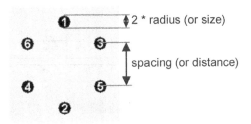

of passing on a reference from an actor to an observer is separated into two parts. Study A was about performing a pointing action, while study B focused on the observation of such an action. The studies were done independently from each other, no direct or mediated verbal communication happened between the actor and the observer, except pointing gestures. It was assumed that the average dwell-times of actors are greater than the average response times of observers or receivers. Instead of imposing a particular dwell-time on the participant by providing a feedback for a selection, the actors performed self-paced, basically driven by their inherent representation of the temporal organization of pointing actions. The idea of the studies was that the results would provide further indications to identify an appropriately time period for feedback for the interaction with computers.

Performing a Pointing Action

The study was conducted in a hand-immersive virtual environment where the participants interacted with a stylus in a 3D scene using shutter glasses providing stereo vision. The input device reliably tracked the participants' interactions. The study was conducted with 15 unpaid participants recruited from the research organisation of the authors. Ten of the participants were male and five female. The task of the participants was to answer questions about the two most common colours of objects by pointing with a tool at the correspondingly coloured objects in the environment. For example: What are the two most common colours of flowers? As a possible answer, the participant pointed at the green objects and then at the red object. Furthermore, participants answered 50 of these questions, each with a different topic and were asked to perform their tasks in a comfortable and relaxed manner. The participants were advised to perform the task so that another person would be able to understand their selections. The participants were given a verbal introduction about the environment. Written instructions about the task were handed out, and questions about the task were discussed. We observed the first few interactions then allowed the participants to finish the study alone.

Figure 4. Histogram of the detected dwell-times of all participants in study A. The histogram is skewed to the right

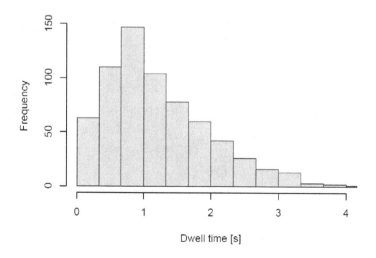

The result of study A can be illustrated in a histogram of the detected dwell-times with an interval width of 333 ms (see Figure 4).

The histogram is right-skewed, because only positive dwell-times can occur. The skewness of the distribution is 0.9602 and standard deviation is 0.7575. Data analysis revealed an average dwell-time of 1.175 s and a median value of 0.999 s. 50 % of the data lies between 0.599 and 1.598 s. Because of the asymmetric shape of the histogram the average value is greater than the median value and the latter is more appropriate for description of the dwell time. The expected numbers of dwell events were 1500, however we collected only 702. Five participants touched target objects rather than pointed at them and were omitted for the analysis. Some dwell actions were insufficiently detected.

Observing a Pointing Action

Study B was done to understand how long observers need to receive the reference of a pointing action by watching the action. A standard desktop computer with a keyboard and an LCD panel was used to collect data about the reactions of the observers. Nine unpaid participants contributed to this study, 2 female and 7 male. The participants were asked to watch on the screen an animated typical trial of one participant of study A. The action was represented only by the replay of the recorded movement of the pointing tool. The task was to press the space bar of the keyboard to confirm the 100 selections that had been made by the person moving the stylus. The participants were asked to perform their tasks in a timely but comfortable and relaxed manner. The participants were given instructions about the task and questions were discussed. We observed the first few reactions then restarted the experiment and the participants finished the study alone. The result of study B is illustrated in a histogram of the detected response times with an interval width of 100 ms (see Figure 5).

In the study 855 confirmations of the 9 participants had been recorded. The missing 45 confirmations are due to the fact that some selections had been overseen by participants probably because of drops in concentration or because of misinterpretations. This inaccuracy of 5 % will be ignored for the following considerations. All confirmations were set into relation to the start

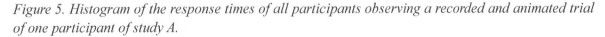

Figure 5. Histogram of the response times of all participants observing a recorded and animated trial of one participant of study A.

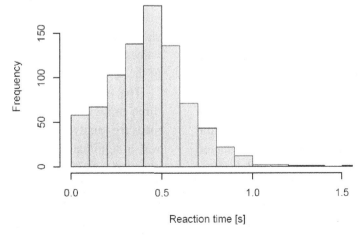

point of the dwelling activity, that is, when stylus started remaining nearly motionless while it was held towards the target object. 17 confirmations (2 %) revealed negative reaction times and were ignored also for further analysis. The histogram of all 838 confirmation time periods can be seen in Figure 5, where 50 percent of the measured reaction times occurred between 0.292 s and 0.552 s. Data analysis revealed an average reaction time of 0.4325 s and the same value as median. The standard deviation is 0.215 and the skewness of the distribution is 0.5484.

The independent studies A and B showed that the median dwell-time (0.999 s) is greater than the median response time (0.4325 s); although there was no feedback given to the pointing participants and the studies were independently conducted. The variances are relatively high compared to those other response time experiments because of the self-paced character of the studies without an explicit feedback stimulus to react to. Nevertheless, the studies indicated a possible existence of a natural dwell-time and suggest a corresponding feedback delay time of about 0.4325 s.

FEEDBACK TIME

Based on the results of the literature review and the exploratory studies hypotheses were formulated. First, feedback delay time above approximately 430 ms is experienced by users to happen late. Second hypothesis, for a feedback delay time above approximately 430 ms users experience waiting for feedback to happen and third, feedback delay below 430 ms is considered by users to be natural as in real life conversations. In order to test the hypotheses the interaction environment of study A was modified to provide a discrete visual feedback. A simple mechanism was implemented to detect dwell events and the feedback delay time was adjustable. The design of the experiment had one within-participant factor, the feedback delay time (FT, see Figure 1) and the study was

conducted with the same 15 participants of study A. The dependant variables were the ratings of a questionnaire.

The task of the participant was similar to that of study A except that they were told that their answers should be confirmed by the computer. As a feedback the colour of the selected object would change to white. The feedback delay time was set in block 1 to 100 ms and was incremented for each block by 250 ms. The last delay time of block 8 was 1850 ms. The participants were not informed about these changes but rather encouraged to act as in study A. After each of the 8 blocks the participants were asked to fill out a questionnaire with possible answers on a 7 point Likert scale. The questions were:

- **Question 1:** Do you have the impression that the system feedback happened in a reasonable time according to your action? Answer: confirmation occurred too fast (1), too late (7).
- **Question 2:** Did you have the feeling to wait for the feedback to happen? Answer: no I didn't have to wait (1), yes, I waited (7).
- **Question 3:** Did you have the impression that the time delay for the feedback was natural? (i.e., as in a real life communication situation) Answer: time delay is not natural (1), quite natural (7).

The average ratings for the three questions are shown in Figure 6. There is a trend in the average values of the ratings under the changing condition of the feedback delay time.

The effects of feedback delay time on the three ratings were tested by one-way repeated measures analysis of variance (ANOVA). There was a significant main effect in the ratings of question 1, $F(7,98) = 11.289$, $p < 0.01$, question 2, $F(7,98) = 6.1828$, $p < 0.01$ and question 3, $F(7,98) = 12.667$, $p < 0.01$. The ratings for questions 1 and 2 increase, while ratings for question 3 decrease with

Figure 6. Results of the questionnaire for the experiment. The ratings show a general trend and the largest changes can be reported between 350 and 600 ms.

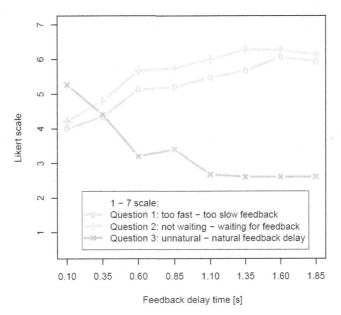

the increasing independent variable. The largest changes of the ratings happen between 350 and 600 ms of feedback delay time (see Figure 6).

We carried out further detailed analysis of the ratings. Several paired t-tests were calculated for the ratings of the questions. The tests revealed that the ratings of question 1 at a feedback delay time of 100 ms are not significantly different to those at 350 ms. In contrast, all other paired t-test between rating of question 1 at 100 ms and those equal and above 600 ms are significantly different. This step of significance between 350 and 600 ms is also valid for the ratings of question 3. The step in ratings of question 2 also exists but the p-values are not significant.

The results of the experiment can be summarized as followed. At a delay time of 100 ms the feedback is rated as neutral (4), i.e., the feedback is neither too fast nor too slow (Question 1). Question 2, waiting for feedback, is also judged neutral. There is a tendency to judge the system feedback as natural at the feedback delay time of 100 ms (Question 3). Towards the delay of 1850 ms

the feedback was rated less natural and feedback time as too slow. On average the participant also rated that they waited for the feedback. At the step in significance between 350 and 600 ms we assume that the judgments of the participants are about to change.

SELECTION GRANULARITY

Another experiment about spatial aspect of pointing was conducted (Chen et al., 2005). Here, twenty unpaid volunteers participated in the experiments, fifteen males and five females, between the ages of 19 and 50. All participants were right-handed. The setup for the experiment was physically very similar to an implementation of transport management application, except a series of simple targets were displayed (Chen et al., 2005). The system comprised a wall-sized rear projection screen and a web cam mounted on a tripod near the user's right arm, within comfortable reach of their right (pointing) hand. A gesture tracking software was run in real time giving users instantaneous position feedback. The screen resolution used throughout the experiments is 1280x1024 pixels.

Subjects were allocated to complete 2 tasks with regard to the selection granularity and the calibration radius. A short questionnaire recording basic subjects' details was completed before starting the experiments. The different tasks were used to gather various types of information on how gesture is used as a selection mechanism. The first task involved pointing and selection of the centre of a circular target. Subjects were presented with a black circular target in the centre of the screen, 20 pixels in radius. They were requested to point to the centre of the target and pause to select it. The trajectory of the gesture was recorded, and from this, two points were recorded: (i) the point in the trajectory with the minimum distance to the centre, and (ii) the distance from the centre of the target at the time of selection. This task was repeated four times, and was considered sufficiently simple to

serve as a gesture practice task for the remainder of the study. This experiment aimed to measure the granularity (minimum selection distance) of gesture selections by monitoring:

- The point in a subject's gesture trajectory that was closest to the centre of the target; and

- The distance of the actual point selected from the centre of the target.

As seen in Figure 7, where the results are averaged across all four repetitions, participants were consistently able to move more closely to the target centre than they were able to select. This is explained by both the difficulty in keeping the hand entirely stationary during the 0.5s selection time and the jitter in cursor position experienced during this interval. From this experiment, the target radius that can accommodate the actual distance at selection appears to be in the range

Figure 7. Average distances from the centre of the target: the closest point the subject came to the centre (black) and the distance at which selection actually occurred (white).

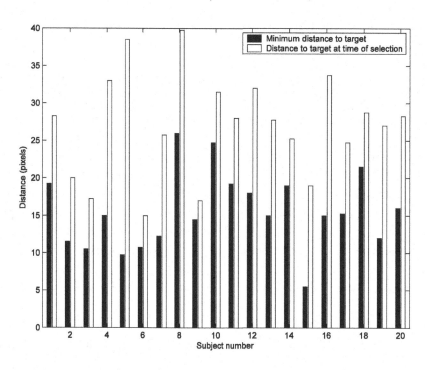

of 15 to 40 pixels, depending on the individual user. Note that selection times are not taken into consideration here, meaning that some subjects may have performed their selection more quickly than others.

CALIBRATION DISTANCE

The second task began with user calibration of a selection area, followed by the sequential selection of circular targets in different configurations on the screen. The first part of each test required the subject to 'calibrate' the selection area for each target. They were asked to designate the radius of a concentric circle around a target to define an area of selection they felt comfortable with for the purposes of reliably selecting that target, which could be anywhere outside the target or within the target. The proposed boundary of the selection area was shown with an outline (see the selection radius in Figure 2).

This 'calibration' was made by the subject using gestures. Multiple attempts at calibration were permitted, and only once they were satisfied was the calibration confirmed by the experimenter and further pointing measurements were taken. The rationale behind the user-calibration method was to gain an insight into user preferences for target size with a device-free gesture pointing device. This second task aimed to gain insight

into user preferences for the required selection area around a target. The calibration distances, i.e. the maximum preferred selection distances from the centres of targets indicated by subjects are shown as a function of both target spacing and radii in Figure 8 and 9, respectively. In Figure 8, experimental results from the first column of Table 1 are given, while in Figure 9, experimental results from the first row of Table 1 are given, averaged across all subjects in each case. A one-way ANOVA analysis showed all these differences to be significant ($p < 0.001$, $F(4,90)=11.58$).

It was expected that for a given target size, subjects would increase the selection area around the target as the distance between targets increased, in order to facilitate the selection as suggested by Fitts' law. It was thought that the lower limit for the selection area would be bounded by the space available between targets and the upper limit would be bounded by subjects' perceptions that they had defined a sufficiently large selection area. Figure 8 seems to confirm this hypothesis, with a monotonically increasing relationship between the calibration radius and spacing between targets, tending towards a more horizontal asymptote for larger spacings. Using Fitts' Index of Difficulty I_d as a coarse indicator (Fitts, 1954), we observed that the selected calibration sizes result in a very mild I_d increase when compared to the I_d derived from the actual target size, confirming our expectations.

Table 1. Target spacings and radii for the calibration task

		Target radius (pixels)				
		9	20	40	70	105
	220	•	•	•	•	•
	150	•	•	•	•	
Target spacing (pixels)	100	•	•	•		
	60	•	•			
	30	•				

Figure 8. Average calibration radius selected by subjects vs. spacing between the centres of each target and corresponding 95% confidence intervals (target radius = 9 pixels)

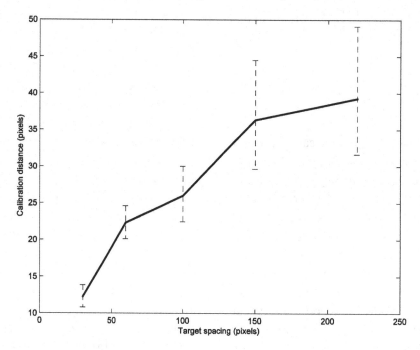

Figure 9. Average calibration radius selected by subjects vs. the radius of each target and corresponding 95% confidence intervals (target spacing = 220 pixels)

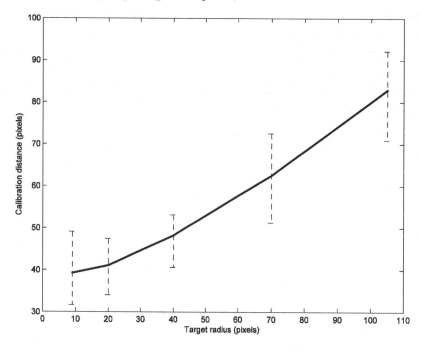

Figure 10. Distance at time of selection vs. calibration distance, for all subjects over all experiments

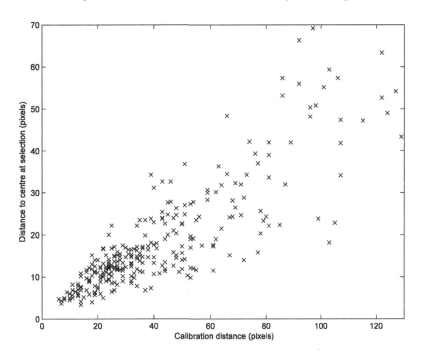

It was also expected that subjects would choose a selection area proportional to the size of the target, with a lower boundary representing an area where the subjects could make gesture selections reasonably quickly. As can be seen in Figure 9, there is an almost linear relationship between the calibration radius and the target size. For target sizes smaller than a 20 pixel radius, a lower threshold of 40 pixels applies for the calibration radius. These values were found to be significantly different by a one-way ANOVA ($p<0.001$, $F(4,90) = 10.451$).

The distances of the selection points from target centres as a function of the calibration distances that subjects selected for the same experiment are shown in Figure 10, across all subjects and all experiment configurations listed in Table 1. Linear regression analysis of these points revealed a gradient of 0.44, indicating that after subjects chose their preferred maximum selection distance during calibration, their actual selection distances during the ensuing tasks were generally around half of this maximum. 95% of all responses fell within a selection distance to calibration distance ratio of between 0.20 and 0.76. For individual users this range was even narrower, for example 0.36 to 0.59 in one user. It appeared that a subset of subjects consistently preferred calibration radii smaller than the target size, while a different subset consistently preferred calibration radii greater than the target size.

DESIGN RECOMMENDATIONS

It is obvious that the results and finding only holds for the particular setup used in the experiments described above. However, the comprehensive literature study and taxonomy of existing approaches make us confident to generalise the findings. Beyond the absolute values gained from the studies, fundamental relationships of aspects of human pointing actions in time and space are an import starting point for the design of hand-free interaction techniques.

Dwell-Time and Feedback Time

The findings of our studies provide empirical evidence that there is a common or *natural dwell-time* in human pointing actions. This dwell-time implies a corresponding delay time for feedback (see also Figure 1). The results of the experiments with controlled feedback time show that for a feedback delay below 600 ms it is likely that the feedback is experienced as natural and that the users rate the feedback neither too fast nor too slow. The significant differences of the ratings at 350 and 600 ms mark an interval in which judgments of the participants are about to change. Furthermore, the interval encloses the average feedback delay time of 430 ms gained from study B and matches some delay times proposed in the literature. However, these had been constrained by technology instead of being based on and informed by empirical evidence. It is clear that the findings strictly hold for the particular environment and task that was used. However, the applications reviewed in the literature resemble in many aspects. We assume that our results might be even compared to those of experiments with manual 2D interaction environments with mouse and pen input devices. Furthermore, the difference of the results of the self-paced study A (dwell-time) and the stimulus-driven study B (reaction or exit time) reveals in alignment with the outcome of the experiment. The difference of dwell and exit time (lead to the feedback time, see Figure 1) of approximately 570 ms lies in the interval of 350 and 600 ms marked by the experiment with controlled feedback.

The detection of a motionless period always requires time and will introduce a temporal delay. A feedback delay time of 350 ms to 600 ms gives detection mechanisms in dwell-based pointing applications enough time to derive the referred object from the real-time processing of the interaction data and to avoid the ambiguity of short dwells. At the same time the acceptance of the feedback based on the rating is still high.

The idea of a natural dwell-time is not entirely new and has been motivated by the research presented in (Peck, 2001; Sibert & Jacob, 2000), (Pöppel, 1997; Schleidt et al., 1987), which favours a universal time constant in short term human actions and by the notion of the Embodiment Level in human behaviour as proposed in (Ballard et al., 1997). Although time periods in human behaviour cannot be literally constant, we argue that the natural dwell-time in pointing could indicate the existence of a particular foundational time scale for human communication. Therefore, it is important to consider the natural dwell time when designing pointing interactions for applications of Human Computer Interaction.

Selection Granularity and Calibration Radius

The results of the experiment addressing the spatial aspect of pointing must also be regarded in the context of our implementation; other implementations may produce different results. However, important findings can be identified beyond the absolute numbers of pixel. The results of form the experiment with the selection granularity reveal that developer are not advised to only rely on the minimum distance to the target during pointing. The distance during the dwell period between the centre of the target and the point at which a user is pointing is often larger than the minimum distance in the period while moving the pointing device towards target. Here the determination of the dwell period helps to improve the selection of the right target. The criteria for the detection of the dwell period depend on the application but the derivative of the target distance, i.e., speed might be used to discriminate the moving from the dwell period.

In the experiment with regard to the calibration radius, it was expected that users would define large selection areas for smaller targets, and relatively smaller selection areas for larger targets. The size of the selection area was expected to be influenced by the proximity of other targets to each other in the configuration; if targets are closer together, the appropriate selection area would be confined to the target limits. The calibration radius is always greater than or equal to the target size, tending towards equality for larger sizes. As observed from Figure 9, on average, the subjects preferred a minimum calibration radius (in this setup of about 40 pixels). Participants select smaller preferred target radii (calibration distances) as both the target spacing and radii are decreased, as seen in Figure 8 and 9. Likewise, subjects perform their selections closer to the target centres as both the target spacing and radii were decreased. This emphasise that not only the target size but also the spacing ahs an effect of the subjective. There appears to be a strong correlation between users' preferred maximum selection distance (calibration distance) and the distance they generally used for selection. Asking users to select their preferred target radius, and adapting the interface to this seems a promising approach, since all subjects studied consistently performed selection at distances between 20% and 76% (typically 44%) of this preferred radius. Similar arguments for user adaptation can be found elsewhere in the multimodal literature, e.g., (Oviatt et al., 2004).

CONCLUSION

The understanding of the organisation of the human pointing gestures in time and space is essential when using hand-free interaction techniques. These are used in many applications of Human Computer Interaction where no explicit and discrete actions, such as button clicks, are practical or available to capture user input. We discussed the role and importance of the dwell period during pointing to express the selection of a target object in order to convey this reference to a communication partner. Experiments revealed that a recommended feedback delay time for

manual pointing actions is approximately 350 to 600 ms, so that 500 ms is a good starting point for the development of interactive applications. This feedback delay is experienced by users as natural and convenient and the majority of observers of pointing actions gave feedback within a similar time span. Any further delay is counterproductive and impedes the progress of a task (Shneiderman, 1984).

With regard to the spatial organisation of pointing, it is not given that the proximity to the target is during the dwell period the closest. Developers have to take into account that a free-had pointing user might be closer to the centre of the target while approaching the target than during the dwell period. Therefore, discrimination has to happen in both, the time and space to gain reliable information about the target selection. The extend of the comfortable area for selection (calibration distance) defined by users itself depends on the size and spatial density of the targets. The calibration distance and the distance to the target are correlated and usually the calibration distance is larger than the distance to the target centre during the selection. The relationship allows taking the user defined calibration to inform and adapt the size of the target selection area.

Finally, we emphasised to concentrate on the requirements of pointing user when developing multimodal interaction techniques. It is not recommended to let technical constraints bias the choice, e.g., for a feedback delay time and selection target size. Instead, the user's behaviour and expectations as presented in this paper should inform the system design to achieve the best interaction quality.

REFERENCES

Ballard, D., Hayhoe, M., Pook, P., & Rao, R. (1997). Deictic codes for the embodiment of cognition. *Behavioral and Brain Sciences, 20*, 723–767.

Bohan, M., Stokes, A.F., & Humphrey, D.G. (1997). An investigation of dwell time in cursor positioning movements. In *Proceedings of the 41st Annual Meeting of the Human Factors Society* (pp. 365–369). Santa Monica, CA: The Human Factors and Ergonomics Society.

Bolt, R.A. (1980). Put-that-there: Voice and gesture at the graphics interface. In *SIGGRAPH '80: Proceedings of the 7th International Conference on Computer Graphics and Interactive Techniques* (pp. 262–270). New York: ACM Press.

Bowman, D., & Hodges, L. (1997). An evaluation of techniques for grabbing and manipulating remote objects in immersive virtual environments. In *Proceedings of the Symposium on Interactive 3D Graphics (1997)* (pp. 35–38).

Bridgeman, B., Peery, S., & Anand, S. (1997). Interaction of cognitive and sensorimotor maps of visual space. *Perception and Psychophysics, 59*(3), 456–469.

Card, S.K., Newell, A., & Moran, T.P. (1983). *The psychology of human-computer interaction.* Mahwah, NJ: Lawrence Erlbaum Associates, Inc.

Chen, F., Choi, E., Epps, J., Lichman, S., Ruiz, N., Shi, Y., Taib, R., & Wu, M. (2005). A study of manual gesture-based selection for the PEMMI multimodal transport management interface. In *ICMI '05: Proceedings of the 7th International Conference on Multimodal Interfaces* (pp. 274–281). New York, NY: ACM Press.

Clark, H., & Wilkes-Gibbs, D. (1986). Referring as a collaborative process. *Cognition, 22*(22), 1–39.

Fitts, P. (1954). The information capacity of the human motor system in controlling the amplitude of movement. *Journal of Experimental Psychology, 47*(6), 381–391.

Haggard, P., Clark, S., & Kalogeras, J. (2002). Voluntary action and conscious awareness. *Nature Neurosciences, 5*(4), 382–385.

Hansen, J., Johansen, A., Hansen, D., Itoh, K., & Mashino, S. (2003). Command without a click: Dwell-time typing by mouse and gaze selections. In *INTERACT '03: Proceedings of the 9th IFIP TC13 International Conference on Human-Computer Interaction* (pp. 121–128). Amsterdam: IOS Press.

ISO (1998). *ISO Report number ISO/TC 159/ SC4/WG3 N147: Ergonomic requirements for office work with visual display terminals (VDTs) - part 9 – Requirements for non-keyboard input devices (ISO 9241-9).* International Organisation for Standardisation.

Jojic, N., Brumitt, B., Meyers, B., Harris, S., & Huang, T. (2000). Detection and estimation of pointing gestures in dense disparity maps. In *Prococeedings of the Fourth International Conference on Automatic Face and Gesture Recognition* (pp. 468–475). Piscataway, NJ: IEEE Computer Society.

Kettebekov, S., & Sharma, R. (2000). Understanding gestures in multimodal human computer interaction. *International Journal on Artificial Intelligence Tools, 9*(2), 205–223.

Kirstein, C., & Müller, H. (1998). Interaction with a projection screen using a camera-tracked laser pointer. In *MMM '98 : Proceedings of the International Conference on Multimedia Modeling* (pp. 191–192). IEEE Computer Society.

Kita, S. (2003). Pointing: A foundational building block of human communication. In S. Kita (Ed.), *Pointing: Where language, culture, and cognition meet* (pp. 1–8). Mahwah, NJ: Lawrence Erlbaum.

Leavens, D.A. (2004). Manual deixis in apes and humans. *Interaction Studies, 5,* 387–408.

Malerczyk, C. (2004). Interactive museum exhibit using pointing gesture recognition. In *WSCG '04 : Proceedings of the 12th International Conference in Central Europe on Computer Graphics, Visualization and Computer Vision* (pp. 165–172).

Maybury, M.T., & Wahlster, W. (1998). Intelligent user interfaces: An introduction. In M.T. Maybury, & W. Wahlster (Eds.), *Readings in intelligent user interfaces* (pp. 1–13). San Francisco, CA: Morgan Kaufmann Publishers Inc.

McNeill, D. (1992). *Hand and mind: What gestures reveal about thought*. Chicago: University of Chicago Press.

Meyer, H., Hänze, M., & Hildebrandt, M. (1999). Das Zusammenwirken von Systemresponsezeiten und Verweilzeiten beim Explorieren von Hypertextstrukturen: Empirische Evidenz für einen zeitlichen Integrationsmechanismus? In *KogWis'99: Proceedings der 4. Fachtagung der Gesellschaft für Kognitionswissenschaft* (pp. 86–91). St. Augustin, Germany: Infix Verlag.

Müller-Tomfelde, C. (2007). Dwell-based pointing in applications of human computer interaction. In *INTERACT '07: Proceedings of the 11th IFIP TC13 International Conference on Human-Computer Interaction* (pp. 560–573). Springer Verlag.

Müller-Tomfelde, C., & Paris, C. (2006). Explicit task representation based on gesture interaction. In *MMUI '05: Proceedings of the 2005 NICTA-HCSNet Multimodal User Interaction Workshop* (pp. 39–45). Darlinghurst, Australia: Australian Computer Society, Inc.

Newell, A. (1990). *Unified theories of cognition*. Harvard University Press.

Nickel, K., & Stiefelhagen, R. (2003). Pointing gesture recognition based on 3D-tracking of face, hands, and head orientation. In *ICMI '03: Proceedings of the 5th International Conference on Multimodal Interfaces* (pp. 140–146). New York: ACM Press.

Nigay, L., & Coutaz, J. (1993). A design space for multimodal systems: Concurrent processing and data fusion. In *INTERCHI '93: Proceedings of the INTERCHI '93 Conference on Human factors in Computing Systems* (pp. 172–178). Amsterdam: IOS Press.

Oviatt, S., Coulston, R., & Lunsford, R. (2004). When do we interact multimodally?: Cognitive load and multimodal communication patterns. In *ICMI '04: Proceedings of the 6th International Conference on Multimodal Interfaces* (pp. 129–136). New York: ACM.

Parker, J.K., Mandryk, R.L., & Inkpen, K.M. (2005). Tractorbeam: Seamless integration of local and remote pointing for tabletop displays. In *GI '05: Proceedings of Graphics Interface 2005* (pp. 33–40). Waterloo, Canada: Canadian Human-Computer Communications Society.

Peck, C.H. (2001). Useful parameters for the design of laser pointer interaction techniques. In *CHI '01: CHI '01 Extended Abstracts on Human factors in Computing Systems* (pp. 461–462). New York: ACM.

Pöppel, E. (1997). A hierarchical model of temporal perception. *Trends in Cognitive Science, 1*, 56–61.

Sato, A., & Yasuda, A. (2005). Illusion of sense of self-agency: Discrepancy between the predicted and actual sensory consequences of actions modulates the sense of self-agency, but not the sense of self-ownership. *Cognition, 94*(3), 241–255.

Schapira, E., & Sharma, R. (2001). Experimental evaluation of vision and speech based multimodal interfaces. In *PUI '01: Proceedings of the 2001 workshop on Perceptive user interfaces* (pp. 1–9). New York: ACM.

Schleidt, M., Eibl-Eibesfeldt, I., & Pöppel, E. (1987). Universal constant in temporal segmentation of human short-term behaviour. *Naturwissenschaften, 74*, 289–290.

Schomaker, L., Nijtmans, J., Camurri, A., Lavagetto, F., Morasso, P., Benoît, C., Guiard-Marigny, T., Le Goff, B., Robert-Ribes, J., Adjoudani, A., Defée, I., Münch, S., Hartung, K., & Blauert, J. (1995). *A taxonomy of multimodal interaction in the human information processing system*. Report of the ESPRIT Project 8579 MIAMI.

Shneiderman, B. (1984). Response time and display rate in human performance with computers. *ACM Computing Surveys, 16*(3), 265–285.

Sibert, L.E., & Jacob, R.J.K. (2000). Evaluation of eye gaze interaction. In *CHI '00: Proceedings of the SIGCHI Conference on Human Factors in Computing Systems* (pp. 281–288). New York: ACM.

Špakov, O., & Miniotas, D. (2004). On-line adjustment of dwell time for target selection by gaze. In *NordiCHI '04: Proceedings of the Third Nordic Conference on Human-Computer Interaction* (pp. 203–206). New York: ACM.

Wang, Y., MacKenzie, C.L., Summers, V.A., & Booth, K.S. (1998). The structure of object transportation and orientation in human-computer interaction. In *CHI '98: Proceedings of the SIGCHI Conference on Human Factors in Computing Systems* (pp. 312–319).

Wilson, A., & Shafer, S. (2003). XWand: UI for intelligent spaces. In *CHI '03: Proceedings of the SIGCHI Conference on Human Factors in Computing Systems* (pp. 545–552). New York: ACM Press.

KEY TERMS AND DEFINITIONS

Deictic Gesture: "How one organism manipulates the visual attention of another to some distant entity" (Leavens, 2004), synonym or similar to pointing

Dwell Time: Special time period during a pointing act where the hand, finger or device remains motion less for a certain time; the dwelling is required to discriminate an intentional pointing form other arbitrary section while moving.

Experiments: The presented findings are based on empirical evidence collected in controlled experiments with participants using generic pointing tasks.

Pointing: The act of using a finger or device to externalise a reference to an object to a communication partner: used in human communication to emphasis the current object of the discourse and to accompany utterances.

Selection Distance: The minimum spatial distance to an area that has to be reached to allow for the detection of a selection of the target in the area.

Section II
From Unimodal to Multimodal Interaction:
Applications and Services

The second section of this book presents chapters describing problems faced when designing, implementing and using multimodal systems. These problems and their solutions are discussed considering specific modal and multimodal applications. An example of solution for ambiguities is provided combining auditive and visual modalities; the problem of accessing objects and services supplied by multimodal mobile applications is faced by multimodal systems in different scenarios using Ontologies permitting interoperability between different environments and semantic interoperability for cooperation. The collaborativeness in designing interactive systems is discussed as a relevant issue to handle specific problems and face them on the field. Finally, the importance to make information and services accessible is highlighted, and one adopted solution for visually impaired people is described.

Chapter X
Speech and Gaze Control for Desktop Environments

Emiliano Castellina
Politecnico di Torino, Italy

Fulvio Corno
Politecnico di Torino, Italy

Paolo Pellegrino
Politecnico di Torino, Italy

ABSTRACT

This chapter illustrates a multimodal system based on the integration of speech- and gaze- based inputs for interaction with a real desktop environment. In this system, multimodal interactions aim at overcoming the instrinsic limit of each input channel taken alone. The chapter introduces the main eye tracking and speech recognition technologies, and describes a multimodal system that integrates the two input channels by generating a real-time vocal grammar based on gaze-driven contextual information. The proposed approach shows how the combined used of auditive and visual clues actually permits to achieve mutual disambiguation in the interaction with a real desktop environment. As a result, the system enables the use of low cost audio-visual devices for every day tasks even when traditional pointing devices, such as a keyboard or a mouse, are unsuitable for use with a personal computer.

INTRODUCTION

In various situations people need to interact with a Personal Computer without having the pos-

sibility to use traditional pointing devices, such as a keyboard or a mouse. People may need both hands free to fulfill other tasks (such as driving or operating some equipment), or may be subject to physical impairment, either temporary or permanent.

In recent years, various alternatives to classical input devices like keyboard and mouse and novel interaction paradigms have been proposed and experimented. Haptic devices, head-mounted devices, and open-space virtual environments are just a few examples. With these futurist technologies, although still far from being perfect, people may receive immediate feedback from a remote computing unit while manipulating common objects. Special cameras, usually mounted on special glasses, allow to track either the eye or the environment, and provide visual hints and remote control of the objects in the surrounding space. More intrusive approaches exploit contact lenses with micro sensors to grasp information about the user's gaze (Reulen & Bakker, 1982). In other approaches special gloves are used to interact with the environment through gestures in the space (Thomas & Piekarski, 2002).

In parallel to computer vision based techniques, voice interaction is also adopted as an alternative or complementary channel for natural human-computer interaction, allowing the user to issue voice commands. Speech recognition engines of different complexity are used to identify words from a vocabulary and to interpret users intentions. These functionalities are often integrated by context knowledge to reduce recognition errors or command ambiguity. For instance, several mobile phones currently provide speech-driven composition of a number in the contact list, which is by itself a reduced contextual vocabulary for this application. Information about the possible "valid" commands in the current context is essential for trimming down the vocabulary size and enhance recognition rate. At the same time, the current vocabulary might be inherently ambiguous, as the same command might apply to different objects or the same object might support different commands: also in this case, contextual information may be used to infer user intentions.

In general most interaction channels, taken alone, are inherently ambiguous, and far-from-intuitive interfaces are usually necessary to deal with this issue (Oviatt, 1999) .

To keep the interaction simple and efficient, multimodal interfaces have been proposed, which try to exploit the peculiar advantages of each input technique, while compensating for their disadvantages. Among these, gaze-, gesture- and speech-based approaches are considered the most natural, especially for people with disabilities.

Particularly, unobtrusive techniques are the most preferred, as they aim at enhancing the interaction experience in the most transparent way, avoiding the introduction of wearable "gadgets" which often make the user uncomfortable. Unfortunately, this is still a strong technical constraint, which mast be softened by some necessary trade-offs. For instance, while speech-recognition may simply require wearing a microphone, eye tracking is usually constrained to using some fixed reference point (e.g., either a head mounted or wall mounted camera), making it suitable only for applications in limited areas. Additionally, the environmental conditions render eye tracking unusable with current mobile devices, which are instead more appropriate for multimodal gesture- and speech-based interaction.

Indeed, the ambient conditions play a major role when choosing the technologies to use and the strategies to adopt, always taking into account the final cost of the proposed solution.

In this context, the chapter discusses a gaze- and speech-based approach for the interaction with the existing GUI widgets provided by the Operating System. While various studies (see the Related Works section) already explored the possibility of integrating gaze and speech information in laboratory experiments, we aim at extending those results to realistic desktop environments. The statistical characteristics (size, labels, mutual distance, overlapping, commands, …) of the widgets in a modern GUI are extremely different from those of specialized applications, and different disambiguation approaches are needed.

One further assumption of this work is the necessity of working with inaccurate eye tracking information: this may be due to a low cost tracking device, or to low-resolution mobile (glass-mounted) cameras, or to calibration difficulties, varying environmental lighting conditions, etc. Gaze information is therefore regarded as a very noisy source of information.

The general approach proposed is based on the following principles:

1. Gaze information is used to roughly estimate the point fixated by the user;
2. All objects in the neighborhood of the fixated point are candidates for being selected by the user, and are the only ones to be recognized by the vocal system;
3. Actual command selection is done by speaking the appropriate command.

As a consequence, and contrarily to related works, the grammar for voice recognition is generated dynamically, depending on the currently gazed area. This improves speech recognition accuracy and speed, and also opens the door to novel disambiguation approaches. In this chapter, a method for analyzing real ambiguity sources in desktop application usage, and an algorithm for disambiguation of vocal commands will be discussed.

BACKGROUND

Eye Tracking

Eye tracking pre-dates the diffusion of personal computers by at least 100 years. As a matter of fact the first research on eye tracking and analysis of the ocular movement goes back to 1878 to Emile Javal (Javal, 1907). The methods used to track, described on this work, were as invasive

as requiring a direct contact with the cornea. The first not invasive technique of eye tracking was developed in 1901 (Dodge & Cline, 1901). This technique allowed to track the horizontal position of the eye onto a photographic film, though the patient was required to be completely immobilized during the analysis of the light reflected by the cornea. In the same period wi find the use of the cinematographer technique which allowed to record the appearance of ocular movements during a time interval (Judd, McAllister, & Steel, 1905). This technique analyzes the reflection produced by the incidental light on a white spot inserted into the eye. These and other researches concerning the study of the ocular movement made further headway during the first half of the 20th Century as techniques combined into different ways.

On 1947 Paul Fitts used the cinematographic technique to study the movement of the military pilots' eyes to understand how controls and instruments on the airplane were observed during landing. Fitts studies represent the first application of eye tracking to the usability discipline. On 1948 Hartridge and Thompson (Hartridge & Thomson, 1948) designed the first eye tracker installed onto a crash helmet. It was rough for our current standards, but this innovation could finally free the users from the strong constraint of head immobility.

The research on ocular movements and eye tracking was reborn in the Seventies, with a big progress both on eye tracking technology and on the psychological theory of the link between cognitive processes and ocular movement models. Most of the work was focused on the research in the psychological and physiological aspect of the structure of human eye, and on the things that it could reveal about cognitive and perceptive processes. The publications made in the Seventies report a sort of stasis in the use of eye tracking applied to ergonomics, probably because of the difficulty in finding and analyzing useful data. Many of the relevant works in those years were technical, and related to improving accuracy and precision of eye trackers.

The discovery that multiple reflections of the human eye could be used to separate ocular rotation from head movement, opened the road to the development of remote systems, without any ties to the users. Since the Nineties, many ideas and techniques for eye tracking have been suggested and developed.

Recent eye tracking systems can be classified according to 3 main aspects:

- The adopted *User Interface*. Eye trackers can be:
  o *Intrusive*, i.e., in direct contact with the users' eyes (e.g., contact lens, electrodes)
  o *Remote*, e.g., a system including a personal computer with one or more video cameras
  o *Wearable*, e.g., small video cameras mounted on a helmet or glasses. Remote eye trackers are the most widespread systems. Wearable eye trackers recently started gaining some popularity, in contrast to invasive methods, typically used in the medical field, which are continuously losing fame.

- The *Applications* that use them as input devices. Eye tracker systems have a great variety of application fields. The first researches, involving eye trackers, were mostly related to the medical and cognitive fields, as they concerned the study of human vision and eye physiology. Recent studies, instead, are rather related to Assistive Technologies and, in general, to Human Computer Interaction, while current eye tracker killer applications seem to be mainly focused on advertising and marketing, aiming at analyzing the area of interest of customers inside either commercial videos or advertising posters. Nowadays the computer game industry is developing more and more innovative interaction and control methods for user inputs. Nevertheless Gaze tracking, that is a fast natural and intuitive input channel, is not exploited in any commercial computer game, yet. Nevertheless, in recent years, several research groups started to study gaze tracking devices applied to computer games.

- The used *technology*. Eye trackers can be based on at least 6 different gaze estimation algorithms that are detailed in subsequent sections.

The aforementioned eye tracking systems classification is summarized in Figure 1.

Figure 1. Eye tracking systems classification

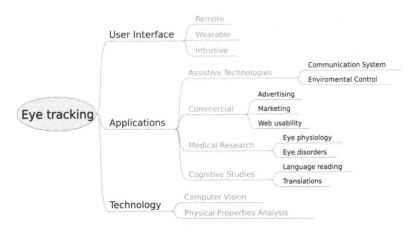

The main eye tracking methods found in literature are six:

- Image analysis
  - o Cornea and pupil reflex
  - o Pupil tracing
  - o Tracing of the corneal reflex through the dual Purkinje image
  - o **Image analysis:** tracing of the limb, the border between iris and sclera
- Physical properties analysis
- **Electro-oculography:** Measurement of the eye electrical potential
- **Scleral coil:** Measurement of the magnetic field produced by the movement of a coil inserted into a user's eye.

Image Analysis

Most computer vision techniques for gaze tracking are based on finding and analyzing the reflex produced by infrared light incident on various parts of the eye.

The tracking of corneal and pupil reflex (Duchowski, 2002) allows determining the gaze direction by comparing the infrared corneal reflex with the pupil position. The corneal reflex tends to stay fixed during pupil movements and is used as a spatial reference for both tracking pupil movements, and for compensating head movements. An eye tracking system using this technique typically consists of a single device composed of one or more infrared light emitters and an infrared-sensitive video camera.

The pupil tracking method (Hansen & Pece, 2005), conversely, uses just the position and the shape of the pupil to infer the gaze direction. This technique is sensitive to head movements and is less accurate in estimating the observed point. Systems adopting this technique, to compensate for head movements, use cameras mounted over glasses worn by the user. Most of the eye tracking systems that use these techniques are composed of one or more infrared light sources to illuminate the eye(s), and one or more infrared cameras to capture eye(s) images.

Physical Properties Analysis

Electro-oculography (Gips, Olivieri, & Tecce, 1993) is based on measuring the electrical potential difference between the cornea and the retina. Typically, pairs of electrodes are placed around the eye. When the eye moves, a potential difference occurs between the electrodes and, considering that the resting potential is constant, the recorded potential measures the eye position.

Scleral coil techniques use a contact lens with a coil to track the eye movements. The coil induces a magnetic field variation while the eye is moving. Scleral coil eye trackers are very intrusive because, typically, the contact lenses are connected to some wire. Only recently a wireless Scleral Coil eye tracker has been developed (Wong, Roberts, & Shelhamer, 2008).

Eye trackers that adopt physical properties analysis are usually composed of a DSP, necessary for data processing, connected to an output channel, which provides the captured samples.

Comparing Eye Tracking Techniques

Table 1 shows a comparison among the previously discussed gaze tracking techniques. It reports, for each eye tracking technology, the type of comapatible devices, the accuracy, and the typical sample frequency range. Accuracy is evaluated as the minimum visual angle, measured in degrees, discriminable by the technique. A visual angle of 0.5° allows to estimate approximately a 20x20 pixels gazed area at the distance of 70 cm.

Speech Recognition

The first studies on speech recognition technologies began as early as 1936 at Bell Labs. In 1939, Bell Labs (Dudley, 1939) demonstrated a speech synthesis machine, simulating talking, at

Table 1. Eye tracking techniques comparison

Technology	Device Type	Accuracy	Sample Frequency
Pupil and Corneal reflection	desktop, weareable	< 0.1°	50 – 100 Hz
Electro-potential	intrusive	0.1 – 0.5°	> 100 Hz
Pupil Tracking	desktop, wearable	0.1 – 0.5°	50 – 100 Hz
Scleral Coil	intrusive	< 0.1°	> 100 Hz
Dual Purkinje Image	desktop, wearable	0.1 – 0.5°	> 100 Hz
Limbus	desktop, wearable	> 0.5°	> 100 Hz

the World Fair in New York. Bell Labs further ceased researches on speech recognition, basing on the incorrect consideration that artificial intelligence would ultimately be necessary for success. Early attempts to design systems for automatic speech recognition were mostly guided by the theory of acoustic-phonetics, which describes the phonetic elements of speech (the basic sounds of the language) and tries to explain how they are acoustically realized in a spoken utterance. These elements include the phonemes and the corresponding place and manner of articulation used to produce the sound in various phonetic contexts. For example, in order to produce a steady vowel sound, the vocal cords need to vibrate (to excite the vocal tract), and the air that propagates through the vocal tract results in sound with natural modes of resonance similar to what occurs in an acoustic tube. These natural modes of resonance, called the formants or formant frequencies, are manifested as major regions of energy concentration in the speech power spectrum. In 1952, Davis, Biddulph, and Balashek of Bell Laboratories built a system for isolated digit recognition for a single speaker (Davis, Biddulph, & Balashek, 1952), using the formant frequencies measured (or estimated) during vowel regions of each digit.

In 1960s the phoneme recognizer of Sakai and Doshita at Kyoto University (Sakai & Doshita, 1962) involved the first use of a speech segmenter for analysis and recognition of speech in different portions of the input utterance. In contrast,

an isolated digit recognizer implicitly assumed that the unknown utterance contained a complete digit (and no other speech sounds or words) and thus did not need an explicit "segmenter". Kyoto University's work could be considered a precursor to a *continuous speech recognition system.*

In 1966, Lenny Baum of Princeton University proposed a statistical method (Baum & Petrie, 1966), namely an Hidden Markov Model (HMM), which was later applied to speech recognition. Today, most practical speech recognition systems are based on the statistical framework and results developed in the 1980s, later significantly improved (Levison, Rabiner & Sondhi, 1983).

In the late 1980s the first platforms were finally commercialized, thanks to the exponentially growing computer processing power. Still, only discrete utterances were successfully recognized, until the mid-'90s when even pauses between words were tolerated. The so called "continuous speech recognition systems" reached an accuracy of 90% and more under ideal conditions.

In the last decade the computational power of personal computer has dramatically increased, thereby allowing the implementation of automatic speech recognizers, which in earlier attempts where hardly feasible even with dedicated hardware devices, such as DSP boards.

Currently, speech recognition technologies offer an effective interaction channel in several application fields, such as:

- **Telephone Services.** Most of telephone companies replace call center operators with speech recognizers to offer real time information services (e.g., forecast information, train and flight timetables and reservations).
- **Computer control.** Recent operative systems integrate native speech recognizer engines that allow disabled people to control the personal computer through vocal commands. In addition, several commercial companies provide special-purpose speech recognizer applications, e.g., voice-to-text editor or converter.
- **Mobile device control.** Several mobile devices can be controlled by *simple* vocal commands. Nowadays, speech recognition in mobile devices is limited to specific functions like contact list management, phone calls, etc., but it is expected to enable more complex activities as the underlying system becomes more performant and less demanding in terms of energy consumption.
- **Automotive control.** Since five years several automobile manufactures integrate speech recognizer systems in the cars. These embedded systems allow drivers to remotely control devices, such as a mobile phone, while keeping the attention to the road, and without taking the hands off the steering wheel.
- **Language learning.** Speech recognition can be used as automatic pronunciation corrector. Some commercial system already allow to propose the correct pronunciation when the spoken words differ too much from the reference samples.

The existing technologies which are currently used in modern applications of ASR (Automatic Speech Recognition) have greatly evolved since their infancy. Yet, a number of factors still make ASR algorithms seriously complex:

- **Speaker independence** Most ASR algorithms require intensive training, which can hardly cover the entire human spectrum. An ideal application would require minimal or no training at all to recognize any user's speech.
- **Continuous speech** It is desirable to allow a user to speak normally, rather than forcing the insertion of pauses to facilitate the identification of word boundaries.
- **Vocabulary size** The range of vocabulary size greatly varies with the application. For instance, only a few words are to be recognized when dealing with simple and limited controls (e.g., an audio player). In contrast, a large vocabulary is necessary for complex communications, although leading to less accurate recognition as a greater number of similar words may occur in the vocabulary.
- **Accuracy** Environmental conditions like noise and even minimal reverberation are likely to lessen accuracy.
- **Delay** The recognition process is not instantaneous. The lag introduced by the algorithms usually grows with the complexity of the application, yielding delayed feedback to the users, which is often annoying.
- **Ergonomy** Typically the microphone has to be placed very near to the mouth for the ASR system to provide accurate results, so limiting the application ranges.
- **User Interface** Two commercial applications for individual voice recognition are already available at low cost, and with a simple interface (namely Dragon Naturally Speaking and IBM Via Voice). Not all the applications provide a practical user interface though.

Given these premises, a multimodal system is presented, which tries to combine the most promising features of the available input channels, while compensating for the disadvantages.

RELATED WORKS

While most of earlier approaches to multimodal interfaces were based on gestures and speech recognition (Bolt, 1980), various speech- and gaze-driven multimodal systems have also been proposed.

In (Miniotas, Spakov, Tugoy, & MacKenzie, 2006), an approach combining gaze and speech inputs is described. An ad-hoc program displays a matrix of fictitious buttons which become colored when spotted through fixation. The test users can then name the color of the desired button to select it via speech recognition, so going beyond the gaze-tracking limits. However, differently from the approach proposed in this paper, the technique has not been applied to real programs, and the color-coding system demonstrated to be somewhat confusing for various users.

In (Zhang, Imamiya, Go, & Gao, 2004), gaze and speech are integrated in a multimodal system to select differently sized, shaped and colored figures in an ad-hoc application. The distance from the fixation point is used to rank the best candidates, while a grammar composed by color, color+shape or size+color+shape is used for speech recognition. The integrated use of both gaze and speech proved to be more robust than their unimodal counterparts, thanks to mutual disambiguation, yet the tests are not based on every-day applications.

Some theoretical directions toward the conversion of unimodal inputs to an integrated multimodal interface are proposed in (Baljko, 2005). The context here is more focused on gaze and speech inputs as Augmentative and Alternative Communication (AAC) channels, which can be the only available ones for several diversely able people. The tests are based on earlier studies which do not involve existing off-the-shelf applications of every-day use.

A multimodal framework for object manipulation in Virtual Environments is presented in (Sharma, Pavlovic, & Huang, 1998). Speech, gesture and gaze input were integrated in a multimodal architecture aiming at improving virtual object manipulation. Speech input uses a Hidden-Markovian-Model (HMM) recognizer, while the hand gesture input module uses two cameras and HMM-based recognition software. The functionality of the gaze input is limited to providing complementary information for gesture recognition. The gaze direction, for example, can be exploited for disambiguating object selection. A test-bench using speech and hand gesture input was implemented for visualization and interactive manipulation of complex molecular structures. The multimodal interface allows a much better interactivity and user control compared with the unimodal, joystick-based, input.

In contrast with most of the mentioned approaches, we base our experimentation on a system for multimodal interaction with every-day and off-the-shelf desktop environments (Microsoft Windows XP was used in the experiments). In particular we want to improve the performance of low-cost eye-gaze trackers and of speech recognition systems when used alone, by using a real-time generated grammar based on the integration of both input channels.

THE PROPOSED SYSTEM

The proposed system (Castellina E., Corno F., & Pellegrino P., 2008), described in this section, aims at extracting the most useful pieces information from the two supported modalities (gaze estimation and voice commands), while at the same time enabling their mutual disambiguation. Gaze is used for setting up a "context" composed of the on-screen object that the user is currently focusing on. Tracking precision is not sufficient for quickly and reliably identifying a single widget, but is sufficient for identifying an area on the screen and for filtering the contained objects. This filtering highly reduces the ambiguity of voice commands, by ruling out most of the selectable actions (since they lie outside the user focus), and by reducing the dictionary size (thus enhancing recognition rate).

The user task considered in this study consists in specifying an object (any selectable element on the screen, i.e., windows, menus, buttons, icons, …) or a command (any action on an object, i.e., open, close, click, drag, …).

Requirements Analysis

In the following sections we describe the simplest situation a user can be involved in: a user is in front of the monitor and wants to select, among various objects, a specific icon (e.g., "firefox"), and to execute a command on it (e.g., "run").

To complete these tasks using visual ad vocal communication tools, the computer-user interaction faces the following issues:

1. **To select available objects within the fixation area.** The eye pointing system determines the area containing the objects to select. As the tracking system is not precise enough to select a single object, the screen analyzes an entire spottable area, which becomes the **context** for the vocal system.

2. **To find a connection between objects and commands pronounced through voice.** Not all the pronounced commands are appropriate for all the objects in the selected area (context), so an algorithm is used to decide the object with which the command is associated, e.g. if a user prounounces the word <<*close*>> that spoken command could be associated only with window application objects.

3. **To disambiguate objects.** In many situations the user requires to select objects on the screen having the same name and belonging to different windows. Users need the chance to refer clearly to a specific object and the application has to deal correctly with ambiguous cases. In other terms, the

systems has to discard those repetitive objects that could create ambiguity errors for the combined use of gaze and voice.

Proposed Solution

In order to take advantage of the concurrent visual and vocal modules, a few basic elements have been defined:

- **Objects** The widgets available on the screen. These may be files represented by an icon and a name, labeled buttons, menu items, window bars and buttons, etc. Each object is characterized by a few properties such as *name*, *role*, state and *actions*. In particular, each object has a default action defined by the system (e.g., open the file with the associated program, show the pop-up menu, etc.).

- **Context** The area spotted by the tracking system, also referred to as Gaze Window (GW), identifies the context of interaction for the vocal system: only the objects within such context will be considered by the vocal system. The context varies as the user's gaze wanders on different areas of the screen.

- **Commands** The words captured by the microphone and recognized by the speech recognition engine. Valid commands are described in the grammar, that is composed of the list of possible commands, corresponding to object names or action names (within the current GW context).

Through the eye motion we track the direction of the gaze as a fixation point on the screen, i.e., the point in which the user is focusing his/her gaze. This point is normally affected by some displacement error due to various factors, so the eye tracker actually identifies an area on the screen rather than a precise point. Thus, the result of the tracking is a GW that may contain several objects. The height and width of the GW around the fixation point are defined by a customizable parameter *GWsize*. In the performed experiments this parameter has been varied automatically, to simulate eye trackers with different accuracy.

While gazing, the user also interacts with the system by uttering a command, i.e., by pronouncing an object name (for the default system action) or a specific action. The vocal platform manages spoken words through a VXML interpreter that is guided by the voiceXML processing unit (Vocal Unit) to completely and accurately interpret the result. The vocal unit interprets messages sent by the vocal platform, processes them and sends the result to the main application unit. This unit is developed in VXML. VXML is the W3C's standard XML format for specifying interactive voice dialogues between a human and a computer. It that allows voice applications to be developed and deployed in an analogous way to HTML for visual applications. After receiving the recognition results, the application matches the received command with the objects selected by the eye tracker.

The rest of this chapter describes in details the various system modules and their functionalities. In particular, we describe a mutual disambigua-

tion algorithm that is based on dynamic grammar generation and is suitable for realistic desktop enviroments. Experimental results will later show quantitative data proving the effectiveness of the disambiguation method with real desktop usage scenarios.

Particularly, the steps required for command recognition and execution can be summarized as follows (Figure 2):

1. Definition of a context as the screen area spotted by the eye-tracking system.
2. Enumeration of the available objects within a given context.
3. Retrieval of object properties, such as name, role, position (with respect to the fixation point), state, default action.
4. Disambiguation of objects having the same name by exploiting positional information.
5. Matching of a pronounced command against object names or actions within a given context
6. Retrieval of the corresponding object and execution of the related action.

Figure 2. System Overview

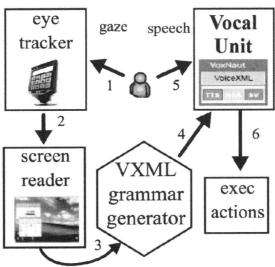

System Architecture

The system is organized as a set of five functional modules, as shown in Figure 2: Eye Tracker, Screen Reader, Grammar Generator, Vocal Unit and Action Executor. Each module is described in the the appropriate sub-section. In particular, the Screen Reader and the Grammar Generator handle object filtering and disambiguation, and real-time generation of the VoiceXML grammar.

Eye Tracker

This module is responsible for the identification of an area of interest on the screen, i.e., of a *Gaze Window*. The eye tracking system, in fact, provides an estimated fixation point that may be affected by some displacement error, strongly dependent on the hardware and software components of the tracker. The actual area location and size are therefore dependent on the fixation point and on the displacement error. Practically, the cursor coordinates at the time of a fixation are used, and are collected as follows:

- If the cursor remains within a small area (a few pixels wide) for at least D seconds (dwell time), a fixation event is raised at the cursor position;
- If the cursor position varies too much before reaching the dwell time threshold, no events are raised.

In case of fixation the Eye Tracker module defines the Gaze Window as a square of size *GWsize* centered on the fixation coordinates and eventually calls the Screen Reader unit.

Screen Reader

The Screen Reader receives the fixated area (GW) as input from the Eye Tracker and retrieves a set of objects on the screen in such area, by interacting with libraries at Operating System level. In particular, this unit enumerates objects within the eye-tracking context and defines for each of them the corresponding name, role, state, default action, and position. The nameless or invisible (background) objects are discarded to get exactly what the user sees on the screen. The retrieved objects are eventually collected into a memory structure and passed to the Grammar Generator unit. The Screen Reader was developed using the Microsoft Active Accessibility SDK and the Win32 Application SDK.

Grammar Generator

This unit generates an appropriate VXML grammar for the speech recognition module of the Vocal Platform by using the objects spotted through the Eye-Tracking system and the Screen Reader. Basically, the grammar defines a set of possible vocal *commands* based on the object names or actions.

The grammar is generated according to the following approach:

- If the object name is unique, a single vocal command is generated, corresponding exactly to that name;
- When 2 to 4 objects share the same name or action, the corresponding commands are disambiguated by exploiting the object locations (left, right, top, bottom). In such a case, the commands entered into the grammar are the disambiguated names, composed of the object name followed by the location direction. For example "firefox left" and "firefox right". Additionally, a final command is also added to the grammar, containing the ambiguous name (e.g., "firefox"): when recognized, the VXML interpreter synthesizes a vocal warning message asking the user to disambiguate it (e.g., *"firefox is ambiguous, please specify left or right"*) to give proper auditory feedback to the user;

- When more than 4 objects are ambiguous, the location-based disambiguation method is ineffective, and in this case a single command is generated with the corresponding name, causing the Vocal Unit to synthesize an error message. The limitation of 4 disambiguation cases is due to the choice of using only 4 relative positions: top, right, left, bottom.

Vocal Unit

The Vocal Platform receives as input the set of possible contextual commands defined by the Grammar Generator, and supplies as output the command pronounced by the user. Every spoken word is processed and interpreted on the basis of the VXML grammar and, still according to the grammar, a vocal message can be synthesized to notify the user of the recognition result: *"command recognized"*, *"ambiguous command identified"*, or *"wrong command"*. When a command is correctly identified, it is passed to the Action Executor unit. The application was developed using a speech processing subsystem based on VoxNauta Lite 6.0 by Loquendo, an Italian company leader on the field of vocal applications and platforms.

Action Executor

It receives as input the command recognized through the Vocal Platform, and executes the associated action. Basically, the object corresponding to the command is retrieved from the data structure previously created by the Screen Reader, by matching the command name with the object name or the available object actions (also considering disambiguation). Then, the specified action (or the default action of the object) is executed through a Microsoft Active Accessibility function.

EXPERIMENTAL EVALUATION

The proposed multimodal system, and in particular the interactive location-based disambiguation mechanism, have been designed for interacting with a real desktop environment. To prove the effectiveness of the approach, we report some experimental results gathered on the Windows XP operating system with the Default Theme and U.S. English localization.

The performed tests have a twofold purpose:

- To analyse the relation between the gaze block size and the number of ambiguous objects and commands, in a realistic desktop environment;
- To analyse the disambiguation efficiency of the location-based method.

The experimentation is based on data about classic Windows XP widgets (e.g., buttons, menu items, etc.) and their locations inside the screen, gathered during both work and personal use of computer. Unlike the other works, that make use of a static pre-generated object disposition or of simple and unusual objects, this work is based on real experimental data. A test-oriented version of the screen reader module has been developed to store screen-shots of the computer desktop taken at predefined time slots (every 3 minutes, provided the user was not idle during that period). Each screen-shot includes a complete list of objects, each object being described by four properties: Name, Role, Rectangle and Window Order.

- The *name* property contains all the text referred to the object, e.g., button title, text area contents, etc.
- The *role* property specifies the object type, e.g., command button, list item, menu item, etc.
- The *rectangle* property represents the location and size of the object.

- The *window order* property indicates the z-order location of the object.

The trials involved 5 unpaid people for about a week. Each person installed the screen reader on his/her own computer and ran it for a week. The gathered data sums to 468 screen-shots involving 144,618 objects, including the hidden ones. These objects have been filtered down through a simple overlap detection algorithm, keeping only the 42,372 (i.e., 29.3% of the total) foreground visible objects, used in all the subsequent test phases.

The tests determine how often the speech recognition system is effective in disambiguating objects, as a function of the Gaze Window size. To speed up analysis, the eye tracking accuracy has been simulated by considering GW with variable dimensions (from 10px to 800px) instead of precise coordinates identifying the objects position. The maximum GW dimensions have been chosen to cover the corner case of a very inaccurate eye tracking with the precision of just two zones (left/right) on a 1600x1200 screen resolution. This correspond to having practically no useful information from the eye tracker.

Two different tests have been performed, each using a different object property to define object *similarity*. In the first test (Name Ambiguity), two objects are considered *similar* if the *name* of the first object is included in (or equal to) the *name* of the second one. In the second test (Role Ambiguity), two objects are considered *similar* if they have the same *role* (e.g., both objects are buttons).

The tests were executed according to Algorithm 1. In particular, the Classification of an object inside a GW (line 6) is organized as follows:

- **Unique object:** there is no other similar object inside the GW.
- **Ambiguous object:** the GW contains two or more objects which are mutually similar.
  - ○ **Discriminable object:** the ambiguous objects within the GW are at most four.
  - ○ **Indiscriminable object:** the ambiguous objects within the GW are more than four.

Algorithm 1: Test Application

```
for each screen-shot S do
  for each target object O in S do
    for each GWsize = 10px . . . 800px
                 step 10px do
      Generate a GW around O with size
                 GWsize x GWsize
      Find the objects (OS) in the GW
                 similar to O
      Classify OS
      Store Statistics
    end for
  end for
end for
```

Name Ambiguity

This test aims at evaluating the number of ambiguous objects having a *name* similar to the target object, within differently sized GWs centered on the object. We neglect the effect of speech recognition errors, and the only sources of imprecision are command ambiguity and large GWs. In this case we reach 100% accuracy if and only if only one object with the same name is found in the considered GW. The test application generated 79 GWs (square, from 10px to 800px wide) for each object and calculated the number of ambiguous objects. Thanks to the vocal localization-based feedback mechanism, discriminable objects may be selected with full precision. Figure 3 illustrates the trend of both the indiscriminable and discriminable ambiguous objects, in function of the GW size.

Experimental results show that the ideal recognition rate is quite high (about 80%) even in case of inaccurate eye tracking device (i.e., wide GW) and no disambiguation. Precision is significantly increased through the localization-based disambiguation method up to 98% in the worst case. A

Figure 3. Name Ambiguity: Unique and ambiguous (Indiscriminable and Discriminable) objects vs. GW size

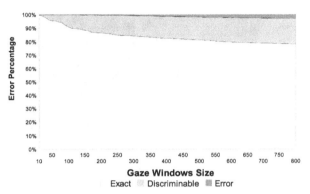

deeper analysis of the results showed that indiscriminable objects are not uniformly distributed here: only the 19.1% of the screen-shots presents indiscriminable objects, and most of them are in an Internet browsing windows. In fact, they are mostly hyperlinks in either Internet Explorer or Mozilla Firefox.

Role Ambiguity

This test aims at evaluating the number of objects having similar *role*, i.e., those objects which support the execution of the same or overlapping set of commands (e.g., all file icons). Even in this case the test application generated 79 GWs (square, from 10px to 800px wide) for each object and computed the number of visible objects with ambiguous role. Figure 4 shows the trend of both the indiscriminable and discriminable ambiguous object roles with various GW sizes.

In this case the ambiguous objects are far more than those obtained by name similarity. Therefore, specifying actions as commands rather than object names can be more error prone in case of low-precision eye trackers: even a 40px GW reduces precision to belows 50%. Even in this case we see the significant effect of location-based disambiguation, that is able to recover all Discriminable cases. In this case, the 50% recognition threshold is reached with a much wider GW, around 150px,

corresponding to a 400% increase in noise rejection of the system to gaze tracking errors.

CONCLUSION

In this study, a system capable of speech recognition and object selection, integrated with an eye-gaze tracker and a vocal platform has been discussed. The system has been proven capable of sustaining user interaction in a real desktop environment, with a very limited error rate, even in presence of inaccurate recognition devices.

The multimodal interaction, which integrates gaze and vocal inputs, proves to overcome the eye tracker imprecision as well as the inherent ambiguity of vocal commands through their combined use. In particular, a VoiceXML grammar is generated in real-time at every fixation to limit the vocabulary size for the speech recognition, based on the objects in the fixated area.

In real-world desktop environments, the names of the objects appear to be a better choice for command disambiguation, while the object actions are far more error prone. The disambiguation method based on relative object location (top, right, left, bottom) allows to discriminate most of the objects which have similar name, while it may not be sufficient for role ambiguity, especially in case of low-precision eye-tracker.

Figure 4. Role Ambiguity: Unique and ambiguous(Indiscriminable and Discriminable) objects vs. GW size

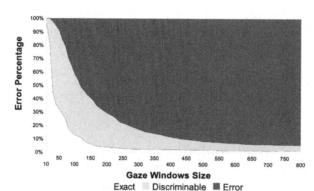

ACKNOWLEDGMENT

This work is partially supported by the European Commission under the IST project COGAIN (*Communication by Gaze Interaction*). The authors would like to thank Loquendo for providing a VoxNauta 6.0 license.

REFERENCES

Baljko, M. (2005). The information-theoric analysis of unimodal interfaces and their multimodal counterparts. *SIGACCESS Conference on Computers and Accessibility* (pp. 28-35). New York: ACM Press.

Baum, L.E., & Petrie, T. (1966). Statistical inference for probabilistic funtions of finite state Markov chains. *Annals of Mathematical Statistics,* 1554-1563.

Bolt, R.A. (1980). Put-that-there: Voice and gesture at the graphics interface. *Computer graphics and interactive techniques* (pp. 262-270). New York: ACM Press.

Castellina E., Corno F., & Pellegrino P. (2008). Integrated speech and gaze control for realistic desktop environments. *ETRA'08: 2008 Symposium on Eye Tracking Research & Applications* (pp. 79-85). New York: ACM Press.

Davis, K.H., Biddulph, R., & Balashek, S. (1952). Automatic recognition of spoken digits. *Journal of the Acoustical Society of America , 24,* 627-642.

Dodge, T.S., & Cline, R. (1901). The angle velocity of eye movements. *Psychological Review,* 145-157.

Duchowski, A.T. (2002). A breadth-first survey if eye tracking applications. *Behavior Research Methods, Instruments, & Computers ,* 455-470.

Dudley, H. (1939). *The Vocoder.* Bell Labs Record.

Gips, J., Olivieri, P., & Tecce, J. (1993). Direct control of the computer through electrodes placed around the eyes. *Fifth Internation Conference on Human-Computer Interaction,* (pp. 630-635).

Hansen, D.W., & Pece, A.E. (2005). Eye tracking in the wild. *Computer Vision Image Understanding,* 155-181.

Hartridge, H., & Thomson, L.C. (1948). Method of investigating eye movements. *British Journal Ophthalmology,* 581-591.

Javal, L.É. (1907). Physiologie de la lecture et de l'écriture. *Bibliography in Annales d'oculistique,* 137-187.

Judd, C.H., McAllister, C.N., & Steel, W.M. (1905). General introduction to a series of studies of eye movements by means of kinetoscopic photographs. *Psychological Review, Monograph Supplements, 7*, 1-16.

Levison, S.E., Rabiner, L.R., & Sondhi, M.M. (1983). An introduction to the application of the theory of probabilistic functions of a markov process to automatic speech recognition. *Bell System Technology Journal*, 1035-1074.

Miniotas, D., Spakov, O., Tugoy, I., & MacKenzie, I.S. (2006). Speech-augmented eye gaze interaction with small closely spaced target. *Symposium on Eye tracking Research and Applications* (pp. 66-72). ACM Press.

Oviatt, S. L. (1999). Mutual disambiguation of recognition errors in a multimodal architecture. *Conference on Human Factors in Computing Systems* (pp. 576-589). ACM Press.

Reulen, J.P., & Bakker, L. (1982). The measurement of eye movement using double magnetic induction. *IEEE Transactions on Biomedical Engineering, 29*, 740-744.

Sakai, J., & Doshita, S. (1962). The phonetic typewriter. *Information Processing*.

Sharma, R., Pavlovic, V., & Huang, T. (1998). Toward multimodal human-computer interface. *IEEE* (pp. 853-869). IEEE.

Thomas, B.H., & Piekarski, W. (2002). Glove based user interaction techniques for augmented reality in an outdoor environment. *Virtual Reality*, 167-180.

Wong, A., Roberts, D., & Shelhamer, M. (2008). A new wireless search-coil system. *Eye Tracking Research and Applications Symposium*, Savannah, GA (pp. 197-204).

Zhang, Q., Imamiya, A., Go, K., & Gao, X. (2004). Overriding errors in speech and gaze multimodal architecture. *Intelligent User Interfaces* (pp. 346-348). ACM Press.

KEY TERMS AND DEFINITIONS

Desktop Enviroment: Graphical user interface based on desktop metophore interaction.

Disambiguation: Uncertainty resolution among overlapping choices.

Eye Tracking: Technique for the estimation of the point of gaze.

Image Analysis: Image processing to retrieve high level information, such as object recognition and tracking.

Multimodal Interaction: Interfacement with a system through multiple alternative input channels.

Screen Reader: Is a software application that retrieves and interprets what is displayed on the screen.

Speech Recognition: Translation of vocal utterances into the corresponding textual representation.

Unobtrusiveness: Property of a device or a technique that do not cause physical trouble to its users.

Z-Order: The order of an object along the Z-axis. It determines which object appears on top among the overlapping others.

Chapter XI
Multimodality and Environment Semantics

Fabio Pittarello
Università Ca' Foscari Venezia, Italy

Augusto Celentano
Università Ca' Foscari Venezia, Italy

ABSTRACT

Safe access to urban environments depends upon a variety of circumstances, among which the abilities of the persons and the complexity of the environment raise interesting issues about design and usability of help systems and information points. This paper proposes a methodology for designing systems able to guide users in finding and accessing the objects and services of a complex environment. The methodology is based on the identification of the user oriented features of the environment and on its mapping onto a semantically enriched 3D virtual world. The physical environment is described at different levels of granularity, functionally and geometrically. Its functional properties are referred to a scene-independent ontology, granting a level of interoperability between different environments. An implementation architecture based on Web standards is proposed for communicating information and signs related to the user location and for generating support to ease the navigation. A case study about the creation of a guided tour through the indoors and outdoors of the town of Venice through a multimodal Web browser is presented.

INTRODUCTION

Proper access to urban environments like streets and squares, buildings, parks, museums, offices, etc., and correct movement inside them are not always simple and straightforward tasks. They are conditioned by a variety of circumstances, biased by the abilities of the visitors and by the complexity of the environments, and raise interesting issues about design and usability of help systems and information points for assistance to people in public places. Physical and cognitive deficiencies could prevent some persons from easily recognizing locations, objects and their relations. Such a situation often leads the visitors of an environment to be unable to get information about objects of interest, to recognize dangerous situations, and to profit from support tools for moving safely, like parapets, traffic-lights, pedestrian crossings, etc..

In this work we discuss the problem of describing complex human environments from a semantic perspective, making explicit the meaning of the environment elements and their relation with the persons moving inside it. We propose a methodology and an implementation architecture to design and build systems able to provide meaningful information to assist people to orient and move. Different persons with different skills need to receive different levels of assistance: for example, elderly people with visual and cognitive deficiencies require proper communication styles and devices, and need more assistance than people with normal physical and cognitive faculties.

Solutions exist, such as GPS based navigators, for guiding people through unknown places to destination, helping them to follow a reasonable path. However, most of them provide a simplified map and suggest direction changes at proper places with standard messages related to streets and roads only, such as "turn left after 50 meters", "go straight", "turn right at the end of the street", and so on. They do not interpret the route in terms of how the user perceives the surroundings, what environment components can be meaningful as landmarks for a visitor, what is their purpose, as a high-level description of the environment could provide. For example, a semantic oriented navigator could suggest directions to a person walking in a town with terms such as "at the traffic-light turn left", or "take the road behind the fountain". In a GPS navigator only a few landmarks, the so

called *Points of Interest* (POI), are marked by type or by touristic relevance and are shown on the map, but they are not used in composing the vocal instructions.

The lack of a complete high-level description of the environment seen by the walker is a consistent limitation that prevents conventional navigation systems to assist the users to identify the relevant objects in the environments as reference points for moving and finding directions, even if this is the usual way humans exchange information when asking for assistance. Indeed, most of the solutions available are unable to contribute to the creation of a mental model of the territory; providing the instructions to reach a destination as a sequence of steps, they miss the big picture in favor of a local perspective.

In addition to providing an environment description based on semantic related concepts, the association of audio signs to different locations could help the user to mark them more clearly and to progressively build an audio, as well as a visual, map of the visited places. Audio marking can be very useful to enable a sudden recognition when the user re-enters the same place.

The methodology we discuss in this chapter takes advantage of a semantic description of the environment mapped onto a virtual 3D counterpart. A system interpreting the two descriptions and aware of the user profile is able to generate multilevel and multimodal messages that guide the user through the environment, describing the environment content about areas and objects in terms related to meaning rather then to geometrical features. Such multilevel description is useful for navigation, since it allows users to understand the role and goal of an object or area within the broader context given by its position in the environment structure. It responds also to specific information needs; for example, a user visiting a palace of artistic relevance might be interested on investigating the architectural details of a building or the technical features of a work of art displayed in a room. Finally, such a representation can be associated with an accurate description of the dangers, of the navigational aids and of the step sequence needed for moving safely through the environment itself. While integration with GPS-enabled devices is not the target of this work, the system architecture we propose may be extended with additional components in order to sense the user in the environment, calculate the user path to destination in real time and give proper assistance.

The remainder of this paper is organized as follows: after presenting the state of art reviewing the relevant literature, we shall describe the requirements guiding our methodology; then, we shall focus on the definition of the semantics for a 3D virtual counterpart mapping the real environment; such high-level description will be used by an implementation architecture for extracting and presenting navigational as well as content information in the form of a multimodal guided tour. We shall support our arguments with a case study related to the urban environment of Venice before drawing the final conclusions.

STATE OF ART

The issue of pedestrian access to and navigation through a complex real environment has been considered by a large number of research works that investigate different aspects of the problem.

Some works focus on the general requirements for navigational aids: an interesting study by May, Ross, Bayer, and Tarkiainen (2003) analyzes the nature of the navigation task and the information needed by users within an urban navigation context, showing that landmarks are the most important navigation cue. The landmarks are visible objects of different sizes that help the user to orient himself/herself inside the environment. The authors suggest also that, where possible, such landmarks should be referred to by using specific semantic information (e.g., "*Mymoney* bank" rather than "building").

Other papers focus on the specific needs of different categories of people. Hub, Diepstraten, and Ertl (2004) point out the importance of informing blind people navigating a real environment about specific features of the scene that may help exploration (e.g., the size of rooms) or situations of danger that may cause severe injuries (e.g., stairs, revolving doors, etc.). Touchable landmarks, which can be any kind of object including light switches or thresholds, are considered an important aid for helping this category of users. Zajicek (2001) investigates interface design issues for older adults. While her work is not directly concerned with navigation in real spaces, it puts in evidence specific disabilities that typically affect adults over 70, including memory and visual impairment. Her analysis will be considered in our work for deriving some important user requirements.

The research area of context-aware systems has approached the problem of effectively guiding the users in new environments. Petrelli, Not, Zancanaro, Strapparava, and Stock (2001) analyze the relations between the user and the environment in museums guides suggesting adaptive description of the museum objects using direct references to the space (e.g., "in front of you", "on the opposite wall"), a solution used also in our proposal.

Concerning the user interface, several systems use audio signals for conveying to users information useful for navigation. AudioGPS (Holland, Morse, & Gedenryd, 2002) uses non-speech spatial audio for communicating information related to direction and distance. The target of such interface are sighted users that do not need too much information about objects and risks of the environment but prefer a simpler interface requiring minimal attention. Several speech based solutions have been proposed for blind users (Hub et al., 2004; Loomis, Golledge, & Klatzky, 2001). Ross and Blasch (2000) propose a multimodal speech and tactile interface for blind people, tested in an urban context, that has shown great usability and flexibility. Our proposal shares with this work the multimodal approach, even if applied in a different way.

Several outdoor navigation applications for blind people use GPS for computing the position of the user and for giving him/her appropriate information. Indoor solutions rely on different technologies (e.g., infrared beacons, WiFi, WLAN based location, etc.) to compensate for the lack of GPS signal.

An interesting indoor solution (Hub et al., 2004) uses a portable sensor equipped with positioning and direction devices for identifying the shape of an object inside the room and matching it with a virtual model that maps the environment. A speech interface presents to the user descriptive information associated to the virtual object mapping the real one. This solution is focused on the identification of landmarks and does not offer to the user explicit suggestions for moving, but shares with our approach the idea of mapping the real environment with a virtual counterpart, including high-level descriptions of the objects contained into the scene.

Although the semantic description of a 3D scene can be useful for deriving high-level information for navigation purposes, it is not a standard feature of 3D environments: often 3D worlds are modeled using low-level geometric primitives such as spheres, cones, etc., that do not contain any reference to the semantics of the objects they represent. Besides, the scene graph used for storing a 3D scene in a hierarchical order is not suited to store semantic information that often has a structure more complex than a hierarchy. A simple yet common example is that of two rooms with a common wall: using a hierarchical description only one room object can be considered as the parent of the wall object, preventing a correct representation of the environment conceptual structure (Halabala, 2003). Recent approaches (Halabala,2003; Mansouri, 2005) solve this problem using the MPEG-7 standard (Nack & Lindsay, 1999a, 1999b) for storing semantic information related to a 3D

world in an external data structure. The limit of these solutions is that the ontologies used for describing the semantic objects and their relations are scene-dependent. Such dependence prevents the progressive building of a set of urban scenes that can be merged and queried using a shared semantic. Our work includes the definition of a scene-independent definition of the environment semantics to overcome this problem.

Most proposals for the semantic annotation of 3D environments focus on the definition of semantic objects rather than on semantic spaces. While a high-level description of the geometry of a given environment is useful for cataloguing the parts composing the 3D scene and can be very useful for searching semantic objects at different levels of granularity, it is not complete because it does not take explicitly into account the use of the space. A simple example is the element *door* that is a semantic object composed by other lower-level semantic objects (e.g., the *handle*), but is also an artifact generating a *space door* with the important function of connecting two different zones of a 3D environment.

Therefore, even though semantic objects generate spaces, there is a strong difference between them that must be considered by the ontologies aiming to give a complete description of the environment useful for navigation. Semantic zones are also a fundamental element for allowing the user to build a mental map of the environment; users attach lower-level semantic objects to space partitions and the association grants a preferential way to recall the objects themselves, as demonstrated also by mnemonic techniques developed by western civilization starting from the Renaissance (Yates, 1966).

The Interaction Locus (IL) concept (Pittarello, 2001, 2003), defined by one of the authors of this work, satisfies the need for an explicit definition of the partitions of space that are designed and recognized as morphologic and functional units, and will be considered as a component of the scene-independent ontology proposal.

The IL was originally introduced as a means for reducing navigational problems in virtual reality worlds due to the lack of details in the 3D scene and to the small view angle for desktop systems. Sounds and textual labels are associated to partitions of space that are semantically relevant for the user (e.g., a square) to improve their identification. In the development of the research on IL, such zones were explicitly associated to the use of space, in terms of sets of allowed and forbidden user interactions. The IL has gradually changed its nature to include not only information necessary for identifying the environment, but also complex content for augmenting the user's knowledge. Currently, the IL is defined as a spatial partition of an environment that is perceived, for morphological reasons, as a specific semantic entity by the humans inhabiting the space. Such partition is associated to a specific use of the space and of its interactive appliances, that may include also a list of forbidden actions or unauthorized users. IL are organized in hierarchies that identify different semantic levels inside an environment. While the concept was introduced at first in the context of the desktop virtual reality, it evolved to bring benefits to all the segments of mixed reality.

The IL is an essential component of the methodology proposed in this paper. It allows a designer to fully define the semantic properties of the environment, a goal that cannot be accomplished without considering the inhabited spaces generated by the objects that make up the environment.

Multimodality is an essential feature of the IL, that takes advantage of both the visual and audio channels for communicating to the user information related to the identity of the location. The use of the audio channels for interaction has been introduced several years ago. Blattner, Sumikawa, and Greenberg (1989) defined the concept of earcons as *"non-verbal audio messages that are used in the computer/user interface to provide information to the user about some computer objects, operations or interaction."* A number of researchers developed the concept and experimented the use of sounds for interaction in different context, including WIMP (*Windows, Icons, Menu and Pointer*) and phone interfaces (Gaver, 1989; Brewster, Wright, & Edwards, 1993). The use of audio signals for improving interaction in 3D environment is more recent (Bowman, Kruijff, La Viola, & Poupyrev, 2000) and has been considered for localizing a user or for transforming information into sound.

In the IL approach sound is used to enhance the perception of locations. The approach has been recently validated (Ardito, Costabile, De Angelis, & Pittarello, 2007), showing than a user aware of the nature of such audio signals may take advantage of them for navigating, since they enforce the creation of a mental map of the environment and help recognition of the places already visited.

Concerning multimodality, there are a few languages that permit to present information to user using different parallel channels. The *XHTML+Voice* (X+V) language (Axelsson et al., 2004), that we consider for the case study described in this work, is an interesting attempt meant for creating multimodal dialogs that use both the visual and the auditory channel in parallel. For the visual channel, X+V takes advantage of the XHTML syntax; for the auditory channel, X+V takes advantage of a subset of VoiceXML 2.0 (Raggett, 2001), an XML language for writing pages with which users can interact by listening to spoken prompts and by issuing vocal commands. X+V supports visual and aural style sheets declared according to CSS2 (Bos, Lie, Lilley, & Jacobs, 1998) in order to style the text source. Finally, the language is supported by the effort of primary players such as IBM and Opera, for creating tools for developing and browsing multimodal content compliant with its specification.

DEFINING THE REQUIREMENTS

Many requirements for presenting navigational information to visitors of a place as a guided tour through the environment derive from the analysis of the state of art proposals and systems, which picture an ample and varying landscape of models, methods and tools. We summarize here the requirements on which our design methodology is built, unifying the many issues discussed in the literature under the perspective of a semantic description of the environment features relevant for user orientation. The requirements, organized in four main areas, take into account both the needs of normally able people and of people with some degree of deficiency. We shall consider three classes of users, representative of various inability types: the elders, the persons with sight deficiencies, and the persons with limited motor abilities. We do not consider, however, persons with strong disabilities, such as blind persons, or persons needing a continuous human assistance; substituting a human assistant with a personal information system, or overcoming blindness with other sensorial stimuli is beyond the scope of this work.

Environment description. The system should provide a high-level description of the objects that populate the environment and have a meaning for the visiting users (*semantic objects*), who must be able to match the description with the objects seen, and to use them as local landmarks. A filter should be provided, considering only near objects local to the current area, avoiding to inform the users about far objects or objects belonging to different, even if visible, locations, such as a skyscraper visible at a distance. While they could be used as generic markers of the landscape, for sight impaired people non local objects could hardly be clearly distinguished, leading to confusion.

The system should provide descriptions organized according to a multilayered view of the environment, to give users the opportunity to ask and receive information at different levels of detail. For example, the user might want to receive information about a museum room, but also details about the contained works of art, or the description of the museum building with details on architectural elements. The multilayered view helps also in locating a specific place in a larger context, such as locating the current room in the building.

Communication and presentation. The system should generate the output through both visual and vocal interfaces and should allow the user to switch seamlessly between the two representations. For example, elderly people might start the tour reading information and later switch to an audio guide, activating a speech engine when they are tired, or when the information becomes complex.

As to the user input, the system should accept both text based input through forms of a graphical interface and speech input through a voice recognition engine, in order to meet different preferences and to overcome specific environment and user conditions, such as traffic noise, or difficulty to use hands.

Concerning the voice interface, the system should clearly specify the words that the user has to pronounce when choosing among different commands and functions. Such requirement, while limiting the user natural expression, greatly reduces the uncertainty related to input interpretation.

Navigation aids. The system should provide timely identification of dangers along the user path, such as staircases, sliding doors, slippery floors, etc., and walking aids, such as rails, chairs for resting, etc., useful mainly for elderly users.

The system should provide a complete yet easy to understand description of the navigation steps inside the current area.

The vocal output system should repeat relevant information at request to compensate for the limits of the vocal output and for the reduced capacity of the elderly to retain information in the short term memory.

User context. The system should provide information about the environment and about navigation from the user subjective perspective. It should refer to object locations with respect to the user point of sight, as a human guide accompanying the user in the tour.

The system should adapt to the user both in terms of preferences expressed in the profile and of preferences inferred from the known user abilities.

Concerning the identification of the user location, which is part of the user context, our approach for supporting navigation does not rely on sophisticated methods for monitoring the user position, but relies on the (even residual) sight of the user to follow the suggestions of the guided tour. An evident limitation of our approach is its inadequacy for, e.g., blind persons, who cannot visually match the information received from the system. Such simplicity, while requiring a more active participation of the users, uses the same suggestions for moving outdoor as well as indoor. Adopting tracking systems effective in both cases would require a costly and complex technological framework, coordinating GPS monitoring with ad-hoc solutions for the building interiors.

Indeed, tracking outdoor navigation is not guaranteed in all urban environments. For example, the town of Venice is characterized by narrow pedestrian streets where a GPS signal can't be reliably received. Precise user tracking would augment the technological requirements with the implementation of an additional costly urban network of sensors placed in public outdoor spaces. This limitation is typical of many old towns, which due to their urban structure often present the most demanding requirements in terms of user assistance.

MAPPING THE REAL WORLD WITH A SEMANTIC VIRTUAL WORLD

Our methodology for improving access to complex physical environments is based on the accurate mapping of the real scene with a virtual model enhanced with semantic information. The map-

Figure 1. A scene with geometric and semantic objects

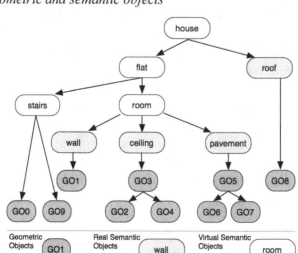

ping includes not only the physical objects that populate the environment, but also the spatial partitions that characterize the real scene.

Mapping Objects

Mapping real objects with a specific meaning for users to the geometric primitives of a 3D model of the scene is not straightforward. In most cases the identifiable geometric components refer only to parts of the objects and not necessarily to components with specific meanings, such as, e.g., a table leg. The lack of a direct mapping is due to the modeling tools, to the habits of the scene modeler, even to the techniques for geometric data acquisition: for example, a 3D scanner may digitize the scene as a point cloud originating a single mesh where the component objects are not split. Besides, the grouping of the geometric objects and their order in the 3D file do not always correspond to criteria of spatial adjacency; again, modeling habits, tools and techniques may prevent or constrain a full correspondence between the geometric and the conceptual structure of the scene components. The recognition of such situation is fundamental for reusing the wide amount of 3D models mapping real world objects that are already available or that may be provided in future by acquisition tools based on geometric features only.

The methodology discussed in this work starts from the identification of the *geometric objects* (GO): basic shapes made of a single geometric primitive, or composed objects, made by aggregation of atomic shapes. Figure 1 shows an example of a scene structure, a hierarchy with the whole scene as root and the elementary objects as leaves. The arcs are relations of type *composedOf*. Geometric objects identified with the labels $GO_1, GO_2 \ldots GO_n$, are hooked to a higher layer of semantic objects mapped to the physical objects recognized in the real world, such as *wall, ceiling, pavement*, etc.. The semantic layer introduced in

the scene description is made of two classes of semantic objects. A *real semantic object* (RSO) corresponds to a single geometric object or to an explicitly declared group of objects to which an identity is assigned as a meaningful part of the scene, such as a mesh or a group of meshes identifying a wall or a ceiling; semantic information is stored as a property of the object. The *virtual semantic object* (VSO) is a means to collect a set of low-level geometric objects that are not explicitly grouped and might be not adjacent in the scene description file, and to associate a semantic to them as a whole. In the scene description file the VSO has a grouping function, acting also as a container of semantic information.

Both real and virtual objects can be organized in a hierarchy: in Figure 1 the RSO *roof* and the VSO *flat* are considered components of the VSO *house*.

Mapping Spaces

The second step of the methodology is the explicit identification of the semantic zones that characterize the human environment. Semantic zones usually are not explicitly defined as entities in the 3D formats that map a real scene; while such choice is reasonable for rendering purposes, it represents a significant drawback from a semantic point of view. Heidegger pointed out that while the concepts of space (*spatium*) and extension (*extensio*) give the opportunity to measure things, they are not able to capture the essence of spaces: "*Spatium and extensio afford at any time the possibility of measuring things and what they make room for, according to distances, spans, and directions, and of computing these magnitudes. But the fact that they are universally applicable to everything that has extension can in no case make numerical magnitudes the ground of the nature of space and locations that are measurable with the aid of mathematics ... Man's relation to locations, and through locations to spaces, inheres in his dwelling. The relationship between man and space is none other than dwelling, strictly thought and spoken."* (Heidegger, 1971)

Indeed, 3D objects generate spaces that are not simply a summa of objects or a collection of Cartesian measures, but are new structural entities enabling humans to inhabit the Earth. Locations are recognized as semantic units, often depending on morphological features, conditioning the human actions organization and more generally the life organization.

We model such structural entities with the *Interaction Locus* (IL) concept, discussed in the state of art review. IL are introduced as explicit entities in files that describe real scenes; such entities are associated to a specific semantics, related to the quality and to the use of space. IL may be organized in hierarchies that identify different semantic levels inside a given environment, such as a set of rooms associated to a flat.

Describing Semantics

The concepts introduced above can be applied to most of the formats available for mapping the real world with a 3D virtual scene. Association of semantic information to objects and spaces follows precise syntactic and structural rules, being specific to format and language. We ground our methodology on existing web standards: X3D (Web3D Consortium, 2004), RDF (Manola & Miller, 2004) and OWL (Smith, Welty, & McGuinness, 2004), in order to maximize the generality of the solution, to minimize the effort related to the creation of tools for manipulating data, and to ease the conversion of existing 3D models and environments mapping the real world.

Semantic information is contained in data structures split across two files: (a) an X3D file describes the objects and the zones that compose the scene, where semantic information is specified in relation to an external scene-independent domain ontology; (b) the domain ontology is de-

fined in OWL, using the RDF Schema syntax for the relations between the environment elements and OWL clauses for the constraints. We have adopted OWL-Full for the ontology specification, despite its complexity with respect to the other two versions, OWL-Lite and OWL-DL, for its higher expressivity in defining relations and constraints, and for the compatibility with RDF Schema, that was used in the early stage of the project development as a self-contained language to express the environment semantics.

The main entities defined by the X3D standard are named *nodes*, used for defining geometric and aural objects, lights, cameras, sensor primitives and scripts. Nodes can be nested generating a complex hierarchical structure. The properties of each node are defined through a set of fields whose value may change as a response to events in the scene and can be transmitted from node to node, generating a dynamic interactive environment. X3D defines also the possibility of inserting metadata nodes, but the standard doesn't suggest any recommendation for their use and content. The methodology described in this work suggests their use for associating geometric objects and semantic objects. While the X3D standard defines several syntax styles for describing its entities, the XML style is preferred since it eases interoperability with other web standards. The examples described below comply with the XML syntax: each node is mapped to a tag and each field is mapped to a tag attribute.

Real Semantic Object. RSO are generated associating to an existing geometry node of the X3D file a **MetadataSet** node containing: (a) the object identification and its relation with the class described in the scene independent ontology; (b) a set of individual properties of the object; (c) the relations with higher level virtual semantic objects if such relations exist.

Example 1. The following X3D fragment defines a simple RSO belonging to the class *wall*, identified as *wall01*; the object is linked with a containment relation to the higher level semantic object *bedroom01*.

```
<Transform ... >
   <MetadataSet name="wall"
      reference="wall01">
   <MetadataString name="containedBy"
      value="bedroom01"/>
      ...
   </MetadataSet>
   <Shape ... >
   ...
   </Shape>
</Transform>
```

Virtual Semantic Object. VSO require the definition of new data structures holding the semantic information, which are nodes according to the X3D standard. In order to minimize the impact on the existing scenes, we add a set of **MetadataSet** nodes to the **WorldInfo** node. Each **MetadataSet** node contains the semantic information related to a specific VSO. Set of ungrouped geometric objects and lower level semantic objects refer to such virtual objects through a **MetadataString**, as shown in Example 1 above.

Example 2. The following X3D fragment defines the VSO *bedroom01*, belonging to class *room* and the associated individual description *"Thomas' bedroom"*. The object is linked with a containment relation to the higher level semantic object *house01*.

```
<WorldInfo ... >
 <MetadataSet name=
   "virtual objects">
 <MetadataSet name="room"
   reference="bedroom01">
 <MetadataString
   name="description"
   value="Thomas' bedroom"/>

   ...
```

```
   <MetadataString name="containedBy"
     value="house1"/>
   </MetadataSet>
   ...
 </MetadataSet>
</WorldInfo>
```

Semantic zone. The explicit definition of semantic areas requires the insertion of new nodes in the existing files for storing spatial information and the associated semantic information. We use **ProximitySensor** nodes because they are the most convenient solution for monitoring the user navigation; by sensing the traversal of different locations, it is possible to trigger internal and external engines for providing information and actions associated with such spaces.

Example 3. The following X3D fragment defines a semantic zone belonging to the class *SestiereSpace*[1], identified as *SanMarcoSpace*.

```
<ProximitySensor ... >
 <MetadataSet name="SestiereSpace"
   reference="SanMarcoSpace">
 </MetadataSet>
</ProximitySensor>
```

Real and virtual semantic objects and semantic zones are associated in the X3D code through the *boundedBy* relation.

Example 4. The following X3D fragment shows the semantic object *San Marco*, belonging to

class *Sestiere*, linked with a *boundedBy* relation to the semantic space

SanMarcoSpace, described in Example 3 above.

```
<MetadataSet name="Sestiere"
   reference="San Marco">
   <MetadataString name="boundedBy"
     value="SanMarcoSpace"/>
</MetadataSet>
```

Environment semantic relations. Information contained in the scene independent ontology completes the semantic definition of the environment, describing the classes of objects of the 3D world and their relations.

Figure 2 illustrates a scene independent ontology that can be used for describing simple worlds made of doors, pavements, walls, rooms, loggias and houses. Some of the objects are associated to semantic spaces; they are evidenced by a strong black border.

The ontology defines different relations between the semantic objects:

- *containedBy*: the object is a component of an higher-level semantic object;
- *sharedBy*: the object is shared between two higher-level semantic objects;
- *boundedBy*: the semantic object has an associated semantic space.

The fragment of RDF Schema in Figure 3 is related to the ontology in Figure 2. The code shows the definitions of the class *wall* and of the relations *containedBy* and *sharedBy*; the OWL restrictions express that the containment relation for an objects belonging to the class *wall* can be defined towards a single object belonging to the class *loggia* or to the class *room* (**maxCardinality**=1), while the sharing relation for the same object can be defined towards two objects belonging to higher-level classes (**maxCardinality**=2).

Semantic objects, described in the X3D file, can be associated to a specific class by setting the field *name* of their **MetadataSet** node to the same value of the class ID; for example, any semantic object belonging to the class *wall*, identified in the RDF file by the ID *wall*, will have the field *name* set to *wall*.

Semantic Description of Urban Environments

While the ontology displayed in Figure 2 offers a sample of the methodological approach for a semantic description of a 3D scene, real environments are characterized by a high number

Figure 2. A simple environment ontology

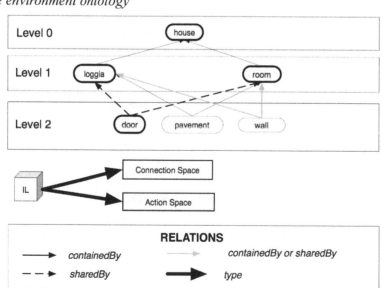

Figure 3. An RDF schema fragment defining the ontology of Figure 2

```
<owl:Class rdf:ID="wall">
<rdfs:subClassOf rdf:resource="&rdfs;Resource"/>

<rdfs:subClassOf>
 <owl:Restriction>
  <owl:onProperty rdf:resource="#containedBy"/>
  <owl:maxCardinality
    rdf:datatype="&xsd;nonNegativeInteger">1
  </owl:maxCardinality>
 </owl:Restriction>
</rdfs:subClassOf>

<rooms:containedBy rdf:resource="&rooms;loggia"/>
<rooms:containedBy rdf:resource="&rooms;room"/>

<rdfs:subClassOf>
 <owl:Restriction>
  <owl:onProperty rdf:resource="#sharedBy"/>
  <owl:Cardinality
    rdf:datatype="&xsd;nonNegativeInteger">2
  </owl:Cardinality>
 </owl:Restriction>
</rdfs:subClassOf>

<rooms:sharedBy rdf:resource="&rooms;loggia"/>
<rooms:sharedByrdf:resource="&rooms;room"/>

</owl:Class>

... <owl:ObjectProperty rdf:ID="containedBy">
  <rdfs:domain rdf:resource="rdf:Class"/>
  <rdfs:range rdf:resource="rdf:Class"/>
</owl:ObjectProperty>
...
<owl:ObjectProperty rdf:ID="sharedBy">
  <rdfs:domain rdf:resource="rdf:Class"/>
  <rdfs:range rdf:resource="rdf:Class"/>
</owl:ObjectProperty>
```

of classes of semantic objects and scenes. New relations need to be defined between objects for taking into account the complexity of a real scene. The resulting multilevel ontology can be described by a complex graph that is not easy to see as a whole. We illustrate the general features of such ontology using two partial views: Figure 4 shows the classes of semantic objects and their relations; Figure 5 shows the classes of semantic spaces and their relations. For the sake of clarity, only the nodes and relations necessary to understand the case study are shown.

The relations *containedBy*, *sharedBy* and *boundedBy* have already been discussed in the simplified ontology of Figure 2; the following relations are needed:

- *subClass*: class specialization;
- *synonym*: relates equivalent terms; for example, in Venice the Italian word *campo* (*field*) is almost always used to denote a *square*;
- *info*: links generic descriptive content about semantic objects;

- *danger*: refers to information about the potential danger represented by the object or more specific classes of users;
- *aid*: refers to information about the potential assistive role that the object can play for one or more classes of users.

The relations *danger* and *aid*, that characterize both semantic objects and spaces, are not explicitly represented in Figures 4 and 5, but they can be associated to any semantic entity.

Semantic zones can be nested, originating a hierarchy of spaces. The property *type* declares

the primary role of such zones: they are classified as *connection spaces* if the main function is connecting other zones; they are considered *action spaces* if they are associated to residential activities. In some cases the role is twofold, e.g., a corridor might be used both for exposing works of art and for connecting rooms.

It is important to note that a containment relation defined for a semantic object doesn't necessarily imply the same relation for the associated semantic zone; for example, the class *door* is contained by the class *room*, but the class *door space* is not contained by the class *room space*;

Figure 4. A view of the ontology for the urban environment centered on semantic objects

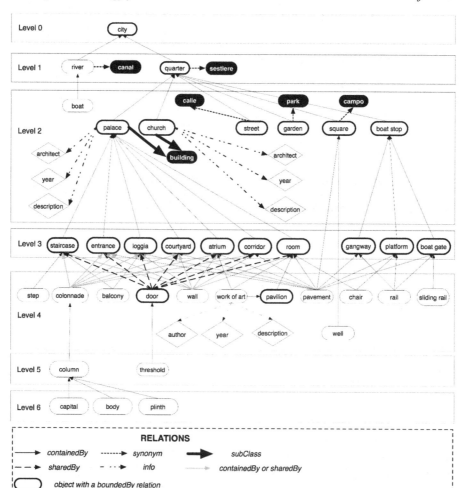

Figure 5. A view of the ontology for the urban environment centered on semantic zones

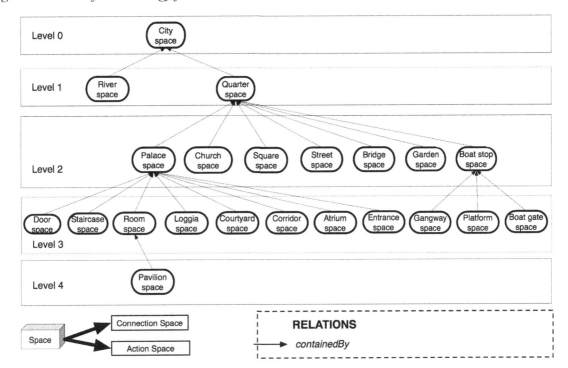

instead it is contained by the higher level class *palace space*.

EXTRACTING AND PRESENTING NAVIGATIONAL INFORMATION

This section and the following one show how the availability of a detailed description of the real environment, including both the geometric and semantic properties, can be the basis for assisting people moving in the environment. This section presents an architecture for extracting information from the environment description and presenting it to the user, in order to assist him/her during navigation. The information presented depends on the knowledge of the environment given by the X3D+RDF description and on the definition of a set of ordered spatial locations that represent the user path through the environment.

The path, as shown in Figure 6a, is defined as a *polyline*, a connected sequence of nodes with a starting and an ending location. Some nodes may be particularly relevant and may be associated to a more detailed description (Figure 6b); we call them *points of interest* (POI), borrowing the terminology from GPS navigators.

The path may be statically defined, as in a guided tour suggested for a museum, or dynamically generated on the basis of the current position of the user and of the navigation target, thus acting as a guide for the forthcoming steps and a user history for the past steps. Several algorithms for route planning are discussed in the literature, starting from the well known Dijkstra's algorithm (1959), that may be used for generating a low-level description of the path; we shall not discuss them, because they are out of the scope of this work.

Figure 7 shows the architecture of a system supporting the methodology described in this paper. The system processes the X3D description of a real environment, the scene-independent ontology for urban environments and the user path. The *generator* component processes the results of other three specialized components: the *metadata extraction* component extracts metadata from the scene geometry; the *structure and information extraction* component extracts semantic information from the ontology; the *positional information creation* component uses the geometrical description of the scene and of the user path for extracting the spatial relations between the user and the scene components. The activity of this component is a prerequisite for giving directions to the user (e.g., *turn right*), for highlighting the position of relevant objects and spaces in relation to the user position (e.g., *the chair in front of you*) and for communicating distances along the path (e.g., *go straight on for 100 meters*).

The generator component outputs a structured XML file containing high-level navigational information, useful for guiding the user through the environment. The XML file is post-processed for generating files compliant with several presenta-tion formats, among which XHTML and X+V are the most relevant in our context.

A prototype of the architecture components has been implemented in Java, chosen for its portability and for the availability of libraries for manipulating XML structures. A specific presentation module was implemented to transform the XML description into a set of files compliant with the X+V profile, for the presentation on multimodal web browsers. The ontology has been developed using Protégé[2] and has been verified for consistency and for conformity to OWL-Full with RacerPro[3].

The integration of the architecture illustrated in Figure 7 with a GPS device monitoring the user position in real time would be useful for assisting the user at a specific location or looking for a destination, without being anchored to a predefined path such as in a guided tour. A complete discussion of such issue is out of the scope of this contribution; however, it is worth to note that such integration is possible, thanks to the design choices about the path description format and the X3D language for describing the geometry. The

Figure 6. The segment-based path

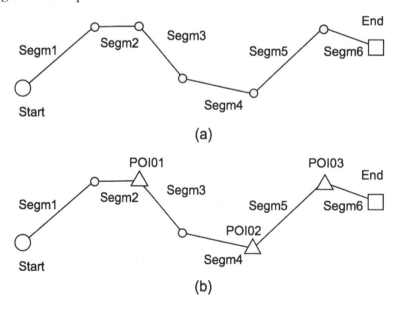

(a)

(b)

Figure 7. The architecture of a system for user navigation assistance

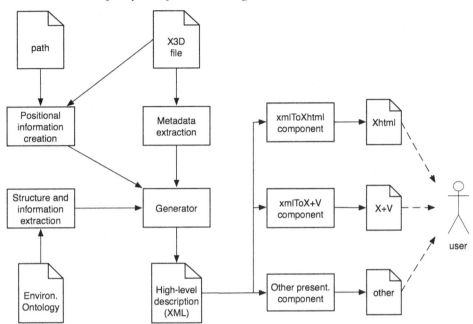

choice of describing the path as a simple polyline simplifies the path computation from the current location sensed by the GPS to the destination, using a route planning algorithm as mentioned above. High-level information can be timely re-generated by the architecture described above for each significant deviation from the planned path. The X3D language provides a way to georefer-ence any model built according to the standard. The geospatial component of X3D describes a set of nodes that can be introduced in any 3D scene to embed geospatial coordinates and to support high-precision geospatial modeling.

Such features help interoperability with infor-mation coming from the GPS device, fastening the data integration process without requiring external components for converting data formats. Also the case of a free user navigation, not an-chored to a specific target, can be supported by the architecture of Figure 7 by using a path with zero length. In this case the system would provide information about the objects, the dangers and the aids that characterize the current location of the user and its immediate surroundings.

A CASE STUDY: NAVIGATING THROUGH VENICE

This section discusses how the methodological approach and the implementation architecture described in previous sections can be used for improving the access to a complex environment in a real case. The case study is related to the town of Venice, covering a part of the urban environ-ment with outdoor and indoor spaces that may require different levels of assistance for users with different abilities.

Figure 8 shows a model of an area of Venice with a square, pedestrian streets and a water chan-nel. The palace facing the square is a complex building hosting an art exhibition. The solid line starting from the left upper corner of Figure 8 and ending at the water boat stop represents the user path that will be considered in the case study. The model has been designed using the methodology described in this paper.

Figure 9 shows an exploded view of the 3D model that maps the palace hosting the art exhibition. The upper three layers display the semantic spaces: the building on top, then the rooms, then the pavilion contained in one of the rooms, according to the layers 2–4 of the ontology in Figure 5. The bottom layer shows the semantic objects mapped by the model: the architectural components of the building and the works of art. All the semantic objects and spaces defined in the model are compliant with the environment ontology illustrated in Figures 4 and 5.

In this case study the X+V files generated for supporting navigation are presented to the user through the visual and aural channels of the Opera Multimodal Browser[4] running on a standard Windows XP notebook or subnotebook.

A typical information sequence presented to the user includes the following content:

a. A synthetic identification of the semantic zone the user is visiting;

b. A list of the dangers that characterize the current zone and the adjacent locations; the user must be aware of all the dangerous situations, even if they are not directly traversed by the path;

c. A list of the navigation aids for the current zone;

d. A multi-level description of the zone; the description can be zoomed out to describe the spatial context that contains the current location or zoomed into X+V files describing in detail the objects contained in the zone and their semantic components;

e. The navigation steps for traversing the location; when a given navigation step leads the user near to a specific danger, its description is preceded by a warning repeating information about such danger and about local aids, if available. Repeating information about critical situations obeys the criterion of supporting the reduced cognitive faculties of elderly people;

f. A link to information related to the next zone; such information is also put at the beginning of the output to allow users not interested in the current zone to switch to information related to the next location.

Indoor Navigation

The first part of the case study, illustrated in Figure 10, focuses on the navigation inside an exhibition room that is part of the palace. The room includes artworks and a chair for the visitors. It is connected to a corridor and to another

Figure 8. A 3D model representing the Venetian environment

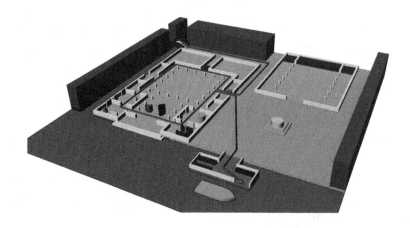

Figure 9. An exploded view of semantic objects and zones of the main Venetian palace

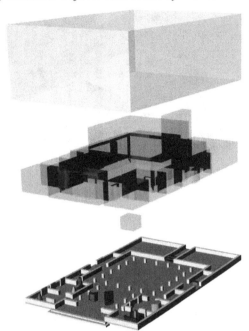

room by two doors. The room has an irregular floor and a damaged threshold.

X+V presents information using both visual and audio communication channels, allowing the user to select the more suited channel. Figure 11 shows a snapshot of the visual presentation adapted to elderly people. Room information comes after a header with a link to information related to the next room, so that visitors not interested in the current room may proceed on.

The information blocks are associated to icons and background colors for easing the identification of the category they belong to. The red background emphasizes dangers (e.g., the irregular floor and the ruined threshold), while the yellow one evidences navigational aids (e.g., a chair for taking a pause). The description of the navigation steps includes directions, such as *go straight*, followed by a measure of distance expressed in meters; such information is not part of the semantic description of the environment but is computed by the components of the implementation architecture.

The description of the semantic objects (work of art, wall, etc.) includes the identification of their position in relation to the user (e.g., in front of you), computed by the implementation architecture. Finally, the visual output includes the possibility to switch to a high-contrast presentation, using a function of the toolbar, that will be shown at the end of this section.

The same information is generated for presentation through a speech interface upon user request. A dialog fragment, related to the same example illustrated in Figure 10, is in Figure 12.

The code in Figure 13 is a fragment of the X+V file; each part of the dialogue requires a speech feedback by the user in order to proceed. The main dialogue partitions are enclosed inside **vxml:field** tags. The first field informs the user about the name of the zone and its dangers; then the user may decide to have detailed information about the room or to proceed. The second **vxml:field** manages information related to the room content; a set of labels are associated

Figure 10. A scheme representing navigation inside the Venetian palace

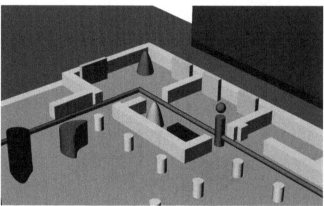

Figure 11. A snapshot of the interface for elderly people

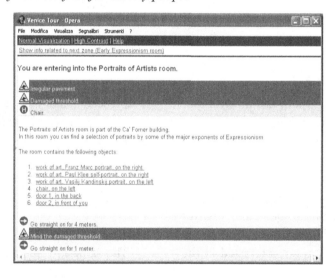

to the different information chunks for allowing the user to choose the desired item. The user may request a repetition of the relevant information, to compensate for the fixed sequentiality that characterizes the speech output. In order to drive the user attention to safety issues, the information related to dangers and aids is presented after a non-speech audio signal, e.g., a bip.

The system generates a different presentation output for non elderly users, compliant with the standard user profile. In this case the users do not need detailed navigation assistance and may be bored by the continuous reference to safety issues they can notice without difficulty. Therefore, while the presentation will keep on being multimodal and will allow the user to select the audio or the visual communication channel, navigation support will not include the information blocks related to dangers and aids advice. Figure 14 shows a sample of this alternative presentation format, referred to the same example and focused on the visual output.

Figure 12. A dialogue fragment about the palace indoor description

COMPUTER: You are entering into the Portraits of Artists room.
[*bip*] There is an irregular floor.
[*bip*] There is a damaged threshold.
…
Would you like some information about this zone? Say `yes' or `no'.

HUMAN: Yes.

COMPUTER: The Portraits of Artists room is part of the Ca' Forner building. The room hosts a selection of portraits by some of the major exponents of Expressionism. The room contains the following objects:

- one, work of art, Franz Marc portrait, on the right
- two, work of art, Paul Klee self-portrait, on the right
- three, work of art, Vasilij Kandinskij portrait, on the right

…

If you want information about an object of the list say the number of the object otherwise say `*next*'; if you want to hear again the list of the objects say `*again*'.

HUMAN: One.

COMPUTER: This work was made by Franz Marc, one of the most eminent representatives of Blaue Reiter …

Outdoor Navigation

The second part of the case study is focused on outdoor navigation. The system supports the user accessing the square, walking from the entrance of the building (Figure 15) to the boat stop on the channel. The environment and its surroundings present a number of dangers: the irregular floor of the square, the mobile floor of the boat stop and the water channel. The user can be helped by a rail for accessing the boat stop. Figure 16 illustrates a fragment of the high-contrast version of the interface, characterized by the definition of larger font sizes and bigger icons, which can be selected by a function of the interface toolbar.

CONCLUSION

In this chapter we have discussed a methodology for designing support systems helping persons with normal abilities, with limited inabilities and elderly people to receive information when visiting complex urban environments. We have also presented the architecture of a system able to provide visitors with personalized messages about places and routes. The methodology is grounded on the description of the semantic properties of the environment through an augmented virtual world mapping the real places. The help system is based on the extraction of high level properties from the virtual world layer, related to the user needs about movement in the real world.

A set of requirements for generating guided tours suitable for elderly people have been defined

Figure 13. A fragment of the X+V file defining the vocal interface

```
<vxml:form id="voice">
<vxml:field name="desc">
  <vxml:grammar src="yes_no.jsgf"/>
  <vxml:prompt> You are entering into the Portraits of Artists room.</vxml:prompt>
  <audio src="danger.wav"/>
  <vxml:prompt> There is an irregular floor.</vxml:prompt>
  <audio src="danger.wav"/>
  <vxml:prompt> There is a damaged threshold.</vxml:prompt>
  ...
  <vxml:prompt> Would you like information about this zone?<break/>
      Say "yes" or "no".
  </vxml:prompt>
  <vxml:catch event="nomatch help">
      If you would like information then say "yes". Otherwise, say "no".
  </vxml:catch>
  <vxml:filled>
     <vxml:if cond="true === desc">
       <vxml:prompt>
         The Portraits of Artists room is part of the Ca' Forner building.
         The room hosts a selection of portraits by some of the major
         exponents of Expressionism.
       </vxml:prompt>
     </vxml:if>
  </vxml:filled>
</vxml:field>

<vxml:field name="objects" xv:id="objects">
  <vxml:grammar>
     <![CDATA[#JSGF V1.0; grammar objects; public <objects> = 1|2|3|4|5|6|again|next;]]>
  </vxml:grammar>
  <vxml:prompt><break/>  The room contains the following objects:
    1, work of art, Franz Marc portrait, on the right;
    2, work of art, Paul Klee self-portrait, on the right;
    3, work of art, Vasilij Kandinskij portrait, on the right.
    If you want information about an object of the list say the number
    of the object otherwise say "next";
    if you want to hear again the list of the objects say "again".
  </vxml:prompt>
  <vxml:filled>
  <vxml:assign name="objVar" expr="objects"/>
  <vxml:if cond="'1' == objVar">
    <vxml:prompt>This work was made by Franz Marc, one of the
      most eminent representatives of Blaue Reiter ...
    </vxml:prompt>
    <vxml:clear namelist="objects"/>
  </vxml:if>
  ...
  <vxml:if cond="'again' == objVar">
    <vxml:clear namelist="objects"/>
  </vxml:if>
    <vxml:if cond="'next' == objVar">
    </vxml:if>
  </vxml:filled>
</vxml:field>
...
</vxml:form>
```

Figure 14. A snapshot of the interface for normal sighted

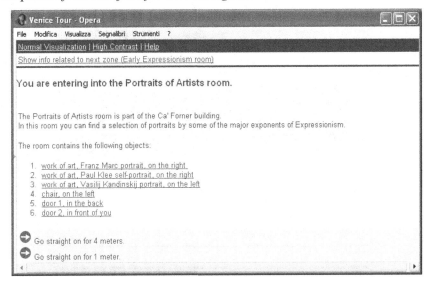

Figure 15. A scheme representing outdoors navigation

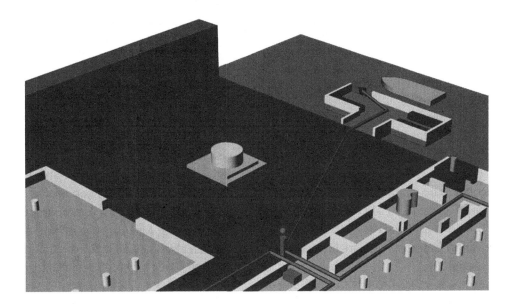

on the basis of the existing literature. Such requirements have influenced the definition of a scene-independent ontology for urban environments, which represents a step further in the state of art about ambient semantic description. The ontology includes a multilevel description of semantic objects and of semantic zones, to support users with variable grained and contextualized information. It provides also the definition of properties related to potential risks, dangers and navigation aids available in the real environment.

Figure 16. A snapshot of the high-contrast interface

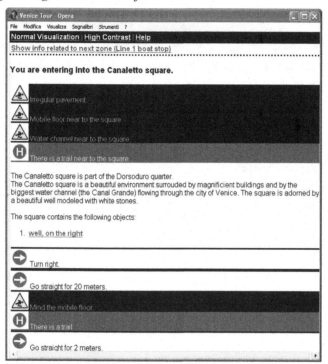

Multimodal communication, based on visual and auditory interaction, allows users to chose the best suited communication channel based on personal abilities and environment properties. We have discussed examples related to normally sighted users, users with visual deficiencies, and elderly people. The multimodal interface has been designed on the XHTML+Voice language using the Opera Multimodal Browser, which have demonstrated to be apt to support the needs of different user profiles.

The case study related to the city of Venice has demonstrated the feasibility of the semantic design on a real urban environment. The experiments are still at an early stage, showing positive comments about the system ability to adapt to different users profiles. The planned future work includes primarily the evaluation of the system in different contexts of use with different users. Following the trend in the spread of personal devices we shall also consider the possibility of porting the help system to small-sized platforms such as palmtops and smart-phones; even if they are limited in the visual output quality, which constrains the use for elder users and users with visual deficiencies, they should well cover the audio communication requirements. As more and more portable devices are equipped with GPS sensors, and new environmental sensors are emerging for supporting context-awareness, we plan also to extend the system architecture to sense the user location in real time.

ACKNOWLEDGMENT

We gratefully acknowledge Alessandro De Faveri, who contributed to the implementation of the ontology and of the prototype for extracting navigational information as part of his Master's Thesis at the Università Ca' Foscari Venezia.

REFERENCES

Ardito, C., Costabile, F., De Angelis, A., & Pittarello, F. (2007). Navigation help in 3D worlds: Some empirical evidences on use of sound. *Multimedia Tools and Applications Journal, 33*(2), 201–216.

Axelsson, J., Cross, C., Ferrans, J., McCobb, G., Raman, T., & Wilson, L. (2004). *XHTML + Voice profile*. Retrieved from http://www.voicexml.org/specs/multimodal/x+v/12/

Blattner, M., Sumikawa, D., & Greenberg, R. (1989). Earcons and icons: Their structure and common design principles. *Human-Computer Interaction, 4*(1), 11–44.

Bos, B., Lie, H.W., Lilley, C., & Jacobs, I. (1998). *Cascading style sheets, level 2 (CSS2) specification - W3C recommendation*. Retrieved from http://www.w3.org/TR/REC-CSS2/

Bowman, D., Kruijff, E., La Viola, J., & Poupyrev, I. (2000). The art and science of 3D interaction. Tutorial notes. In *Proceedings of IEEE International Virtual Reality 2000 conference*. New Brunswick, NJ.

Brewster, S., Wright, P., & Edwards, A. (1993). An evaluation of earcons for use in auditory human-computer interfaces. In *Proceedings of InterCHI'93,* Amsterdam (pp. 222–227).

Dijkstra, E.W. (1959). A note on two problems in connexion with graphs. *Numerische Mathematik, 1*, 269–271.

Gaver, W. (1989). The sonicfinder: An interface that uses auditory icons. *Human-Computer Interaction, 4*(1), 67–94.

Halabala, P. (2003). Semantic metadata creation. In *Proceedings of CESCG 2003: 7ᵗʰ Central European Seminar on Computer Graphics,* Budmerice Castle, Slovakia (pp. 15–25).

Heidegger, M. (1971). Building dwelling thinking. In *Poetry, language, thought*. New York: Harper Colophon Books.

Holland, S., Morse, D., & Gedenryd, H. (2002). AudioGPS: Spatial audio navigation with a minimal attention interface. *Personal and Ubiquitous Computing, 6*(4), 253–259.

Hub, A., Diepstraten, J., & Ertl, T. (2004). Design and development of an indoor navigation and object identification system for the blind. In *Proceedings of the 6ᵗʰ International ACM SIGACCESS Conference on Computers and Accessibility (ASSETS'04)* (pp. 147–152). Atlanta, GA: ACM Press.

Loomis, J., Golledge, R., & Klatzky, R. (2001). GPS based navigation systems for the visually impaired. In W. Barfield & T. Caudell (Eds.), *Fundamentals of wearable computers and augmented reality* (pp. 429–446). Mahwah, NJ: Lawrence Erlbaum.

Manola, F., & Miller, E. (2004). *RDF primer*. Retrieved from http://www.w3.org/TR/rdf-primer/

Mansouri, H. (2005). *Using semantic descriptions for building and querying virtual environments*. Unpublished doctoral dissertation, Vrije Universiteit, Brussel, Belgium.

May, A., Ross, T., Bayer, S., & Tarkiainen, M. (2003). Pedestrian navigation aids: Information requirements and design implications. *Personal and Ubiquitous Computing, 7*(6), 331–338.

Nack, F., & Lindsay, A. (1999a). Everything you wanted to know about MPEG-7 - part 1. *IEEE Multimedia, 6*(3), 65–77.

Nack, F., & Lindsay, A. (1999b). Everything you wanted to know about MPEG-7 - part 2. *IEEE Multimedia, 6*(4), 64–73.

Petrelli, D., Not, E., Zancanaro, M., Strapparava, C., & Stock, O. (2001). Modelling and adapting to context. *Personal and Ubiquitous Computing, 5*(1), 20–24.

Pittarello, F. (2001). *Desktop 3D interfaces for internet users: Efficiency and usability issues.*

Unpublished doctoral dissertation, Department of Computer Science, University of Bologna, Italy.

Pittarello, F. (2003). Accessing information through multimodal 3D environments: Towards universal access. *Universal Access in the Information Society Journal, 2*(2), 189–204.

Raggett, D. (2001). *Getting started with VoiceXML 2.0*. Retrieved from http://www.w3.org/Voice/Guide/

Ross, D., & Blasch, B. (2000). Wearable interfaces for orientation and wayfinding. In *Proceedings of the Fourth International ACM Conference on Assistive Technologies (ASSETS '00)* (pp. 193–200). Arlington, VA: ACM Press.

Smith, M., Welty, C., & McGuinness, D. (2004). *OWL Web Ontology Language guide - W3C recommendation*. Retrieved from http://www.w3.org/TR/owl-guide/

Web3D Consortium. (2004). *Extensible 3D (X3D) ISO/IEC 19775:2004*. Retrieved from http://www.web3d.org/x3d/specifications/ISOIEC-19775-X3DAbstractSpecification/

Yates, F. (1966). *The art of memory*. Chicago: University of Chicago Press.

Zajicek, M. (2001). Interface design for older adults. In *Proceedings of the 2001 EC/NSF Workshop on Universal Accessibility of Ubiquitous Computing* (pp. 60–65). Alcácer do Sal, Portugal: ACM Press.

KEY TERMS AND DEFINITIONS

3D Model: A representation of the geometric properties of the objects that populate a 3D environment. The representation may include different classes of objects, including concrete and aural entities, that have a position and an extension in space. The representation can be used for mapping objects existing in the real world, but it may be also derived from the creative effort of the author, without any correspondence to reality.

Ambient Semantics: The morphological and functional features of an environment, as they are perceived by humans. Such features are referred both to the physical components the environment is made of and to the spatial zones generated by such components.

Multimodality: A communication modality between humans and computer systems that takes advantage of different sensorial channels, used in parallel for the output and/or the input of an interaction process. It differs from the concept of multimediality because information exchanged between the communication actors is used for assisting the interaction process rather than for communicating content.

Navigation: The act of moving through an environment. When referred to a virtual environment the act can be associated to different paradigms, such as "walk", "fly" or "examine", corresponding to the introduction of some constraints for easing the navigation process. Navigation can be further assisted introducing more strict constraints, like predefined paths (the so called *guided tour* mode), comprehensive environment maps or timely information about the features, dangers and aids that can be found in the different locations of the environment.

Ontology: A formal description of a set of concepts related to a specified domain and of the relationships among them. Ontologies are used for representing the knowledge associated to a domain in order to reason about it, for example to derive properties or check the consistency of statements about the domain.

Resource Description Framework (RDF): A set of specifications belonging to the Semantic Web Activity of the W3C Consortium, aimed at defining the semantic properties of resources on the Web through metadata specification. RDF specifications are in the form of *subject, predicate, object* expressions and can be expressed in a variety of syntax styles to allow metadata to be exchanged between applications.

User Profile: The set of properties that describe a user features needed to provide personalized information and interaction. The user profile may contain specifications as spoken (or understood) languages, culture level, physical abilities, preferred interaction styles, interests, etc.

Virtual Reality (VR): A representation, based on an accurate description of a 3D environment, that mimics the appearance of the real world. The representation may appeal to different sensorial channels, including vision, hearing and touch, for giving the user the illusion of being part of the scene. The visual presentation of the environment is done from a subjective point of view corresponding to the user position in the scene and it is usually associated to one or more navigation paradigms (see *Navigation*).

X3D: The ISO standard for describing interactive 3D worlds for the net. The standard includes the definition of concrete objects (i.e., objects with a mass), aural objects, lights, cameras, sensor primitives and scripts. Nodes can be nested generating a complex hierarchical structure. The properties of each node are defined through a set of fields whose value changes as a response to events in the scene and can be transmitted from node to node, generating a dynamic interactive environment.

ENDNOTES

[1]   Sestiere is the Italian word denoting one of the six urban areas of Venice.
[2]   http://protege.stanford.edu/
[3]   http://www.racer-systems.com/
[4]   http://www.opera.com/products/devices/ multimodal/

Chapter XII
An Ontology Supporting an On-Board Vehicle Multimodal Interaction System

Domenico M. Pisanelli
CNR-ISTC, Italy

Claudio De Lazzari
CNR-IFC, Italy

Emilio Bugli Innocenti
Netxcalibur, Italy

Norma Zanetti
Netxcalibur, Italy

ABSTRACT

This chapter introduces a modular ontology supporting an on-board vehichle multimodal interaction system. Such a system is aimed at making road transport more efficient and effective, safer, and more environmentally friendly. The role of the ontology is that of enabling semantic interoperability in order to allow cooperation between the road infrastructure and assisting the driver to perform certain traffic related actions also increasing the infrastructure efficiency. In particular, the project is engaged in the development of applications such as intelligent speed adaptation, including static (new roads, speed limits changed by authorities), temporary (road works, schools), and dynamic (traffic responsive, road and/or weather conditions) speed limits and cooperative early information that is shared in (almost) real time among vehicles and infrastructures in critical conditions. The chapter sketches out the main issues related to ontologies and emphasize the relevance of top-level (i.e., domain independent or foundational) ontologies in order to integrate different domain models. We define five domain ontologies for the purpose of the system: Vehicle Security, Road and Traffic Security, Meteorological, Users' Profiles, and Travel. The last one reports concepts concerning a given travel (departure, destination, vehicle, road) and imports concepts from the other ones. We emphasize the role of ontologies in enabling semantic interoperabilty in such an intensive knowledge-processing contexts.

INTRODUCTION

According to the study made up by the European Commission about the future common transport policy, more than 40 thousand people die on Europe roads each year and, even if the number of fatalities is decreasing, the number of accidents with injuries (about 1,7 million) is still increasing. The costs of these accidents and fatalities in European Union are estimated to be 160 billion € per year, i.e. about the 2% of the Community's Gross National Product.

Another key factor for EU Transport is also mobility. Mobility sector corresponds to more than 10% of gross domestic product (GDP) and employs more than 10 million people. The automobiles are the biggest contributor to mobility (80% of travel calculated in passenger/km is currently by car). Since the demand for transport services continuously, increase, related problems, such as road traffic congestion, will significantly increase by 2010. The effects of road traffic congestion are analysed in the above cited paper and their costs are calculated around the 0.5% of Community GDP; however, these costs are calculated to increase by 142% to reach 80 billion € a year, approximately 1% of Community GDP.

During the last decade, the European Commission together with automotive industries was involved in improving road safety both focusing on drivers (accident prevention and injuries reduction) and on vehicles (passive safety improving and support to active safety systems research). The above cited paper defines some recommendations with the goal to decrease by 50% the road fatalities by 2010 reducing both the number of death and injuries and the number of accidents.

The main strong contribution to this objective, along with infrastructure improvements and enforcement of current safety measures, is doubtless the use of new technologies. The idea is to exploit the benefits of information and communications technologies for safer and more efficient road transports and mobility through Intelligent Co-operative Systems.

Intelligent Co-operative Systems that are based on vehicle-to-vehicle and vehicle-to-infrastructure communications hold the promise of great improvements both in the efficiency of the transport systems and in the safety of road users. They increase the "time horizon", the quality and the reliability of information available to the driver and they offer increased information about the vehicles, their location and road conditions to road operators and infrastructure owners.

Intelligent Co-operative Systems will build and expand on the functionality of the autonomous and stand-alone in-vehicle and infrastructured-based systems, such as Intelligent Vehicle Safety Systems (eSafety systems), including Advanced Driver Assistance Systems (ADAS), traffic control and management systems and motorway management systems (Blythe and Curtis, 2004). The benefits of the Intelligent Co-operative Systems stem from the increased information that is available of the vehicle and its environment. The same set of information can be used for extending the functionality of the in-vehicle safety systems and through vehicle-to-infrastructure communications for more efficient traffic control and management. It is therefore very important to establish a common language, in terms of ontology and vocabulary, to ensure the exchange of information between the world of on-board systems and the world of infrastructure systems and to build context-based eSafety services. In such a context, the ONTOTRAFFIC project is proposing to develop a situation-aware middleware which aims at translating specific contexts into logical situations to enable research on road transport co-operative systems to make one step further.

Intelligent Co-operative Systems are seen all over the world as the next big challenge in automotive electronics and ITS. Activities have been started in USA, Japan and Europe. Europe is well placed in the research on autonomous and stand alone systems that have been developed in EU-funded programs over a decade and have benefited from the support of political initiatives such as eSafety. Now Europe is aiming at taking a lead in the research, standardisation and market introduction of Intelligent Co-operative Systems through several actions listed below, whose objectives will be considered as the context framework for the ONTOTRAFFIC project.

ADVANCED DRIVER ASSISTANCE SYSTEMS

A first step in the direction of Intelligent Co-operative Systems is represented by in-vehicle systems like Advanced Driver Assistance Systems (ADAS), which are able to help in managing several driving functionalities on the basis of data recorded on board.

The term ADAS includes several systems, which have been developed by vehicle manufacturers also with the support of different R&D EU programmes (see for example: www.ist-cover.eu, www.ist-highway.org).

The design and implementation of such systems is aiming at incorporating a wide range of driver support and control functions, in order to providing more acceptable control methods, safety and performance benefits and more relaxing travel experience. Vehicle control assistance includes devices to support and/or control lane position,

overtaking manoeuvres, speed, braking in traffic streams, following. Other "non-critical" driver assistance devices regard intelligent headlamps, intelligent windscreen wipers and intelligent indicators, while technology to monitor driver condition and support appropriate behaviour is on the way.

Vehicle Data

The body of AMI-C work includes a variety of documents describing the very wide range of data types that either currently or eventually will exist in the vehicle. Most of these are not of use to the public sector applications that the Vehicle Infrastructure Integration (VII) architecture is intended to support. There are two types of data that can be used: periodic data and event data. Periodic data includes information that is constantly changing, such as speed and position. Event data only occurs occasionally and is over a very short period, an example of which would be the activation of an antilock braking system. These periodic and event data would be combined to create a probe data message.

The data elements identified as being needed to support the priority vehicle-infrastructure co-operative applications are reported in Annex A.

These vehicle data categories are not yet definitive, nor is it known which model year will incorporate each of the appropriate sensors and systems. However, it is understood from various Original Equipment Manufacturers (OEMs) that the plans for new features do include some subset of the data elements on the list. The probe message is being designed to accommodate new variables within the vehicle as technological improvements take place.

Each vehicle will be equipped with a GPS receiver. To meet the safety requirements, the vehicle must know where it is and have the ability to send and receive this data between itself and the road infrastructure. The GPS unit within the vehicle is likely to not require a differential unit.

It is the intent that the GPS correction signal will be sent over the Dedicated Short Range Communications (DSRC) connection thus simplifying the device within the vehicle. The HMI systems of the vehicle are under development by a wide range of institutions and auto manufacturers. Audible, visual and tactile interfaces are all being investigated.

Adaptive Cruise Control (ACC)

ACC attempts to maintain desired speed (set by the driver) whilst keeping a minimum time gap between the vehicles, typically measured by radar. Operational speed is about 40-50 km/h and the functionalities of the system vary (e.g. engine braking or engine and active braking) according to the control algorithm for managing inter-vehicular separation.

The driver can override the system at any time by activating the brake or the accelerator pedal and can switch it on and off at different stages of the journey.

All ACC systems are fully autonomous and the driver has control of vehicle steering all the time.

An extension of the ACC system is given by Stop&Go, which operates down to zero km/h. The Urban Drive Control Project has extended Stop&Go to involve communication between roadside beacons, to enhance traffic flows through signalised intersections.

Intelligent Speed Adaptation

Intelligent Speed Adaptation (ISA) is a system which can be used to help drivers to control their speeds to prevail speed limits. When equipped with an ISA, the system will respond if the speed limit is exceeded. The responses can take various forms, for example by providing visual or audio warning/advice, some physical resistance for further acceleration, or by making it impossible to drive faster than the speed limit. Three levels are then introduced:

- **Warning:** A visual or audio message is given when speed limit is exceeded.
- **Haptic throttle:** This is also called "active accelerator", i.e. when the driver attempts to exceed the speed limit, additional counterforce is introduced on the accelerator. The driver is informed via a haptic feedback in the accelerator pedal and can override the system by pressing the pedal further.
- **Mandatory:** The vehicle is restricted to speed limit, without possibility of overriding.

As can be seen, these three types of ISA will provide drivers with different levels of assistance to prevent them from exceeding speed limits.

THE ROLE OF ONTOLOGIES

This chapter presents the ontologies defined in the context of the ONTOTRAFFIC project. They are aimed at allowing semantic interoperability for the projects' applications which implements intelligent cooperative systems able to make road transport more efficient and effective, safer and more environmentally friendly.

We sketch out main issues related to ontologies and emphasize the relevance of top-level (i.e. domain independent or foundational) ontologies in order to integrate different domain models (see for example Pisanelli et al 2007 for an application of such principles in the field of medicine).

We define five domain ontologies for the purpose of the ONTOTRAFFIC project: Vehicle Security, Road and Traffic Security, Meteorological, Users' Profiles and Travel. The last one reports concepts concerning a given travel (departure, destination, vehicle, road) and imports concepts from the other four.

The main focus of ONTOTRAFFIC is on the cooperation between the infrastructure and vehicles in order to support or enable the driver and/or the vehicle to perform certain traffic related actions and increase the infrastructure efficiency. In particular, the project is engaged in the development of applications such as intelligent speed adaptation, including static (new roads, speed limits changed by authorities), temporary (road works, schools) and dynamic (traffic responsive, road and/or weather conditions) speed limits and cooperative early information that is shared in (almost) real time among vehicles and infrastructures in critical conditions.

Therefore, ontologies play a relevant role in enabling semantic interoperabilty in such an intensive knowledge-processing contexts.

WHAT IS AN ONTOLOGY?

There is no general agreement on the definition of what is an ontology. Some admit informal descriptions and hierarchies, only aimed at organizing some uses of natural language; others require that an ontology be a theory, i.e. a formal vocabulary with axioms defined on such vocabulary, possibly with the help of some axiom schema, as in description logics.

Ontology as a branch of philosophy is the science of what is, of the kinds and structures of objects, properties, events, processes and relations in every area of reality. 'Ontology' is often used by philosophers as a synonym for 'metaphysics' (literally: 'what comes after the Physics'), a term which was used by early students of Aristotle to refer to what Aristotle himself called 'first philosophy'. The term 'ontology' (or ontologia) was itself coined in 1613, independently, by two philosophers, Rudolf Göckel (Goclenius), in his Lexicon philosophicum and Jacob Lorhard (Lorhardus), in his Theatrum philosophicum. The first occurrence in English recorded by the OED appears in Bailey's dictionary of 1721,

which defines ontology as 'an Account of being in the Abstract'.

The methods of philosophical ontology are the methods of philosophy in general. They include the development of theories of wider or narrower scope and the testing and refinement of such theories by measuring them up, either against difficult counterexamples or against the results of science.

Apart from its definition in a philosophical context - where it refers to the subject of existence - ontology in information science is "a partial specification of a conceptualization", as stated by Guarino, whereas Sowa (2000) proposed the following definition influenced by Leibniz:

The subject of ontology is the study of the categories of things that exist or may exist in some domain. The product of such a study, called an ontology, is a catalogue of the types of things that are assumed to exist in a domain of interest D from the perspective of a person who uses a language L for the purpose of talking about D.

In a pragmatic perspective, an ontology is a formal model which specifies the conceptualization (i.e. the intended meaning) of a lexical item as it is used in a certain domain.

Ontologies are nowadays considered as the basic infrastructure for achieving semantic interoperability. This hinges on the possibility to use shared vocabularies for describing resource content and capabilities, whose semantics is described in a (reasonably) unambiguous and machine-processable form. Describing this semantics, i.e. what is sometimes called the intended meaning of vocabulary terms, is exactly the job ontologies do for semantic interoperability.

What kinds of ontologies do we need? This is still an open issue. In most practical applications, ontologies appear as simple taxonomic structures of primitive or composite terms together with associated definitions. These are the so-called lightweight ontologies, used to represent semantic relationships among terms in order to facilitate content-based access to the (Web) data produced by a given community. In this case, the intended meaning of primitive terms is more or less known in advance by the members of such community. Hence, in this case, the role of ontologies is more that of supporting terminological services (inferences based on relationships among terms – usually just taxonomic relationships) rather than explaining or defining their intended meaning.

ADOPTED DESIGN METHODOLOGY

In order to build a domain ontology, we need an explicit representation of the so-called ontological commitments about the meaning of terms, in order to remove terminological and conceptual ambiguities (Johansson, 1989; Smith, 1995; Guarino and Welty, 2000). A rigorous logical axiomatisation seems to be unavoidable in this case, as it accounts not only for the relationships between terms, but – most importantly – for the formal structure of the domain to be represented. This allows one to use axiomatic ontologies not only to facilitate meaning negotiation among agents, but also to clarify and model the negotiation process itself, and in general the structure of interaction.

Axiomatic ontologies come in different forms and can have different levels of generality, but a special relevance is enjoyed by the so-called foundational ontologies, which address very general domains.

We see the role and nature of foundational ontologies as complementary to that of lightweight ontologies: the latter can be built semi-automatically, e.g. by exploiting machine learning techniques; the former require more painful human labour, which can gain immense benefit from the results and methodologies of disciplines such as philosophy, linguistics, and cognitive science.

These ontologies are the essential "glue" used to integrate different domain ontologies.

A fundamental ontological choice deals with the notion of change. What does it mean for an entity to change? This question raises the problem of variation in time and the related issue of the identity of the objects of experience. In general a 3D option claims that objects are: (a) extended in a three-dimensional space;(b) wholly present at each instant of their life; (c) changing entities, in the sense that at different times they can instantiate different properties (indeed, one could say When I was out in the balcony my hands were colder than now). On the contrary a four-dimensional perspective states that objects are: (a) space-time worms; (b) only partially present at each instant; (c) changing entities, in the sense that at different phases they can have different properties (My hands during the time spent out in the balcony, were colder than now).

The DOLCE (Descriptive Ontology for Linguistic and Cognitive Engineering) foundational ontology contains a description of the basic kinds of entities and relationships that are assumed to exist in some domain, such as process, object, time, part, location, representation, etc. (Masolo et al, 2003). DOLCE is a 3D cognitively-oriented ontology, based on primitive space and time, 3-dimensional intuition (objects are disjoint from processes), distinction between physical and intentional objects, etc. DOLCE is a descriptive ontology, because it helps categorizing an already formed conceptualization: it does not state how things are, but how they can be represented according to some existing knowledge.

Basic elements of DOLCE are *endurants*, *perdurants* and *qualities*.

- Classically, *endurants* (also called continuants) are characterized as entities that are 'in-time', they are 'wholly' present (all their proper parts are present) at any time of their existence.
- On the other hand, *perdurants* (also called occurrents) are entities that 'happen in time',

they extend in time by accumulating different 'temporal parts', so that, at any time t at which they exist, only their temporal parts at t are present. For example, the book you are holding now can be considered an endurant because (now) it is wholly present, while "your reading of this book" is a perdurant because, your "reading" of the previous section is not present now. Note that it is possible to distinguish between 'ordinary objects' (like the book) and 'events or process' (like 'the reading of the book') even when the domain contains perdurants only. In this latter case, one relies on properties that lie outside spatio-temporal aspects. Indeed, one can assume that four-dimensional entities do not need to have different spatio-temporal locations. A person and its life (both taken to be 4D entities) share the same space-time region but differ on other properties since, for instance, color, race, beliefs and the like make sense for person only. Endurants and perdurants can be characterized in a different way. Something is an endurant if (i) it exists at more than one moment and (ii) its parts can be determined only relatively to something else (for instance time). In other words, the distinction is based on the different nature of the parthood relation: endurants need a time-indexed parthood, while perdurants do not. Indeed, a statement like "this keyboard is part of my computer" is incomplete unless you specify a particular time, while "my youth is part of my life" does not require such a specification.

- *Qualities* can be seen as the basic entities we can perceive or measure: shapes, colors, sizes, sounds, smells, as well as weights, lengths, electrical charges.

In order to implement our ontologies, we adopted the OWL language. It is the most recent development in standard ontology languages from the World Wide Web Consortium (W3C). OWL makes it possible to describe concepts but it also provides new facilities. It has a richer set of operators - e.g. and, or and negation. It is based on a different logical model which makes it possible for concepts to be defined as well as described. Complex concepts can therefore be built up in definitions out of simpler concepts. Furthermore, the logical model allows the use of a reasoner which can check whether or not all of the statements and definitions in the ontology are mutually consistent and can also recognise which concepts fit under which definitions. The reasoner can therefore help to maintain the hierarchy correctly.

To create and edit our ontologies, we chose the Protégé tool, which is a free, open source ontology editor and knowledge-base framework. Protégé ontologies can be exported into a variety of formats including RDF(S), OWL, and XML Schema.

Protégé is based on Java, is extensible, and provides a plug-and-play environment that makes it a flexible base for rapid prototyping and application development. It is supported by a strong community of developers and academic, government and corporate users, who are using this tool for knowledge solutions in areas as diverse as biomedicine, intelligence gathering, and corporate modeling (see: protege.stanford.edu)..

At its core, Protégé implements a rich set of knowledge-modeling structures and actions that support the creation, visualization, and manipulation of ontologies in various representation formats. The tool can be customized to provide domain-friendly support for creating knowledge models and entering data. Further, Protégé can be extended by way of a plug-in architecture and a Java-based Application Programming Interface (API) for building knowledge-based tools and applications.

We used the Protégé-OWL editor which enables users to:

- Load and save OWL and RDF ontologies.
- Edit and visualize classes, properties and SWRL rules.
- Define logical class characteristics as OWL expressions.
- Execute reasoners such as description logic classifiers.
- Edit OWL individuals for Semantic Web markup.

Protégé-OWL's flexible architecture makes it easy to configure and extend the tool. Protégé-OWL is tightly integrated with Jena and has an open-source Java API for the development of custom-tailored user interface components or arbitrary Semantic Web services.

In addition to providing an API that facilitates programmatic exploration and editing of OWL ontologies, Protégé-OWL features a reasoning API, which can be used to access an external DIG compliant reasoner, thereby enabling inferences to be made about classes and individuals in an ontology, such as computing the inferred superclasses of a class, determining whether or not a class is consistent (a class is inconsistent if

it cannot possibly have any instances), deciding whether or not one class is subsumed by another, etc. Some of the popular Description Logic reasoners that are available are listed below:

- RACER
- FaCT
- FaCT++
- Pellet

THE ON-BOARD SYSTEM AND ITS ONTOLOGIES

The aim of the on-board system is on the cooperation between the infrastructure and vehicles in order to support or enable the driver and/or the vehicle to perform certain traffic related actions and increase the infrastructure efficiency. In particular, the project is engaged in the development of applications such as intelligent speed adaptation, including static (new roads, speed limits changed by authorities), temporary (road works, schools) and dynamic (traffic responsive, road and/or weather conditions) speed limits and cooperative early information that is shared in (almost)

Figure 1. The architecture of the system

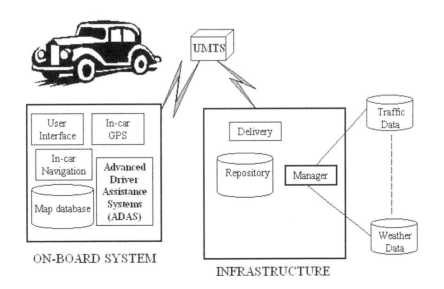

real time among vehicles and infrastructures in critical conditions.

In order to reach such goals, we designed the architecture depicted in figure 1 which shows the on-board system that is connected to the road infrastructure via a GPRS communication system.

To better understand what we mean by cooperation between the infrastructure and the vehicle driver, let us consider the following scenarios:

It is a cloudy day in a winter late afternoon and the temperature is close to zero. The driver is shortsighted and he doesn't like driving with cold temperature. The car's speed is 120 Km/h with the windscreen wiper on. The infrastructure information manager informs the user that a short radius bend climbing down is expected in 4 Km. The on-board system alerts the user about the possibility of finding snow and iced road and that, given the current speed and the weather condition, there is high level of danger.

A user is driving a camper and is travelling on highway viaduct at 100 Km/h. The infrastructure

knows that in that area wind speed is about 60 Km/h. Therefore the on-board system suggests to reduce speed to 70 Km/h.

In order to implement such cooperation we need to collect information related to the user (his/her profile, e.g.: shortsighted, expert, novice ...) and the vehicle itself, both static (e.g.: kind of vehicle, position) and dynamic (e.g.: speed). Road topology has to be represented too, together with metereological entities.

Therefore, we defined five domain ontologies for the purpose of the on-board system. Their scope is depicted in Figure 2. Four of them refer to the different aspects related to driving security:

- The Vehicle Security ontology (**V**)
- The Road and Traffic Security ontology, based on GDF and DATEX standards (**RT**)
- The Meteorological ontology (**M**)
- The Users' Profiles ontology (**U**)

A fifth ontology: The Travel ontology reports entities concerning a given travel (departure,

Figure 2. The scope of the implemented ontologies

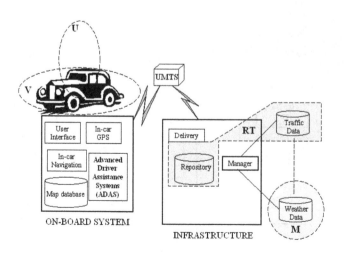

destination, vehicle, road) and imports concepts from the other four ones.

The ontologies are focused on driving safety issues. With respect to other ontologies, they have the following advanced features:

- They are focused on safety issues
- They are based on a top-level domain-independent ontology
- They are richer in axiomatization of concepts (i.e. the formal definitions of concepts is more detailed)
- Their taxonomy is more complex and richer in details.

The Vehicle Security Ontology

This ontology follows the basic distinctions defined by the Dolce top-level, i.e. classes are divided into: *endurants*, *perdurants* and *qualities* (Masolo et al, 2003). Endurant are like objects and perdurants accounts for processes (Hawley, 2001).

The scope of the ontology is not to represent all concepts related to vehicles, but to take into account those concepts that are relevant from the security point of view.

There are four classes of endurants:

- Vehicle (the vehicle itself)
- Vehicle_component
- Vehicle_liquid
- Vehicle_lubricant

Vehicles considered are: cars, motorcycles and trucks (the naming policy is to have name of classes referenced as singular).

The most complex class is " vehicle_component", where all components critical for the vehicle security are represented.

"Vehicle_quality" accounts for "vehicle_data". Data relevant for security purposes are (Figure 3):

- Position
- Acceleration
- Tyre_pressure
- Speed
- Engine_RPM
- Temperature

Figure 3. Vehicle quality

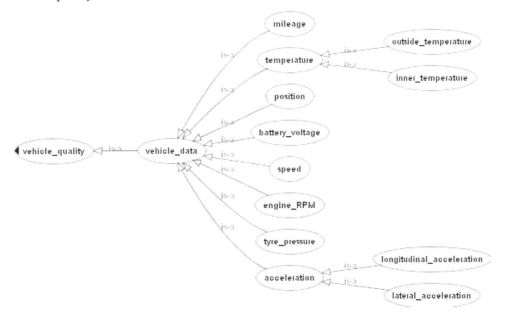

- Battery_voltage
- Mileage

The Road and Traffic Security Ontology

In this ontology too, the basic distinctions defined by the Dolce top-level are followed, i.e. classes are divided into: endurants, perdurants and qualities. Endurant are like objects and perdurants accounts for processes.

Road and traffic concepts related to security issues are represented.

There are four classes of endurants:

- road_typology (i.e. mountain, extra-urban, urban, highway)
- road_element (morphological, permanent and accessory, impairment)
- traffic information
- vehicle_lubricant

Road qualities refer to feature and condition, both of permanent and accessory items.

The Meteorological Ontology

This ontology accounts for the main meteorological phenomena which may affect driving and are related to security issues.

Figure 4. Travel related concepts

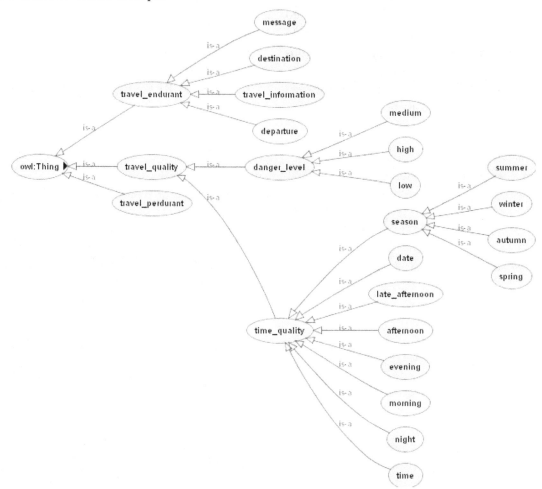

Figure 5. The travel ontology in Protégé

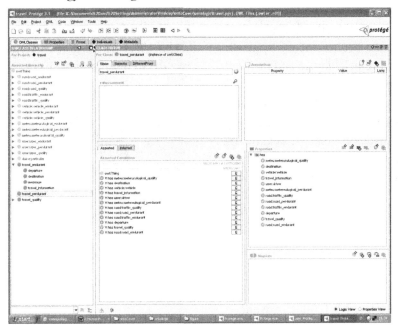

According to the DOLCE paradigm, "rain" itself—for instance—is considered a process (i.e. a perdurant), whereas "raindrop" is and endurant. Relevant qualities are "temperature", wind_speed", "humidity" and so on.

The User Ontology

This ontology represents issues related to users, both drivers and passengers.

According to the DOLCE paradigm, we consider "endurants" people or objects, "perdurants" are processes (e.g. "driving") and qualities account for entities such as user profiles ("novice", "expert"), physical handicaps, uncongenial condition and so on.

The Travel Ontology

This ontology represents issues concerning a particular travel, i.e. an entity having a departure and a destination and related to a vehicle, a user, a given set of roads and meteorological conditions.

Therefore this ontology needs to import concepts from the four ontologies already defined: "road_security&traffic", "vehicle_security", "user" and "meteo".

Figure 4 shows the basic taxonomy, whereas Figure 5 reports a screenshot in Protégé [6] of the ontology, showing also the imported ones.

CONCLUSION

The semantic representation of vehicle and traffic related data is an exciting vision that maximizes the performance of advanced driver assistance systems. Initial results of our work have shown that: ontologies appear to be an excellent approach for integrating information in a computer-interpretable format.

The interconnection of information processing systems, in order to make optimal use of vehicle and traffic data, will be the basis for improved performances and higher efficiency in future advanced driver assistance systems.

In this chapter we have shown how such interconnection may benefit from the design of proper ontologies aimed at allowing semantic interoperability among heterogeneous systems: namely the on-board vehicle device and the road infrastructure system.

As for future work, we are planning to integrate our ontologies into state-of-the-art working advanced driver assistance systems, also in co-operation with the automotive industry. To such an end, it will be crucial to implement solutions capable to process semantic information in real time.

REFERENCES

Blythe, P.T., & Curtis, A.M. (2004). Advanced driver assistance systems: Gimmick or reality? *11ᵗʰ World Congress on ITS*, Nagoya, Japan.

Guarino, N., & Welty, C. (2000). A formal ontology of properties. In R. Dieng, & O. Corby (Eds.), *Knowledge engineering and knowledge management: Methods, models, and tools. 12ᵗʰ International Conference, EKAW2000*. France: Springer Verlag.

Hawley, K. (2001). *How things persist*. Oxford, UK: Clarendon Press.

Johansson, I. (1989). *Ontological investigations. An inquiry into the categories of nature, man, and society*. London: Routledge.

Masolo, C., Borgo, S., Gangemi, A., Guarino, N., Oltramari, A., & Schneider, L. (2003). *The wonder Web library of foundational ontologies. Wonder Web deliverable 18*. Retrieved from http://wonderweb.semanticweb.org

Pisanelli, D.M., Battaglia, M., & De Lazzari, C. (2007). ROME: A Reference Ontology in Medicine. In H. Fujita, & D.M. Pisanelli (Eds.), *New trends in software methodologies, tools, and techniques*. Amsterdam: IOS Press.

Smith, B. (1995). Formal ontology, commonsense, and cognitive science. *International Journal of Human Computer Studies, 43*(5/6).

Sowa, J. (2000). Knowledge representation: Logical, philosophical, and computational foundations. Pacific Grove, CA: Brooks Cole Publishing Co.

KEY TERMS AND DEFINITIONS

Advanced Driver Assistance Systems: Devices used to support drivers and enhancing driving security (e.g. lane position controllers, speed controllers)

Multimodal Interaction System: A system which provides the user with multiple modes of interfacing with a software.

Ontology: A catalog of things that exist or may exist in some domain, together with the definition of formal relationships among these things.

OWL: Ontology Web Language, RDF based formalism to represent the ontologies and share them on the Web.

Chapter XIII
Designing Pervasive and Multimodal Interactive Systems:
An Approach Built on the Field

Barbara R. Barricelli
Università degli Studi di Milano, Italy

Andrea Marcante
Università degli Studi di Milano, Italy

Piero Mussio
Università degli Studi di Milano, Italy

Loredana Parasiliti Provenza
Università degli Studi di Milano, Italy

Marco Padula
*Istituto per le Tecnologie della Costruzione –
Consiglio Nazionale delle Ricerche, Italy*

Paolo L. Scala
*Istituto per le Tecnologie della Costruzione –
Consiglio Nazionale delle Ricerche, Italy*

ABSTRACT

This chapter presents a participatory and evolutionary methodology for pervasive and multimodal interactive systems design that is being developed capitalizing experiences from different target applicative domains. The methodology supports collaborative and evolutionary design of an interactive system; it considers usability problems that users face during the interaction; it is based on a network of software environments, conceived in analogy with the workshop of an artisan, each one customizable to and tailorable by users belonging to different cultures. The requirements, design issues, and a proposal of the architecture of the software environment will be discussed highlighting their pervasiveness, multimodality, and interactivity, the ability offered to users to coordinate desktop and mobile devices, and to access a shared knowledge base. The architecture has been defined and revised exploiting experience gained from different case studies that will be illustrated. The novelty of the approach is that the methodology sprang from empirical experience got by handling problems faced on the field. In the chapter, specific aspects of the presented approach are discussed in relation to the state of the art.

INTRODUCTION

The experiences gained from the field in the development of pervasive and multimodal interactive systems leaded the authors to the definition of a pragmatical approach to virtual systems design that considers the various phenomena characterizing the Human-Computer Interaction (HCI) process (Costabile et al., in press; Costabile, Fogli, Mussio, & Piccinno, 2006): the communication gap between designers and users, tool grain, user diversity, implicit information, tacit knowledge and co-evolution of systems and users. The approach adopts the Software Shaping Workshop (SSW) methodology introduced by Costabile, Fogli, Mussio, and Piccinno (2007). According to the SSW methodology, the design process is carried out by an interdisciplinary design team that includes different stakeholders such as software engineers, HCI experts, and domain experts (Fogli, Marcante, Mussio, & Parasiliti Provenza, 2007). The methodology provides the design team with virtual environments that permit to study, prototype and develop the environment that will be adopted by end users. The virtual environments are tailorable, customizable and adaptive to the context of activity and to community's culture and language. The SSW methodology offers an evolutionary technique for system prototyping in which users can customize and evolve their own workshop. SSWs are virtual interactive environments, which are organized in a network, able to coordinate desktop and mobile devices to allow users to work on a shared knowledge base. The network architecture will be illustrated on the base of the experience gained from different case studies; its accessibility, adaptability, device adaptivity and localization to the specific culture and skills of users will be particularly focused. Localization is a crucial issue because people who use interactive systems for supporting their daily work have different culture, skills, languages, physical abilities and roles and they perform their activities in different contexts. The implemented multimodal interactive environment permits experts to face the problems related to their activity, to update and manage a shared knowledge base and to adapt and evolve their virtual work environment by adding tools becoming unwitting programmer. The novelty of the approach lies in the fact that it is based on practical experience gained on the operative field; this maintains a conceptual connection to real problems and emphasizes the need to support the different actors in their daily work considering the working context, the activities to be performed and the user's culture.

The chapter is organized into five sections. The first section concerns related works. The SSW methodology section presents the design approach, introducing some considerations about the phenomena affecting the HCI process. The third section deals with the system architecture. The fourth section illustrates the annotation primitive operator. The fifth section describes the experiences gained on the field by illustrating several case studies: different scenarios are introduced in which experts have to afford complex problems (e.g. diagnoses, territorial portal organization, tourist guides organization, yard management) in a collaborative asynchronous way and using different devices (e.g. desktop PC, PDAs) to access their SSW from everywhere and in different working contexts. The implemented multimodal interactive environment permits experts to face the problems related to their activity, to update and manage a shared knowledge base and to adapt and evolve their virtual work environment by adding tools becoming unwitting programmer.

RELATED WORKS

The SSW methodology has been influenced by the work performed in EUD-Net, the network of Excellence on End-User Development (EUD), funded by the European Commission during 2002 and 2003 (http://giove.cnuce.cnr.it/eud-net.htm). The term EUD indicates the active participation of end users in the software development process: this can range from providing information about requirements, use cases, and tasks, including participatory design, to activities such as customization, tailoring, and co-evolution. A system acceptable by its users should have a gentle slope of complexity: this means that it should avoid big steps in complexity and keep a reasonable trade-off between ease-of-use and functional complexity. For example, systems might offer end users different levels of complexity in performing EUD activities, going from simply setting parameters, to integrating existing components, up to extending the system by developing new components (Myers, Smith, & Horn, 1992; Wulf and Golombek, 2001). The SSW methodology encompasses all the three levels of tailoring (customization, integration, and extension) proposed by Mørch (1997). It also takes into consideration the results in Mackay (1991) and in Nardi (1993), where empirical studies are reported on the activities end users are willing to perform. The software technology has advanced so that we can build tools that end users can adopt to design systems by interacting with icons and menus in graphical microworlds. Several researchers working on EUD have capitalized on this, and described technologies for component-based design environments, libraries of patterns, and templates (e.g. Mørch and Mehandjiev, 2000). Several design environments have been proposed that allow users to design by instructing the machine to learn by examples (Lieberman, 2001). From this perspective, system workshops devoted to domain experts permit the creation of programs just by visually composing virtual entities selected from repositories; an example will be discussed in relation to the case study in the mechanical engineering field.

Karasti (2001) explores the integration of work practice and system design and insists on increasing the sensitivity of system design towards everyday work practice. She characterizes work practice by describing the complex social organization, technological mediation, knowledge and

meaning as social constructions, and discussing the intertwined nature of the unfolding activities in which all these aspects are connected. Two different bodies of knowledge are explored in Karasti (2001) to make work practice visible and intelligible for system design: knowledge formalized from actual work activity or owned by practitioners and information considered relevant for requirements analysis in system design.

Research with similar interests in work practice has been carried out and presented in studies that intertwine work practice and system design, e.g. Greenbaum and Kyng (1991), Chaiklin and Lave (1993), Button (1993), Engeström and Middleton (1996) and Resnick et al. (1997), and specifically in the field of Computer Supported Cooperative Work (CSCW), e.g. Suchman et al., 1999; Suchman and Trigg, 1991; Goodwin and Goodwin, 1997; Hughes et al., 1992.

The SSW methodology refers to a model of the interaction and co-evolution processes that identifies the causes of usability difficulties affecting interactive systems; it is used to derive design procedures, which permit the implementation of systems in which these difficulties are almost eliminated; it capitalizes on the seminal work by Hutchins, Hollan and Norman (1986) which focuses on the human side of the interaction process and identifies the existence of semantic and articulatory distances in evaluation and execution as the primary sources of usability difficulties.

Moreover, interaction processes are determined by a cognitive system (the human) and a computing system (the computer), which in turn form a unique system that is called "syndetic system" in Barnard, May, Duke and Duce (2000), i.e., a system composed by binding sub-systems of a different nature. To properly describe the interaction process, the computing system must also be modeled highlighting the problems arising on the computer side, i.e., capturing and interpreting the human actions. This stance is clearly posed in the model proposed in Abowd and Beale (1991) and is also adopted by our model.

Rapid prototyping is extensively used in Computer-Aided Design (CAD) and refers to a class of technologies that can automatically construct physical models from CAD data. In the software engineering field, rapid prototyping offers a mean to explore the essential features of a proposed system (Hasselbring, 2000; Luqi, 1992) promoting early experimentation with alternative design choices and allowing engineers to pursue different solutions without any efficiency concerns (Budde, Kuhlenkamp, Mathiassen, & Zullighoven, 1984). Today, while there have been advances in the tools used, user interface prototyping remains the most effective way to gather requirements, communicate concepts between developers and users and evaluate usability in a cost-effective manner. Rapid prototyping is useful in software engineering to show the developed prototypes to the customers, but professional software tools are required to develop such prototypes, which are not easily operated by end users. Each software environment developed according to the SSW methodology actually adopts rapid prototyping techniques, but it is designed and developed to be suitable for end users who are professional people, but not experts in computer science. In Penner and Steinmetz (2002) and Stary (2000), task-based and user-centered development approaches are presented to support the automation of user interface design. The TADEUS project (Stary, 2000) proposes a development methodology starting from a business intelligence model to generate user interfaces or portals by integrating a model-driven, task-based, user-oriented, and object-driven life cycle.

Traditional participatory design approaches exploit techniques derived from social theories (collaborative construction of mock-ups, cooperative prototyping, game-like design session) that support communication and collaboration within an interdisciplinary team (Bodker, Gonnbaek, & Kyng, 1993). In Greenbaum and Kyng (1991), the Future Workshop technique is discussed: it foresees group meetings run by at least two facilitators and having the aim of analyzing common problematic situations, generate visions about the future and discuss how to realize these visions. In this chapter, the term "workshop" is used with the different meaning provided in (Merriam-Webster online, 2008): "a small establishment where manufacturing or handicrafts are carried". "Software Shaping Workshops" refer to software environments that enable users to "shape" virtual tools and data.

Similarly, Cooperative Prototyping is presented (Bodker and Gronbaek, 1991) as an activity where users and designers cooperate. However, prototypes just represent an interactive digital evolution of paper-based mock-ups: real systems are programmed and all modifications require large programming effort that are postponed and made by designers after each session.

The approach presented in this chapter foresees the participation of all the stakeholders in the development of the final system, each one according to their own view, through the use of SSWs which are considered a new technique supporting participatory design. In particular, the use of prototypes permits the participation of end users in the creation of software tools, that they can tailor, customize, and program accordino to participatory programming (Letondal and Mackay, 2004) which exploits traditional techniques of participatory design (in situ observations, interviews, workshops) to allow representatives of end users and software engineers to collaborate in developing and tailoring software tools.

In conclusion, the SSWs methodology simplifies the so-called "translation problem" (DePaula 2004) among different stakeholders, because it allows their participation in the design process to interpret and experiment the workshop being designed from her/his own point of view.

SSW approach is consistent with the concept of meta-design, which is explored in Fischer, Giaccardi, Ye, Sutcliffe, & Mehandjiev, 2004. Meta-design is a process in which users are able to act as designers and contribute to the co-evolution of the system. Meta-design must support humans in shaping their socio-technical environments and empowering the users in adapting their tools to their needs (Fischer et al., 2004). In this perspective, meta-design underlines a novel vision of interactive systems that is adopted by the SSW methodology.

Fischer et al. (2001) propose SER (Seeding, Evolutionary growth, Reseeding), a process model to design systems as seeds, with a subsequent evolutionary growth, followed by a reseeding phase; it is adopted to support meta-design and for the development and evolution of the so-called DODEs (Domain Oriented Design Environments), "software systems that support design activities within particular domains and that are built specifically to evolve" (Fischer et al., 2001) which have been evolved toward meta-design in (Fischer et al., 2004). SER is the base of the work described by Carmien, Dawe, Fischer, Gorman, Kintsch, & Sullivan (2005), where metadesigners (software engineers) develop a system for caregivers who implement scripts supporting people with cognitive disabilities. As in SSW approach, particular attention is paid to the users involved in the domain, and customized environments are provided to them. Co-evolution may also be sustained since tools for automatic feedback and remote observations are used to notify problems to the design team. The SSW approach has some similarities with this work, but it emphasizes the need of providing personalized environments to all stakeholders, in terms of language, notation, layout, and interaction possibilities.

Finally, other works focus on experience-centered domains, requiring six to 12 years of intensive practice before practitioners achieve the most effective levels of skill (Hayes, 1985). In these domains (e.g. medical diagnosis, chess, professional design, planning tasks, etc.), one of the main challenges in decision support is that users, with different levels of domain experience, have often very different needs; for example, a system designed to satisfy domain experts'

specific needs may frustrate novices and vice versa. The SSW methodology emphasizes the need to develop different software environments for end users working in the same domain with different roles.

DAISY (Design Aid for Intelligent Support System), a design methodology for building decision support systems in complex, experience-centered domains (Brodie and Hayes, 2002), provides a technique for identifying the specialized needs of end users within a specific range of domain experience, therefore, it supports the development of customized systems.

DIGBE (Dynamic Interaction Generation for Building Environments) is a system that creates end-user interfaces adapted to the multiple end users with different roles, that collaborate to the management of a building control system (Penner and Steinmetz, 2002). Unlike SSWs, software environments created using DIGBE are adaptive systems that "automatically improve their organization and presentation by learning from visitor access patterns" (Perkowitz and Etzioni, 2000).

SSW approach deals with the problem of digital document management and makes use of the annotation as primitive operator to handle digital documents. Other interesting approaches face these issues.

Annotea is a project in the W3C context (Annotea Project, 2008) proposing a metadata based infrastructure, which allows cooperators to annotate web documents, to share them, to store them in a common repository and retrieve them. Annotea provides protocols for distributed annotation, based on RDF (Resource Description Framework), Xpointer and HTTP, which were adopted in the implementation of Amaya, a browser and editor with a plug-in to manage the annotations, and Annozilla, a Mozilla plug-in for annotating web pages.

Annotations can be visualized in a document context view or in a topic hierarchy view, organized in threads (Koivunen and Swick, 2003). Annotea focuses on the format of annotation and

Table 1. The works related to SSW methodology

TADEUS project (Stary, 2000)	TADEUS is a development methodology conceived from a business intelligence model to generate user interfaces or portals by integrating a model-driven, task-based, user-oriented, and object-driven life cycle.
Cooperative Prototyping (Bodker and Gronbaek, 1991)	In Cooperative Prototyping, prototyping is viewed as a cooperative activity between users and designers.
SER (Fischer et al. 2001)	SER (Seeding, Evolutionary growth, Reseeding) is a process model to design systems as seeds, with a subsequent evolutionary growth, followed by a reseeding phase.
Socio-technical environment for supporting people with cognitive disabilities (Carmien, Dawe, Fischer, Gorman, Kintsch, & Sullivan 2005)	According to this approach, a system is created by metadesigners (software engineers) to be used by caregivers who design and create scripts supporting people with cognitive disabilities.
DAISY (Brodie and Hayes, 2002)	DAISY (Design Aid for Intelligent Support System) is a design methodology for building decision support systems in complex, experience-centered domains.
DIGBE (Perkowitz and Etzioni, 2000)	DIGBE (Dynamic Interaction Generation for Building Environments) is a system that creates end-user interfaces adapted to the multiple end users with different roles that collaborate to the management of a building control system.
Annotea project (Annotea Project, 2008)	Annotea is a metadata based annotation infrastructure for performing and sharing annotations on web documents
MADCOW (Bottoni et al., 2004)	MADCOW (Multimedia Annotation of Digital Content Over the Web) is an environment developed for the annotation of any type of multimedia component of a Web page.
Placeless documents system (Dourish et al. 2000)	Placeless proposes a new paradigm for document management based on document properties, rather than on document organization.
Unifying Reference Framework (Calvary et al. 2003)	The Unifying Reference Framework serves as a reference for classifying user interfaces supporting multiple targets, or multiple contexts of use.

provides a protocol for any annotation performed on a document described according to W3C technologies.

MADCOW (Multimedia Annotation of Digital Content Over the Web) (Bottoni et al., 2004) is an environment developed for annotate any component of a web page. It provides users with a taxonomy of annotation types to help them to classify every annotation. MADCOW has a client-server architecture: the client is a plug-in for a standard web browser and the servers manage repositories of annotations which can be accessed by any client.

In Dourish et al. (2000) a new paradigm for document management is proposed based on document properties, rather than on document organization. Properties (including user categorizations, keywords, links to related items) are the primary, uniform means for organizing, grouping,

managing, controlling and retrieving documents; they are meaningful to users and enable to express system activities, such as sharing criteria, replication management and versioning; therefore, they enable the provision of document-based services on a property infrastructure. An experimental prototype, the Placeless documents system has been developed to experiment the proposed paradigm; it is based on three core features: uniform interaction, user-specific properties and active properties. With the large diffusion of mobile devices such as PDAs, mobile telephones and wireless networks, pervasive systems are becoming the next computing paradigm in which infrastructure and services are seamlessly available anywhere, anytime, and in any format. Pervasive systems are a manifestation of the increasing role played by mobility; Dourish, Anderson, & Nafus (2007) propose an original view of technology and mobility, focusing diversity and agency as central aspects of a socially-responsible approach to mobile computing. This work also connects current research in HCI, ubiquitous computing and human and social geography suggesting a new foundation for design.

In conclusion, the work of Calvary et al. (2003), which can be classified in the field of context-aware computing, aims at describing a framework for classifying user interfaces supporting multiple targets, or multiple contexts of use. Three facets of the context of use are focused: the end user, the computing platform exploited by the user to carry out his/her interactive tasks and the physical environment where the user is working.

THE SSW METHODOLOGY

The Software Shaping Workshop (SSW) methodology (Costabile, Fogli, Mussio and Piccino, 2007) allows to design and develop virtual environments that (a) support the activities of users acting a specific role in their community and having a specific application domain; (b) are tailorable, customizable and adaptive to the working context; (c) support the exchange of information among users belonging to different communities; (d) are multimodal and interactive. The methodology is evolutionary and participatory: the final user can customize and evolve his/her own virtual environment and he/she is involved in each step of the system development. The star life cycle model of the product (Hartson & Hix, 1989) is referred, that covers the entire life of the product: each prototype must be evaluated before its development.

Costabile et al. (2006) identify the major phenomena affecting Human-Computer Interaction process:

- **User diversity:** The non-uniformity of users, in terms of culture, language, skills,

physical and cognitive abilities, needs and preferences have to be considered;
- **Tool grain:** Systems or tools tend to push users toward behaviours that are usually not familiar to them;
- **Communication gap between designers and users:** Designers and users present different cultural backgrounds and due to this fact, they adopt two different approaches to abstraction;
- **Implicit information:** The relevant part of the information spread by a system is embedded in its visual organization, e.g. the use of italics font style to emphasize a concept, and its shape materialization, e.g. icons that may be significant for a specific community but not for another one;
- **Tacit knowledge:** The implicit information, described above, may be interpreted correctly only by the users possessing the knowledge related to that specific application domain;
- **Co-evolution of systems and users:** Users change in result to the use of a system and thereby they use the system in new ways (Nielsen, 1993) forcing the designers to adapt the system to the evolved users and their needs.

All these phenomena influence our design and development approach: users belonging to different communities usually are accustomed to different language, culture, skills, abilities (physical and cognitive), preferences and role. In a working context, the communities' members cooperate performing different tasks and exchanging documents that are part of a shared knowledge base. The correct comprehension of a document depends on the user's application domain and on his/her language and specific dialect (Fogli et al., 2005); therefore, tools are needed, which are customized to user's needs in order to allow communication and comprehension

Figure 1. General SSW network

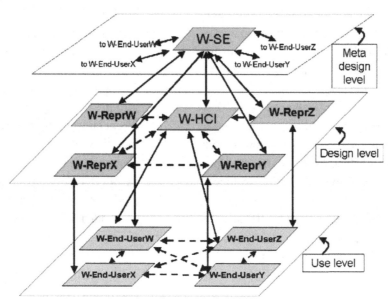

among the different communities they belong to. The systems can be customized to the culture and skills of the target community of practitioners and tailored, customized and adapted to the context of activity.

The SSW methodology considers the development of two different kinds of workshops: the application workshop and the system workshop. The application workshop is a virtual environment customized to each member of the community, according to his/her performing task and role, to his/her abilities (physical and cognitive) and capabilities, and to his/her culture and language. The system workshop is a virtual environment that permits to customize the application workshop to users' preferences, characteristics and needs. As defined in Costabile et al. (2007), we consider meta-design as "a design paradigm that includes end users as active members of the design team and provides all the stakeholders in the team with suitable languages and tools to foster their personal and common reasoning about the development of interactive software systems that support end users' work" (Costabile et al., 2007, p. 50).

With this idea in mind, workshops are organized into a three level network (see Figure 1), in which each member of the design team (software engineers, HCI experts and domain experts) collaborate to design and develop virtual environments customized and tailored for their activity domain and performing tasks:

- At the top, meta-design level, software engineers use a system workshop to create other system workshops in order to permit other software engineers, HCI experts and domain experts to collaborate to design and development of application workshops;
- At the middle, design level, designers collaborate, using their own system workshops, for designing and implementing application workshops;
- At the bottom, use level, domain experts tailor and use application workshops in order to perform their task.

Each expert is a stakeholder that evaluates the system considering it from his/her perspective biased by his/her different cultural backgrounds, experiences and standpoints of problems. Thus, a communication gap arises among the component of the design team: software engineers, HCI and domain experts adopt different approaches to abstraction and follow different reasoning strategies to model, perform and document the tasks to be carried out in a given application domain; furthermore, each expert expresses and describes such tasks adopting his/her own language and jargon (Fogli et al., 2007).

Communication among the application and the system workshops is supported by an annotation tool. At the use level, end users exchange data related to their current task in order to cooperate to achieve a common goal. At the design level, HCI experts and domain experts exchange programs specifying the workshops they are going to develop. HCI and domain experts also communicate with software engineers when it is necessary to develop new tools for supporting their activities. The lower levels are connected to the upper ones by communication paths, allowing end users and designers to interact with other workshops annotating their problems and communicating them to all the experts working in the same SSW network (Costabile et al., 2007).

In the SSW methodology, the principle of symmetry of ignorance is accepted: the software engineers are owners of the technology, the HCI experts are owners of the usability methods and the domain experts are owners of the domain problems. A participatory approach to development is adopted permitting the members of the design team to cooperate: the clash of different cultures that normally determines communication gaps among the design team members is avoided thanks to the localization of each system workshop that supports the stakeholders' activity. That permits the workshops to represent spaces and places that serve as boundary objects where different cultures can meet (Fischer, 2000). As described in Fogli et al. (2007), the SSW methodology is multi-faced because it permits each stakeholder involved in the design process to cope with problems of the

system observing them from the perspective of their own culture.

SYSTEMS' ARCHITECTURE

The SSW methodology allows to design virtual environments in analogy with artisan workshops, i.e. small working environment where artisans such as blacksmiths and joiners manipulate raw materials in order to manufacture their artefacts. Artisans can adapt the environment to their needs by making available all and only the tools they need in the different specific situations. By analogy, the methodology permits to design virtual environments as virtual workshops allowing the user to access sets of virtual tools having a familiar shape and behaviour. Such workshops consent users to perform their tasks and to adapt their virtual working environment using a high-level visual language, manipulating objects in a realistic manner. End users may act a dual role: the role of consumers when they use the tools offered by the system and they match their needs or they may act the role of designers when they need to adapt the tools to their necessities. Two personalization activities have been recognized in Costabile, Fogli, Lanzilotti, Mussio and Piccinno (2005): customization, which is carried out by the design team generating application workshops for a specific users community and tailorization, which is the activity performed by the end users adapting an application workshop to particular activities and work contexts.

A family of multimodal interactive systems, BANCO (Browsing Adaptive Network for Changing user Operativity), has been developed to allow the implementation of the hierarchy of SSWs and their adaptation. It is based on XML (eXtensible Markup Language) and it supports collaborative activities, among users belonging to different communities and cultures, which allow the exchange of multimedial documents and annotations, generate a shared knowledge base and permit to reach a common goal. We propose a technique of interactive systems development based on AJAX (Asynchronous JavaScript and XML). BANCO and AJAX introduce an intermediary engine between client and server (Garrett, 2005). The systems development follows the lines of the semantic Web approach (Berners-Lee, Hendler, & Lassila, 2001), but it stresses the interest on humans accessing, exchanging and understanding documents, not only on machines (Naeve, 2005). The AJAX Web application model involves several technologies: XHTML and CSS for presentation, Document Object Model (DOM) for dynamic display and interaction, XML and XSLT for data interchange and manipulation, XMLHttpRequest for asynchronous data retrieval and JavaScript. The JavaScript AJAX engine is loaded as the session starts; it handles the user interface materialization and the communication with the server. Instead of an HTTP request, a JavaScript call to the AJAX engine is executed as a consequence of user's actions. If data stored on

the server are needed, the engine sends the corresponding requests asynchronously using XML, with no interference with user's interaction.

The architecture of the interactive systems BANCO is shown in Figure 2.

As the session starts, the JavaScript BANCO engine is loaded with the BANCO specification, regarding materialization, localization and content.

The user interface is materialized by a viewer activated by a Web browser; in response to user's actions, JavaScript calls to the BANCO engine are executed. If server-side stored data are needed, the BANCO engine sends a request to the Web server that hosts the BANCO server-side application and the exchange of XML data between the BANCO engine and the Web server do not interfere with user's interaction.

In this paper, we have been coherent with the equation between interacting systems and e-documents presented in (Bottoni et al., in press). They have to be moulded to allow all users, even

Figure 2. High level BANCO architecture

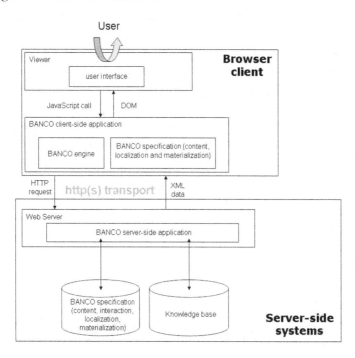

not computer experts, to perceive, understand and handle them in a useful way; e-documents react to user interactions by activating computations and presenting results; they exists as the result of the activity of a program and of the interaction with the user; they include functionalities for the user to operate on them; their functionalities are determined by user needs in specific contexts; in general, they should guarantee and enhance some basic user activities such as annotation, editing and indexing of documents.

BANCO includes a set of document for content, interaction, localization, and materialization specification written in the following languages:

- IM2L (Interaction Multimodal Markup Language), an XML-based markup language for abstract and internationalized specification of interactive systems content, where for content we mean the set of the functional components and its logical structure. IM2L supports annotation and recursive clonation as primitive operators. Aims of IM2L are supporting the participatory design and the innovation: users are seen as knowledge producers thanks to the annotation primitive operator. IM2L permits the recursive annotation, the clonation of some structure (active and passive components) and it is internationalized, allowing a localization concerning order, position, colour, shape, text and sound. In the IM2L-based interactive system specification, we made a distinction between (1) content and organization, (2) localization components, (3) materialization components and (4) interaction components;

- LML (Localization Markup Language) an XML-based markup language for the specification of the localization properties, e.g. properties that characterize geometry, topology, colour representation, shapes and text, considering a particular culture and person with certain physical abilities;

- SVG (Scalable Vector Graphics) the W3C standard that offers a WIMP interaction and direct manipulation in Web applications (Carrara, Fresta, & Mussio, 2001). It is an XML language for describing two-dimensional graphics. SVG allows for three types of graphic objects: vector graphic shapes, images, and text. Furthermore, SVG documents can be interactive and dynamic;

- JavaScript the object-oriented scripting language commonly used in Web development. JavaScript has been standardized by the ECMA with the name ECMAScript and complies an ISO standard. The language is interpreted by the Web browser and the JavaScript code is executed by the client, balancing workload distribution between client and server;

- PHP (PHP Hypertext Preprocessor) is an interpreted scripting language released under open source licence, to realize dynamic Web pages. It is usually adopted for development of server-side Web applications but it could also be used for development of standalone applications and for line-command scripting.

The interaction process of the BANCO Interactive Systems, depicted in Figure 3, involves a set of documents:

- SVG Starter is an SVG document that specifies the documents that the SVG-compliant browser has to interpret in order to generate the whole system;

- System Initial State Specification is the IM2L document that specifies the static part of content and organization of the system initial state;

- Components Initial State Specification is a set of IM2L documents, each one specifying a type of virtual entity that can be instantiated during the interaction process to modify the state of the system;

Figure 3. BANCO interaction process

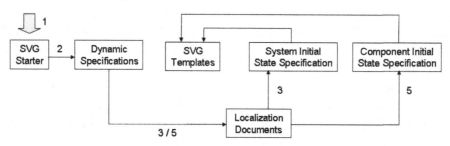

- Localization Documents define how to localize the static part of the system;
- SVG Templates are SVG documents, each one describing the physical materialization of a type of virtual entity composing the system;
- Dynamics Specifications is a set of ECMAScript documents that (a) define how to create the static part of the system and (b) specify the reactions of the system and of the single component to user's actions.

These documents are used at different times during the instantiation process:

- At initialization time, when the user logs to the system, the SVG starter is loaded within the browser. The starter is processed by the XML parser, which creates its DOM (Document Object Model) tree, which is analyzed by an initializing (ECMAScript) function.
- At localization time, the System Initial State Specification, the Localization Document corresponding to the user profile and the SVG templates are loaded in the Web browser and processed by the XML parser. The parser creates the DOM trees for the IM2L and localization documents. These DOM trees are an input for the transformer (an ECMAScript interpreter). The transformer fires the XML parser, having as inputs the SVG templates that correspond to the virtual

entities in the DOM tree of the IM2L document. Each SVG template is processed by the XML parser.

- At interaction time, if user action requires the instantiation of a new component, the Component Initial State Specification document is loaded and processed by the XML parser. The XML parser adds a node in the SVG DOM tree localizing the IM2L Component Initial State Specification document by mean of the localization document DOM tree. The DOM tree of the localization document remains on the client side during the whole session.

The process of BANCO initial state instantiation is described in Figure 4. The initial state creation steps are indicated by ordinal numbers, while the steps involved by events, which cause the modification of the DOM tree, are identified by roman numbers. The process may be described as follows:

- The SVG starter is loaded within the browser and is processed by the XML parser;
- The XML parser generates the DOM (Document Object Model) tree of the SVG starter;
- The DOM tree of the SVG starter is analyzed by the initializator, which loads the IM2L and the LML documents;
- The IM2L and the LML documents are

loaded in the Web browser and are processed by the XML parser. The XML parser creates the DOM trees for the IM2L and the LML documents;

- The DOM trees of the IM2L and LML documents become an input for the transformer (an ECMAScript interpreter) ;
- The transformer calls the XML parser, having as input the set of SVG templates, and it uses the SVG templates that correspond to the virtual entities in the DOM tree of the IM2L document;
- Each SVG template is processed by the XML parser;
- The XML processor produces a DOM tree fragment for each SVG template;
- Each DOM tree fragment of an SVG template is instantiated by the transformer using the information included in the DOM trees of the IM2L and LML documents;
- The transformer embeds each DOM tree fragment of the SVG templates into the full SVG DOM tree;
- The full SVG DOM tree becomes the input of the SVG viewer that materializes on the screen the initial state of the interactive environment.

BANCO systems are interactive, pervasive and multimodal: they permit to adopt different devices and to involve different human senses. These multimodal and pervasive aspects are needed for enable users to access and manage data "on the field", in a specific context of use. Multimodal systems can overcome the problems related to the different users' skills and contexts. The implementation of different interaction modalities increases the usability of the system and allows to take advantage of the tacit knowledge that a suited customization can make to emerge (Fogli, Marcante, Mussio, Oliveri, & Padula, 2006).

Figure 4. BANCO materialization process

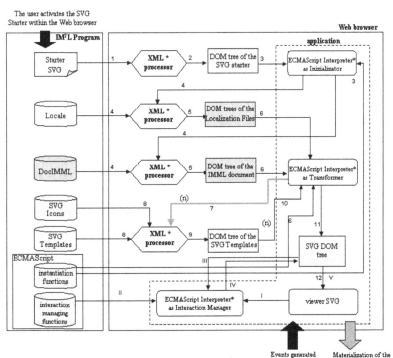

255

ANNOTATION: A PRIMITIVE OPERATOR

We consider annotation a fundamental tool for two-way exchange of ideas in a collaborative work environment and therefore it is defined as a primitive operator in BANCO. It enables all stakeholders in the SSW network to communicate when operating in a same or in different levels, e.g. using application and system workshops. The annotations appended to documents enrich the existing knowledge base, allow users to act both as data consumers by browsing the documents and the existing related annotations, and as data producers, by creating new annotations and consequently enriching the shared knowledge base.

Before the computer-based systems birth and their adoption as groupware for supporting the cooperative work, documents were paper-based: they were interpreted by humans by applying their cognitive criteria and recognizing sets of elementary signs as functional or perceptual units, called characteristic structures (cs) (Fogli, Fresta, Marcante, Mussio, & Padula, 2005). Users associate a particular meaning to each cs producing characteristic patterns (cp). The css can be combined in order to produce complex css (e.g. letters into words, icons into plant maps, etc.) each one associated with a meaning defining complex cps. A document can be seen as a complex cs that becomes a complex cp after its interpretation. Annotation can be seen as a note attached to a part of a document as a comment or an explanation: the annotated portion of document is called the base of the annotation and is made evident by a visual identifier. After the establishment of computer-based systems in support of groups of people involved in common goals and tasks (Ellis, Gibbs, & Rein, 1991), documents and annotations become electronic, i.e. virtual entities that are the results of interpretation of data and programs. In WIMP (Window, Icon, Menu, and Pointer) systems, users access and annotate e-documents and e-annotations thanks to the computational process that generates some physical representations perceivable by them, as functional or perceptual units, i.e. the css.

THE EXPERIENCES GAINED ON THE FIELD

In this section we illustrate the exploratory experiences we grew to satisfy the requests stemmed from different communities of users. Such experiences leaded us to design and develop prototypes according to the SSW methodology previously illustrated.

Basically, we assume a generic scenario in which two users need to access a shared knowledge base in order to perform different tasks. They need to retrieve data stored on the Web using a workshop materialized in their browsers. Programs and data used to materialize workshops and the retrieved documents are stored in a distributed and shared archive. Such a scenario describes a cooperative work environment (Grudin, 1994; Thomas, Bostrom, & Gouge, 2007), in which workers may cooperate to build a shared knowledge base by performing their tasks interacting with other users (Wulf, 1989). The shared knowledge bases, considered in the scenarios described in this chapter, consist in multimedia and multimodal documents accessible and annotable by system's users.

Specific observations and experiences in different target domains leaded us to design and develop prototypes according to the SSW methodology previously illustrated.

A specific BANCO prototype was developed for the building sector. This sector is characterized by the interplay of different users having specific roles, experiences, and skills. This specific scenario considers two principal work places: the firm technical office and the building yard. In the office all documents (electronic and paper-based) are stored in a repository, which represents the knowledge base of the firm: the operator interacts with an archive of documents using a desktop PC on a large-sized display. On the yard, the foreman uses an interactive system running on a mobile device with a small display in which the same document visualized by the operator is represented. Both the operator and the foreman report their activities by annotating the documents on the screen:

- The foreman loads on the mobile device a resized version of the e-document he/she needs (i.e. the technical drawings of a building) according to display specifications;
- The foreman annotates the changes of drawings on the device and can also express his/her system usage difficulties;
- Successively, he/she sends the annotations to the technical office using a wireless connection or a wired one;
- The transferred data are stored in a temporary archive located in the technical office and an operator updates the original e-documents and saves them into the repository. The annotations regarding the usage difficulties of the foreman are stored in a different archive at disposal of HCI experts.

Different modalities for user interaction have been designed: to support the foreman activity in the yard, to support operators in their updating activity and to allow the building surveyors, the building designers and the building administrators to access and manage the data stored in the repository.

The application workshop used on the yard is called building workshop: it is developed for PDA (Personal Digital Assistant) use and provides a set of tools to manage and annotate the e-documents. The foreman can enter in annotation mode by selecting the annotation operator. In this mode, the foreman can perform an annotation on the environment pointing out the problems he/she encounters. The annotations are communicated to the members of the design team in order to support the evaluation of the system. In this way the foreman performs an evolutionary co-evaluation

because (1) he/she is directly involved in the system evaluation and (2) because the system can be evolved in consequence of the collaborative evaluation.

We now introduce another case study with a scenario drawn from an initial analysis of physicians collaborating to achieve a diagnosis (Costabile, Fogli, Fresta, Mussio, & Piccinno, 2002).

We developed some features in order to suport processing, indexing, and retrieval of large collections of e-documents. Indexing tools and metadata specifications lead to efficient information retrieval: we integrated an indexing tool for metadata extraction, and a controlled vocabulary that comprises domain contextual terms. We considered three types of indexes:

- Automatically extracted metadata, such as annotation's creation date and user's identifier;
- Automatically extracted terms from annotation's text comparing it with the controlled vocabulary;
- User's defined keywords assigned to annotations he/she creates.

In this scenario medical doctors need to analyze Magnetic Resonance Images (MRIs) accessed through an interactive system (see Figure 5(a)). The doctor opens the images menu on the right bar and selects the image he/she needs (the MRI of Maria Rossi). The system reacts materializing the image to be operated, along with the tools necessary to work on it in an area called working bench. The buttons on the toolbar over the image are associated with the operations that the medical doctor can perform; in the illustrated case, the doctor selects the tool for creating annotations (clicking on button A in the toolbar) and clicks on the area of interest in the image to annotate it. The system reacts by showing a visual link (the tool with the pencil icon) on the interested area and presenting an annotation manager allowing the user to add annotations. The doctor writes the title and the content of the note in the annotation bench. The user clicks on the I button to assign keywords to the annotation he/she creates. The controlled vocabulary management is possible by clicking on G button. Finally, he/she clicks on 'Chiudi Nota' to close the annotation and save it.

Nowadays, users of information systems working in the same domain and needing to perform similar tasks, often belong to different cultural communities or subcommunities. Hence, according to different cultures and systems of signs, the shared knowledge base should be made accessible and usable to them. The design of BANCO systems copes with these diversities: interactive systems must guarantee access and management of data adaptable to the different users' cultures, languages, and writing systems. These diversities should be considered during design, development, and evolution of systems for supporting users activities. Adaptation to cultural profiles requires to consider different languages, different writing systems, different ways to see the topological and geometrical interface organization, and the different sets of symbols and colours that characterize the system interface through which users and system exchange data. The cultural and linguistic adaptation of a software system needs two processes, the internationalization and the localization process (Esselink, 2000). Internationalization is the process to make the software independent from any cultural specific

information: an internationalized software system can manage different languages and cultural conventions without the need to redesign the system. Localization is the adaptation of the system to the linguistic and cultural conventions of a specific country. Internationalization requires to make the code completely independent from any culture specific information: the information is stored in external data files and loaded at runtime. In literature and experienced cases (Esselink, 2000; Savourel, 2001; Marcus & Baumgartner, 2004), three main software internationalization methods are considered. The first one consists in duplicating the software in many localized copies: this is the simplest method but also the most expensive in terms of resources. In the second method, the software is made neutral creating a unique localization file containing the items' definition (icons, texts, colours and object shape descriptions) defining each locale in the same document: this method is preferred to the previous one, but it is not efficient because the dimention of the localization file depends on the number of languages considered. The third method makes the software neutral by creating a localization file for each locale considered: this is the best method and also the one used for internationalizing the prototypes presented in this chapter. To develop the localization abilities of the workshops, we have contextualized the generic scenario previously

Figure 5. The interactive system localized for (a) the Italian culture and for (b) the Hebrew culture

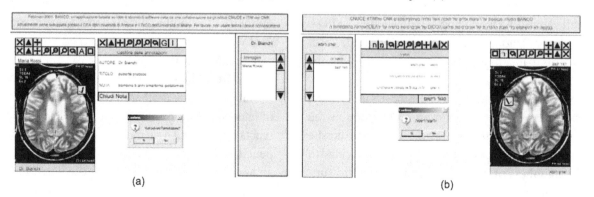

(a)   (b)

described into a specific one in which two medical doctors, one belonging to the Italian culture and the other to the Hebrew one, need to analyse the same MRI (see Figure 5). They access the document through two different workshops localized according to their culture. Each workshop permits a view of the archived data and the use of specialized tools for data analysis. Since Italian and Hebrew languages have different alphabets and different writing systems, a different spatial organization of the interface is required. The writing direction deeply affects the way information is usually placed on the screen: Italian writing system follows the Right-to-Left (RTL) direction, while the Hebrew one follows the LTR (Left-to-Right) direction. In the LTR languages, i.e. western languages, the most important information are usually placed in the top-left area and less important information are placed in the bottom-right area. Therefore, for converting an interface from LTR to RTL reading/writing direction it is necessary to reverse it in a mirror-like manner (Portanieri & Amara, 1996).

In order to experience how culture affects colours meaning, we considered a tourism scenario in which Italian and Japanese users may access information attached on geographical maps using localized workshops. In order to express the emotions they felt visiting tourist attraction, they can choose the best representative emoti-

con among those present in the system toolbar. However, in different cultures the same emotion is showed using different facial expressions, stylized using different graphical signs, i.e. using different shapes, and different colours, because the meaning assigned to a colour depends strictly on the contextual culture. Therefore, emoticons have to be localized choosing colours and shapes according to the different cultures (O'Hagan & Ashworth, 2002). In Figure 6 we illustrate the associations we assume between emotions, cultures and colours.

While colours are univocally associated to the Italian and to the Japanese culture, Japanese users represent faces graphically in two different manners depending on gender: their culture does not allow to women to show their teeth, so it is needed to draw female mouths closed.

We also considered localization per user's role: users may access the system, browse the geographical maps and annotate them using interfaces personalized to their profile. We consider two types of user role: generic and expert. The generic users can retrieve tourist information and annotate maps, the expert users may create and update the system knowledge base according to their competences.

For this case study we extended the BANCO architecture on the server side; we included the eXist Open Source Native XML Database (eXist,

Figure 6. Shape and colours localization in the emoticons case (JPm stands for Japanese man; JPw stands for Japanese woman)

Content	West colours	West shape	JPm colours	JPw colours	JPm shape	JPw shape
Not recommended	red		red			
Disappointing	grey		blue			
Interesting	lightcoral		lightcoral			
Enjoyable	yellow		green			

2008) for documents, annotations and indexes storage, to assures interoperability and platform independence.

In this case study we considered the design of a multimodal system in order to overcoming the hurdles that arise in manipulating and using e-documents in different contexts and with different interaction modes: auditory interaction has, therefore, been enabled. A text-to-speech tool leads the user during his/her work, by converting written annotations to synthesized speech. VoiceXML has been adopted, the W3C standard for text-to-speech conversion (Voice eXtensible Markup Language, 2008) supported by the X+V technology (XHTML+Voice Profile, 2008). The auditory modality permits a user exploring the annotations on an electronic document, in order to fast know how many annotations are in the document and which the content is: the user can see, choose, read, and hear the annotation of interest. In this new BANCO interaction process the SVG Starter component has been substituted by a more complex component, composed by S&B X+V, a X+V document specifying the documents to be interpreted by the VoiceXML-compliant browser to generate the vocal materialization of a particular virtual entity of the system, and the SVG starter.

CONCLUSION

In this chapter, a design methodology (SSW) for pervasive and multimodal interactive systems describing its application has been presented. An architecture for distributed workshops based on SSW methodology allows users to access and annotate a shared knowledge base, acting both as data producer and as data consumer. The novelty of the approach is that the proposed methodology comes from empirical experience gained by handling problems faced on the field. Concrete applications have been presented to discuss the main suggestions we got from real case experi-

ences and to discuss their main aspects; therefore, the discussion has covered topics as design of systems adaptable to users' needs considering their language, writing system, culture and role and, furthermore, annotation, indexing, and information retrieval.

REFERENCES

Abowd, G. D., & Beale, R. (1991). Users, systems, and interfaces: A unifying framework for interaction. In D. Diaper & N. Hammon (Eds.), *Proc. HCI: People and Comput. VI* (pp. 73–87). Cambridge University Press.

Annotea Project. (2008). Retrieved on May 8, 2008, from http://www.w3.org/2001/Annotea

Barnard, P., May, J., Duke, D., & Duce, D. (2000). Systems, interactions, and macrotheory. *ACM Trans. Comput.-Hum. Interact., 7*(2), 222–262.

Berners-Lee, T., Hendler, J., & Lassila, O. (2001, May). The Semantic Web - a new form of Web content that is meaningful to computers will unleash a revolution of new possibilities. *Scientific American*.

Bodker, S., & Gronbaek, K. (1991). Design in action: From prototyping by demonstration to cooperative prototyping. In Greenbaum & Kying (Eds.), *Design at work: Cooperative design of computer systems* (pp. 197-218). Hillsdale, NJ: Lawrence Erlbaum Associates.

Bodker, S., Gronnbaek, K., & Kyng, M. (1993). Cooperative design: Techniques and experiences from the Scandinavian scene. In Schuler & Namioka (Eds.), *Participatory design - principles and practices* (pp. 157-175). Hillsdale, NJ: Lawrence Erlbaum Associates.

Bottoni, P., Civica, R., Levialdi, S., Orso, L., Panizzi, E., & Trinchese, R. (2004). MADCOW: A multimedia digital annotation system. In M.F. Costabile (Ed.), *Proceedings of the Working*

Conference on Advanced Visual Interfaces (pp. 55-62). ACM Press.

Bottoni, P., Ferri, F., Grifoni, P., Mussio, P., Marcante, A., Padula, M., & Reggiori, A. (in press). E-Document management in situated interactivity: The WIL approach. *Universal Access in the Information Society. International Journal.*

Brodie, C.B., & Hayes, C.C. (2002). DAISY: A decision support design methodology for complex, experience-centered domains. *IEEE Trans. on Systems, Man, and Cybernetics - Part A, 32*(1), 50-71.

Budde, R., Kuhlenkamp, K., Mathiassen, L., & Zullighoven, H. (Eds.) (1984). Approaches to prototyping. New York: Springer-Verlag.

Button, G. (Ed.) (1993). Technology in working order: Studies of work, interaction, and technology. New York: Routledge.

Calvary, G., Coutaz, J., Thevenin, D., Limbourg, Q., Bouillon, L., Vanderdonckt, J. (2003). A unifying reference framework for multi-target user interfaces. *Interacting with Computers, 15*(3), 289-308.

Carmien, S., Dawe, M., Fischer, G., Gorman, A., Kintsch, A., & Sullivan, J.F. (2005). Sociotechnical environments supporting people with cognitive disabilities using public transportation. *ACM Transactions on Computer Human Interaction, 12*(2), 233-262.

Carrara, P., Fresta, G., & Mussio, P. (2001). SVG: More than a markup language for vector graphics. In *Proceedings of EuroWeb 2001 - The Web in Public Administration* (pp. 245-257).

Chaiklin, S., & Lave, J. (Eds.) (1993). Understanding practice: Perspectives on activity and context. Cambridge, MA: Cambridge University Press.

Costabile, M.F., Fogli, D., Fresta, G., Mussio, P., & Piccinno, P. (2002). Computer environments for improving end-user accessibility. In *Proceedings*

of 7ᵗʰ ERCIM Workshop User Interfaces For All, Paris, 187-198.

Costabile, M.F., Fogli, D., Lanzilotti, R., Mussio, P., & Piccinno, A. (2005). Supporting work practice through end user development environments (Tech. Rep. 01.10.2005). Bari, Italy: Università degli Studi di Bari, Dipartimento di Informatica.

Costabile, M.F., Fogli, D., Marcante, A., Mussio, P., Parasiliti Provenza, L., & Piccinno, A. (in press). Designing customized and tailorable visual interactive systems. *International Journal of Software Engineering and Knowledge Engineering.*

Costabile, M.F., Fogli, D., Mussio, P., & Piccinno, A. (2006). End-user development: The software shaping workshop approach. In H. Lieberman, F. Paternò & V. Wulf (Eds.), *End user development empowering people to flexibly employ advanced information and communication technology* (pp. 183-205). Dordrecht: Springer.

Costabile, M.F., Fogli, D., Mussio, P., & Piccinno, A. (2007). Visual interactive systems for end-user development: A modelbased design methodology. *IEEE Transactions on Systems, Man and Cybernetics - Part A: Systems and Humans, 37*(6), 1029-1046.

Costabile, M.F., Fogli, D., Lanzilotti, R., Marcante, A., Mussio, P., Parasiliti Provenza, L., & Piccinno, A. (2007). Meta-design to face coevolution and communication gaps between users and designers (LNCS 4554, pp. 46-55).

DePaula, R. (2004). Lost in translation: A critical analysis of actors, artifacts, agendas, and arenas in participatory design. In *Proc. PDC,* Toronto, Canada (pp. 162–172).

Dourish, P., Anderson, K., & Nafus, D. (2007). Cultural mobilities: Diversity and agency in urban computing. In *Proc. IFIP Conf. Human-Computer Interaction INTERACT 2007,* Rio de Janeiro, Brazil.

Dourish, P., Edwards, W.K., Lamarca, A., Lamping, J., Petersen, K., Salisbury, M., Terry, D.B., & Thornton, J. (2000). Extending document management systems with user-specific active properties. *ACM Trans. on Information Systems, 18*(2).

Ellis, C.A., Gibbs, S.J., & Rein, G.L. (1991). Groupware - some issues and experiences. *Communications of the ACM, 34*(1), 39–58.

Engeström, Y., & Middleton, D. (Eds.) (1996). *Cognition and communication at work.* Cambridge: Cambridge University Press.

Esselink, B. (2000). *A practical guide to localization.* John Benjamins Publishing Co.

eXist. (2008). eXist open source native XML database. Retrieved on May 11, 2008, from http://exist.sourceforge.net

Fischer, G. (1998). Seeding, evolutionary growth, and reseeding: Constructing, capturing, and evolving knowledge in domain-oriented design environments. *Automated Software Engineering, 5*(4), 447–468.

Fischer, G. (2000). Symmetry of ignorance, social creativity, and metadesign. *Knowledge-Based Systems, 13*(7-8), 527-537.

Fischer, G., & Giaccardi, E. (2006). Metadesign: A framework for the future of end-user development. In H. Lieberman, F. Paternò & V. Wulf (Eds.), *End user development - empowering people to flexibly employ advanced information and communication technology* (pp. 427-457). Dordrecht, The Netherlands: Kluwer Academic Publishers.

Fischer, G., Giaccardi, E., Ye, Y., Sutcliffe, A.G., & Mehandjiev, N. (2004). Metadesign: A manifesto for end-user development. *Communications of the ACM, 47*(9), 33-37.

Fischer, G., Grudin, J., McCall, R., Ostwald, J., Redmiles, D., Reeves, B., & Shipman, F. (2001). Seeding, evolutionary growth, and reseeding: The incremental development of collaborative design environments. In *Coordination theory and collaboration technology* (pp. 447-472). Mahwah, NJ: Lawrence Erlbaum Associates.

Fogli, D., Fresta, G., Marcante, A., Mussio, P., & Padula, M. (2005). *Annotation in cooperative work: From paper-based to the Web one.* Paper presented at the International Workshop on Annotation for Collaboration, Paris.

Fogli, D., Marcante, A., Mussio, P., Oliveri, E., & Padula, M. (2006). Multimodal interaction for managing knowledge on the field. In *Proceedings of the 1st IEEE Workshop on Multimodal and Pervasive Services*, Lyon, France.

Fogli, D., Marcante, A., Mussio, P., Oliveri, E., Padula, M., & Scaioli, R. (2005). Building yard on line: A distributed and mobile system for supporting building workers. In *Proceedings of the 14th IEEE International Workshops on Enabling Technologies: Infrastructure for Collaborative Enterprise (WETICE)* (pp. 195-200). Linköping: IEEE Computer Society.

Fogli, D., Marcante, A., Mussio, P., & Parasiliti Provenza, L. (2007, May). *Design of visual interactive systems: a multifacet methodology. Workshop: Converging on a science of design through the synthesis of design methodologies.* Paper presented at CHI 2007, San Jose, CA.

Garrett, J.J. (2005). Ajax: A new approach to Web applications. Retrieved on February 18, 2005, from http://www.adaptivepath.com/ideas/essays/archives/000385.php

Goodwin, C., & Goodwin, M.H. (1997). Seeing as a situated activity: Formulating planes. In Y. Engeström & D. Middleton (Eds.), *Cognition and communication at work* (pp. 61-95). Cambridge, MA: Cambridge University Press.

Greenbaum, J., & Kyng, M. (Eds.) (1991). *Design at work: Cooperative design of computer systems.* Hillsdale, NJ: Lawrence Erlbaum.

Grudin, J. (1994). Computer-supported cooperative work: History and focus. *Computer IEEE, 27*(5), 19–26.

Hartson, H.R., & Hix, D. (1989). Human-computer interface development: Concepts and systems for its management. *ACM Computing Surveys (CSUR), 21*(1), 5-92.

Hasselbring, W. (2000). Programming languages and systems for prototyping concurrent applications. *ACM Computing Surveys, 32*(1), 43-79.

Hayes, J.R. (1985). *Three problems in teaching general skills*. Hillsdale, NJ: Lawrence Erlbaum.

Hughes, J.A., Randall, D., & Shapiro, D. (1992). Faltering from ethnography to design. In M. Mantel & R. Baecher (Eds.), *Proceedings of the International Conference on Computer-Supported Cooperative Work (CSCW'92)*, Toronto, Canada (pp. 115-122). New York: ACM Press.

Hutchins, E.L., Hollan, J.D., & Norman, D. (1986). Direct manipulation interfaces. In D. Norman & S. Draper (Eds.), *User centred system design* (pp. 87–124). Hillsdale, NJ: Lawrence Erlbaum.

Karasti, H. (2001). *Increasing sensitivity towards everyday work practice in system design*. Unpublished doctoral dissertation, University of Oulu, Oulu.

Koivunen, M.R., & Swick, R.R. (2003). Collaboration through annotations in the Semantic Web. In S. Handschuh & S. Staab (Eds.), *Annotation for the Semantic Web* (pp. 46-60). Amsterdam: IOS Press.

Letondal, C., & Mackay, W.E. (2004). Participatory programming and the scope of mutual responsibility: Balancing scientific, design, and software commitment. In A. Clement & P. Van den Besselaar (Eds.), *Proceedings of the 8th Conference on Participatory Design Conference (PDC 2004)*, Toronto, Canada (pp. 31-41). New York: ACM Press.

Lieberman, H. (2001). *Your wish is my command: Programming by example*. San Francisco: Morgan Kaufman.

Luqi. (1992). Computer aided system prototyping. In *Proc. 1st Int'l Workshop on Rapid System Prototyping*, Los Alamitos, CA (pp. 50-57).

Mackay, W.E. (1991). Triggers and barriers to customizing software. In *Proc. CHI Human Factors Comput. Syst.*, New Orleans, LA (pp. 153–160).

Marcus, A., & Baumgartner, V.J. (2004). *A practical set of culture dimensions for global user-interface development*. APCHI.

Merriam-Webster online. (2008). Retrieved on May 8, 2008, from http://www.merriam-webster.com

Mørch, A. (1997). Three levels of end-user tailoring: Customization, integration, and extension. In M. Kyng & L. Mathiassen (Eds.), *Computers and Design in Context* (pp. 51–76). Cambridge, MA: MIT Press.

Mørch, A.I., & Mehandjiev, N.D. (2000). Tailoring as collaboration: The mediating role of multiple representations and application units. *Computer Supported Cooperative Work, 9*(1), 75-100.

Myers, B.A., Smith, D.C., & Horn, B. (1992). *Report of the 'end-user programming' working group, languages for developing user interfaces* (pp. 343–366). Boston: Jones & Bartlett.

Naeve, A. (2005). The human Semantic Web – shifting from knowledge push to knowledge pull. *International Journal of Semantic Web and Information Systems (IJSWIS), 1*(3), 1-30.

Nardi, B. (1993). *A small matter of programming: Perspectives on end user computing*. Cambridge, MA: MIT Press.

Nielsen, J. (1993). *Usability engineering*. San Diego, CA: Academic Press.

O'Hagan, M., & Ashworth, D. (2002). *Translation-mediated communication in a digital world facing the challenges of globalization and localization.* Multilingual Matters LTD.

Penner, R.R., & Steinmetz, E.S. (2002). Model-based automation of the design of user interfaces to digital control systems. *IEEE Trans. on Systems, Man, and Cybernetics - Part A, 32*(1), 41-49.

Perkowitz, M., & Etzioni, O. (2000). Towards adaptive Web sites: Conceptual framework and case study. *Artificial Intelligence, 118*(2000), 245–275.

Portanieri, F., & Amara, F. (1996). Arabization of graphical user interfaces. In *International user interfaces.* New York: John Wiley & Sons, Inc.

Resnick, L.B., Saljo, R., Pontecorvo, C., & Burge, B. (Eds.) (1997). *Discourse, tools, and reasoning: Essays on situated cognition.* Berlin, Germany: Springer-Verlag.

Savourel, Y. (2001). *XML internationalization and localization.* SAMS.

Stary, C. (2000). TADEUS: Seamless development of task-based and user-oriented interfaces. *IEEE Trans. on Systems, Man, and Cybernetics - Part A, 30*(5), 509-525.

Suchman, L., Blomberg, J., Orr, J., & Trigg, R. (1999). Reconstructing technologies as social practice. *American Behavioral Scientist, 43*(3), 392-408.

Suchman, L., & Trigg, R.H. (1991). Understanding practice: Video as a medium for reflection and design. In J. Greenbaum & M. Kyng (Eds.), *Design at work: Cooperative design of computer systems* (pp. 65-89). Hillsdale, NJ: Lawrence Erlbaum.

Thomas, D.M., Bostrom, R.P., & G.M. (2007). Making knowledge work in virtual teams. *Communications of the ACM, 50*(11), 85–90.

Voice eXtensible Markup Language Version 2.0, W3C Recommendation. (2008). Retrieved on May 11, 2008, from http://www.w3.org/TR/voicexml20

Wulf, V., & Golombek, V. (2001). Direct activation: A concept to encourage tailoring activities. *Behav. Inf. Technol., 20*(4), 249–263.

Wulf, W.A. (1989). The national collaboratory – a white paper. Appendix A. In *Towards a national collaboratory* (Unpublished report of a National Science Foundation invitational workshop). New York: Rockefeller University.

XHTML+Voice Profile 1.2, W3C. (2008). Retrieved on May 11, 2008, from http://www.voicexml.org/specs/multimodal/x+v/12

KEY TERMS AND DEFINITIONS

Adaptivity: The automatic improving of the organization and presentation of a system by learning from visitor access patterns.

e-Document: Entities that are the results of interpretation of data and programs.

Localization: The adaptation of the system to the linguistic and cultural conventions of a specific country.

Multimodal Systems: Permit to adopt different devices and to involve different human senses.

Participatory Design: Techniques derived from social theories (collaborative construction of mock-ups, cooperative prototyping, game-like design session) that support communication and collaboration within an interdisciplinary team.

Pervasive Systems: Computing paradigm in which infrastructure and services are seamlessly available anywhere, anytime, and in any format.

Software Shaping Workshop: Referring to software environments that enable users to shape virtual tools and data.

Chapter XIV
Making the Web Accessible to the Visually Impaired

Simone Bacellar Leal Ferreira
Universidade Federal do Estado do Rio de Janeiro, Brazil

Denis Silva da Silveira
Programa de Engenharia de Produção - COPPE/UFRJ, Brazil

Marcos Gurgel do Amaral Leal Ferreira
Holden Comunicação Ltda, Brazil

Ricardo Rodrigues Nunes
Universidade Federal do Estado do Rio de Janeiro, Brazil

ABSTRACT

Accessibility is the possibility of any person to make use of all the benefits of society, including the Internet. As the interfaces are typically graphic, sites can be an obstacle for visually impaired persons to access. For a site to be accessible to blind persons it's necessary the information contained in the visual resources be reproduced by means of an "equivalent" textual description, capable of transmitting the same information as the visual resources. This study is aimed at identifying and defining usability guidance compliant with accessibility W3C directives that can facilitate the interaction between visually impaired and Internet and still guarantee sites with understandable navigation content. Towards this end an exploratory study was conducted, comprised of a field study and interviews with visually disabled people from Instituto Benjamin Constant, reference center in Brazil for the education of visually impaired persons, in order to get to know these users better.

INTRODUCTION

Accessibility is the term used to indicate the possibility of any person to make use of all the benefits of society, among which, the use of the Internet. (Nicholl, 2001). Digital accessibility is more specific and refers only to access to computer resources; accessibility to the Internet is the right to use the resources in the worldwide computer Web and accessibility to the Web, or *e-accessibility*, referring specifically to the Web component (Sales, 2003).

The Web component plays a fundamental role in the innovation that the Internet represents in the daily lives of persons with special needs; it facilitates the lives of these people as it allows them to create new ways of relating to others and performing activities previously unattainable (Takagi, 2004) and (Petrie, 2006). But getting digital accessibility is no simple matter; it requires organizations to adapt their resources in order to make the use of the computer accessible to any person (http_1).

In order to be accessed by visually impaired users, the graphic interface of computer systems should be designed with an "equivalent" textual description. These "equivalent" interfaces should be built in such a way that when accessed by support technology, they continue to provide "friendly" interaction, i.e., an interaction focused on usability. Hence, the present study is aimed at identifying and defining usability guidance compliant with accessibility laws, which may facilitate the interaction between those visually impaired and the Web, guaranteeing sites with understandable navigation content. This research is focused on Brazil`s necessities. To achieve this end, a Field work was conducted at the Instituto Benjamin Constant (IBC), an agency of the Ministry of Education of Brazil, and a center of excellence and national reference in matters related to studies of visual impairment (http_6

ACCESSIBILITY TO THE WEB OR E-ACCESSIBILITY

Digital accessibility refers to access to any Information Technology resource, whereas the term accessibility to the Internet is used, widely speaking, to define universal access to all components of the worldwide computer Web, such as chats, e-mail, and so on. The term Web accessibility, or *e-accessibility*, specifically refers to the Web component, which is a set of pages written in HTML language and interconnected by links to the hypertext (Sales, 2003), (Modelo, 2005) and (Nevile, 2005).

Aimed at making the Web accessible to all, W3C (the World Wide Web Consortium), an international committee that regulates matters linked to the Internet, created, in 1999, the WAI (Web Accessibility Initiative), made up of work groups intent on producing guidance to guarantee Web content accessibility to people with disabilities and to people accessing the Web under special conditions related to environment, equipment, navigator and other Web tools (Nevile, 2005), (http_5) and (Enap, 2007).

The members of W3C/WAI put together "W3C Accessibility Guidelines" (WCAG 1.0); this document is the first version for Accessibility to Web Content, released in May 1999, and has been the main reference to Web accessibility until today (http_5). In Brazil, accessibility began to be a part of public policy in the year 2000, when Federal Laws no. 10,048 dated November 8 2000, prioritizing services rendered to people with special needs, and no. 10,098 dated December 19 2000, establishing norms and criteria to guarantee accessibility were promulgated (Enap, 2007). In December 2004 these laws were regulated by decree no. 5,296 that initially established a 12-month deadline for all public administration or public interest sites to undergo an accessibility process; this deadline was subject to prorogation (Queiroz, 2007).

In order to define accessibility guidance at all levels, from physical to virtual spaces, ABNT's CB-40 Committee was put in charge of comparing accessibility norms in various countries and analyzing the guidelines proposed by W3C. As a result, a Brazilian Accessibility Model was designed (e-MAG) so as to generate a set of recommendations that could standardize and harmonize the accessibility process for Brazilian Government sites, enabling easy installation, thereby coherent with Brazilian needs and in conformity with international standards (Model, 2005) and (http_1).

Importance of Internet and Web Accessibility for those with Visual Impairment

The Web plays a fundamental role in the innovation that the Internet represents in the daily lives of those with visual impairment, making their lives easier; it allows them to establish new relationships, find job opportunities and forms of entertainment (Petrie, 2006) and (Queiroz, 2007).

Upon accessing a site, a user with normal eyesight uses a Browser. However, a blind or partially sighted person accessing the Internet would require support technology connected to the Browser, consisting of software called "screen readers", associated to other programs called "voice synthesizers".

Though important, digital accessibility is no simple matter. People with disabilities have sensorial and motor limitations which must be compensated for, one way or another, so as to enable their access to computer resources. With this in mind, organizations need to adapt their systems so that one single computer can be used by any person whatsoever (Harrison, 2005). The problem is that this adaptation requires technical expertise and specialized help, and this is why organizations very often do not make the needed effort to introduce accessibility procedures.

Levels of Accessibility

W3C Accessibility Guidelines (WCAG 1.0) proposed a set of fourteen directives for the Accessibility of Web Content. These directives deal with two generic themes: assure that the sites are accessible in a harmonious way and produce sites with understandable navigational content (http_5). WAI defined verification points for directives; each verification point was attributed a priority level, based on accessibility impact. Three levels of accessibility were defined; the Brazilian model also adopted these same priority levels (Model, 2005).

- **Priority level 1:** Norms and requirements related to verification points that Web designers must comply with so as not to make access unattainable to any group of users.
- **Priority level 2:** Norms and requirements related to verification points that Web designers must comply with so as not to hinder the access of any group of users.
- **Priority level 3:** Norms and recommendations that Web designers can comply with so as not to hinder access to saved files.

Programs for Accessibility Evaluation

Based on W3C/WAI recommendations, programs were designed to evaluate the level of accessibility to the site. These programs detect the HTML code and analyze content, verifying whether it is in compliance with the established set of rules or not; finally, they write reports listing the problems that need to be addressed for the site to be considered accessible (Spelta, 2003).

Some of this software is worth highlighting: *Bobby* (designed by the "Watchfire Corporation"), and *Lift* (designed by "Usablenet"). In Brazil, the *daSilva* program was designed to evaluate sites according to the rules established by WCAG and by e-MAG (http_4). This program was designed by "*Acessibilidade Brasil*", a "Public Interest Corporation" (OSCIP), whose mission is to develop studies for the social and economic insertion of people with impairments (http_1).

METHODOLOGY

The study, exploratory in nature, was carried out in three stages: (*a*) selection of the category of users; (*b*) bibliographic and documental research; (*c*) field work. These stages were accomplished concurrently.

The research work aimed at identifying and defining usability directives that are aligned with accessibility laws and which of these might facilitate the interaction between those visually impaired and the Internet, as well as guaranteeing sites with understandable navigation content.

Stages

a. **Selecting the category of users:** Users with visual impairment were chosen as the object of study of the present work; this decision was made based on the fact that the Internet has done much to contribute to improving the quality of life of those visually impaired, allowing them not only access to information that was previously only attainable with the help of another person, but also providing them with other facilities (Harrison, 2005).

b. **Biographical and documental research**: initially, we sought to understand the principles of accessibility and its implications for Internet sites. During this stage, some institutions provided different software destined for visually impaired users. This software was used to navigate in "common" sites, such as newspapers, and make a deeper observation and analysis of the various aspects brought up in the literature.

c. **Field work**: Field work was conducted at the Instituto Benjamin Constant (IBC), an agency of the Ministry of Education, founded in Rio de Janeiro in 1854 under the name of *Imperial Instituto dos Meninos Cegos*. IBC has become a center of excellence and national reference in matters related to studies of visual impairment. Its main aim is to promote the education and integration of visually impaired persons within a greater framework (http_6). During the field work, which took three months, different sectors of the institute were observed. In addition, several informal interviews and six in-depth interviews were conducted with employees, students and former students at the institution, most of whom are visually impaired and work there nowadays.

MODELS

Mental models are representations existing in the minds of people, which are used to explain, simulate, predict or control objects in the world. These representations are externalized through conceptual models. The elaboration of a user's conceptual model depends on the previous knowledge and experience of each person and is based on the expectations, aims and understanding of the user with regard to the system. Users create models based on "objects" they already know from their daily activities; they try to relate the computer elements to these familiar "objects", in an attempt to understand the machine better (Pressman, 2004).

As the perception of the system is influenced by the experiences of a person, each user creates his/her own conceptual model; since it is highly unlikely that people without special needs undergo similar experiences when surfing the Web as those with deficiencies, the models for disabled people tend to be distinct from the models for non-disabled people (Takagi, 2004). For example, according to Prof. Hercen, who was born blind, the window metaphor (Windows), which indicates the visualization of a work area, has no such meaning for a blind person (Hildebrandt, 2005).

When accessing a system, disabled users make use of a very different environment from non-disabled people. They relate the computer elements to "objects" from their day to day lives, developed to supply their needs. In addition, people with disabilities, such as blind persons, develop special skills, *e.g.*, excellent hearing; they hardly ever sit passively waiting to hear a spoken exit; they move around Web pages using complex combinations of keys. By means of this process, they create their own models and attempt to surf Web pages in a logical way. As these facts increase the level of difficulty when interacting with sites (Hanson, 2004), this ends up influencing their conceptual models (Takagi, 2004).

In systems geared to usability, the perception the user has of the system should be the closest possible to the system *per se*. This is why the designer should know the final users well enough to understand how they perceive the system, *i.e.*, their conceptual models. Thus when dealing with impaired users, it becomes essential to identify what types of impositions and limits they are subject to, in order to understand better their needs and special abilities (Takagi, 2004); an attempt should be made to understand all the hurdles users need to overcome to access information. If these hurdles are understood, it becomes possible to design easy-to-use interfaces for people with special needs as well (Harrison, 2005). The field work for the present study was conducted with this goal in mind.

VISUALLY IMPAIRED-MACHINE INTERACTION

The interface, graphic or otherwise, is the part of the software that users use to communicate with the system in order to perform their tasks;

it should be designed to meet the users' expectations, allowing them to direct their attention to the objects they work with, which in turn reflect the real world (Pressman, 2004).

The interface should allow for user-friendly interaction; its design should be aimed at usability, the characteristic that determines whether the handling of a *product* is easy and quickly learned, difficult to forget, does not provoke operational errors, satisfies its users and efficiently resolves the tasks for which it was designed (Ferreira, 2003) and (Nielsen, 2002). If usability guides the system, users feel comfortable and encouraged to make use of it (Shneiderman, 2004). In order to build systems with sound usability, it is important that they be centered on the user (Norman, 1999); towards this end, one should get to know the final users, know how they perform their tasks, and the types of impositions and limits that they are subject to. Because graphic interfaces are a hurdle for visually challenged users, they must interact with the system using support technology capable of capturing interfaces and making them accessible.

USABILITY

Only recently the matter of usability has been perceived as important to information systems professionals. Driven by the market, organizations are going online in order to position themselves on a new way of performing business. Since the technology infrastructure used to construct Web sites can deal with images, sounds and text composition, it became more evident that the output of information should be treated with care (Ferreira, 2003).

Information system must be designed with the purpose of establishing a productive interaction between the system and their users in order to increase people's productivity while performing their tasks. They must satisfy the expectations and needs of their users. To achieve this end, the NFR (non functional requirement) usability must be present in any method for systems construction.

The communication between users and an Information System (IS) is established by means of the IS interface. A good IS design must guarantee a transparent communication, that is, it must assure that when a user accesses the IS to perform any task, he or she needs only to focus their energy on the intended task (Norman, 1986), (Norman, 1999) & (Jokela , 2004), (Seffah, 2004).

To have users focusing their attention mainly on their tasks, the process of software development must be "user centered", that is, its interface must be designed with the objective of satisfying the expectations and needs of users. The design of an interface that considers user characteristics and the NFR usability is a difficult process for many reasons, but most of this difficulty can be traced to the lack of attention on NFRs during the system definition process. Building systems that take in consideration NFRs, require the availability of a corpus of knowledge to help the engineer in the task of defining the system to comply with those requirements.

Usability Directives Focused on Accessibility

A usability oriented site is not necessarily accessibility oriented, and *vice versa*; a page may be easy to use for ordinary users, but inaccessible for those with special needs (Hanson, 2004). The directives recommend that site administrators check accessibility by accessing them through a screen reader; the problem is that those visually disabled, besides having special abilities, also use certain combinations of keys that a non-disabled person would not be able to simulate; hence, usability aspects differ from one user profile to that of another.

The authors of the current study agree that accessibility should be verified through a screen reader but that in order to obtain a universal access site geared to usability, it is essential that the difficulties and abilities of users be modeled as well, as these guide the mental model of their interactions. With such modeling, it would be possible to obtain usability directives that, in conjunction with the W3C accessibility directives, would provide for harmonious interaction of

Table 1. Usability directives

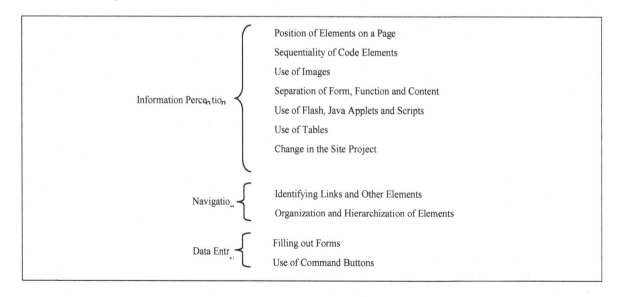

those disabled while guaranteeing understandable navigation sites.

Usability issues occur, generally speaking, due to three reasons: the main aim of accessibility evaluation programs is compliance with directives where usability aspects are overlooked; many evaluation programs rely only on syntax verification techniques for sites and so detectable errors are limited to the tag description layer where the users' mental models are not taken into account (Takagi, 2004).

The literature (Ferreira, 2003), (Pressman, 2004) groups human-machine interaction sequences under two categories: *information visualization* and *data entry*. Based on the field work conducted at the *Instituto Benjamin Constant*, the present study proposes that, in interactions between visually impaired humans and machines, these sequences be grouped under three categories: *information perception, navigation* and *data entry*. After observing these interactions it was possible to identify certain usability directives, shown in the following sections (Table 1).

Information Perception

Users accessing the Web by means of screen readers do not need to listen to all the words contained on the page: they only need to hear enough to determine where they want to go from there. It is, therefore, important that the interfaces be simple, because screen readers process the contents of a site differently from a visual reading process; to use them requires training and experience. Screen readers capture the HTML code, analyze the code and line up elements in the same order they appear in the code. As a result, visually impaired users perceive the page as if it were a text that they can read line by line (by means of arrows) or link by link (by means of the tab key) (Nevile, 2005).

Position of Elements on a Page

The order in which a screen element appears to the user accessing a page by voice reader is not the same order in which it appears visually on a navigator. What determines when it appears on the screen reader is the position it holds in the source code. An important element may very often have a prominent position on the page shown on a navigator, but when analyzed by the screen reader, ends up being one of the last elements users notice, as it is positioned at the end of the code. Aside from losing its prominent position, it will be perceived only after a number of less important information appears (Hildebrandt, 2005).

Sequentiality of Code Elements

Sequentiality is one of the barriers found by those visually disabled when browsing a site with a screen reader (or by means of a program that amplifies the interface): the user is only able to access a limited portion of the screen and, thus, loses out on the idea of the general context of the page at hand (Leporini, 2004). This is why HTML language tags that can be identified by the screen reader become an important element in the information perception process of visually impaired users. They allow the reader to provide information about the structure of the site (Leporini, 2004).

Hence, when designing an interface to be accessed by visually impaired users, one should be careful since many visual characteristics, such as bold, underline, italics, font styles, etc. are not detectable to the reader and so become imperceptible; on the other hand, other invisible elements, such as labels, link titles and alt attributes for images can be used to highlight information (Leporini, 2004).

Use of Images

The W3C 1.1 directive states that all non-textual information must be accompanied by a text. It is recommended that the alt attribute should always be present so that contents can be read by a screen reader. The alt attribute (alternate text) provides an alternative text associated to an image; in most navigators, the alt textual content is shown to the ordinary user when the mouse passes over the image. When the mouse moves away from the image, this window disappears. Likewise, when the page is being downloaded and an image is still being downloaded, the block with the alt text content appears until the final figure is shown.

If the texts for these image attributes are written appropriately, they can provide useful information for disabled users with respect to the meaning of the images being read by the screen readers (Queiroz, 2007), (Hanson, 2004) and (Harrison, 2005).

When a site contains an image without an alt attribute, this image may be detected or not; it will depend on the screen reader program being used. Some readers don't pick up anything, while others may indicate the existence of an "image" to the visually impaired user, but cannot furnish any information about the nature of the figure (Queiroz, 2007).

For instance, an interviewee reported not being able to register with an Internet provider as the link was hidden, probably because it was represented by an image without alt attribute. In her opinion the descriptive text of an image is only useful if it brings relevant information not available in the text (Livramento, 2005).

Interviewees say they prefer texts without images. What is more, they also state they cannot often find subtitles that might justify the presence of the image on the page. Perhaps bad use of alt attributes is in part responsible for the rejection of images, found to be the case in the current research work (Hildebrandt, 2005; Coube, 2005) (Livramento, 2005).

Separation of Form, Function and Content

Although a union of form, function and content are essential to obtain a complete and accessible site, the intersection between these elements may result in inconsistencies among different navigators or even among distinct means of access, as PDAs and cell phones. One should separate these elements, restricting the use of HTML to a description of the content and the use of CSS (Cascading Style Sheets) to the formatting (http_5).

As it offers many more resources for formatting and a more precise control for exhibiting each element in comparison with HTML formatting tags, the CSS standard plays an important role in Web accessibility. When using only CSS to format a page, the HTML code is restricted to the function of gathering and ranking the content, thus enabling navigators that do not depend on formatting – as is the case of screen readers for the visually impaired – to ignore the CSS code and concentrate only on what is contained in the HTML.

Use of Flash, Java Applets and Scripts

As HTML is not a programming language, in order to make sites more interesting, solutions were found to allow them to contain programs. Among these solutions, one can find scripts, small programs incorporated in Web pages with a capacity to generate special animated effects, formatting and forms.

As time passed, more powerful technology, like Flash and Java, began to be used to animate sites, and to make them interactive and more attractive. However, most flash and java applet files cannot be deciphered by screen readers. Though recent versions of Flash include resources that enable integration with accessibility support mechanisms, there are still limits to the relationship between flash components and text navigators, as is the case of certain screen readers. One solution would be to create a link for a text version without these resources (Queiroz, 2007).

Use of Tables

When a screen reader is used, tables are read horizontally, line by line. As visually impaired users cannot visualize the whole table and so have to rely on their memory to know in which position different columns are to be found, it would be preferable to re-read the heading of each column (the first cell of each column) before reading the data contained in each cell (Livramento, 2005). HTML offers resources that allow distinguishing the heading of the remaining cells, paving the way for this type of reading, as long as this distinction is correctly applied in the font code. It is, therefore, good usability practice to identify the names of each column and line by means of the "th" tag (table header).

Change in the Site Project

There are two types of alterations that can be made in sites. The first and more frequent one consists of simply updating the content without modifying the page layout. Newspapers, for example, are updated continually. This does not cause any uneasiness for visually impaired users.

The second and more problematic one occurs when the project of the site is altered. This obliges the visually impaired user to relearn the name and position of all the key elements on the page. Though this was not considered an obstacle, the visually impaired interviewees (Coube, 2005), (Hildebrandt, 2005) and (Livramento, 2005) wished to be notified every time a new version of the site came into effect. One interviewee reported that, when the page of her provider was modified, she and her husband, also blind, had no idea what was going on, unsure of whether it was an error on the part of the program or something they had done wrong (Livramento, 2005). One

suggestion to cater to the needs of the visually impaired user is to put some identification inside the page containing the number and date of the current version.

Navigation

Visually disabled users do not use the mouse to navigate, since this device requires visual coordination (aim) (Queiroz, 2007). They mainly use the tab key and combinations of keys, called *shortcut keys*. These keys can also be used by non-disabled users to expedite certain tasks (Leporini, 2004). Using these keys requires learning one more skill, which leads partially sighted users to prefer using their residual sight (Hanson, 2004). This is why one should select a background color that will create a contrast between the background and the text to facilitate reading (Hanson, 2004).

Identifying Links and Other Elements

When navigating by means of keys, it is essential that the text describing the link be identified in an informative and useful way (Harrison, 2004); this text will be picked up by the screen reader and it is by this means that the disabled user will know what the link is for. So, simply identifying links with words like "click here" or "next" are an obstacle for users who rely on voice readers, as is the case of the visually impaired (http_1).

Organization and Hierarchization of Elements

Screen readers provide functions that enable users to jump directly to the various heading tags, a key element in structuring easy-to-navigate sites. By means of a tag, visually impaired users can navigate using the titles so as to get a general idea of the page (Takagi, 2004).

According to Livramento (2005), sites structured as paragraphs provide more objective navigation. Visually impaired users like to have the option of navigating by jumping from one paragraph to another, only reading through the ones they consider important; experienced users are quickly able to identify if they wish to continue reading a paragraph or skip to another, in this way approximating their method of reading to that of a person with ordinary eyesight (Livramento, 2005).

This is why it is essential to adopt the practice of signaling each paragraph in HTML code by means of a "p" tag instead of a "br" tag, which only enables a line break.

One of the problems in using a screen reader is that navigation on links is sequential (Leporini, 2004). This can slow down navigation. For instance, to return to a link to one's left, one would have to jump over all the links in order to restart reading the page and finally arrive at the desired content. Sites should provide resources that would enable users to jump links repeatedly, accelerating interaction. Hence skip links should be used, speeding up navigation and allowing users to jump links repeatedly and go directly to the desired content (Harrison, 2004). Skip links are not noticeable when a site is exhibited on an ordinary navigator, and are only useful when the site is being accessed by a screen reader (Takagi, 2004).

Data Entry

On entering data, visually impaired users do not use the mouse, but the keyboard, which has become a facilitator capable of being used by any visually disabled user due to an international typing norm: all keyboards produced in conformity with regional technical norms have, on the lower part of the J and F keys (on the alphanumerical side) and 5 (on the numerical side), high-relief to guide blind people when positioning their hands, just as people do when learning to type (Queiroz, 2007).

Relying solely on the keyboard, one could spend a long time choosing commands, typing data and inputting other things. Added measures should be taken to promote accessibility in interfaces dealing with data entry (Ferreira, 2003).

Filling Out Forms

If filling out forms can be a constraint for just any user, it is much worse for those visually impaired, forcing them at times to abandon the site. The simple fact that many sites have restricted access requiring passwords, which, due to security reasons are not spelled out by screen readers, already hinders user access.

One way people send data over the Internet is by filling out forms. Since the user navigates through forms by using the tab key, in order to facilitate data entry, the fields to be filled out and search buttons, if important, should preferentially be located at the top of the page. (Leporini, 2004).

Some interfaces are made in such a way that very often, when a visually impaired user locates the field to be filled out, no voice indication is made to explain what needs to be done; the user only hears a standard notification from the reader: "edit box." The "label" tag would allow placing a text to be read by the user, giving information on what needs to be filled out (Queiroz, 2007). This tag also permits attributing a rapid access key to each field on the form, in addition to enlarging the click field for *selection box* and *radio box*, which would make filling out forms easier for those with only partial visual impairment. One should also avoid using a default value in the field, because even when read by the reader, it would require the user to erase the value (Harrison, 2004).

Another error found in forms is the indication of fields where one is required to make use of different color or font formatting. An alternative to this would be to use an asterisk, but screen reader users often disable the punctuation. Ideally this should be indicated by a letter that would represent the word "obligatory" (Harrison, 2004).

Use of Command Buttons

Another way of sending data is by means of command buttons, such as the "send" or "submit" button; these do not require a "label," since they can be read by means of the "value" attribute; however, one should avoid using words such as "click here" or "continue" with this attribute, because they indicate nothing about the purpose of the button. If the button has an image instead of a text, it would suffice to use the "alt" attribute (Queiroz, 2007).

CONCLUSION

The current paper was motivated by the law decreed and signed in December 2004 that defined a twelve-month deadline for accessibility of public sites. Many organizations were prompted to try to adapt their information systems as a result of this decree in an attempt to obtain the accessibility certification.

Concern over accessibility at the moment of designing or redesigning a site does not guarantee this accessibility is maintained later when the site is updated. Constant and continual verification of accessibility should be made in order to avoid modifications in content or structure that would compromise the initial accessibility of the project. A new challenge emerges: that of designing, administering and maintaining sites in conformity with accessibility directives that are not only current and easy but also attractive.

Field research was conducted at the Instituto Benjamin Constant, the main reference center in Brazil for the education and re-education of those visually impaired, in order to get to know visually disabled users better. The reason for choosing visually disabled people was the fact that the Internet has done much to contribute to the improvement in the quality of their lives, allowing them to engage in new forms of relationships, find work opportunities and alternate forms of entertainment. This research work has prompted the understanding of how these users perceive and interact with sites and has identified certain hurdles that they need to overcome in order to access information. Through the understanding acquired in the field work and based on the literature, different types of impositions and limits that these users are subject to have been identified, enabling a better perception of their needs and special abilities. As a result, impaired user-machine interaction sequences have been grouped together into three categories: *information perception, navigation* and *data entry*. These interactions were observed and analyzed, which enabled the identification of certain usability directives that could contribute to the accessibility of sites in alignment with W3C directives, with emphasis on facilitating visually impaired user access to the Web.

REFERENCES

Enap. (2007, January). Material do curso "e-MAG-Modelo de Acessibilidade de Governo Eletrônico"- ministrado pela Escola Nacional de Administração Pública.

Ferreira, S.B.L., & Leite, J.C.S. (2003). Avaliação da usabilidade em sistemas de informação: o caso do sistema submarino - Revista de Administração Contemporânea - RAC. Publicação da ANPAD, v.7, n 2, - Abril/Junho.

Hanson, V.L. (2004). The user experience: Designs and adaptations. *ACM International Conference Proceeding Series - Proceedings of the International Cross-Disciplinary Workshop on Web Access.*

Harrison, S.M. (2005). Opening the eyes of those who can see to the world of those who can't: A case study. *Technical Symposium on Computer Science Education - Proceedings of the 36th SIGCSE Technical Symposium on Computer Science Education.*

Leporini, B., Andronico, P., & Buzzi, M. (2004). Designing search engine user interfaces for the visually impaired. *ACM International Conference Proceeding Series - Proceedings of the International Cross-disciplinary Workshop on Web Accessibility.*

Modelo de Acessibilidade. (2005). Recomendações de Acessibilidade para a Construção e Adaptação de Conteúdos do Governo Brasileiro na Internet - Departamento de Governo Eletrônico - Secretaria de Logística e Tecnologia da Informação - Ministério do Planejamento, Orçamento e Gestão - Documento de Referência - Versão 2.0 14/12/2005.

Norman, D.A. (1999). *The invisible computer: Why good products can fail, the personal computer is so complex, and information appliances are the solution.* MIT Press.

Nevile, L. (2005, November). Adaptability and accessibility: A new framework. *Proceedings of the 19th Conference of the Computer-Human Interaction Special Interest Group (CHISIG) of Australia on Computer-Human Interaction: Citizens Online: Considerations for Today and the Future,* Canberra, Australia (Vol. 122, pp. 1-10).

Nicholl, A.R.J. (2001). O Ambiente que Promove a Inclusão: Conceitos de Acessibilidade e Usabilidade". Revista Assentamentos Humanos, Marília, v3, n. 2, p49–60.

Nielsen, J., & Tahir, M. (2002). Homepage: Usabilidade – 50 Websites desconstruídos. RJ: Editora Campus.

Petrie, H., Hamilton, F., King , N., & Pavan, P. (2006). Remote - usability evaluations with disabled people. *Proceedings of the SIGCHI Conference on Human Factors in Computing systems,* Canada.

Pressman, R. (2007). *Software engineering - a practioner's approach, 6th ed.* McGraw-Hill, Inc.

Queiroz, M.A. (2007). Material de um curso ministrado no SERPRO RJ por Marco Antonio de Queiroz, especialmente para cegos e pessoas de baixa visão. Tirado 02 de Abril 2003 de 2007 http://www.bengalalegal.com/. 2/4/2007.

Sales, M.B. De, & Cybis, W.de A. (2003). Desenvolvimento de um checklist para a avaliação de acessibilidade da *Web* para usuários idosos - *ACM International Conference Proceeding Series Proceedings of the Latin American Conference on Human-Computer Interaction.*

Shneiderman, B. (2004). *Designing the user interface : Strategies for effective human-computer interaction, 4th ed.* MA: Addison-Wesley.

Spelta, L.L. (2003). O Papel dos Leitores de Tela na Construção de *Sites* Acessíveis - Anais do ATIID 2003, São Paulo-SP, 23–24/09/2003.

Takagi, H., Asakawa, C., Fukuda K., & Maeda J. (2004). Accessibility designer: Visualizing usability for the blind. *ACM SIGACCESS Conference on Assistive Technologies - Proceedings of the ACM SIGACCESS Conference on Computers and Accessibility.*

Web Sites

http1: http://www.acessobrasil.org.br/: March 9, 2007.

http2: http://www.acesso.umic.pcm.gov.pt/: December 11, 2006.

http3: http://www.governoeletronico.gov.br: January 5, 2007.

http4: http://www.*daSilva*.org.br/: April 5, 2007.

http5: http://www.w3.org/WAI/: December 13, 2006.

http6: http://www.ibc.gov.br/: February 5, 2006.

Interviews

Coube, José Elias - Teacher in Informatics of the IBC (blind) – June 31, 2006.

Ferreira, Gerson F. - General Coordinator in Informatics of the IBC (blind) – June 10, 2006.

Hilderbrandt, Hercen - Teacher in Informatics of the IBC (blind) – June 29, 2006.

Cerqueira, Maria de Fátima Carvalhal - ex-learner of the IBC (blind) – July 9, 2006.

Souza, José Francisco - Director of Rehabilitation Division of the IBC (ten percent of vision) – July 22, 2006.

Livramento, Maria Luzia - Text Reviewer of Braille Press of the IBC (blind) – July 5, 2006.

KEY TERMS AND DEFINITIONS

Accessibility: Term used to indicate the possibility of any person to make use of all the benefits of society.

Usability: Term used to denote the ease with which people can employ a particular tool or other human-made object in order to achieve a particular goal.

Visually Impaired: Vision loss that constitutes a significant limitation of visual capability resulting from disease, trauma, or a congenital or degenerative condition that cannot be corrected by conventional means, including refractive correction, medication, or surgery.

Instituto Benjamin Constant (IBC): Center of excellence and national reference in matters related to studies of visual impairment.

World Wide Web Consortium (W3C): The main international standards organization for the World Wide Web (abbreviated WWW or W3).

Web Accessibility Initiative (WAI): An effort to improve the accessibility of the World Wide Web (WWW or Web) for people using a wide range of user agent devices, not just standard Web browsers. This is especially important for people with physical disabilities which require such devices to access the Web.

W3C Accessibility Guidelines (WCAG 1.0): The document is the first version for Accessibility to Web Content, released in May 1999, and has been the main reference to Web accessibility until today.

Chapter XV
Designing Contextualized Interaction for Learning

Marcus Specht
Open University of the Netherlands, The Netherlands

ABSTRACT

In the following chapter, an overview is given over the experiences and design decisions made in the European project RAFT for enabling live distributed collaboration between learners in the field and in the classroom. Beside a context analysis for defining requirements for service needed as an underlying infrastructure user interface design decisions were essential in the project. As a flexible and powerful approach a widget based design for the user interface enable the project to build clients for a variety of hardware and devices in the learning environment ranging from mobile phones, PDAs, tablet PCs, desktop computers, to electronic whiteboard solutions. Enabling consistent and synchronized access to information streams in such a distributed learning environment can be seen one essential insight of the described research.

INTRODUCTION

In the last years the Web 2.0 developments also had an important impact on the e-learning 2.0 approaches and new forms of modular and personal learning environments. These personal learning environments integrate and make use of a variety of learning services and "mash up" those services in individual instantiations of learning environments. Additionally also the field of mobile and ubiquitous computing has established a variety of solutions and best practices bringing e-learning support to the nomadic user. The nomadic user has special requirements and as the user/learner accesses learning support in a variety of context these requirements change. This basically holds both for single users accessing technology and information from different learning contexts as also for collaborative systems that enable distributed learning. As a classical setup for such distribute access to a learning environment we would like to highlight systems for supporting remote collaboration between mobile and classroom settings. The European project RAFT was a project exploring this field for about three years and a lot of lessons have been learned from this project as also empirical studies have demonstrated the effects of well-designed flexible environments supporting such distributed collaboration for learning.

On the one hand these developments describe a trend towards decomposition from highly complex and integrated monolithic learning management systems towards frameworks that enable the dynamic composition of personal learning environments out of a wide range of services and open source systems providing high level functional service interfaces for easy integration (Web-services, APIs). On the other hand the mobility trends and the usability requirements of mobile devices and mobile information access clearly highlight the split of complex e-learning environments into focused small applications of pieces of functionality designed for the context of use referred as widgets or appliances.

This chapter will describe and analyze developments coming from the e-learning 2.0 environments that are composed of Web-services and integrate those services based on flexible and customizable user interfaces that can consume and easily provide personal learning environments. Furthermore the next challenge ahead for making use of such environments is the distribution of such systems between different client systems that can be used mobile, on the desktop, electronic whiteboards, or in embedded displays and interaction devices.

First we will describe the contextual analysis for developing a service portfolio based on a functional specification and a clustering of such functions. The services where also further defined by a description of service orchestration and how the base services have to be combined for higher level use cases and instructional designs.

Second in a mapping between pedagogical roles, the underlying instructional designs, and a variety of mobile, desktop, and whiteboard clients, contextualized user interfaces consisting of widget combinations and customizations where developed based on the described service infrastructure in the European RAFT project.

We will describe developments and design approaches for mobile and contextualized learning support systems and how these systems support nomadic users and the access to functionality from a variety of user interfaces via flexible and dynamically configurable widget frameworks and the underlying service infrastructure.

BACKGROUND AND RELATED WORK

Situated learning as introduced by Lave and Wenger (Wenger & Lave, 1991) states the importance of knowledge acquisition in a cultural context and the integration in a community of practice. Learning in this sense must not only be planned structured by a curriculum but also by the tasks and learning situations and the interaction with the social environment of the learner. This is often contrasted with the classroom-based learning where most knowledge is out of context and presented de-contextualized. On the one hand the process of contextualization and de-contextualization might be important for abstraction and generalization of knowledge on the other hand in the sense of cognitive apprenticeship (Collins, Brown, & Newman, 1989) it is reasonable to guide the learner towards appropriate levels and context of knowledge coming from an authentic learning situation. Contextualized and mobile learning combine the latest developments in ubiquitous and context aware computing with pedagogical approaches relevant to structure more situated and context aware learning support. Searching for different backgrounds of mobile and contextualized learning authors have identified the relations between existing educational paradigms and new classes of mobile applications for education (Naismith, Lonsdale, Vavoula, & Sharples, 2004). Furthermore best practices of mobile learning applications have been identified and discussed in focused workshops (Stone, Alsop, Briggs, & Tompsett, 2002; Tatar, Roschelle, Vahey, & Peunel, 2002). Especially in the area of educational field trips (Equator Project, 2003; RAFT, 2003) in the last years innovative approaches for intuitive usage of contextualized mobile interfaces have been developed.

Many of the field trip support systems have firstly developed new tools for information collection in the field nevertheless a real added value has been shown in connecting the field trip and the classroom via live conferencing and data transmission for shared task work and collaboration (Bergin, 2004). Mostly in newer approaches individual small snippets of functionality or focused applications are provided to individual users or small teams of users with mobile devices, which deliver a part of the complete learning experience and contribute to a bigger shared learning task. The measurements or data from these smaller components are often combined into data streams for allowing analysis, stimulating discussions on multiple perspectives, or reflective learning support. An example for how the functionality for such systems can be split up to support distributed collaborative learning with a variety of devices is described in detail in the next section.

Basically beside the analysis of all activities included in the instructional scenarios a definition of different roles and a split of functionality in the information architecture taking into account the problems of mobile interaction and constraints of mobile user interfaces is essential for the successful design of such contextualized learning support environments. Recent research

in human computer interaction describes several trends in designing new interfaces for interacting with information systems. Benford et al. (Benford et al., 2005) describe four main trends which include growing interest and relevance of sensing technologies, growing diversity in physical interfaces, increasing mobility and physical engagement in HCI, and a shift in types of applications for which innovative interfaces are designed. These developments also have a major impact on the development of new learning solutions and interfaces for explorative and situated learning support.

As context is a broad term we consider different interpretations for contextualized learning here as relevant and also consider different research backgrounds. Nevertheless we understand all different forms of contextualization as an adaptation process to different parameters of a learning situation. The learning environment adapts different adaptation targets (functionality, content, tasks) to different parameters of context (learning task, user characteristics, physical environment). Following Leutner personalization and contextualization can be seen as specialized forms of adaptation. At the core of adaptive systems are adaptive methods, which take an adaptation mean as a certain user characteristic or a part of the current user context and adapt different adaptation targets to this adaptation mean (Leutner, 1992).

For building infrastructures and technical solutions for contextualization relevant work comes from research on context-aware systems (A. Zimmermann, Lorenz, & Specht, 2005) in this interpretation often low level environmental context parameters as location, noise, lighting, temperature, are taken as adaptation means for adapting the learning environment. Considering the adaptation mean Zimmermann et. al distinguish between definitions by synonym or definitions by example which mainly name and describe certain context parameters as location, identity, time, temperature, noise, as well as beliefs, desires, and commitments and intentions

(Andreas Zimmermann, Lorenz, & Oppermann, 2007). Furthermore they introduce an operational definition of context describing following main categories of context information:

- Individuality Context, includes information about objects and users in the real world as well as information about groups and the attributes or properties the members have in common.
- Time Context, basically this dimension ranges from simple points in time to ranges, intervals and a complete history of entities.
- Locations Context, are divided into quantitative and qualitative location models, which allow to work with absolute and relative positions.
- Activity Context, reflects the entities goals, tasks, and actions.
- Relations Context, captures the relation an entity has established to other entities, and describes social, functional, and compositional relationships.

Another approach for using and modelling context information for knowledge worker and learning support is described in (Lokaiczyk et. Al. 2007). The process context allows to take into account the working steps and process progress modelled in working environments often by business process modelling languages. The authors differentiate event-based models and state-based models for process modelling which support different representation of process context information as also different adaptations. Furthermore they differentiate between semiautomatic identification of task context by analysing working documents of users and the user context which is quite similar to the attributes clustered in the individuality context mentioned by Zimmermann et. Al. (2007).

As a relevant approach from the field of instructional design and modelling of learning context

recent approaches for supporting flexible IMS Learning Design deployment environments are important. Recent examples of delivering IMS-LD designs on mobile devices have for example been demonstrated in (Sampson, 2008). Furthermore current developments in authoring environments for instructional design integrate more and more also the integration of mobile learning activities and the delivery of those on different devices. With the splitting of functionality in underlying service frameworks and step from widget based desktop user interfaces towards widget based mobile user interfaces we expect new possibilities for collaborative distributed learning support. First experiences into this direction will be described in this chapter.

A DESIGN METHODOLOGY FOR CONTEXTUALIZED INTERACTION

In the context of the European funded project RAFT - Remotely Accessible Field Trips- the consortium created learning tools for remote field trip support in schools. The system should support a variety of learners with different tasks either in the classroom or in the field.

RAFT envisioned to facilitate field trips for schools and to enable international collaboration of schools. Instead of managing a trip for 30 students, small groups from the RAFT partner schools went out to the field, while the other students and classes from remote schools participate interactively from their classrooms via the Internet. The groups going to the field were equipped with data gathering devices (photographic, video, audio, measuring), wireless communication and a video conferencing system for direct interaction between the field and the classroom.

Field trips are an ideal example for an established pedagogical method that can be enhanced with computer-based tools for new ways of collaboration and individual active knowledge construction. The learners in the field can collect information and contextualize it with their own experiences and in the same time work on tasks with their peers and detect new perspectives and solutions to given problems. To foster the variety of perspectives and activities in the field trip process RAFT developed tools for the focused support of different activities in the field and in the classroom.

Basically from analysing the tasks and activities of users in non-technically supported field trips a role model was developed for roles specializing on different tasks in the field trip. Additionally in a first phase also the usage of out of the box technology (digital cameras, PDAs, GPS devices, Tablet PC) was tested and the usefulness and usability of end users was taken in formal evaluation studies and end user creativity workshops. In a second phase the functionality for technically supporting distributed field trips was specified in a functional description and clustering of the functionality in dedicated appliances. User interfaces for dedicated

roles where then basically developed by analysing, which appliances or end user widgets are necessary for enabling full technical support of the different roles. In a last step the information architectures for different roles where defined and combinations of necessary hardware features and appliances where identified. The different steps are described in the following sections.

Functional Analysis and Service Design

Based on a conceptual model of a field trip different functional clusters where identified ranging from planning activities, coordination and management activities, and field activities as data gathering, tagging, annotation, and in-situ data analysis where identified. In the functional specification a list of activities for the different field trip phases were identified based on scenarios from different subjects and instructional designs for field trips.

Figure 1. Field trip activity clusters from the functional analysis

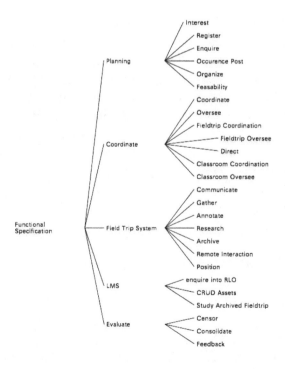

A selection of the found functionality is shown in Figure 1.

To support a wide variety of different learning activities and the usage of interfaces on different devices the user interface of the RAFT system had to be built out of single blocks that support different client technologies and interaction styles. Therefore based on the functional specification coming out of the requirements analysis phase we clustered the functionality into components and recombined those components depending on the task and the interaction device that were foreseen for a certain user role. Additionally a Web service layer was build on the basis of the ALE LCMS (Kravcik & Specht, 2004) which allowed us to give access to a wide variety of interface technologies connecting and implementing the application logic for different activities. Figure 2 gives an overview of the different ALE service frameworks and applications needed for the different phases of the "Interactive Field Trip System" (IFTS) in RAFT. Beside the different tasks for preparation,

evaluation and the field trip activity itself the ALE system provided a basic service infrastructure that needed to be extended with some new functionality for RAFT requirements.

The RAFT services in this sense all build on a common infrastructure with base services as content management, communications support and utilities for administrative support. Furthermore it became clear that a base library for certain interface components was necessary as field trip support applications in most cases had to be adapted to the specific field trip type. Basically the RAFT IFTS integrates all functionality and modules needed for the preparation, the evaluation and the actual field trip. Extending the existing frameworks and functionality with specific functionality and integrating it into a consistent IFTS application provided the basic functionality.

The existing ALE system that was used already provided basic functionality for content interchange, content management, communication and streaming, and basic interface components

Figure 2 gives an overview of the core service frameworks and functional frameworks as also user applications in the different phases

like described in the previous section. In the next section we will give a brief overview of selected RAFT service frameworks that where added.

- **ALE Flexible Metatagging:** Provided data model and functionality to define metadata schemas and to provide metadata sets based on these schemas. The schemas define sets, structures and properties of attributes, which should be entered by users providing metadata. The framework supports multiple and flexible schemas. The schemas are used for easy semi-automatic creation and standard- based support of metadata sets allowing reach flexibility and reuse of existing data. This framework had to be added as new forms of metadata as location data or environmental data had to be added to the content recorded and created live in the field. Furthermore the metadata sets could differ based on the subject and instructional design of the field trip.
- **ALE CTM Connector:** Provided the functionality to communicate with the video conferencing solution (Click To Meet) and create a new videoconference room, get its id and store it as part of a paragraph. This was realized via a Web service enabling the creation and recall of new videoconference rooms from different video conferencing clients. This was also relevant for setting up the field trip and enable flexible access to the video conference from different user interfaces and widgets.
- **ALE Notification:** Handled receiving and distributing notifications between all connected clients and supports the system's awareness functionalities. This was achieved by a central Instant Messaging Server based on the Jabber protocol (http://www.jabber.org, an OpenSource XML based real-time message interchange protocol) who distributes the notifications. Implemented with

Jabber Server and Connection Libraries for Flash, Java, and CE.net. The requirement to synchronize clients components based on different technologies can be seen as an essential element of distributed live collaboration systems.

- **ALE Database / RAFT Database:** Managed all content synchronization and storage in the database. The ALE Database framework holds the basic data model for RLOs specifying the content structure of field trips, content, assessment and exercise elements provided by the ALE system. This framework allowed the usage of the RAFT LMS with different databases and a special RAFT data model that has been developed as extension of the basic content aggregation model.
- **ALE Course Content Management:** Provides logic for combining learning objects in hierarchical or non- hierarchical structures and defines the clusters of content that are defined as high level learning objects, i.e. Courses, Field Trips, Blended Courseware. The framework was extended to handle the new RAFT types like fieldtrip, task, etc.
- **ALE Content Block Management:** Provides all functionality for the management of content blocks, the lowest level of granularity in the ALE content model. A content block can contain canned content like images, text, references, video, animations but also reference to live streams embedded in a content page.
- **ALE User Management:** The user management will allow creation and editing of user accounts, importing user accounts from external data sources like text files or LDAP directories and assigning roles and user rights. It works closely together with the rights management. This framework has been extended to support the role of the user in the fieldtrips.

- **ALE Basic Components:** Basic interface components allow the user interface of ALE to have a consistent handling and user interaction. The framework can be used by applications like an interface widget library with a variety of components like navigations trees, tab components, listings and other. Basically this can be seen as an early version of current development for widget servers that enable to server a library of interface components and flexibly link them to data containers or in this case learning objects of different granularity.

- **ALE Exporter:** The basic exporter framework allowed exporting content into different content interchange formats (CIF). For RAFT mainly standalone formats for schools Web servers and SCORM compatible CIF for integration of RAFT content into standard LMS will be important. For RAFT exporters the following formats have been added:

RAFT standalone (HTML, JavaScript) and RAFT SCORM, RAFT Mobile.

- **ALE Archivist:** The archiving framework provides functionality to store parts of a course, the whole course or several courses into an external format and to retrieve them later into the same or a different database. It will deal also with data integrity and key resolution, for example when primary/ foreign keys already exist in the target database.

- **ALE Communication:** ALE contains basic communication functionality this can be used by any application integrating this framework. It can be used to have forums, chats and other synchronous and asynchronous communication tools. It is based on simple message metaphors that allow communicating via messages with attachments.

- **ALE Streaming:** The ALE streaming framework allows integrating streaming

Figure 3. The basic RAFT infrastructure

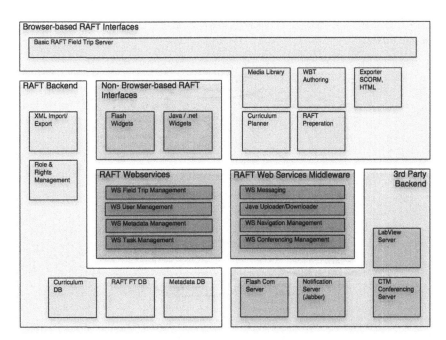

functionality into ALE applications by simply using a preconfigured streaming server. This allows user to integrate live streaming content in RLO pages.

As shown in Figure 3 the different services described above used underlying existing services and tools as a Learning Management System (ALE) and Live Conferencing (Flash Communication Server, Click TO Meet Server, and LabView Server) for integration via the Web services in non-browser based and plain browser based user interfaces.

Towards Nomadic User Interfaces

To develop flexible user interfaces that are focused on specific roles and activities and also fit in the whole distribution of activities and tasks in a second step out of the scenarios in different teaching domains and the functional specification use cases and roles where developed. An example is given in Figure 4.

In parallel to this functional clustering also a role model for different pedagogically motivated roles was developed. An excerpt of those is given in Table 1.

The definition and fine-tuning of the roles enabled by the RAFT system was developed through an iterative approach, based on the observation and involvement of users in order to gain a detailed understanding of requirements. Field trips with school students were held in Scotland, Slovakia, Canada and Germany to identify different activities in the field and in the classroom and to draw first evaluations of critical factors. In line with a contextual inquiry approach (Beyer & Holtzblatt, 1998), our aim was to observe and analyze the users' environment for patterns of collaborative activity, and involve users in the evaluation of technologies.

To provide an example of how our contextual inquiry was conducted, we report our experience in a preliminary field trip trialled on the coast of Tentsmuir together with students from the Harris

Figure 4. Clustered use cases based on roles and phases of activity. The diagram shows teacher field trip preparation use cases.

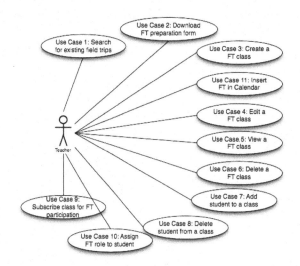

Table 1. Basic functional Roles and their function with examples

Role/Function Description	Functions	Example
Expert Interviews/ Reporter	Structure Interview, Moderate questions from the classroom	A field trip class wants to learn about a defined station in a complex production process
Datagatherer/Annotator: During the field trip the students gather data to support/disprove the proposed hypothesis and to find new interesting aspects. Means of data-gathering examples: video, camera, sensor data	Collect Data, Annotate content with metadata, collect sensor measures, verify concrete hypotheses	Students go to the different phases of the chocolate production process and document the stages with photos.
Analyse: Data gained from site is analysed and discussed in the field trip, in the classroom and post field trip event.	Research online, evaluate incoming data from the field	Students look at the images taken from a biology field trip and assess the quality and if hypotheses can be verified based on the acquired materials.

Academy of Dundee, Scotland. Our aim in this research was to initiate and implement the idea of roles, to gauge the ergonomics of using PDAs in the field, and to test the GPS, GPRS and mapping software during the course of a field trip. In the field, nine 14-years-old students would be using a variety of sampling and gathering techniques to study the development of the dunes that characterize the Tentsmuir Coast.

In a first step, we let the teacher fill the RAFT field trip template, so as to specify pedagogic and curricular goals and indicate tasks. The work involved different learning modules and the students were divided into four groups, engaged in different activities such as landform transect, vegetation survey, soil survey, stream flow measuring. Instructions for each activity were transferred onto PDAs. The roles involved in the RAFT approach were explained and the students were told that they would play Data Gatherers, Scouts and Annotators. This experience suggested that the analyst in the classroom, in charge to analyse and elaborate the raw data collected in the field, has an important function: he/she must check immediately that the data being received is complete and appropriate, so that the data can be recorded

again if necessary, and the opportunity to obtain the necessary data from the field is not lost.

The role-specific information architecture has direct effects on the screen layout of the user interfaces. This suggested us to look for solutions that would adopt design principles such as

scalability, modularity and flexibility. Given the dynamic set of devices that characterizes the RAFT Field Trips, the challenge is to provide a single GUI that runs on all the devices and yet accommodates the input, output and processing capabilities of each device. Our approach in this matter proposes a widget-based scalable and modular interface, which adapts to the role and to the device. The widgets constitute building blocks, functional frames where different components can be placed and displayed, enabling different options. According to the functional components, we defined different widgets that need to adapt to the roles' needs and hardware features.

Based on the role model and the non-functional requirements from the prototyping experiences a basic mapping of functionality and roles was done. Basically by defining such a matrix the focus of the role for a certain task was set and also the cooperation context for different roles was defined.

Table 2. Mapping roles and functional widgets

Role	Task Widget	Navigation Widget	Messaging Widget	Conference Widget
Field Site				
Data Gatherer	+	+	+	-
Annotator	+	-	+	-
Reporter	+	+	+	-
Communicator	+	-	-	+
Classroom				
Task Manager	+	-	+	-
Director	+	+	+	+
Analyst	+	-	+	-

On the one hand learning pairs could be defined by the roles like the Data Gatherer and Annotator pair, which have a clear split of responsibilities: while the navigator knows where to go on the map to collect certain data the annotator looks at the collected data and annotates it with the current context, both roles get their current context by agreeing on a common task. Another example is the Reporter and communicator pair, while the reporter concentrates on the verbal communication between classroom and expert and has a moderating role the communicator focuses on documenting and capturing the communication with the conferencing and recording facilities. On the other hand in the classroom site the director has a moderating role for the whole class and therefore needs all information available on the classroom big screen, while the task manager only concentrates on managing and structuring tasks for the field trip on the fly.

During the field trips in RAFT it became obvious that the roles do not always need to be split between persons but several roles can also be taken over by one person if complexity allows. Additionally it became obvious during ongoing usage studies with out of the box hardware that roles could also be split between different users if the hardware used could be split in a logical way between the task participants working on a certain role. For example the data gathering could be split between handling the GPS device for taking measures of the location and between the personal collecting the data, this was basically dependent on the complexity of collected data and metadata. Therefore in the design further requirements for dynamically configuring user interfaces by splitting up or combining functionality were identified.

For the different roles in the field trip the information architectures for the different appliances where inferred. One example shows the scouting application in Figure 5. According to the related use cases, the Scout searches for interesting points in the field and needs to be informed about tasks; to be able to send information about interesting locations (hotspots); to communicate with other users in the class and in the field. Therefore, the Scout's main interaction widgets are Task, Communication, and Navigation ones, enabling him/her to communicate the personal current position to the other team members and set hotspots for points of interest. A device suiting these requirements is a GPS, GPRS enabled handheld device, providing features of portability and trackability.

Figure 5. The information architecture of the scouting application

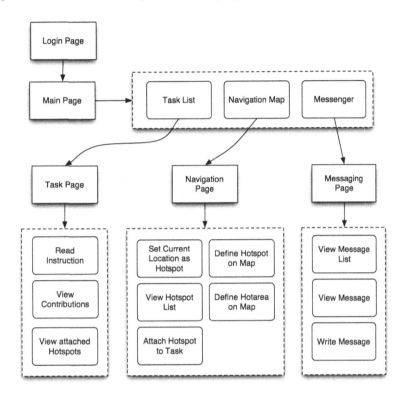

The Scout mainly cooperates with the Task Manager in the classroom and the Data Gathering teams in the field. Therefore, the entities a Scout manipulates go into a consistent field trip object repository and can be seen and manipulated by other team members in the field and in the classroom.

The Scout starts to search for points of interest and scans the environment; as soon as he/she founds something interesting, he/she locks the position and a notification with the Point Of Interest (POI) record is stored in the shared field trip repository. Awareness about changes in the state of tasks and data collections for tasks plays an important role for the collaborative work and the design of the interface. The repository automatically sends a notification to the team members and also to the Task Manager. The Task Manager evaluates the data and the metadata of the Scout and decides if more scouting is needed or the data gathering and annotation can start.

Based on this infrastructure the RAFT partners developed a variety of interface components and widgets based on different technologies like Java, Microsoft .NET, Macromedia Flash and others. Those widgets could then be easily combined in different applications, which allowed a highly focused and contextualized cooperation between different field trip participants.

As an additional problem of designing communication and cooperation between mobile, desktop, and whiteboard clients the problem of multimodal interaction became important. An instantiation of a multimodal communication channel widget is the messaging widget as one component of the RAFT interface. Depending on the input and output characteristics of the device of a user the messaging can be used with classical keyboard input on a classroom role but the back-channel from a mobile user interface in the field has to be based on audio recording as typing not really while walking and collecting data in the field.

Another example is the communication between and archiver who is mainly working with a classical PC terminal and Web access and a data gatherer in the field: As output channel the archiver can use the PC screen and therefore mostly receives text output. On the other hand a scout in the field walking around with a mobile device cannot easily use a text input. Most virtual keyboard input possibilities were quite unusable in the field due to lighting conditions and difficult typing on a mobile device on the move. Therefore the mobile users mostly used scribbles on a notepad like widget and audio input when the environmental conditions allow for.

CONCLUSION AND FUTURE TRENDS

The RAFT project raised a lot of technical and interaction issues relevant for the field of designing learning experiences for mobile and pervasive learning. Beside the backend technology based on an LCMS and Web services that allowed for the combination of different client technologies from electronic whiteboards to mobile telephones the synchronization and notification of heterogeneous clients accessing a persistent and consistent learning object repository became very important.

As we found the field trip a very good example not only the synchronization between different user cooperating on a common task, but also the distribution over the different phases of the field trip (preperation, field trip activitiy, and evaluation) appeared to be an important aspect of nomadic activities for learning and exploration.

Furthermore from the prototyping and analysis of the fieldwork by end users we saw the following main activities for supporting distributed contextualized learning approaches:

Cooperative task work for synchronizing activities and raising interest: The distributed work on a task focuses the interaction and communication between the learners, technology get into the background when the curiosity about the given task and its exploration in physical and knowledge space become the main interest. The context in this sense is an enabling mean that allows the learners to immerse in the learning subject at hand.

Data Gathering for Active Construction of knowledge and learning materials: Users are much more motivated when "self made" learning material get integrated in the curriculum and they have the possibility to extend existing pre-given structures for learning.

Instant and multimodal messaging for a lively experience: The instant exchange of multimodal messages on different service levels was identified as a core requirement to make a live field trip experience happing between the field and the classroom.

Similar to the developments described in this chapter we see comparable trends in a variety of European projects for delivering flexible contextualized user interfaces based on widget approaches. Recently in the TenCompetence integrated project and the MACE project approaches for widget based interfaces and the integration of those widgets with an underlying instructional design engine based on IMS-LD have been developed. In the TENCompetence project a widget server has been developed which allows for the integration of widgets and a control of them based IMS Learning Design. The widget server mainly enables Learning Design authors who wish to use actual services within SleD/Coppercore environment and allows authors to leverage & create new external services and use them in their Learning Designs. The server is based on the draft W3C widget specification and it offers the possibility to add new widget services and make them available to the Learning Design runtime.

Furthermore more and more Web 2.0 services integrate the power of mobile information access and creation any space where learners have access to content and activities can become a learning space on an ad hoc basis. When designing such systems very little is known about how such collaborative learning systems can facilitate people's collaboration in the best way and not to distract and become a hurdle between accessing and experiencing the real world while having digital tool support. Examples that can be found in the literature describing and designing mobile social software as a learning aid have recently been analysed in (De Jong, Specht, & Koper, 2008)

REFERENCES

Benford, S., Schnoedelbach, H., Koleva, B., Anastasi, R., Greenhalgh, C., Rodden, T., et al. (2005). Expected, sensed, and desired: A framework for designing sensing-based interaction. *ACM Trans. Comput.-Hum. Interact., 12*(1), 3-30.

Bergin, D.A., Anderson, A.H., Molnar, T., Baumgartner, R., Mitchell, S., Korper, S., Curley, A., & Rottmann, J. (2004). Providing remote accessible field trips (RAFT): An evaluation study. *Computers in Human Behavior, 23*(1), 192-219.

Beyer, H., & Holtzblatt, K. (1998). *Contextual design: Defining customer-centred systems*. San Francisco: Morgan Kaufmann Publishers Inc.

Collins, A., Brown, J.S., & Newman, S.E. (1989). Cognitive apprenticeship: Teaching the craft of reading, writing, and mathematics. In L.B. Resnick (Ed.), *Knowing, learning, and instruction* (pp. 453-494). Hillsdale, NJ: Lawrence Erlbaum Associates.

De Jong, T., Specht, M., & Koper, R. (2008). A reference model for mobile social software for learning. *International Journal of Continuing Engineering Education and Life-Long Learning (IJCEELL), 18*(1), 118-138.

Equator Project. (2003). The EQUATOR interdisciplinary research collaboration. Retrieved from http://www.equator.ac.uk/

Kravcik, M., & Specht, M. (2004). *Flexible navigation support in the WINDS learning environment for architecture and design*. Paper presented at the Adaptive Hypermedia 2004 Conference, Eindhoven.

Naismith, L., Lonsdale, P., Vavoula, G., & Sharples, M. (2004). *Literature review in mobile technologies and learning* (Literature Review No. 11). University of Birmingham.

RAFT. (2003). RAFT project Website. Retrieved from http://www.raft-project.net

Sampson, D.G., Zervas, P. (2008). *Enabling interoperable mobile learning: Evaluation results from the use of SMILE PDA learning design player*. Paper presented at the WMUTE, Bejing.

Stone, A., Alsop, G., Briggs, J., & Tompsett, C. (2002, June 20-21). *M-Learning and e-learning: A review of work undertaken by the learning technology research group, Kingston University, UK*. Paper presented at the Proceedings of the European Workshop on Mobile and Contextual Learning, The University of Birmingham, England.

Tatar, D., Roschelle, D., Vahey, P., & Peunel, W.R. (2002). *Handhelds go to school: Lessons learned*.

Wenger, E., & Lave, J. (1991). *Situated learning: Legitimate peripheral participation*. Cambridge, New York: Cambridge University Press.

Zimmermann, A., Lorenz, A., & Oppermann, R. (2007). *An operational definition of context*. Paper presented at the Context 07.

Zimmermann, A., Lorenz, A., & Specht, M. (2005). Personalization and context-management. *User Modeling and User Adaptive Interaction (UMUAI), Special Issue on User Modeling in Ubiquitous Computing, 15*(3-4), 275-302.

Section III
Multimodal Interaction in Mobile Environment

The third section of this book discusses of multimodal interaction in mobile environment, according to the devices limitations and the different contexts where people can use them. Some architectural solutions, adaptation methods, and uses to the different contexts are presented. A particular attention was devoted to multimodal interfaces for mobile GIS, due the implicit nature of their spatial and temporal information, the involvement of visual channel, and their tendency to be used in different context by different users. Finally, another emerging scenario discussed by chapters contained in this section deals with the use of multimodal mobile systems for social applications such as e-learning; in particular, specific methods to make adaptable a mobile-learning system and addressing how mobile multimodal interaction is changing many individual and social activities are described.

Chapter XVI
Speech Driven Interaction in Mobile Multimodality

Giovanni Frattini
Engineering IT, Italy

Fabio Corvino
Engineering IT, Italy

Francesco Gaudino
Engineering IT, Italy

Pierpaolo Petriccione
Engineering IT, Italy

Vladimiro Scotto di Carlo
Engineering IT, Italy

Gianluca Supino
Engineering IT, Italy

ABSTRACT

This chapter introduces a possible architecture for building mobile multimodal applications and our experiences in this domain. Mobile devices are becoming increasingly powerful and sophisticated and their use more and more diffused; the need for new and complex services has consequently amplified. New generation mobile applications must be able to manage convenient inputs and outputs modes to make the dialog natural, intuitive, and user centric. Simultaneous use of complementary communication channels (multimodality), such as voice, keyboard, stylus, leads to a more complicated input processing system but it's a way to simplify the interaction. A speech driven interaction between user and service delivery systems may be the ideal solution for the development of ubiquitous and context aware applications: besides being a very instinctive and convenient way to express complex questions, speech is also the best option when eyes and hands are busy.

INTRODUCTION

In this chapter we report some of the experiences we have gained working on a new mobile multimodal speech driven software solution, in a research project called CHAT (Frattini et al. 2006).

More specifically, we have concentrated efforts on mobile multimodal services for supporting cultural heritage fruition (museums, archeological parks, etc.) and e-learning. Multimodal services can be synergic or alternate. Synergic multimodality, which refers to the simultaneous use of different modalities (speech, sketch, handwrite, keyboard) in a single interaction act, could introduce real benefits to mobile users when keyboard-based interaction is difficult. On the other hand, alternate multimodality, which is characterized by a sequence of unimodal messages, has been investigated during past years (Frattini et al. 2006), without an evident commercial success.

A platform for synergic mobile multimodal services is a complex system. Some of the issues discussed in this chapter are well known, others are related to users mobility. We will consider:

- The logic for establishing the user intention and the task to be executed on the server side.
- The target terminals and the client software environment for enabling an optimal user experience.
- The underlying technological infrastructures in terms of network protocols and efficiency.

Synergic multimodality encompasses different processes: one of them, called "fusion", must combine the different modes in order to match the user intention. We can affirm that a software architecture for building multimodal services must have a fusion module (Frattini et al. 2006). Our choice has been to implement a speech-driven fusion process: the role of voice inputs is more relevant than other possible input modalities. Voice is probably the most appropriate and instinctive mean to express complex commands, especially when the information content of user requests becomes more and more rich and complicated. Nevertheless, using complex modalities, like voice, has some important consequences: speech recognition must be as accurate as possible. Furthermore, not all the commercial handsets are able to host a speech recogniser and process vocal inputs locally. Thus, distributing recognition processes can help to improve recognition quality. In particular, as the information content of user requests becomes more and more complicated,

the ideal solution is to acquire and transport vocal signals over a mobile network and, thus processing them on more powerful hardware. Once on the server, different natural language understanding algorithms can be applied. The meaning of linguistic utterances can be derived using formal structures, or meaning representations. The need for these representation models arises while trying to bridge the gap between linguistic inputs and non-linguistic knowledge of the world needed to perform tasks involving the meaning of linguistic inputs. Multimodality can help in formulating more appropriate hypothesis about the context in which the voice command must be placed and could help in improving the machine understanding process.

Simply accessing the phonological, morphological, and syntactic representations of sentences may not be enough in order to accomplish a task. For example, answering questions requires background knowledge about the topic of the question, about the way questions are usually asked and how such questions are usually answered. Therefore the use of domain-specific knowledge is required to correctly interpret natural language inputs.

An empirical approach to constructing natural language processing systems starts from a training corpus comprising sentences paired with appropriate translations into formal queries. Learning algorithms are utilized to analyse the training data and produce a semantic parser that can map subsequent input sentences into appropriate tasks. Some techniques attempt to extend statistical approaches, which have been successful in domains such as speech recognition, to the semantic parsing problem.

In our proposal, the process of semantic inputs disambiguation is based on the collaboration of a stochastic classifier and a rule based engine. A domain specific data corpus has been manually labelled to build the model language while a named entity recogniser works as classifier, in order to extract meaningful semantic contents. This approach allows ignoring false starts or hesitations typical of natural language, focusing on really significant speech fragments. User commands are rebuilt on server side through a frame filling process in which the frame structure is application dependent.

Hidden Markov Model is adopted for modelling user utterances; hidden states of HMM are frame's semantic slots labels, while observed words are the slot filling values (Jurafsky & Martin, 2007). The aim of classifier is to detect the most likely category for a word (or cluster) given the overall sequence of previous words in the sentence.

The task solving process is carried out integrating information fragments included in frame's slots with the ones coming from complementary input channels. Available data are then processed by a rule engine reasoning using inference rules in a forward chain.

In order to overcome issues which could arise from a lack of information due to channel loudness, we also present a possible solution for the recovery of contents affected by different noise sources. The recovery algorithm uses the Levin and Rappaport Hovav *linking theory* (Levin & Rappaport Hovav, 1996). This theory argues that the syntactic realization of predicate arguments is predictable from semantics. Therefore, from a complementary point of view, we expect that fixing the semantic of user's utterance it is possible to gather indications on the syntactic collocation of words, helping in the retrieval of corrupted information fragments. Multimodality can help in establishing the semantic frame of the user utterance and thus formulating more accurate hypothesis on the users' intention.

It is immediate that target terminals are a fundamental piece of the overall system architecture. In order to build a real world multimodal application it is important to understand which kind of devices are currently in use and, possibly, what are the needs that future mobile applications should satisfy. Even though every year new and more powerful devices are appearing (we are talking

also about mobile phones) multimodality can not be easily managed on every kind of terminals. We have considered a minimal set of features that a mobile terminals must have:

- Big screen (to have good fruition of multimedia output),
- Microphone (to acquire audio inputs),
- Touch screen (to manage point/sketch/speak/handwrite interaction),
- Powerful hardware and advanced OS (good software platform, different formats and protocols),
- Battery lifetime.

These are features that are not available on entry level mobile phones at the time being. Thus we have focused our attention toward two main classes of devices: smartphones and PDAs.

We have conducted our experiments using two mobile technologies: J2ME and .NET Compact Framework.

The mobile terminal type and the terminal technologies are not the only constraint and the only choice to undertake. Consider, among the others, the following requirements:

- The ideal mobile multimodal application should be able to update contents without user intervention;
- The ideal mobile multimodal application should be able to understand user will reducing keyboard based interactions;
- The ideal mobile multimodal application should be able to use different modalities, access contents using intelligent matching algorithms, etc.

To match these kinds of requirements a better approach is to consider a so-called thin client approach. In other words, the client logic must be as reduced as possible.

This approach has also disadvantages. Here we enumerate the main ones:

- Band occupation. Such architecture implies the transfer of big amount of information between the two sides. Such solution is possible only with a large band connection (typically WI-FI, UMTS or HSDPA).
- Much slower interaction.
- A more complex architecture.

The use of a thin client/fat server approach implies the use of transfer protocols between the two sides. HTTP is a pillar of modern client/server interactions, but it cannot be left alone. Mixing HTTP with protocols used for IP telephony can boost the application capabilities a step forward. It is possible to stream to the server audio/video signals as long as they are produced, avoiding to store them on the mobile terminal; it is possible to push contents on the client when they are available, etc. In general, since the internet paradigm is more and more "network is the computer", it is of fundamental importance to use as much as possible the available networks.

Last but not least, continuous voice acquisition must be combined with a data transport mechanism. We have used a transport based on the RTP/UDP protocol. Furthermore, using IP signalling (SIP protocol) we have been able to detach the client from the server: the input signals are transferred on the server. When ready, the server calls the terminal and instructs it on how to present the contents. The presentation system, thus, does not use standards like XHTML, SMIL, X+V but extends them. Synergic multimodality implies that classic browsers cannot be used as they are: clients must be able to acquire and present multiple signals at the same time.

BACKGROUND

Synergic multimodality has been investigated in recent years (Nigay & Coutaz, 1993; Oviatt & al.; 1997, Oviatt, 2000). All these works are of fundamental importance to understand the state of art and the research evolution in this domain. The W3C [http://www.w3.org/2002/mmi/] work group has proposed a reference architecture for multimodal systems. A concrete implementation of a full multimodal system is available at [http://www.ravenclaw-olympus.org/]. This work helps in identifying potential improvements in supporting new modes and new clients and more advanced algorithms for fusing modes and render results.

It is true, that simultaneous use of complementary communication channels, leads to a more complicated input processing system. Among others, voice is probably the best option for communicating while eyes and hands are busy and it represents the best mean to express complex questions to a machine. The next generation of voice based user interface technology enables easy-to-use automation of new and existing communication services, achieving a more natural human-machine interaction. However, the main problem in managing human-machine dialog lies in bridging the gap between machine's jargon and natural language. As reported (Gorin et al., 2003), for a determined task, some linguistic events are essential to recognize and understand, others not so. In a user utterance not all words have the same semantic weight and research aims are more and more related with information extraction or part of speech clustering and classification, as shown in (Wright et al., 1997; Arai et al., 1999). Most of the current works on information extraction and dialogue understanding systems are still based on domain-specific frame-and-slot templates. Anyway, this strong link between quality of recognition and restricted application context is the real limit to overcome. So, in (Gidea and Giurasfky, 2002) is proposed a shallow semantic interpreter based on semantic roles that are slightly domain-specific. This work describes an algorithm for identifying the semantic roles filled by constituents in a sentence. Such algorithm leverages on statistical techniques that have been successful for the related problems of syntactic parsing, part of speech tagging, and word sense disambiguation, including probabilistic parsing and statistical classification.

To construct natural language processing systems, most of the empirical approaches start from a training corpus comprising sentences paired with appropriate translations into formal queries. Then statistical methods are used to face the semantic parsing problem (Hwee Tou & Zelle, 1997).Typically statistical algorithms are trained on a hand-labeled dataset; on today, one of the most accurate is the FrameNet database, whose tagset organization is explained in (Johnson & Fillmore, 2000).

Mobile multimodal services are more complex. As discussed in (Yamakami, 2007) mobile multimodal services are very challenging. Furthermore, after a 5-year struggle in OMA (following 2 years in WAP forum), OMA decided to terminate the work item without producing any technical specification except an Architecture document (http://www.openmobilealliance.org/). Thus, while terminals capabilities are increasing, stardardization processes are de facto stopped. It is interesting that, while for alternate multimodality, several mark-up languages have been proposed and adopted industrially (namely X+V [http://www.voicexml.org/specs/multimodal/]) for synergic multimodality a standard language does not exist , even if several researches have addressed the problem proposing possible solutions (Filippo et al., 2003). This is true in general and not only for mobile multimodal applications.

Even if standards are stagnants, commercial products focused on mobile multimodality are available on the market. Kirusa [www.kirusa.com] is a relatively small company that produces multimodal software for Telecommunication operators. Kirusa core product is a solution for Voice SMS, which is a relatively simple multimodal application.

Nuance [www.nuance.com], a well known brand in the speech recognition domain, has recently released a framework for building multimodal mobile applications. This framework is based on standard like X+V and, thus, limited to alternate multimodality, which is not so interesting at the time being. It is worth noting that Nuance has selected a distributed recognition approach limiting the processing on client.

In (Frattini et al., 2006) we discussed and highlighted some of the topics that, in the meantime, the CHAT project has faced . We studied how to extend existing languages (X+V, SALT, SMIL [http://www.w3.org/TR/REC-smil/]) to multimodality, and how to build a new language specific for multimodality. For example, the MONA project (Niklfeld et al., 2005) has produced a multimodal presentation server, whose main features is to support deploy of device independent applications combining graphical user interface and speech input/output. We have found the functionality of pushing pages using the UIML, a markup language for describing user interfaces, particularly interesting. MONA is based on a client side engine that allows the presentation of a non standard mark-up language and the pushing of pages on the mobile device (while for low-end phone they use WAP push messages). However, in CHAT we have developed ((Frattini et al., 2008) multimodal objects able to manage telecommunication protocol for pushing contents. More in detail, we adopt the IP signaling protocol (SIP) that can be used to send unsolicited contents toward final users.

All the past experiences in this domain demonstrate that interfaces must be able to adapt themselves to contents and users' context. The idea of generating UI on the fly is discussed in (Reitter et al., 2004).

Thinlet framework [http://www.thinlet.com/] has inspired us in finding a solution for aggregating multimodal objects in a single UI. In our previous paper (Frattini et al., 2007) we have discussed an embryonic prototype of the J2ME mobile multimodal interface. We have continued on this track working on different operating systems.

For speech recognition we have tested Open Source solutions and commercial ones. Currently we choose the system developed by Loquendo [www.loquendo.com].

For handwriting recognition we have adopted the open source solution Jarnal [http://www.dk-levine.com/general/software/tc1000/jarnal.htm] but we are considering commercial alternatives. We have used software based on algorithms developed by IRPPS (Istituto di Ricerche sulla Popolazione e le Politiche Sociali, Rome) for sketch recognition (Avola, Caschera et al., 2007; Avola, Ferri et al., 2007).

ARCHITECTURE

The figure below shows the system architecture we propose for mobile synergic multimodality.

Such architecture comes from well known patterns [*W3C Multimodal Interaction Activity*. http://www.w3.org/2002/mmi]. The main innovation we have introduced concerns the usage of a mix of web 2.0 and telecommunication technologies; this has produced interesting results. Nevertheless, this approach has different impacts on how software on terminals has to be designed.

In the client/server approach there is still another choice that must be taken; thin client vs. fat client. When speaking about thin vs. fat cli-

ent we do not refer simply to a browser mediated interaction but more in generally to the physical location of the multimodal modules. PDAs and smart-phone are able to run speech recognition applications and TTS application, while other mobile devices are not enabled to run anything but Java applications. Thus, a platform for building a generic multimodal application should be able to receive raw data and pre-processed data, depending on the terminal capabilities. For the client application we follow a thin client approach. So on client side there is only an application able to show a good looking graphical interface, to manage the output channels and to collect the inputs coming from users and context information. We call such application MMUIManager (MultiModal User Interface Manager). The MMUIManager is able to open different input channels toward the server side of the application. Protocols used are HTTP, RTP and SIP

The Front end block contains the interfaces between the MMUIManager and the logic of the architecture. Such interfaces are mainly servlets. Such block has also the task to collect the inputs coming from unimodal channels, send them to recognizers (speech, sketch, handwriting). After the recognition, if successful, each servlet generates an EMMA (Extensible MultiModal Annota-

Figure 1. Overall system architecture (main blocks)

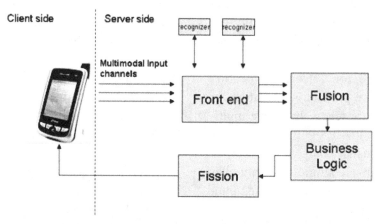

tion markup language, [www.w3.org/TR/emma]) output that is sent toward a fusion module and then forwarded to business logic.

The Fusion module merges contemporary inputs coming from different input channels. It receives different inputs in EMMA format and merges them in a single EMMA file.

The Business Logic block has different tasks to accomplish:

- To maintain/adjourn the status of the interaction for each user;
- To select the contents to send back according to user request, user profile and context.

Fission module has to distribute the contents selected by Business Logic to final users.

MMUIManager

MMUIManager follows a thin client approach. So it is a light client which has to accomplish the following tasks:

- To show a good looking interface built on the fly according to the indication given from the server side business logic;
- To collect multimodal input and show multimedia output to have a good system interaction and content fruition experience.

To reach such goals we have followed a XUL like approach [http://www.mozilla.org/projects/xul/].

Such approach is very flexible and allows a dynamic behaviour according to physical context, interaction type and user profile. The graphical aspect, but the contents too, do not reside in the device, but they are dynamically sent by business logic.

MMUIManager architecture and implementation results are widely reported in (Frattini et al, 2008)

The Front End Module, the Approach to Distributed Recognition

In our architecture we have chosen to distribute the recognition process outside the device to have a light client application as mobile devices have limited hardware resources. So it is suitable to have an abstraction layer among MMUIManager and recognizers. Such layer is the Front End module that essentially has the following tasks to accomplish:

- Redirect input coming from the MMUIManager toward the recognizers, if necessary;
- Send the recognized inputs toward the fusion module in EMMA format;
- Generate some kind of output (TTS).

For Distributed Speech Recognition, as we want to recognize speech in real time, there must be an open streaming channel (RTP protocol) between the device and the recognizer (ASR, Automatic Speech Recognizer). This allows the continuous recognition of the speech. To open such a channel there must be a negotiation process between MMUIManager and recognizer; such negotiations are made using the MRCP protocol (RFC 4463).

For Distributed Sketch/Handwrite Recognition, there's no need of a real time process. After acquisition of InkML traces set, MMUIManager sends it via POST HTTP to the Front end module which forwards it to recognizer (SR, Sketch Recognizer).

Essentially the Front-End has been implemented as a group of cooperating Java servlets deployed on an application server (e.g. Tomcat, JBoss etc.):

- **InitServlet:** This servlet instantiates a SIP communication channel between the ASR and the client device. The init method of the InitSpeechServlet returns to the client the IP of the ASR, the port and the MRCP port in order to open the voice channel.

- **VoiceServlet**: This servlet recognizes the output of the ASR and builds EMMA file to sent to the Fusion.
- **SketchServlet**: This servlet is similar to the SpeechServlet. It builds an EMMA file with the symbol ID and others additional parameters.
- **TTSServlet**: To communicate with TTS engine.

The mechanism for preparation of the voice channel and voice recognition has been implemented as follows:

1. Client invokes the InitServlet in order to open the RTP channel;
2. InitServlet contacts the ASR and returns to the client the specified MRCP port to open a direct RTP channel to the ASR;
3. The client device invokes the ASR with the parameters of the point 2. and opens SIP channel;
4. The ASR tries to recognize each voice input from the device. If a sentence is recognized, the result with a confidence value is sent to the VoiceServlet;

5. The VoiceServlet analyzes the output of the ASR and checks the associate confidence value. If this value is higher than a default value, an EMMA file with the recognized sentence and additional data is built; otherwise a compensation process starts with an action in order to specify to the client an error message using TTSServlet.
6. A complete EMMA file with the recognized sentence is sent to the Fusion.

We report an example of a possible EMMA file as result of the voice recognition process (see Box 1).

We have experimented many recognizers (commercial ones and open source). At the moment our architecture includes:

- ASR Loquendo as engine for speech recognition;
- Jarnal as engine for handwrite recognition;
- Software based on algorithms developed by our partners of IRPPS (Istituto di Ricerche sulla Popolazione e le Politiche Sociali, Rome) for sketch recognition (Avola,

Box 1.

```
<emma:emma version="1.0" xmlns:emma=http://www.w3.org/2003/04/emma>
    <emma:group id="grp">

    <emma:one-of id="oneof">

    <emma:interpretation id="int1"

    emma:confidence="0.9"

    emma:mode="speech"

    emma:start="32324440">

    <user_id>ty90091</user_id>

    <speech> I want information about Giotto</speech>

    </emma:interpretation>

    </emma:one-of>
    </emma:group>
    </emma:emma>
```

Caschera et al., 2007; Avola, Ferri et al., 2007);

- Loquendo TTS, as TTS engine.

Open source solutions have been preferred when available.

Fusion

In multimodal systems, a fusion module has to be designed in order to accomplish the following tasks:

- To merge inputs from complementary channels into a single command;
- To signal and possibly solve ambiguous communication acts from the user.

It's possible to assign different priority level to inputs coming from different communication channels. Thinking about a complex scenario in which user would like to communicate a great amount of information in a restricted time, speech seems to be the main candidate to be the dialog driver input. In fact communicating by voice is probably the best option when eyes and hands are busy. Speech is also the most appropriate and instinctive mean to express complex questions, especially when the information content of user's requests is rich and complicated.

In understanding user's intention some aspects have to be considered:

1. Communication act may result from a combination of inputs coming from different channels and different sources.
2. In the field of human-machine interaction users may want to express their goals with complex sentences answering more than one question at a time.
3. Moreover, a dialog is not a series of unrelated independents acts; instead it's a collective act performed by both participants. Inevitable consequence of this situation is that speaker

and hearer must constantly establish a common ground (Stalnaker, 1978), describing things that are mutually believed by the two parts. The need to achieve a common ground means that hearer system has to be able to collocate the speaker's utterance in a shared context. This context is mainly dependent on the kind of application and environment in which it is used.

Point one of the previous list refers to the issue of consistent inputs correlation. Users interact with devices in a variety of ways (for example submitting a speech command and a selection of an object by a pen pointing) providing an amount of information that the system has to process for detecting the corresponding task (Koons et al., 1993). Inputs could be redundant and contribute to make the level of robustness for the task understanding higher. Often, alternative inputs are used to complete the information content. For example vocal input and sketch may be complementary.

Expressions like *"move this object"* or *"calculate the distance from this point to this other"* can be correctly interpreted from a semantic point of view by an automatic system, but they cannot be mapped on application task until it's not specified what *"this object"* or *"this point"* stands for. So, in particular while dealing with deictic expression, a complementary input seems to be necessary; this introduces another complex question: on which basis inputs could be correlated?

Point two of the list remands us to the analysis of basic dialog systems. User freedom in communicating his intentions depends on the architecture of the dialog system.

Simplest dialogue manager architectures are based on finite-state manager. In this case, the states of the FSA correspond to precise commands, consisting of answers to questions that the dialogue manager asks to the user; the arcs of FSA correspond to the actions to take depending on what the user responds. In these systems the conversation control is completely managed by the system, asking a series of questions and ignoring everything user says that isn't a direct and expected answer.

In these dialog systems, known in literature as *single initiative* systems (or *system initiative*), automatic responder keeps in its hands the dialog control, thought in natural human-human initiative bounces back and forth between the participants. This means that the system could use a restricted language model tuned to expected answers for specific questions, improving the recognition rate of speech recognition engine. In other words, knowing what the user is going to be talking about makes the task of the natural language understanding engine easier.

Indeed this approach is not ideal to take advantage from natural language communications because strong limits are placed to user's expression freedom. Moreover pure single initiative systems require that the user answers exactly the question the system asks and it makes a dialogue unnatural and annoying. To front and get over this limitation mixed initiative dialogue architecture are adopted.

One common mixed initiative dialogue architecture relies on a frame structure to guide the dialogue. Frame could be seen as a conceptual structure containing the pieces of information essential for user's intentions understanding; the frame structure depends on the specific application the system is responsible to fulfil.

These frame-based dialogue managers ask the user questions to complete the frame through a slot filling process, but allow the user to guide the dialogue by giving information that fills other slots in the frame. Each slot may be associated with a question for the user, but he is able to provide more information in a time, submitting a more articulated request. Nonetheless, some parts of the frame may be not necessary and the system must be able to fill the corresponding slots only if the user explicitly specifies them.

This kind of form-filling dialogue manager allows the user not to follow a precise path during

dialog and it does not impose an order for communicating information of interest.

Point three reminds us the matter of context management. This argument concerns the identification of relevant aspects of information in dialogue and how they are updated. Expressions like *information state, conversational score, discourse context* are used to refer the information, increasing while conversation evolves, necessary to distinguish a dialog from another. This amount of information represents the knowledge that every participant carries out and gives an idea of the point that dialog has reached, its recent history and most probable future acts.

In a context in which different communication means between user and system are available, it's necessary to investigate relations among input modes and how to integrate their information contents (Russ et al., 2005). A solution could result from identifying the communication channel that transfers the greater amount of information and let the dialog be led by it.

Following this approach, voice acts are surely the most convenient to drive communication and this implies that a correct understanding of user utterance strongly impacts the overall performances of whole multimodal system. Other input channels are considered complementary to speech input and they are processed and integrated just when user's utterance refers to them, by explicit or implicit way.

The Natural Language Understanding component represents the core component of speech driven multimodal systems. The understanding of natural language has to face the issue of extracting the original semantic content from the utterance. A crucial question for this task is to realize whether each single word has got the same importance in deducing the meaning of user's purpose. We suppose it hasn't.

The idea underlying our approach is that for a given task in a particular context, some linguistic events are crucial to recognize and understand others not so. Hesitations, repetitions or false starts are very common events in natural languages communications and they could be ignored, focusing on really significant speech fragments (Gorin et al., 2003). These situations are more frequent when slightly skilled users deal with new kind of applications or when they use complex services or sophisticated devices.

The actual matter is how really selecting from a user utterance the essential parts to identify the desired task. Simply accessing the phonological, morphological, and syntactic representations of sentences may be not enough, because answering questions requires background knowledge about the topic, about the way questions are usually asked and how they are usually answered. Therefore the use of domain-specific knowledge is required to correctly interpret natural language inputs. An empirical approach to construct natural language processing systems can start from a training corpus comprising sentences paired with appropriate translations into formal queries (Hwee Tou & Zelle, 1997).

Natural language understanding module must produce a semantic representation of user utterance which is appropriate for the task solving step. Many speech driven dialogue systems are based on the frame-and-slot semantics and the result of natural language processing is representing information in a frame-structured way (Minker & Bennacef, 2004).

A frame can be seen as a conceptual structure describing a particular kind of situation, object or event together with its components (other object or situations which contribute to the frame definition). It's hard thinking that a single generic frame could be adopted to model every kind of situation or dialog in user-machine communication context. The choice of most appropriate frame structure is strongly dependent on application and context knowledge. The more the application purpose is general the more a larger range of different frames has to be considered and each different frame is evoked by a target word, a lexical unit that plays a specific rule in the sentence's context. The use

of target words in order to address a specific concept or situation is widespread in systems for telephone call routing, in which a user is allowed to describe, in his own words, what is his question or request. The reception automatic system has to know enough about the domain to redirect the call to the appropriate service extracting from user's utterance words considered salient. Researches in this specific field have revealed that salient clusters of words are preferable to single words, as they show sharper semantics (Gorin et al., 1997).

NLU systems use different ways for turning user's utterances into semantic representations. Semantic grammars are a first possible answer. They are context free grammars in which the node names of parse tree correspond to the semantic categories dealt with in the specific application. The following are possible grammar fragments for a multimodal application devoted to cultural heritage contents retrieving:

GET → *give me* | *show me* | *I'd like to have* | …
INFORMATION → *information* | *details* | …
TOPIC → *about this painting* | *about Caravaggio* | *on this author* | …

Since semantic grammar nodes correspond to the slots in the frame, the frame filling process can be directly activated once the parsing of sentences is completed. Furthermore, simple grammars can be turned into probabilistic semantic grammars by adding probability for specific concepts sequence or combination and it represents and interesting solution to face ambiguities.

Though the semantic grammar approach is widely used, it presents some drawbacks, first of all the necessity to hand-write grammars can be an expensive and slow procedure.

The state of art for recognition of unconstrained spoken language suggests the adoption of stochastic language models, trained on utterance samples paired with related semantic interpretation, by which estimate the probability that a sequence of words occurs. According to this approach, the main effort in extracting semantic meaningful concepts from natural language consists in the hand-labelling of sentences with the concepts/ frame's slot associated with each words cluster.

A widely diffused stochastic algorithm, in particular for named entity extraction, involves the use of semantic HMM (Pieraccini et al., 1991). According to it the hidden states of HMM are the semantic labels assigned to frame slots, while the observed words are the fillers of the slots. Still referring to the retrieval of cultural heritage contents, in the following figure it's shown how a sequence of hidden states can be inferred from clusters of observed words.

Now we describe a possible solution for the implementation of a fusion module containing a natural language processing system core. This component is a part of a server-side platform for synergic multimodal services in a mobile context.

Inputs coming from different sources travel on different non-coupled channels; they are processed by distributed recognisers and integrated by fusion module.

Such process is assumed to be speech driven and the semantic inputs disambiguation is based on the collaboration of a stochastic classifier and a rule based engine. The latter is adopted to match information retrieved from inputs analysis with available tasks.

A domain specific data corpus has been manually labelled to build the model language while a named entity recogniser works as classifier, in order to extract meaningful semantic contents. What is semantically significant and what is not, strongly depends on the application goal and, as a consequence, both language model and frame structure to fill have to be tuned.

For an application which offers different kinds of services to client, a first necessary step is identifying the right context for grounding user's requests, recognizing relevant target words in spoken utterances. That's to say system must be able to select the right semantic frame and language model.

User commands are then rebuilt on server side through a frame filling process. As previously described, frames are schematic representations

Figure 2. Hidden states inferred from observed words in HHM

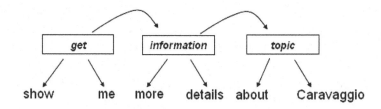

Figure 3. A possible architecture for the fusion module

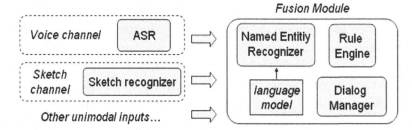

of situations involving various participants, props, and other conceptual roles, each of which is a frame element (Johnson & Fillmore, 2000). In this frame based approach, inputs coming from different modalities are converted in interconnected structures.

Following a stochastic approach a Hidden Markov Model, is adopted for modelling user utterances; hidden states of HMM are frame's semantic slots labels, while observed words are the slot filling values. The aim of classifier is to detect the most likely category for a word (or cluster) given the overall sequence of previous words in the sentence.

Task solving process is carried out integrating information fragments included in frame slots with the ones from complementary input channels. A two steps procedure is adopted in order to integrate inputs coming from different channels:

- First of all, a non-speech input (sketch or handwrite) is integrated with a speech one only if user's utterance refers to it, implicitly or explicitly. Sentences like *"give me information about this painting"* foresee that the topic of information request (*"this painting"*) has to be specified. So, it can happen that a user has to select, among different paintings visualized on his mobile device, the one he'd like to receive info about. Another meaningful example is represented by deictic expressions, in which, the semantic content must be integrated with information related to application context. User's requests like *"please make a zoom here"* can be fulfilled only if the object, or the detail, to enlarge is selected.
- Once it has been verified that vocal command has to be integrated by a complementary input, available alternative inputs are checked. It's essential to underline that every input carries out a timestamp addressing the instant in which it has been acquired by the client device. Through these timestamps it's

possible to verify the temporal correlation between two compatible inputs. A time range is chosen to define the possible mutual delay and this gap is selecting according to the stereotype to which user is assumed to belong (skilled or unskilled, slow or fast in his interaction with the device). Unskilled users may need a longer time to interact with their devices and so the allowed delay has to be extended.

At the end of integration process, available data are submitted to a rule engine, reasoning using inference rules in a forward chain. Task solving step then acts as an ulterior stage in natural language processing and it starts from an appropriate representation of speech communication (in this case a semantic frame based representation).

In the multimodal architecture proposed, a dialog manager module is added for supporting and reinforcing the normal processing of input by opening a direct vocal dialog with the user. Dialog manager acts just to manage particular situations in which user's aim is not clear. Ambiguities in utterance interpretation may happen and so incorrect meaning could be attributed to a user's command. If the semantic frame isn't identified a direct dialog with the user is needed since system isn't able to understand which is the specific conceptual structure to fill. In such cases the system prompts the user for repeating his vocal command, in order to extract an appropriate target word. Another situation that prevents the system to fulfil user request is determined by the lack of one of the slots of semantic frame. Missing frame element may be an optional detail, but it may be not and so the user is asked for completing his request just adding the missing information.

In proposing this architecture we are aware about a crucial issue to overcome: the lack of information due to channel loudness (Hakkani-Tür et al., 2005). Performances of automatic speech recognisers are strongly influenced by noise overlying the meaningful information content, especially while acting in an outdoor context and in a crowded environment. Flaws in quality of communication channels are a well known issue. According to information theory it is possible to model a communication channel in the following way as shown in Figure 4.

The source is described by source probability function P(X) and the channel is characterized by the conditional probability function P(Y|X); X and Y are symbols expressed, respectively, in the input and output alphabet. It's clear that the more noisiness increases the more grows up the possibility to receive a symbol that is different from the one actually produced by the source.

If this situation can be very compromising when the corruption of information involves a large part of user's utterance, there are cases in which the losses can be surrounded. We are studying how to recover contents affected by such problem and our research leverages on the consideration that semantic contents and linguistic features of user's utterances are strongly related, as more as the context of use is well known and restricted.

Already Levin and Rappaport Hovav *linking theory* has dealt with correlation between semantics and syntactic structure of sentences, arguing, in particular, that the syntactic realization of predicate arguments is predictable from semantics. Lexical and syntactic features, including the phrase type of each constituent of utterance, its grammatical function, and its position referred to a target word could be opportunely combined to define the semantic role played by each part of sentence.

Starting from this consideration, and supposing that the overall utterance semantics is known, we expect that some linguistic features are recurrent. Instead of implementing a semantic role labeller starting from linguistic features (Gidea & Giurasfky, 2002), we are confident, fixing the semantic of user's utterance, to be able to retrieve some missing information fragments.

A first step in this direction could be done acting on the grammar adopted by automatic speech recogniser. Assumed that system is aware about the way questions are usually answered and commands are usually submitted, basic grammars could include just words which user is expected to use. But simply listing expected words may be not enough to manage complex, structured utterances and coding a grammar by scheduling all possible combinations of words is expensive and prohibitive when application's context is wide.

A suitable solution may consist in selecting the parts of information we actual care about and dividing possible user's utterances into lexical units to build more complex and flexible grammatical rules. If the approach previously described is correct, we must be able to discover some recurrent sequences or relations among the parts of speech and encode these features in a formal way. Referring to SRGS (Speech Recognition Grammar Specification) it's possible to write rules representing the part of speech of interest. Consider, as an example, the following rows representing a grammar written referring to rules definition for part of speech.

Through this kind of grammar it is possible to define the precise sequence of parts of speech

Figure 4. Example of information channel

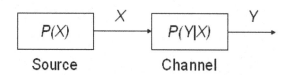

which is expected. Anyway user's expressions may sometimes be unpredictable and it's better simply to define the *most likely* sequence of words. Once analysed a wide corpus of spoken sentences for a specified application, a weight may be provided for any number of alternatives in an alternative expansion for the grammar rules.

Working on grammar is surely a first intuitive solution to improve speech recognition in presence of noise. Another way is acting on automatic

Box 2.

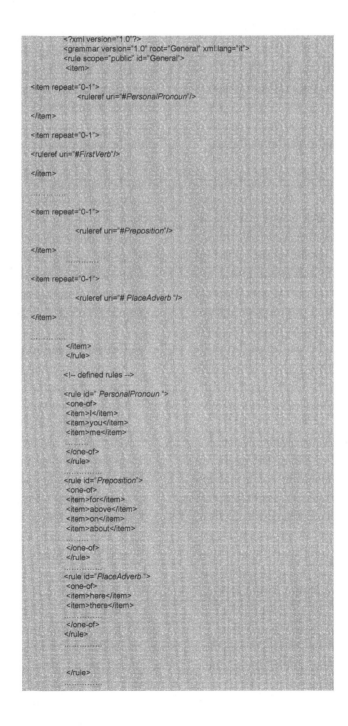

```xml
<?xml version="1.0"?>
<grammar version="1.0" root="General" xml:lang="it">
<rule scope="public" id="General">
  <item>

<item repeat="0-1">
        <ruleref uri="#PersonalPronoun"/>

</item>

<item repeat="0-1">

<ruleref uri="#FirstVerb"/>

</item>


<item repeat="0-1">
        <ruleref uri="#Preposition"/>

</item>

<item repeat="0-1">
        <ruleref uri="# PlaceAdverb "/>

</item>


  </item>
  </rule>

  <!-- defined rules -->

  <rule id=" PersonalPronoun ">
  <one-of>
  <item>I</item>
  <item>you</item>
  <item>me</item>

  </one-of>
  </rule>
  <rule id="Preposition">
  <one-of>
  <item>for</item>
  <item>above</item>
  <item>on</item>
  <item>about</item>

  </one-of>
  </rule>
  <rule id="PlaceAdverb ">
  <one-of>
  <item>here</item>
  <item>there</item>

  </one-of>
  </rule>


  </rule>
```

speech recogniser output, estimating the score attributed to each part of speech recognized. Also in this case a large corpus of typical user's expressions is needed and a deep statistical analysis is necessary.

Business Logic

Essentially the Business Logic has the following goals:

- Maintain/adjourn the status of the interaction for each user;
- Select the contents to send back according to user request, user profile and context.

We are currently working to a content recommendation system in collaboration with Italian universities. The idea we are pursuing is to use context information to feed opportunely an external system that should suggest the best aggregation of modes. Considering what we have discussed above, in our mind a multimodal service is an aggregation of multimodal objects. An issue we are now trying to solve is to push on the user terminal the best aggregation of multimodal objects considering all the possible constraints: user preferred modes, user profile, input/output mode combination, location features (noise, light), etc.

We will not discuss the recommendation system here. It is of worth noting that, the system can use simple rule for task matching. At the moment user requests are associated to annotated web service. Considering that we are using FEDORA, a content repository that allows a semantic information retrieval, once established the user will, contents can be retrieved using sophisticated semantic queries. The minimal business logic, thus, from one side tries to understand the user request and the eventual request parameters, on the other side tries to recover contents or execute a configured task by matching intelligently semantic annotated content or services.

Output Process and Fission

The "Fission" module has the goal to "push" the contents toward final users

For the Fission module we have implemented an asynchronous output system. We want the business logic to have the possibility to modify the interface shown to final users even without an explicit request from the user himself. We want the server side to be able to "push" content toward devices.

Such a feature could be very interesting in prospect to have a real adaptive application, so that the user interface could be modified even without an explicit request coming from the user; for example according to the changes in the context of use (physical, positional, etc...). To implement such a feature we have had to study a particular architecture for the module of Fission.

The multimodal fission component implements appropriate logical distribution of information into one or more outputs in different modalities. The task of a Fission module is composed of three categories (Foster, 2002):

- **Content selection and structuring:** The presented content must be selected and arranged into an overall structure.
- **Modality selection:** The optimal modalities are determined based on the current situation of the environment, for example when the user device has a limited display and memory, the output can be presented as the graphic form such as a sequence of icons.
- **Output coordination:** The output on each of the channels should be coordinated so that the resulting output forms a coherent presentation.

According to the architecture of our system, the tasks of Fission process are linked directly to the business logic layer. The latter has the responsibility to provide an input to the Fission module that contains information taking into account factors such as user's preferences and behavioural characteristics. The Fission module, instead, must be able to send information contents in a coordinated manner: for example, it is responsible for guarantying synchronization between the visual presentation and the audio reproduction of the content. This is done creating an output file (LIDIM, HTML, etc…) to send to MMUIManager.

The Fission module has been designed so that it works in an asynchronous manner towards the requests of the clients; in fact, when the business logic layer has a new content for a specific client, it signals to the Fission through HTTP protocol, independently of the request of the client. So the Fission module notifies the new content to the MMUIManager module through the SIP (Session Initiation Protocol) protocol. Then the MMUIManager module receives from the Fission the new content through a HTTP request.

SIP is the Internet Engineering Task Force's (IETF's) standard for multimedia conferencing over IP. SIP is an ASCII-based, application-layer control protocol (defined in RFC2543) that can be used to establish, maintain, and terminate calls between two or more end points.

The complete Fission architecture is made by the following components:

- The *Dialog Interface* is the module through which the business logic layer talks with the Fission module for the notification of new contents.

- The *Push Manager* is responsible for the notification at the MMUIManager of the presence of new content for a specific client.

- The *Content Interface* is the component through which the MMUIManager module communicates with the Fission module for retrieving new contents.

Box 3.

```
SIP/2.0 200 OK
Via: SIP/2.0/UDP <ip_push_manager>;branch=z9hG4bK-d87543-5f795c5af206133a-1--d87543-;
 received=192.168.1.102;rport=15772
From: "push_manager";tag=11573036
To: " push_manager ";tag=as1647de36
Call-ID: ZGVmYmM0OWRhNzYyMmI5M2FmODIwZjk1YTA2ZTI2Y2I.
CSeq: 2 REGISTER
User-Agent: Asterisk PBX
Allow: INVITE, ACK, CANCEL, OPTIONS, BYE, REFER, SUBSCRIBE, NOTIFY
Expires: 3600
Contact: ;expires=3600
Date: Fri, 21 Dec 2007 22:15:51 GMT
Content-Length: 0
```

```
REGISTER sip:local SIP/2.0
Via: SIP/2.0/UDP <ip_push_manager>;branch=z9hG4bK-d87543-5f795c5af206133a-1--d87543-;rport
Max-Forwards: 70
Contact:
To: " push_manager "
From: " push_manager ";tag=11573036
Call-ID: ZGVmYmM0OWRhNzYyMmI5M2FmODIwZjk1YTA2ZTI2Y2I.
CSeq: 2 REGISTER
Expires: 3600
Allow: INVITE, ACK, CANCEL, OPTIONS, BYE, REFER, NOTIFY, MESSAGE, SUBSCRIBE, INFO
User-Agent: X-Lite release 1011s stamp 41150
Authorization: Digest username="203",realm="asterisk",nonce="29b8191d",uri="sip:<ip_push_manager>",
 response="7306cfba1b131f2f04363b68d908f855",algorithm=MD5
Content-Length: 0
```

As mentioned earlier, contents notification to the MMUIManager, is managed through SIP protocol. The Push Manager, part of fission module, achieves this notification, after a registration process to the SIP server. In fact, when the Fission module started, the PushManger does a registration to the SIP Registrar, a logical element commonly co-located with SIP Server. The registration process gives a unique Universal Resource Identifier (URI) such as, push_manager@xxx. com and after this process its may call the other user agent, for example the MMUIManager. Here is an example that details the previous registration procedure, see Box 3.

The SIP server is not a part of Fission module. This component acts in proxy mode: it is an intermediate device that receives SIP requests from a client and forwards them on the client's behalf.

The Fission module has been designed so that the architecture works in asynchronous way: when the business logic has a new content for a user, it signals to the Fission (HTTP). Then the Fission module notifies the new content to the MMUIManager module through SIP protocol, exactly, in this phase, the PushManager performs a SIP call to MMUIManager which hangs up and gets ready to receive the new contents through a HTTP request. We illustrate the message flow for the SIP call from PushManager to MMUIManager:

1. The PushManager sends an INVITE with Request-URI sip:MMUIManager@xxx. com to the SIP Server. The INVITE request has a unique Call-ID header and a From-Tag. The Contact header in the INVITE request has the address of the UA of PushManager.
2. The SIP Server accepts the INVITE and sends a 100 Trying back to the PushManager.
3. The SIP Server looks up the location server database, gets the address of MMUIManager, and forwards the INVITE to the user agent of MMUIManager.

4. The MMUIManager accepts the incoming INVITE request and sends back 100 Trying to the SIP Server.
5. The user agent of MMUIManager starts and sends 180 Ringing to the SIP Server to indicate the state.
6. The SIP Server forwards the 180 Ringing to the UA of PushManger. After the PushManager gets a 180.
7. MMUIManager answers the call. The MMUIManager sends 200 OK to the SIP Server.
8. The SIP Server forwards the 200 OK to the PushManager.
9. The PushManager acknowledges the 200 OK and sends an ACK directly to the MMUIManager.
10. MMUIManager disconnects the call.
11. The PushManager acknowledges the BYE transaction by sending 200 OK. The push notification is now terminated.

After that, the MMUIManager module calls the Fission, in particular calls the Content Interface module (see figure 10), through a HTTP request for to take the new content.

The following figure shows that the Fission module forwards the new content on different channels through the LIDIM file as shown in Figure 5.

The so-called Voice channel is a voice output channels that allows playing either pre-recorded audio resources or text sources which must be converted in voice (TTS) by a specific engine. According to our light-weight approach, the LIDIM file contains just the information about resource location (an address). Thus, it is MMUIManager responsibility to retrieve the remote resources using HTTP or RTP. For text resources, a TTS engine has the responsibility to transform text to speech accordingly to the MMUIManager request and to stream it on the client. The text Message channel gives the possibility to show popup text message over the interface after the page loading.

Figure 5. Fission and LIDIM file

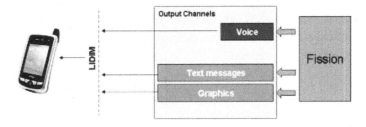

Text messages can be used also for asking user confirmations.

The Graphics channel is the channel that contains information about the graphical interface layout MMUIManager has to show to the user. Notice that such graphical panel can be related to text, audio or even video resources that the MMUIManager loads accordingly with user inputs. All the data on output channels can be included in a LIDIM page. Essentially in our implementation Fission module has the task to send LIDIM page toward MMUIManager.

Content Repository

The architecture described needs another component: a repository for multimedia contents.

Such repository cannot be a simple relational database as it must be able to store different kinds of contents (file audio, file video, text, html). We have experimented the multimodal repository FEDORA (an Open Source by Carnegie Mellon University).

FEDORA shows a web service interface. So to each resource is associated an HTTP url. FEDORA can also make some manipulation of the contents. For example can on the fly, change the format and/or dimensions of image resources.

Business Logic uses data in the repository to construct the output file that must be sent back toward final user. Such file (a LIDIM file in out implementation) will contain only the url of the resources, so when MMUIManager has to build

the interface to show to final user, it will have to send http GET (or POST) toward FEDORA to get the resources.

FUTURE TRENDS

It is difficult to forecast the multimodality future. It is evident that the internet, the most diffused communication channel on earth, will evolve. We believe that more and more the internet and (mobile) telephony will be a perceived as a unique access channel to a large amount of information; in such a framework we believe that multimodality will assume an increasing role in the future. Mobile users are, at the moment, frustrated by difficult interaction modes (small keyboard, slow channels, high latency, etc.) and from very high mobile connectivity costs. It seems that the evolution trends are directed to solve these issues: more and more powerful networks are appearing while connectivity costs are decreasing, and the attention on new and more usable interaction modes is year by year renewed.

Furthermore, it should be considered that probably a deeper collaboration among portable devices, like mobile phones or PDAs, and computers could be a key of the future internet development. More and more, handsets will be considered as personal agents, changing behaviour depending on the user context: sometime acting as personal user sensors, some other time acting as input/output devices for an efficient information retrieval.

It is evident that a lot of work to improve spoken language understanding, sketch and handwriting recognition is still needed. Nevertheless, every single progress on this field will introduce new perspective in human-computer interaction.

CONCLUSION

We have presented our work on mobile multimodality, in particular our approach to multimodality focusing the attention on the fusion and the fission processes. The key ideas are related to mixing telephony and internet protocols for enabling new interaction modes: pushing contents on mobile terminals using SIP and streaming protocols, representing high level content aggregation using a special mark-up language that is able to coordinate so-called multimodal objects. Furthermore we have discussed our approach to fusion, considering that in some case it is possible to use a frame-based approach for enhancing the spoken language understanding success ratio. The overall system has been designed around cultural heritage fruition and e-learning use cases and is now running in the Engineering.IT labs, where the group is still working on further improvements.

REFERENCES

Arai, K., Wright, J.H., Riccardi, G., & Gorin, A. (1999). Grammar fragment acquisition using syntactic and semantic clustering. *Speech Communication, 27*.

Avola, D., Caschera, M.C., Ferri, F., & Grifoni P. (2007). Ambiguities in sketch-based interfaces. *Hawaii International Conference on System Sciences (HICSS 2007). Proceedings of the Hawaii International Conference on System Sciences.* IEEE Computer Society.

Avola, D., Ferri, F. & Grifoni, P. (2007). Formalizing recognition of sketching styles in human centered systems. *11th International Conference on Knowledge-Based and Intelligent Information & Engineering, Systems (KES2007)* (LNAI). Springer-Verlag.

Filippo, F., Krebs, A., & Marsic, I. (2003). A framework for rapid development of multimodal interfaces. *Proceedings of the 5th International Conference on Multimodal Interfaces*, Vancouver, Canada.

Foster, M.E. (2002). State of the art review: Multimodal fission. Retrieved from www.hcrc.ed.ac.uk/comic/documents/deliverables/Del6-1.pdf

Frattini, G., Gaudino, F., & Scotto di Carlo, V. (2007). Mobile multimodal applications on mass-market devices: Experiences. *18th International Workshop on Database and Expert Systems Applications (DEXA 2007)* (pp. 89-93).

Frattini, G., Romano, L., Scotto di Carlo, V., Petriccione, P., Supino, G., & Leone, G. (2006). Multimodal architectures: Issues and experiences. *OTM Workshops (1)*, 974-983.

Frattini, G., Ceccarini, F., Corvino, F., De Furio, I., Gaudino, F., Petriccione, P., Russo, R., Scotto di Carlo, V., & Supino, G. (2008). *A new approach toward a modular multimodal interface for PDAs and smartphones VISUAL 2008* (pp. 179-191).

Gorin, A.L., Alonso, T., Abella, A., Riccardi, G., & Wright, J.H. (2003). Semantic information processing of spoken language - how may I help you? In *Pattern recognition in speech and language processing*. CRC Press.

Gorin, A.L., Riccardi, G., & Wright, J.H. (1997). How may I help you? *Speech Communication, 23*, 113-127.

Hakkani-Tür, D., Tur, G., Riccardi, G., & Hong Kook Kim (2005). Error prediction in spoken dialog: From signal-to-noise ratio to semantic confidence scores. In *Proceedings of ICASSP-2005, IEEE International Conference on Acoustics, Speech, and Signal Processing*, Philadelphia, PA.

Hwee Tou Ng, & Zelle, J.M. (1997). Corpus-based approaches to semantic interpretation in NLP. *AI Magazine, 18*(4), 45-64.

Johnson, C.R., & Fillmore, C.J. (2000). The frameNet tagset for frame-semantic and syntactic coding of predicate-argument structure. In *Proceedings of the 1st Meeting of the North American Chapter of the Association for Computational Linguistics (ANLP-NAACL 2000)*, Seattle, WA (pp. 56-62).

Jurafsky, D. & Martin, J.H. (2007). *Speech and language processing: An introduction to natural language processing, computational linguistics, and speech recognition.*

Koons, D.B., Sparrell, C.J., & Thorisson, K.R. (1993). Integrating simultaneous input from speech, gaze, and hand gestures. In M. Maybury (Ed.), *Intelligent multimedia interfaces*. Menlo Park, CA: MIT.

Levin, B., & Rappaport Hovav, M. (1996). Lexical semantics and syntactic structure. In S. Lappin (Ed.), *The handbook of contemporary semantic theory*. Oxford, UK: Blackwell.

Minker, W., & Bennacef, S. (2004). *Speech and human-machine dialog*. Boston: Kluwer Academic Publishers.

Nigay, L., & Coutaz, J. (1993). A design space for multimodal systems: Concurrent processing and data fusion. In *Proceedings of the INTERACT '93 and CHI '93 Conference on Human Factors in Computing Systems*, Amsterdam, The Netherlands (pp. 172-178).

Niklfeld, G., Anegg, H., Pucher, M., Schatz, R., Simon, R., Wegscheider, F., et al. (2005, April). Device independent mobile multimodal user interfaces with the MONA multimodal presentation server. In *Proceedings of Eurescom Summit 2005*, Heidelberg, Germany.

Oviatt, S., DeAngeli, A., & Kuhn, K. (1997). Integration and synchronization of input modes during multimodal human compute interaction. In *Proceedings of the SIGCHI conference on Human Factors in Computing Systems*, Atlanta, GA (pp. 415-422).

Oviatt, S. (2000). Multimodal system processing in mobile environments. In M.S. Ackerman & K. Edwards (Eds.), *Proceedings of the 13th Annual ACM Symposium on User Interface Software and Technology*, San Diego, CA (pp. 21-30).

Pieraccini, R., Levin, E., & Lee, C.H. (1991). Stochastic representation of conceptual structure in the ATIS task. In *Proceedings DARPA Speech and Natural Language Workshop*, Pacific Grove, CA (pp. 121–124).

Reitter, D., Panttaja, E., & Cummins, F. (2004). UI on the fly: Generating a multimodal user interface. In *Proceedings of Human Language Technology Conference 2004 / North American Chapter of the Association for Computational Linguistics (HLT/NAACL-04)*.

Russ, G., Sallans, B., & Hareter, H. (2005). *Semantic based information fusion in a multimodal interface*. CSREA HCI.

Stalnaker, R.C. (1978). Assertion. In P. Cole (Ed.), *Pragmatics: Syntax and semantics* (Vol. 9, pp. 315–332). Academic Press.

Wright, J.H., Gorin, A.L., & Riccardi, G. (1997). Automatic acquisition of salient grammar fragments for call-type classification. In *Proceedings of 5th European Conf. Speech Communication and Technology, International Speech Communication Association*, Bonn, Germany (pp. 1419-1422).

KEY TERMS AND DEFINITIONS

ASR: Automatic Speech Recognizers. Software component that is able to acquire speech input and transform it in text.

Fusion: Process that combines different input modes (e.g. point, speak, handwrite…) in order to match the user intention.

LIDIM: LInguaggio di Definizione Interfaccia Multimodale (Language for definition of multimodal interface). Our own language able to describe structure and contets of a multimodal/multimedia interface.

MMUIManager: MultiModal User Interface Manager. Application running on the client side able to render a multimodal/multimedia interface.

Natural Language Processing: (NLP) is a field of computer science concerned with the interactions between computers and human (natural) language.

Push: Process to send contents without an explicit request from final users. Our process uses SIP protocol.

Synergic Multimodality: Simultaneous use of different modalities (speech, sketch, handwrite, keyboard) in a single interaction act

Chapter XVII
Providing Mobile Multimodal Social Services Using a Grid Architecture

Stefania Pierno
Engineering IT, Italy

Vladimiro Scotto di Carlo
Engineering IT, Italy

Massimo Magaldi
Engineering IT, Italy

Roberto Russo
Engineering IT, Italy

Gian Luca Supino
Engineering IT, Italy

Luigi Romano
Engineering IT, Italy

Luca Bevilacqua
Engineering IT, Italy

ABSTRACT

In this chapter, we describe a grid approach to providing multimodal context-sensitive social services to mobile users. Interaction design is a major issue for mobile information system not only in terms of input-output channels and information presentation, but also in terms of context-awareness. The proposed platform supports the development of multi-channel, multi-modal, mobile context aware applications, and it is described using an example in an emergency management scenario. The platform allows the deployment of services featuring a multimodal (synergic) UI and backed up on the server side by a distributed architecture based on a GRID approach to better afford the computing load generated by input channels processing. Since a computational GRID provides access to "resources" (typically computing related ones) we began to apply the same paradigm to the modelling and sharing of other resources as well. This concept is described using a scenario about emergencies and crisis management.

INTRODUCTION

The penetration of mobile device in western countries is high and still increasing. At the same time new generation terminals feature ever increasing computing power, opening new possibilities for innovation, especially in service delivery.

One emerging trend in service evolution is for services to cater not only to individuals but also to communities of users. Communities are a social phenomenon where people with common interests, experiences, and objectives are brought together. They provide a social place where individuals exchange and share information, knowledge, emotions and jointly undertake activities. Managing the creation or deletion of flexible communities improves the user experiences in communities (NEM, 2006).

MoSoSo (Mobile Social Software), is a class of mobile applications that aims to support social interaction among interconnected mobile users (Lugano, G., 2007). While existing Internet-based services have already shown the growing interest in communication support for communities, *MoSoSo* adds additional dimensions to group communication by exploiting contextual data such as the user geographical position (Counts, S., 2006).

When designing MoSoSo applications, three important differences between desktop and mobile environments should be taken into account:

- The physical context of use is no longer static and poses some constraint to user attention;

- The social context is also dynamic: mobile communities member are tied up by common interest and contextual information, like location and time;

- MoSoSo applications are designed not just for communication but for usage in everyday life situations: users are always socially connected.

In our vision the MoSoSo concept could also benefit "public" (e-Government) services leading to innovative, more effective mobile services, able to leverage on dynamic management of *ad-hoc* communities, context-awareness (i.e. time and location), user profile management and multimodal interaction.

One domain where such benefits will matter most will be emergencies and crisis management. In fact, the response to such situations typically implies the coordination of physical resources, (emergency services personnel, often belonging to different organizations, or even possibly volunteers) in hardly predictable environments in situations where ineffective operations can cause the loss of lives.

From an IT standpoint, implementing such a vision requires coordination of services and sharing of resources among different organizations that typically operate heterogeneous hardware and software environments. The Virtual Organizations paradigm address this issue: "VOs enable disparate groups of organizations and/or individuals to share resources in a controlled fashion, so that members may collaborate to achieve a shared goal" (Foster I., 2001). In those circumstances dynamism, flexibility and interoperability become essential requirements.

Interoperability, in particular, is a key issue in the e-Government domain due to the increasing demand for integrated services. We aim to integrate MoSoSo users into a typical Grid resource management model. To this end, we designed an experimental platform to support the development of multimodal MoSoSo application, allowing an easy integration of mobile community users into a Grid based VO.

OGSA (Open Grid Service Architecture (Foster, I., 2006), a refinement of the SOA concept, allows the interoperability of "resources". In fact the OGSA specification allows each resource to be seen as a service with a standard interface. In the WS-Resource framework conceptual model, a Web service is a stateless entity that acts upon, provides access to, or manipulates a set of logical stateful resources (documents) based on the messages it sends and receives (WSRF, 2006) (Foster I , 2004).

Obviously, to evolve from SOA to OGSA, all architectural components must be extended to deal not only with services but also with resources. For example, as far as process execution is concerned, the workflow engine has to be able to compose both services and resources. Similarly a logical enhancement to the UDDI registry is required to store information about WS-Resources too.

Whereas there are interesting technology products (both commercial and open sources) dealing with multimodal client interfaces (EIF, 2004) (Frissen, V)(I.D.A.B.C) (Berners-Lee, Tim, 2001) and grid middleware (Foster, I., 2001) (Foster, I., 2006) (OASIS , 2006)(Mark Little, 2004), the innovative idea proposed in this article is to bring them together to enable innovative social services (multimodal emergency services being an example) and reduce digital divide.

The rest of this chapter is organized as follows. In the next section we will describe the multimodal part of the overall architecture (front-end). Then we will describe the back-end grid based architecture. Final remarks in the last section conclude the chapter.

MULTIMODAL ARCHITECTURE OVERVIEW

The multimodal part of the overall architecture (Figure 1, Figure 3), is composed by the following modules (Frattini G, 2006),(Frattini G, 2008):

- **Client side application (MMUIManager, MultiModal User Interface Manager):** shows an appealing graphical interface to the user, manages the output channels and collects the inputs from the user and context information.
- **Front end:** collects input from clients and routes it to distributed back-end recognizers (speech, sketch and handwriting recognizers);
- **Fusion:** semantically merges recognized input fragments coming from different channels;
- **Business Logic:** selects appropriate contents;
- **Fission:** sends the selected content to final users.

Building upon a fairly established conceptual multimodal reference architecture (W3C), we enriched it with web 2.0 (Frattini, G, 2008),

Figure 1. Architecture overview

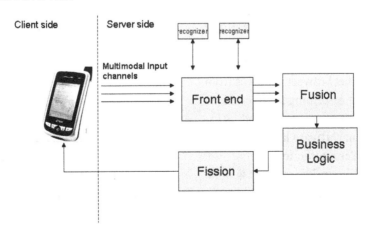

telecommunication & grid technologies, open to community model based interaction. We think the final result is interesting.

In the next sections we will expand on this evaluation. We will first describe our approach to assemble on-the fly mobile multimodal user interfaces using a thin client that exploits resources available on the network. Then, we will present the back-end architecture that deals with the induced computational load.

We focused on using commonly available mobile devices (PDAs or smart phones), and tried to avoid installing specific sw environments. Hence we had to develop a very light software framework for building multimodal interfaces. The framework exploits several standard protocols, over commonly available networks, to interact with both local environment and remote servers (Frattini G, 2007).

Being multimodal, such interfaces have to be able to:

- Collect multimodal input from different channels: speech, point, sketch, handwrite;
- Render outputs selecting the best possible channels (multimedia output);
- Exploit local resources to create an appropriate context for service fruition.

Since we chose to use light, standard "thin" terminals, all collected input fragments have to be routed to network based modal recognizers . All those functions are grouped in a small footprint application: the MMUIManager. The MMUIManager, operating in a fashion conceptually similar to an Internet browser, receives from servers the information describing the UI contents (images, text, audio/video resources), loading locally just the minimum software layer needed to support the desired user interaction.

Such an approach is similar to what is done fore other languages (XUL).

Implementing this concept was a not trivial task. Suffice it to say that, since a standard markup language to describe synergic mobile multimodal UI had not yet emerged, we had to develop our own: an XML based markup language for aggregating multimodal objects: LIDIM (from the Italian Linguaggio di Definizione Interfacce Multimodali, - language for designing multimodal interfaces).

LIDIM is a tag language that by exploiting alsoresources provided by a general multimodal framework is able to handle any potential combination of input modes and to compose multimodal output objects.

The thin client approach implies that the MMUIManager cannot carry out recognition tasks locally on the user terminal but instead it has to rely on back end recognition server distributed over the network, by streaming input fragments to them. To optimize this task, avoiding local buffering of input signals, we adopted the telecommunication protocols SIP/RTP and developed special multimodal objects able to manage streaming protocols in both input and output.

Mobile Interface: The Thin Client Approach

To reach such goals we have followed an XUL like approach. We defined the LIDIM language to describe the multimodal mobile interface built the support for LIDIM in our MMUIManager (MMUIManager acts as a browser for LIDIM building the multimodal interface on the fly and rendering it for user fruition). Such approach enables a very flexible interface design: a specific multimodal applicative frame can be dynamically built adapting to device capabilities, physical context, interaction type, user profile. Not only the graphical aspect, but also content fragments, need not to reside in the device. They reside on optimised content servers and are dynamically selected and streamed to the mobile device .

In short our MMUIManager had to be able to collect multimodal input fragments and send them to back end servers for recognition while at the same time managing multimedia output (text, image, audio, video) composed on the fly.

To be able to handle those tasks, rather than building a monolithic MMUIManager we chose to develop a multimodal framework : a rather comprehensive set of Multimodal elementar objects that can be composed into a coherent multimodal interface. At this moment available alements are buttons, textboxes, html browsers, imageboxes, audio/video panels (able to play audio/video resources) etc.

Those elements can be enriched with specific input modalities, like speech, stylus touch, or draw. For example it is possible to use an "image box" element, and make it sensible to stylus input. In this way the element can allow for an interface in which the user can draw free hand sketches and/or handwriting on top of a picture.

In the specific example ink traces are saved in InkML standard format and sent over the network to appropriate recognition servers, as soon as possible (as soon as a recognition fragment is completed by the user).

Audio acquisition is different: since it is much more difficult to relate a speech fragment a specific interface object "a priori" (i.e. by not considering the semantic content of the speech utterance itself) such input is captured by the MMUIManager itself. This acquisition process is done continuously and the acquired utterances are continuosly streamed over RTP to backend speech recognizers.

As already anticipated we chose to introduce a specific language to describe modular, multimodal/multimedia interfaces: LIDIM.

An alternative choice could have been to extend an existing language to our requirements.

Since we wanted to be able to achieve synergic coordinated multimodal input and multimedia output in a modular interface, the existing technologies/standards proved overly difficult to extend: SMIL conceived for output was too difficult to adapt to input, while X+V and SALT showed the limits inherited from their design that did not consider synergic multimodal input over simultaneously active input channels.

LIDIM manages the following output channels:

- Graphic modular panel interface;
- Audio (pre-recorded sources and TTS);
- Text Messages (Pop up message).

For each resource of the modular interface one or more output media (image, audio, video, text) and input modalities (point, sketch) can be specified. Note that LIDIM just describes the output interface, while the MMUIManager builds the interface and manages the input/output channels.

Let us give an example of how it is possible to build an object having point and sketch as input mode and media text, image and audio as possible output.

```
<object id="78678687">
    <output_media>
        <text uri="http://...."/>
        <image uri=" http://...."/>
        <audio uri=" http://...."/>
    </output_media>
    <input_mode>
        <point isActive="true"/>
        <sketch isActive="true"/>
    </input_mode>
</object>
```

Like HTML, LIDIM does not include the resources (images, text, audio/video resources) which compose the interface; it just contains the addresses where the MMUIManager can get them.

The language is template based, hence leaving to the MMUIManager to dispose the objects on the screen. The current version cannot synchronize different output resources. Future releases are planned to remove such limitation.

We built two MMUIManager prototypes on top of J2ME and .NET Compact Framework software environments.

This was motivated by two someway opposite requirements:

- The possibility to run on almost every commercial devices;
- The necessity to exploit all the hardware and OS capabilities of the devices.

The current .NET implementation is more advanced, for its support of streaming for audio input/output. The J2ME lacks this feature (handling only discrete speech utterances via HTTP) since J2ME lacks standard support for RTP protocol.

The main MMUIManager tasks are:

- Build the graphic interface using an XML user interface language;

Figure 2. Example of client interface

- Manage the input and output channels on the device;

The UI needs to be able to simultaneously collect multimodal input and show multimedia output according to instructions coming from the server.

This approach has a significant advantage: the very same MMUI manager can be used in very different applications contexts content or logic change will be only necessary on server side.

It is a crucial advantage for portable terminals whose users are not, and need not to become, used to installing and configuring local sw applications

According to our goals, the MMUIManager must be based on an engine for interpreting an XML language for creating multimodal/multimedia interface on the fly. Considering this, we have designed and developed a framework for aggregating multimodal objects. A composition of multimodal objects creates a complete multimodal user interface.

The interaction modes enabled by our multimodal framework are, at the moment, the following:

- Point on specific buttons (ex. a "Back" button) and point on object;
- Draw/handwrite on the screen;
- speak.
- Output media supported are: image, text, Html, audio, video.

INPUT CHANNELS

To deliver synchronous coordinate synergic multimodality, the client has first to collect simultaneously different input channels ,which currently are:.

- Speech
- Pointing

- Sketch
- Handwriting

To overcome the constraints posed by the somewhat limited hardware resources of mobile devices we chose to distribute the recognition process over back end recognisers.

To optimise this distribution we found useful to design an intermediate layer between the MMUIManager and the recognizers. This layer (that we call "Front End module") essentially manages the redirection of input from the MMUIManager toward the recognizers allowing for some location independence, failover and load balancing).

It also takes care of sending recognized input fragments to the fusion module in standard (EMMA) format, and for the TTS channel generate the output.

The Front-End was implemented as a set of cooperating Java servlets deployed on an application server (e.g. Tomcat, JBoss etc.).

The acquisition of the "pointing" modality is the simplest. Every time the user touches a sensible on screen object an HTTP call containing the object identifier is sent to the server to be merged with other concurrent modal fragments.

The acquisition of sketch/handwring is more complex. But still there is no need for a real time process.

The client side framework offers multimodal objects sensible to stylus inputs and traces. Acquired traces are buffered locally and then sent to the front-end server via HTTP using a standard format (InkML). The Front-end server, in turn, routes the acquired input to recognizer and fusion modules.

Speech Recognition is the most complex.

To recognize speech in real time by using distributed Speech Recognizers, an open streaming channel (RTP protocol) between the device and the recognizer (ASR, Automatic Speech Recognizer) has to be established.

This channel allows continuous recognition of the user speech and we chose to have it established through a direct negotiation process between the MMUIManager and the recognizer; such negotiations are made using the MRCP protocol (RFC 4463).

Figure 3. Sample of draw acquisition

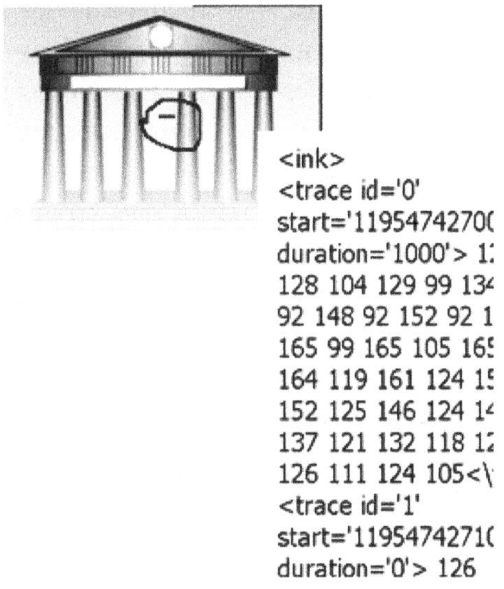

```
<ink>
<trace id='0'
start='11954742700(
duration='1000'> 1:
128 104 129 99 13∢
92 148 92 152 92 1
165 99 165 105 16!
164 119 161 124 1!
152 125 146 124 1∢
137 121 132 118 1:
126 111 124 105<\
<trace id='1'
start='11954742710(
duration='0'> 126
```

To trigger the recognition process start we introduced a special "start" keyword such as "computer"; so when a user utters "computer,.. do this" the recognition process starts. Obviously any other keyword can be chosen. A recognition fragment isidentified when the user pauses his speech.

OUTPUT PROCESS

In our architecture, the output process is managed by a business logic layer and by the Fission component. The former provides to thelatter application specific information (also taking into account factors such as user's preferences and behavioural patterns) while the Fission module, takes care of the technical coordination of the output. For example the Fission module guarantees synchronization between the visual presentation and the audio reproduction of the content. To do that the Fission module creates a specific LIDIM output file that is sent to the MMUIManager for rendering.

The Fission was designed to treat asynchronously clients' requests; when the business logic layer has new content for a specific client, it signals this availability to the Fission module by using the HTTP protocol and this may happen independently from client requests (for example because an element in the environment changesornew data becomes available). The Fission module notifies the MMUIManager that updated content issvailable by using the SIP (Session Initiation Protocol) protocol. Then the MMUIManager receives from the Fission module the new content through an HTTP request.

SIP is the Internet Engineering Task Force's (IETF's) standard for multimedia conferencing over IP. SIP is an ASCII-based, application-layer control protocol (defined in RFC2543) that can be used to establish, maintain, and terminate calls between two or more end points.

The complete Fission architecture is illustrated in Figure 4.

Figure 4 shows the following components:

- The *Dialog Interface* is the module by which the business logic layer talks with the Fission module for the notification of new contents.
- The *Push Manager* is responsible for notifying the MMUIManager about the availability of new content for a specific client.
- The *Content Interface* is the component by which the MMUIManager module communicates with the Fission module for retrieving new contents.

As previously mentioned, contents notification to the MMUIManager, is managed through SIP protocol. The Push Manager, part of the fission module, achieves this notification, after a registration process to the SIP server.

To complete contents notification, the PushManager performs a SIP call to the MMUIManager, that in turn hangs up and gets ready to receive the contents.

Figure 5 shows the steps just described.

The SIP server is not part of Fission module, but rather it is a component of the overall system. This component acts in proxy role: it is an intermediate device that receives SIP requests from a client and forwards them on the client's behalf.

The output channels that the MMUIManager can process are depicted in Figure 6.

Figure 4. Fission module internal architecture

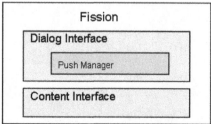

Figure 5. Asynchronous push

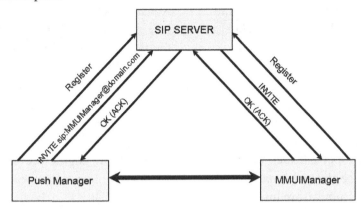

Figure 6. Output channels schema

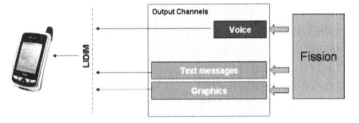

The voice output channel can play either pre-recorded audio streams or text streams converted to voice by a TTS engine.

The LIDIM file just contains information about resource location (an address). The MMUIManager fetches such content by using HTTP or RTP.

The text Message channel allows popup text messages that can also be used for asking user confirmations.

The Graphics channel instructs the MMUIManager about the graphical interface layout to be shown. All the output information are included in a LIDIM page and the Fission module takes care of sending it to the MMUIManager.

It is worth noticing that the fission module is completely asynchronous. This is an important feature: real adaptive services must be able to react by adapting the user interface to context changes, even without an explicit user request,

typically to react to usage context changes (noise or lightning conditions).

BACK-END ARCHITECTURAL OVERVIEW

Figure 7 shows the logical view of our back-end architecture (Pierno S, 2008).

The applications, being highly service specific, will not be discussed.

The Workflow Management System (WFMS) takes care of e-Government processes, dealing with process flow design and execution.

The Workflow Engine component belonging to WFMS, has to aggregate both WS and WS-Resources. Our architecture, as well as the functionalities of the components of the Grid oriented workflow system, are based on the model proposed by the Workflow Management Coalition (WfMC) (Yu, Jia , 2005)(Globus Alliance).

To enable processes combining both WS and WS-Resources, we selected, in the J2EE domain, JBOSS Jbpm as the workflow engine and bpel as the script language.

We are hence investigating how to extend them to fully support WSRF-compliant services (PVM) (Dörnemann T, 2004).

Processes that can be fully defined at design time do not pose significant research challenges, hence we concentrated our research efforts on processes that need to be planned dynamically at execution time. To this aim we are investigating different artificial intelligence techniques that will leverage semantic descriptions of both services and resources. This automatic process planning would either adapt an existing template (stored in a repository) or try to compose it ex novo.

A Service Flow Planner component in the WFMS (Pierno S, 2008) is devoted to this task while a Match-Maker component cooperates with it by finding the best service/resource available (early binding).

In more detail, the Service Flow Planner will be able to automatically plan a process from domain ontology in OWL and service descriptions in OWL-S into Planning Domain Definition Language PDDL.

In choosing the planner, we selected OWLS-Xplan because of its PDDL 2.1 compliance. The language PDDL2.1 is an extension of PDDL for temporal expressions.(Hoffmann, J, 2000) (Hoffmann, J, 2001) (Hoffmann, J, 2003) (Klusch Matthias). By exploiting this feature, the planner can chose the best service/resource according to QoS parameters.

To integrate the Service Flow Planner with the workflow engine previously described, we are developing a component that will be able to convert PDDL2.1 in both BPEL (OASIS) and JPDL languages.

The Match-Maker component (Pierno, S, 2008) can be used during process execution to find the best service at run time (process planning / re-planning) or, at build time, for discoverying service in the service registry. Our Match-Maker prototype does not depend on either language description, service registry, or matching strategies.

We are building upon the Match-Maker architecture proposed by Paolucci by extending it with the addition of other domain matching strategies such as e-Government QoS matching strategies. These extensions are very important in crisis management scenarios, where processes need to be highly dynamic.

Figure 7. Back-End (SIEGE) architecture

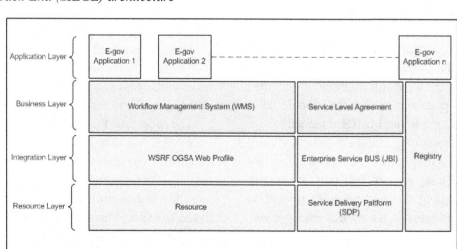

The Service Flow Planner and the Match-Maker have the objective of increasing the capabilities of Workflow Management Systems for the autonomous self-management of composite processes, reducing human intervention to the minimum, primarily in the critical phases of process definition, execution and evolution.

In order to obtain such a result, we are starting from the body of research about Autonomic Web Processes. Autonomic Web Processes research aims to extend the Autonomic Computing model to the execution phase of Web Processes, with the objective of defining a model that extends autonomic self-management to the design, execution and post-execution phases.

In order to achieve such a result (that we define as Autonomic Workflow (Tretola Giancarlo, September 2007) we are proposing autonomic components for supervising a generic process, decreasing the need for human intervention, even during the design and supervision phases. (Tretola Giancarlo, April 25-29, 2006) (Tretola Giancarlo, February 7-9, 2007).

We are currently investigating how to integrate the JBOSS Process Virtual Machine (PVM) with Service Flow Planner and Match-Maker to fully support Autonomic Web Processing (Miers Derek (2005) (Tretola Giancarlo, March 26-30,

2007) (Tretola Giancarlo, June 19-20, 2007), (Tretola Giancarlo, July 9-13, 2007). While the Workflow Management System takes care of the high level coordination of services it does not need to concern itself with lower level details.

Functions such as data transformation, intelligent routing based on message content, protocol translation, message AAA (authentication, authorization, accounting) management, transaction management are best taken care of by a specialized component: the Enterprise Service Bus. We chose JBoss ESB because it is an ESB compliant with the Java Business Integration (JBI) standard.

WMS can invoke (via ESB) internal or external services and resources. The Service Delivery Platform (SDP), includes a library of loosely coupled services and it is responsible for their management and lifecycle control (Pierno, S, 2008).

The OGSA environment allows the use of resources and their lifecycle management Since the Globus Toolkit 4 (Globus Alliance) is one of OGSA most mature implementations (and one which is being evolved in parallel with OGSA specification), we selected it as a starting point for our investigations.

Figure 8. Match-Maker

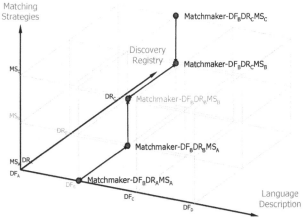

325

In distributed heterogeneous systems, mechanisms and technologies able to support a fast and effective services/resources discovery (an effective discovery mechanism has to deal with services/resources capabilities and resources status) are fundamental. In literature the use of semantic description is widely considered as the most promising approach about this. In particular the Semantic-OGSA (Oscar Corcho, 2006) proposal treats metadata as a first class citizen while defining a set of services suited for metadata management (lifetime management, change notification, etc).

Semantic-OGSA is particularly interesting because it provides for a flexible introduction of semantic data in the architecture: grid resources extended with semantic descriptions may operate together with grid resources that do not receive such an extension. With this approach Semantic-OGSA semantically enables basic OGSA services.

The Registry is another key architectural element. A decentralized hierarchical structure is well suited to the e-Government domain where some kind of hierarchical topology of organizations (national, regional, local) often exists.

We hence started our studies by investigating the UDDI 3.0 registries federation. specification

(federation of registries) and developed a framework that allows the navigation of its hierarchical structure. In other words, our framework enables *distributed queries*. It is based on an algorithm that, using configurable parameters, allows the best path for querying the federated registries to be selected.

We foresee future work to further extend our framework to enable *match-making* of services/resources in federated environments.

By so doing our framework will eventually enable *semantic distributed queries*.

Since we intend to use federated UDDI registries to discovery both WS and WS-Resources we need a mechanism to "refresh" resource status across the whole domain: whenever the status of a specific resource changes, the federated registry structure as a whole must be made aware of it.

For this function we are developing the architectural component named SLA (whose main functions are in fact retrieving the state of all services/grid resources and refresh the service registries).

To obtain a registry able to manage all the needed information, it is necessary to extend the registry with metadata annotations. We will follow this approach to add semantic Web capabilities to UDDI registries (Paolucci, M., 2002).

Figure 9. Client application: Collecting useful information

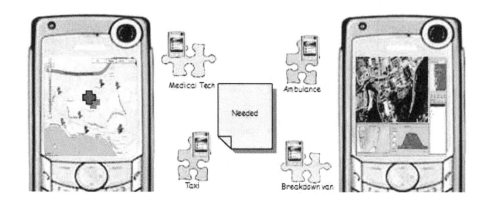

Figure 10. Server side: Information management

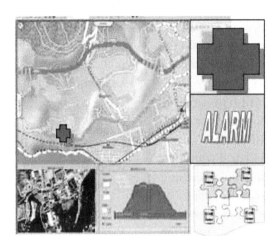

SCENARIO

In a crisis, several organizations must work together as a virtual organization, sharing resources across organizational boundaries to deal with the complexities of such situations. In those scenarios resources are mainly physical ones: police cars, ambulances, emergency professionals and volunteers. Disaster response VO are hence characterized by resource heterogeneity and must rapidly reconfigure (structural and functional changes) to adapt to the changing communication and control demands which may be needed to handle such events (Sharad Mehrotra, 2008).

All this requires dynamic and adaptive workflows, able to coordinate fixed and mobile resources on the basis of their readiness, availability and capabilities.

In our scenario, local Emergency Operations Centers (ECOs) are in charge of collecting information and coordinating operations. To facilitate communication between VO members (EOC chief, workers and volunteer), our solution provides multimodal interaction support for the mobile devices of the operators involved in the operations, exploiting a "point and sketch" interaction mode, which is particularly useful in on-field mobile operation.

In case of emergency, mobile social community users, are asked by a Resource Planning Support (RPS) service to be involved in the operation and eventually integrated into an *ad-hoc* emergency VO created by the EOC. In this way, we may be able to augment the on-field operator team with additional resources. Furthermore, accessing community member profiles, the RPS service can organize operations considering user's skills and assigning the best task to each VO member.

Let's suppose, for example, that after an earthquake some teams are involved in on-site damage control on the affected area, may be requesting assistance.

Imagine that some team's member with medical skill identifies the symptoms of an heart attack for a citizen asking help. He can use his multimodal mobile device to request intervention of a properly equipped ambulance by indicating the location pointing to a map on the screen (Lugano G, 2007). Through support services, every organization in the VO that can provide ambulance resources, will be asked to return availability, location, capabilities (equipment and crew) and other relevant information.

The available resources will be discovered on the (federated) registry and the best matching one will be called upon to accomplish the task at hand.

CONCLUSION AND FUTURE WORK

So far the research activities already carried out show that the described approach is feasible, although it places high demands (in terms of computing power) to back end systems.

In particular the availability of suitable distributed input processing software for voice recognition on large scale is still elusive.

Future research activities will deal with solving those aspects and improving the processing of context sensitive but user unaware input. For example in case of an unexpected raise in temperature an environment sensor may signal the risk of a fire inception even if no user recognizes visually a fire yet.

REFERENCES

Berners-Lee, T., Hendler, J., & Lassila, O. (May). The Semantic Web. *Scientific American Magazine*. Retrieved on March 26, 2008.

Counts, S., Hofter, H., & Smith, I. (2006). Mobile social software: Realizing potential, managing risks. *Workshop at the Conference on Human Factors in Computing Systems (CHI '06)* (pp.1703-1706).

Dörnemann T., Friese, T., Herdt, S., Juhnke, E., & Freisleben, B. (2007). Grid workflow modelling using grid-specific BPEL extensions. *German E-Science*.

EIF. (2004). *European interoperability framework for pan-European e-government services version 1.0*. Brussels. Retrieved from http://europa.eu.int/idabc/en/document/3761

Foster, I., Kesselman, C., Tuecke, S. (2001). The anatomy of the grid: Enabling scalable virtual organizations. *International J. Supercomputer Applications, 15*(3).

Foster, I., Kishimoto, H., Savva, A., Berry, D., Djaoui, A., Grimshaw, A., Horn, B., Maciel, F., Siebenlist, F., Subramaniam, R., Treadwell, J., & Von Reich, J. (2006). The open grid services architecture, version 1.5. *Open Grid Forum*, Lemont, IL. GFD-I.080.

Foster I., Frey, J., Graham, S., Tuecke, S., Czajkowski, K., Ferguson, D., Leymann, F., Nally, M., Sedukhin, I., Snelling, D., Storey, T., Vambenepe, W., & Weerawarana, S. (2004). *Modeling statefull fesources with Web services v.1.1.*

Frattini, G., Romano, L., Scotto di Carlo, V., Pierpaolo, P., Supino, G., Leone, G, & Autiero, C. (2006). Multimodal architectures: Issues and experiences. *OTM Workshops, (1)*, 974-983.

Frattini, G., Gaudino, F., Scotto di Carlo, V. (2007). Mobile multimodal applications on mass-market devices: Experiences. *DEXA Workshops 2007* (pp. 89-93).

Frattini, G., Petriccione, P., Leone, G., Supino, G., & Corvino, F. (2007, September). Beyond Web 2.0: Enabling multimodal web interactions using VoIP and Ajax. In *Security and Privacy in Communications Networks and the Workshops, 2007. SecureComm 2007. Third International Conference* (pp. 89-97).

Frattini, G., Ceccarini, F., Corvino, F., De Furio, I., Gaudino, F., Petriccione, P., Russo, R., Scotto di Carlo, V., & Supino, G. (2008). *A new approach toward a modular multimodal interface for PDAs and smartphones*. VISUAL: 179-191.

Frissen, V., Millard, J., Huijboom, N., Svava Iversen, J., Kool, L., & Kotterink, B. In D. Osimo, D. Zinnbauer & A. Bianchi (Eds.), *The future of e-government: An exploration of ICT-driven models of e-government for the EU in 2020*. Retrieved from http://ipts.jrc.ec.europa.eu/publications/pub.cfm?id=1481

Globus Alliance. *Globus toolkit*. Retrieved from http://www.globus.org/toolkit/

Hoffmann, J., & Nebel, B. (2001). The FF planning system: Fast plan generation through heuristic search. *Journal of Artificial Intelligence Research, (14),* 253–302.

Hoffmann, J. (2000). A heuristic for domain indepndent planning and its use in an enforced hill-climbing algorithm. In *Proceedings of 12th Intl Symposium on Methodologies for Intelligent Systems.* Springer Verlag.

Hoffmann, J. (2003). The metric-FF planning system: Translating ignoring delete lists to numeric state variables. *Artificial Intelligence Research (JAIR), 20.*

BPEL. Retrieved from http://www.jboss.org/jbossjbpm/bpel/

JPDL. Retrieved from http://www.jboss. org/jbossjbpm /jpdl

PVM. Retrieved from http://www.jboss.org/jbossjbpm/pvm/

I.D.A.B.C. *Interoperable Delivery of European E-Government Services to Public Administrations, Businesses, and Citizens.* Retrieved from http://ec.europa.eu/idabc/en/document/5101

Klusch, M., & Schmidt, M. *Semantic Web service composition planning with OWLS-Xplan.* Retrieved from www-ags.dfki.uni-sb.de/~klusch/i2s/owlsxplan-3.pdf

Lugano, G. (2007). Mobile social software: Definition, scope, and applications. *EU/IST E-Challenges Conference,* The Hague, The Netherlands.

Lugano, G., & Saariluoma, P. (2007). *Share or not to share: Supporting the user decision in mobile social software applications.*

Little, M., Webber, J., & Parastatidis, S. (2004). Stateful interactions in Web services. A comparison of WSContext and WS-Resource framework. *SOA World Magazine,* April.

Miers, D. (2005). *Workflow handbook, workflow management coalition.* UK: Enix Consulting.

NEM. (2006, August). *Strategic research agenda, version 4.0.*

OASIS. (2006). *Reference model for service oriented architecture 1.0.*

OASIS. *Web services business process execution language.* Retrieved from http://www.oasisopen.org/committees/tc_home.php?wg_abbrev=wsbpel

Corcho, O., Alper, P., Kotsiopoulos, I., Missier, P., Bechhofer, S., & Goble, C. (2006). An overview of S-OGSA: A reference semantic grid architecture. *Web Semantics: Science, Services, and Agents on the World Wide Web, 4*(2).

Paolucci, M., Kawamura, T., Payne, T., & Sycara, K. (2002). Importing the Semantic Web in UDDI. In *Web Services, e-business, and Semantic Web workshop.*

Paolucci, M., Kawamura, T., Payne, T., Sycara, R., & Katia, P. (2002). Semantic matching of Web services capabilities. *International Semantic Web Conference* (pp. 333-347).

Pierno, S., Romano, L., Capuano, L., Magaldi, M., Bevilacqua, L. (2008). Software innovation for e-government expansion. In R. Meersman & Z. Tari (Eds.), *OTM 2008, Part I* (LNCS 5331, pp. 822–832). Springer-Verlag Berlin Heidelberg Computer Science.

Mehrotra, S., Znati, T., & Thompson, C.W. (2008). Crisis management. *IEEE Internet Computing Magazine.*

Tretola, G. (2007). *Autonomic workflow management in e-collaboration environment.* Department of Engineering University of Sannio, Benevento.

Tretola, G., & Zimeo, E. (2006, April 25-29). Workflow fine-grained concurrency with automatic continuations. In *Proceedings of the IEEE IPDPS 06, 20th International Parallel and Distributed Processing Symposium,* Rhodes Island, Greece.

Tretola, G., & Zimeo, E. (2007, February 7-9). Activity pre-scheduling in grid workflow. In *Proceedings of the 15ᵗʰ Euromicro International Conference on Parallel, Distributed and Networkbased Processing (PDP).*

Tretola, G., & Zimeo, E. (2007, March 26-30). Client-side implementation of dynamic asynchronous invocations for Web services. In *Proceedings of the IEEE IPDPS 07, 21ˢᵗ International Parallel and Distributed Processing Symposium*, Long Beach, CA.

Tretola, G., & Zimeo, E. (2007, June 19-20). Structure matching for enhancing UDDI queries results. In *Proceedings of the IEEE International Conference on Service-Oriented Computing and Applications (SOCA'07)*, Newport Beach, CA.

Tretola, G., & Zimeo, E. (2007, July 9-13). Extending Web services semantics to support asynchronous invocations and continuation. In *Proceedings of the IEEE 2007 International Conference on Web Services (ICWS)*, Salt Lake City, UT.

W3C. *Multimodal interaction activity.* Retrieved from http://www.w3.org/2002/mmi/

WSRF. (2006). *Web services resource framework 1.2 TC.* OASIS.

Yu, J., & Buyya, R. (2005). *A taxonomy of workow management systems for grid computing* (Tech. Rep.). Grid Computing and Distributed Systems Laboratory, University of Melbourne, Australia.

Chapter XVIII
Benefits, Challenges, and Research in Multimodal Mobile GIS

Julie Doyle
University College Dublin, Ireland

Michela Bertolotto
University College Dublin, Ireland

David Wilson
University of North Carolina at Charlotte, USA

ABSTRACT

The user interface is of critical importance in applications that provide mapping services. It defines the visualisation and interaction modes for carrying out a variety of mapping tasks, and ease of use is essential to successful user adoption. This is even more evident in a mobile context, where device limitations can hinder usability. In particular, interaction modes such as a pen/stylus are limited and can be quite difficult to use while mobile. Moreover, the majority of GIS interfaces are inherently complex and require significant user training, which can be a serious problem for novice users such as tourists. In this chapter, we review issues in the development of multimodal interfaces for mobile GIS, allowing for two or more modes of input, as an attempt to address interaction complexity in the context of mobile mapping applications. In particular, we review both the benefits and challenges of integrating multimodality into a GIS interface. We describe our multimodal mobile GIS CoMPASS which helps to address the problem by permitting users to interact with spatial data using a combination of speech and gesture input, effectively providing more intuitive and efficient interaction for mobile mapping applications.

INTRODUCTION

Verbal communication between humans is often supplemented with additional sensory input, such as gestures, gaze and facial expressions, to convey emotions. Multimodal systems that process two or more naturally co-occurring modalities, aim to emulate such communication between humans and computers. The rationale for multimodal HCI is that such interaction can provide increased naturalness, intuitiveness, flexibility and efficiency for users, in addition to being easy to learn and use. As such, there has been a growing emphasis in recent years on designing multimodal interfaces for a broad range of application domains.

Significant advances have been made in developing multimodal interfaces since Bolt's original 'Put-that-there' demonstration (Bolt, 1980), which allowed for object manipulation through a combination of speech and manual pen input. This has been due, in large part, to the multitude of technologies available for processing various input modes and to advances in device technology and recognition software. A varied set of multimodal applications now exist that can recognise and process various combinations of input modalities such as speech and pen (Doyle et al, 2007), speech and lip movements (Benoit et al, 2000), tilting (Cho et al, 2007), and vision-based modalities including gaze (Qvarfordt & Zhai, 2005), head and body movement (Nickel & Stiefelhagen, 2003), and facial features (Constantini et al, 2005).

In addition to intuitive input modalities, the large range of relatively inexpensive mobile devices currently available, ensure applications supporting multimodality are available to a broad range of diverse users in society. As such, multimodal interfaces are now incorporated into various applications contexts, including healthcare (Keskin et al, 2007), applications for vision-impaired users (Jacobson, 2002), independent living for the elderly (Sainz Salces et al, 2006), and mobile GIS to name but a few. This latter application area represents the focus of our re-

search and the subject of this chapter. Multimodal interfaces can greatly assist users in interacting with complex spatial displays in mobile contexts. Not only do such interfaces address the limited interaction techniques associated with mobile usage, but they provide the user with flexibility, efficiency and, most importantly, an intuitive, user-friendly means of interacting with a GIS. This is particularly beneficial to non-expert GIS users, for whom traditional GIS interfaces may be too difficult to operate.

This chapter presents an account of the most significant issues relating to multimodal interaction on mobile devices that provide geospatial services. In particular we focus on speech and pen input, where speech may take the form of voice commands or dictation, while pen input includes gestures, handwriting or regular stylus interaction to communicate intention. The contribution of this chapter is two-fold. First, we discuss the benefits of multimodal HCI for mobile geospatial users, in addition to providing an account of the challenges and issues involved in designing such interfaces for mobile GIS. Secondly, we provide a review of current state of the art in the area of multimodal interface design for mobile GIS. This includes a discussion of CoMPASS (Combining Mobile Personalised Applications with Spatial Services), the mobile mapping system that we have developed for use on a Tablet PC. We also present an account of comparable systems in the literature and discuss how these contrast with CoMPASS.

The motivation behind our research is to overcome some of the challenges of mobile systems and issues of complexity of GIS interfaces. Supporting multiple input modalities addresses the issue of limited interaction capabilities and allows users to choose the mode of interaction that is most intuitive to them, hence increasing user-friendliness of a mobile geospatial application.

The remainder of this chapter is organised as follows. The next section presents a detailed account of the benefits, challenges and issues arising when designing multimodal interfaces for mobile GIS. We introduce CoMPASS in the following section, and describe the design and implementation of the multimodal interface for the CoMPASS client component. In the 4th section we outline a representative survey of related research in the area of multimodal geospatial system design, and provides a comparison of such systems with CoMPASS. Finally, we conclude and outline some areas of future work.

MOBILE GIS INTERFACE DESIGN: BENEFITS AND CHALLENGES OF MULTIMODAL INTERACTION

A Geographic Information System is a computer system for capturing, storing, querying, analysing and displaying geographic data (Chang, 2002). While many traditional GIS applications are desktop-based, significant benefits of such systems can often be gained through field use. Mobile GIS refers to the acquisition and use of GIS functionality through mobile devices and in a mobile context. In recent years, mobile GIS usage has moved from exclusively professional spatial applications (such as cartography and geography) to wider contexts. As such, users of mobile GIS now include professional GIS experts such as cartographers and surveyors, in addition to non-expert users such as tourists, outdoor enthusiasts such as fishermen and non-expert professionals such as electricians who may use mobile GIS frequently for their work.

The integration of GIS functionality into diverse application contexts poses a new set of challenges when designing interfaces for such applications. If interfaces are too specialised, the chances are high that few people will be able to operate them without the burden of much user training (Blaser et al, 2000). As such, designing interfaces that are highly user-friendly, learnable and intuitive to a diverse range of users, is indis-

pensable for the adoption and usability of mobile mapping applications.

A further hindrance to mobile GIS stems from the mobile context of use of such applications. This relates to both mobile devices and the problem of interacting whilst moving. While the availability and usage of mobile devices has increased significantly in recent years, alongside advances in device technology, there are still many limitations associated with such devices which can have negative effects on the usability of mobile GIS. A significant problem with mobile devices is that they attempt to give people access to powerful computing services through small interfaces, which typically have extremely small visual displays, poor input techniques and limited audio interaction facilities. Furthermore, use in motion affects the usability of mobile GIS as it may be difficult to interact with such an application using a pen and virtual keyboard. These limitations create the need to address human computer interaction challenges associated with mobile device technology and mobile contexts when designing interfaces for mobile geospatial applications.

Research has shown that multimodal interfaces can aid in considerably reducing the complexity of GIS interfaces (Doyle et al, 2007), (Fuhrmann et al, 2005), (Oviatt, 1996a). Interest in multimodal interface design is motivated by the objective to support more efficient, transparent, flexible and expressive means of human computer interaction (Oviatt et al, 2000). Multimodal interaction allows users to interact in a manner similar to what they are used to when interacting with humans. Using speech input, gesture input and head and eye tracking, for example, allows for more natural interaction. However, there are also a number of challenges associated with designing multimodal interfaces which interaction designers should keep in mind to ensure a successful, robust system. This section discusses both the benefits and challenges of integrating multimodal interaction, particularly speech and pen input, into the design of mobile GIS.

Benefits of Multimodal Interaction for Mobile GIS

The benefits of multimodal interfaces, particularly within mobile geospatial environments, are numerous. These include:

- Flexible interaction in mobile contexts.
- Increased access to spatial information for non-professional user groups.
- Novel visualisation and interaction and increased efficiency for professional user groups.
- Increased robustness of geospatial applications and
- The majority of users prefer to interact multimodally.

Traditional input techniques, such as a keyboard and mouse, are unsuitable in mobile contexts. To counteract this problem, mobile devices are equipped with a pen/stylus and virtual keyboard for interaction and data entry. However, given that mobile users are continuously in motion when carrying out field-based geospatial tasks, it is likely that their hands and eyes will be busy fulfilling their tasks. In such situations, another input modality might be an attractive alternative over the stylus. For example, it is more natural for users to speak or gesture whilst moving than it is to point or enter text whilst moving. Furthermore, such impoverished input techniques as a stylus and virtual keyboard may not be sufficiently expressive to convey the geospatial intentions of mobile users, who may be required to point precisely to small interface objects, or to input text. Such interaction modalities might be cumbersome or frustrating for many users, as they do not lend themselves to user-friendliness or efficiency. Multimodal interfaces allow users to choose the most appropriate modality for carrying out varied spatial tasks in contrasting environments, which provides users greater freedom to exercise control over how they interact. Therefore, they can choose to use the modality that not only is more suited to their current task, but also is most intuitive to them for this task. This has the benefit of greatly increasing the accessibility of multimodal applications to a wider range of users in various application contexts.

Mobile geospatial applications have recently surged in popularity among a wide range of non-professional user groups. This includes, for example, tourists who use such applications to navigate an area, get directions, locate points of interest (POI) and discover information regarding these POIs. Such tourists may include people from different walks of society, such as those with limited computer knowledge, the elderly or disabled people. Designing multimodal interfaces for mobile geospatial applications results in increased access to spatial information for this large group of potential users and as such, helps to promote universal access. For those users with little computing experience of using buttons and menus to navigate and query, voice commands and pointing gestures may provide a more natural and intuitive means of communication with a GIS. In addition, information presented through different modalities allows a user to adapt to the format of information display that suits their own cognitive learning style, or that they have sensory access to (Wickens & Baker, 1995). For example, non-visual interfaces, using tactile, haptic and auditory modalities, can potentially increase the use of spatial applications to vision-impaired users. As such, multimodal interfaces can help to ensure mobile geospatial applications are accessible to people irrespective of skill level, age or sensory impairment.

The integration of multiple modalities into mobile GIS can also afford many benefits to professional GIS users such as geographers, surveyors and cartographers. Enhanced editing capabilities in the field are one such advantage. When, for example, a cartographer is collecting data in the field, he/she may want to annotate this data with their own notes. A multimodal system that recognises dictation of speech can allow such a task to be performed more easily and more efficiently than with pen and keyboard input. Indeed, increased efficiency of interaction is another advantage held by multimodal systems over their unimodal counterparts (Doyle et al, 2007), (Oviatt, 1996a) and is of great importance for GIS professionals who must work under time constraints.

A particularly advantageous aspect of multimodal interaction is that it can lend itself to more robust performance of geospatial applications. During such interaction, information from different input sources is merged thus allowing the rectification of errors made by individual modalities. This process is known as mutual disambiguation of input modalities (Oviatt, 1999). This paradigm is particularly useful in certain environments where one input modality might be predominantly weak (for example, speech in a noisy environment). Even more beneficial for multimodal applications is the ability to support multimodal error correction, which has been shown to be superior to unimodal error correction both in terms of avoidance of and recovery from errors (Suhm, Myers & Weibel, 2001), (Oviatt, Bernard & Levow, 1999).

A final noteworthy benefit of designing multimodal interfaces for mobile GIS is users' strong preferences to interact multimodally (Doyle et

al, 2007). This may be attributed to feelings of increased control over how one can interact, increased flexibility, increased efficiency and more intuitive interaction.

Potential Limitations of Integrating Multimodality into an Interface

When designing a multimodal interface that includes speech, the designer must be aware not only of the advantages of speech technology which may enhance the user's interaction, but also of its limitations. There are a number of factors that can contribute to the failure of a speech application, the most notable being that of background noise which can disrupt a speech signal, making it more difficult to process and decreasing recognition rates. Indeed reducing the speech recogniser's error rate under all environmental contexts remains one of the greatest challenges facing speech recognition manufacturers (Deng & Huang, 2004). Table 1 lists some suggestions of when to use speech recognition and when to avoid it.

Oviatt (2000a) identifies two primary sources of speech degradation in noisy acoustic environments:

- Additive noise which can contaminate a speech signal and
- In noisy environments people change how they speak in an effort to be understood.

Table 1. When to Use Speech Recognition

Use When	Avoid When
Task requires the user's hands to be occupied so they cannot use a keyboard or mouse.	Task requires users to talk to other people while using the application.
Commands are embedded in a deep menu structure.	Users work in a very noisy environment.
Using a keyboard and mouse is not feasible (e.g. in a mobile context).	Task can be accomplished more easily using a mouse and keyboard (e.g. in an office environment).
Users have a physical disability.	Speech may be inappropriate (e.g. in a museum context).
Users are unable to type, or are uncomfortable with typing.	Trying to express location. Pen input is better suited to this.

Additive noise can, for example, result from other people speaking in close proximity to the speech recognition application. This background noise can often be interpreted as words which then get positively matched against the words in the application's rule grammar. Methods can be implemented to deal with this source of error. Developers can add commands to their application's rule grammar which effectively put the microphone 'to sleep' when the user issues the appropriate command, and 'wake it up' when necessary. In addition, headsets are available with an on/off switch fitted to the microphone allowing users to simply switch off speech recognition functionality should they require it.

People tend to speak differently in different environments - in a noisy environment people will speak louder and slower and may even change the pitch of their speech in an effort to be understood by the system (Junqua, 1993). Speech modifications in such environments are an automatic normalisation response known as the "Lombard Effect". This can result in recognition errors as speech recognition training is designed and trained in a controlled environment. So while speech recognition technology performs well in idealised conditions, it is estimated that there is a 20% to 50% decrease in recognition rates when speech recognition is implemented in a natural field environment (Oviatt, 2000b).

The emotive content of a person's voice can also cause problems for speech recognition engines, as speech recognition software has no means to detect and adapt to a person's mood (Shneiderman, 2000). Also, in a training environment a user is reading from a training script and so their voice contains no emotive content.

A large percentage of recognition errors in speech recognition systems result from dictation input. When a user enters dictation input to a recognition system the words spoken are not matched against a rule grammar, but rather a dictation grammar. Dictation grammars impose fewer restrictions on what a user can say and

so can ideally provide free-form speech input. However, this comes at a cost, as dictation grammars require higher quality audio input, more computing resources and they tend to be more error-prone. This has implications on how interfaces for recognition systems that process dictation should be designed, as such interfaces should allow users to intuitively correct errors resulting from dictation.

Issues in Designing Multimodal Interfaces for GIS that Incorporate Speech

The functionality and ease of use of GUIs does not scale well on small, mobile and wearable devices (Sawhney & Schmandt, 2000). As devices get smaller it gets increasingly difficult to use input methods such as keyboards and pens for interaction and speech is an attractive alternative. On the other hand, in certain situations such as noisy outdoor environments, it is not always feasible to use voice recognition as input, and in such circumstances it is necessary to use traditional input methods. Therefore, it is important to design a versatile multimodal interface which allows for various types of interaction. A speech interface should only be available to users should they explicitly request to use it - responsive yet unobtrusive.

Commercial speech recognition software packages are readily available and can be easily plugged into existing applications. However, a number of challenges arise when integrating speech technology into an interface to ensure it is beneficial for all users. Primarily, it must be evident to users that speech input is an available modality at the interface, as an alternative to traditional input methods. Furthermore, it is necessary to ensure that the process of how to turn speech recognition on and off is highly intuitive to the user. If the user cannot see how to turn such functionality on they might either waste time trying to figure this out, or carry out their tasks without using speech functionality and as such they might not reap the full benefits of the application they are using. It is equally important however that users can easily switch speech functionality off. This is important in situations where speech input and output may not be appropriate, for example for tourist users visiting a church or a museum.

A further issue concerning the integration of speech into an application are the possible errors which might result from its use. While speech recognition technology has advanced significantly in recent years, speech recognition errors remain a serious impediment in the design of user interfaces that integrate speech. Some typical sources of speech recognition errors are provided in Table 2. Much research has been conducted into designing speech interfaces that address error avoidance by attempting to minimise user errors. Within a multimodal interface, Oviatt (1999) outlines four factors which are capable of both better error avoidance and better recovery from errors:

1. *Users will select the input mode that they judge to be less error prone for particular lexical content, which leads to error avoidance.* For example, users will identify that it is easier, and more accurate, to describe spatial locations using pen/gesture input as opposed to verbal input i.e. that speech input is an ineffective pointing device (Haller et al, 1984).

2. *Users' language is simplified when interacting multimodally, which reduces the complexity of natural language processing and avoids errors.* It has been shown (Oviatt & Kuhn, 1998) that when interacting multimodally, users speak fewer words, have fewer spoken disfluencies and voice less complex spatial descriptions than when interacting unimodally through speech input, leading to a reduction in system recognition errors.

3. *Users tend to switch modes after system errors, facilitating error recovery.* If the system fails to recognise a user's voice command after two or three attempts, the user is likely to switch modality and carry out the action using an alternative input mode. In this way, a user's task can be completed regardless of initial errors.

4. *Users report less subjective frustration with errors when interacting multimodally, even when errors are as frequent as in a unimodal interface.* One of the reasons for this may be that users are free to exercise selection and control over how they interact within a multimodal system, so if they experience errors with one mode of interaction they are aware that they can simply switch modes to recover from such errors.

In addition to the user-centred methods of error avoidance and correction above, it is necessary to have specific methods of error correction in systems providing a dictation interface. Multimodal error correction has been suggested as a solution to avoiding repeated errors during dictation tasks (Suhm, Meyers & Weibel, 2001). The most obvious advantage of continuous speech dictation input to a system is the increase in efficiency over traditional input methods (such as pen and keyboard) for entering large amounts of text. However, this efficiency gain can significantly diminish if interactive and efficient methods are not provided to correct dictation errors. Multimodal error correction - allowing the user to switch modality to correct a dictation error - can be more accurate and efficient than repeating the dictation through continuous speech (Wang et al 2006). While re-speaking is the preferred mode of repetition in human-human interaction it is not the most intuitive or efficient mode for interaction with a dictation system. If the speech recognition system did not correctly recognise all words of a dictation input on the first attempt, it is unlikely that 100% recognition will be achieved on a second attempt. Furthermore, while users may initially prefer speech input for dictation, they learn to avoid ineffective correction modalities with experience (Suhm, Meyers & Weibel, 2001).

Providing alternative methods of correction increases user satisfaction with the system's error handling facilities, leading to an overall augmentation in system usability. Figure 1 depicts the typical flow of processes in a continuous speech dictation system. When a user dictates input to a system, the dictation is processed and feedback in visual or audio form is provided to the user. The user is asked to confirm whether the recognised input is correct and if it is the dictation is stored in the system. Otherwise, the user must choose a method of correction to correct the errors. Typical methods include repeated continuous speech, handwriting, pen and keyboard input and repeating only those words that were incorrectly recognised. The repeated input is presented to the user again for confirmation, after which the process begins once more. The process of multimodal error correction in CoMPASS is described in Section 3.

A further issue in designing multimodal interfaces is that strategies are required for coordinating input modalities and for resolving issues related to integration and synchronisation of input modes. Hickey (2000) outlines three main classes of multimodality integration:

- **Sequential**, whereby only one modality is available at a time. With sequential integration, there is no requirement for inputs to be active simultaneously. In any given state, only one input mode will be active when the user takes some action. Furthermore, inputs from different modalities are interpreted separately by the system's inference engine.

- **Simultaneous Uncoordinated**, whereby several modalities are available but only one modality is interpreted at any given time. While input modalities are simultaneously active, there is no requirement that these modalities are interpreted together.

- **Simultaneous Coordinated**, whereby several modalities are coordinated and are interpreted together. This is the most advanced type of multimodal integration.

However, although a common belief, multimodal signals will not always occur co-temporally. Research has shown that for map-based tasks using speech and pen input, as few as 25% of user's multimodal commands actually contain overlapping inputs; rather, they are sequential with a lag of one or two seconds between inputs (Oviatt, DeAngeli & Kuhn, 1997). As such, multimodal

Table 2. Possible sources of Speech Recognition Errors

Problem	Cause
Rejection or Mis-recognition	- User speaks one or more words not in the vocabulary. - User's words do not match any interactive grammar. - User speaks before system is ready to listen. - Words in active vocabulary sound alike and are confused (e.g. "too", "two"). - User pauses too long in the middle of input. - User speaks with a disfluency (e.g. restarts input, stumbles with input, "umm", "eh"). - User's voice trails off at the end of input. - User has an accent or a cold - User's voice is substantially different from stored voice model. - Computer's audio is not properly configured. - User's microphone is not properly adjusted.
Misfire	- Non-speech sound (cough or laugh). - Background speech triggers recognition. - User is talking with another person whilst computer is listening.

Figure 1. Flowchart of Multimodal Error Correction Process

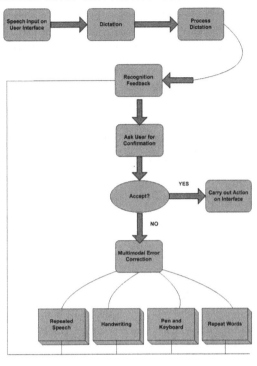

interface designers for mobile GIS must decide which of the above integration types will work best for the system they want to develop.

THE COMPASS MULTIMODAL INTERFACE

The focus of our own research has been the design and implementation of an intuitive, user-friendly interface for mobile GIS applications. The development of the client module for CoMPASS has provided the case study for such research. CoMPASS is a mobile, multimodal Geographic Information System (GIS) that has been developed on a Tablet PC, for delivering personalised, vector-based spatial data to various types of users (Weakliam et al, 2005), (Doyle et al, 2006). CoMPASS allows users to connect to a remote server and download vector maps in GML file

format over wireless connections, to mobile devices. Users can then dynamically interact with these maps through pen and voice input modes. Available interactions include zooming and panning, querying and spatial annotating. Users can also manipulate the visual display by turning on/off features and changing the appearance of map features. Furthermore, they can attach annotations to both spatial locations and features.

A Tablet PC is an ideal platform for the development of CoMPASS as it provides all the power of a desktop computer on a mobile device. As such, it enabled us to develop an interface which can support all the functionality that CoMPASS provides. This would not be possible on smaller mobile devices such as PDAs or Smart Phones as they simply are not yet sufficiently advanced to support such a complex GIS. Constraints of PDAs, such as limited computational power, limited memory capacity, limited user interface space and limited interaction techniques could be overcome on a Tablet PC. Moreover, GIS professionals, one of our target groups of users, would require the more advanced Tablet PC for everyday use. While many non-professionals may not currently be Tablet PC users, we envision that in the near future Tablet PCs will replace Laptop computers as the mobile computer of choice, significantly widening our range of users.

The following system architecture is proposed for delivering personalised geo-spatial data using non-proprietary software and to efficiently represent maps in either Web or mobile environments. The scope of the system's functionality ranges from geospatial information handling and transmission over slow communication links to personalisation techniques and human-computer interaction (HCI). In order to fulfil the requirements of the system in a distributed computing environment, the system architecture comprises an n-tier client-server application structure (Figure 2). The architecture encompasses three aspects: (1) a map server, (2) a service provider and (3) a data deployment component. Of most interest to us for this chapter are the HCI handling service of the Services Layer and the Deployment Layer.

Design of the Mobile Client

Processing at the client corresponds to the HCI handling service of Figure 2. The client can handle and process interactions in the form of gesture, speech and handwriting (Figure 3). Separate recognisers are responsible for recognition of each mode of input. The processing and interpretation of speech-based input has been our primary focus with regard to providing an alternative interaction mode to pen-based input. Commercial speech software packages which process both speech recognition and synthesis are readily available and such packages can easily plug-in to existing applications. Despite this, there are, however, a number of issues involved in integrating speech software into an interface and these were discussed in Section 2.3. The software package used within CoMPASS is IBM's ViaVoice, release 10 (IBM, 2005).

Two modes of speech input are available when interacting with the CoMPASS interface - voice commands and dictation. Voice commands consist of short phrases made up of one or two words. We felt that keeping voice commands short would

Figure 2. CoMPASS Architecture

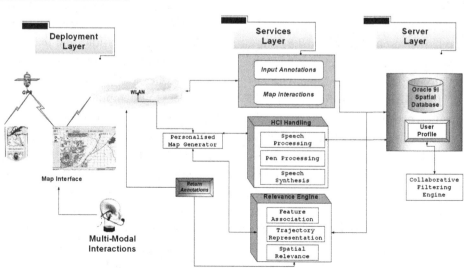

reduce the time to learn these commands and hence increase the efficiency of the system, as users would not be reliant on the CoMPASS help menu to look up commands. Such phrases are matched against a specified rule grammar, which contains a list of all possible voice commands available for interacting with the system. Providing a specific set of voice commands ensures more precise and robust recognition, as an interface action will only be carried out if the command associated with the action has been recognised and determined as being a legitimate voice command.

Currently there are approximately 350 commands that CoMPASS recognises. The vast majority of these commands contain a feature name, combined with another word for performing some action on that feature. The structure of these commands within the rule grammar is shown in Table 3. To toggle a layer, for example, the rule requires a member of <Layer> followed by a member of <Toggle> whereby <Layer> contains a list of all map features such as streets, parks etc. and <Toggle> is either the command 'on' or 'off'. So issuing the command 'lakes on' results in the lakes feature being toggled on, if lakes are currently not visible on the map. Voice commands can be used within CoMPASS for navigating, feature manipulation, querying and carrying out additional actions at the interface such as asking for help, switching speech recognition off and exiting the application.

An important aspect of our client interface is that the user receives visual feedback after they have issued a command. The command is displayed on the left hand side of the information bar allowing the user to check that their command

Figure 3. Structure of the Client Module

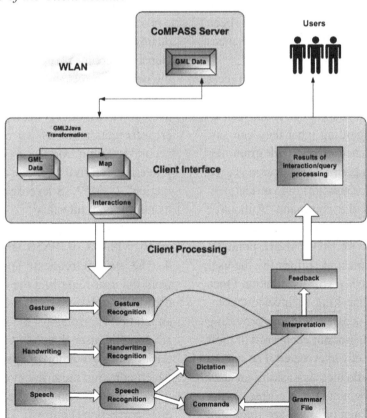

Table 3. Voice Command Structure

Action	Rule	Commands
Navigate	<Action Direction> = <Action><Direction>	<Action> = Zoom | Pan <Direction> = In | Out | North | Southeast etc.
Layer On/Off	<Layer Toggle> = <Layer><Toggle>	<Layer> = Highways | Lakes | Streets etc. <Toggle> = On | Off
Change Layer Colour	<Change Colour> = <Layer><Colour>	<Layer> = Highways | Lakes | Streets etc. <Colour> = Blue | Green | Red etc.
Highlight Query	<Highlight Layer> = <Highlight><Layer>	<Highlight> = Highlight <Layer> = Highways | Lakes | Streets etc.

has been interpreted correctly. Similarly, once the required action has been carried out on the interface, a message is displayed on the right hand side of the information bar to notify the user of such. Providing some form of feedback to users plays a crucial role in assuring them that their intentions have been interpreted correctly and that the task they were hoping to achieve has been completed successfully. This in turn enhances system usability and intuitiveness.

The CoMPASS speech module can process dictation entered by a user. Dictation is essentially free-form speech and so enforces fewer restrictions on the user regarding what they can say. Such input is not matched against a rule grammar, but rather a dictation grammar. Dictation is used within CoMPASS for annotating map features. Once a user issues the command 'Annotate', the rule grammar is disabled and the dictation grammar becomes active. CoMPASS responds by delivering an audio message informing the user that they should input their voice annotation. Once the user has finished speaking, their voice annotation is displayed in a separate window, providing feedback as to whether or not each word of their annotation was correctly interpreted. The system delivers a second audio message asking the user to confirm that their annotation is correct. If the user provides confirmation, they are requested

to pick a point on the map to assign the annotation to, whereupon the annotation and its spatial location are recorded by the system.

However, as dictation grammars contain no specific rules pertaining to what the user can say, they tend to be more error prone. It is likely, particularly in outdoor mobile environments, that a relatively high percentage of the words spoken during dictation will not be recognized correctly. Hence, it becomes crucial to provide methods for the user to correct their voice annotation if necessary. It has been recognised that allowing the user to switch modality during continuous speech error correction can result in increased correction accuracy (Suhm, Meyers & Weibel, 2001). This process is referred to as "multimodal error correction". CoMPASS leverages this technique in its multimodal interface.

The process involved in correcting dictation errors within CoMPASS is described in Table 4. The system requests spoken confirmation from the user regarding the correctness of their dictated annotation. If the user indicates that the annotation is erroneous, the system responds by advising the user that they can now correct any errors. A new window is displayed, one part of which contains the original erroneous dictation while the other contains the possible modes of error correction (Figure 4). The user must choose

Table 4. The Error Correction Process

- If dictation is incorrect output audio message requesting the user to choose a mode of input to correct the dictation.

- Display window with original (incorrect) dictated input and buttons for corrections.

- If choice is 'Pen and Keyboard' - Open virtual keyboard application; Open Annotation Window; Request user to input annotation through keyboard and save within Annotation Window.

- If choice is 'Voice Record' - Open voice record window; Ask user to record their annotation as a voice memo and save it.

- If choice is 'Handwriting' – Open handwriting application; Open Annotation window; Request user to input annotation using the handwriting application.

from re-entering the annotation using the pen and virtual keyboard of the Tablet PC, recording a voice memo or handwriting. We chose not to provide an option to 're-speak' the dictation as we felt that if the dictation was erroneous the first time round, it is highly unlikely that it would be 100% accurate the second time round. Hence the user was required to switch modality.

When creating an annotation within CoM-PASS, users can associate an image with the annotation before saving it and assigning it to a feature. In addition, users can record annotations in the form of 'sound bytes'. The user simply presses 'Record' at the interface, speaks their annotation and presses 'Stop' when their annotation is complete. The user can then playback their recorded annotation, save it and assign it to a feature on the map, thus creating a geo-referenced voice memo. Other CoMPASS users can subsequently listen to this annotation through audio output. While this correction method has the advantages of efficiency and accuracy, such a 'sound byte' file can be quite large, typically ranging between 1 and 2 megabytes for an annotation consisting of about 18 words. Additionally, the recorded annotation is simply stored as a sound file: it is not converted to text and hence we cannot associate keywords with it for annotation indexing and retrieval, the process of which is outside the scope of this chapter.

Handwriting is another possible choice of modality to correct errors during dictation of annotations. Pressing the 'Handwriting' button on the Error Correction window opens the handwriting application. The in-built handwriting recogniser of the Tablet PC can process both block and cursive handwriting. If a handwritten word is misinterpreted, the user can choose from a list of alternatives simply by clicking on the word. The efficiency of and preference for handwriting as a mode of error correction within CoMPASS, was demonstrated in a previous evaluation (Doyle et al, 2008).

In addition to voice commands and dictation, the CoMPASS multimodal interface also recognises and processes interactions in the form of gestures. Gestures can take the form of 'intra-gestures' i.e. pointing or selecting with the stylus to locations or objects on the Tablet PC screen. 'Extra-gestures' that allow users to point to surrounding objects in their current environment are not supported. Intra-gestures can take two forms within CoMPASS: pointing and dragging. Users can point at objects to re-centre the map at this point, to discover the name and type of objects, to specify what feature they would like to query or what feature they would like to annotate. Dragging gestures specify a 'zoom in' on the area over which the pen is dragged or, when used in conjunction with a query, to specify the area of interest for the query.

With regard to the development of the interface for the CoMPASS client, our primary objective was to provide users with an interface that enhanced, rather than impeded, our users' experience when viewing and interacting with geospatial data in a mobile context. Contributing factors to an enhanced geospatial experience include, but are not limited to, ease and efficiency of task completion as well as overall user satisfaction. The CoMPASS system has now been fully implemented and evaluated. Evaluations of the client served to demonstrate that we have achieved our objectives for tasks involving all possible CoMPASS functionality through the provision of a multimodal interface. Our results showed that our multimodal interface supports more efficient and effective interaction than a unimodal interface and that the ability to switch between modes of interaction for different types of tasks significantly increases ease of task completion. Furthermore, our multimodal interface elicited strong positive feedback from our users. Details of CoMPASS client evaluations can be found in (Doyle et al, 2007), (Doyle et al, 2008).

RELATED RESEARCH

The array of available multimodal applications providing geospatial services has broadened widely, and ranges from city navigation and wayfinding for tourists, to emergency planning and military simulation. In this section, we provide a representative survey of the state of the art within the research realm of multimodal mobile GIS. We focus our attention on multimodal systems that process active forms of input i.e. speech and pen. We feel such input modalities are more reliable regarding user intention than vision-based (passive) methods which require no input from the user, but instead implicitly monitor their movements to infer recognition.

A characteristic of mobile applications is the continually changing environmental context, and hence changing noise levels, which can have a serious impact on multimodal applications that include speech. Research by Wasinger et al (2003) outlines a mobile architecture for pedestrian navigation, designed to support multimodal input and

Figure 4. Error Correction Interface

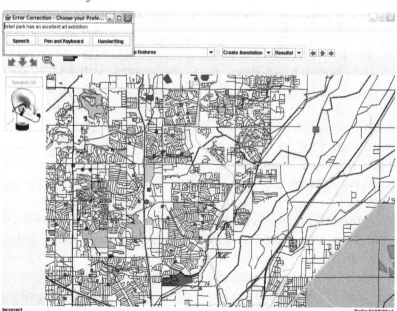

the aim of which is to increase speech recognition rates in environments where noise levels are high and user contexts are continuously changing. The authors suggest that the fusion of inputs, including speech, gesture and keyboard/mouse produce more robust recognition rates than when inputs are used separately. In addition, multimodal output is supported in the form of a speech synthesizer that provides audio route instructions to aid users in navigating to a desired location.

In (Charaniya & Lodha, 2003) the authors extend their existing system of a visual interface for querying GIS (Lodha et al, 2003), to include a speech interface. Their speech interface includes both speech recognition and synthesis capabilities. The speech interface can work as part of the visualisation interface, or alternatively, as an independent entity. Certain queries are supported by both interfaces and so overlap. This redundancy of queries was found to be useful to users in heightening their geospatial awareness. Initial user testing proved the speech interface to be effective when used both independently and in combination with the visual interface.

DeepMap (Malaka & Zipf, 2000) is a prototype tourist guide system that has two facets. Firstly, users can plan their upcoming trip through DeepMap's web-based interface, from their home. DeepMap consequently provides such users with a mobile-based version of their prototype which can be used as a tourist guide for navigating the city of Heidelberg. One of the primary goals of the DeepMap mobile tourist guide is to provide users with a user interface that is both intuitive and allows easy access to spatial information. The authors strive to achieve this goal through the use of both a 3D visualisation (in addition to 2D visualisations) and by providing multiple modes of input and output for interaction. However, the 3D visualisation is not feasible on a mobile device such as a PDA due to computational performance restrictions. With regard to the multimodal interaction, a natural language interface is provided that allows free speech and real dialogs. Unlike

CoMPASS however, no command grammars are used. Grammars are important in any application providing speech recognition as they support more robust and accurate recognition.

The issue of the complexity of GIS interfaces is addressed in (Rauschert et al, 2002), which describes DAVE_G (Dialogue-Assisted Visual Environment for Geoinformation), a system which uses a combination of speech and gesture to aid users in collaborative group work when responding to a crisis situation in the context of emergency management. As such, DAVE_G is a professional GIS application. However, its target users are those without special GIS training, therefore addressing complexity is vital to the usability of the system. The authors found that for a task such as querying, using speech and gestures is more efficient, and natural, than traditional querying methods and hence more user-friendly. Results for such queries are instant and such efficiency is a necessity for applications such as emergency management. Moreover, the advantage of using gestures in addition to speech is that speech may not be completely accurate when spatial information such as location needs to be specified. However, such research is carried out on a large screen display, rather than on a mobile device. Despite this, the DAVE_G system demonstrates that multimodal interaction can reduce the complexity of a user's task during an emergency management situation.

Multimodal interaction research tends to focus on how best to enhance an application by using different input modalities. Very little research has been conducted into multimodal feedback, however. The use of combining oral messages with visual modalities for aiding target location tasks is described in (Keiffer & Carbonell, 2006). The authors present an experimental evaluation the aim of which is to assess the efficiency, accuracy and usability of oral system messages, including brief spatial information, to help users locate objects on crowded displays with minimal effort. The experiment consisted of locating a pre-viewed photograph in a scene and selecting it as quickly as possible using the mouse. Oral messages to help users were composed of short phrases such as "On the left (of the screen)" or "At the bottom". Providing oral feedback as a supplement to visual stimuli proved to be both more efficient and accurate than no oral output. Moreover, evaluation subjects expressed preference for the inclusion of oral messages for such a task. While this experiment was not spatially-based, it demonstrates the utility of speech output for locating objects in a scene, and hence could be applied to GIS.

Multimodal feedback/output within CoM-PASS takes the form of confirmation messages (for example when a voice command has been interpreted correctly) printed to an unobtrusive information bar at the bottom of the screen. In addition, audio prompts are output to aid the user in completing complex tasks. Such audio prompts consume less cognitive resources than pop-up windows displaying information messages, as the user must pause their task to read the message. Pop-up windows also take up a lot of screen space on small devices and so temporarily obstruct the user's view of their map. Speech prompts on the other hand do not distract from the user's main task, allowing them to continue to carry out their task while they receive instructions to assist them further.

Comparatively few systems integrate handwriting recognition as an input modality in a multimodal system. However, such an input mode can prove particularly efficient and accurate for inputting textual information such as annotations. An evaluation to determine user preference of a number of modalities, including handwriting recognition, for interacting with a mobile shopping assistant is presented in (Wasinger & Kreuger, 2005). Subjects were required to trial 23 different modality combinations, including both unimodal (e.g. handwriting only) interaction and conflicting multimodal combinations (e.g. speech and handwriting together), for the task of buying a digital camera. While each individual modality

presented both advantages as well as disadvantages, a number of problems were reported with regard to handwriting recognition. It was commonly expressed that writing took too long and that the display area for writing was too small. In addition, users reported feeling self-conscious that their handwriting would not be recognised, even though results proved that recognition was high. One of the noted benefits of handwriting, however, was that it was unobtrusive to the user and would be suitable in situations where privacy was required. With regard to the combination of speech and handwriting, it was generally felt that such a multimodal approach was not efficient as it caused users to slow down and slur their speech input.

Handwriting might be seen as more suitable for the input of annotations than pen/keyboard or speech input in a system such as CoMPASS. Results of CoMPASS user evaluations demonstrate that for annotation tasks, pen and keyboard input is perceived as cumbersome and time consuming by our users, whereas speech input via dictation, while efficient, is too erroneous to be considered an acceptable input mode (Doyle et al, 2008). Handwriting can provide a more balanced approach to inputting textual annotations, combining the accuracy of pen input with the efficiency of speech input. As such, handwriting is an integrated modality within CoMPASS supporting the input of annotations.

While each of the systems presented in this Section provide relevant research into the area of multimodal GIS, they also suffer from certain limitations which we attempt to address within CoMPASS. These limitations are summarised below:

The vast majority of current mobile GIS applications are targeted at tourists and as such support only limited geospatial functionality such as way-finding and accessing semantic information regarding Points of Interest.

Such systems are typically implemented on PDA devices. While these devices have the advantage of being small and lightweight, the available screen space for displaying maps is extremely limited which can have effects on complexity and the cognitive resources required to read mobile maps.

There is a distinct lack of novel interaction techniques to support and enhance interaction with such systems in a mobile context. Supporting multiple input modes increases the flexibility and choice users have in interacting and consequently can enhance usability and efficiency.

Many of those systems that do support multimodal interaction tend to lack other features which CoMPASS provides. For example, the multimodal tour guide applications presented lack full geospatial functionality providing only navigation and information viewing, but not spatial annotation functionality, for example. These systems target primarily tourist or similar non-expert users, while other multimodal systems have been developed solely for use in a professional context (e.g. DAVE_G). Moreover, whether developed for professional or non-professional use, many of the multimodal systems presented are based on handheld devices such as PDAs. Apart from the cognitive issues of map reading associated with such hardware devices, they lack the sophistication to allow professional users to carry out their work efficiently and effectively in mobile contexts. Finally, the majority of systems presented do not support either feedback or multimodal error correction, which are essential to ensure a robust multimodal application.

We address the above limitations through the CoMPASS client interface. Primarily, CoMPASS is a multi-functional GIS supporting not only navigation and information retrieval but also manipulation, customisation, querying and annotating of maps and map features. CoMPASS also incorporates personalisation of map detail for users in addition to progressive vector transmission techniques, both of which contribute to less irrelevant detail being sent to users and hence reduce the complexity of navigation. Moreover,

CoMPASS targets both professional and non-expert users alike, providing both groups with a friendly, usable and efficient environment for the completion of geospatial tasks. As CoMPASS is implemented on a Tablet PC our users (particularly professional users) benefit further from this superior mobile device.

CoMPASS leverages full advantage of the multimodal paradigm. It provides a multimodal system that not only supports multimodal input, allowing users to carry out any geospatial task through speech or pen/gesture input, but which also provides multimodal feedback to users in addition to methods for multimodal error correction. Overall, CoMPASS provides our users with an enhanced geospatial experience.

CONCLUSION AND FUTURE WORK

Mobile GIS has, in recent years, been afforded a significant increase in popularity and has expanded greatly from its traditional context of use i.e. solely GIS professionals. Given that a much wider and diverse range of users now depend on mobile geospatial applications, it is critical to address issues of complexity surrounding current GIS interfaces.

This chapter has presented a review of multimodal interfaces for mobile GIS. Such interfaces significantly assist in increasing the flexibility and robustness of mobile GIS and in addition have been shown to enhance the usability of such applications for a broad range of users. In addition to the many benefits afforded by a multimodal interface, the main challenges in the design of such interfaces have also been highlighted. We have also described the multimodal interface we have developed for the mobile GIS CoMPASS. Such an interface is flexible and intuitive to use and allows for an easy switch between different input modalities. CoMPASS has been evaluated with a number of users, the results of which were presented in previous publications (Doyle et al, 2008). Our main findings demonstrate that the multimodal interface we developed played a significant role in contributing to the overall intuitiveness, user-friendliness, efficiency and flexibility of our mobile GIS application, for both novice and professional user groups. Moreover, multimodal (as opposed to unimodal) interaction was rated highly by users as the preferred mode of interaction for mobile geospatial tasks. We expect, therefore, that as mobile mapping applications become more widely available in the near future, an application such as CoMPASS will play a vital role in improving interaction with and usability of such systems.

Notwithstanding the many advantages of such an interface, it can be enhanced in several ways. For example, it currently only supports sequential multimodal input. In the future we intend to provide synchronous fusion of input. We are also investigating the use of multimodal feedback for different users (expert, non-expert, etc.). Transferring the functionality to a lighter mobile device (PDA) is also on-going.

REFERENCES

Benoit, C., Martin, J.C., Pelachaud, C., Scho-maker, L., & Suhm, B. (2000). Audio-visual and multimodal speech-based systems. In D. Gibbon, I. Mertins & R. Moore (Eds.), *Handbook of multimodal systems and spoken dialogue systems: Resources, terminology, and product evaluation.* Kluwer Academic Publishers.

Blaser, A.D., Sester, M., & Egenhofer, M. (2000). Visualization in an early stage of the problem solving process in GIS. *Computer and GeoSciences, Special Issue on GeoScientific Visualization, 26*(1), 57-66. Elsevier Science.

Bolt, R. (1980). Put-that-there: Voice and gesture at the graphics interface. In *7th International Conference on Computer Graphics and Interactive Techniques* (pp. 262-270). Seattle, WA: ACM Press.

Chang, K.T. (2002). Introduction to geographic information systems. New York: McGraw Hill.

Charaniya, A.P., & Lodha, S.K. (2003). Speech interface for geospatial visualization. *Computer Graphics International.* Acta Press.

Cho, S.J., & Murray-Smith, R., & Kim, Y.-B. (2007). Multicontext photo browsing on mobile devices based on tilt dynamics. In *Mobile HCI '07,* Singapore.

Constantini, E., Pianesi, F., & Prete, M. (2005). Recognising emotions in human and synthetic faces: The role of the upper and lower parts of the face. In *10th International Conference on Intelligent User Interfaces,* San Diego, CA (pp. 20-27). ACM Press.

Deng, L., & Huang, X. (2004). Challenges in adopting speech recognition. *Communications of the ACM, 47*(1), 69-75. ACM Press.

Doyle, J., Bertolotto, M., & Wilson, D. (2007). A survey of multimodal interfaces for mobile mapping applications. In L. Meng, A. Zipf & S. Winter (Eds.), *Map-based mobile services–interactivity and usability.* Springer-Verlag.

Doyle, J., Bertolotto, M., & Wilson, D. (in press). Evaluating the benefits of multimodal interface design for CoMPASS–a mobile GIS. In *GeoInformatica.*

Doyle, J., Weakliam, J., Bertolotto, M., & Wilson, D. (2006). A multimodal interface for personalising spatial data in mobile GIS. In *ICEIS, 8th International Conference on Enterprise Information Systems,* Paphos, Cyprus (pp. 71-78).

Fuhrmann, S., MacEachren, A., Dou, J., Wang, K., & Cox, A. (2005). Gesture and speech-based maps to support use of GIS for crisis management: A user study. In *AutoCarto 2005.* Las Vegas, NV: Cartography and Geographic Information Society.

Haller, R., Mutschler, H., & Voss, M. (1984). Comparison of input devices for correction of typing errors in office systems. In *INTERACT '84, the 1st IFIP Conference on Human Computer Interaction* (pp. 218-223). London: North Holland.

Hickey, M. (2000). Multimodal requirements for voice mark-up languages. *W3C working draft*. Retrieved on March 18, 2008, from http://www.w3.org/TR/multimodal-reqs

IBM ViaVoice. (2005). Retrieved on October 2005, from http://www-306.ibm.com/software/voice/viavoice/

Jacobson, R.D. (2002). Representing spatial information through multimodal interfaces. In *6th International Conference on Information Visualization* (pp. 730-734). IEEE press.

Junqua, J.C. (1993). The Lombard reflex and its role on human listeners and automatic speech recognisers. *Acoustical Society of America, 93*(1), 510-524.

Keiffer, S., & Carbonell, N. (2006). Oral messages improve visual search. In *AVI '06, the Working Conference on Advanced Visual Interfaces* (pp. 369-372). Venice, Italy: ACM Press.

Keskin, C., Balci, K., Aran, O., Sankar, B., & Akarun, L. (2007). A multimodal 3D healthcare communication system. In *3DTV Conference*. Kos, Greece: IEEE press.

Lodha, S.K., Faaland, N.M., Wong, G., Charaniya, A.P., Ramalingam, S., & Keller, A.M. (2003). Consistent visualization and querying of GIS databases by a location-aware mobile agent. *Computer Graphics International*. Acta Press.

Malaka, M., & Zipf, A. (2000). DEEP MAP–challenging IT research in the framework of a tourist information system. In *7th International Congress on Tourism and Communication Technologies in Tourism (ENTER '00)* (pp. 15-27). Barcelona, Spain: Springer LNCS.

Nickel, K., & Stiefelhagen, R. (2003). Pointing gesture recognition based on 3D-tracking of face, hands, and head orientation. In *5th International*

Conference on Multimodal Interfaces (pp. 140-146). Vancouver, Canada: ACM Press.

Oviatt, S. (1996). Multimodal interfaces for dynamic interactive maps. In *SIGCHI Conference on Human Factors in Computing Systems,* Vancouver, Canada (pp. 95-102).

Oviatt, S. (2000a). Multimodal system processing in mobile environments. In *13th Annual ACM Symposium on User Interface Software and Technology,* CA (pp. 21-30).

Oviatt, S. (1999). Mutual disambiguation of recognition errors in a multimodal architecture. In *Conference on Human Factors in Computing Systems (CHI '99),* Pittsburgh, PA (pp. 576-583).

Oviatt, S. (2000b). Taming recognition errors with a multimodal interface. In *Communications of the ACM, 43*(9), 45-51. ACM Press.

Oviatt, S., Bernard, J., & Levow, G. (1999). Linguistic adaptation during error resolution with spoken and multimodal systems. *Language and Speech (special issue on Prosody and Conversation), 41*(3-4), 415-438.

Oviatt, S., Cohen, P., Wu, L., Vergo, J., Duncan, L., Suhm, B., Bers, J., Holzman, T., Winograd, T., Landay, J., Larson, J., & Ferro, D. (2000). Designing the user interface for multimodal speech and pen-based gesture applications: State-of-the-art systems and future research directions. *Human-Computer Interaction, 15*(4), 263-322.

Oviatt, S., DeAngeli, A., & Kuhn, K. (1997). Integration and synchronization of input modes during multimodal human computer interaction. In *Conference on Human Factors in Computing Systems (CHI, 97)* (pp. 415-422). Atlanta, GA: ACM Press.

Oviatt, S., & Kuhn, K. (1998). Referential features and linguistic indirection in multimodal language. In *International Conference on Spoken Language Processing,* Sydney, Australia (pp. 2339-2342).

Qvarfordt, P., & Zhai, S. (2005). Conversing with the user based on eye-gaze patterns. In *SIGCHI Conference on Human Factors in Computing Systems,* Portland, OR (pp. 221-230).

Rauschert, I., Sharma, R., Fuhrmann, S., Brewer, I., & MacEachren, A. (2002). Approaching a new multimodal GIS interface. In *2nd International Conference on GIS (GIScience),* CO.

Sainz Salces, F.J., Baskett, M., Llewellyn-Jones, D., & England, D. (2006). Ambient interfaces for elderly people at home. In J.G. Carbonell & J. Siekmann (Eds.), *Ambient intelligence in everyday life* (pp. 256-284). Springer LNCS.

Sawhney, N., & Schmandt, C. (2000). Nomadic radio: Speech and audio interaction for contextual messaging in nomadic environments. *ACM Transactions on Computer-Human Interaction, 7*(3), 353-383. ACM Press.

Shneiderman, B. (2000). The limits of speech recognition. *Communications of the ACM, 43*(9), 63-65. ACM Press.

Suhm, B., Myers, B., & Weibel, A. (2001). Multimodal error correction for speech user interfaces. *ACM Transactions on Computer-Human Interaction, 8*(1), 60-98, ACM Press.

Wang, X., Li, J., Ao, X., Wang, G., & Dai, G. (2006). Multimodal error correction for continuous handwriting recognition in pen-based user interfaces. In *11th International Conference on Intelligent User Interfaces (IUI '06),* Sydney, Australia (pp. 324-326).

Wasinger, R., & Kreuger, A. (2005). Modality preference–learning from users. In *Workshop on User Experience Design for Pervasive Computing (Experience) at Pervasive 05*. Munich, Germany: Springer LNCS.

Wasinger, R., Stahl, C., & Kreuger, A. (2003). Robust speech interaction in a mobile environment through the use of multiple and different input types. In *EuroSpeech 2003-InterSpeech 2003, the 8th European Conference on Speech Communication and Technology* (pp. 1049-1052).

Weakliam, J., Lynch, D., Doyle, J., Bertolotto, M., & Wilson, D. (2005). Delivering personalized context-aware spatial information to mobile devices. In *W2GIS '05 - The 5th International Workshop on Web and Wireless Geographical Information Systems.* (pp. 194-205). Lausanne, Switzerland: Springer LNCS.

Wickens, C.D., & Baker, P. (1995). Cognitive issues in virtual reality. In T.A. Furness & W. Barfield (Eds.), *Virtual environments and advanced interface design* (pp. 514-541). Oxford University Press.

KEY TERMS AND DEFINITIONS

GIS: A computer system for capturing, storing, querying, analysing and displaying geographic data.

Mobile GIS: The acquisition and use of GIS functionality through mobile devices and in a mobile context.

Multimodal Error Correction: Allowing the user to switch modality to correct an error relating to a particular modality.

Multimodal Interaction: Provides a user with multiple modes of interfacing with a system beyond the traditional keyboard and mouse input and output.

Speech Recognition: Converts spoken words to machine-readable input.

State-of-the-Art: The highest level of development of a device, technique or scientific field, achieved at a particular time.

User Interface: The means by which people interact with a system, machine or computer program.

Chapter XIX
Adapted Multimodal End–User Interfaces for XML–Content

Benoît Encelle
University Claude Bernard - Lyon 1, LIRIS, France

Nadine Baptiste-Jessel
University Paul Sabatier, France

Florence Sèdes
University Paul Sabatier, France

ABSTRACT

Personalization of user interfaces for browsing content is a key concept to ensure content accessibility. This personalization is especially needed for people with disabilities (e.g,. visually impaired) and/or for highly mobile individuals (driving, off-screen environments) and/or for people with limited devices (PDAs, mobile phones, etc.). In this direction, we introduce mechanisms, based on a user requirements study, that result in the generation of personalized user interfaces for browsing particular XML content types. These on-the-fly generated user interfaces can use several modalities for increasing communication possibilities: in this way, interactions between the user and the system can take place in a more natural manner.

ADAPTED MULTIMODAL END-USER INTERFACES FOR XML-CONTENT

Currently, Web content providers mainly drive the presentation of content and the end-user navigation (i.e. scanning) possibilities within this content. As a result, user interfaces for browsing this content—with common Web browsers—remain almost identical, using the same modes of interaction whatever the user.

However, people with special needs (e.g. visually impaired users or highly mobile individuals) that cannot access Web content using traditional modes of interaction (e.g. visual mode) require a customized presentation and adapted scanning possibilities to access this content.

For instance, in order to easily access available information, blind users need a fine-tailored multimodal browsing system that takes advantage of several modalities/media (e.g. a text-to-speech synthesizer and a Braille display) for communicating the content.

These additional functionalities not only depend on a user profile, on his preferences but also depend on the content type that has to be browsed (Schweikhardt, Bernareggi, Jessel, Encelle, & Gut, 2006): for instance, presentation intents (e.g. modalities that have to be used) and scanning possibilities will not be the same if the user browses a mathematical content or a musical content.

In order to fulfil these requirements, we develop a user profile model for representing for each content type, users preferences in terms of content presentation and scanning possibilities inside content. For a given type of content, a transformation process is generated with the help of such a user profile. Finally, an adapted content browsing user interface is generated thanks to this transformation process (Encelle, 2005).

In this paper, the problem of content accessibility is addressed using personalization mechanisms.

We firstly introduce the context of our work and the terminology we use. In the following two sections, we discuss related work and we introduce some guidelines for designing personalization systems. In the following section, we identify end-users' personalization requirements for a content browsing system and we introduce the model and mechanisms we developed for specifying these requirements (section "The Concepts of Profile..."). Two representations of the end-user browsing requirements are also described: a user-friendly one and a system-friendly one. In the following section, the transformation process, from the end-user browsing requirements to the generation of personalized user interface is explained. We present the results of utility and usability evaluations of the proposed mechanisms for personalizing content browsing (section "Evaluation") and we conclude.

CONTEXT OF WORK AND TERMINOLOGY

XML is currently the well established standard for representing and exchanging semi-structured documents or data. The XML philosophy is to separate style (i.e. presentation) from substance (i.e. content). Thanks to this separation principle, the same content can be presented in several different ways (using a visual, an auditory or a tactile presentation). This possibility of giving multiple presentations of the same content increases its accessibility. As a consequence, our work tends to personalize XML content browsing.

By "browsing" we mean, from a user point of view, the task of "active" reading of a given content. From a system point of view, this activity is broken up into two types of task: a task that consists in a content presentation to the user, and a navigation task that targets, according to a user action, a particular XML element in order to present it in detail. As a consequence, a "browsing" activity is viewed as a series of coupled tasks (presentation, navigation).

Moreover, communication modalities[1] used to facilitate content browsing have to be indicated by the user. For a given device, we assume that its communication modalities are always available.

RELATED WORK

In order to make Web content accessible, transformations (i.e. adaptations) of content must be performed. We distinguish two kinds of adaptations: adaptation performed at authoring-time (i.e. during the writing of documents) and adaptation performed at run-time (i.e. during content consultation).

Authoring-Time Content Adaptation

Authoring-time adaptation firstly results in a set of "accessibility" rules/guidelines that developers of authoring tools or user agents and authors of Web documents have to follow. To this end, the Web Accessibility Initiative (WAI) (WAI, 2008) from the W3C wrote a set of guidelines.

Moreover, for visually impaired users or highly mobile individuals, audio browsable Web content has been developed. For this purpose, several markup languages such as VoiceXML, SALT (Speech Application Language Tags), XHTML+Voice and voice browser systems have emerged.

Although WAI and development of specialized languages are very promising and necessary, adapting content using guidelines or adapting it to voice browser technology still remains a significant burden for many content providers and can prove costly.

Run-Time Adaptation

The second kind of adaptation (Run-Time Adaptation) consists in preserving Web content as it is and results in the development of assistive technologies (e.g. screen readers, JAWS) or Web browsers dedicated to people with special needs (e.g. HearSay (Ramakrishnan, Stent, & Yan, 2004), IBM HomePageReader). Using this kind of software, the user browses content though multiple modalities. However, most assistive technologies and dedicated Web browsers do not provide the end-user with sufficient filtering options for eliminating unwanted information (Ramakrishnan et al., 2004; Theofanos & Redish, 2003). Generally speaking, due to the fact that this kind of software is already designed for a highly specific group of users, the personalization or customization aspect (i.e. the adaptation to each user's needs) is often a bit limited.

Stylesheets can be employed for personalizing the presentation of particular kinds of documents (i.e. HTML and XML documents). In theory, an end-user could describe documents presentation intents using CSS (Cascading Style Sheets) (W3C, 1998; Wium Lie, 2005). Two others "actors" could

also suggest presentation intents using CSS: the author of the document and the user agent (e.g. the browser). Each of these actors can specify different presentation intents for the same content element (or set of content elements). In this case, applied presentation intents (these coming from the user / the author or the user agent) is determined using the "cascade" rule.

In our opinion, the idea of separating presentation intents according to the different abilities of actors is interesting. However, the mechanism for selecting the presentation intents that will be applied does not seem to be fully relevant. Indeed, default priority is given to the presentation intents of the author.

CSS can only personalize the presentation of content: navigation possibilities inside this content cannot be personalized. Moreover, CSS was not designed to allow different presentation levels of a given content: formatting is done in one go for the whole content.

CSS only decorates the logical structure of a document and does not provide features for transforming this logical structure. The formatting tree containing presentation objects remains very similar to the logical structure tree. As a result, if an element B is a descendant of an element A in the logical structure of a document, B could not be presented using CSS before A. For instance, this means that unordered bibliography entries could not be presented in alphabetical order.

Even if CSS permits one to obtain media-specific document presentations (i.e. on screen, using vocal synthesis, etc.), CSS does not benefit from media objects synchronization features. As a consequence, CSS can not be used for producing multimodal presentation of content.

Finally, from a utility point of view, CSS presentation intents are "low-level" content formatting rules (i.e. media specific formatting rules).

Even if CSS benefits from a simple syntax, its vocabulary is a bit large (many formatting properties): CSS learning is time-consuming. CSS language usability, as far as we know, has never been evaluated. In our opinion, the major drawback of the CSS language is that it is not designed to be used by "end-users".

DESIGN GUIDELINES FOR PERSONALIZATION SYSTEMS

In our opinion, several design guidelines have to be followed during the development of a personalization system: the more these guidelines are followed, the more the system will be useful and usable. In our case, utility (Nielsen, 2003; Senach, 1990) qualifies the adequacy between personalization possibilities of a given system and users' requirements. In our case, usability, the ability to use the utility (Nielsen, 2003), qualifies the ease of use of available personalization mechanisms.

- **Guideline n°1 (G1):** *Identification of activities, tasks that have to be personalized (Utility)*
- **Guideline n°2 (G2):** *To unburden the end-user for each activity or task that has to be personalized, actors involved in the requirements specification have to be well identified. (Usability)*

To be quickly usable by all kinds of end-users, a personalization system has to be directly usable: the end-user has to be able to take advantage of the system without having to set up all his preferences. The more complete the personalization is, the more difficult it will be for the user to fully control it (e.g. costly learning time, etc.). A solution consists in distinguishing and separating specification requirements well according to actors' skills: requirements that have to be described by experts (experts of a given disability, device experts, Web designers, etc.) and requirements that have to be described by end-users themselves.

- **Guideline n°3 (G3):** *For each actor, available mechanisms for describing requirements have to be suitable. (Usability)*

Available mechanisms for describing requirements have to suit actors' abilities. As a consequence, usability of these mechanisms according to the kind of people that will employ them has to be evaluated: this is especially required for description mechanisms handled by end-users.

In this article, when propositions follow one or more of the previously stated guidelines, they will be indicated in brackets.

IDENTIFICATION OF TASKS AND CONNECTED PERSONALIZATION REQUIREMENTS (G1)

For determining personalization requirements for content browsing activities we used the reference study of Theofanos & Redish (2003). Two tasks (content presentation and navigation) have to be personalized in order to improve communication between a system and its end-user.

End-User Personalization Requirements

From the System to the End-Users (Task: Content Presentation)

- Requirement 1 (**R1**): *content filtering*
  For each type of element of the logical structure (or set of element types), the user must have the ability to choose the descendant element types that will really be presented by the system.
- Requirement 2 (**R2**): *choice of modalities for presenting the content and choreography*
  For each type of selected descendant element, the user must have the ability to choose the right output modalities. Moreover, the user

has to indicate the choreography that will be carried out for presenting these element types.

From the End-Users to the System (Task: Navigation Inside Content)

- Requirement 3 (**R3**): *choice of navigation/ scanning possibilities*
  For each type of element of the logical structure (or set of element types), the user must have the ability to specify inside-element and outside-element navigation / scanning possibilities.
- Requirement 4 (**R4**): *choice of input modalities that trigger navigation action*
  For each navigation (i.e. scanning) possibility, the user must have the ability to choose the right input modalities that trigger the navigation action.

These personalization requirements are qualified as "high-level" requirements.

Deduced Requirement (R5)

According to R2 and R4, an adaptation of communication modalities/media between the end-user and the system is required. As a result, the content has to be adapted to a media-readable format in order to be transmitted. The adaptation requirement, connected to a specific modality or media, is qualified as "low-level" requirement. Indeed, its specification implies the knowledge and the implementation of specific formatting rules or particular recognition grammars.

Advantage of Our Approach

Several presentation levels and scanning levels can be specified for a given content. For instance, the first presentation level for *RSS* (Really Simple Syndication) documents (Berkman Center for Internet & Society, 2003), specified for the *rss* element type (root element of an RSS document) could only present the title of each news item (*title* child element of each *item* element). Accessing a particular news item could be done using a specific navigation action. A particular news item could be presented in the following way: its description will be presented and so on.

In this way, presentation intents (and navigation possibilities) are not associated with the whole document (the case in CSS) but can be different for each type of element to present (the presentation and navigation context is defined by the element). This approach permits to firstly present the content deemed essential by the user (e.g. only news headlines – no news descriptions) and then, according to the user's interests, subsequently present detailed content (e.g. the description of a particular news item).

In this way, from an accessibility point of view, the user will not be lost in the mass of details obtained.

THE CONCEPTS OF PROFILE, POLICY AND THEIR REPRESENTATIONS FOR XML (G2)

In order to represent preceding identified requirements, we introduce the concept of profile and the concept of policy.

Profiles

In order to personalize system reactions to each user, individual needs or preferences are gathered into a *profile* (Kobsa, 1994). The use of profiles upgrades the 'one-size-fits-all' approach to a 'one-to-one' approach (Fink & Kobsa, 2000). In order to separate the profile components that can be described by the end-users themselves and those that have to be specified by an expert, we suggest the following structure (cf. figure 1).

According to this architecture, an entity called User Global Profile is made up of the specifications of all personalization requirements. This architecture brings to light several classifications of profile components.

Stereotype-Based and Personalized Profiles

User adaptable or adaptive systems like Adaptive Hypermedia Systems (A.H.S)(Chen & Magoulas, 2005) often initialize a user profile using a stereotype-based profile (Boyle & Encarnacion, 1994). A stereotype-based profile corresponds to average preferences of a set of users that share common characteristics (Rich, 1989; Fink, Kobsa & Nill, 1998).

Stereotype-based profiles have to be set up by experts that have a good knowledge of a specific domain (e.g. a given disability, a given job).

Using stereotype-based profiles, the user takes advantage of the system directly without having to set up all his preferences. A stereotype profile only represents preference tendencies: because individual needs and requirements are diverse and can be difficult to anticipate (Brown & Robinson, 2004), a personalized profile, gathering user-specific preferences is needed too.

Content and Device Profiles

All identified "high level" requirements can be specified by the end-user himself. However, "low-level" requirement R5 rather requires the technical skills of an expert. As a result, requirement specifications are split up, according to actors skills (G2), into two distinct profiles: content ("high-level" requirements) and device ("low-level" requirement).

Application Policies

Definition

In previous works (Encelle & Jessel, 1-2004, 2-2004, 2006), we introduced the concept of application policies. An *Application Policy* is connected to a specified kind of content (e.g. an XML application: XHTML, MathML, RSS, etc.) and represents preferences associated with the different types of element that compound this application. Contrary to application policy, a default policy is not connected to a particular XML application but to XML-conformant content. The goal of a default policy is to go easy with the end-user (G2): when the user wants to browse a content that is not connected with a dedicated application policy, default policy will be applied.

Classifications of Applications Policies

The notion of application policy has been specialized for each task that has to be personalized. As a result, the notions of presentation application policy and navigation application policy extend (object oriented meaning) the notion of application policy.

- **Application presentation policies:** An application presentation policy (e.g. RSS presentation policy) specifies preferences connected to "high level" requirements R1 and R2. These preferences have to be applied to present a content coming from this application.
- **Application navigation policies:** An application navigation policy describes preferences connected with the "high-level" requirements R3 and R4.
- **Media-specific application policies:** A media-specific application presentation policy represents preferences connected to "low-level" requirement R5.

Context Representation

The notion of context was introduced in ubiquitous computing or pervasive computing. In fact, ubiquitous or pervasive environments use "context-aware" systems that adapt their behaviours according to their contexts of use (Schilit, Adams, & Want, 1994; *Dey, 2001*).

For instance, the user's location, lighting, noise level and network connectivity are parameters that can influence the behaviour of a context-aware system.

According to content browsing, an end-user may have different expectations in terms of content presentation and scanning possibilities according to his device or "ambient environment".

For instance, content scanning using an automatic speech recognizer in a noisy environment is prohibited and haptic scanning possibilities may be more appropriated in such a situation. Moreover, user's content presentation policies may be different according to the size of the screen of the device used (e.g. mobile phone vs. desktop computer).

As a result, we have extended our model in order to integrate presentation and scanning policies of several user devices.

Currently, our context parameter is the user device and the following section describes how a device and its corresponding policies can be specified.

Device Specification Architecture

According to the suggested architecture (cf. Figure 1), a device is represented using a *Device Profile* that is made up of several "*Media policies*". A media corresponds to either a formatter (i.e. an effector): a content formatting software component, or to a listener (i.e. a sensor): a user events listener software component. For instance, a vocal synthesis is a formatter and an Automatic Speech Recognizer (ASR) is a listener.

Sometimes, the same software component can be both a formatter and a listener (i.e. an HTML content browsing software component).

According to our architecture, media policies have to be described by experts. A media policy represents transformation rules for adapting content in a media-readable format (R5). For instance, an RSS presentation policy for an HTML content viewer takes in input RSS content and outputs HTML content according to specified transformation rules.

An ASR takes in input, a user oral production and a grammar and outputs the most probabilistic predefined grammar rules that match the user production.

As a result, media formatters and listeners can be viewed as a transformation process. The Figure 2 illustrates this point: *Formatter* and *Listener* abstract classes extend a *Media* abstract class. *ASR* class extends the *Listener* class and *VocalSynthesis* class extends the *Formatter* one.

Figure 1. Architecture of profiles/application policies

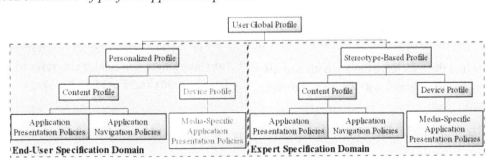

Figure 2. Media classes diagram

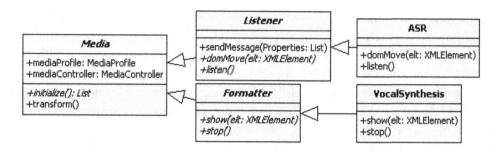

Representation of Profiles/ Application Policies for XML-Conformant Content

Two representations of profiles of policies have been developed: a user-friendly one and a system-friendly one. Profiles structure application policies and this section deals with the representation of application policies (i.e. browsing preferences for a given type of content).

User-Friendly Representation of Policies

In order to give users the possibility of writing their own applications policies, two description languages - one for each kind of application policy – have been developed using LL(1) grammars (Aho, Sethi, & Ullman, 1986) written in JavaCC (CollabNet, 2008).

Using these description languages, the user can describe policy components R1, R2 for a presentation policy and R3, R4 for a navigation policy.

Example: RSS Presentation Policy for Limited Device
We assume that the user has a device with a small screen (e.g. mobile phone) and wants to browse RSS content.

His preferences according to this context and concerning the list of news are the following: For news, only headlines (i.e. title element of a news item) have to be presented on the screen. Simultaneously, each headline has to be presented using a Text-To-Speech (i.e. TSS) engine.

According to previously stated preferences, using the language for describing presentation policies the user will write the following line:

rss : (item/title : screen | item[title : TTS]);

- " **rss :** " means that the following presentation preferences are specified for presenting an *rss* element type ;
- " **item/title : screen** " means that element types *title*, children of element types *item,* have to be presented using the screen ;
- " **|** " means "simultaneously" ;
- " **item [title : TTS]** " means that each item has to be presented in sequence and that Text-To-Speech has to be used for presenting the titles of items.

For further details concerning these description languages, the reader can refer to Encelle & Jessel (2006) and Encelle (2005).

System-Friendly Representation of Policies

From a system point of view, application policies are represented and structured using dedicated XML elements. In more details, an application policy is identified both with its type (i.e. presentation or navigation) and with its associated application (URI of the application namespace). The body of an application presentation/navigation policy is represented using an XSLT stylesheet (W3C, 1-1999). Each XSLT template rule corresponds to preferences for an application element type (or set of element types). This element type (or set of element types) is determined using an XPath expression (W3C, 2-1999).

These two representations are studied in depth in Encelle (2005). With the help of these preferences representations, personalized browsing user interfaces can be generated.

FROM THE END-USER REQUIREMENTS TO THE GENERATION OF ADAPTED USER INTERFACES

From the End-User Representation to the System Representation of Policies

The parsing of the end-user representation of an application policy generates its corresponding system representation (i.e. transformation rules) (Encelle & Jessel, 2007).

This resulting system representation is stored in the content profile of the personalized profile (cf. Figure 1).

From the System Representation of a Policy to the User Interface Generation

For a given context (a task (i.e. presentation/navigation), an XML application and an element *e*), e.g. the presentation of the XHTML element *Title*, presentation and navigation directives will be computed and then interpreted. This process transforms *e* according to the rules stated for the given context. For presentation for instance, two chained transformations are realized (cf. Figure 3).

The first level of transformation converts *e* using "high level" preferences (i.e. coming from a content profile policy). This results in a first document (doc. 1). Next to that, this resulting document is transformed this time using "low-level" preferences (i.e. coming from device profiles). This second level of transformation results in another document (doc. 2). Finally, this resulting document is interpreted in order to present *e*.

The first transformation level (doc. 1) indicates the choreography that has to be realized for presenting *e*: temporal chain (in sequence, in parallel) of couples (descendant element to be presented, presentation media). The second transformation level adds the formatting rules that have to be

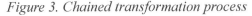

Figure 3. Chained transformation process

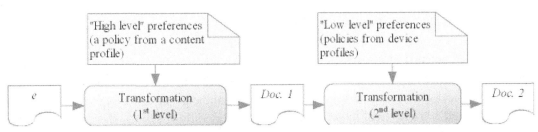

applied in order to correctly present the relevant element on the relevant media.

In order to determine the most suitable preferences to be applied for each transformation level, a matching process is performed.

Matching Process

This process logic firstly considers personalized preferences. If personalized preferences match the context, they will be applied. Otherwise, if stereotypical preferences match the context, they will be applied.

A given set of preferences, stored in the body of an XSLT template, will match a given context only if it successfully checks the pattern of the template rule (constraints on the logical structure and possibly on the content) represented using an XPath expression.

If no personalized preferences are specified for the content type and if default personalized preferences have been indicated (i.e. preferences specified for XML-conformant content), these default preferences will be applied.

Results

In the worst case scenario, a content browsing user interface based on the default policies of the stereotyped profile will be suggested to the end-user. As a consequence, the end-user will always have access to the content, whatever its type. For instance, for a visually impaired user or a user having a screen-less device, elements that compound an XML document could be presented vocally. The user could for instance navigate form one element to another using a keyboard (e.g. with the arrows keys).

If policies are specified for a content type, a more suitable access to the content will be provided to the end-user. For instance, a mathematical content (e.g. MathML content) - an equation – could be displayed on a Braille line and simultaneously presented using vocal synthesis. End-user vocal commands like "left", "right" will target either the left part or the right part of the equation.

In the following section, suggested personalization mechanisms are evaluated. On the one hand, the first objective is to know whether suggested personalization mechanisms correspond to user requirements in terms of personalization of content browsing user interfaces (i.e. utility evaluation). The second objective, on the other hand, is to know whether end-users could easily understand and handle these personalization mechanisms (i.e. usability evaluation).

EVALUATION

Evaluation Context

Generally speaking, an interactive system in the HCI field is evaluated by measuring its utility and its usability. In short, the utility of a system generally refers to the fact that it allows the user to complete relevant tasks (Senach, 1990), while the usability of a system refers to the ease and efficiency with which its user interface can be operated (Nielsen, 2003).

As the proposed concepts tend to generate a personalized user interface for browsing XML content according to user preferences (i.e. profile of policies), measuring the utility and usability of a specifically generated user interface does not seem to be relevant.

As a consequence, the evaluation of our proposition will measure the utility and usability of the mechanisms for describing user interfaces (i.e. mechanisms for describing policies).

Utility Evaluation

Principle

Firstly, the expressivity power of policy mechanisms for describing user interfaces was estimated. The goal is to know the kinds of user interfaces that can be generated using these mechanisms.

Generally speaking, the goal of these generated user interfaces is to improve content accessibility in using multimodal communication possibilities.

As a result, utility evaluation qualifies the kind of multimodal interactions that can be described in these generated user interfaces. To qualify the kind of cooperation between modalities that such generated user interfaces can support, the CARE Framework and properties (Coutaz et al., 1995) are used. The CARE properties define a framework for characterizing different forms of multimodal usages of an interactive application.

Results

Interpretation of the results leads to the conclusion that all CARE properties can be instantiated using the policy description languages except one. This property is the equivalence property in the following direction: from the system to the end-user. In fact, this property can not be instantiated according to our context of works (Encelle & Jessel, 2006).

Usability Evaluation

Principle

This evaluation is mandatory according to the third rule for designing personalization systems: *"usable mechanisms for describing requirements have to be available."*

In order to evaluate the usability of policy description languages, the usability of each language (presentation/navigation) has to be measured. Our goal is to know if any *a priori* novice end-user is able to use the description language.

Usability tests have been performed, asking the end-users to accomplish a set of representative tasks.

The ease of use of a description language has been quantified according to the following hypothesis: a language can be described as easily

usable if two sets of users, one initially tagged as novice and the other initially tagged as expert, handle the language after X usages with roughly the same ease of use (X must be quite small).

Three exercises (i.e. task: the writing of an application policy) were given to 20 subjects (10 experts/ 10 novices).

A short tutorial (15 min.) concerning the writing of application policies was presented to the subjects before the first exercise.

Parameters

Subjects

In order to maximize the probability of having expert and novice subjects, we made the following assumption: "someone who has programming skills has more chance of being an expert in the writing of application policies than someone who does not know anything about programming". As a result, subjects were students with different levels of knowledge of programming. However, expert and novice groups of subjects were established after the results of the first exercise.

Tasks

Each exercise (i.e. task) consisted, according to a given textual description of end-user "browsing preferences" for a specific application (e.g. RSS), in the writing of the corresponding policy. The objective was to evaluate the subjects' understanding and their ease of use of the different concepts of a policy description language through the writing of the different syntactic constructions of this language. Concerning the presentation policy description language for instance, the following concepts were identified (cf. section "End-user Personalization Requirements" for corresponding end-user requirements R): declaration of presentation intents for an element type (R1-R2), specification of content filters (R1), coordination of the presentations of parts of content over time (R1-R2).

Table 1. Usability Evaluation Results

Marks (/6) and %	1st Exercise	2nd Exercise	3rd Exercise
Expert: average	5.800	5.925	5.960
Expert: std. deviation	0.209	0.112	0.089
Novice: average	2.400	5.150	5.875
Novice: std. deviation	1.353	0.652	0.125
Averages difference	3.400	0.775	0.085
Ratio[1]* (%)	**100**	**22.800**	**2.500**

Results

According to data analysis, the difference between the expert group's average and the novice group's average tends to decline progressively.

For the final exercise, the ratio[2] (2.5%) seems to be trifling: distinction between a novice and an expert user is increasingly difficult to make. Moreover, the standard deviation by group decreases progressively: for each group, the level of users tends to become increasingly homogeneous.

The initial question was: "*Is any* a priori *novice end-user able to use a policy description language?*" According to the assumption we made, the conclusion is that a novice subject is quickly able to employ a policy description language because he tends to become an expert after using the language only three times.

CONCLUSION

People with special needs (e.g. highly mobile people, blind people) require fine-tailored multimodal browsing user-interfaces to easily access content. These user interfaces must be personalized according to the end-user preferences/requirements and according to the content type.

In this article, we introduced a set of design guidelines for developing personalization systems. From our point of view, these guidelines have to be followed in order to develop a useful and usable personalization system. The specific end-user requirements concerning a personalization system for browsing semi-structured content are studied and we suggested a model for structuring and for representing the end-user preferences corresponding to these requirements.

The concept of application policy we introduced results in the representation of end-user preferences in terms of presentation and navigation (scanning) possibilities of content encoded by a particular XML application (e.g. XHTML, MathML, RSS, SVG and so on). These application policies are stored in profiles.

Two representations of these application policies have been developed: a user-friendly one and a system-friendly one. The body of the system representation of an application policy is an XSLT stylesheet. Using this kind of representation, personalized user interfaces for browsing content can be generated on-the-fly with the help of a content transformations sequence.

In order to determine the most suitable preferences (i.e. policies) for a given usage context (e.g. a specific content that has to be browsed by the end-user), a matching process was described.

Utility of application policies for generating adapted multimodal user interfaces has been evaluated. Furthermore, the usability of the policy description mechanisms has been estimated. On the one hand, results of these evaluations show that these generated user interfaces can practically support every kind of cooperation between modalities. On the other hand, policy description languages, according to the usability tests we performed, are user-friendly (e.g. simple and quick to apply).

Personalizing user interfaces for browsing content using multimedia/multimodal possibilities is very interesting not only for disabled people or older people but also for highly mobile individuals and people with limited devices (PDAs, mobile phones, etc.). Moreover, due to the emergence of the Semantic Web (W3C, 2008), dedicated applications frequently appear (e.g. MathML, MusicXML, CML (Chemical Markup Language), RSS, XMLTV, etc.): the use of such policies is resulting in the rapid development of user interfaces for browsing content coded with these applications.

REFERENCES

Aho, A., Sethi, R., & Ullman, J. (1986). *Compilers, principles, techniques, and tools.* Addison-Wesley.

Berkman Center for Internet & Society. (2003). *Really simple syndication (RSS).* Retrieved on October 27, 2008, from http://cyber.law.harvard.edu/rss/rss.html

Boyle, C., & Encarnacion, A.O. (1994). Metadoc: An adaptive hypertext reading system. *User Modeling and User-Adapted Interaction, Kluwer Academic, 4*(1), 1–19.

Brown, S.S., & Robinson, P. (2004). Transformation frameworks and their relevance in universal design. *Universal Access in the Information Society, 3.3*(4), 209-223.

Chen,Y. S., & Magoulas, G.D. (2005). *Adaptable and adaptive hypermedia systems.* IRM Press. CollabNet. (2008). JavaCC-java compiler compiler (JavaCC)-the java parser generator. Retrieved on October 27, 2008, from https://javacc.dev.java.net/

Coutaz, J., Nigay, L., Salber, D., Blandford, A., May, J., & Young, R. (1995). Four easy pieces for assessing the usability of multimodal interaction: The CARE properties. *InterAct '95,* Lillehammer (pp. 115-120).

Dey, A.K. (2001). *Understanding and using context. Personal Ubiquitous Computing, 5*(1), 4-7.

Encelle, B., & Jessel, N. (2007). Personalization of user interfaces for browsing XML content using transformations built on end-user requirements. In *Proceedings of the 2007 International Cross-Disciplinary Conference on Web Accessibility (W4A), ACM International Conference Proceeding Series* (Vol. 225, pp. 58-64).

Encelle, B., & Jessel, N. (2006). Personalization of information browsing user interface: Evaluation of the user policies concepts. *ICWI'06: IADIS International Conference WWW/Internet.*

Encelle, B. (2005). *Accessibilité aux documents électroniques: Personnalisation de la présentation et de l'interaction avec l'information.* Unpublished doctoral dissertation, University Paul Sabatier, Toulouse, France.

Encelle, B., & Jessel, N. (2004). Adapting presentation and interaction with XML documents to user preferences. In *ICCHP'04: International Conference on Computers Helping People with Special Needs* (LNCS 3118, pp. 143-150). Springer.

Encelle, B., & Jessel, N. (2004). Using the concept of user policies for improving HTML documents accessibility. *ICWI'04 Vol. 2, IADIS International Conference WWW/Internet* (pp. 835-839).

Fink, J., & Kobsa, A. (2000). A review and analysis of commercial user modeling servers for personalization on the World Wide Web. *User Modeling and User-Adapted Interaction. Kluwer Academic, 10,* 209-249.

Fink, J., Kobsa, A., & Nill, A. (1998). Adaptable and adaptive information provision for all users, including disabled and elderly people. *New Review of Hypermedia and Multimedia, 4,* 163-188.

Kobsa, A. (1994). User modeling and user-adapted interaction. In *CHI' 94 Tutorial.*

Martin, J.C. (2004). Introduction aux interfaces homme-machine multimodales. *Conférence invitée. Actes des entretiens de l'Institut de Garches. Innovations technologiques et Handicap* (pp. 25-26). Retrieved on October 27, 2008, from http://www.limsi.fr/Individu/martin/research/articles/martin-garche.pdf

Nielsen, J. (2003). *Usability 101: Introduction to usability.* Retrieved on October 27, 2008, from http://www.useit.com/alertbox/20030825.html

Ramakrishnan, I., Stent, A., & Yang, G. (2004). Hearsay: Enabling audio browsing on hypertext content. *World Wide Web Conference (WWW)* (pp. 80-89).

Rich, E. (1989). Stereotypes and user modeling. *User Models in Dialog Systems,* 35-51.

Senach., B. (1990). *Evaluation ergonomique des interfaces homme-machine : Une revue de la litterature.* (Tech. Rep.). National Institute for Research in Computer and Control Sciences.

Schilit, B.N., Adams, N.I., & Want, R. (1994). Context-aware computing applications. In *Proceedings of the Workshop on Mobile Computing Systems and Applications, IEEE Computer Society* (pp. 85-90).

Schweikhardt, W., Bernareggi, C., Jessel, N., Encelle, B., & Gut, M. (2006). LAMBDA: A European system to access mathematics with Braille and audio synthesis. In *ICCHP '06: International Conference on Computers Helping People with Special Needs* (LNCS 4061, pp. 1223-1230).

Theofanos, M.F., & Redish, J.G. (2003). Bridging the gap: Between accessibility and usability. *Interactions, X6,* 36-51.

W3C. (2008). *Semantic Web.* Retrieved on October 27, 2008, from http://www.w3.org/2001/sw/

W3C. (1999). *XSL transformations (XSLT).* Retrieved on October 27, 2008, from http://www.w3.org/TR/xslt

W3C. (1999). *XML path language (XPath).* Retrieved on October 27, 2008, from http://www.w3.org/TR/xpath

W3C. (1998). *Cascading style sheets, level 2.* Retrieved on October 27, 2008, from http://www.w3.org/TR/REC-CSS2/

WAI. (2008). *Web accessibility initiative.* Retrieved on October 27, 2008, from http://www.w3.org/WAI

Wium Lie, H. (2005). *Cascading style sheets.* Unpublished doctoral dissertation, Faculty of Mathematics and Natural Sciences, University of Oslo, Norway.

KEY TERMS AND DEFINITIONS

Accessibility: Accessibility is a general term used to describe the degree to which a product (e.g., device, service, environment) is accessible by as many people as possible. Accessibility can be viewed as the "ability to access" the functionality, and possible benefit, of some system or entity. Accessibility is often used to focus on people with disabilities and their right of access to entities, often through use of assistive technology.

Context-Aware Systems: Context-aware systems refers to a class of systems that tries to determine their context of use and adapt their behavior accordingly.

Multimodal User Interfaces, Multimodal Interaction: Multimodal interaction provides the user with multiple modes of interfacing with a system beyond the traditional keyboard and mouse input/output. The most common such interface combines a visual modality (e.g. a display, keyboard, and mouse) with a voice modality (speech recognition for input, speech synthesis and recorded audio for output). However other modalities, such as pen-based input or haptic input/output may be used. Multimodal user interfaces are a research area in human-computer interaction (HCI). The advantage of multiple modalities is increased usability: the weaknesses of one modality are offset by the strengths of another. Multimodal user interfaces have implications for accessibility: a well-designed multimodal application can be used by people with a wide variety of impairments.

XML: The Extensible Markup Language (XML) is a general-purpose specification for creating custom markup languages. It is classified as an extensible language because it allows its users to define their own elements. Its primary purpose is to help information systems share structured data, particularly via the Internet. It started as a simplified subset of the Standard Generalized Markup Language (SGML), and is designed to be relatively human-legible. By adding semantic constraints, application languages can be implemented in XML. These include XHTML, RSS, MathML, GraphML, Scalable Vector Graphics, MusicXML, and thousands of others. XML is recommended by the World Wide Web Consortium (W3C). It is a fee-free open standard. The recommendation specifies both the lexical grammar and the requirements for parsing.

XPath: XPath (XML Path Language) is a language for selecting nodes from an XML document. In addition, XPath may be used to compute values (strings, numbers, or boolean values) from the content of an XML document. XPath was defined by the World Wide Web Consortium (W3C).

XSLT: Extensible Stylesheet Language Transformations (XSLT) is an XML-based language used for the transformation of XML documents into other XML or "human-readable" documents. The original document is not changed; rather, a new document is created based on the content of an existing one. XSLT is most often used to convert data between different XML schemas. As a language, XSLT is influenced by functional languages, and by text-based pattern matching languages. XSLT can also be considered as a template processor. XSLT relies upon the W3C's XPath language for identifying subsets of the source document tree, as well as for performing calculations.

ENDNOTES

[1]   We used the definitions given by Martin (1994): media—physical support for transmitting information (e.g. loudspeakers). Modality—way of using a media (e.g. vocal synthesis).

[2]   Difference between expert and novice averages for the nth exercise divided by the same difference for the 1st exercise.

Chapter XX
Mobile Virtual Blackboard as Multimodal User Interface

Sladjana Tesanovic
GISDATA Skopje, Macedonia

Danco Davcev
University "Ss Cyril and Methodius", Macedonia

Vladimir Trajkovik
University "Ss Cyril and Methodius", Macedonia

ABSTRACT

Multimodal mobile virtual blackboard system is made for consultation among students and professors. It is made to improve availability and communication using mobile handheld devices. Our system enables different forms of communication: chat, VoIP, draw, file exchange. Providing greater usability on small screens of mobile devices can be done by adaptation of the features in an application according to the specific user preferences and to the current utilization of the application. In this chapter, we describe our mobile virtual table consultation system with special attention to the multimodal solution of the user interface by using XML agents and fuzzy logic. The general opinion among the participants of the consultations lead on this mobile system is positive. Participants mark this system as user friendly, which points out that our efforts in development of adaptable user interface can serve as good practice in designing interfaces for mobile devices.

INTRODUCTION

The emerging advancement of various technologies (computers, handheld devices, cell phones, communication networks) is going in the direction to provide same services to be available from many different interfaces. Today, it is expected television to provide dynamic and interactive content, laptops to access the Internet through various network connections, and the cell phones do not provide voice telephony solely, but they also begin to provide greater interaction with services and information sharing using the Internet. In very near future, it is expected all these three types of communication to be able to provide the same services, using different ways to accomplish this task. Obviously, the carriers of the communication will be different. Television, as immovable device, uses fixed infrastructure as cable and fiber optics. Mobile devices use various types of networks, such as wireless networks for mobile telephony, GPRS, Wi-Fi, 3G. Laptops use communication through fixed and wireless networks (PSTN, ADSL, Wi-Fi, WiMax, LANs, WANs, cable networks). The convergence of the utilization of different devices, such as TV, computer and cell phone, produces many variations of devices, as well as many variations of the way how the communication is carried. Besides providing same services through different forms of the communications, new, modern utilizations emerge from this multi-connected information world. Some of the modern utilizations of the multi-connected world are: e-Commerce, teleconference, e-Learning, online banking, personal communication through messengers, various communities, gaming etc. A slightly different, new way of providing various kinds of services is the mobile environment. A new, logical requirement imposes in front of the human development: everything should be available everywhere, at any moment. Mobile devices are developed to provide more and more services, previously available only through personal computers and television. So, m-Commerce is becoming reality, websites are customized and displayed through mobile web browsers. Personal communication and businesses are advanced through mobility and availability of the person at any moment. A person can call, send SMS, MMS, IM, e-mail, voice and video calls through his/her mobile device, and in that way he/she can stay available even when out of the office, on a journey or else. Besides the existing services that are being mapped from the desktop to the mobile environment, new kinds of services are being developed. Navigation and global positioning have become widely available. Location Based Services (LBS) are in their rising phase of development and discovering new usages. They will advance the enterprise, entertainment, public and other sectors.

In this pool of new services that are emerging through the mobile technology, one of the most honorable utilizations of the mobile environment is mobile learning [Luchini, Quintana, & Soloway, 2004]. Mobile learning is a new way of acquiring knowledge, which is highly adaptable [Glavinic, Rosic, & Zelic, 2007], [Jeong & Lee, 2007] to different kinds of student profiles [Misfud & Morch, 2007], from people that do not have time to attend normal courses to a practical enhancement of ordinary courses with additional access to the knowledge. Mobile learning is appropriate for acquiring small pieces of knowledge at a time. Persistent use of this source of learning contents can lead to a great amount of acquired knowledge. Everybody can use it to fulfill his/her knowledge in this world of fast changes where success depends on information. Besides the static contents that are provided by books and different digital multimedia [Gang & Zongkai, 2005] that just reside passively on servers, very important aspect of learning is exchange of knowledge and consultation process among student participants and available expert authority (professor/instructor) [Chang & Ishii, 2006].

Our project, Mobile Virtual Blackboard is developed for student - professor communication, for achieving availability in any situation. Besides the development of the various means of communication, such as VoIP, text messages, drawing on the dashboard, we had to take into the consideration the intuitiveness of the user interface and make the interface behave in the manner the user expects and interacts with it. For the purpose of achieving usable interface on small screens, we have made improvements in layout adaptation of the most frequently used features at the time within our application. We have developed a multimodal user interface that can automatically switch from one view to another, according to the specific user preferences and the current usage of the specific media. Our multimodal knowledge – based interface is managed by three XML agents and fuzzy logic.

The second heading is about the utilization and manipulation of multimedia contents on mobile devices and new services that emerge from the benefits that the mobility offers. Also, it is pointed that the complex applications should be available in mobile environments also, but a great efforts must be done with the user interfaces, because it is obvious that simple copying of the user interface behavior from the desktop environments is not suitable for small devices. The third heading shows how our work is related to other similar projects. In the fourth and fifth heading, the architecture and the design of the Mobile Virtual Blackboard are presented. The Multimodal agent-based user interface management is explained in the sixth heading. The implementation of the applications is described in the seventh heading. Evaluation of the Mobile Virtual Blackboard consultation system is given in the heading chapter, and the conclusion comes in the ninth. Finally, in the tenth heading are the references.

MULTIMEDIA COMMUNICATION AND USER INTERFACE

There are many desktop applications that support real time multimedia communication among participants. However, in the sphere of mobile handheld devices, a communication among several participants that includes multimedia transfer is at the beginning of the development and utilization. Mobile handheld devices' primary use was personal assistance, making and using schedules, notes, and voice communication. New demands are imposed to these devices: greater processing power to support real time multimedia transfer (video stream, voice stream, exchange of files), greater memory space and data transfer. Modern,

feature rich applications demand a lot of space on the screen for displaying available features. Position and use of the features demand special attention for handheld devices. User interface designers have to consider introduction of many various ways of presenting the contents to the user as well as user's interaction with the application. Advancement of handheld devices is a turning point where multimodality can give more efficient and more diverse user input and output options. Besides the new techniques of managing the 2D contents on the screen, also voice commands and automatic readers are becoming more interesting. The sound interface is in its beginning phase. New generation of smart phones with operating systems (Nokia E71, HP Voice Messenger, HTC etc.) offer voice commands for dialing a number and also have functions for pronunciation of the contents.

The user interface of the mobile devices has become a necessary challenge for development. Multimodal user interfaces bring new quality experience and intuitive interaction with the services. They help in providing easy and natural user interaction. Actually, a good user interface is mandatory requirement for successful utilization of any application, whether it is on desktop or mobile device. There is still much work to do in order to provide a satisfactory experience for the consumers of mobile applications. A good organization of the interface is important, especially when the complexity of a service developed for desktop environment is transferred to the mobile environment. Also, much consideration must be taken so these different environments (desktop and mobile) can have mutual collaboration. If a user can approach to an online service from various devices and environments, some kind of synchronization should be provided for the services. Typical example is using mailboxes that should be synchronized across different devices or provision of various documents on each device that the user uses. Another aspect of accessing the same service from different environments is to use common application interface or access to the database.

Alternative user inputs are introduced into the new generation of mobile devices, such as Voice commands for dialing a number, optical stylus, and touch screen instead of classic buttons. They make quite a revolution in improvement of the user interface on mobile handheld devices.

Also, there is an improvement of the devices for the people with special needs. The Mobile Reader Product Line from knfbReading Technologies, Inc. presents a major advancement in portability and functionality of print access for the blind, the vision impaired and those with reading difficulties. The knfbReader Mobile and kReader Mobile software packages run on a multifunction cell phone that allow the user to read mail, receipts, handouts and many other documents wherever the user happens to be. This is a pocket-sized solution to reading on the go. The kReader Mobile is designed for people who have difficulty reading due to learning or language problems.

Artificial intelligence and machine learning can be used in order to accommodate the interface of an application to the needs of a specific user. An example of this kind of using of the artificial intelligence is a module that constantly learns the habits of the user and adapts the position and visibility of the features displayed on the interface. Every user has own affinities for use of the offered features in an application. For example, in order to read the contents of a website, someone can customize his/her web browser by changing the text size or the color of the background. Some features are useful to a specific kind of a user, but the same features do not have to be necessarily useful for everybody. That is why a customization for each user cannot be made before the delivery of the software product. The preferences can be deduced from the user's experience. A specific interaction with the controls can provide the way how the user wants the interface of the application to behave. So, application should record the behavior of the user, and according to his specific interaction with the application it should correct the interface to reflect users' preferences.

Mobile learning is a new, convenient way of acquiring knowledge. Small pieces of knowledge should be available at any time when a person feels a need to learn a specific topic. In an era of developing technologies and sciences, there are a lot of facts to be learned just to keep up with the developing society. It is widely accepted that learning and education should not stop with finishing a formal kind of education. A person must learn constantly, not regarding the age or profession. M-learning systems represent a convenient way for acquiring knowledge at any time, any place and in situations when the specific knowledge is needed. Access to the internet and online content, such as Wikipedia, "HowStuffWorks", "WhatIs?", various dictionaries and great number of educational sites is a good way of acquiring knowledge. But also, m-Learning can offer very useful interaction among students and professors in formal education. It became obvious that collaboration and team work is very important even in learning process. Students have access to the global knowledge through the Internet. There are many situations when a student can present a new piece of knowledge to the professor and other students. So, the communication plays very important role in spreading knowledge. There are specialized web applications where the main goal is sharing knowledge and interaction regarding learning topics. With a proper adaptation of the browsers for mobile devices, these learning sites will become available to the mobile user.

RELATED WORK

In [Luchini et al., 2004] learner-centered handheld tools were presented. We have designed similar tools, but we have extended their usability. Our set of tools can be used for more diverse cases, since they support upload of various types of files such as bitmap picture or text and allow drawing and making notes on the blackboard. Creations of new sketches from scratch are also possible, while participating in the consultations and discussions with other participants.

In [Glavinic et al., 2007] an intelligent tutoring system was presented. It is different from our system because we have introduced static agents whose purpose is to intelligently adapt the user interface to the preferences of each user.

In [Jeong & Lee, 2007] an adaptation of the user interface was elaborated based on the used device in the learning process. In our case, we have developed context aware learning system which determines the features of the user interface according to the learning contents for the specific learning session. It can be also used to dynamically reconfigure the user interface according to the user preferences and the learning contents.

The system that stimulates students' active involvement in learning process by using the manual personalization of PDA devices and organization of folders is elaborated in [Misfud & Morch, 2007]. In our approach, we propose agent based adaptive personalization in the learning process.

Instead of using hardware-based personalization [Chang, & Ishii, 2006] we try to achieve similar effects by applying adaptive interfaces on the standard devices.

The agent-based approach that uses fuzzy logic to determine importance of certain information is elaborated in [Camacho, Hernandez, & Molina, 2001]. We use similar approach to determine importance of user interface features in regards to user preferences and media contents used in current session.

Effect of Input Mode on Inactivity and Interaction Times of Multimodal Systems [Perakakis & Potamianos, 2008] is another research that pays attention to the experience of the users in using various offered modes of interaction with the user interface. We also have made tests to understand the affinity of the usage of our application's features.

We continued developing our Mobile Virtual Blackboard [Trajkovik, Gligorovska, & Davcev, 2007] by adding the user interface management system in order to improve the user experience with applications for mobile devices. In [Lu, Kitagata, Suganuma, & Kinoshita, 2003] an agent based adaptive user interface control for desktop applications is presented. We share similar ideas, focused on handheld devices. Part of our researches were inspire also by [Liu, Wong, & Hui, 2003] where adaptive user interface is elaborated and a great accent is put to the personalized learning. We were also aware of the current trends in adaptive user interfaces [Alvarez-Cortes, Zayas-Perez, Zarate-Silva, Ramirez, & Uresti, 2007]. Also, empirical study design for adaptive user interfaces in an e-Learning system is related work to ours, except that we focus on mobile environment, instead of desktop [Granic & Nakic, 2007].

Some of the roots of the idea for Mobile Virtual Blackboard come from [Adewunmi et al., 2003] where enhancement of the learning process in the classroom using wireless technology is presented, as well as the expansion of the research ideas on our university [Kulakov, 2001].

MOBILE VIRTUAL BLACKBOARD ARCHITECTURE

The Mobile Virtual Blackboard is developed for attending consultations using mobile devices, more precisely pocket PCs. The mobile virtual blackboard was inspired by the necessity for ubiquitous access to information using the convenience of the mobile handheld devices. When compared to other kinds of distance learning methods, mobile learning should be used in a manner to give fast and exact answers to needed questions. Consultations in a group create implicit collaboration among the students, which can increase the quality of obtained knowledge.

Our Mobile Virtual Blackboard consultation system is implemented using a client - server architecture that provides less communication load on the client devices. This kind of thin client architecture is chosen because mobile devices have limited memory and processor power. The server part is implemented as desktop PC application, because serving the clients demands a system with high performances and data throughput. The entire communication and synchronization among the clients is carried out through the server application. The architecture of the system is presented on the Figure 1.

Figure 1 represents the design architecture of the consultation system. The client applications reside on pocket PCs and they have three main parts: Active user agent, VoIP client, and the set of the client features for drawing and messaging. Active user agent manages the user's interaction within the application regarding the interface layout, visibility and dimensions of certain controls. This agent counts the number of hits to each control of the application (message window, blackboard, etc). VoIP client serves the voice transfer. The client application represents all the features that student or professor can use in their mutual communication: chat, draw, voice, upload and download of files. Both kinds of clients (student and professor) have the same general architecture.

The communication is realized through wireless area networks connected to the Internet. The server is on a desktop machine and it contains the following parts: Passive User Agent, Media Agent, XML data storage, VoIP Server and UDP server application. For the purpose of memory saving and avoiding overload to the processing power of the clients' handheld devices, Passive User Agents and Media Agent reside on the server side. The messages with whom the agents communicate are XML based, and also, the data types that describe the user profiles stored in the database, are also XML based.

The first client is instructor application, which controls the resources in the group, and represents the source of relevant knowledge. The second type of a client is student application, which is dedicated to ask and fetch the knowledge provided from the instructor, during the communication and consulting. There is only one instructor and many students in one consultation session. Network communication is realized in a way that clients send UDP datagrams to the server, and the server forwards these UDP datagrams to specified clients, according to the contents of the received message. Streaming is used for voice transfer. Desktop based clients can also be con-

Figure 1. Architecture of the Mobile blackboard system

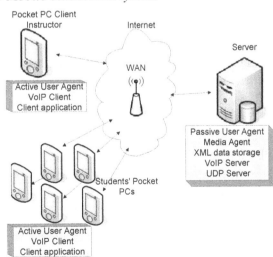

nected to the server. The instructor has the role of a moderator of the consultation process. He/she can give the control over the public drawing on the blackboard and reclaim the control later. The same procedure is used for the control over the speaking.

Interactivity of the consultation mobile system is the most important feature. The limitations of the user interface must be overcome. The new technologies should improve the student-professor interaction. Different variations of the user interface must not discourage the utilization of the system. Many messengers available today, have accustomed the people to use this special kind of communication and collaboration. Implementing messengers and consultations on pocket PCs provides convenience by making people more available. Another important point is that the student's focus of attention (blackboard, where the topic is being explained) is at the same place where the student takes notes, or draws own scenario to show to the rest of the group. Traditionally, the professor draws on a table or paper, or explains certain topic on a projected fixed picture on the wall and students watch and take notices in their notebooks. Merging the two attention focuses into one provides prompt discussions and greater attention. Speaking, combined with drawing, where the students largely participate, should be the most advanced way of conducting conversation and explaining learning topics.

Figure 2 shows the Use Case of the Wireless virtual blackboard consulting process. The student can post a question by using several ways of communication: send textual messages, draw on blackboard, or point to a specific part of the picture on the blackboard, and by speaking. The instructor can explain the topic by sending textual messages, drawing or showing on the blackboard, or he/she can speak. The instructor listens to the questions of the students by reading the incoming messages, watching the blackboard if the control over it has been previously given to some student, or listens while a student speaks. Logically, the drawing

on the blackboard would be followed by textual or voice explanation. In order all the participants in the consultation process to see the picture that the instructor uses in his explanations, a feature for file transfer is needed. Only the instructor can upload a file on the server, while the download of the files can be done by all clients. At any moment of explanation and drawing, users can save the modified picture locally. Because the blackboard and the speaking are the resources that cannot be used by many users at the same time, a control of using of VoIP and the blackboard is included on the instructor's side. Initially, the instructor can use the blackboard and the voice. If the student needs these features, he/she can send request for the blackboard, or request for speaking. The instructor can give the control over the blackboard (or speaking) to the student, and reclaim the control later, after the student has ended with his question or his part of the discussion. The instructor can check information on every logged student.

Students can pose questions and discuss using textual messages, speaking, showing or drawing on the table. For using the blackboard so that everybody can see where the student draws or points, he/she must ask for the control over the table. If the student needs to discuss over the VoIP, he/she should ask for the control over VoIP from the instructor. Students can learn from the instructor's explanations by reading the chat messages, by listening and watching graphic explanations on the blackboard. For reminding of important graphic notes later, the student can save the snapshot of the blackboard at any moment. The instructor can save the picture on the blackboard at any moment as well, so he can reuse the important explanations on his next consultations.

MOBILE VIRTUAL BLACKBOARD DESIGN

The user interface for mobile devices should have two main characteristics:

Figure 2. Use Case diagram of the Mobile Virtual Blackboard

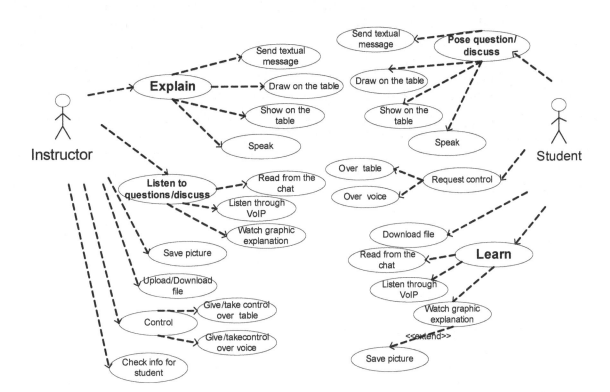

1. Capacity to present the learning contents in an appropriate way (clear, understandable, with appropriate size);
2. The user interface should be adaptable to the user.

Our mobile virtual blackboard system enables different forms of communication: chat, VoIP, draw, file exchange. A user or the whole consultation group can focus on the specified set of possible features. For example, consultations can be lead by using VoIP and draw, ignoring the chat utility. Here, we can see how multimodality of input and output features helps keeping the communication fast and convenient. VoIP, chat and blackboard provide users to express their knowledge or question in the most appropriate way. In the case of handheld devices, where screen surface is a scarce resource, a feature that is not used at the moment, should be invisible or with minimized dimensions in order to relinquish the space to a more frequently utilized feature. This is why the necessity of multimodal user interfaces is obvious. We have incorporated three different agents into our virtual blackboard consultation system for the purposes of management of the user interface. These agents monitor user interaction with the available features in the application, scan the media contents used in the particular consultation session, update users' profiles and calculate the visualization of features on the user's interface. In this way, we propose highly adaptable multimodal user interface for handheld devices that can bring benefits to application developers for mobile software environment, to users of mobile learning systems and finally, to all mobile device users.

Figure 3 represents activity diagrams of the virtual blackboard client and the server applications. The server application has to be started first. The IP address of the server host and the port number on which the server listens are necessary for establishing communication. Valid login name and password must be provided for fulfillment of the login form in order to proceed to the virtual blackboard system. If the login succeeds, the list of all logged clients is received, and the virtual blackboard client interface is shown to the user. The client program has three interface points which serve the interaction with the outside world, providing the necessary communication.

The login form and the virtual blackboard form are two points of the human user interface, and the third one is for the communication with the server. The user interface is represented with common controls like textboxes and buttons, a pen with several colors and a rectangular space on the form where drawing can be done. The interface to the server represents the means of communication with other machines and applications. This interface is represented with UDP socket procedures Send and Receive. The asynchronous UDP socket was used, so the clients can do many tasks simultaneously, and because of the natural unreliability of the wireless networks. After the

Figure 3. The mobile blackboard activity diagrams

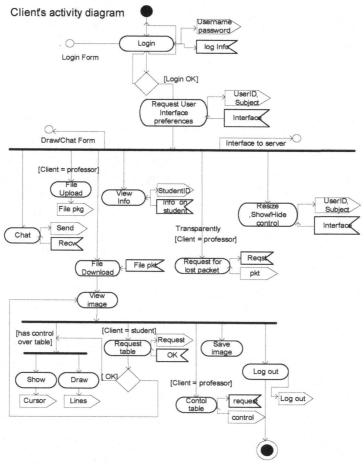

continued on following page

Figure 3. continued

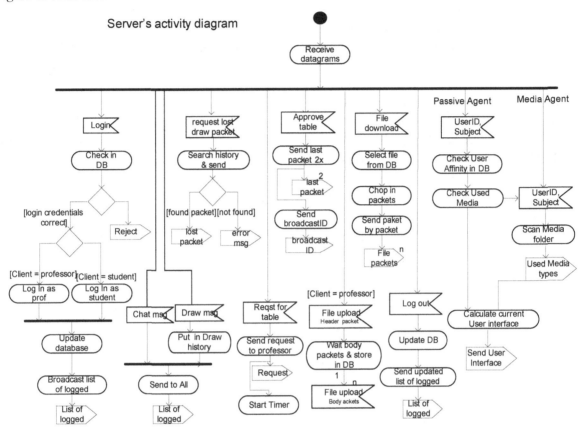

Server's activity diagram

successful login, Active User Agent sends information about the current subject and the current user and waits for the information about the user interface appearance from the Passive User Agent on the server. On every user interaction regarding the position and the size of some control, as well as the usage of the features, Active User Agent sends this information to the server where the user preferences are updated. If the user preferences change, new information about the user interface is sent back to the agent. The Server's activity diagram shows that the server executes an operation when some client sends a message. Client can make several types of communication with the server: login, logout, resend chat or draw message, resend request and approval for the table or voice, upload and download of a file. Actions that are taken without the direct intention of the

user are request for resending of lost packages and user interface management. The server application communicates with the database. Specialized functions that take care of the user interface of each participant are named Passive User Agent and Media User Agent.

The part of the client's application that implements the chat feature is designed in such way that the conversation with all clients is visible in the same window. This method is known as conference chat. Everybody can post messages and all the others can read them. Although, the primary use of the chat is that the questions are intended for the instructor and the relevant answer is expected from this same authority. The server resends the incoming messages to all the clients that are logged in, providing the senders' names.

In the file upload operation, the file is chopped in pieces with size of 500 bytes and sent packet by packet to the server. Every packet has a unique ID. The file is stored in the database on the server machine. When the client wants to see the picture that is stored on the server, the file is downloaded (packet by packet) to the client's pocket PC and the picture is shown on the virtual blackboard area. The client that has the public control over the blackboard (initially the professor) can draw on it with several colors and several thicknesses of the line. While drawing, the points that are drawn, containing absolute position on the blackboard and on the bitmap, with appropriate color are sent to the server. Sending the packets with drawing are triggered either by timer (in case a smaller number of points are drawn) or when 40 points are drawn.

The student can send request for public drawing on the blackboard. A datagram with appropriate structure is sent (containing information for the blackboard request and identification of who precedes the request). When triggering the request, a timer for this event is started. In a predefined amount of time, if the instructor returns the approval, the student gets the public control over the blackboard. Now, the student with the control over the blackboard can draw or point on it, and every logged person can see the changes. If the timer counts down, the request is discarded. The request for the blackboard is shown in the instructor's application by showing and blinking of the student's name. Sending approval for the public use of the blackboard is triggered by the button click event. If a message is not sent, this means that the blackboard is not approved or the instructor is busy. The server application makes the transfer of the control from the student application to the instructor's.

Every client can draw, and make notes on the blackboard without broadcasting the drawing (if the client hasn't control). In this way, the student can make notes specific to him and if needed, he/she can save his own drawing. The client can

log out at any time. In that case, a message for logout is sent. The list of logged users is updated in the database.

The process that goes on automatically, without any concern of the clients, is the management of lost packets. This feature applies only for drawing packets, because of their large number and the fact that the meaning of the picture would not be understood without all of the pieces that the instructor or a student would have drawn. The necessity for this feature has been practically proven. When the testing of the application was conducted, many UDP datagrams had been lost during the communication. Every client that is drawing publicly, keeps the history of last ten drawing UDP datagrams. Every drawing datagram has its own ID, and if the server receives a datagram with ID that is larger than the last accepted at least for 2, then request for lost datagram with the known ID is sent. The server keeps history of last 100 drawing datagrams. If client's application doesn't receive a datagram (and datagram with larger number is received), the client application sends request to the server for the datagram with the precise ID. Similar management of non received datagrams is provided for uploading and downloading files.

The communication in the mobile blackboard system is realized with relatively simple scenario. The server receives UDP datagrams, checks them, and resends them to appropriate recipient(s). The files are kept on the server, and the clients can download them when they need them. The server's activity diagram shows that the server application listens for the incoming datagrams, reads their headings, and initiates actions according to their contents. The datagrams come in simultaneously from every client that initiates some action as log in, send chat message, request for blackboard, download and upload a file or speak. The server has two interfaces. One interface serves the communication with the clients' applications. Similar to the client's applications, this interface is represented with the procedures for receiving and sending datagrams. The server has one UDP socket

Figure 4. The mobile virtual blackboard collaboration diagram

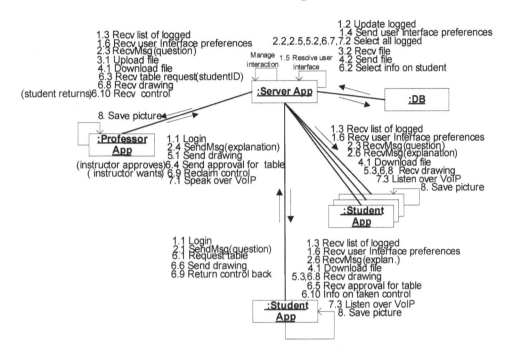

on which it receives and resends the datagrams from and to all the clients. The host's IP address and the port number are the key parameters for communication with clients. The second interface is reserved for the communication with the database. A proper connection string has to be provided for connecting to the database, where the files and the users' information are stored. Voice conversation includes a feature for recording and sending voice in real time, and the part for reproducing the voice. These features are set in the clients' applications, while the server has the special part which takes care of resending the voice data to online recipients.

Different aspects of collaboration are of recognized in the Mobile Virtual Blackboard System. Our attention is focused on the forms and methods of communication that modern pocket PCs can offer, combined with the development environments designed for them. The first aspect of collaboration is the communication between the instructor and the student. The Mobile Virtual Blackboard is made for providing another com-

munication bridge between the two communities, the community that teaches, and the community that needs to learn. Another aspect of collaboration is that many students participate in one consultation session. In this way, during the consultation process, students have the opportunity to remind themselves to the things they know and deepen the knowledge on the known theme, or they can learn new topics.

The collaboration diagram on the Figure 4 shows the interaction among the different applications used in our system. This collaboration diagram reflects the technical possibilities of the system that can be used for the collaboration among the participants in a consultation process.

Every communication message in the collaboration diagram is marked with one or more numbers. The first number signifies the scenario, such as question and answer through the chat (the lines that begin with 1), or drawing (lines begin with 4). The first scenario is Login. Student or professor Log on the server. The server updates the list of the logged clients. The clients receive the list of all logged clients. The server also sends user interface preferences to each client separately, after reading the users preferences from the database and scanning of the media folder for the current subject (1.4 and 1.5). The clients receive the information about the preferred user interface (1.6). The second scenario, posing question and answering begins with 2.1 SendMsg (question) which is sent by a student. The student's application sends this chat message to the server. The server queries the database, in order to get all logged clients (2.2). When the server application receives the list of all clients that are logged in, it resends the message to all the logged participants. The instructor also receives the question (2.3) and sends the explanation in a text message (2.4). The database is queried again for the logged clients (2.5) and the message with the explanation is resent to all logged clients (2.6). The database keeps the info on clients' logs. The clients can login and logout at any time, so checking of all logins is necessary before every resending of a message. Since only one person can draw at a time, it is made that the instructor controls the use of the blackboard. If a student has the necessity to draw some example that needs an explanation, he/she can send a request for public drawing on the blackboard (5.1). The personal information about the student is provided from the database (5.2) and the request is resent to the instructor (5.3). If the instructor approves the student's request, on the press of the button, the message with the approval is sent to the student (5.4). Public drawing on his blackboard is enabled and the student can now draw on the virtual blackboard. The messages that contain the points drawn by the student are sent to all logged clients (first to the server (5.6), and then the server resends them to all the logged clients (5.8)). The instructor can upload files. This kind of a communication is lead between the instructor's application, and the database, through the server application (2.1, 2.2). File download is the reverse process (3.1, 3.2). When a login occurs (6.1), the server application queries the database to check if there is a user with the specified credentials (6.2). If the login succeeds, the list of the users that are logged in is updated and sent to all participants (6.3). The last presented scenario is saving the snapshot from the blackboard as a bitmap picture (7). The client can save the picture that is being drawn on the virtual blackboard at any moment. This task doesn't require communication with the server or other clients. Clients may draw on their own blackboards without public display of their changes, in the case when they don't have the control over the blackboard. When the client saves the picture, he actually saves his own version of the picture. In this way, a student may draw specific notes on his own blackboard and save it for further reference.

MULTIMODAL AGENT-BASED USER INTERFACE MANAGEMENT

Readability and good usability of the screen is of a great importance for handheld devices and demands great developer attention, since the success of the application depends on the users' positive experience with the application interface. Every particular user can have preferences on using of the available features in the application, and the consultation session can vary according to those preferences and the material that is to be presented to the students. Regarding the dimensions of the user interface on handhelds, a management of the interface is required, in order to expose only the currently used features. We have created multimodal user interface that exposes only the currently used features on the display, while the unused controls are being minimized or hidden. The management of the controls on the interface is carried by three agents: Passive agent, Media agent and Active agent.

The XML structure of our user-interface agents and the data of the user's profile is shown below.

The Active user agent resides on the client's side, and monitors the user's interaction with the features in the application. After the user has logged in on the consultation session, Active user agent in his application communicates with the Passive user agent on the server. The Passive agent retrieves the information from the Media agent about the type of the materials that are being used in the current consultation session. The Media agent monitors the specificly assigned folder with the materials for the consultation session, and sends the information about the contents of the folder to the Passive agent. The Passive agent uses this information as one of the inputs for the calculation of the user interface. The information

that the Media agent provides consists of the types of the documents that are stored in the folder for the specific consultation session. The second input data that the Passive agent uses is the history of interface affinities for the particular user. This information is stored in the database for every user. The Passive agent processes these data inputs and sends the corresponding information for the type of the user interface to the Active agent. Then, the Active agent adapts the user interface according to this information. The profiles with personal information for each user are stored in the database in XML format. Additionally, a history of affinities is stored for every user. According to this history of affinities and the data stored

Table 1. XML structure for user profiles

Table 2. XML code for Passive agent

```
<INTERFACE_MGMT_SM>
 <profiles>

  <USERPROFILE UserID ="">
   <name></name>
   <e-mail></e-mail>
   <chat_aff></chat_aff>
   <draw_aff></draw_aff>
   <speak_aff></speak_aff>
  </USERPROFILE>

  <HISTORY>
   <HISTORY_USER UserID ="">
    <SESSION SessionID="">
     <chat_aff></chat_aff>
     <draw_aff></draw_aff>
     <speak_aff></speak_aff>
     <U_A></U_A>
    </SESSION>
   </HISTORY_USER>
  </HISTORY>

 </profiles>
 ...
</INTERFACE_MGMT_SM>
```

```
<PASSIVE_AGENT>
 <AFFINITIES afID="">
  <AFF UserID="" SessionID="" chat_aff=""
draw_aff="" speak_aff="">
   <U_A> </U_A>
   <M_P> </M_P>
   <I></I>
  </AFF >
 </AFFINITIES>

 <RULES>
  <IF U_A="CHAT" M_P ="TEXT"/>
   <ASSIGN I="INCREASE_CHAT"/>
  <IF U_A="CHAT" M_P ="DRAWING"/>
   <ASSIGN I="THE_SAME"/>
  <IF U_A="CHAT" M_P ="SOUND"/>
   <ASSIGN I="INCREASE_CHAT"/>
  <IF U_A="DRAW" M_P ="TEXT"/>
   <ASSIGN I="THE_SAME"/>
  <IF U_A="DRAW" M_P ="DRAWING"/>
   <ASSIGN I="INCREASE_DRAW"/>
  <IF U_A="DRAW" M_P ="SOUND"/>
   <ASSIGN I="INCREASE_DRAW"/>
  <IF U_A="VOIP" M_P ="TEXT"/>
   <ASSIGN I="INCREASE_CHAT"/>
  <IF U_A="VOIP" M_P ="DRAWING"/>
   <ASSIGN I="INCREASE_DRAW"/>
  <IF U_A="VOIP" M_P ="SOUND"/>
   <ASSIGN I="THE_SAME"/>
 </RULES >
 ...
</PASSIVE_AGENT>
```

for the current conslutation session, the Passive agent adapts the user interface at the beginning of the consultation session for each user. Redesign of the interface can be done at any time during the session. This activity is triggered when the user resizes or moves a control on the screen, or simply with using or not using of some features, the Active agent sends messages to the server where the affinities are being updated.

The part of the XML structure of the Passive User Agent is shown above. It is composed of two parts: Affinities, which contains the data about user's affinity, and Rules, according to which, the passive agent decides the type of the user interface.

There are three predefined user interfaces, which can be preloaded on the client's device, according to his preferences and the media contents for the current consultation session. The first interface has chat on the larger part of the screen, the second one has larger drawing blackboard on the screen, and the third one has equal space for the chat and the blackboard. VoIP feature doesn't occupy much space on the screen, so the buttons for voice can always be displayed.

Since there is no universal conclusion for making decisions about which user interface should be preloaded, i.e. which interface mode should be used; the fuzzy logic approach is used to model this kind of the imprecise information [Camacho et al., 2001]. In order to create a fuzzy expert system for calculation of the user interface visual features, fuzzy variables are defined for this expert system. The linguistic variable LEVEL accepts values from the set of terms {high, medium, low} as shown on Figure 5. It can be used to represent chat, draw and voice affinity.

The interaction made by the user upon the features in the application (chat, draw and voice feature), is represented as a vector (chat_aff, draw_aff, sound_aff). A linguistic variable named *RESULT_PREFERENCE* is introduced, and can accept values from the set of terms {increase_chat, increase_draw (=reduce_chat)}. This variable represents the visualization of the user interface, produced by the user interaction with the interface and also according to the contents of the media folder.

The proposed expert system has two variables: U_A (user affinity) which presents the most used feature by the user, i.e. it has the greatest affinity for the feature; M_P (media profile) presents the profile of the interface that should be used according to the media contents. The output variable named I (interface) presents the necessary interface to be preloaded onto the user's device screen, according to the input variables.

Figure 5. Graphic representation of the defined fuzzy functions

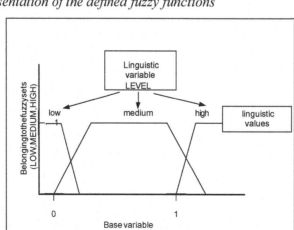

The system contains Active agents on each client handheld machine and one Passive User Agent and also a Media Agent on the server machine. Media Agent monitors the specific folder with the materials for the consultation session. Passive User Agent serves all the Active User Agents in one consultation session. Interaction among the three clients is shown on the Figure 6. In this class diagram, the used attributes along with the methods are shown for each agent.

Passive User Agent uses the following attributes: UserProfile, MediaProfile and UserInterface. MediaProfile is variable which contains the information of the prepared media contents for the specific consultation session. Regarding the contents of the folder where the uploaded files are stored, MediaProfile can be text, drawing, or sound. The necessity of introduction of this variable can be shown with a simple example: user might not prefer to draw, but the explanations are done with the help of the drawings. Therefore, drawing surface should be shown on the screen. Passive User Agent's main task is to calculate the appropriate user interface, according to user's affinity and contents of the media for the current consultation session. Active User Agent monitors

user's utilization of the media features (responds to user's interaction on the interface: whether it uses the draw function, or chat or voice). After the user action, Active User Agent updates the user's profile and triggers the Passive User Agent to reconsider the user's interface type with the updated data. The interaction among agents and the user interface is shown on the Figure 7.

The multimodal structure of the user interface is made with the help of these three autonomous agents that serve only for user interface purposes.

MOBILE BLACKBOARD IMPLEMENTATION

The applications for Wireless Mobile Virtual Blackboard are first made in C++ Visual Studio .NET 2005 development environment. Operating system used on the pocket PCs was Windows Mobile 2003. The application is upgraded to the Visual Studio 2008, and the Pocket PC operating system is changed to Windows Mobile 5. The operating system for desktop machines on

Figure 6. Agents' class model

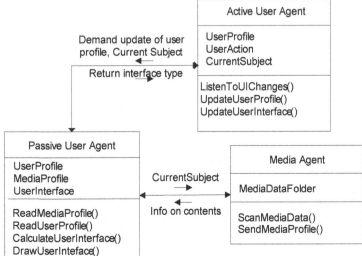

which the application is practically deployed, is Windows XP SP2.

Two instances of instructor's interface are shown on Figure 5. The control of the blackboard is represented with the button named "get control". The chat module consists of the input text box as well as display text box, where all chat messages are written, and the send button. The button named "Chat" enables seeing the chat on the full screen. The buttons named "fUp" and "fDown" serve for upload and download. The rectangular space on the screen where the graphics is shown is called the virtual blackboard. This is the place where the downloaded files are opened and where notes can be added using colors and pens with different

thickness. The "Clean" button serves for clearing the blackboard. With clicking on the "Save" button, the contents shown on the virtual blackboard can be saved as a bitmap file.

Student's user interface is very similar to the professor's except that it has a button to send drawing and voice request; it does not have the authority control, and does not have the ability for upload.

Figure 8 shows two types of user interfaces, managed and adjusted by the user interface management system with the three presented agents. Real demonstration of our Virtual Mobile Blackboard system is presented on the Figure 9.

Table 3. Communication example. A simple scenario for exchange of messages among the agents

Active Agent	Passive Agent	Media Agent
<message ID = "0" SessionID = "434" recipient ="passive_ agent017"> < userID> Peter </ userID > < action >start_app</ action > </message>	< message ID = "1" SessionID = "434" recipient ="media_agent001"> </message> <!--processing info with passive_agent XML code--> < message ID = "4" SessionID = "434" recipient ="active_agent017"> < userID> Peter </ userID > <interface> draw</ interface > </message>	< message ID = "3" SessionID = "434" recipient = "passive_ agent001" > <media_contents>draw</media_contents > </message>

Figure 7. Agents' collaboration diagram

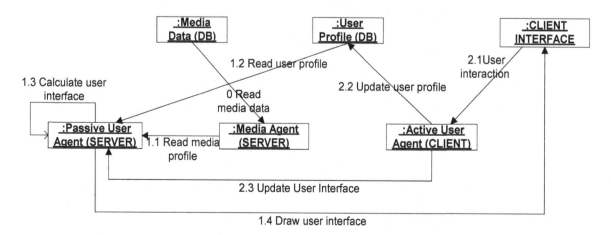

EVALUATION OF THE MOBILE VIRTUAL BLACKBOARD

The Mobile Virtual Blackboard was evaluated by 24 students at their last year of undergraduate studies in Information Technologies. The evaluation still proceeds and the students are encouraged to use this mobile system. The students were asked to assess whether the mobile blackboard would be useful for their studies. The questionnaire given to the students was separated in three logical parts: (1) Experience with the mobile devices, ((2) Interface usability and (3) Features of the application.

The questions list that examines the participants experience and acceptability of our mobile Distance Education Systems are:

- Do you own Pocket PC device?
- Do you have any experience with Pocket PC devices?
- Do you think that Mobile Virtual Blackboard makes the learning process easier?

- Have you used applications with similar purpose before?

The Y axis in Chart 1 represents questions with the same number from questionnaire above.

Results show that most of the examinees have previous experience with Pocket PC application. All of them agreed that Mobile Virtual Blackboard could make learning process easier and more convenient. The only fact that concerns is that the Pocket PCs are not yet that widely spread among the students population (probably because of their high price).

The questions that examine the system interface usability and provide information for future upgrades are:

- Is the number of different colors that can be selected for the drawing pens satisfying?
- Are you satisfied with the layout presentation on the blackboard?
- What do you think about the giving drawing controls to more than one user?

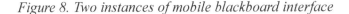

Figure 8. Two instances of mobile blackboard interface

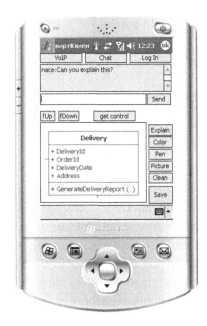
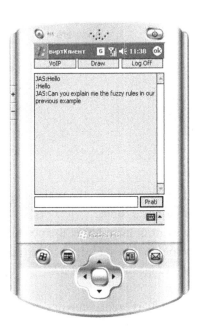

Figure 9. Live demonstration of Mobile Virtual Blackboard

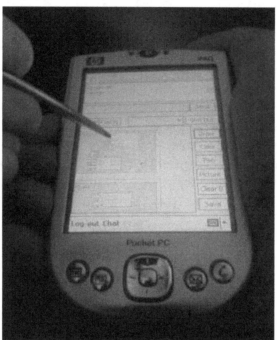

Chart 1. Results from experience part of questionnaire

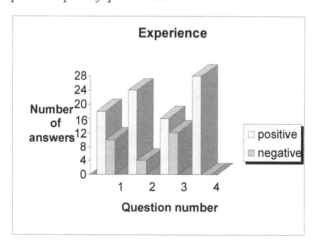

- What is your opinion about the logging concept on the system?
- What is your opinion about the position of the controls on the user interface and do you have any suggestions about it?

The Y axis in Chart 2 represents questions with the same number from questionnaire above.

The general opinion among the participants about the interface usability is positive. The interface appears to the examinees as functional and some suggestions about the position of the controls will be included in the future project. The option that will allow more than one user to have the public control over the drawing on the blackboard is divided among the participants.

Chart 2. Results from interface usability part of questionnaire

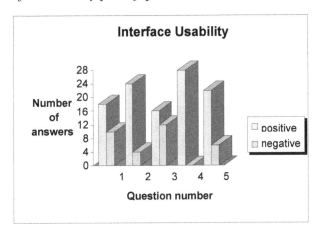

The current system design left this option to the instructor who can decide about the number of holders of the drawing controls.

The questions used prior our newest version of the Virtual Mobile Blackboard which helped us introduce new features to our system and according to which, we made our future directions are:

• Do you think that an option for sending files should be provided?
• Do you think that an option for VOIP communication should be provided?
• Do you think that an option to save current image on the blackboard should be provided?
• Do you think that an option to save chat history should be provided?
• What is your opinion on providing communication between mobile phones and virtual blackboard using MMS and SMS messages?

The Y axis in Chart 3 represents the questions with the same number from questionnaire above.

The research on students' interest on adopting handheld mobile devices in educational context shows that most of the students have positive opinion about the introduction of mobile virtual blackboard into the educational process. The specific suggestions and critics that are not represented graphically refer to the position of the chat visual components and the need for an option for automatic drawing of geometrical shapes. The general opinion of all examinees is that the virtual mobile blackboard could increase the effectiveness of the learning process.

The information provided from our research shows that there is a place for new extensions of the project, like implementing MMS and SMS communication that will enable students with mobile phones to interact and be part of the virtual blackboard. But also, in very near future, cheaper wireless access to the Internet will be available to the mobile phones, such as Wi-Fi and 3G, so we conclude that we have to put accent to the Internet Protocols, and the selection of a carrier should be user's preference. The newly produced mobile phones come with advanced platforms, mobile operating systems that support installation of custom applications, so this kind of applications and many others are going to be normal reality in the very near future, we can even say now.

Chart 3. Results from "mobile blackboard features" part of questionnaire

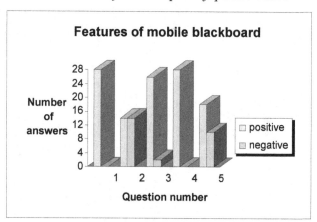

CONCLUSION

This chapter presents our project named Mobile Virtual Table, with great accent on multimodal features implemented on the user interface. In order to achieve efficient multimodal interface we have used XML based agents and fuzzy logic. We have developed context aware learning system which determines the exposure of the features on the interface according to the learning contents prepared for each specific learning session. The system can dynamically reconfigure the user interface according to the user preferences, also. The fuzzy logic approach is used to model the user affinities towards the different features of the application (chat, draw, VoIP). In this way, we have proposed highly adaptable user interface for handheld devices which brings benefits to the application developers in this software environment, to users of mobile learning systems and at the end, to all mobile device users. The general opinion among the participans about the interface usability is positive. We expect and encourage our mobile consultation system to be widely used in our campus. With dedicating a lot of time and attention to the usability of the interface, by introducing multimodal user interaction with other participants, our Virtual Mobile Blackboard has evolved to a convenient user friendly system, and can be used for further direction of developing and advancing of the user interface for mobile handheld devices.

REFERENCES

Adewunmi, A., et al. (2003). Enhancing the in-classroom teaching/learning experience using wireless technology. In *Proc. of 33rd ASEE/IEEE Frontiers in Education Conference*, Boulder, CO (pp. S4E-20-5).

Alvarez-Cortes, V., Zayas-Perez, B., Zarate-Silva, E., Ramirez, V.H., & Uresti, J.A. (2007, September 25-28). Current trends in adaptive user interfaces: Challenges and applications. *Electronics, Robotics, and Automotive Mechanics Conference, CERMA 2007* (pp. 312-317).

Camacho, D., Hernandez, C., & Molina, J.M. (2001). Information classification using fuzzy knowledge based agents, (Vol. 4, pp. 2575-2580).

Chang, A., & Ishii, H. (2006). Personalized interactions with reality based interfaces. *CHI 2006 Workshop "What is the Next Generation of Human-Computer Interaction?"*

Gang, Z., & Zongkai, Y. (2005, October 19-22). Learning resource adaptation and delivery framework for mobile learning. *Frontiers in Education, 2005. FIE apos;05. Proc. 35th Annual Conference.*

Glavinic, V., Rosic, M., & Zelic, M. (2007). Agents in m-learning Systems based on intelligent tutoring. *HCI, (7).*

Granic, A., & Nakic, J. (2007, June 25-28). Meeting user individual characteristics through adaptive interface of an e-learning system: An empirical study design. *Information Technology Interfaces, 2007. ITI 2007. 29th International Conference,* Cavtat, Croatia (pp. 333-338).

Jeong, C., & Lee, E. (2007). Context aware human computer interaction for ubiquitous learning. *HCI, 9* (LNCS 4558).

Kulakov. (2001). Virtual classroom and virtual laboratory. In *Proc. of the 20th World Conference on Open Learning and Distance Education,* Dusseldorf, Germany. CD Rom Publication.

Liu, J., Wong, C.K., & Hui, K.K. (2003). An adaptive user interface based on personalized learning. *Intelligent Systems,* 52-57.

Lu, L., Kitagata, G., Suganuma, T., & Kinoshita, T. (2003). Adaptive user interface for multimedia communication system based on multiagent. In *Proc. of the 17th International Conference on Advanced Information Networking and Applications, IEEE Computer Society* (pp. 53-58).

Luchini, K., Quintana, C., & Soloway, E. (2004). Design guidelines for learner-centered handheld tools. *CHI 2004,* Vienna, Austria (Vol. 6, pp. 135-142).

Misfud, L., & Morch, A.I. (2007). 'That's my PDA!' The role of personalization for handhelds in the classroom. In *Proc. of the Fifth IEEE International Conference on Pervasive Computing and Communications Workshops* (pp. 187-192).

Perakakis, M., & Potamianos, A. (2008). The effect of input mode on inactivity and interaction times of multimodal systems. *ACM,* 102-109.

Trajkovik, V., Gligorovska, S., & Davcev, D. (2007, July 5-7). Mobile virtual blackboard. In *Proc. of IADIS International Conference on Mobile Learning 2007,* Lisbon, Portugal.

Yoshino, et al. (2003). Group digital assistant: Shared or combined PDA screen. *IEEE Transactions on Consumer Electronics, 49*(3), 524-529.

KEY TERMS AND DEFINITIONS

Client-Server: Software architecture model that distinguishes client systems from server systems, which communicate over a computer network. A client-server application is a distributed system comprising both client and server software. A client software process may initiate a communication session, while the server waits for requests from any client.

Fuzzy Logic is a problem-solving control system methodology that lends itself to implementation in systems ranging from simple, small, embedded micro-controllers to large, networked, multi-channel PC or workstation-based data acquisition and control systems. It can be implemented in hardware, software, or a combination of both. Fuzzy logic provides a simple way to arrive at a definite conclusion based upon vague, ambiguous, imprecise, noisy, or missing input information. Fuzzy logic's approach to control problems mimics how a person would make decisions, only much faster.

Mobile Device (also known as cellphone device, handheld device, handheld computer, "Palmtop" or simply handheld) is a pocket-sized computing device, typically having a display screen with touch input or a miniature keyboard. In the case of the personal digital assistant

(PDA) the input and output are combined into a touch-screen interface.

Mobile Learning: (M-learning) refers to the use of mobile and handheld IT devices, such as Personal Digital Assistants (PDAs), mobile telephones, laptops and tablet PC technologies, in teaching and learning. M-learning, or "mobile learning", now commonly abbreviated to "mLearning", has different meanings for different communities. Although related to e-learning and distance education, it is distinct in its focus on learning across contexts and learning with mobile devices. One definition of mobile learning is: *Learning that happens across locations, or that takes advantage of learning opportunities offered by portable technologies.* In other words, mobile learning decreases limitation of learning location with the mobility of general portable devices.

Multimodal: Multiple access to data or ways of interacting with a computer.

Multimodal Interaction: Provides the user with multiple modes of interfacing with a system beyond the traditional keyboard and mouse input/output. The most common such interface combines a visual modality (e.g. a display, keyboard, and mouse) with a voice modality (speech recognition for input, speech synthesis and recorded audio for output). However other modalities, such as pen-based input or haptic input/output may be used. Multimodal user interfaces are a research area in human-computer interaction (HCI).

Multimodal Technology: Allows users to utilize multiple forms of input and output – including voice, keypads and stylus – interchangeably.

Pocket PC: Abbreviated P/PC or PPC, is a hardware specification for a handheld-sized computer (Personal digital assistant) that runs the Microsoft Windows Mobile operating system. It may have the capability to run an alternative operative system like NetBSD, Linux, Android or others. It has many of the capabilities of modern desktop PCs.

XML Agents: Software agents that use XML (eXtensible Markup Language) for communication and are are used widely as an enabling technology for building collaborative applications. They are usually intelligent entities. They can autonomously achieve assigned collaborative tasks without human instructions, and they adapt dynamically to different environments to maintain the optimal solution to the collaborative tasks.

Chapter XXI
Mobile Devices to Support Advanced Forms of E-Learning

Alessia D'Andrea
Istituto di Ricerche sulla Popolazione e le Politiche Sociali-Consiglio Nazionale delle Ricerche, Italy

Fernando Ferri
Istituto di Ricerche sulla Popolazione e le Politiche Sociali-Consiglio Nazionale delle Ricerche, Italy

Leopoldina Fortunati
Università degli Studi di Udine, Italy

Tiziana Guzzo
Istituto di Ricerche sulla Popolazione e le Politiche Sociali-Consiglio Nazionale delle Ricerche, Italy

ABSTRACT

This chapter describes changes that mobile devices, such as mobile phones, PDAs, iPods and smart phones improve on the learning process. The diffusion of these devices has drastically changed learning tools and the environment in which learning takes place. Learning has moved outside the classroom becoming "mobile." Mobile learning provides both learners and teachers with the capability to collaborate and share data, knowledge, files, and messages everywhere and everytime. This allows learners and teachers to microcoordinate activities withoutlimitation of time and space.

INTRODUCTION

Learning, in its most natural form, is the way in which knowledge is acquired by individuals. The diffusion of mobile devices has changed tools and modalities of transmission/acquisition of knowledge and the contextual environments in which learning takes place. Learning has moved outside the classroom into the learner's environment becoming "mobile".

Mobile Learning is not a simple extension of E-learning, but "it is often highly dynamic, targeted to the user's current context and learning needs in respect to e-learning" (Parsons, 2006). Mobile Learning uses advantages of mobile devices (such as mobile phones, handheld computers, personal digital assistants and so on) and permits learners to complete activities in a variety of settings and according to different cadences.

The aim of this chapter is to describe changes mobile devices improve on the learning process. In particular the chapter introduces a specification of Mobile Learning by describing the different properties of mobile devices. Mobile devices promote the every-where and every-time conversation and collaboration between learners and teachers, enabling them to share knowledge, files and messages. This allows learners to informally acquired knowledge while being away from their computers and classrooms when and where it is convenient for them by using a collaborative approach. However the use of mobile devices for learning activities presents also disadvantages, the most important concern the technological limitations due to the small screen size of these devices, limitations of the keyboard, difficulty of navigation, limited battery power and little memory storage. Despite disadvantages, there is a growing interest in using Mobile Learning in different contexsts of use (e.g., in educational, in business as well as in tourism field). This flexibility of Mobile Learning has determined a growing interest in developing Mobile Learning Systems (MLSs). These Systems permit truly to implement

the concept of an anywhere/anytime learning that can enrich, enliven or add variety to conventional lessons or courses. The diffusion of MLSs has promoted the development of a more interactive communication between learners and teachers. However during the interaction process learners and teachers have different needs and different features. These features produce the need for User Interfaces that are usable, multimodal and personalized to the greatest extent possible for each user. Multimodal User Interfaces support this purpose because they give learners and teachers the possibility to use several modalities such as visual information (involving images, text, and so on) voice or gestures that provide flexible and powerful dialog approaches, enabling them to choose one or more of the multiple interaction modalities.

BACKGROUND

The learning of the future will be characterized by a growing need among learners to access local content and to develop both personal and global knowledge in different social contexts and environments. There are many different situations of learning outside the classroom and the workplace that could employ chunks of knowledge that are produced and shared through social learning experiences. This scenario has been envisaged and supported by several methodological studies and European research projects.

Many methodological studies have shown that a variety of approaches and best practices concerning the use of mobile devices to support learners are being applied, however some of them lack of a sound analysis from a pedagogical and human-computer interaction point-of-view.

The pedagogical point-of-view addresses the process of designing, communicating and presenting new content and learning resources on small devices for different users with different needs in different contexts. These include identifying appropriate conceptual organisational frameworks for content and specifying the range of interaction modes made possible in different contexts and using different devices. Furthermore robust pedagogical theories of how mobile media mediate the learning process are still lacking in much of the research and development literature.

The human-computer interaction point-of-view addresses how different interaction modalities are used (by the user) to select and (by the system) to present the content on small devices. Results of many studies underline the necessity to support users (in the selection of the content) and system (in the presentation of the content) with multimodal interaction facilities. Multimodal interaction provides the user with a way to interface with a system in both input and output. Multimodality allows user and system to exchange information using several modalities such as speech, gesture, eye tracking, keyboarding, etc.

The processing of the pedagogical and human-computer interaction points-of-view has determined the interest toward different research themes developed by several European research projects. In particular, three of these projects were supported by the Leonardo Da Vinci programme of the European Union. The first project called *"From e-learning to m-learning"* (http://learning. ericsson.net/mlearning2/project_one/book.html), led by Ericsson Education Dublin, addressed the development of courseware for mobile phones, smart-phones and PDAs. In particular the project analysed the main pedagogical problems of developing Mobile Learning for PDAs. The second project called *"Mobile Learning: the next generation of learning" (http://learning.ericsson.net/ mlearning2)*, led by Ericsson Education Ireland, aimed to achieve the production of acceptable courseware for smart-phones in XHTML. In this project the next generation of Mobile Learning course development was based on FlashLite (a toned down version of Flash designed for mobile devices). The third project called *"The incor-*

poration of Mobile Learning into mainstream Education and training" (http://www.ericsson. com/ericsson/ corpinfo/programs/incorporating_mobile_learning_into_mainstream_education/), led by Ericsson Education Ireland, asserted that "it is now time for Mobile Learning to emerge from its project status and enter into mainstream education and training – as the related fields of distance education and e-learning have done before it". For the first time a Mobile Learning project is focused on the field as a whole and not on the development of Mobile Learning for an institution or a group of institutions.

Other two projects were supported by the IST programme. The first project called *"M-Learning"* (http://www.m-learning.org/reports.shtml), led by the United Kingdom government Learning and Skills Development Agency (LSDA), had an important social dimension. It recognised that there were (in the United Kingdom) many 16 to 20 year old youths who were unemployed and had urgent needs for additional training, but who refused to attend a training centre or college. They all had, however, a mobile phone, which they used constantly. The project, therefore, set out to develop courses for them on their mobile phones in the fields of literacy, numeracy and social skills. The second project called *"MOBILearn" (http://www. mobilearn.org/)*, led by Giunti Ricerca of Genoa (Italy), was a very large project led from Italy and counted a wide range of at least 20 European universities among its members. The objectives of this project were the definition of theoretically supported and empirically-validated models for effective learning/teaching/tutoring in a mobile environment.

Both methodological studies and European research projects, developed along this decade, have shown the necessity to analyse mobile devices properties in order to evaluate changes that these devices improve on the learning process. In the two following paragraphs the chapter provides an analysis of these properties and an evaluation of advantages and limitations of Mobile Learning.

Afterward the chapter illustrates the collaborative approach of Mobile Learning and discusses tree different contexts of use of Mobile Learning. Furthermore the chapter describes MLSs and Multimodal Interfaces. The chapter concludes with a classification of existing MLSs according to the different contexts of use.

MOBILE LEARNING: THE NEXT GENERATION OF LEARNING

In the "E-Learning Guild Research 3600 Report on Mobile Learning" the Mobile Learning is defined as *"any activity that allows individuals to be more productive when consuming, interacting with, or creating information, mediated through a mobile device that the individual carries on a regular basis, has reliable connectivity, and fits in a pocket or purse"* (Wexler et al. 2007).

Many are the mobile devices that are used to improve learning activities such as mobile phones, PDAs, iPods and smarth phones. These different devices allow to perform different kind of learning activities.

For Example, mobile phones are useful for:

- Establishing voice communications with learners and teachers;

- Sending and receiving SMS or MMS (e.g. for glossary information, reminders and alerts);
- M-blogging (use of phones to blog).

PDAs with their larger screen sizes are useful for:

- Consulting contents in different formats such as: text documents, flash-based content, video or audio;
- Sending and receiving instant messaging and emailing.

iPods are useful for:

- Downloading podcasts of instructional materials along with video and audio lectures;
- Providing visual step-by-step directions that are difficult to convey with words only.

Finally smarth phones summarise the features of the previous cited kinds of tools.

Being mobile adds a new dimension to learning activities both because of mobile devices properties and because of the kinds of interaction that these devices can support. Several studies individuate and classify mobile devices properties.

Table 1. Mobile devices properties

Connectivity	Social Interactivity	Individuality	Context sensitivity	Portability
A shared network can facilitates the connection mobile devices to other devices or to a common network.	Mobile devices satisfy the anthropological need of individuals to communicate.	Mobile devices provide the development of personalized adaptive learning..	By using mobile devices, people can gather and respond to data to the current environment and time.	Thanks to the small size and weight of mobile devices it is possible to take them to different sites.

In particular Klopfer et al. (2004) classify the following five property classes, shown in Table 1, to characterise mobile devices: Connectivity, Social interactivity, Individuality, Context sensitivity and Portability.

These properties, that characterise the Mobile Learning process, are strictly related to several key elements: the user device, the user, user communities, the Network and the context. In this scenario, connectivity represents the interaction between the user device and the Network, many devices are characterised by a high connectivity (smart phones) other by a limited capability (PDAs). The Social interactivity represents the interaction between the user device and user communities that satisfy user need to communicate, this property class is strongly related to the previous connectivity class. The Individuality represents the interaction between the user device and its user and allows to adapt content according to the users needs and characteristics. The Context sensitivity represents the interaction between the user device and the external environment and permits to adapt content according to the context characteristics. Finally Portability represents the property to establish interactions between the user device and all others actors every-where and every-time.

These different properties suggest that the nature of learning process is changing. Mobile devices is providing a new way of conversation and collaboration between learners and teachers giving at the same time the possibility to undertake new kinds of learning activities. According to the conversation theory (Pask, 1976) "learning is a continual conversation with the external word and its artefacts with oneself, with other learners and with teachers". Thus it is through conversation and collaboration that learners come to a shared understanding of the world. In this perspective, mobile devices support learning experiences that are collaborative and integrated with the world beyond the classroom. Through mobile devices anywhere and anytime learners could contact and

collaborate with their colleagues to discuss their course materials or to find someone else in their same situation that might help them by solving a doubt or just by providing the feeling that they are not "the only ones". This flexibility of mobile devices provides the possibility to undertake different kinds of learning activities. Many studies underline several theory-based categories of learning activities by using mobile devices, and identify a number of examples of the use of these devices in each of them. In particular Naismith et al. (2004) distinguish the following categories:

- **Behaviourist:** That promotes learning as a change in observable actions. An example of the implementation of behaviourist principles with mobile devices is the content delivery by text messages to mobile phones.
- **Constructivist:** That encourages learners to discover principles for themselves in order "to transform them from passive recipients of information to active constructors of knowledge". An example of the implementation of constructivist principles with mobile devices come from a learning experience called "participatory simulations", where learners take part of an immerse recreation of a dynamic system.
- **Situated:** That requires knowledge to be presented in authentic context and learners to participate within a community of practice. Mobile devices are well suited to context-aware applications; in fact they are available in different contexts, and so they can allow on those contexts to enhance the learning activities.
- **Collaborative:** That promotes learning through social interactions. Mobile devices can support collaborative learning (as discussed in the following paragraphs) and provide another means of coordination.
- **Informal/lifelong:** That supports learning outside dedicated environments. Mobile devices allow to support learning outside

the classroom by embeding learning in everyday life.

- **Support/coordination:** That assists in the coordination of learners and resources. Mobile devices can be used by teachers for reviewing student marks, attendance reporting, accessing of central school data and managing them more effectively.

This range of learning activities that is possible to carry out by using mobile devices has determined the academic interest about how effectively making links between what is going on around the learner and what the learner is doing with their mobile device. At the same time, a real need is growing to evaluate the advantages and limitations of Mobile Learning in order to provide the educators with the confidence needed to support the advancement of this new learning approach.

MOBILE LEARNING: ADVANTAGES AND LIMITATIONS

The challenge of Mobile Learning is to enhance the advantages of this new form of learning and to reduce the technological limitations that restrict their use.

The mobility is the key factor of Mobile Learning, that allows to gain the advantages introduced

in Table 2, that summarizes several considerations of Clarke (2003).

These advantages derive from the properties of mobile devices: Connectivity, Social interactivity, Individuality, Context sensitivity and Portability previously shown in Table 1.

Connectivity and Portability give the advantages of Ubiquity and Convenience. Advantages of Mobile Learning in fact, mainly consist in the access to information where previously it was not possible without being limited to time and space. Convenience and ubiquity in fact mean that teachers and learners can interact at any time from anywhere. Context sensitivity gives the advantage of localization that allows to provide services that are targeted to the user's current locality. Social Interactivity and Individuality give the advantage of personalization that offers the opportunity to access to resources and learning materials adapting them to the specific needs of the learners, respecting individual learning rhythm. For example learners with physical disabilities or learners that live in a remote area can benefit of these features.

It is needed to consider besides advantages also disadvantages of Mobile Learning, among these there are technological limitations: the less functionality than desktop computers due to small screen size of mobile devices, limitations of the keyboard, difficulty of navigation, limited

Table 2. Advantages of mobile devices for learning

Ubiquity	Convenience	Localisation	Personalization
Access to learning contents anywhere.	Access to learning contents at any time.	Access to learning on the basis of learner's position.	Access to learning by learners whit different needs.

Table 3. Properties and advantages of mobile devices

	Ubiquity	Convenience	Localisation	Personalization
Connectivity	X	X		
Social Interactivity				X
Individuality				X
Context sensitivity			X	
Portability	X	X		

battery power, little memory storage. The size of the text, always uncomfortable for limited space on the mobile devices displays, makes difficult reading for prolonged periods. Moreover size and portability of mobile devices are subject to damage, easy to lose and more likely to be stolen than desktop systems.

According to Robertson et al. (1997) without a direct relationship between teachers and learners, problems of the integration of computers into education will continue. In Mobile Learning courses more feedback and assessment is needed in order to stimulate the learners and maintain interest and enthusiasm. Moreover while young people accept very well the use of mobile devices in the learning process, to the contrary older people have problems to use mobile devices in their work or education. Another problem is tied to user data privacy and learning materials security because new technologies are more vulnerable to attacks by intruders. Moreover issues of authentication and authorization are critical for successful education and development of effective Mobile Learning System. (Yordanova, 2007).

A study of Stanford University's Language lab (Qingyang, 2003) provides some insights into the fragmented experience of learning with mobile device. The mobility in fact is subject to noise situations (on a train, in a café, in the street) that reduce concentration and reflection, increasing distractions.

One of the most important disadvantages is economic cost of mobile devices. Providing each learner of a high tech device also means to invest in software, care services and maintenance repairs upgrades. Implementing this kind of learning method or policy means to take a compelling business case.

Mobile Learning has both many advantages in terms of the quality of the learning experience and many technical limitations. To completely evaluate this technology, it is important to consider the acceptance by users. Learners accept Mobile Learning if it meets their own needs.

Wilson et al. (2001), starting from the work of Rogers, list six features in order to determine the acceptance in educational technology innovations: simplicity, trialability, observability, relative advantage, compatibility and support:

- **Simplicity:** Concerns the aspect that the innovation is easy to understand, maintain, use and explain to others.
- **Trialability:** Concerns the testing and use of the innovation.
- **Observability:** Concerns that the innovation is visible to others, so that the users can see how it works and observe the consequences.

- **Relative Advantage:** Concerns that the innovation is the better technology in economical, socially prestigious, convenient, satisfying terms.
- **Compatibility:** Concerns the satisfaction of the values, past experiences, and needs of the potential adopters.
- **Support:** Concerns the availability of time, energy, money, resources, administrative and political support, to ensure the project's success.

There are several researches that have shown that Mobile Learning is very accepted by users. For example a study by Ericsson (2002) showed that users who use a simple Wireless Access Protocol (WAP) browser interface, consider Mobile Learning a quality experience. In this study, 77% of participants answered that the equipment in Mobile Learning course was easy to use and they stated that would take another Mobile Learning course if it was relevant to their learning needs. The 66% would recommend to others learners, Mobile Learning as a method of study. The 99% affirmed that Mobile Learning increases access to education and training. The most part stated that the learning experience could be improved by the use of graphics and illustrations, 33% of participants considered that this was not of fundamental importance.

The main motivations to use Mobile Learning, such as palmtop computers, is that it assists learners, encouraging a sense of responsibility, helping organisational skills in independent and collaborative learning and tracking student's progress. The relatively low cost in respect to palmtop computer enables 'ownership' of the computer and continuous access both in school and out. (Savill-Smith, 2003).

In their study Wang et al. (2008) research the determinants of Mobile Learning acceptance and their relations with age or gender. The results by data collected from 330 respondents in Taiwan indicate that performance expectancy, effort expectancy, social influence, perceived fun, and self-management of learning are all significant determinants of behavioural intention to use Mobile Learning. They also stated that age differences moderate the effects of effort expectancy and social influence on Mobile Learning use intention, and that gender differences moderate the effects of social influence and self-management of learning on Mobile Learning use intention.

In another study of Fung et al. (1998) the researchers recorded the attitudes of learners aged 15-16 before and after their use of palmtops. The learners have individuated the following advantages of pocketbook computing (Savill-Smith, 2003): facility of storage and portability, increase of motivational stimulus, development of computer knowledge, improvement and easier to produce written work, availability at all times and a range of useful functions.

According to Soloway et al. (2001), personal computers have changed professional's work making it more productive and effective, but in the schools they don't have large success due to low 'personal' access to networked desktop computers by learners and teachers. The palmtops 'ready-at-hand' can change this situation and can increase learning (Soloway et al. 2001), because they are not bound to the access to a computer laboratory but consent to reflect in flexible time and to collaborate and share with other learners via infra-red. (Perry, 2003). Collaboration is another important feature of Mobile Learning to be considered. Mobile devices in fact allow users to collaborate every where in real time by exchanging text and multimedial contents.

COLLABORATIVE APPROACH OF MOBILE LEARNING

Crucial point of each learning process is interaction. Learning is a social process; many researches have demonstrated that in group learning is better.

Learning should be examined as the process of meaning making through social interaction between learners and their peers. The social aspect of learning is understood as a process of social negotiation and joint knowledge construction. In the context of collaborative learning, negotiation is viewed as a process by which learners attempt to attain agreement on aspects of the learning task and on certain aspects of the interaction itself (Dillenbourg, 1996).

According to Vygotsky (1978), "collaboration, as part of the social constructivism theory, emphasises the importance of intrinsic learning through social interactions", and more "this learner-centred interaction results in learners being more engaged and helps to develop personal intellectual structures that foster a deeper understanding of the content at hand" (Stahl et al., 1995). Another positive issue about this learner-centred collaborative approach, is that it allows learners to discuss complex situations and to resolve ambiguities, common in these domains (Spiro et al., 1991).

Collaborative Mobile Learning gives learners and teachers the opportunity to enrich their experience. In a collaborative scenario, face-to-face interactions are essential for a learning process, anyway online communities have allowed learners and teachers to be far from each other and their working online is not bounded on a physical proximity in the same place.

Some important topics in Collaborative Learning are to make learners able in the virtual learning environments to feel the social presence of others and to not feel alone in their problems and tasks.

These concepts are achievable in a virtual community of practice. Wenger et al. (2002) defined the term "community of practice" (CoP) as a community that "binds together groups of people who share a concern, a set of problems, or a passion about topic, and who deepen their knowledge and expertise by interacting on an ongoing basis".

Mobile Learning communities of practice allow learners to collaboratively acquire knowledge by sharing ideas, contents, problems and solutions, moreover mobile devices can be used for several collaborative activities in learning context, such as: gathering responses from learners (classroom response systems), participatory simulations, and for collaborative data-gathering.

The main features of a community of practice in fact are:

- Social or professional cohesion
- Direct collaboration
- Enrichment by time and experience
- Motivation to learning
- To contribute to growing community.

Empirical studies state that mobile devices support collaborative activities in different ways: by strengthening the organization and the structure of the learning material and information, by supporting communication among peers and by helping the coordination of the learning activities and by helping the work of the moderator of the community (or the teacher). Other issues reported in different studies about Mobile Learning are: more student engagements, increased interaction among learners and between learners and moderator, enhancing the collaborative environment.

An important element is social interaction in particular for learners who cannot meet in the conventional classroom, campus or coffee shops. Learners talking and communicating with others peers, feel part of a community, support in times of need and acquire trust in the group members (Haythornthwaite, 2000). In general, both moderators (teachers) and learners have found Collaborative Mobile Learning very efficient because mobile devices contributed positively to learners' autonomy, anonymity and motivation.

New technologies in general are very important for Collaborative Mobile Learning. In their paper, Grew and Pagani (2005) analyse e-learning inside university campus by proposing an original platform based on wireless technology and mobile devices to support learning communities. Their project would improve ubiquitous interactivity and cooperation among teachers and learners, that can get online, and interact anywhere and anytime. The services they describe are designed to offer four main functions: (i) to encourage cooperation and interaction among learners and teachers, during the lessons but also outside of the classroom, (ii) to support learners in their training process, (iii) to provide learners with an enhanced information-distribution system for items of interest and (iv) to allow learners access to campus facilities.

This collaborative approach caused a growing interest in using Mobile Learning in different contexts of use, besides educational also in business as well as in tourism field.

DIFFERENT CONTEXTS OF USE OF MOBILE LEARNING

After illustrating the advantages and the social in this paragraph, the different contexts of use,

where it is possible to utilize this new kind of learning, are described.

In particular there are three main fields of use:

- Mobile Learning for education: the goal is to make learning more rapid, efficient and accessible anytime and anywhere.
- Mobile Learning for business: the goal is to reach commercial aims, for training of employees, for professional refresher courses.
- Mobile Learning for social life: the goal is to share information and not formal knowledge in real time with other people, to learn about own interests such as: sport, music, games, cultures, places and so on.

In Table 4, the main contexts of use and the main goal in the respective field are shown.

In the following sections a detailed description of these contexts is given.

Table 4. Contexts of use of Mobile Learning

GOAL	MAIN CONTEXTS OF USE		
	EDUCATION	BUSINESS	SOCIAL LIFE
TO EXCHANGE INFORMATION	To share tasks and home works	To share professional knowledge	To share personal experience or knowledge with others
TO IMPROVE SOCIAL ENGAGEMENT	To have human contact to be not isolated and to sustain impaired	To promote social inclusion of unemployed or people with low skills	Keep in touch for cultural exchanges
TO SUPPORT FRIENDSHIP	To enhance relationship with other learners	To create conditions for ongoing collaboration	To meet people with similar interests
FOR ENTERTAINMENT	Social games	Recreation and after work activities	Relax
TO DEVELOP A COMMON INTERESTS	To improve learning process	Economic, time and resources saving	To enhance knowledge about own interests and hobby

Mobile Learning for Education

Mobile Learning represents a focal element for students, that are involved in different facets (both formal and informal) of educational activities. Mobile phones are becoming social places, where people access daily (the phenomenon is particularly relevant for young people) due to the ubiquity of mobile phones among students and their interactive potential. Internet connection enables users to meet in a virtual place such as: blog, forum, wiki, creating a social network. In particular, the transformation from Web 1.0 to Web 2.0, and their passage on mobile devices, is promoting an interactive approach with which people create, publish, exchange, and share, contents. Indeed, it represents a complete change for communication, because it enables people not only to access and browse contents, but also to create and share them. For these reasons students can interact with other students and contemporaneously be learners as well as authors, stimulating the same learning process. In this way they can also enthusiastically share tasks and homeworks. Mobile Learning has an important role in supporting education to learner, because it enables both to reach a wide segment of people in each place and in each time, and it enables to have a user generated educational content. Students can exchange information files, prepare exams and share project results, collaborate on projects providing visual step-by-step directions. Moreover Mobile Learning helps students to have human contacts with peer and don't feel isolated enhancing interaction and social relations with other. It is clear that young people enthusiasm for mobile phones and other communication and entertainment devices can be used to engage them in learning activities.

An example of use of Mobile Learning in educational field are medical students, that spend a lot time in hospital and they need to consult reference information about diseases, drugs, and create a work collaborative environment.

Mobile Learning for Business

The economy, in our society, is based on knowledge, therefore there is a continous need of formation and orientation. The modern economic system requires adaptation, flexibility and constant updating of knowledge. In this context, the concept of lifelong learning playes an important role. Lifelong learning, according to Smith and Spurling (1999), "relates to people learning consistently throughout their lifespan, and which may start at any age".

The Learning process on Mobile devices allows people to enhance continuously their knowledge and their skills, not at school or college, but providing people of all ages an open access to learning opportunities in a variety of contexts throughout their lifetimes (Bentley, 1998). This method of learning have the advantage of flexibility, accessibility, convenience, allowing lerners to progress according to their schedue. (Benedek, 2003).

In a business context, it is fundamental to improve the skills, update knowledge, manage professionalism. Lifelong learning on mobile devices can be used both by employees to enhance their employment prospects, and by employers to enhance their efficiency.

All companies invest on education and training of their employees in order to improve their performance over the medium and long term, and increase competitiveness on the market. The Mobile Learning can be of great help in this field by facilitating: economic, time and resources saving.

- **Economic saving:** Employees are not forced to long travel to attend courses; moreover it is possible to save on teacher's offsite.
- **Time saving:** Learning "anywhere, anytime" gives the possibility for users to attend refresher course at any place and at any time while they are in business trip, in train, in hotel.

- **Resources saving:** The interaction is managed by the user, the employee decides the rhythm of interaction, he establishes when to study and for how long.

Moreover Mobile Learning allows privacy, each employee don't have worry about the judgement of their colleagues, because he can attend the course in a private environment.

In our modern society where the single person cannot know everything about a particular domain, sharing information and cooperating is of foremost importance for the advance of the society. Complex tasks often require the combined contribution of different kinds of specialized knowledge and are also often more easily achieved as a collaborative activity. Nowadays, the concept of collaboration is itself undergoing a transformation driven by the new-networked technologies. In particular, collaboration, which is unplanned, decentralized and beyond the formal organisation structure has become a valuable resource. Mobile Learning can give a great opportunity for sharing of professional knowledge with far colleagues and to create conditions for ongoing collaboration.

Mobile Learning in business field can be used for social inclusion of unemployed or people with low skills and who are outside of formal education. These people, always, have lack access to computer but use daily mobile phones. Learning on mobile phones can improve basic skills of disadvantaged worker by creating new workplaces and reducing the social exclusion that create new forms of poverty.

A challenge for mobile devices is the retention and reintegration of people off work due to disabilities, thanks to personalization of training process, times flexibility in according to individual learning rhythm, wide accessibility through different media.

Mobile Learning for Social Life

Mobile Learning is also well used for personal knowledge and for own hobby and entertainment. People, in fact can use advanced tools such as: wikis, blog, personal spaces, mush-up on mobile devices to relate to each other's and learn about their own interests.

Wiki, for example, allows users to add contents and also to edit contents supporting collaborative writing, opening discussions and interaction (Desitlets, 2005). Everybody can write everything about music, country, sport and so on and can read everything, or improve what is already written. Wiki is the most important example of collaborative online community and gives to everyone the chance to share their own experience and to collaborate with other members.

A great use is growing in particular in tourism field. Mobile devices make available tools to plan the complete travel and the localization of the places of interest. Among these devices we find the digital interactive maps that supply information on the hotel proximity, restaurants, stores, services, monuments, situated historians, archaeological sites. It is also possible to know the territory classified in different topics (sport, well-being, wine and food, information on traffic, weather forecast). The customer can generate personalized itineraries, search useful services and visualize more specific information on places of interest.

Another chance for learning in tourism is given by portable mp3 devices. In fact, they allow tourists but also learners in travel school, to bring with them, in a very low weight, a large amount of video or audio files, such as thematic guides. Some operators have also started to provide their customers, with mp3 devices already filled by guides about the subject of the travel (a museum tour, a walk in the historical centre of a town, and so on).

The main reasons that allow the tourism to benefit from the use of mobile devices are the new services to travellers on the move. Actually, social network accessible by mobile devices can provide more timely and complete information than paper guidebooks. In fact, a community member can receive an updated answer to her/his question, better than if s/he uses a paper guidebook.

In the future will be more and more use of devices such as a PDA or a Smart Phone that thanks to GPS system, localize not only the tourist on the territory, but also the cultural heritage of the location, by sending users, on their wireless devices, the geo-referenced information with geographic route to reach that particular cultural heritage. The information sent to tourists can be personalized, integrated, complete, clear and multimedia: it can be communicated by text, but also map, video clip, 3D images and audio files. Mobile Learning represents a great chance for tourism field and enhances the information quality that they need.

The widespread diffusion of Mobile Learning in these different contexts of use has determined a growing interest in developing MLSs in the educational process, that are described in the following paragraph.

MOBILE LEARNING SYSTEMS AND MULTIMODAL USER INTERFACES

In literature there are different classifications of MLSs. In particular a way to classify these Systems is to consider two different points-of-view: technological and pedagogical. The technological point-of-view considers the Information and Communication Technologies, on the contrary pedagogical point-of-view considers Educational Technologies (as shown in Figure 1).

According to the technological point-of-view the Information and Communication Technologies of the MLSs, are classified by the type of Mobile devices (ex. Phones, Pdas and IPods) and the type of Communication Technology used to access learning materials (ex. Bluethooth, Irda, GPRS).

According to the pedagogical point-of-view the Education Technologies of the MLSs are classified in the following kinds:

- Technologies, which support synchronous education by giving learners the possibility to communicate in real time with other learn-

Figure 1. A Mobile Learning System classification

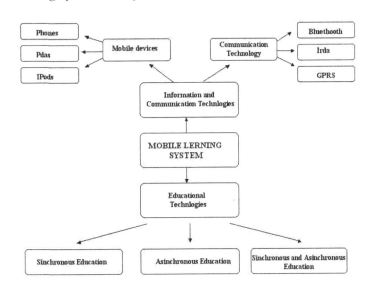

ers or with teachers by voice communication or chat

- Technologies, which support asynchronous education. In these systems learners can not communicate in real time with other learners or with teachers. More often SMS or E-Mail are used to send asynchronous information
- Technologies, which support synchronous and asynchronous education

MLSs implement a different philosophy of learning by making it "situated nowhere" (it occurs everywhere) and transforming interpersonal roles and communications (they are independent from the fixed location or roles). The ubiquitous form of communication allows learners and teachers to micro-coordinate activities without prearranging an agreed-upon time and space. This enhances capabilities for learners to participate in continuous education at a time and location convenient for them, along with useful communication and knowledge-sharing.

The implementation of this philosophy requires to develop an easy and natural interaction. Multimodal User Interfaces support this purpose because they enable users to choose one or more of the multiple interaction modalities according to their needs. The use of multimodal interfaces leads to three benefits over unimodality. First, multimodality improves accessibility to the device, as it provides users with the means to choose among available modalities according to the device's specific usability constraints. Second, multimodality improves accessibility by encompassing a broader spectrum of users, enabling those of different ages and skill levels as well as users with disabilities to access technological devices. Finally, it offers improved flexibility, usability and interaction efficiency. User Interfaces give learners and teachers the possibility to produce, manage and access information, by using several modalities that provide flexible and powerful dialog approaches, enabling users to choose one or more

of the multiple interaction modalities. This allows to enhance naturalness and intuitivity in human machine interaction. Intelligent User Interfaces have the ability to adapt the output to the level of understanding and interests of individual users, typically served by adaptivity and adaptability. Adaptivity is defined as one form of adaptation or as a quality of a system to automatically and autonomically regulate and organise its functioning, appearance and the (order of) information it offers. In contrast to adaptivity, adaptability refers to a possibility of a learner to adapt the system to make it work better. Adaptive factors such as: user profile and context- awareness are on the basis of the development of a personalized learning. Personalized learning aims to engage each student in the learning process in the most productive way to optimise each student's learning potential and success. In order to provide personalized learning is important to first identify characteristics, needs, preferences and behaviours of the user that concur to define his/her profile and affect very much the strategy to respond to his/her stimuli, since they determine what content should be provided and how. Simplest user profiles are the forms that users have to fill before getting access to the learning materials. Another important requirement of personalized learning is the context that we can define as the circumstances in which a learning activity occurs. In literature current research in context-awareness for mobile computing define context as an important focus to learning, because particular services are more important in particular context than others. The situational context knowledge is very important because it allows to adapt the Mobile Learning system to the situation. In particular, a situation is defined by a set of contexts over a period of time, which is relevant to future device actions, and they can be atomic or composite. In detail, an atomic situation is composed of contexts in terms of context operators, including function, arithmetic or comparison operators, and time constraints. By placing mobility of learning, as the object of analysis, is important to better understand how knowledge and skills can be extended across contexts such as home, school, and workplace, and how learning can be managed across life transitions. This will inform how system can be designed to provide pervasive and seamless support for a continuity of learning across physical and social settings. The context specifies *what parameters* the application should adapt. One of the primary aims is to generate both objective and subjective metadata automatically, based on the current context. This will enable more precise retrieval of the data when learning materials are processed or elaborated by learners and teachers.

EXISTING MOBILE LEARNING SYSTEMS

Today a variety of MLSs exists which are used in different spheres of daily life - in the Education, in the Business and in the Social Life. In the following paragraphs we classify existing MLSs according to the different contexts of use.

Educational Context

Typical examples of MLSs used in the Educational context are WELCOME and MobiLP. WELCOME System (Lehner et al. 2002), implemented by the University of Regensburg, aims to support both teachers and students in an innovative way. It can be used as a fundamental software architecture for all wireless learning and administrative services and also for the distribution of learning materials and personalization. The System provides access via WLAN but also using technologies such as WAP, Short Message Service (SMS), AvantGo or Voice XML.

MobiLP (Chan et al. 2003) is a System that aims to provide educational contents and communication services to teachers and learners anytime, anywhere. The different functions of this System are classified into three different classes:

- User functions (available to learners) that include the display of Web materials specified by the teachers, the online quiz system and online chat rooms.
- User functions (available to teachers) that include the input of teacher-specified Web materials, online quiz management, online chat rooms, user profile management and data logs analysis
- Administrator functions that include all management functions such as access control and user account management.

Business Field Context

Two MLSs particular relevant in the business context are GoBinder 2006 and Exact-Mobile. GoBinder 2006 (http://www.agilix.com/www/mobilizer.html) is a System designed to help students to learn more effectively. It enables learners to bring learning contents with them, to take digital notes and annotate and search learning content. It also includes an electronic calendar, assignment manager and contact database to help students stay organized. Students can easily share personal notes and captured content with peers through email. Even part of database can be exported to easily share with other students. GoBinder is so effective that a lot of professionals use it as well (about 35%). The System is designed for expansion through an open architecture, Agilix, that provides APIs (application program interfaces) and the GoBinder SDK (software development kit) that enable GoBinder to be further enhanced.

Exact-Mobile (http://www.learnexact.com/Brochure_exactMobile.pdf) is a System that aims to enable context-aware learning content delivery anywhere and any time. It is the perfect learning solution for all your mobile learners. In fact it is ideal for:

- Sales force education;
- Industrial training and maintenance support;

- Continuous medical and pharmaceutical education;
- Cultural heritage edutainment;
- Blended academic learning programmers.

Social Life Context

MLSs developed to this context are Urban Tapestries and Mobile ELDIT.

Urban Tapestries (http://urbantapestries.net) is a Proboscis project System that explores social and cultural uses of the convergence of place and mobile devices through transdisciplinary research. The system allows to explore and share experience and knowledge of the environment around them. People can author their own virtual annotations of the city, which are accessed via handheld devices such as PDAs and mobile phones.

Mobile ELDIT (Trifonova et al. 2004) is a language translation system. The System is a good tool for studying German and/or Italian languages with PDA devices and for the preparation for the exams in bilingualism in the South Tyrol region. MOBILedit consist of an electronic learner's dictionary (to reduce the load of vocabulary acquisition) a text corpus (that contains all the texts of exams in bilingualism), a tandem module, quizzes and an adaptive tutor.

CONCLUSION

The chapter has described changes that mobile devices improve on the learning process.

Firs of all the chapter has analysed advantages and limitations of Mobile Learning. Many are the advantages both in terms of product quality and in terms of the quality of the learning experience. Mobile Learning offers learners and teachers the possibility of ubiquitous computing: they are in the central focus in a computing environment, flexible access to computing, providing augmented reality. However many are the technological limitation: the size of the text is always uncomfortable for

limited space on the mobile devices displays makes difficult reading for prolonged periods. Until now little attention has been paid to these technological limitations. In this sense future works on this field could be focused on designing recommendations to effectively deal with the issues of main technical features of mobile devices.

Furthermore the chapter has provided a description of different contexts of use of Mobile Learning. Today we can say that the Mobile Learning in the educational field cannot replace an entire traditional course, but it can be well used as support and integration outside the school. Mobile Learning enables to share tasks and homework enthusiastically and can be considered an excellent tool for cohesion and interaction among students by improving social relations.

In business field, Mobile Learning meet requirements of workers mobility and their need to update also allowing economic, time and resources savings to companies.

The field that better responds to this technology is linked to informal, linked to increasing personal knowledge about their free time, their hobbies, their interests. In particular, the field in which these concepts are better applied is the tourism field. Today there are always more tools able to answer all the information needs of tourists on the move: mp3 audio, Personal Digital Assistant (PDA) ecc.

Furthermore the chapter has described MLSs and Multimodal Interfaces. The diffusion of MLSs, has promoted the development of a more natural way for interactive communication because these devices offer new means of interaction. However during the interaction process people have different needs and different features so it is necessary to offer them an easy and natural interaction. Multimodal User Interfaces support this purpose because they have the ability to adapt the output to the level of understanding and interests of individual users. Adaptive factors such as: user profile and context-awareness are on the basis of the development of a personalized adaptive learning. Personalized adaptive learning aims to engage each student in the learning process in the most productive way to optimise each student's learning potential and success.

Finally the chapter has provided a classification of existing MLSs according to the different contexts of use.

REFERENCES

Benedek, A. (2003). Mobile learning and lifelong knowledge acquisition. In K. Nyíri (Ed.), *Mobile studies paradigms and perspectives*. Passagen Verlag.

Bentley, T. (1998). *Learning beyond the classroom: education for a changing world*. London: Routledge.

Chan, Y.Y., Leung, C.H., & Wu, A.K.W., & Chan, S.C. (2003). MobiLP: A mobile learning platform for enhancing lifewide learning. In *Proceedings on the 3rd IEEE International Conference on Advanced Learning Technologies 2003*, Athens, Greece (pp. 457-457).

Clarke, I., Flaherty, T., & Madison, J. (2003). Mobile portals: The development of m-commerce. In B. Mennecke & T. Strader (Eds.), *Mobile commerce: Technology, theory, and applications*. Hershey, PA: IRM Press.

Desilets, A., Paquet, S., & Vinson, N. (2005, October 16-18). Are wikis usable? In *WikiSym Conference*, San Diego, CA.

Dillenbourg, P., Baker, M., Blaye, A., & O'Malley, C. (1996). The evolution of research on collaborative learning. In E. Spada & P. Reiman (Eds.), *Learning in humans and machine: Towards an interdisciplinary learning science*. Oxford, UK: Elsevier.

Ericsson. (2002). *Mobile learning in action: Report on the use of mobile telephones for training*. Retrieved on January 24, 2006, from http://learning.ericsson.net/mlearning2/project_one/mobile_learning.html

Fung, P., Hennessy, S., & O'Shea, T. (1998). Pokketbook computing: A paradigm shift? *Computers in the Schools, 14* (3/4), 109–118.

Grew, P., & Pagani, E. (2005). Towards a wireless architecture for mobile ubiquitous e-learning. *Workshop on Learning Communities in the Era of Ubiquitous Computing*, Milan, Italy.

Haythornthwaite, C., Kazmer, M.M., Robins, J., & Shoemaker, S. (2000). Community development among distance learners: Temporal and technological dimensions. *Journal of Computer Mediated Communication*.

Klopfer, E., Squire, K., & Jenkins, H. (2004). Environmental detectives: PDAs as a window into a virtual simulated world. In M. Kerres, M. Kalz, J. Stratmann & de Witt, C. (Eds.).

Lehner, F., Nösekabel, H., et al. (2002). Wireless e-learning and communication environment. *WELCOME at the University of Regensburg, Workshop on M-Services, 2002*, Lyon, France.

McGreal, R., & Roberts, T. (2001). *A primer on metadata for learning objects*. Retrieved from http://www.elearningmag.com/issues/Oct01/learningobjects.asp.

Naismith, L., Lonsdale, P., Vavoula, G., & Sharples, M. (2004). *Mobile technologies and learning*. Retrieved on April 29, 2005, from http://www.nestafuturelab.org/research/lit_reviews.htm#lr11

Naismith, L., Lonsdale, P., Vavoula, G., & Sharples, M. (2004). *Literature review in mobile technologies and learning* (Lit. Rev. No. 11), University of Birmingham.

Parsons, D., & Ryu, H. (2006). A framework for assessing the quality of mobile learning. In *Proceedings of the 11th International Conference for Process Improvement, Research, and Education (INSPIRE)*, Southampton Solent University, UK.

Pask, G. (1976). *Conversation theory: Applications in education and epistemology.* Amsterdam and New York: Elsevier.

Perry, D. (2003). *Handheld computers (PDAs) in schools.* British Educational Communications and Technology Agency (Becta). Coventry, UK.

Qingyang, G. (2003). *M-Learning: A new development towards more flexible and learner-centred learning.* IATEFL Poland Computer Special Interest Group, Teaching English with Technology.

Robertson, S., Calder, J., Fung, P., Jones, A., & O'Shea, T. (1997). The use and effectiveness of palmtop computers in education. *British Journal of Educational Technology, 28*(3), 177-189.

Rumetshofer, H., & Wöß, W. (2003). XML-based adaptation framework for psychologicaldrivene-learning systems. *Educational Technology & Society, 6*(4), 18-29.

Savill-Smith, C., & Kent, P. (2003). *The use of palmtop computers for learning. A review of the literature* (Lit. Rev.), Learning and Skills Development Agency.

Sharma, S.K., & Kitchens, F.L. (2004). Web services architecture for m-learning. *Electronic Journal on E-Learning, 2*(1), 203–216.

Soloway, J.E., Norris, M.C., Jansen, R.J., Krajcik, R.M., Fishman, B., & Blumenfeld, P. (2001). Making palm-sized computers the PC of choice for K-12. *Learning & Leading with Technology, 28* (7), 32–34, 56–57.

Spiro, R.J., Feltovich, P.J., Jacobson, M.J., & Coulson, R.L. (1991). Cognitive flexibility, constructivism, and hypertext. *Educational Technology,* 24-33.

Stahl, G., Sumner, T., & Repenning, A. (1995). Internet repositories for collaborative learning: Supporting both students and teachers. In *Proceedings of the Computer Supported Collaborative Learning Conference.* Retrieved on May 20, 2004.

Trifonova, A., Knapp, J., Ronchetti, M., & Camper, J. (2004, June 21-26). Mobile ELDIT: Transition from an e-learning to an m-learning system. In *Proceedings of the World Conference on Educational Multimedia, Hypermedia, and Telecommunications (ED-MEDIA 2004),* Lugano, Switzerland (pp. 188-193).

Vygotsky, L. (1978). *Mind in society: The development of higher psychological processes.* Boston: Harvard University Press.

Wang, Y.S., Wu, M.C., & Wang, H.Y. (2008). Investigating the determinants and age and gender differences in the acceptance of mobile learning. *British Journal of Educational Technology.*

Wenger, E., McDermott, R., & Snyder, W.M. (2002). *Cultivating communities of practice: A guide to managing knowledge.* Harvard Business School Press.

Wexler, S., et al. (2007). *The e-learning guild research 3600 report on mobile learning.*

Wilson, B., Sherry, L., Dobrovolny, J., Batty M., & Ryder, M. (2001). Adoption of learning technologies in schools and universities. In H. Adelsberger, B. Collis & J. Pawlowski (Eds.), *Handbook on information technologies for education and training.* New York: Springer-Verlag.

Yordanova, K. (2007). Mobile learning and integration of advanced technologies. In *Education, International Conference on Computer Systems and Technologies-CompSysTech.*

KEY TERMS AND DEFINTIONS

Educational Technology: The study and ethical practices of facilitating learning and improving performance by creating, using and managing appropriate technological processes and resources.

E-Learning: Refers to the delivery of a learning or education program by electronic means. It involves the use of a computer or electronic device (e.g. a mobile phone) in some way to provide training, educational or learning material.

Human-Computer Interaction: Discipline concerned with the design, evaluation and implementation of interactive computing systems for human use and with the study of major phenomena surrounding them.

Information and Communication Technologies: Is an umbrella term that includes all technologies for the manipulation and communication of information.

Mobile Devices: A parent category for mobile telephony, mobile computing, and miscellaneous portable electronic devices, systems, and networks

Mobile Learning: Refers to any activity that allows individuals to be more productive when consuming, interacting with, or creating information, mediated through a mobile device that the individual carries on a regular basis, has reliable connectivity, and fits in a pocket or purse.

Multimodal Interfaces: Refers to systems that allow input and/or output to be conveyed over multiple channels such as speech, graphics, and gesture.

Section IV
Standards, Guidelines, and Evaluation of Multimodal Systems

This section presents the emerging standards and guidelines for mobile multimodal applications design and usability evaluation. Standards for multimodal interaction provided by W3C are described and a visual interaction design process for mobile multimodal systems is sketched. Finally, a selection of "classical" methods and some new developed methods for testing usability in the area of multimodal interfaces are given.

Chapter XXII
Standards for Multimodal Interaction

Deborah A. Dahl
Conversational Technologies, USA

ABSTRACT

This chapter discusses a wide variety of current and emerging standards that support multimodal applications, including standards for architecture and communication, application definition, the user interface, and certifications. It focuses on standards for voice and GUI interaction. Some of the major standards discussed include the W3C multimodal architecture, VoiceXML, SCXML, EMMA, and speech grammar standards. The chapter concludes with a description of how the standards participate in a multimodal application and some future directions.

INTRODUCTION

This chapter will discuss the topic of standards for multimodal interaction. We begin by briefly defining several different categories of standards and talk about the reasons that standards are especially helpful in multimodal systems. There will also be a short discussion of the role of tools in standards and a discussion of requirements for multimodal standards, such as support for distributed systems, extensibility to new modalities, and the ability to support a variety of platforms, such as different types of mobile devices.

Most of the chapter will be focused on specific standards for multimodal interaction and their relationship to each other. We conclude with a few examples of present and future standards-based multimodal systems.

BACKGROUND

Essentially a standard represents an agreement among a community about the meaning of a term or on a way of doing things. In some cases standards are arbitrary, for example, which side of the road you drive on, and in some cases standards represent an agreement on best practices. A standard might be enforced legally, such as building codes, or food safety, or it might just be an agreement within an industry on how to do things. In this section we present a classification of the different types of standards which will lay the groundwork for the discussion of specific standards in the later sections.

Architecture: Components and Communication

Architectural standards define the overall organization of a system, its components, their functions, and how they communicate. In the context of multimodality, we will discuss the World Wide Web Consortium's Multimodal Architecture and Interfaces standard (Barnett, Dahl et al., 2008) and the older DARPA Communicator standard (Bayer, 2005) and describe their commonalities and differences.

Architectural standards describe how functions are allocated among specific hardware/software components and how they communicate. The goal of architectural standards is to ensure interoperability of components, even if they are developed completely independently. The World Wide Web is an excellent example of an architecture which supports independent servers, clients and applications with a high level of interoperability

Carefully-defined communication standards are critically important if components developed by different organizations are to interoperate. Communication takes place at several levels. The underlying protocols, such as TCP/IP and HTTP, will not be discussed here since they are not specific to multimodal systems, but do need to be referenced in multimodal standards in order to insure interoperability. Higher level communication protocols specific to multimodal systems, which we will discuss here, include the high level multimodal interaction life cycle events defined in (Barnett, Dahl et al., 2008) as well as standards defining the format of data payloads for the representation of user input. These include the Extensible MultiModal Annotation (EMMA) specification (Johnston et al., 2007) and InkML (Chee, Froumentin, & Watt, 2006) for representing stylus traces. We will also discuss the Media Resources Control Protocol (MRCP) (Shanmugham & Burnett, 2008). MRCP controls speech media servers which perform the functions of speech recognition, speech synthesis, and speaker recognition. Finally, we discuss some biometric standards, such as the BioAPI, being developed by the BioAPI Consortium.

Application Definition

The next type of standard is a standard language for defining an application, especially through the use of standardized markup. The goal of markup standards is to make applications easier to build by:

- Abstracting away as many procedural details of the application as possible so that the developer can concentrate on functionality
- Supporting reuse

The best-known standardized markup, which defines GUI web applications, is HTML. XML (W3C, 2000), which might be considered a meta-markup, is used as a tool to define other modality-specific markups. This chapter assumes some basic knowledge of XML. We will not discuss these well-known formats in detail. In the specific area of multimodal interaction, we will discuss the following:

State Chart XML (SCXML) (Barnett, Akolkar et al., 2008): A language for defining state charts which is useful for describing the flow of interaction in a multimodal application.

VoiceXML (McGlashan et al., 2004; Matt Oshry et al., 2004): A language for describing spoken dialogs.

Speech Recognition Grammar Specification (SRGS)(Hunt & McGlashan, 2004), Semantic Interpretation for Speech Recognition (SISR) (Van Tichelen & Burke, 2007), Speech Synthesis Markup Language (SSML) (Burnett, Walker, & Hunt, 2004)and Pronunciation Language Specification (PLS)(Paolo Baggia & Scahill, 2004): lower level languages for defining speech resources.

The User Interface

The next type of standard we will discuss has to do with the multimodal user interface. User interface standards are much less rigid than standards that define communication between software components, and are perhaps better described as best practices. User interface standards, unlike architecture and application definition standards, can be less rigid because one side of the interaction involves a human user, who is much more flexible and capable of dealing with ambiguity or fuzziness than the computers involved the other categories. However, while on the one hand human users are much more flexible than computers, on the other hand, the design of the human side of an interaction must take into account specific properties of human beings, such as their physical, perceptual and cognitive capabilities, that are very difficult, if not impossible, to change. Aesthetic and social factors are also important to human users.

Examples of guidelines for multimodal user interfaces include (Larson, 2005), a standard for Mobile Web Best Practices (Rabin & McCathieN-evile) and standards for accessible user interfaces, for example (Caldwell, Cooper, Reid, & Vander-heiden, 2007), all published by the W3C.

Certification

The final category we will discuss is *certification standards*, which define a name or attribute, possibly legally. Certification standards ensure that products with a designated name or attribute have known properties. Measurements are a good example of certification standards in everyday life. For example, because a "meter" has a standard definition, we can know exactly what is meant when we hear that an item is "a meter long". The fact that there are standardized names for food leads to product descriptions such as "chocolaty" or "buttery" when a product doesn't actually legally qualify as "chocolate" or "butter". Certification is generally a process applied to standards in the other categories. For example, the VoiceXML language is a markup language used for defining applications, but the VoiceXML Forum also has a process for certifying VoiceXML platforms and VoiceXML developers. We will discuss certifications only briefly because they are not yet common in the multimodal and voice industries.

The Role of Tools

Another way that standards make applications easier to develop is by promoting the development of tools. When a standard becomes widespread, tool vendors begin to find a market in creating tools to support development using the standard. In addition, tools speed up the development process because they can provide visualizations of the developing application that make it easier for the developer to understand the application as a whole (Dahl, 2005), and they can also automate the generation of some of the routine markup. However, while it's relatively easy to design graphical tools that look attractive and include some of the functionality of the native markup, it's more difficult to make sure that the high level application visualization is truly usable for real applications and has all the functionality of the native markup. Consequently, it's a mistake to assume that tools can always compensate for complex or badly-designed markup languages.

Tools are most commonly used with application definition standards, such as VoiceXML.

The Importance of Standards for Multimodality

Applications involving multimodal functions especially benefit from standards because of the potential complexity of these applications. In a multimodal application, each modality can be very complex in itself, and may require significant expertise in that modality. For example, the voice component of a multimodal application might include complex grammars and prompts. Standards allow modality components to be developed independently by experts and used as components in multimodal systems. Standards that describe generally how to define components also make it possible to extend applications to future modality components.

Requirements for Multimodal Standards

The W3C Multimodal Interaction Working Group has published requirements for multimodal standards(Maes & Saraswat, 2003). Some of the more important requirements include support for distributed applications, extensibility to new modalities, support for accessibility, and the ability to support a variety of platforms, such as different types of mobile devices.

ARCHITECTURE AND COMMUNICATION STANDARDS

Multimodal Architecture

One of the most important standards in multimodal applications is the overall architecture — what components are present, what their functions are, and how they communicate. There must be a balance between an architecture that is general enough for extensibility but at the same time specific enough to support interoperability.

A key early standard for distributed speech applications was the Galaxy Communicator architecture (Bayer, 2005). The architecture, which was intended to be general enough to also support multimodal applications, included a variety of components doing specialized tasks such as speech recognition, dialog management, and language generation, communicating through standardized messages to a central Hub component which coordinated communication among the components. This design enabled different developer to contribute components but did not support distributed web-based applications.

More recently, the W3C Multimodal Interaction Working Group has published a specification for a multimodal architecture (Barnett, Dahl et al., 2008). Figure 1 is an overall picture of the Multimodal Interaction (MMI) Architecture, showing the Runtime Framework, the Interaction Manager, and the Modality Components.

This architecture has some similarities to the Communicator architecture in that it is organized around a central coordinating component, the Runtime Framework (RF), which communicates with modality specific components, called Modality Components (MC's). The MC's are black boxes from the point of view of the RF. The RF and the MC's communicate through a specific set of messages called the Life-Cycle events, listed in Table 1. All of the communication is asynchronous and event-based. All communication goes through the RF; that is, MC's do not communicate directly with each other. This ensures that the RF is aware of the overall state of the application in order to maintain a consistent user interface.

When two or more modalities need to have a tightly-coupled interface (for example, a visual avatar that must be coordinated with a text-to-speech component to display appropriate speech-related

Figure 1. The Multimodal Architecture

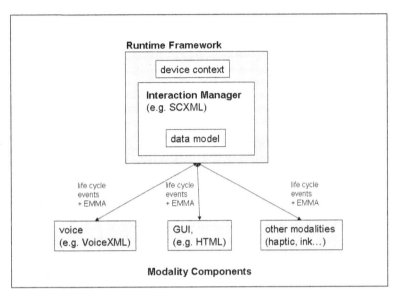

facial movements), they can be combined into a *nested* MC that behaves like a single component from the point of view of the architecture.

The encapsulation of MC's protects individual component data. It also enhances extensibility to new modalities because the interface between the RF and MC's is clean and well-defined.

Another key component of the Multimodal Architecture is the Interaction Manager (IM), which controls the overall flow of the application and provides coordination among components. The IM also is responsible for maintaining a global data model. The format of the data model is not defined in the MMI Architecture, but is expected to be part of the IM. Finally, the device context component maintains information about the device, its properties such as screen size and audio capabilities, and its current state (for example, microphone muted). The device context component uses the Delivery Context: Client Interfaces specification (DCCI) (Waters et al., 2007).

Examples of Life Cycle Event Syntax

The MMI Architecture specification provides examples of the XML syntax for the Life Cycle

events. Here we look at three key events, startRequest, startResponse, and extensionNotification. Examples of the full set of events, as well as an XML Schema defining the event syntax, are contained in the specification.

startRequest (from RF to MC)

The startRequest event is a request from the RF to an MC to start running. Through the "context" attribute, it is associated with a specific session, or *context,* since the MC may be running multiple sessions. The "contentURL" element includes a URI that points to the location of markup to run when the component starts. Alternatively, markup may be included inline in the startRequest event as in the following shown in Box 1.

startResponse (from MC to RF)

The MC is required to respond to the startRequest event with a startResponse event. This is to inform the RF either that the component has started, or that it failed to start due to some error. This example

Box 1.

```
<mmi xmlns="http://www.w3.org/2008/04/mmi-arch" version="1.0">
     <mmi:startRequest source="someURI" context="URI-1" requestID="request-1">
        <mmi:contentURL href="someContentURI" max-age="" fetchtimeout="1s">
     </mmi:startRequest>
  </mmi:mmi>
```

shows a failure, with detailed failure information contained in the statusInfo element.

```
<mmi  xmlns="http://www.w3.org/2008/04/
mmi-arch" version="1.0">
     <mmi:startResponse source="someURI"
context="someURI"  requestID="request-1"
status="failure">
        <mmi:statusInfo>
             NotAuthorized
        </mmi:statusInfo>
     </mmi:startResponse>
  </mmi:mmi>
```

extensionNotification

The extensionNotification event is the point of extensibility for the life cycle events. Information that isn't covered by the other events, in particular most application-specific information, is handled by the extension event. Extensibility is also provided by an optional "data" field which is available in every life cycle event, which carries any additional information about the event. We will see some examples of how the data field of an extensionNotification event is usedbelow. The full set of life cycle events is shown in Table 1.

Extensible MultiModal Annotation (EMMA): Representing User Input

So far we've discussed the events that communicate between components, but what is it that they're communicating? In many cases, the message is about what the user said or did at the user interface. EMMA (Johnston et al., 2007) is designed to represent user inputs in a modality-independent way, especially inputs using human languages, such as speech, typing, handwriting and sign languages.

Key features of EMMA include:

1. Decoupling of speech recognition from a spoken dialog manager.
2. Providing a uniform interpretation of inputs that were created by speech, typing, or text, so that the interaction manager doesn't have to deal with modality-specific details.
3. Making it easier to deal with composite multimodality—two or more simultaneous inputs in different modalities, such as a combination of voice and pointing.
4. Because EMMA allows inputs to be annotated, for example with confidences, it can be used to represent the level of uncertainty of an input as well as alternate possibilities. This is familiar with this in speech and handwriting recognition, but it can also be used in traditional GUI applications, in particular for accessibility. For example, the exact location of a mouse click might be uncertain if the user has a tremor.
5. Standardized archiving format for user inputs.

With respect to the life cycle events, EMMA data is typically contained in the "data" tag of the extension or done life cycle events.

EMMA is currently being used in a variety of language projects. For example, the XM-flow language (Li, Cao, Chou, & Liu, 2006) uses EMMA

Table 1. Full Set of MMI Life Cycle Events

Event	From	To	Purpose
newContextRequest	Modality	Runtime Framework	Request new context
newContextResponse	Runtime Framework	Modality	Send new context id
prepareRequest	Runtime Framework	Modality	Pre-load markup
prepareResponse	Modality	Runtime Framework	Acknowledge prepareRequest
startRequest	Runtime Framework	Modality	Run markup
startResponse	Modality	Runtime Framework	Acknowledge startRequest
done	Modality	Runtime Framework	Finished running
cancelRequest	Runtime Framework	Modality	Stop processing
cancelResponse	Modality	Runtime Framework	Acknowledge cancelRequest
pauseRequest	Runtime Framework	Modality	Suspend processing
pauseResponse	Modality	Runtime Framework	Acknowledge prepareRequest
resumeRequest	Runtime Framework	Modality	Resume processing
resumeResponse	Modality	Runtime Framework	Acknowledge resumeRequest
extensionNotification	either	either	Send data values
clearContext	Runtime Framework	Modality	Deactivate context
statusRequest	Runtime Framework	Modality	Request component status
statusResponse	Modality	Runtime Framework	Acknowledge statusRequest

to represent multimodal semantics in a portable and extensible fashion. West, et. al. (West, Apted, & Quigley, 2004) describe a system where input agents send application defined, modality neutral, input to application agents in the form of EMMA. In the SmartWeb Project ("SmartWeb: Mobile Broadband Access to the Semantic Web,"), the internal communication format is a derivative of the EMMA standard, as described, for example in (Porzel, Zorn, Loos, & Malaka, 2006). EMMA is also being used to represent information in the MI-MUS (MultIModal, University of Seville) corpus, which is the result of multimodal Wizard of Oz (WOZ) experiments conducted at the University of Seville (Portillo, Valdés, Carredano, & Pérez García, 2006). From these examples of recent papers, it is clear that EMMA is increasingly being used throughout the research community as a standard for language annotation. In addition, the EMMA format is now available in commercial

speech recognition technology as an option for processors conforming to Media Resource Control Protocol Version 2, (MRCP v2) a standard from the Internet Engineering Task Force used for distributed speech processing (Shanmugham & Burnett, 2008).

Figure 2 shows an example of how EMMA could be used to represent the utterance "play something by Beethoven". The "composer", "action" and "name" tags indicate the application semantics portion of the EMMA document, which represents the interpretation of the utterance created by the processor of the utterance. There is also an <info> section with general information about the application, and a <model> section, which provides a data model for the utterance. The fourteen attributes of the <interpretation> element contain standard annotations about the utterance, including timestamps ("start" and "end"), the language ("en-us"), and the processor

Figure 2. EMMA for "play something by Beethoven"

```
<emma:emma version="1.0"  xmlns:emma="http://www.w3.org/2003/04/emma"
xmlns:xsi="http://www.w3.org/2001/XMLSchema-instance"
xsi:schemaLocation="http://www.w3.org/2003/04/emma  http://www.w3.org/TR/2007/CR-
emma-20071211/emma.xsd" xmlns="http://www.example.com/example">
 <emma:info>
   <application>music</application>
 </emma:info>
 <emma:model id="musicModel">
  <model class="music">
   <action></action>
   <composer></composer>
   <name></name>
   <artist></artist>
   <id>musicModel</id>
  </model>
 </emma:model>
 <emma:interpretation
        id="interp18"
        emma:duration="3305"
        emma:model-ref="musicModel"
        emma:confidence="1.0"
        emma:medium="acoustic"
        emma:mode="speech"
        emma:verbal="true"
        emma:start="1207938164320"
        emma:uninterpreted="false"
        emma:function="dialog"
        emma:dialog-turn="5"
        emma:end="1207938167625"
        emma:lang="en-us"
        emma:tokens="play something by Beethoven">
      <composer>ludwig_van_beethoven</composer>
      <action>play</action>
      <name>anything</name>
  </emma:interpretation>
 </emma:emma>
```

confidence (in this case 1.0). The application-specific sections allow the developer to include arbitrary information about the utterance, and thus provides extensibility. Because the "mode" attribute can be any string, EMMA can represent new modes that weren't anticipated when EMMA was designed.

EMMA also contains some interesting provisions for representing composite multimodal inputs, such as speech combined with a pointing gesture, as in "draw a circle here". Each individual modality, speech and pointing, would generate an EMMA document. The grammar for the speech component would contain a special token "emma:hook", which indicates that the semantics of that position is to be provided by a non-speech modality. These two EMMA documents would be combined by means of another processor to create a third, composite document, where the "mode" attribute would be "emma:mode="speech gui". The composite document can optionally either contain or refer to the two original documents.

A final capability of EMMA worth noting is the ability to represent lattices of alternative speech or gesture results., as shown in Figure 3. A lattice is a much more compact representation of alternatives than an nbest list because duplicates are largely eliminated. It is especially useful for representing multimodal inputs where there are many alternatives and an n-best list would consequently be very large.

InkML: A Format for StylusInput

Pen or stylus input is often used in multimodal applications, particularly those involving mobile devices or tablets. It is particularly useful when the user is standing or walking and has to hold the device with one hand, when the device is very small, such as a PDA or a mobile phone, or when the input is graphical, as in the case of a sketch. InkML is an XML-based standard under development by the W3C Multimodal Interaction Working Group which focuses on standard representations of the electronic ink created by a stylus or other

pointing device. The InkML standard can be employed in multimodal applications for functions like text input, signature verification, and shared whiteboards. Figure 4 shows the InkML representing a handwritten word "hello". Each <trace> element represents a single stroke, and contains the coordinates of points along the stroke.

For more information on InkML, see (Chee et al., 2006; Watt, 2007).

MRCP: Messages to and from Speech Engines

Media Resources Control Protocol (MRCP) (Shanmugham & Burnett, 2008) is a protocol for controlling remote speech resources, including recording, speech recognition, text-to-speech and speaker verification. This protocol allows, for example, an application to reside on a client or on a different server from the speech services it needs. Some of the types of functions that MRCP provides include setting parameters like confidence thresholds, timeouts, grammars and maximum length of a returned nbest list. MRCP servers can also generate events like "start of input" and "recognition complete".

Figure 3. EMMA representation of a lattice

```
<emma:lattice initial="1" final="8">
    <emma:arc from="1" to="2">flights</emma:arc>
    <emma:arc from="2" to="3">to</emma:arc>
    <emma:arc from="3" to="4">boston</emma:arc>
    <emma:arc from="3" to="4">austin</emma:arc>
    <emma:arc from="3" to="4">houston</emma:arc>
    <emma:arc from="3" to="4">anchorage</emma:arc>
    <emma:arc from="4" to="5">from</emma:arc>
    <emma:arc from="5" to="6">portland</emma:arc>
    <emma:arc from="5" to="6">oakland</emma:arc>
    <emma:arc from="6" to="7">today</emma:arc>
    <emma:arc from="7" to="8">please</emma:arc>
    <emma:arc from="6" to="8">tomorrow</emma:arc>
</emma:lattice>
```

Figure 4. InkML representation of "hello"

```
<ink>
  <trace>
    10 0, 9 14, 8 28, 7 42, 6 56, 6 70, 8 84, 8 98, 8 112, 9 126, 10 140,
    13 154, 14 168, 17 182, 18 188, 23 174, 30 160, 38 147, 49 135,
    58 124, 72 121, 77 135, 80 149, 82 163, 84 177, 87 191, 93 205
  </trace>
  <trace>
    130 155, 144 159, 158 160, 170 154, 179 143, 179 129, 166 125,
    152 128, 140 136, 131 149, 126 163, 124 177, 128 190, 137 200,
    150 208, 163 210, 178 208, 192 201, 205 192, 214 180
  </trace>
  <trace>
    227 50, 226 64, 225 78, 227 92, 228 106, 228 120, 229 134,
    230 148, 234 162, 235 176, 238 190, 241 204
  </trace>
  <trace>
    282 45, 281 59, 284 73, 285 87, 287 101, 288 115, 290 129,
    291 143, 294 157, 294 171, 294 185, 296 199, 300 213
  </trace>
  <trace>
    366 130, 359 143, 354 157, 349 171, 352 185, 359 197,
    371 204, 385 205, 398 202, 408 191, 413 177, 413 163,
```

Biometric Standards

Biometric technologies enable computers to recognize people on the basis of their physical or behavioral properties. Biometric technologies include speaker recognition, face recognition, fingerprint identification, iris recognition, and a wide variety of other ways of identifying people. Biometrics will increasingly become part of multimodal applications. Speaker recognition in particular, lends itself well to applications that include speech. See (Wayman, Jain, Maltoni, & Maio, 2005) for an overview of biometric technologies and (Markowitz, 2005) for a review of using speaker recognition and speaker identification in speech applications. Biometric components can be treated as Modality Components in the MMI Architecture, for example, by using the "function" attribute of EMMA to designate an input as "verification" or "identification".

APPLICATION DEFINITION

So far the discussion has focused on the architectural components and communication among these components in multimodal systems. The next question is, once an architecture has been defined, how are actual applications built? Clearly, applications can be built with procedural programming languages, but basing applications on declarative markup can greatly simplify their development. Consequently, this section will focus on approaches for defining multimodal applications based on markup languages, in most cases XML-based markup.

Two markup-based approaches to defining multimodal applications combining speech with HTML interfaces were published in 2001, XHTML+Voice (Cross, Axelsson, McCobb, Raman, & Wilson, 2003) and Speech Application Language Tags (SALT)(SALT Forum, 2002). While these approaches served to stimulate interest in multimodal standards, they were both limited by lack of support for distributed applications and not being extensible to other modalities.

Flow Control and Interaction Management

State Chart XML (SCXML) (Barnett, Akolkar et al., 2008) is an important new standard for describing the flow of an application and for managing interactions among components, and is a natural choice for the Interaction Manager in a Multimodal Architecture implementation. SCXML is an XML syntax for describing state machines with the semantics of Harel State Charts (Harel & Polti, 1998). In SCXML, an application is represented as a set of states and transitions. By sending life cycle events to MC's, an SCXML interpreter can start and stop modalities and receive back user input. The SCXML interpreter can transition to other states through an application, based on user input. The Call Control Markup Language (CCXML) (Auburn, 2007) can also be used to control the flow of an application, although its primary function is to control telephony functions.

The Voice Modality

In this section we discuss components that can be used to build the voice component of a multimodal system. Voice modality components might be as basic as just a speech recognizer or a text to speech synthesizer, they could combine speech recognition and speech synthesis or audio playback, or they could also include dialog management and flow control in addition to purely speech functions. VoiceXML (Hocek & Cuddihy, 2002; Larson, 2003; McGlashan et al., 2004; Miller, 2002; Matt Oshry et al., 2007; Sharma & Kunins, 2002; Shukla, Dass, & Gupta, 2002) is a well-known and widely used XML language for developing speech applications that includes support for speech recognition, speech synthesis, audio playback, DTMF interpretation and dialog management.

A VoiceXML application consists of a set of related VoiceXML *forms*. A form is very much like a frame in a frame-based dialog system. It consists of a set of fields, each containing a prompt and possibly a speech recognition grammar. At a high level, when the user speaks an utterance in response to the prompt for a field, a field variable is set with the value of the field based on the spoken utterance. When all of the fields in a form have been filled, the field variables and their values are submitted to a web server for further action. At a more detailed level, the behavior of a VoiceXML application is determined by an algorithm called the Form Interpretation Algorithm (FIA), which performs the basic tasks of interacting with the user; gathering field values, handling errors, reprompting a user who doesn't speak, and transitioning to other forms.

VoiceXML was designed for speech-only applications. As a consequence, VoiceXML 2.1 (the most recent version) is not a good fit for multimodal applications, primarily for two related reasons:

It cannot in general receive events from external software, specifically software functioning as the IM in the MMI Architecture

It assumes that the VoiceXML application is the controller of the overall dialog, whereas in a multimodal application, the IM is the overall controller.

The second drawback isn't as serious as the first one, because a specific VoiceXML form used in a multimodal application could be written as single-field forms, thus eliminating most of the dialog control functionality of the VoiceXML component, and using VoiceXML basically as a speech controller. However, the first one is quite serious, because it means that the VoiceXML component cannot receive the life cycle events. In the short term, VoiceXML can be used in multimodal applications through a Call Control Markup Language (CCXML)(Auburn, 2007) shell that can receive events and which can stop and start VoiceXML sessions. In the long term, future versions of VoiceXML may eventually include the ability to receive external events directly, which would make VoiceXML much more suitable for multimodal applications.

Two earlier languages, XHTML+Voice (IBM, 2003) and the Speech Applications Language Tags (SALT) (SALT Forum, 2002) were proposed as standards for combining voice and GUI; however, they are limited to applications that require only the speech and GUI modalities, and where all resources are located locally on the client.

The MRCP protocol, as discussed above, could also provide the basis for a speech modality component through middleware that supports the life cycle events.

SRGS and SISR: Defining Grammars and Semantics for Speech Recognizers

Speech recognizers require some form of a *language model,* or a description of the words and phrases that the recognizer can recognize. The language model can be a grammar or a statistical model, based on word patterns collected by analyzing large corpora of text. The statistical approach has not been standardized, although one initial effort at standardization is available in (Brown, Kellner, & Raggett, 2001). Here we will focus on grammar standardization. One early proposal for a standard grammar format was the format used in the Java Speech API (JSAPI) ("Java Speech API," 1998), the Java Speech Grammar Format (JSGF). This was an Augmented BNF format for context-free grammars. The JSGF format was the basis of the W3C's Speech Recognition Grammar Specification (SRGS) (Hunt & McGlashan, 2004), which includes both an ABNF format and an XML format.

Returning values from matched grammar rules is a way to support many different ways of saying the same thing in an application, without requiring the application logic to handle all the variations itself. Return values can also translate phrases that a user might utter, such as "Chicago airport", into phrases that a user is unlikely to utter but which are more meaningful to the application, like "ORD". Semantic Interpretation for Speech Recognition (SISR) (Van Tichelen & Burke, 2007) is a standard format for representing the values to be returned after a speech grammar match. SISR semantic tags are based on the ECMAScript Compact Profile ("Standard ECMA-327 ECMAScript 3rd Edition Compact Profile," 2001).Figure 5 shows an example of one rule of an SRGS grammar that recognizes the phrase *I would like a small coca cola and three large pizzas with pepperoni and mushrooms*, taken from the SISR specification. We see one rule, the "order" rule, which refers to two other rules, "drink" and "pizza", found elsewhere in the document.

Speech Synthesis Markup Language (SSML)

Text to speech engines have internal techniques to determine how to pronounce words, but sometimes it's desirable to adjust the default pronunciations of the engines by marking up text with pronunciation annotations. Speech Synthesis Markup Language (SSML) (Burnett et al., 2004) is a standard for defining pronunciations for text to speech engines. Using SSML, developers can specify the natural language of the text to be spoken, the speaking rate, pitch, breaks, prosody, different voices, volume, emphasis and other attributes of the text. In addition, if it is necessary to provide a precise pronunciation of a particular word, phonemes can also be represented in SSML. SSML documents can either stand alone or they can be incorporated into a document defining a spoken dialog, such as a VoiceXML document. Figure 6 shows an example from the SSML spec illustrating the markup for "emphasis". As in the case of many subjective aspects of TTS, the exact meaning of "emphasis" is determined by the synthesizer, taking into account such considerations as the language and the specific voice being used.

Figure 5. SISR Tags

```
"I would like a small coca cola and three large pizzas with pepperoni and mushrooms."
<rule id="order">
    I would like a
    <ruleref uri="#drink"/>
    <tag>out.drink = new Object();      out.drink.liquid=rules.drink.type;
        out.drink.drinksize=rules.drink.drinksize;</tag>
    and
    <ruleref uri="#pizza"/>
    <tag>out.pizza=rules.pizza;</tag>
```

Figure 6. SSML markup for emphasis

```
<?xml version="1.0"?>
<speak version="1.0" xmlns="http://www.w3.org/2001/10/synthesis"
        xmlns:xsi="http://www.w3.org/2001/XMLSchema-instance"
        xsi:schemaLocation="http://www.w3.org/2001/10/synthesis
            http://www.w3.org/TR/speech-synthesis/synthesis.xsd"
        xml:lang="en-US">
    That is a <emphasis> big </emphasis> car!
    That is a <emphasis level="strong"> huge </emphasis>
    bank account!
</speak>
```

PLS: Defines How Words are Pronounced

The last voice modality specification we will discuss is the Pronunciation Lexicon Specification (PLS) (Paolo Baggia, Bagshaw, Burnett, Carter, & Scahill, 2008). PLS is a format for a lexicon of pronunciations of words. It is not language-specific, and it would generally be used in a multimodal application as an adjunct to a speech recognizer or text to speech system. PLS implementations must support at a minimum pronunciations written in the International Phonetic Alphabet (IPA) ("International Phonetic Alphabet,"). Figure 7 show a sample PLS entry for the Japanese word "nihongo", showing how three different graphemes can be associated with one pronunciation.

The Visual Modality

The best-known markup for defining a visual interface is HTML, the language used for web pages. We won't discuss HTML in detail here because there are many other resources for learning about HTML. It's worth pointing out; however, that HTML lacks certain features that would be desirable in a visual modality component within the MMI Architecture, specifically the ability to receive events from a server. Newer technologies like the server-sent events proposed for HTML 5 (Hickson & Hyatt, 2008) may address this problem, but in the meantime, techniques like having the browser poll the server for pending Interaction Manager generated life cycle events can be used to address this issue.

Figure 7. Sample PLS entry (from the PLS spec)

```
<?xml version="1.0" encoding="UTF-8"?>
<lexicon version="1.0"
    xmlns="http://www.w3.org/2005/01/pronunciation-lexicon"
    xmlns:xsi="http://www.w3.org/2001/XMLSchema-instance"
    xsi:schemaLocation="http://www.w3.org/2005/01/pronunciation-lexicon
      http://www.w3.org/TR/2007/CR-pronunciation-lexicon-20071212/pls.xsd"
    alphabet="ipa" xml:lang="jp">
 <lexeme>
  <grapheme>nihongo<!-- "Romaji" --></grapheme>
  <grapheme>日本語<!-- "Kanji" --></grapheme>
  <grapheme>にほんご<!-- "Hiragana" --></grapheme>
  <phoneme>ɲihoŋo
    <!-- IPA string is: "&#x0272;iho&#x014B;o --></phoneme>
 </lexeme>
</lexicon>
```

Figure 8. SVG markup for "Hello, out there"

```
<?xml version="1.0" standalone="no"?>
<!DOCTYPE svg PUBLIC "-//W3C//DTD SVG 1.1//EN"
 "http://www.w3.org/Graphics/SVG/1.1/DTD/svg11.dtd">
<svg width="10cm" height="3cm" viewBox="0 0 1000 300"
    xmlns="http://www.w3.org/2000/svg" version="1.1">
  <desc>Example text01 - 'Hello, out there' in black</desc>
  <text x="250" y="150"
      font-family="Verdana" font-size="55" fill="black" >
   Hello, out there
  </text>
  <!-- Show outline of canvas using 'rect' element -->
  <rect x="1" y="1" width="998" height="298"
      fill="none" stroke="black" stroke-width="2" />
        </svg>
```

Another possibility for a standard approach to the visual modality is Scalable Vector Graphics (SVG)(Ferraiolo, Fujisawa, & Jackson, 2003). SVG is a markup for vector graphics, and it can be used to define displays of graphical elements, text and animations. SVG can be displayed in many browsers, or in standalone applications and can be combined with HTML. Ferraiolo, Fuijisawa, & Jackson, 2003. shows the SVG markup for the text "Hello, out there", rendered in Figure 9.

Building New Modality Components

A very interesting feature of the MMI architecture results from the fact that the API between the RF and the MC's is generically defined as consisting of the life cycle events and EMMA. This means that to define a new type of modality component, an implementer has a fairly well-defined task; that is, to specify any modality-specific extension-Notification events and/or data fields required by

Figure 9. Rendered SVG

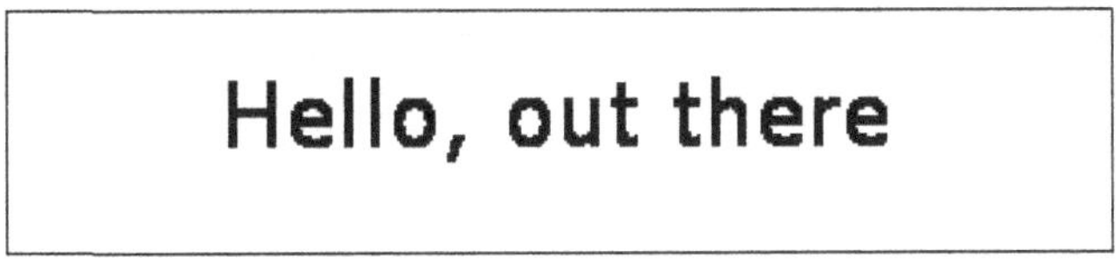

Hello, out there

the modality. This may be a complex task, but in many cases API's to modality components may already exist that can form the basis for defining a modality component. For example, for speech components, API's like the Java Speech API (JSAPI)("Java Speech API," 1998), the Microsoft Speech API (SAPI) (Microsoft, 2007) and MRCP (Shanmugham & Burnett, 2008) have already been defined. Instructions for defining modality components and an example are included in the MMI Architecture specification (Barnett, Dahl et al., 2008)

THE MULTIMODAL USER INTERFACE

As mentioned above, recommendations for user interfaces tend to be best practices or guidelines rather than strict standards. They can be more flexible because users are more able to deal with variation than software. It is often difficult to give hard and fast rules for applications that is are complex as a multimodal user interface.

(Larson, 2006) addresses the topic of multimodal user interfaces. This paper presents four major principles of multimodal user interaction.

1. Satisfy real-world constraints (for example, if the user's hands are busy, use speech)
2. Communicate clearly, concisely, and consistently with users (for example, phrase all prompts consistently)
3. Help users recover quickly and efficiently from errors (for example, present words recognized by the speech recognition system on the display)

4. Make users comfortable (for example, always present the current system status to the user).

Accessibility is often mentioned as a motivation for multimodal applications. While not dealing specifically with multimodal applications, (Caldwell et al., 2007) presents good general accessibility guidelines that are often relevant to multimodal applications.

Another commonly mentioned motivation for multimodality is the small screens and keypads found on today's mobile devices make GUI interaction difficult. The Mobile Web Best Practices Working Group at the W3C has prepared a specification on best user interface practices for the mobile web (Rabin & McCathieNevile, 2006), focusing on the GUI interface.

CERTIFICATION STANDARDS

There are few certification programs that are relevant to multimodality, largely because the field is relatively new. We will briefly mention two certifications here.

For certifying that an application's user interface is appropriate for mobile devices, (Owen & Rabin, 2007) provides tests for certifying that an application is "MobileOK", based on the Mobile Web Best Practices specification (Rabin & McCathieNevile, 2006) described in Section 0.

The VoiceXML Forum (www.voicexmlforum. org) has developed programs for certifying platforms as VoiceXML compliant and for certification of VoiceXML developers.

PUTTING IT ALL TOGETHER: A VOICE SEARCH APPLICATION

As an example of putting standards together to create applications, we can consider a multimodal voice search application. This kind of application would enable the user to ask for a particular type of information, for example, "Where's the nearest parking garage?", or "Where's the nearest Italian restaurant?" This is a good multimodal application in mobile environments because speech input allows the user to cut through layers of menus and to avoid using the tiny keypads found on mobile devices. On the other hand, graphical display of the information retrieved in the search has two advantages: first, it enables complex information to persist and second, it is also possible to provide maps and images as part of the search results that would be impossible to convey by voice alone. The application might also make use of the haptic modality by allowing the user to scroll through a list of results with a back and forth motion of the device. This hypothetical application would go through the following steps:

1. Startup
    a. User clicks a button on a web page to request a session
    b. The SCXML Interaction Manager (IM) on the server starts the application
    c. The IM sends an HTML page to web browser on the user's device through a life cycle event (startRequest)
    d. The IM issues another startRequest which sends a VoiceXML page to a remote voice browser. This page defines the voice portion of the multimodal interaction
2. Basic Search Operation
    a. The user speaks a search request "show me parking garages near here"
    b. The voice browser converts this request to EMMA and sends it back to the IM as part of a "done" life cycle event

c. The IM submits the request to a search engine
d. The IM receives the search results as an HTML page
e. The IM sends the new HTML page with search results to the web browser
f. The user moves the device back and forth to page through results. The user's motions are interpreted by the haptic modality interpreter located on the device. An extensionNotification event is sent to the IM requesting a new result after each motion.
g. The search ends when the user says "that one", which sends an extensionNotification event to the IM indicating the user's choice.
h. The IM submits a request to a routing server, receives a page, and then sends the new HTML page with the route to the requested location to the user's device.

FUTURE TRENDS

Distributed Applications

Yudkowsky (Yudkowsky, 2005) discusses the concept of "disaggregation"; that is, how breaking down systems previously considered to be monolithic into components creates market opportunities. Standards are a key aspect of disaggregation, because they promote the independent development of interoperable components. As an example, standards could support multilingual dialog applications like the one shown in Figure 10. Figure 10 shows a configuration of web services cooperating to provide distributed multilingual speech recognition, handwriting recognition, and natural language parsing services for French and English inputs, as well as language-independent dialog management and archiving. Because each service uses the EMMA language for representing

Figure 10. Distributed multimodal application

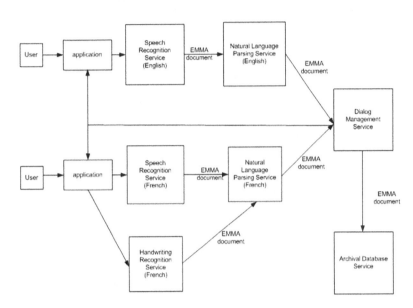

user inputs, the components could be developed independently, by language and modality experts, and hosted on different servers.

Future Modalities

A key requirement for multimodal standards is to be able to accommodate future modalities. Because of the modality-independent nature of the MMI Architecture and EMMA, they are both very adaptable to future modalities. In the near future, haptic, or motion-based user inputs will become more common. Systems integrating ink and speech, for example, as described in (Adler & Davis, 2007), are being explored. Biometric inputs are also becoming important in general, and the variety of biometrics is also increasing rapidly. Simple brain-wave interpreters are also possible now and could potentially be integrated into future multimodal systems.

CONCLUSION

There exists a wide range of standards, both well-established and emerging, that are applicable to the development of multimodal applications. Together this set of standards provides a comprehensive suite of capabilities for enabling multimodal applications based on both current and future modalities. Table 2 summarizes the standards discussed in this chapter, along with the organizations that are responsible for them as well as their current standardization status. It is hoped that these standards will lay the foundation for many valuable current and future multimodal applications.

ACKNOWLEDGMENT

I would like to thank the members of the W3C Multimodal Interaction Working Group and the W3C Voice Browser Working Group for many

Table 2. Summary of multimodal standards

Standard	Organization	Status
Architecture and Communication		
MMI Architecture	W3C (Multimodal Interaction WG)	W3C Working Draft
EMMA	W3C (Multimodal Interaction WG)	W3C Candidate Recommendation
InkML	W3C (Multimodal Interaction WG)	W3C Last Call Working Draft
MRCPv2	IETF (SpeechSC WG)	Internet Draft
Biometrics	Various (ANSI, ISO)	Various
Application Definition		
VoiceXML 2.0 and 2.1	W3C (Voice Browser WG)	W3C Recommendation
SRGS/SISR	W3C (Voice Browser WG)	W3C Recommendation
SSML	W3C (Voice Browser WG)	W3C Recommendation
PLS	W3C (Voice Browser WG)	W3C Recommendation
SCXML	W3C (Voice Browser WG)	W3C Working Draft
SVG	W3C (SVG WG)	W3C Recommendation
(X)HTML	W3C (HTML and XHTML WG's)	W3C Recommendation
User Interface		
MMI Guidelines	W3C (Multimodal Interaction WG)	W3C Note
Web Content Accessibility Guidelines 2.0 (WCAG 2.0)	W3C (Web Content Accessibility Guidelines WG)	W3C Candidate Recommendation
Mobile Web Best Practices	W3C (Mobile Web Best Practices WG)	W3C Recommendation
Certifications		
MobileOK tests	W3C (Mobile Web Best Practices WG)	W3C Last Call Working Draft
VoiceXML Platform Certification	VoiceXML Forum	Program is in place
VoiceXML Developer Certification	VoiceXML Forum	Program is in place

interesting standards discussions over the past nine years which have lead to the development of many of the standards discussed in this chapter. I would also like to thank the World Wide Web Consortium for its support of this work.

REFERENCES

Adler, A., & Davis, R. (2007, August 2-3). *Speech and sketching: An empirical study of multimodal interaction.* Paper presented at the Fourth Eurographics Conference on Sketch Based Interfaces and Modeling, Riverside, CA.

Auburn, R.J. (2007, June). *Voice browser call control: CCXML version 1.0.* Retrieved from http://www.w3.org/TR/ccxml/

Baggia, P., Bagshaw, P., Burnett, D., Carter, J., & Scahill, F. (2008). *Pronunciation lexicon specification (PLS) version 1.0.* Retrieved from http://www.w3.org/TR/pronunciation-lexicon/

Baggia, P., & Scahill, F. (2004). *Pronunciation lexicon specification (PLS) version 1.0 requirements.* Retrieved from http://www.w3.org/TR/2004/WD-lexicon-reqs-20041029/

Barnett, J., Akolkar, R., Bodell, M., Burnett, D.C., Carter, J., McGlashan, S., et al. (2008). *State chart XML (SCXML): State machine notation for control abstraction*. Retrieved from http://www.w3.org/TR/scxml/

Barnett, J., Dahl, D.A., Kliche, I., Tumuluri, R., Yudkowsky, M., Bodell, M., et al. (2008, April 14). *Multimodal architecture and interfaces*. Retrieved from http://www.w3.org/TR/mmi-arch/

Bayer, S. (2005). Building a standards and research community with the galaxy communicator software infrastructure. In D.A. Dahl (Ed.), *Practical spoken dialog systems* (Vol. 26, pp. 166-196). Dordrecht: Kluwer Academic Publishers.

Brown, M.K., Kellner, A., & Raggett, D. (2001). *Stochastic language models (n-gram) specification*. Retrieved from http://www.w3.org/TR/ngram-spec/

Burnett, D.C., Walker, M.R., & Hunt, A. (2004). *W3C speech synthesis markup language (SSML)*. Retrieved from http://www.w3.org/TR/speech-synthesis/

Caldwell, B., Cooper, M., Reid, L.G., & Vanderheiden, G. (2007). *Web content accessibility guidelines 2.0*. Retrieved from http://www.w3.org/TR/2007/WD-WCAG20-20071211/

Chee, Y.-M., Froumentin, M., & Watt, S.M. (2006). *Ink markup language*. Retrieved from http://www.w3.org/TR/InkML

Cross, C., Axelsson, J., McCobb, G., Raman, T.V., & Wilson, L. (2003). *XHTML + voice profile 1.1*. Retrieved from http://www-306.ibm.com/software/pervasive/multimodal/x+v/11/spec.htm

Dahl, D.A. (2005). Visualization tools for designing spoken dialogs. In D.A. Dahl (Ed.), *Practical spoken dialog systems*.

Ferraiolo, J., Fujisawa, J., & Jackson, D. (2003). *Scalable vector graphics (SVG) 1.1 specification*. Retrieved from http://www.w3.org/TR/SVG11/

Harel, D., & Polti, M. (1998). *Modeling reactive systems with statecharts: The statemate approach*. New York: McGraw-Hill.

Hickson, I., & Hyatt, D. (2008). *HTML 5 a vocabulary and associated APIs for HTML and XHTML*. Retrieved from http://www.w3.org/TR/html5/

Hocek, A., & Cuddihy, D. (2002). *Definitive voiceXML*. Prentice-Hall.

Hunt, A., & McGlashan, S. (2004). *W3C speech recognition grammar specification (SRGS)*. Retrieved from http://www.w3.org/TR/speech-grammar/

IBM. (2003). *X + V 1.1*. Retrieved from http://www-3.ibm.com/software/pervasive/multimodal/x+v/11/spec.htm

International Phonetic Alphabet. Retrieved from http://www.arts.gla.ac.uk/ipa/index.html

Java Speech API. (1998). Retrieved from http://java.sun.com/products/java-media/speech/

Johnston, M., Baggia, P., Burnett, D., Carter, J., Dahl, D.A., McCobb, G., et al. (2007). *EMMA: Extensible multimodal annotation markup language*. Retrieved from http://www.w3.org/TR/emma/

Larson, J.A. (2003). *VoiceXML: Introduction to developing speech applications*. Upper Saddle River, NJ: Prentice Hall.

Larson, J.A. (2005). Voice user interface design for novice and experienced users. In D.A. Dahl (Ed.), *Practical spoken dialog systems*. Kluwer Academic Press.

Larson, J.A. (2006). *Common sense suggestions for developing multimodal user interfaces*. Retrieved from http://www.w3.org/TR/2006/NOTE-mmi-suggestions-20060911/

Li, L., Cao, F., Chou, W., & Liu, F. (2006, October 3-6). *XM-flow: An extensible micro-flow for multimodal interaction*. Paper presented at the

International Workshop on Multimedia Signal Processing, Victoria, Canada.

Maes, S.H., & Saraswat, V. (2003). *Multimodal interaction requirements*. Retrieved from http://www.w3.org/TR/mmi-reqs/

Markowitz, J. (2005). Designing for speaker authentication. In D.A. Dahl (Ed.), *Practical spoken dialog systems* (pp. 123-139). Heidelberg, Germany: Springer.

McGlashan, S., Burnett, D.C., Carter, J., Danielsen, P., Ferrans, J., Hunt, A., et al. (2004, March 16. *Voice extensible markup language (voiceXML 2.0)*. Retrieved from http://www.w3.org/TR/voicexml20/

Microsoft. (2007). *Microsoft speech API 5.3 (SAPI)*. Retrieved from http://msdn2.microsoft.com/en-us/library/ms723627.aspx

Miller, M. (2002). *VoiceXML: 10 projects to voice-enable your Web site*. New York: Wiley Publishing, Inc.

Oshry, M., Auburn, R.J., Baggia, P., Bodell, M., Burke, D., Burnett, D.C., et al. (2007, March 24). *Voice extensible markup language (voiceXML) 2.1*. Retrieved from http://www.w3.org/TR/voicexml21/

Oshry, M., Auburn, R.J., Baggia, P., Bodell, M., Burke, D., Burnett, D. C., et al. (2004, July 28). *Voice extensible markup language (voiceXML) 2.1*. Retrieved from http://www.w3.org/TR/2004/WD-voicexml21-20040728/

Owen, S., & Rabin, J. (2007). *W3C mobileOK basic tests 1.0*. Retrieved from http://www.w3.org/TR/mobileOK-basic10-tests/

Portillo, P.M., Valdés, C.d.S., Carredano, G.d.A., & Pérez García, G. (2006). *The MIMUS corpus*. Paper presented at the LREC-06 International Workshop on Multimodal Corpora from Multimodal Behaviour Theories to Usable Models, Genoa, Italy.

Porzel, R., Zorn, H.-P., Loos, B., & Malaka, R. (2006, August 28). *Towards A separation of pragmatic knowledge and contextual information*. Paper presented at the ECAI-06 Workshop on Contexts and Ontologies, Riva del Grada, Italy.

Rabin, J., & McCathieNevile, C. (2006). *Mobile Web best practices 1.0*. Retrieved from http://www.w3.org/TR/mobile-bp/

SALT Forum. (2002). *Speech application language tags (SALT)*. Retrieved from http://www.saltforum.org

Shanmugham, S., & Burnett, D.C. (2008, June 23). *Media resource control protocol version 2 (MRCPv2)*. Retrieved from http://tools.ietf.org/html/draft-ietf-speechsc-mrcpv2-16

Sharma, C., & Kunins, J. (2002). *VoiceXML*. New York: John Wiley and Sons, Inc.

Shukla, C., Dass, A., & Gupta, V. (2002). *VoiceXML 2.0 developer's guide: Building professional voice-enabled applications with JSP, ASP, & Coldfusion*. New York: McGraw-Hill Osborne Media.

SmartWeb: Mobile Broadband Access to the Semantic Web. Retrieved from http://smartweb.dfki.de/main_pro_en.pl?infotext_en.html

Standard ECMA-327 ECMAScript 3rd Edition Compact Profile. (2001). Retrieved from http://www.ecma-international.org/publications/standards/Ecma-327.htm

Van Tichelen, L., & Burke, D. (2007, April 5). *Semantic interpretation for speech recognition*. Retrieved from http://www.w3.org/TR/semantic-interpretation/

W3C. (2000). *Extensible markup language (XML) 1.0 (second edition)*. Retrieved from http://www.w3.org/TR/REC-xml

Waters, K., Hosn, R.A., Raggett, D., Sathish, S., Womer, M., Froumentin, M., et al. (2007). Delivery context: Client interfaces (DCCI) 1.0 accessing static and dynamic delivery context properties. Retrieved from http://www.w3.org/TR/DPF/

Watt, S.M. (2007, September 23-26). *New aspects of InkML for pen-based computing.* Paper presented at the International Conference on Document Analysis and Recognition, (ICDAR), Curitiba, Brazil.

Wayman, J., Jain, R., Maltoni, D., & Maio, D. (2005). *Biometric systems: Technology, design, and performance.* London: Springer-Verlag.

West, D., Apted, T., & Quigley, A. (2004, September 7). *A context inference and multimodal approach to mobile information access.* Paper presented at the AIMS 2004: Artificial Intelligence in Mobile Systems, Nottingham, UK.

Yudkowsky, M. (2005). *The pebble and the avalanche.* San Francisco: Berrett-Koehler Publishers, Inc.

KEY TERMS AND DEFINITIONS

Application Definition Standards: Markup-based standards for defining application, for example, a standard format for writing speech recognition grammars.

Architectural Standards: Standard ways of dividing functions among system components and standard communication protocols among system components

Certification Standards: Standards which provide a formal definition of a term, such as "VoiceXML Platform" and certify that a system meets that definition.

Extensible MultiModal Annotation (EMMA): An XML-based language for representing user inputs and communicating them among system components.

Semantic Interpretation for Speech Recognition (SISR): A language for associating speech grammar rule results with return values.

Speech Recognition Grammar Specification (SRGS): A language for defining grammars for speech recognizers.

State Chart XML (SCXML): An XML language for defining state machines.

Speech Synthesis Markup Language (SSML): A standard markup language for speech synthesis

User Interface Standards: Standards for the user interface, intended to help systems accommodate human physical, perceptual, and cognitive capabilities.

VoiceXML: An application definition standard for voice dialogs.

Chapter XXIII
Visualising Interactions on Mobile Multimodal Systems

Kristine Deray
University of Technology, Sydney, Australia

Simeon Simoff
University of Western Sydney, Australia

ABSTRACT

The purpose of this chapter is to set design guidelines on visual representations of interactions for mobile multimodal systems. The chapter looks at the features of interaction as process and how these features are exposed in the data. It presents a three layer framework for designing visual representations for mobile multimodal systems and a method that implements it. The method is based on an operationalisation of the source-target mapping from the contemporary theory of metaphors. Resultant design guidelines are grouped into (i) a set of high-level design requirements for visual representations of interactions on mobile multimodal systems; and (ii) a set of specific design requirements for the visual elements and displays for representing interactions on mobile multimodal systems. The second set then is considered subject to an additional requirement – the preservation of the beauty of the representation across the relevant modalities. The chapter is focused on the modality of the output. Though the chapter considers interaction data from human to human interactions, presented framework and designed guidelines are applicable towards interaction in general.

INTRODUCTION

Contemporary information and communications technology (ICT) offer an unprecedented degree of mobility, affecting the operating environments of human endeavours. These environments may span multiple and changing contexts, be that offices, homes, outdoors, hospitals or any other environments where ICT is embedded in the processes that operate in such environments. The concept of mobility of a device spans a range of platforms with different sizes, capabilities and interfaces. On the one end are familiar compact devices, such as mobile phones, personal digital assistants (PDAs) and integrated ICT devices, such as iPhone, when on the other end are emerging technologies of larger size, but still mobile and embedded in the environment, for instance, digital tables like Microsoft Surface platform[1] which can be moved around in the physical environment in the same way as we arrange conventional furniture. Such systems, due to their spatial presence and relatively large interaction area, enable rich multimodal interaction (Tse *et al.*, 2008), hence, require the development and support of efficient multimodal interfaces (Oviatt, 2003). Such interfaces require the development of new interaction paradigms in order to facilitate the design. Successful interface paradigms are recognised by their consistency and respective intuitive behaviour – a result of well-understood underlying metaphors and corresponding design patterns that can be articulated independently of any single application (Raman, 2003)

Many application areas, that utilise mobile systems, require communication of information about the interaction process. The way interactions unfold can tell us a lot about both the process and the outcomes of the interactions. For example, in health care, the treatment process is expected to benefit if we are able to present the information about how patient-practitioner interactions unfold, and if, based on that representation, one can judge about whether there has been a good communication or not, and if not, where were the bottlenecks (Deray and Simoff, 2007). In design, the participatory design process may benefit if we can present the information about how client-designer interactions unfold and if, based on that representation, one can judge about whether design communication has been good or not, and align interaction patterns with the emergence of design solutions in order to revisit intermediate design solutions (Simoff and Maher, 2000). In interna-

tional negotiations, the negotiation process may benefit if we can present the information about how the interaction between negotiating parties unfolds, in order to monitor the flow of these interaction and provide indicators to a third-party trusted mediator to interfere before negotiations reach a deadlock (Simoff *et al.*, 2008).

These examples emphasise the interplay between information about interaction and informed decision making in respective application domains. Such interplay set the key goals in the pursuit of efficient and effective means for information communication in mobile multimodal systems, in particular: (i) enabling information fusion naturally into human communication and human activities; (ii) increasing the reliability of interactions within the information-rich environments; (iii) delivering information at the right level of granularity, depending on the context of the decision making process; (iv) enabling visual analytics based on communicated information through the different modality channels. In order to address these goals it is important to develop methods of encoding information about the way interactions unfold that both humans and mobile systems are able to process and utilise in order to improve interactions and respective processes.

Further in this chapter we consider the specifics of interactions from the point of view of their visual representation in multimodal systems. The term "multimodal" has been broadly used in a number of disciplines. For the purpose of this chapter we adapt the definition of multimodal HCI system in (Jaimes and Sebe, 2007) to mobile systems. Multimodal mobile system is a mobile system that can respond to human inputs in more than one modality and can communicate its output to humans in more than one modality.

In this chapter we take the stance that a design of visual representations of interactions in multimodal mobile systems that is based on the principles of natural (physical) systems offers seamless and consistent interface, allowing the human to concentrate on the task at hand. Though the framework of the underlying natural system may limit the range of visualisation elements and their operations when representing interactions, it ensures the consistency of the representations and the consistent integration of the visual representation in the existing interface. We then formulate a set of high-level design requirements for visual representations of interactions on mobile multimodal systems and a set of ten rules as specific design requirements for visual elements and displays for representing interactions on mobile multimodal systems. The chapter also briefly considers aspects of beauty that cut cross the design guidelines.

INTERACTIONS FROM A PERSPECTIVE OF VISUALISATION ON MOBILE MULTIMODAL SYSTEMS

Interactions in real world scenarios are usually placed in the context of those scenarios. Following the examples in the previous section, in health care, patient-practitioner interaction is placed in the context of current patient condition, the medical history of the patient, previous interactions with the same practitioner and/or other practitioners, work conditions, family conditions and other possible factors that can influence the treatment process. In participatory design, the interaction between designers and the client is placed in the context of client's requirements, designers' experience, background knowledge of both parties, project budget, the outcomes of previous interactive sessions and other factors that can influence the participatory design process. In international negotiations, interaction between negotiators is placed in the context of current relations between negotiating parties, the regional and overall international arena, the history of the region, the outcomes of previous interactions and other factors that can influence the negotiation process. These examples illustrate the key features of interactions

that need to be presented in multiple modalities. Interactions

- Are inherently dynamic and depend on the information transfer between involved parties;
- Unfold in specific temporal spatial frames of reference that provide the context of enactment;
- Are embedded in collaborative and generative processes;
- Carry essential information about the process they are embedded into;
- Create channels that have certain characteristics in terms of information fusion;
- Operate through different modalities.

Figure 1 presents a framework for designing visual representations for mobile multimodal systems. The framework provides high level links of the key concepts involved in modelling interactions, expanded in the "Interaction Modelling Layer", with the formation of the underlying representation constructs catering for multiple modalities (the "Representation Constructs Layer") and the formation of respective visual language (the "Visualisation Layer") – all these operating under the guidelines for designing visual representations and the guidelines for multimodal interface design. For the purpose of this chapter we adapt the approach towards modelling interactions presented in (Pinhanez, 1999). Within the framework actions are the building (unit) blocks of interactions. An action is a discrete unit of intentional behaviour that involves change in a given context. Actions are performed by individual parties. Then interaction is a series of actions between two parties that produce reciprocal effects as perceivable outcomes. In terms of communication, interaction is a two-way process, which involves an exchange of messages, the sequence of which forms a dialogue, not a semantically disconnected set of actions. Interactions unfold in time forming an interaction space - a collection of interactions

Figure 1. Framework for designing visual representations for mobile multimodal systems

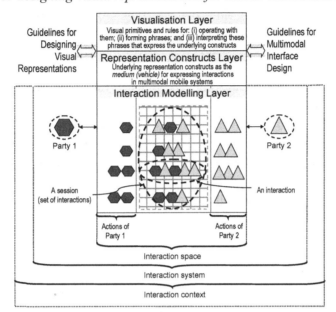

over a given period of time. Collection of interactions, bounded by a common task and/or time constraint, forms a session. Each session has an entry action, which is incorporated in the first interaction in the sequence and an exit action, which is incorporated in the last interaction in the session. An interaction space is bounded by the parties involved and can include one or more sessions. An interaction system encompasses the interaction space and the parties involved in it. Further the interaction system is embedded in the interaction context, which has components that are internal and components that are external to the interaction system. For instance, with respect to an individual interaction, the previous interactions within the interaction space between the same parties can be considered as a context. Interactions or relations of the parties, bounded by the interaction space, with other parties that are not part of the same interaction space are example of external components of the interaction context.

This interaction model, which presents interactions as a physical system, provides the features of the interactions necessary for formulating the requirements towards representation constructs from a computational perspective. From a physical system point of view interactions can be described through their:

- Intensity, which indicates the strength of the structural coupling between the individual actions in a resultant interaction;

- Information fusion, which indicates the quality of communication;

- Decision path, which indicates the type of decision making that takes place during the interaction;

- Common ground, which indicates the amount of co-referencing, coordination and agreed event structure (see Coiera, 2001) for a formalised definition of common ground as the intersection of the internal models of two communicating parties;

- Dialogue features, which indicate the dynamics of the interaction sequences through a session.

Representational constructs that can express these features from computational perspective require some form of quantification. (Acampora *et al.*, 2006) provide an interesting approach considering symbolic representations for modelling human interactions within environments populated with sensors and actuators. (McCowan *et al.*, 2003) provide an approach for looking at multimodal interaction and group actions, that is helpful when considering interaction at a higher level of granularity

As a sequence of actions, interactions can be described through the various time-based statistics of actions. These include the length of each action, the average length and variance of actions of each party in an interaction, the frequency of turn taking and other similar parameters. Similarly, the interaction space can be described in similar parameters at the interaction level. These parameters describe interactions as a physical system and allow us to specify a guiding process of how to populate the Representation Constructs Layer in Figure 1.

The design of visual representations, in broad sense, is the definition of the rules for conversion of data into graphics (graphical forms). Formal approaches utilise the concept of semantic visualisation, defined as a visualisation method, which establishes and preserves the semantic link between form of the visual elements and their function in the context of the visualisation metaphor (Simoff, 2008). The operationalisation of the framework in Figure 1 utilises the contemporary view of metaphors in cognitive linguistics (Lakoff and Johnson, 1980; Lakoff, 1993; Turner, 1994). These mechanisms of the metaphors are described in cognitive linguistics through the terms *source* and *target*, referring to the conceptual spaces connected by the metaphor. (In the research literature the target is variously referred to as the primary system or the topic, and the source is often called the secondary system or the vehicle). The target is the conceptual space that is being described, and the source is the space that is being used to describe the target (Lakoff, 1993; Turner, 1994). Correct mapping requires that the structure of the source domain is projected onto the target domain in a way that is consistent with inherent target domain structure (Lakoff, 1993; Turner, 1994). The model reflects the phenomena that humans usually use well known concepts from one (the source) domain when describing less (or even new) concepts in another (the target) domain.

For the purpose of this chapter we consider conceptual spaces that describe physical systems, which usually include some formal description of such systems and a formal representation (language) for describing the systems. If both domains can be represented as physical systems then inherent features of the physical system in the source domain can be used to develop formal representation of the physical system in the target domain. The idea of the source-target mapping between the conceptual spaces that describe physical systems is illustrated in Figure 2 with an example of looking for concepts in human movement (the source domain) to be used to describe interactions (the target domain). These concepts then are formalised to construct representations for mobile multimodal systems. On the left-hand side is the source domain, which, in this example, describes human movement, on the right-hand side is the target domain that, in this example, will use constructs from human movement to describe interactions. The translational mapping is illustrated at three levels. The labels in the sections in the diagram for each level are indexed with "S" and "T", indicating respectively "source" and "target".

The two physical systems are compared in terms of their features and dynamics in order to identify the underlying correlations and derive the concepts in one of the systems that are suitable to express the properties of the other. Diagram sections a_S and a_T in Figure 2 show the similarity between "human movement" from a physical system perspective. They show that both dancing and interactions can be structured as a sequence of states

$S_{[t_1]}, S_{[t_2]}, ..., S_{[t_n]}$ of the system in respective time intervals $[t_1], [t_2], ..., [t_n]$. Diagram section a_T shows that the states of the system $S_{[t_1]}, S_{[t_2]}, ..., S_{[t_n]}$ depend on the sequences of activities of the interacting parties

$$\left\{ P_1^{[t_1]}, P_2^{[t_1]} \right\} \left\{ P_1^{[t_2]}, P_2^{[t_2]} \right\} ..., \left\{ P_1^{[t_n]}, P_2^{[t_n]} \right\}$$

during the respective time intervals $[t_1], [t_2], ..., [t_n]$. In this example in the source domain the "Movement observation science" (Newlove and Balby, 2004) has been selected as the formal system for conceptualising human movement (diagram section b_S). The physical constituents in the source domain, for example, effort and flow, and their expression are constructed through the behaviour of respective elements, in this example, through the behaviour of shaping affinities of elasticities and qualities. The temporal expressions of the concepts from the source domain, the effort and flow in this case, can be interpreted as shape deformations. These expressive properties of the physical systems suitable for the source domain are the enablers of the translation into the target domain, where the morphodynamics of interactions now can be expressed through the changing geometry of the models of elasticities and qualities (for details see (Deray and Simoff, 2007)). Morphodynamics here is used in a non-geological sense, to label the evolution of the interaction landscape (i.e. treating interaction as a single entity) as a result of the contributions of participating parties. This derivation is schematically illustrated in diagram section b_T, Figure 2. The upper part shows visualisation elements that reflect the underlying computational models of elasticities and qualities, catering for literal interpretation of the term "geometry of interactions". The lower part shows an audio reflection of the underlying computational models of elasticities and qualities, enabling another mode for representing interactions in a multimodal system. The introduction of multiple modalities is enabled by the introduction of the common computational representation that then maps on to specific visual, audio or other modal representation.

Diagram sections c_S and c_T in Figure 2 show that in some cases the analogical mapping between the systems could extend even to the level of the formalisms used – in our example scores are used both in the source and target domain. The score in the source domain in diagram section c_S is a fragment of Labanotation. It is mainly used at theatres to archive most commonly ballet,[2] however, there has been an increasing interest in it from the field of human-computer interaction spanning from motion segmentation (Bouchard and Badler, 2007) to enabling affective modality (Fagerberg *et al.*, 2003). The scores in the target domain in diagram section c_T are following the two modalities of presentation: visual, generated according to the visual language described in (Deray and Simoff, 2007) and adapted for mobile devices in (Deray and Simoff, 2008) and audio, which, only for illustrative purposes is shown as a visualisation with the mapping used by WolframTones[3]. The sheet music scores and Tibetan musical scores illustrate the idea of having multiple possible formal representations, depending on the specific implementation of the modality input. In other words, the different scores are generated from data about interactions kept and updated at the Representation Constructs Layer in the framework in Figure 1.

Design Guidelines for Visualisation of Interactions on Mobile Multimodal Systems

We synthesise the design guidelines in the context of our framework in Figure 1. The guidelines are a synthesis, which also incorporates elements from:

- The principles for designing visual languages for representing interactions, formulated

Figure 2. Operationalisation of the framework in Figure 1

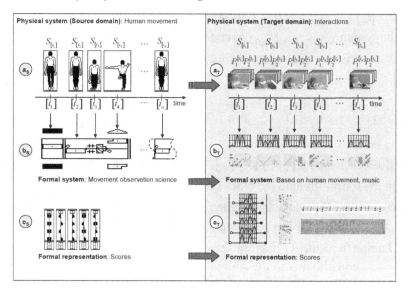

in (Deray and Simoff, 2007) and extended to mobile systems in (Deray and Simoff, 2008);

• The guidelines for multimodal user interface design, presented in (Reeves *et al.*, 2004) and the user interface principles for multimodal interaction in (Raman, 2003);

• The discussions of user and task modeling, multimodal fusion, taxonomy of techniques, as well as the broad consideration of the body, gesture, gaze, and affective interaction in (Jaimes and Sebe, 2007);

High-Level Design Requirements for Visual Representations of Interactions on Mobile Multimodal Systems

This section addresses the high-level design guidelines. (Reeves *et al.*, 2004) suggest that the interface design for multimodal systems should cater for broadest range of users and contexts of use. Consequently, (Reeves *et al.*, 2004) suggest that designers should become familiar with users' psychological characteristics. Further we discuss

specific requirements along these lines and the guidelines that address them.

Consistency relates to common features in the design that can accommodate different tasks by using dimensions that reference similar phenomenal experience. Choosing these dimensions provides consistency of the geometrical or topological structures (Gärdenfors, 2000; Gärdenfors, 2005). In turn this partially depends on what modalities are assumed to be used and their function. Within the framework proposed in this chapter this requirement is addressed through the selection of the source domain. For instance, the design of spring-based visualisations of graphs uses the physics of spring model as the source domain to specify the visual representation components, the relations and behaviours in the visualisation (target) domain. In Figure 2 we have used the human movement domain as a source for describing interactions. The fundamental premise behind such choice is the research in embodied cognition according to which intelligence has a bodily basis of thought (Pheifer and Bongard, 2007). (Deray and Simoff, 2007; Deray and Simoff, 2008) demonstrated the feasibility of such approach for developing mechanisms for visualisation of interactions in general, including mobile systems. As requirements evolve in time, the source-target approach offers also a set of constraints in terms of consistency against which the design solutions that address such evolving requirements are tested.

Adaptivity can only be consistently supported if users can identify the logic for the adaptation, to say, a different interaction context (e.g. visualising healthcare interactions during a patient visit and during a lecture to medical students) or a different user (e.g. visualising interactions to a patient or to a doctor). Having a common formal representation (see Figure 2) enables adaptivity.

The above two requirements for consistency and adaptivity lead to the requirement for **synchronising multiple modalities**. Though this chapter is limited to the discussion of output modalities, it's worth considering (Raman, 2003) points about the temporal and spatial dimensions of interaction, which, in some sense, reflect its sequential and parallel (multimodal) nature, respectively. In some we can speculate about a "second order" multiple modality, i.e. we have to be able to represent in our multimodal outputs data about multimodal interactions themselves. For instance, a phone interview is primarily characterised by the sequence of speech utterances over the phone – the sequence in turn-taking and the content of the individual speech acts. An interaction in a face-to-face interview may include also passing information on a shared document through pointing, gestures over specific parts of the document and other activities part of interaction. Extending this to the interactions during the deliberations of the selection committee leads to parallel streams of utterances and spatial elements (e.g. committee member can point to a particular paragraph and figure in the document that another member is looking at) within the same time interval. In terms of design requirements, in order to enable synchronisation between multiple modalities in the output, *representation of interactions should*

be capable of capturing both the temporal and spatial dimensions, as well as parallel communications. Within the framework of this chapter this is achieved with the design of a common formal representation, from which then are generated respective modality outputs. In essence each modality should interact with a common underlying representation of interactions.

Having common underlying representation will enable also **smooth transition between presentation modalities**. This element of the guidelines not only reflects the natural change in the modalities of human interaction, but also the change in the environment in which a multimodal mobile system operates. For example, designers will need to cater for changes not only in the bandwidth for communication between the mobile device and the user (e.g. screen size, audio level in comparison to surrounding noise), but also for the bandwidth of communication between the mobile device and the network, when switching between different networks. In other words, in a collaborative session the selection of a high resolution visualisation of the interactions may be inappropriate if it is shared between two devices that are on heavily loaded network. In some sense, this extends the adaptability requirement in terms of adapting to users environment and to the operational environment.

Figure 3 illustrates aspects of compliance with the above discussed guidelines on an example from visualising interactions in healthcare. The underlying representation of interactions uses a score type of formal representation, allowing the generation of visual and audio output modalities. Within the visual modality, depending on the context in which the user operates the system can shift to different displays combining text, table, graphics and video display. In a scenario, when specialists provide remote consultation, the choice of the combination of displays between Figure 3a – Figure 3c may depend on the current task, as well as the network connection.

Further we present a set of specific requirements for the construction of the visual elements and combinations of such elements, which constitute the following section.

Specific Design Requirements for Visual Elements and Displays for Representing Interactions on Mobile Multimodal Systems

The guidelines for the design of visual elements and combinations of them are necessary for the development of specific visual primitives and their behaviour, so that they can support the tasks considered in the system design specifications. These guidelines are synthesised including requirements specified in (Deray and Simoff, 2007) (based on adaptation of requirements enlisted in (Pretorius, 2005) and requirements extension in (Deray and Simoff, 2008). The specific design requirements are formulated as ten rules. The aspects of beauty in human-computer interactions that should be taken in consideration in the design are then discussed across these ten rules:

- **Rule 01–*Symmetry***: The argument for the symmetry comes from our view at the interaction as single object whose parameters are defined by the combined activities of contributing parties. Symmetry is expected to allow users to identify "balanced" interactions on each visual axes and to discover interaction patterns typical for particular scenarios and situations. The description of such set of patterns is a requirement in these guidelines.

- **Rule 02 – *Regularity***: The composition rules that are used to integrate visual elements should produce visual phrases with regular (normalised) structures. Such format of the visual phrase enables the comparison of visual elements within and between visual phrases.

- **Rule 03– *Similarity***: The visual elements should have similar appearances in terms of colour and shape. The size should be normalised and its value should be generated based on the output from the common representational layer (see Figure 1).

Figure 3. Examples of a single visual modality with different combinations of displays

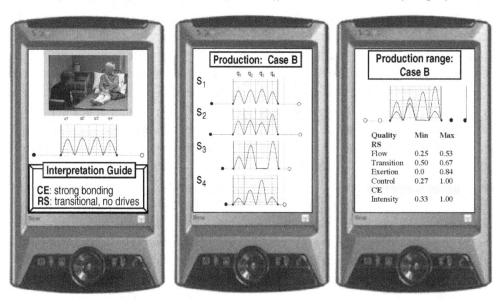

a. Text, graphics and video displays   b. Graphics display   c. Table data and graphics displays

- **Rule 04–*Connectivity***: The visualisation elements should be conceptually connected, ideally forming a visual language as mobile multimodal systems are expected to support analysis of interaction in variety of situations and contexts.
- **Rule 05–*Legend***: In general, the visual representation should be equipped with algorithms for attaching semantic labels to the visual components when required by the task or the user.
- **Rule 06–*Containment and Aggregation***: The visual representation should incorporate rules for aggregating visualisation elements for representing interactions at different levels of granularity. Membership to an element to an upper level is represented by containment. For example, in the visual language for representing interactions in (Deray and Simoff, 2007) the production range element is visually similar to the production element for achieving cognitive consistency. When catering views of large amounts of interaction data, aggregations also reduce the visual cluttering of the display.
- **Rule 07–*Transparency***: This design principle is used for enabling comparison of visual elements and respective analysis by aligned superimposing of the elements. This feature is useful when analysing discrete snapshots of collections of interactions over specific time intervals or interactions with similar structures of participating parties obtained over the same time interval. Transparency can also be used to emphasise the elements in focus, or to reduce the visual cluttering when displaying many scores.
- **Rule 08–*Complexity***: This design principle aims at achieving low representational complexity, so that through the visual representation the development and unfolding of interactions can be monitored in real-time on a mobile device.
- **Rule 09–*Expandability***: This design principle enables the development of a visuali-

sation that can accommodate change in the representation of interaction information. In other words, visual elements should be designed in a way to accommodate gradual expansion. This principle is key to the gradual incorporation of data from multiple interaction modalities in the visual representation.

- **Rule 10–*Scalability***: This design principle addresses not only the size of the interaction data displayed, but the diversity of screens in mobile multimodal systems on which visualisation can appear, so that the displayed components remain recognisable under projective transformations, such as scaling, rotation, translation or if presented in perspective.

The underlying representation of interactions *should preserve beauty across different modalities*. This means that a visual aesthetics should be preserved if the information is presented in audio form. In other words the consistency of aesthetics in representations needs to be carried over different modalities. This principle is separate from the ten rules as it cuts across them. Rule 01 Symmetry and Rule 02 Regularity are enabling features of a visual design that complies with the beauty requirement. In the rest of the rules the compliance with the beauty comes as a constraint on the forms, proportions, ratios and other features in the representation. The six articles in the special volume 19 of the *Journal of Human-Computer Interaction* (HCI) for 2004, devoted to the different aspects and perspectives of beauty in HCI, is a must reading to be considered when thinking through the design of the visual representations of interactions.

CONCLUSION

The importance of interactions as a source of information has been recognised in many areas of human endeavour. This recognition includes not only the content of the interactions (for instance, the numerous transcripts of conversations) but also the information about how the interactions unfold. The later information has been given less attention in terms of the development of technologies that capture such information. In the chapter we illustrated these aspects with examples from the fields of health care, design and negotiation. The advent of mobile multimodal systems offers platforms for capturing and presenting this information. The chapter has focussed specifically on the formulation of a framework for designing visual representations of information about the interaction process in a way that such information can be used in the decision making process in respective fields. The chapter analysed the process of unfolding interactions and the features of that process from a visualisation perspective. We have presented a model of the interaction space and three layer framework for designing visual representations for mobile multimodal systems. Further we discussed a method that enables the implementation of the framework. The method is based on the work in the contemporary theory of metaphors and the source-target operational model (Lakoff, 1993; Turner, 1994). The design guidelines are focused on the modality of the output. They have been presented in two sets: (i) a set of high-level design requirements for visual representations of interactions on mobile multimodal systems; and (ii) a set of ten specific design requirements for the visual elements and displays for representing interactions on mobile multimodal systems. We discuss the preservation of beauty across the visualisation elements as a constraint across the design requirements.

When making decisions it is worth recalling the 10 myths of multimodal interaction (Oviatt, 1999). In particular, when it comes to design decisions on supporting multiple modalities for representing interactions it is worth taking in consideration the following myths:

- Myth #1 ("If you build a multimodal system, users will interact multimodally");
- Myth #6 ("Multimodal integration involves redundancy of content between modes")
- Myth #10 ("Enhanced efficiency is the main advantage of multimodal systems")

The myths are cited as formulated in (Oviatt, 1999) – keep in mind that each myth is formulated as the opposite of the actual point that is made.

ACKNOWLEDGMENT

This research is supported by University of Technology, Sydney and University of Western Sydney, Australia.

REFERENCES

Acampora, G., Loia, V., Nappi, M., & Ricciardi, S. (2006, October 8-11). A semantic view for flexible communication models between humans, sensors, and actuators. In *Proceedings of the IEEE International Conference on Systems, Man, and Cybernetics,* Taipei, Taiwan (pp. 3640-3646). IEEE Press.

Bouchard, D., & Badler, N. (2007, September 17-19). Semantic segmentation of motion capture using laban movement analysis. In *Intelligent Virtual Agents, Proceedings of the 7th International Conference IVA 2007,* Paris, France (pp. 37-44). Heidelberg: Springer.

Coiera, E. (2001). Mediated agent interaction. In *Proceedings of the 8th Conference on Artificial Intelligence in Medicine Europe, AIME 2001.*

Deray, K., & Simoff, S.J. (2007). Designing a visual language for interaction representation based on aspects of human movement. In F. Ferri (Ed.), *Visual Languages for Interactive Computing: Definitions and Formalizations* (pp. 205-231). Hershey, PA: IGI Global.

Deray, K., & Simoff, S.J. (2008, October 20-23). Visualising the dynamics of unfolding interactions on mobile devices. *Advances in Conceptual Modeling-Challenges and Opportunities, Proceedings of the ER 2008 International Workshop on Modeling Mobile Applications and Services (M2AS'08)*, Barcelona, Spain (pp. 238-247). Springer.

Fagerberg, P., Ståhl, A., & Höök, K. (2003). Designing gestures for affective input: An analysis of shape, effort, and valence. In *Proceedings of the International Conference Mobile Ubiquitous and Multimedia MUM 2003*, Norrköping, Sweden (pp. 57-65). ACM Press.

Gärdenfors, P. (2000). *Conceptal spaces*. Cambridge, MA: MIT Press.

Gärdenfors, P. (2005). *The dynamics of thought*. Heidelberg: Springer.

Jaimes, A., & Sebe, N. (2007). Multimodal human-computer interaction: A survey. *Computer Vision and Image Understanding, 108*, 116-134.

Lakoff, G. (1993). The contemorary theory of metaphor. In A. Ortony (Ed.), *Metaphor and thought* (pp. 202-251). Cambridge, MA: Cambridge University Press.

Lakoff, G., & Johnson, M. (1980). *Metaphors we live by*. Chicago, IL: University of Chicago Press.

McCowan, I., Bengio, S., Gatica-Perez, D., Lathoud, G., Monay, F., Moore, D., Wellner, P., & Bourlard, H. (2003). Modeling human interaction in meetings. In *Proceedings of ICASSP 2003, IEEE Press: IV-748 - IV-751*.

Newlove, J., & Balby, J. (2004). *Laban for all*. London: Nick Hern.

Oviatt, S. (1999). Ten myths of multimodal interaction. *Communications of the ACM, 42*(11), 74-81.

Oviatt, S.L. (2003). Multimodal interfaces. In J. Jacko & A. Sears (Ed.), *The human-computer interaction handbook: Fundamentals, evolving technologies, and emerging applications* (pp. 286-304). Mahwah, NJ: Lawrence Erlbaum.

Pheifer, R., & Bongard, J. (2007). *How the body shapes the way we think*. Cambridge, MA: MIT Press.

Pinhanez, C.S. (1999). *Representation and recognition of action in interactive spaces*. Unpublished doctoral dissertation, Cambridge, MA, Massachusetts Institute of Technology.

Pretorius, A.J. (2005). Visual analysis for ontology engineering. *Journal of Visual Languages and Computing, 16*, 359-381.

Raman, T.V. (2003). User interface principles for multimodal interaction. *Workshop on Principles for Multimodal User Interface Design, CHI 2003*. Retrieved from http://www.almaden.ibm.com/cs/people/tvraman/chi-2003/mmi-position.html

Reeves, L.M., Lai, J., Larson, J.A., Oviatt, S., Balaji, T.S., Buisine, S., Collings, P., Cohen, P., Kraal, B., Martin, J.-C., McTear, M., Raman, T., Stanney, K.M., Su, H., & Wang, Q.Y. (2004). Guidelines for multimodal user interface design. *Communications of the ACM, 47*(1), 57-59.

Simoff, S.J. (2008). Form-Semantics-Function-a framework for designing visual data representations for visual data mining. In S.J. Simoff, M.H. Böhlen & A. Mazeika (Eds.), *Visual data mining: Theory, techniques, and tools for visual analytics* (LNCS 4404, pp. 30-45). Heidelberg: Springer Verlag.

Simoff, S.J., & Maher, M.L. (2000). Analysing participation in collaborative design environments. *Design studies, 21*, 119-144.

Simoff, S.J., Sierra, C., & López de Mántaras, R. (2008, September 17). Requirements towards automated mediation agents. In *Pre-proceedings of the*

KR2008-Workshop on Knowledge Representation for Agents and MultiAgent Systems (KRAMAS), Sydney, Australia (pp. 171-185).

Tse, E., Greenberg, S., Shen, C., Forlines, C., & Kodama, R. (2008, February 25-27). Exploring true multiuser multimodal interaction over a digital table. In *Proceedings of DIS 2008,* Cape Town, South Africa (pp. 109-118).

Turner, M. (1994). Design for a theory of meaning. In W. Overton & D. Palermo (Eds.), *The nature and ontogenesis of meaning* (pp. 91-107). Lawrence Erlbaum Associates.

KEY TERMS AND DEFINITIONS

Common Ground is an aggregated measure of the intersection of the internal models of two communicating parties and includes co-referencing, coordination and agreed event structure.

Conceptual space in this work is a space built up on key quality dimensions that describe and structure the physical system needed for representing concepts.

Dialogue Features indicate the dynamics of the interaction sequences through a session.

Interaction is a series of actions between two parties that produce reciprocal effects as perceivable outcome.

Metaphor in this work is the system and process of understanding and representing one idea, or conceptual domain, in terms of another

Multimodal Mobile System is a mobile system that can respond to human inputs in more than one modality and can communicate its output to humans in more than one modality.

Physical System is a system that operates on natural principles and is the portion of the physical material world chosen for analysis.

Semantic Visualisation is a method that establishes and preserves the semantic link between form of the visual elements and their function in the context of the visualisation metaphor.

Translational Mapping is the term applied collectively to the levels of mapping from the source to the target domain

ENDNOTES

[1] http://www.microsoft.com/surface/index.html

[2] See "Introduction to Labanotation" [http://user.uni-frankfurt.de/~griesbec/labane.html] for a quick introduction of how the notation looks like and how the notation analyses movement.

[3] http://tones.wolfram.com/

Chapter XXIV
Usability Evaluation of Multimodal Interfaces

Regina Bernhaupt
IRIT, IHCS, Toulouse, France

ABSTRACT

In order to develop easy-to-use multimodal interfaces for mobile applications, effective usability evaluation methods (UEMs) are an essential component of the development process. Over the past decades various usability evaluation methods have been developed and implemented to improve and assure easy-to-use user interfaces and systems. However, most of the so-called 'classical' methods exhibit shortcomings when used in the field of mobile applications, especially when addressing multimodal interaction (MMI). Hence, several 'classical' methods were broadened, varied, and changed to meet the demands of testing usability for multimodal interfaces and mobile applications. This chapter presents a selection of these 'classical' methods, and introduces some newly developed methods for testing usability in the area of multimodal interfaces. The chapter concludes with a summary on currently available methods for usability evaluation of multimodal interfaces for mobile devices.

INTRODUCTION

Designing and developing usable interfaces and interaction techniques is one of the main goals in the area of human-computer interaction. The goal of easy-to-use interfaces is achieved by applying iterative and user-centered development. During the various stages of the product development several forms of evaluation take place,

aiming to inform the product design to increase the usability (and today also the user experience) of the product.

The classical forms of usability evaluation methods were developed starting in the early 1980ies. Main goal was to increase the usability of desktop applications. These applications were typically used by a more or less clearly described user group, used in a fixed (working) environment with the goal to support the productivity of the user by achieving goals fast, efficient and easy. Today the rapid development of mobile services and devices asks for new forms of usability evaluation: mobile applications are used by "almost" everyone, in all kinds of places—public or private, for business, leisure or entertainment, to achieve clear goals or to simply be entertained during a waiting period, together or with a group of people—in the same location or even shared remotely.

This multitude of usage scenarios explains why mobile devices today try to use multimodal interaction techniques. Multimodal interaction techniques and interfaces (MMI) are seen as a good way to increase customer satisfaction, user experience and comfort by providing a more natural interaction (Boldt, 1992). Besides that, multimodal interaction can increase the bandwidth between the user and the system. Modalities are often complementary, thus multimodal interfaces can help to clarify and reinforce the communication between the user and the system (Oviatt, 1999).

Mobile devices and services on the other side suffer sometimes from limited communication bandwidth like small screens or non-availability of keyboards, and communication between user and system is extremely influenced by contextual factors, like usage location, usage alone or in groups, usage time or users pre-knowledge. Based on the benefits multimodal interaction is promising, it has become common to use multimodal interfaces in mobile applications to extend the sometimes limited communication bandwidth, for example Pirhonen, Brewster and Holguin (2002) using gesture and non-speech iconography to improve the user interface.

To develop easy-to-use multimodal interfaces for mobile applications continuous usability evaluation within the (most often) user-centered and iterative development process is a necessity. When evaluating multimodal interaction with mobile

devices the specifities of mobile usability evaluation and multimodal usability evaluation have to be taken into account.

The evaluation must take into account that usability problems might be influenced by the current location of the user, a multimodal interface including sound (e.g. earcons) as feedback might not be appropriate if the current environment is noisy. Thus new forms of evaluation are needed to investigate the real usage of the system. In-situ methods can help to investigate the real usage of the system in the field. Using prototypes in the field might help to discover new forms of usability problems – on the other side a fully functional prototype must be available to use this kind of usability evaluation methods.

This chapter will describe these specifities of evaluating multimodal interaction techniques and interfaces for mobile applications and devices and how the possible methodological shortcomings can be coped with by using a mix of methods and approaches. The next section will give an overview on usability evaluation methods used for mobile applications, next an introduction on usability evaluation for multimodal interfaces is given. A short case-study shows how to apply a methodological mix of usability evaluation methods for the development of a mobile tourist guide including multi-modal interaction. Finally the chapter is concludes summarizing the most important decision criteria for choosing the right kind of evaluation method.

USABILITY EVALUATION OF MOBILE APPLICATIONS

During the evaluation of mobile applications and services it is typical to focus on providing solutions for technical problems. In-depth studies on what kind of classical methodologies for usability evaluation can be used and how these classical methods have to be adopted for usage in mobile scenarios are rare. But it is commonly accepted that data collection for evaluation of mobile devices and applications is a central challenge, and that novel methods must be found for that (Isomursu, Kuutti & Värinämo, 2004).

Jones and Marsden (2006) provide in their introductory book on mobile interaction design an overview of currently applied evaluation methods. For early stages within the development cycle, they name a form of ethnography ("Quick and Dirty"), conceptual model extraction, direct observation (often called usability studies or usability testing), interviews, questionnaires, and experiments. Other methods listed that are not involving the user are heuristic evaluation and theoretical models.

Looking at the real distribution of evaluation forms in scientific literature Kjeldskov and Graham (2003) conducted one of the most comprehensive reviews on evaluation methods used in HCI. They selected papers focusing on mobile HCI from relevant conferences over the past years and classified them according to the described research methods. The findings show that the prevalent mobile HCI research falls into the applied category (55%) followed by laboratory experiments (31%). On the bottom portion of the scale, only three and four (out of 102) research methods were conducted as case and field studies respectively. These findings imply that there is a strong tendency towards environment independent and artificial settings in HCI research.

This lack of real-use-contexts and natural setting research could be justified by the fact that mobile HCI has strong roots in the field of computer sciences and HCI. These fields have a strong bias towards engineering and evaluation methodology. In addition, the methods stemming from the social sciences are normally more costly and resource intensive.

Bernhaupt, Mihalic and Obrist (2008) summarize usability evaluation methods for mobile application and services in four classes:

- User testing (Thinking aloud protocol, Wizard of Oz, Log file analysis, field observation, laboratory observation, …);
- Inspection oriented methods (like heuristic evaluation, cognitive walkthrough or guideline review);
- Self-reporting and inquiry oriented methods (like diaries and interviews, cultural probes, user experience sampling);
- Analytical modeling (task model analysis and performance models).

This classification is based on traditional classifications for UEMs and our experience in the field of evaluating mobile applications and services. More general classifications for methods in the field of mobile HCI are available focusing on the way data is collected (Hagen, Robertson, Kon & Sadler, 2005).

In the field of mobile applications most of the above mentioned methods are used to some extent, with analytical modeling being used only in some specialized areas (saftety-critial applications).

User Testing or usability studies typically are conducted in the laboratory, involving a user, who is performing a set of typical tasks. The users are asked to think aloud while performing the tasks. The system tested can be a real functional system, or the system is just acted out or a Wizard-of-Oz setting is used to pretend the multimodal capabilities of the system (Salber & Coutaz, 1993). The performance of the users (in terms of problem solution, clicks/key-presses, chosen combination of modalities) is most often logged or observed. Observation can take place by some experimenters/researchers or by using cameras in the test-setting. Evaluating the usability of mobile applications a usability study in a lab might not be sufficient. To investigate the real usage context, testing in the field or in "real situations" is necessary to learn about possible usage problems.

Inspection-oriented methods on the other side involve an expert. The experts are using existing guidelines and they try to judge possible usability problems based on their experience. Expert methods are most often referred to as easy, fast and cheap, but they require a trained expert (Nielsen & Mack, 1994). The results heavily depend on the expert's knowledge and experience. If you want to learn more about how to conduct a usability evaluation for mobile devices, the introductory text book of Jones & Marsden (2006) is helpful.

The group of self-reporting and inquiry oriented methods is an emerging set of usability evaluation methods that is useful for investigating usage of mobile devices and services. Users typically interact with their mobile devices in daily life, and at the same time report their experiences, problems and insights to help inform the product development process.

The last group of analytical models is used especially to evaluate possible interaction techniques for mobile devices. Based on some general laws (e.g. Fitts law) the time, duration, or mean-error rate can be computed. This helps to get a better understanding of the implications the selection of an interaction technique might have for daily usage.

When selecting an appropriate evaluation method for mobile devices and systems we have to take into account the following specifities (Jones & Marsden, 2006):

- **End-users or experts:** Who is going to conduct the evaluation, will it be a "real" user or an expert based evaluation?
- **Context:** Where will the evaluation take place? We have to realize that what is useful and what is perceived as problematic from a user perspective is influenced by the real usage conditions and the development of the usage over time. Studies in the lab started to simulate the context of usage and expert-oriented evaluation methodologies have been varied, to enable the inclusion of the usage context.

- **Results:** The various forms of evaluation will inform the design process in different ways depending on the stage of the development (low vs. high fidelity prototypes).

Evaluation of usability in mobile settings is thus influenced by the method selected, and results can only be useful if the appropriate method is chosen in the respective development stage. A good starting point for the discussion on what kind of data can be gathered with user testing during which step of development process is the SEM-CPU approach (Lee, Hong & Smith-Jackson, 2005). The authors are proposing a systematic evaluation method for cell phone user interfaces, showing clearly the different kind of data that can be gathered during an experimental usability study for each step of the development process.

USABILITY EVALUATION METHODS FOR MULTIMODAL INTERACTION

Evaluating the usability of a multimodal system can be conducted with any of the above listed methods. In the following we briefly describe each category and some specific methods used to evaluate multimodal interaction. A more detailed description of usability evaluation for MMI can be found in Bernhaupt, Navarre, Palanque and Winckler (2008).

To investigate usability and user experience of multimodal interfaces, in general user testing is applied. The observation and recording of user's activity helps to understand how different modalities can be used beneficial by the user and what kind of possibilities and restrictions arise from the combination of various input and output modalities. Several types of user testing have been conducted both in usability laboratories and in field studies. Studies in the lab or in the field are neither good nor bad, but must be selected based on research question, focus of investigation and intended results usability.

Evaluation based on inspection methods are conducted by a usability expert and rely on the expert's knowledge on usability or existing guidelines with recommendations. This category includes Cognitive Walkthrough (Lewis, Polson & Wharton, 1990), formative evaluation and heuristic evaluation (Nielsen & Mack, 1994) and also benchmarking approaches covering issues such as ISO 9241 usability recommendations or conformance to guidelines (Bach & Scapin, 2003).

Expert based evaluation methods are rarely used in the area of multimodal interfaces, as there seems to be a lack of ergonomic knowledge. Knowledge is not only missing in terms of experts experience for the design of multimodal systems but also due to the lack of guidelines to cover all potential modalities and modality combinations that might be encountered in multimodal interfaces. The proposed methods, especially cognitive walkthroughs, are designed to assess the achievement of goals focusing on the goal-structure of the interface rather than on interaction techniques.

Questionnaires have been extensively employed to obtain qualitative feedback from users (e.g. satisfaction, perceived utility of the system, user preferences for modality). When investigating cognitive workload of MMI the NASA-TLX method is helpful (Brewster, Wright & Edwards, 1994), and was already adopted for MMI in mobile settings (Prihonen, Brewster & Holguin, 2002).

More recently, simulation and model-based checking of system specifications have been used to predict usability problems such as unreachable states of the systems or conflict detection of events required for fusion. Bernhaupt, Navarre, Palanque and Winckler (2008) proposed to use formal specification techniques in combination with traditional usability evaluation methods like user testing or cognitive walkthroughs to support the evaluation of multimodal interaction techniques, to enable a detailed verification and analysis of usability problems, related to the fission and fusion of modalities.

EVALUATING MULTIMODAL INTERFACES IN MOBILE SETTINGS

For the evaluation of multimodal interaction techniques (MM) for mobile devices we have to take into account the shortcomings and difficulties from the two respective areas. Related to the mobile nature, we have to carefully investigate the possible usage contexts that might affect the usability of the product (Taminnen, Oulasvirta, Toiskallio & Kankainen, 2003). The physical context is typically described as the location where the user is currently interacting, the technological context is the context of technology currently available to the user (e.g. the network, additional input or output devices like keyboards or screens), and the social context, representing all kind of situations influenced by social connections (like being upset that someone does not call). Please note, that the usability of a system is reasonable reflected, when you consider the above three contexts (Jones & Marsden, 2006). Other models of context typically refer to other settings like the home and are helpful to understand the adoption and long-term usage of a product (e.g. Venkatesh, 2006).

Following you find a list of evaluation methods that can be helpful for investigating MMI for mobile devices. Each method is briefly explained and their benefits and shortcomings for evaluation of mobile MMI are given.

User Testing of Mobile MMI

Usability tests, user studies and experiments conducted in the lab are performance measurements to determine whether usability goals have been achieved. The usability evaluation of mobile devices with MMI in the lab has several advantages: the conditions for conducting the test can be controlled; all participants experience the same setting leading to higher quality data. On the other hand, user testing in the field allows discovery of usability problems related to the context of use.

Pascoe, Ryan and Morse (2000) studied the effects of using mobile devices while on the move, especially HCI related issues involved in using mobile devices in a real world (field) environment. The main factors which influence the interaction between users and mobile device include contextual awareness, task hierarchy, visual attention, hand manipulation, and mobility. These are critical issues of usability and mobile application design. Testing in a real environment means that test users are able to behave as they would normally, to the extent that they need not to be told to do so (Bernhaupt, Mihalic & Obrist, 2008).

Especially when investigating MMI for mobile services, studies conducted in the field might help to discover new forms of usage problems. Sound output might not be possible in noisy environments, or are socially not accepted. The current situation (like standing in a bus for local transportation) might not allow usage of all types of modalities. Field studies help to discover usability problems that are not discovered with other methods.

Whether usability studies should be conducted in the lab or in the field is still a matter of discussion and needs further research. How to conduct usability testing in "real-world" situations is also addressed in other areas of HCI. For example Bennett, Lindgaard, Tsuji, Conelly and Siek (2006) conducted a workshop on how testing in non-traditional environments can be conducted. Experts from domains like military, healthcare or mobile devices discussed on how methods have to be adopted to address testing in non-traditional environments. The general agreement was that only a mix of several methods during design and evaluation can help to ensure usability of the product.

To summarize, user testing is helpful to gather insights on the real usage of the product and related usability problems. Especially when looking at multi-modal interaction, the usage context is a typical source of usability problems, as certain modalities might not be used in vari-ous usage situations. A user testing should thus take into account the usage context, by either simulating the real usage situation or testing in the field. To overcome limitations of user testing a combination with inspection oriented methods and self-reporting methods during early design phases is helpful.

Inspection Oriented Methods

Industry typically relies on expert or inspection oriented usability evaluation methods, as they are said to be fast and cheap. A prominent inspection oriented method is the so called heuristic evaluation (see Nielsen & Mack, 1994 for a description on how to conduct the method and its benefits and shortcomings). Other methods focus on special aspects of usability, for example the cognitive walkthrough focuses on the learn-ability of the system (Nielsen & Mack, 1994). When applied to evaluating mobile (multimodal) systems, inspection-oriented methods lack validity. These methods do not take into account the contextual factors that affect user-system interaction (Johnson, 1998; Kjeldskov & Graham, 2003). Inspection oriented methods thus depend on the expert's ability to interpret the context of use, the difficulties of the usage of the various modalities and their interdependencies.

To overcome the shortcomings of the interpreting the usage context, Gabrielli, Mirabella, Kimani and Catarsi (2005) enhanced the cognitive walkthrough method including videos describing the usage context or by simply performing the cognitive walkthrough in a typical environment. They found that providing evaluators with a video recorded usage of the system in a real environment or doing the evaluation in a real context increases the number of problems detected by 63 % and 68 % respectively, compared to conducting a normal heuristic evaluation. However, they also found that the number of problems discovered in the video enhanced situation compared to the real context situation, did not differ. Nevertheless, usage of video or performing the evaluation method in a real setting helps to discover context-related usability problems.

Po, Howard, Vetere and Skov (2004) enhanced Nielsen's heuristic evaluation to include usage scenarios and varied the extended methodology to be conducted either in the lab or in the field. The enhanced heuristic evaluation helps to find usability problems which are related to timing sequences and that usability problems found in the extended methodology condition are typically more severe than problems found with the "normal" heuristic evaluation.

The modification of inspection oriented methods helps evaluators to combine the advantages of these methods and reduce the shortcomings of the methods when applied in the field of mobile systems and applications. On the other hand, these methods rely on the knowledge and expertise of the experts. As detailed ergonomics on multi-modal interaction with all their possible combinations are missing, usage of inspection-oriented methods for evaluation is limited in the area of multimodal interaction for mobile systems, and most HCI oriented research is still conducted using user studies (Jones, Buchanan, Thimbelby, 2002; Mizobuchi, Mai Ren & Michaki, 2002).

Self Reporting and Inquiry

To overcome the shortcomings of several usability evaluations methods not being able to take into account the usage context, so called in-situ, self reporting or inquiry-based evaluation methods have been developed and adopted.

In-situ methods describe all kinds of methods that can be used to evaluate a system or prototype in its real usage context. During field usability studies or trials, questionnaires and self-reporting methods are used to evaluate possible usage difficulties or hindering effects. In-situ methods typically include ethnographic studies, (video) observation, contextual inquiries, or interviews. All these methods have in common, that they

try to explore usage of the (multimodal mobile) system in the real usage context, by investigating possible usage problems. One of the most prominent self-reporting approaches (Sanders, 2002) are the various forms of probing – cultural probing (Gaver, Dunne & Pacenti, 1999), technology probing (Hutchinson et al., 2003) or playful probing and creative cultural probing (Bernhaupt et al., 2007).

Cultural probes were developed by Gaver et al. (1999) and can be used to investigate early design phases, mainly gathering insights on the users' context in order to better inform the design process in an early stage (Gaver et al., 1999; Jääskö & Mattelmäki, 2003). To investigate usage of a (functional) prototype or system, technology probes were invented. Technology probes involve the deployment and evaluation of a new technology or application into a real use context (Hutchinson et al., 2003). The main advantage of this approach for usability evaluation purposes is providing real life insights on a number of usability issues (e.g. how users choose to interact with a certain device in a special context), which have to be considered in the user-centered design and development process of new products and applications.

Shortcomings of laboratory user testing of mobile devices and applications can be overcome by using technology probes. Users can explore the technology in their real life setting without being directly observed by the evaluator. By using self-reporting materials (mainly diaries and photos) the user becomes the evaluator herself over a specified period of time (e.g. two or more weeks).

Results of technology probes are typically qualitative. When conducting a usability evaluation using technology probes the functional prototype is given to the users. Technology probe studies last from days to weeks. The users note usability and usage problems (either in diary format, with photos or videos, using special probing material like post-cards, cards or simple post-its.) while using the product in their daily life. After the usage phase, interviews are conducted with the participants, to examine the gathered probing material. One of the main challenges of probe studies related to mobile applications is to motivate people to complete the probe material in mobile contexts. In order to address this shortcoming, other methods can be used, especially the experience sampling method (ESM).

The main goal of experience sampling is to understand and gather information about people's daily routines, their feelings and emotions. Typically participants are asked to write down what they are doing at a special period or point in the day. To adopt ESM for mobile usage participants get signals by chance (most commonly on their mobile phones). After they received a signal they either have to write down what they where currently doing (where, what context), or to answer some questions (typically also on the mobile phone). ESM allows to collect qualitative and quantitative data, and can be helpful in understanding typical usages and influencing factors for usability problems. The main qualities of experience sampling are that usability and user experience factors can be studied within a natural setting, in real time, on repeated time occasions and by request (Vermeeren & Kort, 2006). Conner, Barrett, Bliss-Moreau, Lebo and Kaschub (2003) provides additional information on ESM procedures and Van Esch-Bussemakers, Neerincx, Lindenberg and Streefkerk (2005) report experiences about the combination of ESM with classical usability evaluation methods. Future usability evaluations of mobile applications should also consider context-aware experience tools as well as the combination and triangulation of different in-situ methods (Intille, Rondoni, Kukla, Iacono & Bao, 2003).

Analytical Modeling

In addition to the aforementioned user and expert centered usability evaluation methods and adopted methods for user inquiries we should not forget traditional usability evaluation methods originally applied in the field of software engineering, like automatic testing, formal descriptions of user and task models, model-based evaluations or critical incident and accident analysis. The authors are not aware of a broad usage of these methods in the field of mobile devices and applications, although one example in reference to Lee et al. (2005) was proposed in the SEM-CPU approach of a critical incident analysis. Usage of formal descriptions in multi-modal interfaces are more common, but are not typically used when evaluating multimodal interfaces for mobile devices.

A model-based evaluation for MMI that might be also useful for evaluating multimodal mobile devices and services was described by Bernhaupt, Navarre, Palanque and Winckler (2008). Model-based evaluation helps to inform traditional usability evaluation methods by providing information from the formal specification.

Model-based evaluation might be helpful in the context of multimodal interfaces for mobile systems, as the evaluation of multimodal interfaces is difficult to realize with current usability methods. The different modalities can only be tested using a huge number of experiments (conducted in lab and field). With model-based evaluation the typical usability problems related to the multimodality could be found more easily. Model-based evaluation can be used in combination with any other usability evaluation method.

When testing multimodal interfaces with a usability study, the following characteristics have to be taken into account:

- Which pairs of (device, interaction technique) have to be tested?
- How can users address the system using the various communication channels and which channel can be used in the various contexts (tasks)?
- What types of fission and fusion can be tested (especially in the case of safety critical systems)?

- How can the various dimension affecting usability evaluation of MMIs be addressed (Usage and interpretation of modalities, individual user preferences, context-of-use and activities supported by the system, etc.).

The goal of a usability test is typically to identify major usability problems within the interface. When conducing usability tests, the most frequently performed tasks (extracted from task analysis for instance) are commonly included in the usability test. Having a system that is described in a formal notation (unfortunately this is most often only the case for safety-critical systems), it is possible to identify not only the "minimum" number of scenarios to be tested but also to select more rationally the tasks that are to be focused on. This selection can be done using analysis techniques on the models that will help designer to identify complex or cumbersome behaviours that have been modelled and might require more specific usability testing.

When testing multimodal interfaces, selection of scenarios reaches a higher level of complexity due to the significant number of possible combinations of input modalities. In order to test all (or most) of these combinations it is required to provide usability tests scenarios at a much lower level of description than what is usually done with systems featuring more classic interaction techniques.

When setting up the usability test for multimodal interfaces the selection of tasks must be informed by the models. Tasks with high complexity in the low-level multimodal interaction must be listed exhaustively. Up to now, this comprehensive list has to be done by the expert describing the tasks to be evaluated. In addition, the frequency of highly-complex low-level interactions has to be estimated, based on the task-models. In the case study, the number of synergistic usages of speech and two mice has been counted. Based on this information the tasks for the usability test representing the low-level interaction are

selected. Additionally high-level tasks are selected to conduct the usability test.

This way of selecting the tasks for the usability test, helps to represent all levels of multi-modal interaction. Thus the results of the usability test are more informative and connected to the precise design of the system.

Model-based evaluation helps to support standard usability evaluation methods to overcome their reported weaknesses when testing multimodal interfaces. Provided with the adequate tools for editing models and generated marking graphs, the above descriptions might sound easy to follow. Of course the method will only show its benefits, when the method is carefully set up and conducted.

A CASE STUDY: EVALUATING A TOURIST GUIDE

To exemplify how to combine various forms of usability evaluation within a product development cycle we want to use an example of a mobile tourist guide. The mobile tourist guide called "Sound of Music" enables tourists of the city of Salzburg to visit the original locations of the film scenes and to get information about that original location (sound, short videos, text). To determine the location a new form of GPS program enhancing pedestrian navigation (Kappacher, 2007). In the final version of the system users can access content either using the hierarchical menu or via pen-input. Output is given as sound feedback, visual feedback and includes also multimedia content. Currently there is no option to connect for additional information to the internet.

Setting up a new tourist guide first an extensive literature review on touristic needs in that region was performed. A thorough user and task analysis including persona description was done. To investigate if the first (low fidelity) screen design would fit the user needs, if it enables the user to navigate and to find their way, and additionally it enables a thorough user experience, an expert analysis was conducted. The experts performed a heuristic evaluation in the real locations of the tourist guide (walking through the city), trying to understand how users would find their way through the city and use the information on site. This form of expert evaluation in the field was chosen as it allows performing the evaluation at an early stage of the development. Conducting the evaluation in the field improves additionally the findings of the experts (Po et al., 2004).

The prototype was improved based on the findings of the expert analysis, including some extensions of functionality, especially a new way of triangulation to support navigation of pedestrians.

Once a first version of the functional prototype is available, user studies can be performed. The lab allows more technical flexibility for the mock-up and it limits possible influencing factors of the trial situation (network problems in the field, by-passers in the street disturbing, difficult observation conditions, limited ability to mock-up a system for usage in the field). In the usability lab study it is easier to investigate how users will be using the new navigation system and how they will perceive the multimodal output. Input was limited (due to the used cell phone for the prototype stage) to navigation in a hierarchical menu with the navigation keys and numeric keys (T9).

To investigate usability problems that might be influenced by contextual facts a field trial was used. Using an improved technical prototype, including most of the functionality of the final system, we conducted a usability test in the field. While walking to the typical locations of the Sound of Music Tour people can experience difficulties when using the local GPS system, to orientate themselves, while watching the content, or to simply try to look at the content together with other tourist (which might bring difficulties if someone else is starting to do some pen-interaction, while the other one uses the navigation of the mobile phone to select content).

During the different evaluation phases we learned that problems initially appearing in the lab, where no problems in the real setting (especially tasks related to orientation and navigation), while problems that where found in the real world study, did not appear during the lab evaluation (the co-cooperation for input, the difficulties in listening to the content in a more noisy environment, the visibility of some design elements with very bright sunshine, the difficulties arising when a way – that was initially shown by the GPS – was blocked due to a festival).

The combination of three evaluation methods helps to discover various forms of usability problems that a single method would not reveal. Especially the combination of lab and field user studies helps to understand what kind of usability problems users will face, once using the product in the real usage situation.

SUMMARY AND OUTLOOK

This chapter presented an overview on currently used usability evaluation methods in the field of multimodal interaction techniques and in the field of mobile applications and services. It presents a methodological framework to describe different classes of usability evaluation methods and how these methods can be used to evaluate usability for mobile systems with multimodal interfaces. A listing of several methods available helps the reader to select an appropriate selection to test their development. Finally a short case-study description is given, to describe more detailed typical shortcomings and advantages of some of the methods and the influence of context on usability evaluation.

The development pace of new forms of interaction techniques and new ways of mobile services is fast. From the methodological viewpoint only few studies investigate in detail the benefits and difficulties of the methods used to evaluate usability and how the combination of methods helps to find more (or more efficient) usability problems. Especially in areas that go beyond any industrial set of mobile devices (pervasive computing, ubiquitous computing) and in areas that typically push the limits of technologies (games) or invent new forms of interaction techniques like exertion interfaces (Mueller, Agamanolis & Picard, 2003) evaluation of usability is still difficult due to a lack of suitable evaluation methods.

REFERENCES

Bach, C., & Scapin, D. (2003). Ergonomic criteria adapted to human virtual environment interaction. In M. Rauterberg, M. Menozzi & J. Wesson (Eds.), *IFIP Conference on Human-Computer Interaction (INTERACT'2003)* (pp. 880–883). Zurich: IOS Press.

Bennett, G., Lindgaard, G., Tsuji, B., Connelly, K.H., & Siek, K.A. (2006). Reality testing: HCI challenge in non-traditional environments. In *Proceedings of CHI 2006, Extended Abstracts* (pp. 1679-1682). New York: ACM Press.

Bernhaupt, R., Weiss, A., Obrist, M., & Tscheligi, M. (2007). Playful probing: Making probing more fun. In *Proceedings of Interact 2007* (pp. 606–619). Heidelberg: Springer LNCS.

Bernhaupt, R., Mihalic, K., & Obrist, M. (2008). Usability evaluation methods for mobile applications. In J. Lumsden (Ed.), *Handbook of research on user interface design and evaluation for mobile technology* (pp. 745-758). Hershey, PA: IGI Global.

Bernhaupt, R., Navarre, D., Palanque, P., & Winckler, M. (2008). Model-based evaluation: A new way to support usability evaluation of multimodal interactive applications. In E. Law, E. Hvannberg, G. Cockton & J. Vanderdonckt. (Eds.), *Maturing usability: quality in software, interaction, and quality* (pp. 96-122). Heidelberg: Springer.

Brewster, S.A., Wright, P.C., & Edwards, A.D.N. (1994). The design and evaluation of an auditory-enhanced scrollbar. In *Proceedings of the SIGCHI Conference on Human factors in computing systems (CHI '94)* (pp. 173-179). New York: ACM Press.

Bolt, R.E., & Herranz, E. (1992). Two-handed gesture in multimodal natural dialog. In J. Mackinlay & M. Green (Eds.), *Proceedings of the Symposium on User Interface Software and Technology (UIST'92)* (pp. 7-14) New York: ACM Press.

Conner, T., Barrett, L.F., Bliss-Moreau, E., Lebo, K., & Kaschub, C. (2003). A practical guide to experience-sampling procedures. *Journal of Happiness Studies, 4,* 53-78.

Gabrielli, S., Mirabella, V., Kimani, S., & Catarsi, T. (2005). Supporting cognitive walkthrough with video data: A mobile learning evaluation study. In M. Tscheligi, R. Bernhaupt & K. Mihalic (Eds.), *Proceedings of the Conference on Human Computer Interaction with Mobile Devices and Services (MobileHCI 2005)* (pp. 77–82). ACM Press.

Gaver, B., Dunne, T., & Pacenti, E. (1999). Design: Cultural probes. *Interactions, 6*(1), 21-29.

Hagen, P., Robertson, R., Kan, M., & Sadler, K. (2005). Emerging research methods for mobile technology use. In *Proceedings of CHISIG Australia* (pp. 1- 10). ACM Press.

Hutchinson, H., Mackay, W., Westerlund, B., Bederson, B.B., Druin, A., Plaisant, C., Beaudouin-Lafon, M., Conversy, S., Evans, H., Hansen, H., Roussel, N., Eiderbäck, B., Lindquist, S., & Sundblad, Y., (2003). Technology probes: Inspiring design for and with families. In *Proceedings of the SIGCHI Conference on Human Factors in Computing Systems (CHI'03)* (pp. 17-24). ACM Press.

Intille, S.S., Tapia, E.M., Rondoni, J., Beaudin, J., Kukla, C., Agrwal, S., Bao, L., & Larson, K.

(2003). Tools for studying behavior and technology in natural settings. In *Proceedings of Ubiquitous Computing 2004* (pp. 157–174). Springer LNCS 3205.

Isomursu, M., Kuutti, K., & Väinämö, S., (2004). Experience clip: Method for user participation and evaluation of mobile concepts. In *Proceedings Participatory Design Conference 2004*, Toronto, Canada (pp. 83-92).

Jääskö, V., & Mattelmäki, T., (2003). Observing and probing. In *Proceedings of Designing Pleasurable Products and Interfaces Conference (DPPI'03)*, Pittsburgh, PA (pp. 126-131).

Johnson, P. (1998). Usability and mobility: Interaction on the move. In *Proceedings of First Workshop on Human-Computer Interaction with Mobile Devices*, Glasgow, UK (pp. 39-25).

Jones, M., Buchanan, G., & Thimbleby, H. (2002). Sorting out searching on small screen devices. In F. Paterno (Eds.), *Proceedings of the Conference on Human Computer Interaction with Mobile Devices and Services (MobileHCI 2002)* (pp. 81-94). Berlin: Springer.

Jones, M., & Marsden, G. (2006). *Mobile interaction design*. West Sussex, UK: John Wiley.

Kappacher, M. (2007). *Empirische Untersuchung einer GPS gestützten Filmtour für mobile Endgeräte am Beispiel des Films The Sound of Music*. Master thesis, FH Salzburg, Austria.

Kjeldskov, J., & Graham, C. (2003). A review of mobile HCI research methods. In L. Chittaro (Ed.), *Proceedings on the Conference on Human-Computer Interaction with Mobile Devices and Services (MobileHCI 2003)* (pp. 317-335). Berlin: Springer.

Lee, Y.S., Hong, S.W., Smith-Jackson, T.L., Nussbaum, M.A., & Tomioka, K. (2005). Systematic evaluation methodology for cell phone user interfaces. In *Interacting with Computers, 18*(2), 304-325.

Lewis, C., Polson, P., & Wharton, R. (1990). Testing a walkthrough methodology for theory-based design of walk-up-and-us interfaces. In J.C. Chew & J. Whiteside (Eds.), *Proceedings of the SIGCHI Conference on Human Factors in Computing Systems (CHI'90)* (pp. 235-241). Seattle, WA: ACM Press.

Mizobuchi, S., Mori, K., Ren, X., & Michiaki, Y. (2002). An empirical study of the minimum required size and the minimum number of targets for pen input on the small display. In F. Paterno (Ed.), *Proceedings of the Conference on Human Computer Interaction with Mobile Devices and Services (MobileHCI 2002)* (pp. 184-194). Berlin: Springer.

Mueller, F., Agamanolis, S., & Picard, R. (2003). Exertion interfaces: Sports over a distance for social bonding and fun. In *Proceedings of the SIGCHI Conference on Human Factors in Computing Systems (CHI 2003)* (pp. 561-568). ACM Press.

Nielsen, J., & Mack, R. (1994). *Usability inspection methods*. New York: Wiley.

Oviatt, S. (1999). Ten myths of multimodal interaction. *Communications of the ACM, 42*(11), 74–81.

Pascoe, J., Ryan, N., & Morse, D. (2000). Using while moving: Human-computer interaction issues in fieldwork environments. *Transactions on Computer-Human Interaction, 7*(3), 417-437.

Pirhonen, A., Brewster, S., & Holguin, C. (2002). Gestural and audio metaphors as a means of control for mobile devices. In *Proceedings of the SIGCHI Conference on Human Factors in Computing Systems (CHI 2002)* (pp. 291-298). New York: ACM.

Po, S., Howard, S., Vetere, F., & Skov, M.B. (2004). Heuristic evaluation and mobile usability: Bridging the realism gap. In S. Brewster & M. Dunlop (Eds), *Proceedings of the Conference on Human*

Computer Interaction with Mobile Devices and Services (MobileHCI 2004) (pp. 49–60). Berlin: Springer.

Sanders, E. (2002). Ethnography in NPD research. How applied ethnography can improve your NPD research process. Retrieved on October 8, 2006, from http://www.pdma.org/ visions/apr02/applied.html

Salber, D., & Coutaz, J. (1993) Applying the Wizard of Oz technique to the study of multimodal systems. *Human-computer interaction* (LNCS 753, pp. 219-230). Heidelberg: Springer.

Tamminen, S., Oulasvirta, A., Toiskallio, K., & Kankainen, A. (2003). Understanding mobile contexts. In L. Chittaro (Ed.), *Proceedings of the Conference on Human-Computer Interaction with Mobile Devices and Service (MobileHCI 2003)* (pp. 17-31). Berlin, Springer.

Van Esch–Bussemakers, M.P., Neerincx, M.A., Lindenberg, J., & Streefkerk, J.W. (2005). User experience testing in context: Attentive services for the police. In *CHI2005 Workshop Usage Analysis: Combining Logging and Qualitative Methods*, Portland, ME.

Venkatesh, A. (2006). Introduction to the special issue on ICT in everyday life: Home and personal environments. *The Information Society Journal, 22,* 191-194.

Vermeeren, A., & Kort, J. (2006). Developing a testbed for automated user experience measurement of context aware mobile applications. In *Proceedings of the Workshop User Experience–Towards a Unified View*. Retrieved from http://141.115.28.2/cost294/ux-workshop-nordichi2006/nordichi-userexperience-workshop.html

KEY TERMS AND DEFINITIONS

Context: Mobile services and devices can be used in various places and situations, by a single user or involving others. These circumstances are described as context of use or usage context.

Experience Sampling Method (ESM): An in-situ method especially suitable for collecting quantitative and qualitative data with mobile and ubiquitous systems. ESM studies user experience factors in a natural setting, in real time, and over a longer period of time.

In-Situ Evaluation Methods: Set of methods used to evaluate a system or prototype in its real usage context.

Inspection-Oriented UEMs: Set of methods used by experts and most commonly based on guidelines to investigate possible usability problems.

Usability Evaluation Methods (UEMs): A set of methods used to evaluate a system, mockup, or prototype in terms of usability.

Usability Test: Performance measurements of users to determine whether usability goals have been achieved.

Compilation of References

Abacy, T., Cyger, J., & Thalmann, D. (2005). Action semantics in smart objects. In *Workshop Towards SVE* (pp. 1-7).

Abascal, J., & Civit, A. (2001). Universal access to mobile telephony as a way to enhance the autonomy of elderly people. *WUAUC 2001.* Alcacer so Sal. Portugal.

Abowd, G. D., & Beale, R. (1991). Users, systems, and interfaces: A unifying framework for interaction. In D. Diaper & N. Hammon (Eds.), *Proc. HCI: People and Comput. VI* (pp. 73–87). Cambridge University Press.

Acampora, G., Loia, V., Nappi, M., & Ricciardi, S. (2006, October 8-11). A semantic view for flexible communication models between humans, sensors, and actuators. In *Proceedings of the IEEE International Conference on Systems, Man, and Cybernetics*, Taipei, Taiwan (pp. 3640-3646). IEEE Press.

Adewunmi, A., et al. (2003). Enhancing the in-classroom teaching/learning experience using wireless technology. In *Proc. of 33rd ASEE/IEEE Frontiers in Education Conference*, Boulder, CO (pp. S4E-20-5).

Adler, A., & Davis, R. (2007, August 2-3). *Speech and sketching: An empirical study of multimodal interaction.* Paper presented at the Fourth Eurographics Conference on Sketch Based Interfaces and Modeling, Riverside, CA.

Aggelidis, V.P., & Chatzoglou, P.D. (2008). Using a modified technology acceptance model in hospitals. *International Journal of Medical Informatics,*.doi:10.1016/j.ijmedinf.2008.06.006

Agrawal, R., & Srikant, R. (1995). Mining sequential patterns. In *Proceedings of the International Conference on Data Engineering (ICDE95)* (pp. 3-14).

Agrawal, R., Manilla, H., Srikant, R., Toivonen, H., & Verkamo, A. (1996). Fast discovery of association rules. In U. Fayyad, G. Piatetsky-Shapiro, P. Smyth, & R. Uthurusamy (Eds.), *Advances in knowledge discovery and data mining* (pp. 307-328). AAAI Press.

Aho, A., Sethi, R., & Ullman, J. (1986). *Compilers, principles, techniques, and tools.* Addison-Wesley.

Alshawi, H., & Crouch, R. (1992). Monotonic semantic interpretation. In *the Proceedings of the 30th Annual Meeting of the Association for Computational Linguistics.*

Alvarez-Cortes, V., Zayas-Perez, B., Zarate-Silva, E., Ramirez, V.H., & Uresti, J.A. (2007, September 25-28). Current trends in adaptive user interfaces: Challenges and applications. *Electronics, Robotics, and Automotive Mechanics Conference, CERMA 2007* (pp. 312-317).

Ambler, S. (2004). *Object primer, the agile model-driven development with UML 2.0.* Cambridge University Press.

American Psychological Association. (1994). *Publication manual of the American Psychological Association (4th ed.).* Washington, DC.

Andre, M., Popescu, V.G., Shaikh, A., Medl, A., Marsic, I., Kulikowski, C., & Flanagan J.L. (1998, January). Integration of speech and gesture for multimodal human-computer interaction. In *Second International Conference on Cooperative Multimodal Communication*, Tilburg, The Netherlands (pp. 28-30).

Annotea Project. (2008). Retrieved on May 8, 2008, from http://www.w3.org/2001/Annotea

Arai, K., Wright, J.H., Riccardi, G., & Gorin, A. (1999). Grammar fragment acquisition using syntactic and semantic clustering. *Speech Communication, 27*.

Ardissono, L., Gena, C., Torasso, P., Bellifemmine, F., Difino, A., & Negro, B. (2004). *Personalized digital television –targeting programs to individual viewers* (Vol. 6, pp. 3-26). Springer.

Ardito, C., Costabile, F., De Angelis, A., & Pittarello, F. (2007). Navigation help in 3D worlds: Some empirical evidences on use of sound. *Multimedia Tools and Applications Journal, 33*(2), 201–216.

Arens, Y., & Hovy, E. (1990). How to describe what? Towards a theory of modality utilization. In *Proceedings of the 12ᵗʰ Conference of the Cognitive Science Society* (pp. 18-26).

Arning, K., & Ziefle, M. (2007). Understanding age differences in pda acceptance and performance. *Computers in Human Behaviour, 23*, 2904-2927.

Auburn, R.J. (2007, June). *Voice browser call control: CCXML version 1.0*. Retrieved from http://www.w3.org/TR/ccxml/

Augusto, J.C., & Nugent, C.D. (Eds.) (2006). *Designing smart homes, the role of artificial intelligence* (LNCS 4008). Springer.

Avola D., Caschera, M.C., & Grifoni, P. (2006). Solving ambiguities for sketch-based interaction in mobile enviroments. *Workshop on Mobile and Networking Technologies for social applications (MONET 06), Springer-Verlag,* (LNCS 4278, pp. 904-915).

Avola, D., Caschera, M.C., Ferri, F., & Grifoni P. (2007). Ambiguities in sketch-based interfaces. *Hawaii International Conference on System Sciences (HICSS 2007). Proceedings of the Hawaii International Conference on System Sciences*. IEEE Computer Society.

Avola, D., Ferri, F. & Grifoni, P. (2007). Formalizing recognition of sketching styles in human centered systems. *11ᵗʰ International Conference on Knowledge-Based and Intelligent Information & Engineering, Systems (KES2007)* (LNAI). Springer-Verlag.

Axelsson, J., Cross, C., Ferrans, J., McCobb, G., Raman, T., & Wilson, L. (2004). *XHTML + Voice profile*. Retrieved from http://www.voicexml.org/specs/multi-modal/x+v/12/

Bach, C., & Scapin, D. (2003). Ergonomic criteria adapted to human virtual environment interaction. In M. Rauterberg, M. Menozzi & J. Wesson (Eds.), *IFIP Conference on Human-Computer Interaction (INTERACT'2003)* (pp. 880–883). Zurich: IOS Press.

Bachvarova, Y.S., van Dijk, E.M.A.G., & Nijholt, A. (2007, January 25-26). Towards a unified knowledge-based approach to modality choice. In *Proceedings Workshop on Multimodal Output Generation (MOG 2007)*, Aberdeen, Scotland (pp. 5-15).

Baggia, P., & Scahill, F. (2004). *Pronunciation lexicon specification (PLS) version 1.0 requirements*. Retrieved from http://www.w3.org/TR/2004/WD-lexicon-reqs-20041029/

Baggia, P., Bagshaw, P., Burnett, D., Carter, J., & Scahill, F. (2008). *Pronunciation lexicon specification (PLS) version 1.0*. Retrieved from http://www.w3.org/TR/pronunciation-lexicon/

Baggia, P., Burnett, D.C., Carter, J., Dahl, D.A., McCobb, G., & Raggett, D. (2007). EMMA: Extensible multimodal annotation markup language, W3C recommendation. Retrieved from http://www.w3.org/TR/emma/

Baldi, R.A. (1997). Training older adults to use the computer. Issues related to the workplace, attitudes, and training. *Educational Gerontology, 23*, 453-465.

Baldridge, J., & Kruijff, G. M. (2002, July 6-12). Coupling CCG and hybrid logic dependency semantics. In *Proceedings of ACL 2002*, Philadelphia, PA. ACL.

Baldridge, J., Kruijff, G., & White, M. (2003). *OpenCCG*. Retrieved from http://openccg.sourceforge.net

Baljko, M. (2005). The information-theoric analysis of unimodal interfaces and their multimodal counterparts. *SIGACCESS Conference on Computers and Accessibility* (pp. 28-35). New York: ACM Press.

Ballard, D., Hayhoe, M., Pook, P., & Rao, R. (1997). Deictic codes for the embodiment of cognition. *Behavioral and Brain Sciences*, *20*, 723–767.

Bangalore, S., & Johnston, M. (2000, October 16-20). Integrating multimodal language processing with speech recognition. In *Proceedings of ICSLP 2000*, Beijing, China. ISCA.

Barnard, P., May, J., Duke, D., & Duce, D. (2000). Systems, interactions, and macrotheory. *ACM Trans. Comput.-Hum. Interact.*, *7*(2), 222–262.

Barnett, J., Akolkar, R., Bodell, M., Burnett, D.C., Carter, J., McGlashan, S., et al. (2008). *State chart XML (SCXML): State machine notation for control abstraction*. Retrieved from http://www.w3.org/TR/scxml/

Barnett, J., Dahl, D.A., Kliche, I., Tumuluri, R., Yudkowsky, M., Bodell, M., et al. (2008, April 14). *Multimodal architecture and interfaces*. Retrieved from http://www.w3.org/TR/mmi-arch/

Baum, L.E., & Petrie, T. (1966). Statistical inference for probabilistic funtions of finite state Markov chains. *Annals of Mathematical Statistics*, 1554-1563.

Bayer, S. (2005). Building a standards and research community with the galaxy communicator software infrastructure. In D.A. Dahl (Ed.), *Practical spoken dialog systems* (Vol. 26, pp. 166-196). Dordrecht: Kluwer Academic Publishers.

Beckett, D. (Ed.). (2004). RDF/XML syntax specification (rev.), W3C recommendation. Retrieved from http://www.w3.org/TR/rdf-syntax-grammar/

Benedek, A. (2003). Mobile learning and lifelong knowledge acquisition. In K. Nyíri (Ed.), *Mobile studies paradigms and perspectives*. Passagen Verlag.

Benford, S., Schnoedelbach, H., Koleva, B., Anastasi, R., Greenhalgh, C., Rodden, T., et al. (2005). Expected, sensed, and desired: A framework for designing sensing-based interaction. *ACM Trans. Comput.-Hum. Interact.*, *12*(1), 3-30.

Bennett, B., Cohn, A.G., Wolter, F., & Zakharyaschev, M. (2002). Multi-dimensional modal logic as a framework for spatio-temporal reasoning. *Applied Intelligence*, *17*(3), 239-251.

Bennett, G., Lindgaard, G., Tsuji, B., Connelly, K.H., & Siek, K.A. (2006). Reality testing: HCI challenge in non-traditional environments. In *Proceedings of CHI 2006, Extended Abstracts* (pp. 1679-1682). New York: ACM Press.

Benoit, C., Martin, J.C., Pelachaud, C., Schomaker, L., & Suhm, B. (2000). Audio-visual and multimodal speech-based systems. In D. Gibbon, I. Mertins & R. Moore (Eds.), *Handbook of multimodal systems and spoken dialogue systems: Resources, terminology, and product evaluation*. Kluwer Academic Publishers.

Bentley, T. (1998). *Learning beyond the classroom: education for a changing world*. London: Routledge.

Bergin, D.A., Anderson, A.H., Molnar, T., Baumgartner, R., Mitchell, S., Korper, S., Curley, A., & Rottmann, J. (2004). Providing remote accessible field trips (RAFT): An evaluation study. *Computers in Human Behavior*, *23*(1), 192-219.

Berkman Center for Internet & Society. (2003). *Really simple syndication (RSS)*. Retrieved on October 27, 2008, from http://cyber.law.harvard.edu/rss/rss.html

Berners-Lee, T., Hendler, J., & Lassila, O. (2001, May). The Semantic Web - a new form of Web content that is meaningful to computers will unleash a revolution of new possibilities. *Scientific American*.

Bernhaupt, R., Mihalic, K., & Obrist, M. (2008). Usability evaluation methods for mobile applications. In J. Lumsden (Ed.), *Handbook of research on user interface design and evaluation for mobile technology* (pp. 745-758). Hershey, PA: IGI Global.

Bernhaupt, R., Navarre, D., Palanque, P., & Winckler, M. (2008). Model-based evaluation: A new way to support usability evaluation of multimodal interactive applications. In E. Law, E. Hvannberg, G. Cockton & J. Vanderdonckt. (Eds.), *Maturing usability: quality in software, interaction, and quality* (pp. 96-122). Heidelberg: Springer.

Bernhaupt, R., Weiss, A., Obrist, M., & Tscheligi, M. (2007). Playful probing: Making probing more fun. In *Proceedings of Interact 2007* (pp. 606–619). Heidelberg: Springer LNCS.

Bernsen, N.O. (1994). Foundations of multimodal representations: A taxonomy of representational modalities. *Interacting With Computers, 6*(4).

Berry, D.M., Kamsties, E., Kay, D.G., & Krieger, M.M. (2001). *From contract drafting to software specification: Linguistic sources of ambiguity* (Tech. Rep.). Canada: University of Waterloo.

Beyer, H., & Holtzblatt, K. (1998). *Contextual design: Defining customer-centred systems*. San Francisco: Morgan Kaufmann Publishers Inc.

Bierbaum, A., Just, C., Hartling, P., Meinert, K., Baker, A., & Cruz-Neira, C. (2001). Vr juggler: A virtual platform for virtual reality application development. In *Proceedings of Virtual Reality 2001 Conference*, Yokohama, Japan (pp. 89-96).

Bille, W., Pellens, B., Kleinermann, F., & De Troyer, O. (2004). Intelligent modelling of virtual worlds using domain ontologies. In *Proceedings of the Workshop of Intelligent Computing (WIC), held in conjunction with the MICAI 2004 Conference*, Mexico City, Mexico (pp. 272-279).

Blackburn, P. (2000). Representation, reasoning, relational structures: A hybrid logic manifesto. *Journal of the Interest Group in Pure Logic, 8*(3), 339-365.

Blaser, A.D., Sester, M., & Egenhofer, M. (2000). Visualization in an early stage of the problem solving process in GIS. *Computer and GeoSciences, Special Issue on GeoScientific Visualization, 26*(1), 57-66. Elsevier Science.

Blattner, M., Sumikawa, D., & Greenberg, R. (1989). Earcons and icons: Their structure and common design principles. *Human-Computer Interaction, 4*(1), 11–44.

Blythe, P.T., & Curtis, A.M. (2004). Advanced driver assistance systems: Gimmick or reality? *11th World Congress on ITS*, Nagoya, Japan.

Bodker, S., & Gronbaek, K. (1991). Design in action: From prototyping by demonstration to cooperative prototyping. In Greenbaum & Kying (Eds.), *Design at work: Cooperative design of computer systems* (pp. 197-218). Hillsdale, NJ: Lawrence Erlbaum Associates.

Bodker, S., Gronnbaek, K., & Kyng, M. (1993). Cooperative design: Techniques and experiences from the Scandinavian scene. In Schuler & Namioka (Eds.), *Participatory design - principles and practices* (pp. 157-175). Hillsdale, NJ: Lawrence Erlbaum Associates.

Bohan, M., Stokes, A.F., & Humphrey, D.G. (1997). An investigation of dwell time in cursor positioning movements. In *Proceedings of the 41st Annual Meeting of the Human Factors Society* (pp. 365–369). Santa Monica, CA: The Human Factors and Ergonomics Society.

Bolt, R.A. (1980). Put-that-there: Voice and gesture at the graphics interface. In *SIGGRAPH '80: Proceedings of the 7th International Conference on Computer Graphics and Interactive Techniques* (pp. 262–270). New York: ACM Press.

Bolt, R.E., & Herranz, E. (1992). Two-handed gesture in multimodal natural dialog. In J. Mackinlay & M. Green (Eds.), *Proceedings of the Symposium on User Interface Software and Technology (UIST'92)* (pp. 7-14) New York: ACM Press.

Bos, B., Lie, H.W., Lilley, C., & Jacobs, I. (1998). *Cascading style sheets, level 2 (CSS2) specification - W3C recommendation*. Retrieved from http://www.w3.org/TR/REC-CSS2/

Bottoni, P., Civica, R., Levialdi, S., Orso, L., Panizzi, E., & Trinchese, R. (2004). MADCOW: A multimedia digital annotation system. In M.F. Costabile (Ed.), *Proceedings of the Working Conference on Advanced Visual Interfaces* (pp. 55-62). ACM Press.

Bottoni, P., Ferri, F., Grifoni, P., Mussio, P., Marcante, A., Padula, M., & Reggiori, A. (in press). E-Document management in situated interactivity: The WIL approach. *Universal Access in the Information Society. International Journal*.

Botwinick, J. (1967). *Cognitive processes in maturity and old age*. Springer.

Bouchard, D., & Badler, N. (2007, September 17-19). Semantic segmentation of motion capture using laban movement analysis. In *Intelligent Virtual Agents, Proceedings of the 7th International Conference IVA 2007*, Paris, France (pp. 37-44). Heidelberg: Springer.

Bouchet, J., Nigay, L., & Ganille, T. (2004). Icare software components for rapidly developing multimodal interfaces. In *Proceedings of the 6th International Conference on Multimodal Interfaces (ICMI '04)*, New York, NY (pp. 251-258). ACM.

Bowman, D., & Hodges, L. (1997). An evaluation of techniques for grabbing and manipulating remote objects in immersive virtual environments. In *Proceedings of the Symposium on Interactive 3D Graphics (1997)* (pp. 35–38).

Bowman, D., Kruijff, E., La Viola, J., & Poupyrev, I. (2000). The art and science of 3D interaction. Tutorial notes. In *Proceedings of IEEE International Virtual Reality 2000 conference*. New Brunswick, NJ.

Boyle, C., & Encarnacion, A.O. (1994). Metadoc: An adaptive hypertext reading system. *User Modeling and User-Adapted Interaction, Kluwer Academic, 4*(1), 1–19.

BPEL. Retrieved from http://www.jboss.org/jbossjbpm/bpel/

Brajnik, G., & Tasso, C. (1992). A flexible tool for developing user modeling applications with nonmonotonic reasoning capabilities. In *Proceedings of the Third International Workshop on User Modeling*, Dagstuhl, Germany (pp. 42-66).

Bratko, I. (2001). *Prolog programming for artificial intelligence, 3rd ed.* Boston: Addison-Wesley Longman Publishing Co., Inc.

Brewster, S. (2002). Overcoming the lack of screen space on mobile computers. *Personal and Ubiquitous Computing, 6*(3), 188-205.

Brewster, S., Wright, P., & Edwards, A. (1993). An evaluation of earcons for use in auditory human-computer interfaces. In *Proceedings of InterCHI'93*, Amsterdam (pp. 222–227).

Brewster, S.A., Wright, P.C., & Edwards, A.D.N. (1994). The design and evaluation of an auditory-enhanced scrollbar. In *Proceedings of the SIGCHI Conference on Human factors in computing systems (CHI '94)* (pp. 173-179). New York: ACM Press.

Bridgeman, B., Peery, S., & Anand, S. (1997). Interaction of cognitive and sensorimotor maps of visual space. *Perception and Psychophysics, 59*(3), 456–469.

Brodie, C.B., & Hayes, C.C. (2002). DAISY: A decision support design methodology for complex, experience-centered domains. *IEEE Trans. on Systems, Man, and Cybernetics - Part A, 32*(1), 50-71.

Brown, M.K., Kellner, A., & Raggett, D. (2001). *Stochastic language models (n-gram) specification*. Retrieved from http://www.w3.org/TR/ngram-spec/

Brown, S.S., & Robinson, P. (2004). Transformation frameworks and their relevance in universal design. *Universal Access in the Information Society, 3.3*(4), 209-223.

Brusilovsky, P., Kobsa, A., & Nejdl, W. (Eds.) (2007). *The adaptive web: Methods and strategies of Web personalization* (LNCS). Berlin: Springer.

Budde, R., Kuhlenkamp, K., Mathiassen, L., & Zullighoven, H. (Eds.) (1984). Approaches to prototyping. New York: Springer-Verlag.

Buisine, S., & Martin, J. (2003). Design principles for cooperation between modalities in bidirectional multimodal interfaces. In *CHI'2003 Workshop on Principles for Multimodal User Interface Design*, Florida (pp. 5-10).

Buring, D. (2007). Intonation, semantics, and information structure. In G. Ramchand, & C. Reiss (Eds.), *The Oxford handbook of linguistic interfaces.*

Burke, D.M., & Mackay, D.G. (1997). Memory, language, and ageing. *Philosophical Transactions of the Royal Society B: Biological Sciences, 352*(1363), 1845-1856.

Burnett, D.C., Walker, M.R., & Hunt, A. (2004). *W3C speech synthesis markup language (SSML)*. Retrieved from http://www.w3.org/TR/speech-synthesis/

Burnett, D.C., Walker, M.R., & Hunt, A. (Ed.). (2004). Speech synthesis markup language (SSML), version 1.0, W3C recommendation. Retrieved from http://www.w3.org/TR/speech-synthesis/

Button, G. (Ed.) (1993). Technology in working order: Studies of work, interaction, and technology. New York: Routledge.

Buvac, S. (1996). Resolving lexical ambiguity using a formal theory of context. In K. Van Deemter, & S. Peters (Eds.), *Semantic ambiguity and underspecification.* CSLI Publications.

Caldwell, B., Cooper, M., Reid, L.G., & Vanderheiden, G. (2007). *Web content accessibility guidelines 2.0.* Retrieved from http://www.w3.org/TR/2007/WD-WCAG20-20071211/

Calvary, G., Coutaz, J., Thevenin, D., Limbourg, Q., Bouillon, L., & Vanderdonckt, J. (2003). A unifying reference framework for multi-target user interfaces. *Interaction with Computers, 15*(3), 289-308.

Camacho, D., Hernandez, C., & Molina, J.M. (2001). Information classification using fuzzy knowledge based agents, (Vol. 4, pp. 2575-2580).

Card, S.K., Newell, A., & Moran, T.P. (1983). *The psychology of human-computer interaction.* Mahwah, NJ: Lawrence Erlbaum Associates, Inc.

Carmien, S., Dawe, M., Fischer, G., Gorman, A., Kintsch, A., & Sullivan, J.F. (2005). Sociotechnical environments supporting people with cognitive disabilities using public transportation. *ACM Transactions on Computer Human Interaction, 12*(2), 233-262.

Carpenter, B. (1992). *The logic of typed feature structures.* UK: Cambridge University Press.

Carr, D. (1997). Interaction object graphs: An executable graphical notation for specifying user interfaces. In *Formal methods for computer-human interaction* (pp. 141-156). Springer-Verlag.

Carrara, P., Fresta, G., & Mussio, P. (2001). SVG: More than a markup language for vector graphics. In *Proceedings of EuroWeb 2001 - The Web in Public Administration* (pp. 245-257).

Carrozzino, M., Tecchia, F., Bacinelli, S., Cappelletti, C., & Bergamasco, M. (2005). Lowering the development time of multimodal interactive application: The real-life experience of the xvr project. In *Proceedings of the International Conference on Advances in Computer Entertainment Technology*, Valencia, Spain (pp. 270-273).

Caschera, M.C., Ferri, F., & Grifoni, P. (2007). An approach for managing ambiguities in multimodal interaction. *OTM Workshops*, (1), 387-397.

Caschera, M.C., Ferri, F., & Grifoni, P. (2007). *Management of ambiguities. Visual languages for interactive computing: Definitions and formalizations.* Hershey, PA: IGI Publishing.

Caschera, M.C., Ferri, F., & Grifoni, P. (2007). Multimodal interaction systems: Information and time features. *International Journal of Web and Grid Services, 3*(1), 82-99.

Cassell, J., Vilhjalmsson, H. (1999). Fully embodied conversational avatars: Making communicative behaviors autonomous. *Autonomous Agents and Multiagent Systems, 2*, 45-64.

Castellina E., Corno F., & Pellegrino P. (2008). Integrated speech and gaze control for realistic desktop environments. *ETRA'08: 2008 Symposium on Eye Tracking Research & Applications* (pp. 79-85). New York: ACM Press.

Chai, J.Y., Hong, P., & Zhou, M.X. (2004). A probabilistic approach to reference resolution in multimodal user interfaces. In *Proceedings of 9th International Conference on Intelligent User Interfaces (IUI)* (pp. 70-77).

Chai, J.Y., Prasov, Z., & Qu, S. (2006). Cognitive principles in robust multimodal interpretation. *Journal of Artificial Intelligence Research, 27*, 55-83.

Chaiklin, S., & Lave, J. (Eds.) (1993). Understanding practice: Perspectives on activity and context. Cambridge, MA: Cambridge University Press.

Chan, Y.Y., Leung, C.H., & Wu, A.K.W., & Chan, S.C. (2003). MobiLP: A mobile learning platform for enhancing lifewide learning. In *Proceedings on the 3ʳᵈ IEEE International Conference on Advanced Learning Technologies 2003*, Athens, Greece (pp. 457-457).

Chang, A., & Ishii, H. (2006). Personalized interactions with reality based interfaces. *CHI 2006 Workshop "What is the Next Generation of Human-Computer Interaction?"*

Chang, K.T. (2002). Introduction to geographic information systems. New York: McGraw Hill.

Charaniya, A.P., & Lodha, S.K. (2003). Speech interface for geospatial visualization. *Computer Graphics International.* Acta Press.

Chee, Y.-M., Froumentin, M., & Watt, S.M. (2006). *Ink markup language*. Retrieved from http://www.w3.org/TR/InkML

Chen, F., Choi, E., Epps, J., Lichman, S., Ruiz, N., Shi, Y., et al. (2005, October 4-6). A study of manual gesture-based selection for the PEMMI multimodal transport management interface. In *Proceedings of ICMI2005*, Trento, Italy.

Chen, Y. S., & Magoulas, G.D. (2005). *Adaptable and adaptive hypermedia systems.* IRM Press. CollabNet. (2008). JavaCC-java compiler compiler (JavaCC)-the java parser generator. Retrieved on October 27, 2008, from https://javacc.dev.java.net/

Cheverst, K., Davies, N., Mitchell, K., Friday, A., & Efstratiou, C. (2000). Developing a context-aware electronic tourist guide: Some issues and experiences. In *CHI'00: Proceedings of the SIGCHI conference on Human factors in computing systems*, New York (pp. 17-24). ACM.

Chismar, W.G., & Wiley-Patton, S. (2003). Does the extended technology acceptance model apply to physicians? In *Proceedings of the 36ᵗʰ Annual Hawaii International Conference on System Sciences*, doi 10.1109/HICSS.2003.1174354.

Chittaro, L. (2006). Visualizing information on mobile devices. *IEEE Computer, 39*(3), 40-45.

Cho, S.J., & Murray-Smith, R., & Kim, Y.-B. (2007). Multicontext photo browsing on mobile devices based on tilt dynamics. In *Mobile HCI '07,* Singapore.

Chok, S.S., & Marriott, K. (1995). Automatic construction of user interfaces from constraint multiset grammars. In *11ᵗʰ International IEEE Symposium on Visual Languages* (pp. 242-245.

Chomsky, N. (1971). Deep structure, surface structure, and semantic interpretation. In D.D. Steinberg, & L.A. Jakobovits (Eds.), *Semantics. An interdisciplinary reader in philosophy, linguistics, and psychology* (pp. 183-216). MA: Cambridge University Press.

Christensen, E., Curbera, F., Meredith, G., & Weerawarana, S. (2001). Web services description language (WSDL) 1.1, W3C note. Retrieved from http://www.w3.org/TR/wsdl

Chu, S.M., Libal, V., Marcheret, E., Neti, C., & Potamianos, G. (2004, June 27-30). Multistage information fusion for audio-visual speech recognition. In *Proceedings of the (IEEE) International Conference on Multimedia and Expo 2004, (ICME '04)*, New York, NY (Vol. 3, pp.1651-1654).

Cimiano, P., Eberhart, A., Hitzler, P., Oberle, D., Staab, S., & Studer, R. (2004). *The smartweb foundational ontology* (Tech. Rep. AIFB). University of Karlsruhe, Germany, SmartWeb Project.

Clark, H., & Wilkes-Gibbs, D. (1986). Referring as a collaborative process. *Cognition, 22*(22), 1–39.

Clarke, I., Flaherty, T., & Madison, J. (2003). Mobile portals: The development of m-commerce. In B. Mennecke & T. Strader (Eds.), *Mobile commerce: Technology, theory, and applications*. Hershey, PA: IRM Press.

Clerckx, T., Luyten, K., & Coninx, K. (2004). Dynamo-AID: A design process and a runtime architecture for dynamic model-based user interface development. In *9ᵗʰ IFIP Working Conference on Engineering for Human-Computer Interaction jointly with 11ᵗʰ International*

Workshop on Design, Specification, and Verification of Interactive Systems EHCI-DSVIS 2004, Hamburg, Germany (pp. 77-95). Springer-Verlag.

Clerckx, T., Vandervelpen, C., & Coninx, K. (2007). Task-based design and runtime support for multimodal user interface distribution. In *Engineering Interactive Systems 2007; EHCI/HCSE/DSVIS,* Salamanca, Spain.

Cohen, P., Johnston, M., McGee, D., Oviatt, S., Pittman, J., Smith, I., Chen, L., & Clow, J. (1997, November 9-13). QuickSet: Multimodal interaction for distributed applications. In *Proceedings of the 5th ACM International Conference on Multimedia,* Seattle, WA (pp. 31-40).

Coiera, E. (2001). Mediated agent interaction. In *Proceedings of the 8th Conference on Artificial Intelligence in Medicine Europe, AIME 2001.*

Collins, A., Brown, J.S., & Newman, S.E. (1989). Cognitive apprenticeship: Teaching the craft of reading, writing, and mathematics. In L.B. Resnick (Ed.), *Knowing, learning, and instruction* (pp. 453-494). Hillsdale, NJ: Lawrence Erlbaum Associates.

Collins, M. (1997). Three generative, lexicalised models for statistical parsing. In *Proceedings of the 35th Meeting of the Association for Computational Linguistics and the 7th Conference of the European Chapter of the ACL* (pp. 16-23).

Coninx, K., Cuppens, E., De Boeck, J., & Raymaekers, C. (2006). Integrating support for usability evaluation into high level interaction descriptions with NiMMiT. In *Proceedings of 13th International Workshop on Design, Specification and Verification of Interactive Systems (DSVIS'06),* Dublin, Ireland (Vol. 4385).

Coninx, K., De Troyer, O., Raymaekers, C., & Kleinermann, F. (2006). VR-DeMo: A tool-supported approach facilitating flexible development of virtual environments using conceptual modelling. In *Virtual Concept 2006 (VC 06),* Cancun, Mexico.

Coninx, K., Van Reeth, F., & Flerackers, E. (1997). A hybrid 2D/3D user interface for immersive object modeling. In *Proceedings of Computer Graphics International '97,* Hasselt and Diepenbeek, BE (pp. 47-55).

Conner, T., Barrett, L.F., Bliss-Moreau, E., Lebo, K., & Kaschub, C. (2003). A practical guide to experience-sampling procedures. *Journal of Happiness Studies, 4,* 53-78.

Constantini, E., Pianesi, F., & Prete, M. (2005). Recognising emotions in human and synthetic faces: The role of the upper and lower parts of the face. In *10th International Conference on Intelligent User Interfaces,* San Diego, CA (pp. 20-27). ACM Press.

Conti, G., Ucelli, G., & De Amicis, R. (2006). "Verba volant scripta manent" a false axiom within virtual environments. A semiautomatic tool for retrieval of semantics understanding for speech-enabled vr applications. *Computers & Graphics, 30*(4), 619-628.

Cook, D.J. (2006). Health monitoring and assistance to support aging in place. *The Journal of Universal Computer Science, 12*(1),15-29.

Corcho, O., Alper, P., Kotsiopoulos, I., Missier, P., Bechhofer, S., & Goble, C. (2006). An overview of S-OGSA: A reference semantic grid architecture. *Web Semantics: Science, Services, and Agents on the World Wide Web, 4*(2).

Corradini, A., Mehta, M., Bernsen, N.O., & Martin, J.-C. (2003). Multimodal input fusion in human-computer interaction on the example of the ongoing NICE project. In *Proceedings of the NATO-ASI Conference on Data Fusion for Situation Monitoring, Incident Detection, Alert, and Response Management,* Yerevan, Armenia.

Corradini, A., Wesson, R., Cohen, P. (2002, October 14-16). A map-based system using speech and 3D gestures for pervasive computing. In *Proceedings of the 4th IEEE International Conference on Multimodal Interfaces (ICMI'02),* Pittsburgh, PA (pp. 191-196) .

Costabile, M.F., Fogli, D., Lanzilotti, R., Marcante, A., Mussio, P., Parasiliti Provenza, L., & Piccinno, A. (2007). Meta-design to face coevolution and communication gaps between users and designers (LNCS 4554, pp. 46-55).

Costabile, M.F., Fogli, D., Mussio, P., & Piccinno, A. (2007). Visual interactive systems for end-user development: A modelbased design methodology. *IEEE*

Transactions on Systems, Man and Cybernetics - Part A: Systems and Humans, 37(6), 1029-1046.

Costabile, M.F., Fogli, D., Fresta, G., Mussio, P., & Piccinno, P. (2002). Computer environments for improving end-user accessibility. In *Proceedings of 7ᵗʰ ERCIM Workshop User Interfaces For All*, Paris, 187-198.

Costabile, M.F., Fogli, D., Lanzilotti, R., Mussio, P., & Piccinno, A. (2005). Supporting work practice through end user development environments (Tech. Rep. 01.10.2005). Bari, Italy: Università degli Studi di Bari, Dipartimento di Informatica.

Costabile, M.F., Fogli, D., Marcante, A., Mussio, P., Parasiliti Provenza, L., & Piccinno, A. (in press). Designing customized and tailorable visual interactive systems. *International Journal of Software Engineering and Knowledge Engineering*.

Costabile, M.F., Fogli, D., Mussio, P., & Piccinno, A. (2006). End-user development: The software shaping workshop approach. In H. Lieberman, F. Paternò & V. Wulf (Eds.), *End user development empowering people to flexibly employ advanced information and communication technology* (pp. 183-205). Dordrecht: Springer.

Counts, S., Hofter, H., & Smith, I. (2006). Mobile social software: Realizing potential, managing risks. *Workshop at the Conference on Human Factors in Computing Systems (CHI '06)* (pp.1703-1706).

Coutaz, J., & Caelen, J. (1991, November). A taxonomy for multimedia and multimodal user interfaces. In *Proceedings of the 1ˢᵗ ERCIM Workshop on Multimedia HCI*, Lisbon.

Coutaz, J., Nigay, L., & Salber, D. (1993). The MSM framework: A design space for multisensori-motor systems. In L. Bass, J. Gornostaev, C. Unger (Eds.), *Human computer interaction. In 3ʳᵈ International Conference EWHCI'93, East/West Human Computer Interaction*, Moscow (LNCS 753). Springer Verlag.

Coutaz, J., Nigay, L., Salber, D., Blandford, A., May, J., & Young, R.M. (1995). Four easy pieces for assessing the usability of multimodal interaction: The CARE properties. In *Proceedings of INTERACT95*, Lillehammer (pp. 115-120).

Cross, C., Axelsson, J., McCobb, G., Raman, T.V., & Wilson, L. (2003). *XHTML + voice profile 1.1*. Retrieved from http://www-306.ibm.com/software/pervasive/multimodal/x+v/11/spec.htm

Cuppens, E., Raymaekers, C., & Coninx, K. (2004). VRIXML: A user interface description language for virtual environments. In *Developing user interfaces with XML: Advances on user interface description languages* (pp. 111-117). Gallipoli, Italy.

D'Ulizia, A., Ferri, F., & Grifoni, P. (2007, November 25-30). A hybrid grammar-based approach to multimodal languages specification. In *OTM 2007 Workshop Proceedings*, Vilamoura, Portugal (LNCS 4805, pp. 367-376). Springer-Verlag.

D'Ulizia, A., Grifoni, P., & Rafanelli, M. (2007). Classification of ambiguities. In *Visual languages for interactive computing: Definitions and formalizations*. Hershey, PA: IGI Publishing.

Dahl, D.A. (2005). Visualization tools for designing spoken dialogs. In D.A. Dahl (Ed.), *Practical spoken dialog systems*.

Davis, F.D. (1989). Perceived usefulness, perceived ease of use, and user acceptance of information technology. *MIS Quarterly, 13*(3), 319-340.

Davis, K.H., Biddulph, R., & Balashek, S. (1952). Automatic recognition of spoken digits. *Journal of the Acoustical Society of America , 24*, 627-642.

De Boeck, J., Gonzalez Calleros, J.M., Coninx, K., & Vanderdonckt, J. (2006). Open issues for the development of 3D multimodal applications from an MDE perspective. In *MDDAUI Workshop 2006*, Genova, Italy.

De Boeck, J., Raymaekers, C., & Coninx, K. (2007). Comparing NiMMiT and data-driven notations for describing multimodal interaction. In *Proceedings of TAMODIA 2006* (LNCS, pp. 217-229).

De Boeck, J., Vanacken, D., Raymaekers, C., & Coninx, K. (2007). High-level modeling of multimodal interaction techniques using nimmit. *Journal of Virtual Reality and Broadcasting, 4*(2).

De Jong, T., Specht, M., & Koper, R. (2008). A reference model for mobile social software for learning. *International Journal of Continuing Engineering Education and Life-Long Learning (IJCEELL), 18*(1), 118-138.

Dehaspe, L., & Toivonen, H. (1999). Discovery of frequent datalog patterns. *Data Mining and Knowledge Discovery, 3*(1), 7-36.

Deng, L., & Huang, X. (2004). Challenges in adopting speech recognition. *Communications of the ACM, 47*(1), 69-75. ACM Press.

DePaula, R. (2004). Lost in translation: A critical analysis of actors, artifacts, agendas, and arenas in participatory design. In *Proc. PDC*, Toronto, Canada (pp. 162–172).

Deray, K., & Simoff, S.J. (2007). Designing a visual language for interaction representation based on aspects of human movement. In F. Ferri (Ed.), *Visual Languages for Interactive Computing: Definitions and Formalizations* (pp. 205-231). Hershey, PA: IGI Global.

Deray, K., & Simoff, S.J. (2008, October 20-23). Visualising the dynamics of unfolding interactions on mobile devices. *Advances in Conceptual Modeling-Challenges and Opportunities, Proceedings of the ER 2008 International Workshop on Modeling Mobile Applications and Services (M2AS'08)*, Barcelona, Spain (pp. 238-247). Springer.

Desilets, A., Paquet, S., & Vinson, N. (2005, October 16-18). Are wikis usable? In *WikiSym Conference*, San Diego, CA.

Dey, A.K. (2001). Understanding and using context. Personal Ubiquitous Computing, 5(1), 4-7.

Dey, A.K., Salber, D., & Abowd, G.D. (2001). A conceptual framework and a toolkit for supporting the rapid prototyping of context-aware applications. In T.P. Moran, & P. Dourish (Eds.), *Human-Computer Interaction, 16*(2-4), 97-166.

Dijkstra, E.W. (1959). A note on two problems in connexion with graphs. *Numerische Mathematik, 1*, 269–271.

Dillenbourg, P., Baker, M., Blaye, A., & O'Malley, C. (1996). The evolution of research on collaborative learning. In E. Spada & P. Reiman (Eds.), *Learning in humans and machine: Towards an interdisciplinary learning science*. Oxford, UK: Elsevier.

Dix, A., Finlay, J., Abowd, G., & Beale, R. (1993). *Human-computer interaction*. Englewoods Cliffs: Prentice Hall.

Dodge, T.S., & Cline, R. (1901). The angle velocity of eye movements. *Psychological Review*, 145-157.

Dolog, P., Henze, N., Nejdl, W., & Sintek, M. (Eds.) (2003). Towards the adaptive Semantic Web. *First Workshop on Principles and Practice of Semantic Web Reasoning*.

Dörnemann T., Friese, T., Herdt, S., Juhnke, E., & Freisleben, B. (2007). Grid workflow modelling using grid-specific BPEL extensions. *German E-Science*.

Dourish, P., Anderson, K., & Nafus, D. (2007). Cultural mobilities: Diversity and agency in urban computing. In *Proc. IFIP Conf. Human-Computer Interaction INTER-ACT 2007*, Rio de Janeiro, Brazil.

Dourish, P., Edwards, W.K., Lamarca, A., Lamping, J., Petersen, K., Salisbury, M., Terry, D.B., & Thornton, J. (2000). Extending document management systems with user-specific active properties. *ACM Trans. on Information Systems, 18*(2).

Doyle, J., Bertolotto, M., & Wilson, D. (2007). A survey of multimodal interfaces for mobile mapping applications. In L. Meng, A. Zipf & S. Winter (Eds.), *Map-based mobile services–interactivity and usability.* Springer-Verlag.

Doyle, J., Bertolotto, M., & Wilson, D. (in press). Evaluating the benefits of multimodal interface design for CoMPASS–a mobile GIS. In *GeoInformatica*.

Doyle, J., Weakliam, J., Bertolotto, M., & Wilson, D. (2006). A multimodal interface for personalising spatial data in mobile GIS. In *ICEIS, 8th International Conference on Enterprise Information Systems,* Paphos, Cyprus (pp. 71-78).

Dragicevic, P., & Fekete, J.-D. (2004). Support for input adaptability in the ICON toolkit. In *Proceedings of the 6th International Conference on Multimodal Interfaces (ICMI04)*, State College, PA (pp. 212-219).

Dubois, E., Gray, P., Trevisan, D., & Vanderdonckt, J. (2004). Exploring the design and engineering of mixed reality systems. In *Proceedings of International Conference on Intelligent User Interfaces*Funchal, Madeira (pp. 374-375).

Duchowski, A.T. (2002). A breadth-first survey if eye tracking applications. *Behavior Research Methods, Instruments, & Computers* , 455-470.

Dudley, H. (1939). *The Vocoder.* Bell Labs Record.

Dunlop, M., & Brewster, S. (2002). The challenge of mobile devices for human computer interaction. *Personal and Ubiquitous Computing, 6*(4), 235–236.

Earley, J. (1970) An efficient context-free parsing algorithm. *Communication of ACM 13, 2,* 94-102. New York.

Eickeler, S., Kosmala, A., & Rigoll, G. (1998). Hidden Markov model based continuous online gesture recognition. In *Proceedings of International Conference on Pattern Recognition, 2,* 1206-1208.

EIF. (2004). *European interoperability framework for pan-European e-government services version 1.0.* Brussels. Retrieved from http://europa.eu.int/idabc/en/document/3761

Ellis, C.A., Gibbs, S.J., & Rein, G.L. (1991). Groupware - some issues and experiences. *Communications of the ACM, 34*(1), 39–58.

Enap. (2007, January). Material do curso "e-MAG-Modelo de Acessibilidade de Governo Eletrônico"- ministrado pela Escola Nacional de Administração Pública.

Encelle, B. (2005). *Accessibilité aux documents électroniques: Personnalisation de la présentation et de l'interaction avec l'information.* Unpublished doctoral dissertation, University Paul Sabatier, Toulouse, France.

Encelle, B., & Jessel, N. (2004). Adapting presentation and interaction with XML documents to user preferences. In *ICCHP'04: International Conference on Computers Helping People with Special Needs* (LNCS 3118, pp. 143-150). Springer.

Encelle, B., & Jessel, N. (2004). Using the concept of user policies for improving HTML documents accessibility. *ICWI'04 Vol. 2, IADIS International Conference WWW/Internet* (pp. 835-839).

Encelle, B., & Jessel, N. (2006). Personalization of information browsing user interface: Evaluation of the user policies concepts. *ICWI'06: IADIS International Conference WWW/Internet.*

Encelle, B., & Jessel, N. (2007). Personalization of user interfaces for browsing XML content using transformations built on end-user requirements. In *Proceedings of the 2007 International Cross-Disciplinary Conference on Web Accessibility (W4A), ACM International Conference Proceeding Series* (Vol. 225, pp. 58-64).

Engel, F.L., Goossens, P., & Haakma, R. (1994). Improved efficiency through I- and E-feedback: A trackball with contextual force feedback. *International Journal Man-Machine Studies, 41,* 949-974.

Engel, R., & Sonntag, D. (2007). Text generation in the smartWeb multimodal dialogue system. In *KI 2007* (pp. 448-451).

Engeström, Y., & Middleton, D. (Eds.) (1996). *Cognition and communication at work.* Cambridge: Cambridge University Press.

Equator Project. (2003). The EQUATOR interdisciplinary research collaboration. Retrieved from http://www.equator.ac.uk/

Ericsson. (2002). *Mobile learning in action: Report on the use of mobile telephones for training.* Retrieved on January 24, 2006, from http://learning.ericsson.net/mlearning2/project_one/mobile_learning.html

Esselink, B. (2000). *A practical guide to localization.* John Benjamins Publishing Co.

eXist. (2008). eXist open source native XML database. Retrieved on May 11, 2008, from http://exist.sourceforge.net

Fagerberg, P., Ståhl, A., & Höök, K. (2003). Designing gestures for affective input: An analysis of shape, effort, and valence. In *Proceedings of the International Confer-*

ence Mobile Ubiquitous and Multimedia MUM 2003, Norrköping, Sweden (pp. 57-65). ACM Press.

Fensel, D., Hendler, J.A., Lieberman, H., & Wahlster, W. (Eds.). (2003). Spinning the Semantic Web: Bringing the World Wide Web to its full potential. In D. Fensel, J.A. Hendler, H. Lieberman, & W. Wahlster (Eds.) *Spinning the Semantic Web*. MIT Press.

Ferraiolo, J., Fujisawa, J., & Jackson, D. (2003). *Scalable vector graphics (SVG) 1.1 specification.* Retrieved from http://www.w3.org/TR/SVG11/

Ferreira, S.B.L., & Leite, J.C.S. (2003). Avaliação da usabilidade em sistemas de informação: o caso do sistema submarino - Revista de Administração Contemporânea - RAC. Publicação da ANPAD, v.7, n 2, - Abril/Junho.

Fife, E., & Pereira, F. (2005, June 2-3). Global acceptance of technology (gat) and demand for mobile data services. *Hong Kong Mobility Roundtable.*

Figueroa, P., Green, M., & Hoover, H.J. (2002). InTml: A description language for VR applications. In *Proceedings of Web3D'02*, AZ (pp. 53-58).

Filippo, F., Krebs, A., & Marsic, I. (2003). A framework for rapid development of multimodal interfaces. *Proceedings of the 5th International Conference on Multimodal Interfaces*, Vancouver, Canada.

Finin, T.W. (1989). Gums: A general user modeling shell. In A. Kobsa, & W. Wahlster (Eds.), *User models in dialog systems* (pp. 411-430).

Fink, J., & Kobsa, A. (2000). A review and analysis of commercial user modeling servers for personalization on the World Wide Web. *User Modeling and User-Adapted Interaction. Kluwer Academic, 10*, 209-249.

Fink, J., Kobsa, A., & Nill, A. (1998). Adaptable and adaptive information provision for all users, including disabled and elderly people. *New Review of Hypermedia and Multimedia, 4*, 163-188.

Fischer, G. (2000). Symmetry of ignorance, social creativity, and metadesign. *Knowledge-Based Systems, 13*(7-8), 527-537.

Fischer, G., & Giaccardi, E. (2006). Metadesign: A framework for the future of end-user development. In H. Lieberman, F. Paternò & V. Wulf (Eds.), *End user development - empowering people to flexibly employ advanced information and communication technology* (pp. 427-457). Dordrecht, The Netherlands: Kluwer Academic Publishers.

Fischer, G., Giaccardi, E., Ye, Y., Sutcliffe, A.G., & Mehandjiev, N. (2004). Metadesign: A manifesto for end-user development. *Communications of the ACM, 47*(9), 33-37.

Fischer, G., Grudin, J., McCall, R., Ostwald, J., Redmiles, D., Reeves, B., & Shipman, F. (2001). Seeding, evolutionary growth, and reseeding: The incremental development of collaborative design environments. In *Coordination theory and collaboration technology* (pp. 447-472). Mahwah, NJ: Lawrence Erlbaum Associates.

Fitts, P. (1954). The information capacity of the human motor system in controlling the amplitude of movement. *Journal of Experimental Psychology, 47*(6), 381–391.

Fogli, D., Fresta, G., Marcante, A., Mussio, P., & Padula, M. (2005). *Annotation in cooperative work: From paper-based to the Web one.* Paper presented at the International Workshop on Annotation for Collaboration, Paris.

Fogli, D., Marcante, A., Mussio, P., & Parasiliti Provenza, L. (2007, May). *Design of visual interactive systems: a multifacet methodology. Workshop: Converging on a science of design through the synthesis of design methodologies.* Paper presented at CHI 2007, San Jose, CA.

Fogli, D., Marcante, A., Mussio, P., Oliveri, E., & Padula, M. (2006). Multimodal interaction for managing knowledge on the field. In *Proceedings of the 1st IEEE Workshop on Multimodal and Pervasive Services*, Lyon, France.

Fogli, D., Marcante, A., Mussio, P., Oliveri, E., Padula, M., & Scaioli, R. (2005). Building yard on line: A distributed and mobile system for supporting building workers. In *Proceedings of the 14th IEEE International Workshops on Enabling Technologies: Infrastructure for Collaborative Enterprise (WETICE)* (pp. 195-200). Linköping: IEEE Computer Society.

Foster I., Frey, J., Graham, S., Tuecke, S., Czajkowski, K., Ferguson, D., Leymann, F., Nally, M., Sedukhin, I., Snelling, D., Storey, T., Vambenepe, W., & Weerawarana, S. (2004). *Modeling statefull fesources with Web services v.1.1.*

Foster, I., Kesselman, C., Tuecke, S. (2001). The anatomy of the grid: Enabling scalable virtual organizations. *International J. Supercomputer Applications, 15*(3).

Foster, I., Kishimoto, H., Savva, A., Berry, D., Djaoui, A., Grimshaw, A., Horn, B., Maciel, F., Siebenlist, F., Subramaniam, R., Treadwell, J., & Von Reich, J. (2006). The open grid services architecture, version 1.5. *Open Grid Forum*, Lemont, IL. GFD-I.080.

Foster, M.E. (2002). State of the art review: Multimodal fission. Public deliverable 6.1, COMIC project.

Foster, M.E. (2002). State of the art review: Multimodal fission. Retrieved from www.hcrc.ed.ac.uk/comic/documents/deliverables/Del6-1.pdf

Frattini, G., Ceccarini, F., Corvino, F., De Furio, I., Gaudino, F., Petriccione, P., Russo, R., Scotto di Carlo, V., & Supino, G. (2008). *A new approach toward a modular multimodal interface for PDAs and smartphones VISUAL 2008* (pp. 179-191).

Frattini, G., Gaudino, F., & Scotto di Carlo, V. (2007). Mobile multimodal applications on mass-market devices: Experiences. *18ᵗʰ International Workshop on Database and Expert Systems Applications (DEXA 2007)* (pp. 89-93).

Frattini, G., Petriccione, P., Leone, G., Supino, G., & Corvino, F. (2007, September). Beyond Web 2.0: Enabling multimodal web interactions using VoIP and Ajax. In *Security and Privacy in Communications Networks and the Workshops, 2007. SecureComm 2007. Third International Conference* (pp. 89-97).

Frattini, G., Romano, L., Scotto di Carlo, V., Petriccione, P., Supino, G., & Leone, G. (2006). Multimodal architectures: Issues and experiences. *OTM Workshops (1)*, 974-983.

Frissen, V., Millard, J., Huijboom, N., Svava Iversen, J., Kool, L., & Kotterink, B. In D. Osimo, D. Zinnbauer & A. Bianchi (Eds.), *The future of e-government: An exploration of ICT-driven models of e-government for the EU in 2020*. Retrieved from http://ipts.jrc.ec.europa.eu/publications/pub.cfm?id=1481

Fuhrmann, S., MacEachren, A., Dou, J., Wang, K., & Cox, A. (2005). Gesture and speech-based maps to support use of GIS for crisis management: A user study. In *AutoCarto 2005*. Las Vegas, NV: Cartography and Geographic Information Society.

Fung, P., Hennessy, S., & O'Shea, T. (1998). Pocketbook computing: A paradigm shift? *Computers in the Schools, 14* (3/4), 109–118.

Futrelle, R.P. (1999). Ambiguity in visual language theory and its role in diagram parsing. *IEEE Symposium on Visual Languages, IEEE Computer Society*, Tokyo (pp. 172-175).

Gabrielli, S., Mirabella, V., Kimani, S., & Catarsi, T. (2005). Supporting cognitive walkthrough with video data: A mobile learning evaluation study. In M. Tscheligi, R. Bernhaupt & K. Mihalic (Eds.), *Proceedings of the Conference on Human Computer Interaction with Mobile Devices and Services (MobileHCI 2005)* (pp. 77–82). ACM Press.

Gaitanis K., Vybornova, M.O., Gemo, M., & Macq, B. (2007). Multimodal high level fusion of input commands as a semantic goal-oriented cooperative process. *12ᵗʰ International Conference "Speech and Computer" (SPECOM 2007)*.

Gang, Z., & Zongkai, Y. (2005, October 19-22). Learning resource adaptation and delivery framework for mobile learning. *Frontiers in Education, 2005. FIE apos;05. Proc. 35ᵗʰ Annual Conference.*

Gangemi, A., Guarino, N., Masolo, C., Oltramari, A., & Schcneider, L. (2002). Sweetening ontologies with DOLCE. In *13ᵗʰ International Conference on Knowledge Engineering and Knowledge Management (EKAW02)*, Spain (LNCS 2473, p. 166).

Gärdenfors, P. (2000). *Conceptal spaces*. Cambridge, MA: MIT Press.

Gärdenfors, P. (2005). *The dynamics of thought*. Heidelberg: Springer.

Garg, A., Pavlovic, V., & Rehg, J.M. (2003). Boosted learning in dynamic bayesian networks for multimodal speaker detection. In *Proceedings IEEE* (No. 9, pp.1355-1369).

Garrett, J.J. (2005). Ajax: A new approach to Web applications. Retrieved on February 18, 2005, from http://www.adaptivepath.com/ideas/essays/archives/000385.php

Gavalda, M., & Waibel, A. (1998). Growing semantic grammars. In *Proceedings of ACL/ Coling 1998*, Montreal, Canada.

Gaver, B., Dunne, T., & Pacenti, E. (1999). Design: Cultural probes. *Interactions, 6*(1), 21-29.

Gaver, W. (1989). The sonicfinder: An interface that uses auditory icons. *Human-Computer Interaction, 4*(1), 67–94.

Gibson, J.J. (1979). *The ecological approach to visual perception*. Boston: Houghton Mifflin.

Gips, J., Olivieri, P., & Tecce, J. (1993). Direct control of the computer through electrodes placed around the eyes. *Fifth Internation Conference on Human-Computer Interaction*, (pp. 630-635).

Girard, J.-Y. (1987). Linear logic. *Theoretical Computer Science, 50*, 1-102.

Glavinic, V., Rosic, M., & Zelic, M. (2007). Agents in m-learning Systems based on intelligent tutoring. *HCI*, (7).

Globus Alliance. *Globus toolkit*. Retrieved from http://www.globus.org/toolkit/

Goodwin, C., & Goodwin, M.H. (1997). Seeing as a situated activity: Formulating planes. In Y. Engeström & D. Middleton (Eds.), *Cognition and communication at work* (pp. 61-95). Cambridge, MA: Cambridge University Press.

Goody, J., & Watt, I. (1968). *The consequences of literacy, in literacy in traditional societies*. Cambridge University Press, Goody Ed.

Gorin, A.L., Alonso, T., Abella, A., Riccardi, G., & Wright, J.H. (2003). Semantic information processing of spoken language - how may I help you? In *Pattern recognition in speech and language processing*. CRC Press.

Gorin, A.L., Riccardi, G., & Wright, J.H. (1997). How may I help you? *Speech Communication, 23*, 113-127.

Granic, A., & Nakic, J. (2007, June 25-28). Meeting user individual characteristics through adaptive interface of an e-learning system: An empirical study design. *Information Technology Interfaces, 2007. ITI 2007. 29th International Conference*, Cavtat, Croatia (pp. 333-338).

Greenbaum, J., & Kyng, M. (Eds.) (1991). *Design at work: Cooperative design of computer systems*. Hillsdale, NJ: Lawrence Erlbaum.

Greenberg, S. (1988). *Using unix: Collected traces of 168 users* (Res. Rep. No. 88/333/45). Alberta, Canada: University of Calgary, Department of Computer Science.

Grew, P., & Pagani, E. (2005). Towards a wireless architecture for mobile ubiquitous e-learning. *Workshop on Learning Communities in the Era of Ubiquitous Computing*, Milan, Italy.

Grosz, B., & Sidner, C. (1986). Attention, intentions, and the structure of discourse. *Computational Linguistics 12*(3), 175-204.

Grudin, J. (1994). Computer-supported cooperative work: History and focus. *Computer IEEE, 27*(5), 19–26.

Guarino, N., & Welty, C. (2000). A formal ontology of properties. In R. Dieng, & O. Corby (Eds.), *Knowledge engineering and knowledge management: Methods, models, and tools. 12th International Conference, EKAW 2000*. France: Springer Verlag.

Gupta, A.K., & Anastasakos, T. (2004, October 4-8). Dynamic time windows for multimodal input fusion. In *Proceedings of the 8th International Conference on Spoken Language Processing (INTERSPEECH 2004 - ICSLP)*, Jeju, Korea (pp. 1009-1012).

Gustafson, J. (2002). Developing multimodal spoken dialogue systems. Empirical studies of spoken human-computer interaction. Doctoral dissertation.

Gutiérrez, M., Thalmann, D., & Vexo, F. (2005). Semantic virtual environments with adaptive multimodal interfaces. In *Proceedings of the 11th International Multimedia Modeling Conference 2005* (pp. 277-283).

Haddon, L. (2003). Domestication and mobile telephony. In *Machines that become us: The social context of personal communication technology* (pp. 43-56). New Brunswick, NJ: Transaction Publishers.

Hagen, P., Robertson, R., Kan, M., & Sadler, K. (2005). Emerging research methods for mobile technology use. In *Proceedings of CHISIG Australia* (pp. 1- 10). ACM Press.

Haggard, P., Clark, S., & Kalogeras, J. (2002). Voluntary action and conscious awareness. *Nature Neurosciences, 5*(4), 382–385.

Hakkani-Tür, D., Tur, G., Riccardi, G., & Hong Kook Kim (2005). Error prediction in spoken dialog: From signal-to-noise ratio to semantic confidence scores. In *Proceedings of ICASSP-2005, IEEE International Conference on Acoustics, Speech, and Signal Processing*, Philadelphia, PA.

Halabala, P. (2003). Semantic metadata creation. In *Proceedings of CESCG 2003: 7th Central European Seminar on Computer Graphics*, Budmerice Castle, Slovakia (pp. 15–25).

Haller, R., Mutschler, H., & Voss, M. (1984). Comparison of input devices for correction of typing errors in office systems. In *INTERACT `84, the 1st IFIP Conference on Human Computer Interaction* (pp. 218-223). London: North Holland.

Halliday, M.A.K. (1967). Notes on transitivity and theme in English, part II. *Journal of Linguistics, 3*, 199-244.

Hansen, D.W., & Pece, A.E. (2005). Eye tracking in the wild. *Computer Vision Image Understanding*, 155-181.

Hansen, J., Johansen, A., Hansen, D., Itoh, K., & Mashino, S. (2003). Command without a click: Dwell-time typing by mouse and gaze selections. In *INTERACT '03: Proceedings of the 9th IFIP TC13 International Conference on Human-Computer Interaction* (pp. 121–128). Amsterdam: IOS Press.

Hanson, V.L. (2004). The user experience: Designs and adaptations. *ACM International Conference Proceeding Series - Proceedings of the International Cross-Disciplinary Workshop on Web Access*.

Harel, D. (1987). Statecharts: A visual formalism for complex systems. *Science of Computer Programming, 8*, 321-274.

Harel, D., & Polti, M. (1998). *Modeling reactive systems with statecharts: The statemate approach*. New York: McGraw-Hill.

Harper, M.P. (1994). Storing logical form in a shared-packed forest. *Computational Linguistics, 20(4)*, 649-660.

Harper, M.P., & Shriberg, E. (2004). Multimodal model integration for sentence unit detection. *ICMI 2004* (pp. 121-128).

Harrison, S.M. (2005). Opening the eyes of those who can see to the world of those who can't: A case study. *Technical Symposium on Computer Science Education - Proceedings of the 36th SIGCSE Technical Symposium on Computer Science Education*.

Hartridge, H., & Thomson, L.C. (1948). Method of investigating eye movements. *British Journal Ophthalmology*, 581-591.

Hartson, H.R., & Hix, D. (1989). Human-computer interface development: Concepts and systems for its management. *ACM Computing Surveys (CSUR), 21*(1), 5-92.

Hasselbring, W. (2000). Programming languages and systems for prototyping concurrent applications. *ACM Computing Surveys, 32*(1), 43-79.

Hauptmann, A.G. (1989). Speech and gestures for graphic image manipulation. In *SIGCHI Conference on Human Factors in Computing Systems: Wings for the Mind*, (pp. 241-245). New York: ACM Press.

Hawley, K. (2001). *How things persist*. Oxford, UK: Clarendon Press.

Hayes, J.R. (1985). *Three problems in teaching general skills*. Hillsdale, NJ: Lawrence Erlbaum.

Haythornthwaite, C., Kazmer, M.M., Robins, J., & Shoe-maker, S. (2000). Community development among distance learners: Temporal and technological dimensions. *Journal of Computer Mediated Communication.*

Heidegger, M. (1971). Building dwelling thinking. In *Poetry, language, thought.* New York: Harper Colophon Books.

Heierman III, E.O., & Cook, D.J. (2003, December 19-22). Improving home automation by discovering regularly occurring device usage patterns. In *Proceedings of the 3rd IEEE International Conference on Data Mining (ICDM 2003),* Melbourne, FL (pp. 537-540). IEEE Computer Society.

Heinrich, M., Winkler, M., Steidelmuller, H., Zabelt, M., Behring, A., Neumerkel, R., & Strunk, A. (2007). Mda applied: A tas-model driven tool chain for multimodal applications. *Task Models and Diagrams for User Interface Design (TAMODIA'07)* (pp. 15-27).

Hickey, M. (2000). Multimodal requirements for voice mark-up languages. *W3C working draft.* Retrieved on March 18, 2008, from http://www.w3.org/TR/multimodal-reqs

Hickson, I., & Hyatt, D. (2008). *HTML 5 a vocabulary and associated APIs for HTML and XHTML.* Retrieved from http://www.w3.org/TR/html5/

Hirschberg, J., Litman, D., Pierrehumbert, J., & Ward, G. (1987). Intonation and the intentional discourse structure. In *Proceedings of the Tenth International Joint Conference on Artificial Intelligence,* Milan, Italy (pp. 636-639).

Hirst, G. (1987). Semantic interpretation and the resolution of ambiguity. Cambridge, UK: Cambridge University Press.

Hocek, A., & Cuddihy, D. (2002). *Definitive voiceXML.* Prentice-Hall.

Hoffmann, J. (2000). A heuristic for domain indepndent planning and its use in an enforced hill-climbing algorithm. In *Proceedings of 12th Intl Symposium on Methodologies for Intelligent Systems.* Springer Verlag.

Hoffmann, J., & Nebel, B. (2001). The FF planning system: Fast plan generation through heuristic search. *Journal of Artificial Intelligence Research, (14),* 253–302.

Holland, S., Morse, D., & Gedenryd, H. (2002). AudioGPS: Spatial audio navigation with a minimal attention interface. *Personal and Ubiquitous Computing, 6*(4), 253–259.

Holzapfel, H., Nickel, K., & Stiefelhagen, R. (2004, October 13-15). Implementation and evaluation of a constraint-based multimodal fusion system for speech and 3D pointing gestures. In *Proceedings of ICMI 2004,* State College, PA.

Holzinger, A., Searle, G., Kleinberger, T., Seffah, A., & Javahery, H. (2008). Investigating usability metrics for the design and development of applications for the elderly. *ICCHP 2008, LNCS, 5105,* 98-105.

Hu, J., Brown, M.K., & Turin, W. (1994). Handwriting recognition with hidden Markov models and grammatical constraints. *Fourth International Workshop on Frontiers of Handwriting Recognition,* Taipei, Taiwan.

Huang, X., Oviatt, S., & Lunsford, R. (2006). Combining user modeling and machine learning to predict users' multimodal integration patterns. In S. Renals, S. Bengio, & J.G. Fiscus (Eds.), *MLMI 2006* (LNCS 4299, pp. 50-62). Heidelberg: Springer.

Hub, A., Diepstraten, J., & Ertl, T. (2004). Design and development of an indoor navigation and object identification system for the blind. In *Proceedings of the 6th International ACM SIGACCESS Conference on Computers and Accessibility (ASSETS'04)* (pp. 147–152). Atlanta, GA: ACM Press.

Hughes, J.A., Randall, D., & Shapiro, D. (1992). Faltering from ethnography to design. In M. Mantel & R. Baecher (Eds.), *Proceedings of the International Conference on Computer-Supported Cooperative Work (CSCW'92),* Toronto, Canada (pp. 115-122). New York: ACM Press.

Huls, C., Claassen, W., & Bos, E. (1995). Automatic referent resolution of deictic and anaphoric expressions. *Computational Linguistics, 21*(1), 59–79.

Hunt, A., & McGlashan, S. (2004). *W3C speech recognition grammar specification (SRGS)*. Retrieved from http://www.w3.org/TR/speech-grammar/

Huot, S., Dumas, C., Dragicevic, P., Fekete, J.-D., & Hegron, G. (2004). The magglite post-wimp toolkit: Draw it, connect it, and run it. In *Proceedings of the 17th ACM Symposium on User Interface Software and Technologies (UIST 2004)*, Santa Fe, NM (pp. 257-266).

Hutchins, E.L., Hollan, J.D., & Norman, D. (1986). Direct manipulation interfaces. In D. Norman & S. Draper (Eds.), *User centred system design* (pp. 87–124). Hillsdale, NJ: Lawrence Erlbaum.

Hutchinson, H., Mackay, W., Westerlund, B., Bederson, B.B., Druin, A., Plaisant, C., Beaudouin-Lafon, M., Conversy, S., Evans, H., Hansen, H., Roussel, N., Eiderbäck, B., Lindquist, S., & Sundblad, Y., (2003). Technology probes: Inspiring design for and with families. In *Proceedings of the SIGCHI Conference on Human Factors in Computing Systems (CHI'03)* (pp. 17-24). ACM Press.

Hwee Tou Ng, & Zelle, J.M. (1997). Corpus-based approaches to semantic interpretation in NLP. *AI Magazine, 18*(4), 45-64.

Hyyppä, K., Tamminen, S., Hautala, I., & Repokari, L. (2000, October 23-25). *The effect of mental model guiding user's action in mobile phone answering situations.* Paper presented at the Electronical Proceedings from the 1st Nordic Conference on Computer Human Interaction, Stockholm, Sweden.

I.D.A.B.C. *Interoperable Delivery of European E-Government Services to Public Administrations, Businesses, and Citizens.* Retrieved from http://ec.europa.eu/idabc/en/document/5101

Iacucci, G. (2001). Bridging observation and design in concept development for mobile services. In *Third international symposium on human computer interaction with mobile devices, ihm-hci.* Lille, France.

IBM ViaVoice. (2005). Retrieved on October 2005, from http://www-306.ibm.com/software/voice/viavoice/

IBM. (2003). *X + V 1.1.* Retrieved from http://www-3.ibm.com/software/pervasive/multimodal/x+v/11/spec.htm

International Phonetic Alphabet. Retrieved from http://www.arts.gla.ac.uk/ipa/index.html

Intille, S.S., Tapia, E.M., Rondoni, J., Beaudin, J., Kukla, C., Agrwal, S., Bao, L., & Larson, K. (2003). Tools for studying behavior and technology in natural settings. In *Proceedings of Ubiquitous Computing 2004* (pp. 157–174). Springer LNCS 3205.

Irawati, S., Calder'on, D., & Ko., H. (2005). Semantic 3D object manipulation using object ontology in multimodal interaction framework. In *Proceedings of ICAT'05* (pp. 35-39).

Irawati, S., Calder'on, D., & Ko., H. (2006). Spatial ontology for semantic integration in 3D multimodal interaction framework. In *ACM International Conference on VRCIA* (pp. 129-135).

ISO (1998). *ISO Report number ISO/TC 159/SC4/WG3 N147: Ergonomic requirements for office work with visual display terminals (VDTs) - part 9 – Requirements for non-keyboard input devices (ISO 9241-9).* International Organisation for Standardisation.

Isomursu, M., Kuutti, K., & Väinämö, S., (2004). Experience clip: Method for user participation and evaluation of mobile concepts. In *Proceedings Participatory Design Conference 2004*, Toronto, Canada (pp. 83-92).

Ivory, M.Y., & Hearst, M.A. (2001). The state of the art in automating usability evaluation of user interfaces. *ACM Computing Surveys, 33*(4), 470-516.

Jääskö, V., & Mattelmäki, T., (2003). Observing and probing. In *Proceedings of Designing Pleasurable Products and Interfaces Conference (DPPI'03)*, Pittsburgh, PA (pp. 126-131).

Jackson, G.R., & Owsley, C. (2003). Visual dysfunction, neurodegenerative diseases, and aging. *Neurology and Clinical Neurophysiology, 21*(3), 709-728.

Jacobs, N. (2004). *Relational sequence learning and user modelling.* Unpublished doctoral dissertation, K.U. Leuven, Leuven, Belgium.

Jacobs, N., & Blockeel, H. (2001). From shell logs to shell scripts. In C. Rouveirol, & M. Sebag (Eds.), *Proceedings of the 11ᵗʰ International Conference on Inductive Logic Programming* (Vol. 2157, pp. 80-90). Springer.

Jacobson, R.D. (2002). Representing spatial information through multimodal interfaces. In *6ᵗʰ International Conference on Information Visualization* (pp. 730-734). IEEE press.

Jaimes, A., & Sebe, N. (2007). Multimodal human-computer interaction: A survey. *Computer Vision and Image Understanding, 108*, 116-134.

Java Speech API. (1998). Retrieved from http://java.sun.com/products/java-media/speech/

Javal, L.É. (1907). Physiologie de la lecture et de l'écriture. *Bibliography in Annales d'oculistique*, 137-187.

Jeong, C., & Lee, E. (2007). Context aware human computer interaction for ubiquitous learning. *HCI, 9* (LNCS 4558).

Jiang, W., Sun, Z. (2005, August 18-21). Hmm-based online multistroke sketch recognition. In *Proceedings of the Fourth International Conference on Machine Learning and Cybernetics*, Guangzhou (pp. 4564-4570).

Johansson, I. (1989). *Ontological investigations. An inquiry into the categories of nature, man, and society.* London: Routledge.

Johnson, C.R., & Fillmore, C.J. (2000). The frameNet tagset for frame-semantic and syntactic coding of predicate-argument structure. In *Proceedings of the 1ˢᵗ Meeting of the North American Chapter of the Association for Computational Linguistics (ANLP-NAACL 2000)*, Seattle, WA (pp. 56-62).

Johnson, P. (1998). Usability and mobility: Interaction on the move. In *Proceedings of First Workshop on Human-Computer Interaction with Mobile Devices*, Glasgow, UK (pp. 39-25).

Johnston, M., Cohen, P.R., McGee, D., Oviatt, S.L., Pittman, J.A., & Smith, I. (1997, July 7-12). Unification-based multimodal integration. In *Proceedings of the 35ᵗʰ Annual Meeting of the Association for Computational Linguistics and 8ᵗʰ Conference of the European Chapter of the Association for Computational Linguistics*, Madrid, Spain (pp. 281-288). ACL.

Johnston, M. (1998, August 10-14). Unification-based multimodal parsing. In *Proceedings of the 36ᵗʰ Annual Meeting of the Association for Computational Linguistics and 17ᵗʰ International Conference on Computational Linguistics (COLING-ACL '98)*, Montreal, Canada (pp. 624-630).

Johnston, M., & Bangalore, S. (2000, July 31-August 4) Finite-state multimodal parsing and understanding. In *Proceedings of COLIN2000*, Saarbrücken, Germany.

Johnston, M., & Bangalore, S. (2005). Finite-state multimodal integration and understanding. *Journal of Natural Language Engineering 11.2*, 159-187.

Johnston, M., & Bangalore, S. (2005). Combining stochastic and grammar-based language processing with finite-state edit machines. In *Proceedings of IEEE Automatic Speech Recognition and Understanding Workshop.*

Johnston, M., Baggia, P., Burnett, D., Carter, J., Dahl, D.A., McCobb, G., et al. (2007). *EMMA: Extensible multimodal annotation markup language.* Retrieved from http://www.w3.org/TR/emma/

Jojic, N., Brumitt, B., Meyers, B., Harris, S., & Huang, T. (2000). Detection and estimation of pointing gestures in dense disparity maps. In *Prococeedings of the Fourth International Conference on Automatic Face and Gesture Recognition* (pp. 468–475). Piscataway, NJ: IEEE Computer Society.

Jones, M., & Marsden, G. (2005). *Mobile interaction design.* Hoboken, NJ: John Wiley and Sons.

Jones, M., Buchanan, G., & Thimbleby, H. (2002). Sorting out searching on small screen devices. In F. Paterno (Eds.), *Proceedings of the Conference on Human Computer Interaction with Mobile Devices and Services (MobileHCI 2002)* (pp. 81-94). Berlin: Springer.

Joshi, A.K., Marcus, M.P., Steedman, M., & Webber, B.L. (1991). Natural language research. In *Proceedings of HLT.*

JPDL. Retrieved from http://www.jboss. org/jbossjbpm /jpdl

Judd, C.H., McAllister, C.N., & Steel, W.M. (1905). General introduction to a series of studies of eye movements by means of kinetoscopic photographs. *Psychological Review, Monograph Supplements, 7,* 1-16.

Junqua, J.C. (1993). The Lombard reflex and its role on human listeners and automatic speech recognisers. *Acoustical Society of America, 93*(1), 510-524.

Jurafsky, D. & Martin, J.H. (2007). *Speech and language processing: An introduction to natural language processing, computational linguistics, and speech recognition.*

Kaiser, E., Olwal, A., McGee, D., Benko, H., Corradini, A., Li, X., Cohen, P., et al. (2003, November 5-7). Mutual disambiguation of 3D multimodal interaction in augmented and virtual reality. In *Proceedings of the 5th International Conference on Multimodal Interfaces,* Vancouver, Canada. ACM.

Kaiser, E., Demirdjian, D., Gruenstein, A., Li, X., Niekrasz J., Wesson, M., et al. (2004, October 13-15). Demo: A multimodal learning interface for sketch, speak, and point creation of a schedule chart. In *Proceedings of ICMI 2004*, State College, PA.

Kallmann, M., & Thalmann, D. (1999). Direct 3D interaction with smart objects. In *Proceedings of the ACM symposium VRST* (pp. 124-130).

Kaplan, C., Fenwick, J., & Chen, J. (1993). Adaptive hypertext navigation based on user goals and context. *User Modeling and User-Adapted Interaction, 3*(3), 193-220.

Kappacher, M. (2007). *Empirische Untersuchung einer GPS gestützten Filmtour für mobile Endgeräte am Beispiel des Films The Sound of Music.* Master thesis, FH Salzburg, Austria.

Karasti, H. (2001). *Increasing sensitivity towards everyday work practice in system design.* Unpublished doctoral dissertation, University of Oulu, Oulu.

Kay, J. (1994). Lies, damned lies, and stereotypes: Pragmatic approximations of users. In A. Kobsa, & D. Litman (Eds.), *Proceedings of the 4th International Conference on User Modeling UM94* (pp. 175-184). MITRE, UM Inc.

Keiffer, S., & Carbonell, N. (2006). Oral messages improve visual search. In *AVI '06, the Working Conference on Advanced Visual Interfaces* (pp. 369-372). Venice, Italy: ACM Press.

Keskin, C., Balci, K., Aran, O., Sankar, B., & Akarun, L. (2007). A multimodal 3D healthcare communication system. In *3DTV Conference.* Kos, Greece: IEEE press.

Kettebekov, S. (2004, October 13-15). Exploiting prosodic structuring of coverbal gesticulation. In *Proceedings of the 6th International Conference on Multimodal Interfaces (ICMI 2004)*, State College, PA (pp. 105-112). New York: ACM Press.

Kettebekov, S., & Sharma, R. (2000). Understanding gestures in multimodal human computer interaction. *International Journal on Artificial Intelligence Tools, 9*(2), 205–223.

Kiljander, H. (2004). *Evolution and usability of mobile phone interaction styles.* Unpublished doctoral dissertation, Helsinki University of Technology, Helsinki.

Kirstein, C., & Müller, H. (1998). Interaction with a projection screen using a camera-tracked laser pointer. In *MMM '98 : Proceedings of the International Conference on Multimedia Modeling* (pp. 191–192). IEEE Computer Society.

Kita, S. (2003). Pointing: A foundational building block of human communication. In S. Kita (Ed.), *Pointing: Where language, culture, and cognition meet* (pp. 1–8). Mahwah, NJ: Lawrence Erlbaum.

Kjeldskov, J., & Graham, C. (2003). A review of mobile HCI research methods. In L. Chittaro (Ed.), *Proceedings on the Conference on Human-Computer Interaction with Mobile Devices and Services (MobileHCI 2003)* (pp. 317-335). Berlin: Springer.

Klopfer, E., Squire, K., & Jenkins, H. (2004). Environmental detectives: PDAs as a window into a virtual simulated world. In M. Kerres, M. Kalz, J. Stratmann & de Witt, C. (Eds.).

Klusch, M., & Schmidt, M. *Semantic Web service composition planning with OWLS-Xplan*. Retrieved from www-ags.dfki.uni-sb.de/~klusch/i2s/owlsxplan-3.pdf

Kobsa, A. (1990). Modeling the user's conceptual knowledge in BGP-MS, a user modeling shell system. *Computational Intelligence, 6*(4), 193-208.

Kobsa, A. (1994). User modeling and user-adapted interaction. In *CHI' 94 Tutorial.*

Kobsa, A., & Pohl, W. (1995). The user modeling shell system bgp-ms. *User Modeling and User-Adapted Interaction, 4*(2), 59-106.

Koivunen, M.R., & Swick, R.R. (2003). Collaboration through annotations in the Semantic Web. In S. Handschuh & S. Staab (Eds.), *Annotation for the Semantic Web* (pp. 46-60). Amsterdam: IOS Press.

Komagata, N. (1997). Efficient parsing for CCGs with generalized type-raised categories. In *Proceedings of the 5th International Workshop on Parsing Technologies*, Boston, MA (pp. 135-146). ACL/SIGPARSE.

Komagata, N. (1999). *Information structure in texts: A computational analysis of contextual appropriateness in English and Japanese.* Unpublished doctoral dissertation, University of Pennsylvania, PA.

Koons, D.B., Sparrell, C.J., & Thorisson, K.R. (1993). Integrating simultaneous input from speech, gaze, and hand gestures. In M. Maybury (Ed.), *Intelligent multimedia interfaces*. Menlo Park, CA: MIT.

Kravcik, M., & Specht, M. (2004). *Flexible navigation support in the WINDS learning environment for architecture and design.* Paper presented at the Adaptive Hypermedia 2004 Conference, Eindhoven.

Kulakov. (2001). Virtual classroom and virtual laboratory. In *Proc. of the 20th World Conference on Open Learning and Distance Education*, Dusseldorf, Germany. CD Rom Publication.

Kurniawan, A. (2007). Interactions. *Mobile Phone Design for Older Persons, July & Aug*, 24-25.

Kwon, H.S., & Chidambaram, L. (2000). A test of the technology acceptance model: The case of cellular telephone adoption. In *Proceedings of the 33rd Hawaii International Conference on System Sciences*, Hawaii (Vol. 1). IEEE Computer Society.

Lakoff, G. (1993). The contemorary theory of metaphor. In A. Ortony (Ed.), *Metaphor and thought* (pp. 202-251). Cambridge, MA: Cambridge University Press.

Lakoff, G., & Johnson, M. (1980). *Metaphors we live by.* Chicago, IL: University of Chicago Press.

Lambrecht, K. (1994). *Information structure and sentence form.* London: CUP.

Larson, J.A. (2003). *VoiceXML: Introduction to developing speech applications.* Upper Saddle River, NJ: Prentice Hall.

Larson, J.A. (2005). Voice user interface design for novice and experienced users. In D.A. Dahl (Ed.), *Practical spoken dialog systems.* Kluwer Academic Press.

Larson, J.A. (2006). *Common sense suggestions for developing multimodal user interfaces*. Retrieved from http://www.w3.org/TR/2006/NOTE-mmi-suggestions-20060911/

Latoschik, M.E. (2005, October 4-6). A user interface framework for multimodal VR interactions. In *Proceedings of ICMI'05*, Trento, Italy (pp. 76-83). ACM.

Latoschik, M.E., & Frolich, C. (1986). Semantic reflection for intelligent virtual environments. In *Virtual Reality Conference, 2007 (VR '07)* (pp. 305-306). IEEE.

Lau, C.W., Ma, B., Meng, H.M., Moon, Y.S., & Yam, Y. (2004). Fuzzy logic decision fusion in a multimodal biometric system. In *Proceedings of the 8th International Conference on Spoken Language Processing (ICSLP)*, Korea.

Lavrac, N., & Dzeroski, S. (1994). *Inductive logic programming: Techniques and applications.* New York: Ellis Horwood.

Leavens, D.A. (2004). Manual deixis in apes and humans. *Interaction Studies, 5,* 387–408.

Lee, Y.S. (2007). *Older adults' user experiences with mobile phone: Identification of user clusters and user requirements.* VA: Virginia Polytechnic Institute and State University.

Lee, Y.S., Hong, S.W., Smith-Jackson, T.L., Nussbaum, M.A., & Tomioka, K. (2005). Systematic evaluation methodology for cell phone user interfaces. In *Interacting with Computers, 18*(2), 304-325.

Lehner, F., Nösekabel, H., et al. (2002). Wireless e-learning and communication environment. *WELCOME at the University of Regensburg, Workshop on M-Services, 2002,* Lyon, France.

Lemmelä, S. (2008). Selecting optimal modalities for multimodal interaction in mobile and pervasive environments. *IMUx (Improved Mobile User Experience) Workshop, Pervasive 2008 (Sixth International Conference on Pervasive Computing),* Sydney, Australia.

Leporini, B., Andronico, P., & Buzzi, M. (2004). Designing search engine user interfaces for the visually impaired. *ACM International Conference Proceeding Series - Proceedings of the International Cross-disciplinary Workshop on Web Accessibility.*

Letondal, C., & Mackay, W.E. (2004). Participatory programming and the scope of mutual responsibility: Balancing scientific, design, and software commitment. In A. Clement & P. Van den Besselaar (Eds.), *Proceedings of the 8ᵗʰ Conference on Participatory Design Conference (PDC 2004),* Toronto, Canada (pp. 31-41). New York: ACM Press.

Levin, B., & Rappaport Hovav, M. (1996). Lexical semantics and syntactic structure. In S. Lappin (Ed.), *The handbook of contemporary semantic theory.* Oxford, UK: Blackwell.

Levison, S.E., Rabiner, L.R., & Sondhi, M.M. (1983). An introduction to the application of the theory of probabilistic functions of a markov process to automatic speech recognition. *Bell System Technology Journal,* 1035-1074.

Lewis, C., Polson, P., & Wharton, R. (1990). Testing a walkthrough methodology for theory-based design of walk-up-and-us interfaces. In J.C. Chew & J. Whiteside (Eds.), *Proceedings of the SIGCHI Conference on Human Factors in Computing Systems (CHI'90)* (pp. 235-241). Seattle, WA: ACM Press.

Lewis, T.W., & Powers, D.M.W. (2002). Audio-visual speech recognition using red exclusion and neural networks. In *Proceedings of the 25ᵗʰ Australasian Conference on Computer Science. Australian Computer Society, Inc.,* Melbourne, Australia (pp. 149-156).

Li, L., Cao, F., Chou, W., & Liu, F. (2006, October 3-6). *XM-flow: An extensible micro-flow for multimodal interaction.* Paper presented at the International Workshop on Multimedia Signal Processing, Victoria, Canada.

Liang, J., & Green, M. (1994). JDCAD: A highly interactive 3D modeling system. *Computer and Graphics, 18*(4), 499-506.

Liao, L., Patterson, D., Fox, D., & Kautz, H.A. (2007). Learning and inferring transportation routines. *Artificial Intelligence, 171*(5-6), 311-331.

Lieberman, H. (2001). *Your wish is my command: Programming by example.* San Francisco: Morgan Kaufman.

Ling, R. (2001). *The diffusion of mobile telephony among Norwegian teens: A report from after the revolution.* Paper presented at ICUST, Paris. Telenor R&D.

Little, M., Webber, J., & Parastatidis, S. (2004). Stateful interactions in Web services. A comparison of WSContext and WS-Resource framework. *SOA World Magazine,* April.

Liu, J., Wong, C.K., & Hui, K.K. (2003). An adaptive user interface based on personalized learning. *Intelligent Systems,* 52-57.

Lodha, S.K., Faaland, N.M., Wong, G., Charaniya, A.P., Ramalingam, S., & Keller, A.M. (2003). Consistent visualization and querying of GIS databases by a location-aware mobile agent. *Computer Graphics International.* Acta Press.

Loomis, J., Golledge, R., & Klatzky, R. (2001). GPS based navigation systems for the visually impaired. In W. Barfield & T. Caudell (Eds.), *Fundamentals of wearable computers and augmented reality* (pp. 429–446). Mahwah, NJ: Lawrence Erlbaum.

Loomis, J.M., & Leederman, S.J. (1986). Tactual perception. In *Handbook of Perception and HumanPperformance* (p. 31).

Lu, L., Kitagata, G., Suganuma, T., & Kinoshita, T. (2003). Adaptive user interface for multimedia communication system based on multiagent. In *Proc. of the 17th International Conference on Advanced Information Networking and Applications, IEEE Computer Society* (pp. 53-58).

Luchini, K., Quintana, C., & Soloway, E. (2004). Design guidelines for learner-centered handheld tools. *CHI 2004*, Vienna, Austria (Vol. 6, pp. 135-142).

Lugano, G. (2007). Mobile social software: Definition, scope, and applications. *EU/IST E-Challenges Conference*, The Hague, The Netherlands.

Lugano, G., & Saariluoma, P. (2007). *Share or not to share: Supporting the user decision in mobile social software applications.*

Luqi. (1992). Computer aided system prototyping. In *Proc. 1st Int'l Workshop on Rapid System Prototyping*, Los Alamitos, CA (pp. 50-57).

Luyten, K., Clerckx, T., Coninx, K., & Vanderdonckt, J. (2003). Derivation of a dialog model from a task model by activity chain extraction. In *Proceedings of 10th International Conference on Design, Specification, and Verification of Interactive Systems DSVIS 2003*, Madeira (LNCS 2844, pp. 203-217). Berlin: Springer–Verlag.

Mackay, W.E. (1991). Triggers and barriers to customizing software. In *Proc. CHI Human Factors Comput. Syst.*, New Orleans, LA (pp. 153–160).

MacKenzie, I.S., & Chang, L. (1999). A performance comparison of two handwriting recognisers. *Interacting with Computers, 11*, 283-297.

Maes, S.H., & Saraswat, V. (2003). *Multimodal interaction requirements*. Retrieved from http://www.w3.org/TR/mmi-reqs/

Malaka, M., & Zipf, A. (2000). DEEP MAP–challenging IT research in the framework of a tourist information system. In *7th International Congress on Tourism and Communication Technologies in Tourism (ENTER '00)* (pp. 15-27). Barcelona, Spain: Springer LNCS.

Malerba, D., & Lisi, F. (2001). Discovering associations between spatial objects: An ilp application. In *Proceedings of the 11th International Conference on Inductive Logic Programming* (LNCS 2157, pp. 156-166). Springer.

Malerczyk, C. (2004). Interactive museum exhibit using pointing gesture recognition. In *WSCG'04: Proceedings of the 12th International Conference in Central Europe on Computer Graphics, Visualization and Computer Vision* (pp. 165–172).

Malhotra, Y., & Galletta, D.F. (1999). Extending the technology acceptance model to account for social influence: Theoretical bases and empirical validation. In *Proceedings of the 32nd Annual Hawaii International Conference on System Sciences* (Vol. 1). IEEE.

Mallenius, S., Rossi, M., & Tuunainen, V.K. (2007). Factors affecting the adoption and use of mobile devices and services by elderly people – results from a pilot study. *6th Annual Mobile Round Table*. Los Angeles, CA.

Mankoff, J., Hudson, S.E., & Abowd, G.D. (2000a). Providing integrated toolkit-level support for ambiguity in recognition-based interfaces. *CHI 2000*, 368-375.

Mankoff, J., Hudson, S.E., & Abowd, G.D. (2000b). Interaction techniques for ambiguity resolution in recognition-based interfaces. *UIST 2000*, 11-20.

Mann, W.C., & Thompson, S.A. (1987). *Rhetorical structure theory: A theory of text organization*. USC/Information Sciences Institute (Tech. Rep. No. RS-87-190). Marina del Rey, CA.

Manola, F., & Miller, E. (2004). *RDF primer.* Retrieved from http://www.w3.org/TR/rdf-primer/

Mansouri, H. (2005). *Using semantic descriptions for building and querying virtual environments.* Unpublished doctoral dissertation, Vrije Universiteit, Brussel, Belgium.

Marcus, A., & Baumgartner, V.J. (2004). *A practical set of culture dimensions for global user-interface development*. APCHI.

Markowitz, J. (2005). Designing for speaker authentication. In D.A. Dahl (Ed.), *Practical spoken dialog systems* (pp. 123-139). Heidelberg, Germany: Springer.

Martin, D., Burstein, M., Hobbs, J., Lassila, O., McDermott, D., McIlraith, S., Narayanan, S., Paolucci, M., Parsia, B., Payne, T., Sirin, E., Srinivasan, N., & Sycara, K. (2004). OWL-S: Semantic markup for Web services, W3C member submission. Retrieved from http://www.w3.org/Submission/OWL-S/

Martin, J.C. (1997). Toward intelligent cooperation between modalities: The example of a system enabling multimodal interaction with a map. In *Proceedings of the International Conference on Artificial Intelligence (IJCAI'97) Workshop on Intelligent Multimodal Systems*, Nagoya, Japan.

Martin, J.C. (1999). Six primitive types of cooperation for observing, evaluating, and specifying cooperations. In *Proceedings of AAAI*.

Martin, J.C. (2004). Introduction aux interfaces homme-machine multimodales. *Conférence invitée. Actes des entretiens de l'Institut de Garches. Innovations technologiques et Handicap* (pp. 25-26). Retrieved on October 27, 2008, from http://www.limsi.fr/Individu/martin/research/articles/martin-garche.pdf

Martin, J.C., Grimard, S., & Alexandri, K. (2001). On the annotation of the multimodal behavior and computation of cooperation between modalities. In *Proceedings of the Workshop on Representing, Annotating, and Evaluating Non-Verbal and Verbal Communicative Acts to Achieve Contextual Embodied Agents*, Montreal, Canada (pp. 1-7).

Martınez, J. I. (2004). *An intelligent guide for virtual environments with fuzzy queries and flexible management of stories*. Unpublished doctoral dissertation, Universidad de Murcia.

Masolo, C., Borgo, S., Gangemi, A., Guarino, N., Oltramari, A., & Schneider, L. (2003). *The wonder Web library of foundational ontologies. Wonder Web deliverable 18*. Retrieved from http://wonderweb.semanticweb.org

May, A., Ross, T., Bayer, S., & Tarkiainen, M. (2003). Pedestrian navigation aids: Information requirements and design implications. *Personal and Ubiquitous Computing, 7*(6), 331–338.

Maybury, M.T., & Wahlster, W. (1998). Intelligent user interfaces: An introduction. In M.T. Maybury, & W. Wahlster (Eds.), *Readings in intelligent user interfaces* (pp. 1–13). San Francisco, CA: Morgan Kaufmann Publishers Inc.

McCarthy, J., & Hayes, P. (1969). Some philosophical problems from the standpoint of artificial intelligence. In B. Meltzer, & D. Michie (Eds.), *Machine Intelligence 4* (pp. 463-502). Edinburgh University Press.

McCowan, I., Bengio, S., Gatica-Perez, D., Lathoud, G., Monay, F., Moore, D., Wellner, P., & Bourlard, H. (2003). Modeling human interaction in meetings. In *Proceedings of ICASSP 2003, IEEE Press: IV-748 - IV-751*.

McGlashan, S., Burnett, D.C., Carter, J., Danielsen, P., Ferrans, J., Hunt, A., et al. (2004, March 16. *Voice extensible markup language (voiceXML 2.0)*. Retrieved from http://www.w3.org/TR/voicexml20/

McGreal, R., & Roberts, T. (2001). *A primer on metadata for learning objects*. Retrieved from http://www.elearningmag.com/issues/Oct01/learningobjects.asp.

McKeown, M.G. (1985). The acquisition of word meaning from context by children of high and low ability. *Reading Research Quarterly, 20*, 482-496.

McNeill, D. (1992). *Hand and mind: What gestures reveal about thought*. Chicago: University of Chicago Press.

McNeill, D., & Duncan, S. (2000). Growth points in thinking-for speaking. In D. McNeill (Ed.), *Language and Gesture*. Cambridge, MA: Cambridge University Press.

Mehrotra, S., Znati, T., & Thompson, C.W. (2008). Crisis management. *IEEE Internet Computing Magazine*.

Meier, U., Stiefelhagen, R., Yang, J., & Waibel, A. (2000). Towards unrestricted lip reading. *International Journal of Pattern Recognition and Artificial Intelligence, 14*(5), 571-585.

Merriam-Webster online. (2008). Retrieved on May 8, 2008, from http://www.merriam-webster.com

Meyer, H., Hänze, M., & Hildebrandt, M. (1999). Das Zusammenwirken von Systemresponsezeiten und Verweilzeiten beim Explorieren von Hypertextstrukturen: Empirische Evidenz für einen zeitlichen Integrationsmechanismus? In *KogWis'99: Proceedings der 4. Fachtagung der Gesellschaft für Kognitionswissenschaft* (pp. 86–91). St. Augustin, Germany: Infix Verlag.

Microsoft. (2007). *Microsoft speech API 5.3* (SAPI). Retrieved from http://msdn2.microsoft.com/en-us/library/ms723627.aspx

Miers, D. (2005). *Workflow handbook, workflow management coalition*. UK: Enix Consulting.

Miller, M. (2002). *VoiceXML: 10 projects to voice-enable your Web site*. New York: Wiley Publishing, Inc.

Miniotas, D., Spakov, O., Tugoy, I., & MacKenzie, I.S. (2006). Speech-augmented eye gaze interaction with small closely spaced target. *Symposium on Eye tracking Research and Applications* (pp. 66-72). ACM Press.

Minker, W., & Bennacef, S. (2004). *Speech and human-machine dialog*. Boston: Kluwer Academic Publishers.

Misfud, L., & Morch, A.I. (2007). 'That's my PDA!' The role of personalization for handhelds in the classroom. In *Proc. of the Fifth IEEE International Conference on Pervasive Computing and Communications Workshops* (pp. 187-192).

Mizobuchi, S., Mori, K., Ren, X., & Michiaki, Y. (2002). An empirical study of the minimum required size and the minimum number of targets for pen input on the small display. In F. Paterno (Ed.), *Proceedings of the Conference on Human Computer Interaction with Mobile Devices and Services (MobileHCI 2002)* (pp. 184-194). Berlin: Springer.

Modelo de Acessibilidade. (2005). Recomendações de Acessibilidade para a Construção e Adaptação de Conteúdos do Governo Brasileiro na Internet - Departamento de Governo Eletrônico - Secretaria de Logística e Tecnologia da Informação - Ministério do Planejamento, Orçamento e Gestão - Documento de Referência - Versão 2.0 14/12/2005.

Mørch, A. (1997). Three levels of end-user tailoring: Customization, integration, and extension. In M. Kyng & L. Mathiassen (Eds.), *Computers and Design in Context* (pp. 51–76). Cambridge, MA: MIT Press.

Mørch, A.I., & Mehandjiev, N.D. (2000). Tailoring as collaboration: The mediating role of multiple representations and application units. *Computer Supported Cooperative Work, 9*(1), 75-100.

Mori, G., Patern`o, F., & Santoro, C. (2002). CTTE: Support for developing and analyzing task models for interactive system design. *IEEE Transactions on Software Engineering, 28*(8), 797-813.

Mori, G., Patern`o, F., & Santoro, C. (2004). Design and development of multidevice user interfaces through multiple logical descriptions. *IEEE Transactions On Software Engineering, 30*(8), 1- 14.

Moyle, S., & Muggleton, S. (1997). Learning programs in the event calculus. In *Proceedings of the 7th International Workshop on Inductive Logic Programming* (pp. 205-212). Springer.

Mueller, F., Agamanolis, S., & Picard, R. (2003). Exertion interfaces: Sports over a distance for social bonding and fun. In *Proceedings of the SIGCHI Conference on Human Factors in Computing Systems (CHI 2003)* (pp. 561-568). ACM Press.

Muggleton, S., & De Raedt, L. (1994). Inductive logic programming: Theory and methods. *Journal of Logic Programming, 19/20*, 629-679.

Müller-Tomfelde, C. (2007). Dwell-based pointing in applications of human computer interaction. In *INTERACT '07: Proceedings of the 11th IFIP TC13 International Conference on Human-Computer Interaction* (pp. 560–573). Springer Verlag.

Müller-Tomfelde, C., & Paris, C. (2006). Explicit task representation based on gesture interaction. In *MMUI '05: Proceedings of the 2005 NICTA-HCSNet Multimodal User Interaction Workshop* (pp. 39–45). Darlinghurst, Australia: Australian Computer Society, Inc.

Myers, B.A., Smith, D.C., & Horn, B. (1992). *Report of the 'end-user programming' working group, languages for developing user interfaces* (pp. 343–366). Boston: Jones & Bartlett.

Nack, F., & Lindsay, A. (1999a). Everything you wanted to know about MPEG-7 - part 1. *IEEE Multimedia, 6*(3), 65–77.

Naeve, A. (2005). The human Semantic Web – shifting from knowledge push to knowledge pull. *International Journal of Semantic Web and Information Systems (IJSWIS), 1*(3), 1-30.

Naismith, L., Lonsdale, P., Vavoula, G., & Sharples, M. (2004). *Literature review in mobile technologies and learning* (Literature Review No. 11). University of Birmingham.

Naismith, L., Lonsdale, P., Vavoula, G., & Sharples, M. (2004). *Mobile technologies and learning.* Retrieved on April 29, 2005, from http://www.nestafuturelab.org/research/lit_reviews.htm#lr11

Nardi, B. (1993). *A small matter of programming: Perspectives on end user computing.* Cambridge, MA: MIT Press.

National Instruments. (2006, June). National instruments lab view. Retrieved from http://www.ni.com/

Navarre, D., Palanque, P., Bastide, R., Schyn, A., Winckler, M., Nedel, L., & Freitas, C. (2005). A formal description of multimodal interaction techniques for immersive virtual reality applications. In *Proceedings of Tenth IFIP TC13 International Conference on Human-Computer Interaction*, Rome, Italy.

Neal, J.G., & Shapiro, S.C. (1991). Intelligent multimedia interface technology. In J. Sullivan, & S. Tyler (Eds.), *Intelligent user interfaces* (pp. 11-43). New York: ACM Press.

NEM. (2006, August). *Strategic research agenda, version 4.0.*

Nevile, L. (2005, November). Adaptability and accessibility: A new framework. *Proceedings of the 19th Conference of the Computer-Human Interaction Special Interest Group (CHISIG) of Australia on Computer-Human Interaction: Citizens Online: Considerations for Today and the Future,* Canberra, Australia (Vol. 122, pp. 1-10).

Newell, A. (1990). *Unified theories of cognition.* Harvard University Press.

Newlove, J., & Balby, J. (2004). *Laban for all.* London: Nick Hern.

Nicholl, A.R.J. (2001). O Ambiente que Promove a Inclusão: Conceitos de Acessibilidade e Usabilidade". Revista Assentamentos Humanos, Marília, v3, n. 2, p49–60.

Nickel, K., & Stiefelhagen, R. (2003). Pointing gesture recognition based on 3D-tracking of face, hands, and head orientation. In *ICMI '03: Proceedings of the 5th International Conference on Multimodal Interfaces* (pp. 140–146). New York: ACM Press.

Nickel, K., & Stiefelhagen, R. (2003). Pointing gesture recognition based on 3D-tracking of face, hands, and head orientation. In *5th International Conference on Multimodal Interfaces* (pp. 140-146). Vancouver, Canada: ACM Press.

Nielsen, J. (1986). A virtual protocol model for computer-human interaction. *International Journal Man-Machine Studies, 24*, 301-312.

Nielsen, J. (1993). *Usability engineering.* San Diego, CA: Academic Press.

Nielsen, J. (2003). Usability 101: Introduction to usability. Retrieved on October 27, 2008, from http://www.useit.com/alertbox/20030825.html

Nielsen, J., & Mack, R. (1994). *Usability inspection methods.* New York: Wiley.

Nielsen, J., & Tahir, M. (2002). Homepage: Usabilidade – 50 Websites desconstruídos. RJ: Editora Campus.

Nigay, L., & Coutaz, J. (1993). A design space for multimodal systems: Concurrent processing and data fusion. In *INTERCHI '93: Proceedings of the INTERCHI '93 Conference on Human factors in Computing Systems* (pp. 172–178). Amsterdam: IOS Press.

Nigay, L., & Coutaz, J. (1995). A generic platform for addressing the multimodal challenge. In *Proceedings of the Conference on Human Factors in Computing Systems*. ACM Press.

Niklfeld, G., Anegg, H., Pucher, M., Schatz, R., Simon, R., Wegscheider, F., et al. (2005, April). Device independent mobile multimodal user interfaces with the MONA multimodal presentation server. In *Proceedings of Eurescom Summit 2005*, Heidelberg, Germany.

Niles, I., & Pease, A. (2001, October). Towards a standard upper ontology. In C. Welty, & B. Smith (Eds.), *Proceedings of the 2nd International Conference on Formal Ontology in Information Systems (FOIS-2001)*, Ogunquit, ME.

Norman, D.A. (1999). *The invisible computer: Why good products can fail, the personal computer is so complex, and information appliances are the solution*. MIT Press.

O'Hagan, M., & Ashworth, D. (2002). *Translation-mediated communication in a digital world facing the challenges of globalization and localization*. Multilingual Matters LTD.

OASIS. (2006). *Reference model for service oriented architecture 1.0.*

OASIS. *Web services business process execution language*. Retrieved from http://www.oasisopen.org/committees/tc_home.php?wg_abbrev=wsbpel

Obrenovic, Z., Abascal, J., & Starcevic, D. (2007). Universal accessibility as a multimodal design issue. *Communications of the ACM, 50*, 83-88. New York: ACM.

Orwant, J. (1995). Heterogeneous learning in the doppelgänger user modeling system. *User Modeling and User-Adapted Interaction, 4*(2), 107-130.

Oshry, M., Auburn, R.J., Baggia, P., Bodell, M., Burke, D., Burnett, D.C., et al. (2007, March 24). *Voice extensible markup language (voiceXML) 2.1*. Retrieved from http://www.w3.org/TR/voicexml21/

Osman, Z., Maguir, M., & Tarkiainen, M. (2003). Older users' requirements for location based services and mobile phones. *LNCS, 2795*, 352-357.

Otto, K. A. (2005). The semantics of multiuser virtual environments. In *Workshop towards SVE* (pp. 35-39).

Oviatt, S. (1996). Multimodal interfaces for dynamic interactive maps. In *SIGCHI Conference on Human Factors in Computing Systems,* Vancouver, Canada (pp. 95-102).

Oviatt, S., DeAngeli, A., & Kuhn, K. (1997). Integration and synchronization of input modes during multimodal human compute interaction. In *Proceedings of the SIGCHI conference on Human Factors in Computing Systems*, Atlanta, GA (pp. 415-422).

Oviatt, S., & Kuhn, K. (1998). Referential features and linguistic indirection in multimodal language. In *International Conference on Spoken Language Processing*, Sydney, Australia (pp. 2339-2342).

Oviatt, S. (1999). Ten myths of multimodal interaction. *Communications of the ACM, 42*(11), 74-81.

Oviatt, S. (1999, May 15-20). Mutual disambiguation of recognition errors in a multimodal architecture. In *Proceedings of the SIGCHI Conference on Human Factors in Computing Systems: The CHI is the Limit,* Pittsburgh, PA (pp. 576-583). ACM.

Oviatt, S., Bernard, J., & Levow, G. (1999). Linguistic adaptation during error resolution with spoken and multimodal systems. *Language and Speech (special issue on Prosody and Conversation), 41*(3-4), 415-438.

Oviatt, S. (2000). Multimodal system processing in mobile environments. In M.S. Ackerman & K. Edwards (Eds.), *Proceedings of the 13th Annual ACM Symposium on User Interface Software and Technology*, San Diego, CA (pp. 21-30).

Oviatt, S. (2000). Taming recognition errors with a multimodal interface. In *Communications of the ACM, 43*(9), 45-51. ACM Press.

Oviatt, S., & Cohen, P. (2000). Multimodal interfaces that process what comes naturally. *Communications of the ACM, 43*(3), 45-53.

Oviatt, S., Cohen, P., Wu, L., Vergo, J., Duncan, L., Suhm, B., Bers, J., Holzman, T., Winograd, T., Landay, J., Larson, J., & Ferro, D. (2000). Designing the user interface for multimodal speech and gesture applications: State-of-the-art systems and research directions for 2000 and beyond.

Oviatt, S., Cohen, P., Wu, L., Vergo, J., Duncan, L., Suhm, B., Bers, J., Holzman, T., Winograd, T., Landay, J., Larson, J., & Ferro, D. (2000). Designing the user interface for multimodal speech and pen-based gesture applications: State-of-the-art systems and future research directions. *Human-Computer Interaction, 15*(4), 263-322.

Oviatt, S., Coulston, R., & Lunsford, R. (2004, October 13-15). When do we interact multimodally? Cognitive load and multimodal communication pattern. In *the 6th International Conference on Multimodal Interfaces (ICMI 2004)*, State College, PA (pp. 129-136). New York: ACM Press.

Oviatt, S., Coulston, R., Tomko, S., Xiao, B., Lunsford, R., Wesson, M., & Carmichael, L. (2003, November 5-7). Toward a theory of organized multimodal integration patterns during human-computer interaction. In *the 5th International Conference on Multimodal Interfaces (ICMI 2003)*, Vancouver, Canada (pp. 44-51). New York: ACM Press.

Oviatt, S.L. (2002). Multimodal interfaces. In J. Jacko, & A. Sears (Eds.), *Handbook of human-computer interaction*. New Jersey: Lawrence Erlbaum.

Oviatt, S.L. (2003). Multimodal interfaces. In J. Jacko & A. Sears (Ed.), *The human-computer interaction handbook: Fundamentals, evolving technologies, and emerging applications* (pp. 286-304). Mahwah, NJ: Lawrence Erlbaum.

Owen, S., & Rabin, J. (2007). *W3C mobileOK basic tests 1.0.* Retrieved from http://www.w3.org/TR/mobileOK-basic10-tests/

OWL Web Ontology Language. (2008, January). OWL. Retrieved from http://www.w3.org/TR/owl-features/

Paiva, A., & Self, J. (1994). Tagus: A user and learner modeling system. In *Proceedings of the Fourth International Conference on User Modeling*, Hyannis, MA (pp. 43-49).

Palanque, P., & Bastide, R. (1994). Petri net based design of user-driven interfaces using the interactive cooperative objects formalism. In *Interactive systems: Design, specification, and verification* (pp. 383-400). Springer-Verlag.

Pantic, M., Pentland, A., Nijholt, A., & Huang, T. (2006). Human computing and machine understanding of human behavior: A survey. In *Proceedings of the 8th International conference on Multimodal Interfaces (ICMI '06)*, New York, NY (pp. 239-248). ACM Press.

Paolucci, M., Kawamura, T., Payne, T., & Sycara, K. (2002). Importing the Semantic Web in UDDI. In *Web Services, e-business, and Semantic Web workshop*.

Paolucci, M., Kawamura, T., Payne, T., Sycara, R., & Katia, P. (2002). Semantic matching of Web services capabilities. *International Semantic Web Conference* (pp. 333-347).

Parker, J.K., Mandryk, R.L., & Inkpen, K.M. (2005). Tractorbeam: Seamless integration of local and remote pointing for tabletop displays. In *GI '05: Proceedings of Graphics Interface 2005* (pp. 33–40). Waterloo, Canada: Canadian Human-Computer Communications Society.

Parsons, D., & Ryu, H. (2006). A framework for assessing the quality of mobile learning. In *Proceedings of the 11th International Conference for Process Improvement, Research, and Education (INSPIRE)*, Southampton Solent University, UK.

Pascoe, J., Ryan, N., & Morse, D. (2000). Using while moving: Human-computer interaction issues in fieldwork environments. *Transactions on Computer-Human Interaction, 7*(3), 417-437.

Pask, G. (1976). *Conversation theory: Applications in education and epistemology.* Amsterdam and New York: Elsevier.

Paterno, F. (2000). *Model-based design and evaluation of interactive applications.* Springer-Verlag.

Pavlovic, V.I., Berry, G.A., & Huang, T.S. (1997). Integration of audio/visual information for use in human-computer intelligent interaction. In *Proceedings of the 1997 International Conference on Image Processing (ICIP '97)*, (Vol. 1, pp. 121-124).

Peck, C.H. (2001). Useful parameters for the design of laser pointer interaction techniques. In *CHI '01: CHI '01 Extended Abstracts on Human factors in Computing Systems* (pp. 461–462). New York: ACM.

Pedersen, E. (2005). Adoption of mobile internet services: An exploratory study of mobile commerce early adopters. *Journal of Organizational Computing and Electronic Commerce, 15*(3), 203-222.

Penner, R.R., & Steinmetz, E.S. (2002). Model-based automation of the design of user interfaces to digital control systems. *IEEE Trans. on Systems, Man, and Cybernetics - Part A, 32*(1), 41-49.

Perakakis, M., & Potamianos, A. (2008). The effect of input mode on inactivity and interaction times of multimodal systems. *ACM,* 102-109.

Pérez, G., Amores, G., & Manchón, P. (2005). Two strategies for multimodal fusion. In *Proceedings of Multimodal Interaction for the Visualization and Exploration of Scientific Data*, Trento, Italy (pp. 26-32).

Perkowitz, M., & Etzioni, O. (2000). Towards adaptive Web sites: Conceptual framework and case study. *Artificial Intelligence, 118*(2000), 245–275.

Perry, D. (2003). *Handheld computers (PDAs) in schools.* British Educational Communications and Technology Agency (Becta). Coventry, UK.

Petrelli, D., Not, E., Zancanaro, M., Strapparava, C., & Stock, O. (2001). Modelling and adapting to context. *Personal and Ubiquitous Computing, 5*(1), 20–24.

Petri, C.A. (1962). Fundamentals of a theory of asynchronous information flow. In *IFIP Congress* (pp. 386-390).

Petrie, H., Hamilton, F., King, N., & Pavan, P. (2006). Remote - usability evaluations with disabled people. *Proceedings of the SIGCHI Conference on Human Factors in Computing systems*, Canada.

Pfeiffer, T., & Latoschik, E. (2004). Resolving object references in multimodal dialogues for immersive virtual environments. In *Proceedings of the IEEE VR2004*, Chicago, IL (pp. 35-42).

Phang, C.W.J., Sutano, A., Kankanhalli, L., Yan, B.C.Y., & Teo, H.H. (2006). Senior citizens' acceptance of information systems: A study in the context of e-government services. *IEEE Transactions on Engineering Management.*

Pheifer, R., & Bongard, J. (2007). *How the body shapes the way we think.* Cambridge, MA: MIT Press.

Phillips, L., & Sternthal, B. (1977). Age differences in information processing: A perspective on the aged consumer. *Journal of Marketing Research, 14*(2), 444-457.

Pieraccini, R., Levin, E., & Lee, C.H. (1991). Stochastic representation of conceptual structure in the ATIS task. In *Proceedings DARPA Speech and Natural Language Workshop*, Pacific Grove, CA (pp. 121–124).

Pierno, S., Romano, L., Capuano, L., Magaldi, M., Bevilacqua, L. (2008). Software innovation for e-government expansion. In R. Meersman & Z. Tari (Eds.), *OTM 2008, Part I* (LNCS 5331, pp. 822–832). Springer-Verlag Berlin Heidelberg Computer Science.

Pierrehumbert, J., & Hirschberg, J. (1990). The meaning of intonational contours in the interpretation of discourse. In P. Cohen, J. Morgan, & M. Pollarck (Eds.), *Intentions in communication* (pp. 271-311). Cambridge, MA: MIT Press.

Pinhanez, C.S. (1999). *Representation and recognition of action in interactive spaces.* Unpublished doctoral dissertation, Cambridge, MA, Massachusetts Institute of Technology.

Pinto, H., Han, J., Pei, J., Wang, K., Chen, Q., & Dayal, U. (2001). Multi-dimensional sequential pattern mining. In *CIKM '01: Proceedings of the Tenth International Conference on Information and Knowledge Management*, New York (pp. 81-88). ACM Press.

Pirhonen, A., Brewster, S., & Holguin, C. (2002). Gestural and audio metaphors as a means of control for mobile devices. In *Proceedings of the SIGCHI Conference on Human Factors in Computing Systems (CHI 2002)* (pp. 291-298). New York: ACM.

Pisanelli, D.M., Battaglia, M., & De Lazzari, C. (2007). ROME: A Reference Ontology in Medicine. In H. Fujita, & D.M. Pisanelli (Eds.), *New trends in software methodologies, tools, and techniques*. Amsterdam: IOS Press.

Pittarello, F. (2001). *Desktop 3D interfaces for internet users: Efficiency and usability issues.* Unpublished doctoral dissertation, Department of Computer Science, University of Bologna, Italy.

Pittarello, F. (2003). Accessing information through multimodal 3D environments: Towards universal access. *Universal Access in the Information Society Journal, 2*(2), 189–204.

Po, S., Howard, S., Vetere, F., & Skov, M.B. (2004). Heuristic evaluation and mobile usability: Bridging the realism gap. In S. Brewster & M. Dunlop (Eds), *Proceedings of the Conference on Human Computer Interaction with Mobile Devices and Services (MobileHCI 2004)* (pp. 49–60).

Popelínsky, L. (1998). Knowledge discovery in spatial data by means of ILP. In *Proceedings of the Second European Symposium on Principles of Data Mining and Knowledge Discovery* (pp. 185-193). Springer.

Pöppel, E. (1997). A hierarchical model of temporal perception. *Trends in Cognitive Science, 1*, 56–61.

Portanieri, F., & Amara, F. (1996). Arabization of graphical user interfaces. In *International user interfaces*. New York: John Wiley & Sons, Inc.

Portillo, P.M., Garcia G.P., & Carredano, G.A. (2006). Multimodal fusion: A new hybrid strategy for dialogue systems. In *Proceedings of ICMI'06*, Banff, Canada. ACM.

Portillo, P.M., Valdés, C.d.S., Carredano, G.d.A., & Pérez García, G. (2006). *The MIMUS corpus.* Paper presented at the LREC-06 International Workshop on Multimodal Corpora from Multimodal Behaviour Theories to Usable Models, Genoa, Italy.

Porzel, R., Zorn, H.-P., Loos, B., & Malaka, R. (2006, August 28). *Towards A separation of pragmatic knowledge and contextual information.* Paper presented at the ECAI-06 Workshop on Contexts and Ontologies, Riva del Grada, Italy.

Preece, J., Sharp, H., & Rogers, Y. (2002). *Interaction design--beyond human-computer interaction.* New York: John Wiley & Sons, Inc.

Pressman, R. (2007). *Software engineering - a practioner's approach, 6th ed.* McGraw-Hill, Inc.

Pretorius, A.J. (2005). Visual analysis for ontology engineering. *Journal of Visual Languages and Computing, 16*, 359-381.

PVM. Retrieved from http://www.jboss.org/jbossjbpm/pvm/

Qingyang, G. (2003). *M-Learning: A new development towards more flexible and learner-centred learning.* IATEFL Poland Computer Special Interest Group, Teaching English with Technology.

Queiroz, M.A. (2007). Material de um curso ministrado no SERPRO RJ por Marco Antonio de Queiroz, especialmente para cegos e pessoas de baixa visão. Tirado 02 de Abril 2003 de 2007 http://www.bengalalegal.com/. 2/4/2007.

Quek, F., McNeill, D., Bryll, B., Duncan, S., Ma, X., Kirbas, C., McCullough, K.-E., & Ansari, R. (2002, September). Multimodal human discourse: Gesture and speech. *ACM Transactions on Computer-Human Interaction (TOCHI), 9*(3).

Quek, F., McNeill, D., Bryll, R., Kirbas, C., Arlsan, H., McCullough, K.E., Furuyama, N., & Gesture, A.R. (2000, June 13-15). Speech and gaze cues for discourse segmentation. In *IEEE Conference on computer Vision and Pattern Recognition (CVPR 2000)*, Hilton Head Island, SC (pp. 247-254).

Quesada, J. F., Torre, D., & Amores, G. (2000). Design of a natural command language dialogue system. Deliverable 3.2, Siridus Project.

Qvarfordt, P., & Zhai, S. (2005). Conversing with the user based on eye-gaze patterns. In *SIGCHI Conference on Human Factors in Computing Systems,* Portland, OR (pp. 221-230).

Rabin, J., & McCathieNevile, C. (2006). *Mobile Web best practices 1.0.* Retrieved from http://www.w3.org/TR/mobile-bp/

Rabiner, L. (1990). A tutorial on hidden Markov models and selected applications in speech recognition (pp. 267-296).

Rabiner, L.R. (1989). A tutorial on hidden Markov models and selected applications in speech recognition. In *Proceedings of the IEEE, 77,* 257-285.

RAFT. (2003). RAFT project Website. Retrieved from http://www.raft-project.net

Raggett, D. (2001). *Getting started with VoiceXML 2.0.* Retrieved from http://www.w3.org/Voice/Guide/

Ramakrishnan, I., Stent, A., & Yang, G. (2004). Hearsay: Enabling audio browsing on hypertext content. *World Wide Web Conference (WWW)* (pp. 80-89).

Raman, T.V. (2003). User interface principles for multimodal interaction. *Workshop on Principles for Multimodal User Interface Design, CHI 2003.* Retrieved from http://www.almaden.ibm.com/cs/people/tvraman/chi-2003/mmi-position.html

Randell, C., & Muller, H. (2000). Context awareness by analysing accelerometer data. In B. MacIntyre, & B. Iannucci (Eds.), *Proccedings of the 4th International Symposium on Wearable Computers* (pp. 175-176). IEEE Computer Society.

Rao, S.P., & Cook, D.J. (2004). Predicting inhabitant action using action and task models with application to

smart homes. *International Journal on Artificial Intelligence Tools, 13*(1), 81-99.

Rauschert, I., Sharma, R., Fuhrmann, S., Brewer, I., & MacEachren, A. (2002). Approaching a new multimodal GIS interface. In *2nd International Conference on GIS (GIScience),* CO.

Raymaekers, C., & Coninx, K. (2001). Menu interactions in a desktop haptic environment. In *Proceedings of Eurohaptics 2001*, Birmingham, UK (pp. 49-53).

Raymaekers, C., Coninx, K., Boeck, J.D., Cuppens, E., & Flerackers, E. (May 12-14). High-level interaction modelling to facilitate the development of virtual environments. In *Proceedings of Virtual Reality International Conference,* Laval, France.

Reeves, L.M., Lai, J., Larson, J.A., Oviatt, S., Balaji, T.S., Buisine, S., et al. (2004). Guidelines for multimodal user interface design. *Communications of the ACM, 47,* 57-59. New York: ACM.

Reeves, L.M., Lai, J., Larson, J.A., Oviatt, S., Balaji, T.S., Buisine, S., Collings, P., Cohen, P., Kraal, B., Martin, J.-C., McTear, M., Raman, T., Stanney, K.M., Su, H., & Wang, Q.Y. (2004). Guidelines for multimodal user interface design. *Communications of the ACM, 47*(1), 57-59.

Reitter, D., Panttaja, E., & Cummins, F. (2004). UI on the fly: Generating a multimodal user interface. In *Proceedings of Human Language Technology Conference 2004 / North American Chapter of the Association for Computational Linguistics (HLT/NAACL-04).*

Renaud, K., & Van Biljon, K. (2008). Predicting technology acceptance by the elderly: A qualitative study. In C. Cilliers, L. Barnard, & R. Botha (Eds.), *Proceedings of SAICSIT 2008* (Vol. 1, 210-219). Wildernis, South Africa: ACM Conference Proceedings.

Resch, B. Hidden Markov models-a tutorial for the courses computational intelligence. Retrieved from http://www.igi.tugraz.at/lehre/CI

Resnick, L.B., Saljo, R., Pontecorvo, C., & Burge, B. (Eds.) (1997). *Discourse, tools, and reasoning: Essays on situated cognition.* Berlin, Germany: Springer-Verlag.

Reulen, J.P., & Bakker, L. (1982). The measurement of eye movement using double magnetic induction. *IEEE Transactions on Biomedical Engineering, 29*, 740-744.

Rich, E. (1979). *Building and exploiting user models.* Unpublished doctoral dissertation, Pittsburgh, PA.

Rich, E. (1989). Stereotypes and user modeling. In A. Kobsa, & W. Wahlster (Eds.), *User models in dialog systems* (pp. 35-51). Berlin, Heidelberg: Springer.

Rich, E. (1998). User modeling via stereotypes. In *Readings in intelligent user interfaces* (pp. 329-342). San Francisco: Morgan Kaufmann Publishers Inc.

Robertson, S., Calder, J., Fung, P., Jones, A., & O'Shea, T. (1997). The use and effectiveness of palmtop computers in education. *British Journal of Educational Technology, 28*(3), 177-189.

Rodríguez, J., Alonso, C., & Böstrom, H. (2000). Learning first order logic time series classifiers. In J. Cussens, & A. Frisch (Eds.), *Proceedings of the 10th International Workshop on Inductive Logic Programming* (pp. 260-275). Springer.

Rogers, E.M. (2003). *Diffusion of innovations* (5th ed.). New York: The Free Press.

Rosenberg, A.L. (1964). On n-tape finite state acceptors. *FOCS*, 76-81.

Ross, D., & Blasch, B. (2000). Wearable interfaces for orientation and wayfinding. In *Proceedings of the Fourth International ACM Conference on Assistive Technologies (ASSETS'00)* (pp. 193–200). Arlington, VA: ACM Press.

Rousseau, C., Bellik, Y., Vernier, F., & Bazalgette, D. (2006). A framework for the intelligent multimodal presentation of information. *Signal Processing, 86*(12), 3696-3713.

Rudzicz, F. (2006, July). Clavius: Bi-directional parsing for generic multimodal interaction, In *Proceedings of COLING/ACL 2006*, Sydney, Australia.

Ruiz, N., Taib R., & Chen, F. (2006, November 20-24). Examining redundancy in multimodal input. In *Proceedings of OZCHI 2006*, Sydney, Australia.

Rumetshofer, H., & Wöß, W. (2003). XML-based adaptation framework for psychologicaldrivene-learning systems. *Educational Technology & Society, 6*(4), 18-29.

Russ, G., Sallans, B., & Hareter, H. (2005, June 20-23). Semantic based information fusion in a multimodal interface. *International Conference on Human-Computer Interaction (HCI'05)*, Las Vegas, NV (pp. 94-100).

Sainz Salces, F.J., Baskett, M., Llewellyn-Jones, D., & England, D. (2006). Ambient interfaces for elderly people at home. In J.G. Carbonell & J. Siekmann (Eds.), *Ambient intelligence in everyday life* (pp. 256-284). Springer LNCS.

Sakai, J., & Doshita, S. (1962). The phonetic typewriter. *Information Processing.*

Salber, D., & Coutaz, J. (1993) Applying the Wizard of Oz technique to the study of multimodal systems. *Human-computer interaction* (LNCS 753, pp. 219-230). Heidelberg: Springer.

Sales, M.B. De, & Cybis, W.de A. (2003). Desenvolvimento de um checklist para a avaliação de acessibilidade da *Web* para usuários idosos - *ACM International Conference Proceeding Series Proceedings of the Latin American Conference on Human-Computer Interaction.*

SALT Forum. (2002). *Speech application language tags (SALT).* Retrieved from http://www.saltforum.org

Salthouse, T.A. (1985). Speed of behavior and its implications for cognition. In J.E. Birren, & K.W. Schaie (Eds.), *Handbook of the psychology of aging* (2nd ed.). New York: Van Nostrand Reinhold.

Sampson, D.G., Zervas, P. (2008). *Enabling interoperable mobile learning: Evaluation results from the use of SMILE PDA learning design player.* Paper presented at the WMUTE, Bejing.

Sanders, E. (2002). Ethnography in NPD research. How applied ethnography can improve your NPD research process. Retrieved on October 8, 2006, from http://www.pdma.org/ visions/apr02/applied.html

Sarker, S., & Wells, J.D. (2003). Understanding mobile handheld device use and adoption. *Communications of the ACM, 46*(12), 35-40.

Sato, A., & Yasuda, A. (2005). Illusion of sense of self-agency: Discrepancy between the predicted and actual sensory consequences of actions modulates the sense of self-agency, but not the sense of self-ownership. *Cognition, 94*(3), 241–255.

Savill-Smith, C., & Kent, P. (2003). *The use of palmtop computers for learning. A review of the literature* (Lit. Rev.), Learning and Skills Development Agency.

Savourel, Y. (2001). *XML internationalization and localization*. SAMS.

Sawhney, N., & Schmandt, C. (2000). Nomadic radio: Speech and audio interaction for contextual messaging in nomadic environments. *ACM Transactions on Computer-Human Interaction, 7*(3), 353-383. ACM Press.

Schapira, E., & Sharma, R. (2001). Experimental evaluation of vision and speech based multimodal interfaces. In *PUI '01: Proceedings of the 2001 workshop on Perceptive user interfaces* (pp. 1–9). New York: ACM.

Schilit, B.N., Adams, N.I., & Want, R. (1994).Context-aware computing applications. In *Proceedings of the Workshop on Mobile Computing Systems and Applications, IEEE Computer Society* (pp. 85-90).

Schleidt, M., Eibl-Eibesfeldt, I., & Pöppel, E. (1987). Universal constant in temporal segmentation of human short-term behaviour. *Naturwissenschaften, 74*, 289–290.

Schomaker, L., Nijtmans, A.J., Camurri, F. Lavagetto, P., Morasso, C., Benoit, T., et al. (1995). A taxonomy of multimodal interaction in the human information processing system. *Multimodal Integration for Advanced Multimedia Interfaces (MIAMI). ESPRIT III, Basic Research Project 8579.*

Schweikhardt, W., Bernareggi, C., Jessel, N., Encelle, B., & Gut, M. (2006). LAMBDA: A European system to access mathematics with Braille and audio synthesis. In *ICCHP '06: International Conference on Computers Helping People with Special Needs* (LNCS 4061, pp. 1223-1230).

Senach.,B. (1990). *Evaluation ergonomique des interfaces homme-machine : Une revue de la litterature.* (Tech. Rep.). National Institute for Research in Computer and Control Sciences.

Sezgin, T.M., & Davis, R. (2005). HMM-based efficient sketch recognition. In *Proceedings of the 10th International Conference on Intelligent User Interfaces (IUI 05)* (pp. 281-283). ACM Press.

Shanmugham, S., & Burnett, D.C. (2008, June 23). *Media resource control protocol version 2 (MRCPv2)*. Retrieved from http://tools.ietf.org/html/draft-ietf-speechsc-mrcpv2-16

Sharma, C., & Kunins, J. (2002). *VoiceXML*. New York: John Wiley and Sons, Inc.

Sharma, R., Pavlovic, V.I., & Huang, T.S. (1998). Toward multimodal human-computer interface. In *Proceedings of the IEEE, Special Issue on Multimedia Signal Processing, 86*(5), 853-869.

Sharma, R., Zeller, M., Pavlovic, V.I., Huang, T.S., Lo, Z., Chu, S., Zhao, Y., Phillips, J.C., & Schulten, K. (2000). Speech/gesture interface to a visual-computing environment. *IEEE Computer Graphics and Applications, 20*(2), 29-37.

Sharma, S.K., & Kitchens, F.L. (2004). Web services architecture for m-learning. *Electronic Journal on E-Learning, 2*(1), 203–216.

Shneiderman, B. (1984). Response time and display rate in human performance with computers. *ACM Computing Surveys, 16*(3), 265–285.

Shneiderman, B. (2000). The limits of speech recognition. *Communications of the ACM, 43*(9), 63-65. ACM Press.

Shneiderman, B. (2004). *Designing the user interface : Strategies for effective human-computer interaction, 4th ed.* MA: Addison-Wesley.

Shukla, C., Dass, A., & Gupta, V. (2002). *VoiceXML 2.0 developer's guide: Building professional voice-enabled applications with JSP, ASP, & Coldfusion*. New York: McGraw-Hill Osborne Media.

Si, H., Kawahara, Y., Morikawa, H., & Aoyama, T. (2005). A stochastic approach for creating context-aware services based on context histories in smart home. In *ECHISE2005, Pervasive 2005 Proceeding* (pp. 37-41).

Sibert, L.E., & Jacob, R.J.K. (2000). Evaluation of eye gaze interaction. In *CHI '00: Proceedings of the SIGCHI Conference on Human Factors in Computing Systems* (pp. 281–288). New York: ACM.

Siewiorek, D., Smailagic, A., Furukawa, J., Krause, A., Moraveji, N., Reiger, K., Shaffer, J., & Wong, F.L. (2003). Sensay: A context-aware mobile phone. In *Proceedings of the 7th IEEE International Symposium on Wearable Computers (ISWC'03)*, Los Alamitos, CA (p. 248). IEEE Computer Society.

Silverstone, R., & Haddon, L. (1996). Design and the domestication of information and communication technologies: Technical change and everyday life. In *Communication by design: The politics of information and communication technologies* (pp. 44-74). Oxford, UK: Oxford University.

Simoff, S.J. (2008). Form-Semantics-Function-a framework for designing visual data representations for visual data mining. In S.J. Simoff, M.H. Böhlen & A. Mazeika (Eds.), *Visual data mining: Theory, techniques, and tools for visual analytics* (LNCS 4404, pp. 30-45). Heidelberg: Springer Verlag.

Simoff, S.J., & Maher, M.L. (2000). Analysing participation in collaborative design environments. *Design studies, 21*, 119-144.

Simoff, S.J., Sierra, C., & López de Mántaras, R. (2008, September 17). Requirements towards automated mediation agents. In *Pre-proceedings of the KR2008-Workshop on Knowledge Representation for Agents and MultiAgent Systems (KRAMAS),* Sydney, Australia (pp. 171-185).

SmartWeb: Mobile Broadband Access to the Semantic Web. Retrieved from http://smartweb.dfki.de/main_pro_en.pl?infotext_en.html

Smith, B. (1995). Formal ontology, commonsense, and cognitive science. *International Journal of Human Computer Studies, 43*(5/6).

Smith, M., Welty, C., & McGuinness, D. (2004). *OWL Web Ontology Language guide - W3C recommendation.* Retrieved from http://www.w3.org/TR/owl-guide/

Soloway, J.E., Norris, M.C., Jansen, R.J., Krajcik, R.M., Fishman, B., & Blumenfeld, P. (2001). Making palm-sized computers the PC of choice for K-12. *Learning & Leading with Technology, 28* (7), 32–34, 56–57.

Sonntag, D., Engel, R., Herzog, G., Pfalzgraf, A., Pfleger, N., Romanelli, M., & Reithinger, N. (2007). SmartWeb handheld - multimodal interaction with ontological knowledge bases and Semantic Web services. *Artifical Intelligence for Human Computing 2007*, 272-295.

Souchon, N., Limbourg, Q., & Vanderdonckt, J. (2002). Task modelling in multiple contexts of use. In *DSV-IS '02: Proceedings of the 9th International Workshop on Interactive Systems. Design, Specification, and Verification*, London (pp. 59-73). Springer-Verlag.

Sowa, J. (2000). Knowledge representation: Logical, philosophical, and computational foundations. Pacific Grove, CA: Brooks Cole Publishing Co.

Špakov, O., & Miniotas, D. (2004). On-line adjustment of dwell time for target selection by gaze. In *NordiCHI '04: Proceedings of the Third Nordic Conference on Human-Computer Interaction* (pp. 203–206). New York: ACM.

SPARQL Query Language for RDF. (2008, January). SPARQL. Retrieved from http://www.w3.org/TR/rdf-sparqlquery/

Spelta, L.L. (2003). O Papel dos Leitores de Tela na Construção de *Sites* Acessíveis - Anais do ATIID 2003, São Paulo-SP, 23–24/09/2003.

Spiro, R.J., Feltovich, P.J., Jacobson, M.J., & Coulson, R.L. (1991). Cognitive flexibility, constructivism, and hypertext. *Educational Technology,* 24-33.

Stahl, G., Sumner, T., & Repenning, A. (1995). Internet repositories for collaborative learning: Supporting both students and teachers. In *Proceedings of the Computer Supported Collaborative Learning Conference.* Retrieved on May 20, 2004.

Stalnaker, R.C. (1978). Assertion. In P. Cole (Ed.), *Pragmatics: Syntax and semantics* (Vol. 9, pp. 315–332). Academic Press.

Standard ECMA-327 ECMAScript 3rd Edition Compact Profile. (2001). Retrieved from http://www.ecma-international.org/publications/standards/Ecma-327.htm

Stary, C. (2000). TADEUS: Seamless development of task-based and user-oriented interfaces. *IEEE Trans. on Systems, Man, and Cybernetics - Part A, 30*(5), 509-525.

Steedman, M. (1990). Structure and intonation in spoken language undestanding. *ACL 1990*, 9-16.

Steedman, M. (2000). Information structure and the syntax-phonology interface. *Linguistic Inquiry, 31*, 649-689.

Steedman, M. (2000). *The syntactic process.* Cambridge, MA: The MIT Press.

Steedman, M. (2003). Information-structural semantics for English intonation. *LSA Summer Institute Workshop on Topic and Focus*, Santa Barbara.

Steedman, M., & Kruijff-Korbayová, I. (2001). Introduction two dimensions of information structure in relation to discourse structure and discourse semantics. In I. Kruijff-Korbayová & Steedman (Eds.), *Proceedings of the ESSLLI 2001 Workshop on Information Structure.*

Stolze, M., Riand, P., Wallace, M., & Heath, T. (2007). Agile development of workflow applications with interpreted task models. *Task Models and Diagrams for User Interface Design (TAMODIA'07)* (pp. 8-14).

Stone, A., Alsop, G., Briggs, J., & Tompsett, C. (2002, June 20-21). *M-Learning and e-learning: A review of work undertaken by the learning technology research group, Kingston University, UK.* Paper presented at the Proceedings of the European Workshop on Mobile and Contextual Learning, The University of Birmingham, England.

Sturm, J., Bakx, I., Cranen, B., Terken, J., & Wang, F. (2002). The effect of prolonged use on multimodal interaction. In *Proceedings of ISCA Workshop on Multimodal Interaction in Mobile Environments*, Kloster Irsee, Germany.

Suchman, L., & Trigg, R.H. (1991). Understanding practice: Video as a medium for reflection and design. In J. Greenbaum & M. Kyng (Eds.), *Design at work: Cooperative design of computer systems* (pp. 65-89). Hillsdale, NJ: Lawrence Erlbaum.

Suchman, L., Blomberg, J., Orr, J., & Trigg, R. (1999). Reconstructing technologies as social practice. *American Behavioral Scientist, 43*(3), 392-408.

Suhm, B., Myers, B., & Weibel, A. (2001). Multimodal error correction for speech user interfaces. *ACM Transactions on Computer-Human Interaction, 8*(1), 60-98, ACM Press.

Sun, Y., Chen, F., Shi, Y.D., & Chung, V. (2006). A novel method for multisensory data fusion in multimodal human computer interaction. In *Proceedings of the 20th Conference of the Computer-Human Interaction Special Interest Group (CHISIG) of Australia on Computer-Human Interaction: Design, Activities, Artefacts, and Environments*, Sydney, Australia (pp. 401-404).

Sun, Y., Shi, Y., Chen, F., & Chung, V. (2007, November 28-30) An efficient unification-based multimodal language processor in multimodal input fusion. In *Proceedings of OZCHI2007*, Adelaide, Australia. ACM.

Takagi, H., Asakawa, C., Fukuda K., & Maeda J. (2004). Accessibility designer: Visualizing usability for the blind. *ACM SIGACCESS Conference on Assistive Technologies - Proceedings of the ACM SIGACCESS Conference on Computers and Accessibility.*

Tamminen, S., Oulasvirta, A., Toiskallio, K., & Kankainen, A. (2003). Understanding mobile contexts. In L. Chittaro (Ed.), *Proceedings of the Conference on Human-Computer Interaction with Mobile Devices and Service (MobileHCI 2003)* (pp. 17-31). Berlin, Springer.

Tan A.H. (1995). Adaptive resonance associative map. *Neural Networks Archive, 8*(3), 437-446. Vijay-Shanker, K., & Weir, D. (1990). Polynomial time parsing of combinatory categorical grammars. In *Proceedings of ACL'90*, Pittsburgh, PA. ACL.

Tatar, D., Roschelle, D., Vahey, P., & Peunel, W.R. (2002). *Handhelds go to school: Lessons learned.*

Taylor, M.M. (1988). Layered protocol for computer-human dialogue. *International Journal Man-Machine Studies, 28*, 175-218.

Theofanos, M.F., & Redish, J.G. (2003). Bridging the gap: Between accessibility and usability. *Interactions, X6*, 36-51.

Thomas, B.H., & Piekarski, W. (2002). Glove based user interaction techniques for augmented reality in an outdoor environment. *Virtual Reality*, 167-180.

Thomas, D.M., Bostrom, R.P., & G.M. (2007). Making knowledge work in virtual teams. *Communications of the ACM, 50*(11), 85–90.

Thórisson, K.R. (1999). A mind model for multimodal communicative creatures and humanoids. *International Journal of Applied Artificial Intelligence, 13*(4-5), 449-486.

Toyama, K., & Horvitz, E. (2000). Bayesian modality fusion: Probabilistic integration of multiple vision algorithms for head tracking. In *Proceedings of the Fourth Asian Conference on Computer Vision*, Tapei, Taiwan.

Trajkovik, V., Gligorovska, S., & Davcev, D. (2007, July 5-7). Mobile virtual blackboard. In *Proc. of IADIS International Conference on Mobile Learning 2007*, Lisbon, Portugal.

Tretola, G. (2007). *Autonomic workflow management in e-collaboration environment.* Department of Engineering University of Sannio, Benevento.

Tretola, G., & Zimeo, E. (2006, April 25-29). Workflow fine-grained concurrency with automatic continuations. In *Proceedings of the IEEE IPDPS 06, 20th International Parallel and Distributed Processing Symposium*, Rhodes Island, Greece.

Tretola, G., & Zimeo, E. (2007, February 7-9). Activity pre-scheduling in grid workflow. In *Proceedings of the 15th Euromicro International Conference on Parallel, Distributed and Networkbased Processing (PDP).*

Tretola, G., & Zimeo, E. (2007, July 9-13). Extending Web services semantics to support asynchronous invocations and continuation. In *Proceedings of the IEEE 2007 International Conference on Web Services (ICWS)*, Salt Lake City, UT.

Tretola, G., & Zimeo, E. (2007, June 19-20). Structure matching for enhancing UDDI queries results. In *Proceedings of the IEEE International Conference on Service-Oriented Computing and Applications (SOCA'07)*, Newport Beach, CA.

Tretola, G., & Zimeo, E. (2007, March 26-30). Client-side implementation of dynamic asynchronous invocations for Web services. In *Proceedings of the IEEE IPDPS 07, 21st International Parallel and Distributed Processing Symposium*, Long Beach, CA.

Trifonova, A., Knapp, J., Ronchetti, M., & Camper, J. (2004, June 21-26). Mobile ELDIT: Transition from an e-learning to an m-learning system. In *Proceedings of the World Conference on Educational Multimedia, Hypermedia, and Telecommunications (ED-MEDIA 2004)*, Lugano, Switzerland (pp. 188-193).

Tsai, W.H., & Fu, K.S. (1979). Error-correcting isomorphism of attributed relational graphs for pattern analysis. *IEEE Transactions on Systems, Man, and Cybernetics, 9*, 757-768.

Tse, E., Greenberg, S., Shen, C., Forlines, C., & Kodama, R. (2008, February 25-27). Exploring true multiuser multimodal interaction over a digital table. In *Proceedings of DIS 2008*, Cape Town, South Africa (pp. 109-118).

Turner, M. (1994). Design for a theory of meaning. In W. Overton & D. Palermo (Eds.), *The nature and ontogenesis of meaning* (pp. 91-107). Lawrence Erlbaum Associates.

Ullman, J. (1988). *Principles of database and knowledge-base systems, vol. I.* Computer Science Press.

Van Biljon, J.A. (2007). *A model for representing the motivational and cultural factors that influence mobile phone usage variety.* (Doctoral dissertation, University of South Africa, Pretoria). Retrieved from http://etd.unisa.ac.za/ETD-db/theses/available/etd-09062007-131207/unrestricted/thesis.pdf

Van Esch–Bussemakers, M.P., Neerincx, M.A., Lindenberg, J., & Streefkerk, J.W. (2005). User experience testing in context: Attentive services for the police. In *CHI2005 Workshop Usage Analysis: Combining Logging and Qualitative Methods*, Portland, ME.

Van Tichelen, L., & Burke, D. (2007, April 5). *Semantic interpretation for speech recognition*. Retrieved from http://www.w3.org/TR/semantic-interpretation/

Vanacken, L., Cuppens, E., Clerckx, T., & Coninx, K. (2007). Extending a dialog model with contextual knowledge. In M. Winckler, H. Johnson, & P.A. Palanque (Eds.), *TAMODIA* (LNCS 4849, pp. 28-41). Springer.

Vanacken, L., Raymaekers, C., & Coninx, K. (2007). Automatic speech grammar generation during conceptual modelling of virtual environments. In *Intuition 2007*, Athens, Greece.

Vanacken, L., Raymaekers, C., & Coninx, K. (2007). Introducing semantic information during conceptual modelling of interaction for virtual environments. In *WMISI '07: Proceedings of the 2007 Workshop on Multimodal Interfaces in Semantic Interaction* (pp. 17-24).

Vanderdonckt, J. (2005). A MDA compliant environment for developing user interfaces of information systems. In *Proceedings of 17th Conference on Advanced Information Systems Engineering CAiSE'05*, Porto, Portugal (pp. 16-31).

Vanderdonckt, J., Limbourg, Q., Michotte, B., Bouillon, L., Trevisan, D., & Florins, M. (2004). Usixml: A user interface description language for specifying multimodal user interfaces. In *Proceedings of W3C Workshop on Multimodal Interaction WMI'2004*, Sophia Antipolis (pp. 35-42).

Venkatesh, A. (2006). Introduction to the special issue on ICT in everyday life: Home and personal environments. *The Information Society Journal, 22,* 191-194.

Venkatesh, V., Morris, M.G., Davis, G.B., & Davis, F.D. (2003). User acceptance of information technology: Toward a unified view. *MIS Quarterly, 27*(3), 425-478.

Vermeeren, A., & Kort, J. (2006). Developing a testbed for automated user experience measurement of context aware mobile applications. In *Proceedings of the Workshop User Experience–Towards a Unified View*. Retrieved from http://141.115.28.2/cost294/ux-workshop-nordichi2006/nordichi-userexperience-workshop.html

Virtools Inc. (2008, April). Virtools Dev. Retrieved from http://www.virtools.com

Vo, M.T. (1998). *A framework and toolkit for the construction of multimodal learning interfaces.* Unpublished doctoral dissertation, Carnegie Mellon University, Pittsburgh, PA.

Vo, M.T., & Wood, C. (1996, May 7-10). Building an application framework for speech and pen input integration in multimodal learning interfaces. In *Proceedings of the Acoustics, Speech, and Signal Processing (ICASSP'96), IEEE Computer Society* (Vol. 6, pp. 3545-3548).

Voice eXtensible Markup Language Version 2.0, W3C Recommendation. (2008). Retrieved on May 11, 2008, from http://www.w3.org/TR/voicexml20

Vygotsky, L. (1978). *Mind in society: The development of higher psychological processes.* Boston: Harvard University Press.

W3C. (1998). *Cascading style sheets, level 2.* Retrieved on October 27, 2008, from http://www.w3.org/TR/REC-CSS2/

W3C. (1999). *XML path language (XPath).* Retrieved on October 27, 2008, from http://www.w3.org/TR/xpath

W3C. (1999). *XSL transformations (XSLT).* Retrieved on October 27, 2008, from http://www.w3.org/TR/xslt

W3C. (2000). *Extensible markup language (XML) 1.0 (second edition).* Retrieved from http://www.w3.org/TR/REC-xml

W3C. (2008). *Semantic Web.* Retrieved on October 27, 2008, from http://www.w3.org/2001/sw/

W3C. *Multimodal interaction activity.* Retrieved from http://www.w3.org/2002/mmi/

Wachsmuth, I., Lenzmann, B., & Cao, Y. (1995). *VIENA: A Multiagent Interface to a Virtual Environment (ICMAS 1995)* (p. 465).

Wachsmuth, I., Lenzmann, B., Jörding, T., Jung, B., Latoschik, M.E., & Fröhlich, M. (1997). A virtual interface agent and its agency. *Agents 1997*, 516-517.

Wahlster, W., Reithinger, N., & Blocher, A. (2001). SmartKom: Multimodal communication with a life-like character. In *Proceedings of Eurospeech*, Aalborg, Denmark.

WAI. (2008). *Web accessibility initiative*. Retrieved on October 27, 2008, from http://www.w3.org/WAI

Wang, X., Li, J., Ao, X., Wang, G., & Dai, G. (2006). Multimodal error correction for continuous handwriting recognition in pen-based user interfaces. In *11th International Conference on Intelligent User Interfaces (IUI '06)*, Sydney, Australia (pp. 324-326).

Wang, Y., MacKenzie, C.L., Summers, V.A., & Booth, K.S. (1998). The structure of object transportation and orientation in human-computer interaction. In *CHI '98: Proceedings of the SIGCHI Conference on Human Factors in Computing Systems* (pp. 312–319).

Wang, Y.S., Wu, M.C., & Wang, H.Y. (2008). Investigating the determinants and age and gender differences in the acceptance of mobile learning. *British Journal of Educational Technology*.

Ware, C., & Osborne, S. (1990). Exploration and virtual camera control in virtual three dimentional environments. *Computer Graphics, 24*.

Wasinger, R., & Kreuger, A. (2005). Modality preference–learning from users. In *Workshop on User Experience Design for Pervasive Computing (Experience) at Pervasive 05*. Munich, Germany: Springer LNCS.

Wasinger, R., Stahl, C., & Kreuger, A. (2003). Robust speech interaction in a mobile environment through the use of multiple and different input types. In *EuroSpeech 2003-InterSpeech 2003, the 8th European Conference on Speech Communication and Technology* (pp. 1049-1052).

Waters, K., Hosn, R.A., Raggett, D., Sathish, S., Womer, M., Froumentin, M., et al. (2007). Delivery context: Client interfaces (DCCI) 1.0 accessing static and dynamic delivery context properties. Retrieved from http://www.w3.org/TR/DPF/

Watt, S.M. (2007, September 23-26). *New aspects of InkML for pen-based computing*. Paper presented at the International Conference on Document Analysis and Recognition, (ICDAR), Curitiba, Brazil.

Wayman, J., Jain, R., Maltoni, D., & Maio, D. (2005). *Biometric systems: Technology, design, and performance*. London: Springer-Verlag.

Weakliam, J., Lynch, D., Doyle, J., Bertolotto, M., & Wilson, D. (2005). Delivering personalized context-aware spatial information to mobile devices. In *W2GIS '05 - The 5th International Workshop on Web and Wireless Geographical Information Systems.* (pp. 194-205). Lausanne, Switzerland: Springer LNCS.

Web3D Consortium. (2004). *Extensible 3D (X3D) ISO/IEC 19775:2004*. Retried from http://www.web3d.org/x3d/specifications/ISOIEC-19775-X3DAbstractSpecification/

Wenger, E., & Lave, J. (1991). *Situated learning: Legitimate peripheral participation*. Cambridge, New York: Cambridge University Press.

Wenger, E., McDermott, R., & Snyder, W.M. (2002). *Cultivating communities of practice: A guide to managing knowledge*. Harvard Business School Press.

West, D., Apted, T., & Quigley, A. (2004, September 7). *A context inference and multimodal approach to mobile information access*. Paper presented at the AIMS 2004: Artificial Intelligence in Mobile Systems, Nottingham, UK.

Wexler, S., et al. (2007). *The e-learning guild research 3600 report on mobile learning*.

Wickens, C.D., & Baker, P. (1995). Cognitive issues in virtual reality. In T.A. Furness & W. Barfield (Eds.), *Virtual environments and advanced interface design* (pp. 514-541). Oxford University Press.

Wilson, A., & Shafer, S. (2003). XWand: UI for intelligent spaces. In *CHI '03: Proceedings of the SIGCHI Conference on Human Factors in Computing Systems* (pp. 545–552). New York: ACM Press.

Wilson, B., Sherry, L., Dobrovolny, J., Batty M., & Ryder, M. (2001). Adoption of learning technologies in schools and universities. In H. Adelsberger, B. Collis & J. Pawlowski (Eds.), *Handbook on information technologies for education and training*. New York: Springer-Verlag.

Wium Lie, H. (2005). *Cascading style sheets*. Unpublished doctoral dissertation, Faculty of Mathematics and Natural Sciences, University of Oslo, Norway.

Wong, A., Roberts, D., & Shelhamer, M. (2008). A new wireless search-coil system. *Eye Tracking Research and Applications Symposium,* Savannah, GA (pp. 197-204).

WordNet. (2008, January). Retrieved from http://wordnet.princeton.edu/

Wright, J.H., Gorin, A.L., & Riccardi, G. (1997). Automatic acquisition of salient grammar fragments for call-type classification. In *Proceedings of 5th European Conf. Speech Communication and Technology, International Speech Communication Association*, Bonn, Germany (pp. 1419-1422).

WSRF. (2006). *Web services resource framework 1.2 TC*. OASIS.

Wulf, V., & Golombek, V. (2001). Direct activation: A concept to encourage tailoring activities. *Behav. Inf. Technol., 20*(4), 249–263.

Wulf, W.A. (1989). The national collaboratory – a white paper. Appendix A. In *Towards a national collaboratory* (Unpublished report of a National Science Foundation invitational workshop). New York: Rockefeller University.

XHTML+Voice Profile 1.2, W3C. (2008). Retrieved on May 11, 2008, from http://www.voicexml.org/specs/multimodal/x+v/12

Yates, F. (1966). *The art of memory*. Chicago: University of Chicago Press.

Yordanova, K. (2007). Mobile learning and integration of advanced technologies. In *Education, International Conference on Computer Systems and Technologies-CompSysTech*.

Yoshino, et al. (2003). Group digital assistant: Shared or combined PDA screen. *IEEE Transactions on Consumer Electronics, 49*(3), 524-529.

Young, T. (2003). Software interface design for small devices. Retrieved on October 12, 2006, from http://www.cs.ubc.ca/~trevor/writings/SmallScreenDesign.pdf

Younger, D.H. (1967). Recognition and parsing of context-free languages in time $O(n^3)$. *Information and Control, 10*, 189-208.

Yu, J., & Buyya, R. (2005). *A taxonomy of workow management systems for grid computing* (Tech. Rep.). Grid Computing and Distributed Systems Laboratory, University of Melbourne, Australia.

Yuan, Y., & Zhang, J.J. (2003). Towards an appropriate business model for m-commerce. *Mobile Communications, 1*(1-2), 35-56.

Yudkowsky, M. (2005). *The pebble and the avalanche*. San Francisco: Berrett-Koehler Publishers, Inc.

Zadeh, L. (1978). Fuzzy sets as a basis for a theory of possibility. *Fuzzy Sets and Systems, 1*,3-28.

Zajicek, M. (2001). Interface design for older adults. In *Proceedings of the 2001 EC/NSF Workshop on Universal Accessibility of Ubiquitous Computing* (pp. 60–65). Alcácer do Sal, Portugal: ACM Press.

Zhang, Q., Imamiya, A., Go, K., & Gao, X. (2004). Overriding errors in speech and gaze multimodal architecture. *Intelligent User Interfaces* (pp. 346-348). ACM Press.

Zhang, Q., Imamiya, A., Go, K., & Mao, X. (2004). Resolving ambiguities of a gaze and speech interface. In Proceedings of the 2004 Symposium on Eye Tracking Research & Applications, San Antonio, TX (pp. 85-92). ACM.

Zhihong, Z., Yuxiao, H., Ming, L., Yun, F., & Huang, T.S. (2006). Training combination strategy of multi-stream fused hidden Markov model for audio-visual affect recognition. In *Proceedings of the 14th Annual ACM International Conference on Multimedia*, Santa Barbara, CA (pp. 65-68).

Ziefle, M., & Bay, S. (2004). Mental models of a cellular phone menu. Comparing older and younger novice users. In *Lecture Notes in Computer Science: Mobile Human-Computer Interaction (MobileHCI 2004),* (LNCS 3160/2004, pp. 25-37).

Zimmermann, A., Lorenz, A., & Oppermann, R. (2007). *An operational definition of context.* Paper presented at the Context 07.

Zimmermann, A., Lorenz, A., & Specht, M. (2005). Personalization and context-management. *User Modeling and User Adaptive Interaction (UMUAI), Special Issue on User Modeling in Ubiquitous Computing, 15*(3-4), 275-302.

About the Contributors

Patrizia Grifoni is a researcher at the National Research Council of Italy since 1990, where she works within the staff researchers of MultiModal Laboratory of the Institute of Research on Population and Social Policies. She received her degrees in electronics engineering at the University of Rome "La Sapienza". From 1994 to 2000 she was professor of "Elaborazione digitale delle immagini" at the University of Macerata. She is author of more than 70 papers in international journals, books and conferences. She served as referee of several international conferences, books and journals and is co-organiser of international research workshops and events. Her scientific interests have evolved from query languages for statistical and geographic databases to human-computer interaction, multimodal interaction and languages, visual languages, visual interfaces, sketch-based interfaces, Web technologies, social networks. She was responsible for several projects funded by Italian and International Institutions.

* * *

Simone Bacellar Leal Ferreira is an information systems scholar (graduate and post-graduate) at the Department of Applied Computer Sciences of the Federal University of the State of Rio de Janeiro (Universidade Federal do Estado do Rio de Janeiro - UNIRIO). She holds a Master's degree (graphic computing) and a PhD (software engineering) in computer sciences from PUC-Rio. Her areas of expertise are usability, accessibility, human-computer interaction, information systems, color theory, entrepeneurship, eBusiness and environmental management.

Barbara Rita Barricelli obtained a Bachelor's degree in digital communication and a Master's degree in information and communication technologies at the Department of Computer Science and Communication of Università degli Studi di Milano (Italy). Currently she is a PhD student of the Doctoral School for Computer Science at Università degli Studi di Milano. Her research topics are end-user development and specification, design and development of internationalized and localizable visual interactive systems.

Teresa M.A. Basile got the Laurea degree in computer science at the University of Bari, Italy (2001). In March 2005 she obtained the PhD at the University of Bari defending a dissertation titled *"A Multistrategy Framework for First-Order Rules Learning."* Since April 2005, she is a researcher at the Computer Science Department of the University of Bari. Her research interests concern the investigation of symbolic machine learning techniques. She is author of about 60 papers published on National and International journals and conferences/workshops proceedings and was/is involved in various National and European projects.

Regina Bernhaupt is currently on a sabbatical leave at the University of Toulouse III, IRIT-LIIHS to accomplish her habilitation. Since 2002 she is working as an assistant professor at the University of Salzburg on usability and user experience evaluation in non-traditional environments. Some of her recent publications include the usage of usability evaluation and user experience evaluation methods for non-traditional environments. She was involved in several (industrial) projects focusing on usability evaluation and user experience evaluation in environments like the home, public places, games or even human-robot interaction in industrial settings. She was organizing conferences like MobileHCI 2005, ACE 2007, Euroitv2008 and she acts as a reviewer for several journals and conferences.

Michela Bertolotto received a PhD in computer science from the University of Genoa (Italy) in 1998. Subsequently she worked as a postdoctoral research associate in the National Center for Geographic Information and Analysis (NCGIA) at the University of Maine. Since 2000 she has been a faculty member at the School of Computer Science and Informatics of University College Dublin. Her research interests include Web-based and wireless GIS, spatio-temporal data modelling and 3D interfaces.

Luca Bevilacqua, born in Naples 1965, got his graduate degree in electronic engineering in 1989 from the Naples University and his Master in Business Administration degree in 1992 from SDA of the Bocconi University in Milan. He has been working in big IT company since 1993 (Olivetti, Getronics, Sema, Atos Origin and Engineering) and since1996 he specialized in the field of R&D project, cofinanced by public bodies. He has been and still is scientific coordinator for several relevant R&D projects with cumulative budgets in excess of 20 mln €.

Judy van Biljon is an associate-professor in the School of Computing at the University of South Africa. Starting her career as mathematics teacher she obtained a Master's degree in computer science on the design of intelligent tutoring systems and a Doctoral degree on technology adoption in the field of human-computer interaction.

Emilio Bugli Innocenti (1958) received MSc in physics at University of Florence in 1983. Over the last 20 years, he has been devoting his drive and enthusiasm to research and innovate information technology in different sectors ranging from software engineering to application fields such as health systems, automotive and mobile location-based services. He has been R&D director at large and medium-sized IT companies in Italy and lately he has been launching his own venture. Project manager of research projects at national and international level, he is author of several IEEE and ACM papers.

Maria Chiara Caschera received her degree in computer science engineering at the University of Rome 'La Sapienza'. She is actually a young research at CNR-IRPPS (National Research Council, Institute Of Research On Population And Social Policies). She is also a doctoral researcher in computer science at the 'Roma Tre' University sponsored by the MultiMedia & Modal Laboratory (M3L) of the National Research Council of Italy. She is mainly interested in human-computer interaction, multimodal interaction, visual languages, visual interfaces and sketch-based interfaces.

Augusto Celentano is full professor of Information Systems at Università Ca' Foscari Venezia, Italy. He received a Master's Degree in electronic engineering from Politecnico di Milano. He has been deputy rector for information technology at Università Ca' Foscari Venezia, member of scientific committees in research and educational centers of the Politecnico di Milano, and consultant and scientific coordinator of research projects of the European Union. His current research interests are in mobile, pervasive and context-aware information systems, in multimedia systems and in human computer interaction.

Fang Chen joined NICTA in 2004 and is currently a senior principal researcher and the research group manager for the Making Sense of Data research theme at the ATP Laboratory. Dr. Chen has received conjoint professor and honorary associate positions with the University of New South Wales and the University of Sydney. Her main research interests is human machine interaction, especially in multimodal systems, ranging from speech processing, natural language dialogue, user interface design and evaluation, and cognitive load modelling. She has more than 80 publications in peer reviewed journals and conferences. She has also filed 19 patents in US, Australia, Europe, China, Japan, South Korea and Mexico.

Karin Coninx gained a PhD in computer science following a study into human-computer interaction in immersive virtual environments. Since 1998 she has worked as a full-time professor at the Hasselt University and in that capacity lectures on various general computer science subjects and specialized subjects relating to man-machine interaction. As group leader of the human-computer interaction group of the Expertise Centre for Digital Media at the Hasselt University, she is responsible for various research projects relating to interaction in virtual environments, mobile and context-sensitive systems, interactive work spaces, user-centred development and the model-based realization of user interfaces.

Fulvio Corno (PhD) is an associate professor at the Department of Computer Science and Automation of Politecnico di Torino. He received his MS and PhD degrees in electronics and computer science engineering from Politecnico di Torino in 1991 and 1995, respectively. He is (or was) involved in several European research projects (in the 4th, 5th and 6th Framework Programmes and in e-learning projects) as well as national and regional ones. His current research interests include the application of Semantic Web technologies to information systems engineering, the conception and design of intelligent domotic environments, and advanced multimedia and multi-modal interfaces for alternative access to computer systems. He published more than 150 papers at international conferences and 15 on international journals.

Fabio Corvino was born in Caserta, Italy, in 1975. He received the engineer degree in electronic engineering at Second University of Naples in 2004, with a thesis in *"Authentication and Authorization Mechanisms for Web Services"*. He works in Research & Development department of Engineering.IT in Pozzuoli (Italy) and he has been working in multimodality on mobile devices since 2006.

Danco Davcev obtained the degree of Engineer in electronics and computer science from the Faculty of Electrical Engineering at the University of Belgrade in 1972. He received the "Doctor – Ingenieur" degree in Computer Science from the University of ORSAY (Paris, France) in 1975 and PhD degree in Informatics from the University of Belgrade in 1981. From 1984 -1985 and 2001-2002 he was a Fulbright postdoctoral research scientist and visiting professor at the University of California, San Diego (USA). He is currently a full professor and head of the Computer Science Department at the University "Sts. Cyril & Methodius", Skopje (Macedonia). He has more than 250 research papers presented on International Conferences or published in International Journals in Computer Science and Informatics.

Alessia D'Andrea: she received her degree in Communication Science at the University of Rome 'La Sapienza'. She is being a PhD student in multimedia communication at the University of Udine sponsored by the IRPPS of the National Research Council of Italy. She is mainly interested in communication science, social science, risk management, virtual communities, mobile technologies and health studies.

Deborah Dahl is a consultant in speech and natural language understanding technologies, with over 25 years of experience. Her interests are in practical spoken and multimodal dialog systems and related standards. She serves as chair of the World Wide Web Consortium (W3C) Multimodal Interaction Working Group. Dr. Dahl is an editor of the EMMA standard, and contributed to the W3C standards for spoken dialog (VoiceXML) and speech grammars (SRGS). She has published over 50 technical papers, and is the editor of the book, *Practical Spoken Dialog Systems*. Dr. Dahl received her PhD in linguistics from the University of Minnesota in 1984.

Joan De Boeck obtained an Engineering degree from the 'Katholieke Hogeschool Kempen' in 1996. He also obtained a Master degree in computer science (with an applied mathematics component) as an additional study in 1997. He started his part-time research career at the UHasselt in 1998 (while conducting several commercial projects elsewhere). He obtained his PhD in 2007. Now he is a post-doctoral researcher at the EDM and a teacher at the engineering department of the 'Katholieke Hogeschool Kempen'. His research interests include virtual environments, human computer interaction, haptic interaction and multimodal interfaces.

Kristine Deray is a senior lecturer in design at the University of Technology, Sydney. She has an interdisciplinary background of design, design computing, dance and movement studies and visualization//visual representation of the moving image. Together these contribute to her unique approach and focus on conceptual modelling of interaction, human centred design and computing, visualization, and designing for interaction, interactive spaces. She is a core member of the Centre for Digital Design (CDD) Research Group, and of the Contemporary Design Practice Research Group at UTS, with her specific focus being developing frameworks for explaining the mechanisms and (reciprocal) effects in interactions based on mappings derived from physical systems. Her research interests include human usability technologies for consumer /patient empowerment in health care and pervasive service industries. Kristine is a chief investigator on a governmental community health project with Health Services Network, (HsNET) focused on the social construction of knowledge and community participation in health services, derived from digital stories.

Julie Doyle received a PhD in computer science from University College Dublin, Ireland. Her thesis focused on improving the usability and interactivity of mobile geospatial applications. Subsequently she worked as a postdoctoral fellow at the School of IT and Engineering, University of Ottawa, Canada, where she developed a framework to ensure the long term preservation of 3D digital data. Currently she is a postdoctoral fellow in HCI and Systems Engineering in the UCD School of Computer Science and Informatics. Her main research interests include the design of interfaces for mobile geospatial applications, multimodal HCI, usability and long term data preservation.

Arianna D'Ulizia received her degree in computer science engineering at the University of Rome 'La Sapienza'. She is actually young researcher at the Institute of Research on Population and Social Policies of the National Research Council of Italy. She is also doctoral researcher in computer science at the 'Roma Tre' University. She is the author of more than 20 papers on books and conferences. She is mainly interested in human computer interaction, multimodal interaction, visual languages, visual interfaces and geographical query languages.

Castellina Emiliano (MS) is a PhD candidate at the Department of Computer Science and Automation of Politecnico di Torino. He received his MS degree in computer science engineering from the same institution in 2005.His current research interests include eye tracking (analysis and studies on gaze tracking algorithms), computer assistive technologies (development of special software applications for disabled people) and domotic systems.

Benoît Encelle PhD in computer science (University Paul Sabatier – Toulouse III). I am an assistant professor in computer science at the IUT B of the Claude Bernard Lyon 1 University (France) and i do my research at the LIRIS research center. My main research interests are engineering for human-computer interaction (EHCI) and information system. More precisely, i work in the field of context-aware adaptation of content browsing. During and after my PhD, I contribute to the developments of three European projects in the field of accessibility (projects Contrapunctus, Lambda, Play2).

Floriana Esposito, ECCAI Fellow, is since 1994 full professor of computer science at the University of Bari. Among her scientific interests there are similarity based learning, integration of numerical and symbolic methods in learning and classification, logical foundations of conceptual learning techniques, revision of logical theories by incremental learning, multistrategy learning, inductive logic programming. The major application fields are document processing and digital libraries and, recently, bioinformatics. She is author of more than 250 papers which published in international journals and Proceedings. She is in the PC of the most important scientific conferences on machine learning and artificial intelligence.

Stefano Ferilli was born in 1972. He got a PhD in computer science at the University of Bari, and is currently an associate professor at the Computer Science Department of the University of Bari. His research interests include logic and algebraic foundations of machine learning, inductive logic programming, multistrategy learning, knowledge representation, digital document processing and digital libraries. He participated in various national and European (ESPRIT e IST) projects on these topics, and is a (co-)author of more than 100 papers published on journals, books and proceedings of national and international workshops/conferences.

Fernando Ferri: he received the degrees in electronics engineering and the PhD in medical informatics. He is actually senior researcher at the National Research Council of Italy. From 1993 to 2000 he was professor of "Sistemi di Elaborazione" at the University of Macerata. He is the author of more than 100 papers in international journals, books and conferences. His main methodological areas of interest are: human-computer interaction visual languages, visual interfaces, sketch-based interfaces, multimodal interfaces, data and knowledge bases, geographic information systems and virtual communities. He has been responsible of several national and international research projects.

Leopoldina Fortunati: since 20/02/2002 was the Italian representative at the COST Technical Committee on Social Sciences and Humanities and then since 24 March 2006 at the COST Domain Committee INSCH (Individuals, Societies, Cultures and Health), where she was elected as a member of the Executive group. She was part of the European funded research project SIGIS "Strategies of Inclusion: Gender and the Information Society", August 1 2002- 31 January 2004, where she did 9 case studies on the social construction of femininity and masculinity in relation to the acquisition and use of the information technologies. She had an Outstanding Research Award from Rutgers University in 2001. For 15 years she was in the Advisory Board of the journal *New Media & Society*, she is an associate editor of the journal *The Information Society* and she serves as reviewer several journals. She founded, with others, in June 2003, *The society for the social study of mobile communication* (SSSMC – www. sociomobile.org) of which she is co-chair.

Francesco Gaudino earned a Master's degree in physics from University of Naples Federico II in 1999 (specialization in cybernetics and artificial intelligence), with a final dissertation about hypermedia knowledge acquisition and BDI agent for navigation assistance. He has been studying multimodality applications on mobile devices for the last two years. He works in Research & Development department of Engineering.IT in Pozzuoli (Italy).

Marcos Gurgel do Amaral Leal Ferreira is a freelance Web designer with over ten years experience catering to a wide range of companies and professionals, from actors and record labels to law firms and private clinics. His work employs simplicity and objectivity to create functional and easy-to-navigate Web sites. His current interests are usability, color theory, Web standards and programming for Web applications.

Giovanni Frattini received his Laurea degree in physics from University of Naples in 1995. He has worked for several companies with different roles. From 2000 his focus is on value added services. He has been delivery unit manager of Atos Origin Italia from 2002 to 2004. Currently he is chief architect of several projects providing is contribution to operational and research team. As researcher is main focus is currently on multimodal mobile services.

Tiziana Guzzo: she received her degree in sociology and the PhD in theory and social research at the University of Rome "La Sapienza". She is actually young researcher at the National Research Council of Italy. From 2005 to 2008 she was professor of Sociology at the University of Catanzaro. She is mainly interested in social science, new technologies, communication, mobile technologies, social networks, risk management, environment and tourism.

Nadine JESSEL, PHD in computer sciences. I am an assistant professor in the teacher training centre in Toulouse. (IUFM Midi pyrénées). My research centre is the IRIT (Research Institute in computer science of Toulouse) and my research concerns the representation of literature, scientific and musical documents for their accessibility by a blind person. At the moment, I focus my research on graphical (musical and mathematical) documents, and their accessibility by a blind user with the help of Braille editors or using haptic devices. I am involved in European projects LAMDBA project (http://www. lambdaproject.org) and Contrapunctus project (http://www.punctus.org)

Claudio De Lazzari (1956) received his *laurea* degree in Electronic Engineering (Automatic Controls) from the University of Rome "La Sapienza". He is currently a Researcher of Italian National Council for Research (CNR) at the Institute of Clinical Physiology in Rome (IFC). His main scientific interests include: modelling of the cardiovascular system and different mechanical circulatory assist devices, simulation and optimisation of ventilatory assistance and ontologies in medicine. He is author of over 110 scientific papers published in international journals and conferences. He is involved in several scientific committee of international congresses and journals (on computer science in medicine). He recently edited the books *"Modelling Cardiovascular System and Mechanical Circulatory Support"*, published by Italian National Research Council.

Massimo Magaldi received his degree in computer and automation engineering from University of Naples in 1998. From 1998 to 2000 he worked for Cap Genimi Italy, where he was involved in software systems for the telecommunication industries. In 2000 he joined Sema Group Italy (now Engineering IT), where he was involved in several telecom projects with different roles. Since 2003 he is working in the R&D area of the Telecom division. His research interests are in WFMS, BRMS, SOA, WS, Semantic and security. He is currently involved in a research project aiming to improve e-government efficiency leveraging Semantic grid Computing.

Andrea Marcante, PhD in information society, has worked since 2003 with the Computer Semiotics Laboratory at the Dept. of Informatics and Communication of the University of Milano. His research focuses on human-computer interaction, and in particular on the issues related to multimodal and multi-media interaction with digital documents accessible via Web. He is a teaching assistant in fundamentals of digital communication and HCI in the digital communication course and in computer science course at the University of Study of Milano. He is also a Web consultant for publishing companies.

Nicola Di Mauro got the Laurea degree in computer science at the University of Bari, Italy. In March 2005 he discussed a PhD thesis in computer science at the University of Bari titled *"First Order Incremental Theory Refinement"* facing the problem of incremental learning in ILP. Since January 2005, he is an assistant professor at the Department of Computer Science, University of Bari. His research activities concern relational learning. He is author of about 60 papers published on international and national journals and conference proceedings. He took part to European and national projects.

Christian Müller-Tomfelde is a researcher at the CSIRO ICT Centre in Sydney. His expertise lies in the research area of human computer interaction and virtual and hybrid environments focusing on the support of co-located and remote collaboration. His interests also include novel forms of interaction, multimodal interaction such as sound feedback. He studied electrical engineering at the University of Hamburg-Harburg and worked at the Center for Art and Media Technology (ZKM) in Karlsruhe (1994). In 1997 he joined the GMD-IPSI's division AMBIENTE "Workspaces of the Future" in Darmstadt/ Germany. He was involved in the i-LAND project and in the design and development of the Roomware components.

Piero Mussio is full professor of computer science at the University of Milano (Italy), where he is the head of the Computer Semiotic Laboratory. His research interest include human computer interaction, visual communication and interaction design. He published more than 150 scientific papers in international journal and conference proceedings. He served as scientific coordinator and principal investigator of national, regional and local research units in several international and national projects and industrial contracts . He is Fellow IAPR, member of the ACM, member of the Pictorial Computing Laboratory; associate editor of *Journal of Visual Languages and Computing.*

Marco Padula, graduated in mathematics at the State University of Milan; is a senior researcher in information technology at the ITC - CNR, Milan and professor of system usability design at the Catholic University of Brescia; took part in the on line management of the national earthquake catalogues for the National Group for the Defence from the Earthquakes, in national projects on document indexing for on line management, in the EU projects *Aquarelle: A system for on line exploitation of cultural heritage, C-Web: A generic platform supporting community-webs, CONNIE (CONstruction News and Information Electronically.*

Stefano Paolozzi: he received his degree in informatic engineering at the University of "ROMA TRE". He is a PhD student in computer science at the "ROMA TRE" University under supervision of Prof. Paolo Atzeni. His research activity with Multi Media & Modal Laboratory (M3L) of the IRPPS-CNR of Italy is sponsored by a fellowship (assegno di ricerca). He is mainly interested in model management, multimodal interaction, multimedia database, temporal database, ontology alignement, ontology versioning, NLP.

Loredana Parasiliti Provenza holds a post-doc position at the department of Computer Science and Communication (DICO) of the University of Milan (Italy). She received the Laurea degree in mathematics with full marks from the University of Messina (Italy) in 2001 and the Master's degree in information and communication security from the University of Milan in 2002. In 2006 she received her PhD in computer science at the University of Milan. Her current research interests include specification, design and development of visual interactive systems, theory of visual languages, W3C technologies, XML security and privacy preserving data mining.

Paolo Pellegrino is a postdoctoral researcher at the Department of Computer Science and Automation of Politecnico di Torino. He received his MS and PhD degrees in computer science engineering from Politecnico di Torino in 2004 and 2008, respectively. He has taken part in European, national and regional projects. His current research interests focus on knowledge representation systems, human-computer interaction and intelligent environmental control. He has published papers at international conferences and a book chapter in an international journal.

Pierpaolo Petriccione received a MS degree in telecommunications engineering at University of Naples Federico II (2003) and a Master's degree in "software technologies" at the University of Sannio, Benevento (2004). From 2004 to 2007 he worked at the research department of Atos Origin Italia. Since 2007, he has been working at Engineering.IT and his main research interests are in the multimodality on mobile devices, content provisioning and GRID.

Stefania Pierno got her graduate degree in mathematics at the "Federico II" University of Naples, in March 1993 with a final dissertation about stochastic processes. In 1996 he attended the Doctor's degree from the High Mathematics National Institute (INDAM) of the "La Sapienza" University in Rome. She has been working in big IT company since 1997 (IBM Research Centre, Selfin, Sema, and Atos Origin). She currently works for Engineering in Research & Development department as technical director. Her research interests include innovative architecture as service oriented architecture and grid computing.

Fabio Pittarello is a researcher at the Computer Science Department of Università Ca' Foscari Venezia, Italy, where he teaches Web design and human computer interaction for the computer science curriculum. His current research interests include both theoretical and application oriented aspects of HCI in Web-based and ubiquitous contexts, with a particular reference to interaction in 3D environments, adaptivity, multimodality and universal access to information.

Domenico M. Pisanelli (1959) graduated in electronic engineering (computer science in medicine) at the University of Rome in 1986. Since 1987 he is researcher at CNR (National Research Council). His main research interest is in the field of medical informatics (expert systems in medicine, computerized guidelines, and ontologies in medicine). From 1990 to 2001 he held an appointment at University of L'Aquila for teaching computer science in the Engineering Faculty, since 2004 he teaches "biolanguages and bioarchives" at Milan Polytechnic University. He is involved in several national and international projects on computer science in medicine and in European working groups on standardization in health care. He acted as project evaluator and reviewer in the UE e-Health sector. He recently edited the books "*Ontologies in Medicine*", published by IOS-Press and "*New Trends in Software Methodologies, Tools and Techniques*" (the latter with Hamido Fujita).

Chris Raymaekers is an assistant professor in computer science. His research is situated in the domain of human-computer interaction, more specifically interaction in virtual environments and usability. He obtained his PhD in 2002. He supports Prof. Dr. K. Coninx in managing the Human-Computer Interaction (HCI) group of EDM, where he concentrates on technical management of the research with regard to HCI in Virtual Environments. In this capacity, he aids in the management of several research projects (with national and European funding). His research interests include virtual environments, human-computer interaction, mixed reality, tangible and multi-modal interfaces, haptic interaction and haptic rendering.

Karen Renaud is a computer scientist, and lectures in the Computing Science Department at the University of Glasgow. She has a keen interest in mobile phone usage and in developing an understanding of, and solutions for, older technology users. Renaud was previously a professor at the University of South Africa and the work reported in this chapter is the result of a continuing collaboration with Judy van Biljon.

Ricardo Rodrigues Nunes is a professor (graduate and post-graduate) of digital design at Infnet Institute (Rio de Janeiro - Brazil). He is attending the Master's Program of post-graduate in Information Systems at the Federal University of the State of Rio de Janeiro (Universidade Federal do Estado do Rio de Janeiro - UNIRIO). His areas of expertise are groupware, CSCW (computer supported cooperative work), virtual worlds, usability, accessibility, human-computer interaction, multimedia, information systems and e-learning.

Luigi Romano received his Laurea degree in physics from University of Naples in 1996. In 1997 he attended the Pre-Doctoral School in Communication Systems at the Swiss Federal Institute of Technology Lausanne (EPFL). From 1997 on he was engaged in different roles for several telecommunication operators and in 2000 he started working in the system integration area of Sema Group. In the 2003 he was involved in a research project, in Engineering IT, attempting to ground mobile value added services in innovative architectures. He followed other research projects related to multimodal systems and artificial intelligence and he is currently involved in a project aiming to explore the potential of Semantic Grid Computing in e-government applications.

Roberto Russo was born in 1974, degree in computer science at Federico II University of Naples. Since 1999 he has been working for Engineering.IT (ex Atos Origin Italia) with different roles. Currently he is team leader of several projects; his research interests include human-computer interaction, mobile application and architectures. He has been involved in several research projects such as SERVICEWARE and WISE and was author of several papers.

Paolo Luigi Scala obtained a Bachelor's degree in information technology at the Università degli Studi di Milano (Italy) in 2005, and is currently studying for his Master's degree in information and communication technologies. He is a research cooperator at the ITC - CNR, Milan working as a software developer. His areas of interest are software I18N and L10N, industrial processes automation and geographic information systems.

Vladimiro Scotto di Carlo earned a degree in physics (astrophysics) summa cum laude in 1998 at the Naples University Federico II. He has been working in multimodality on mobile devices since 2005. He works in Research & Development department of Engineering.IT in Pozzuoli (Italy). He lives in Naples with his wife and a son.

Florence Sèdes is full professor in computer sciences, University of Toulouse. Her main research topics are about multimedia documents and semi-structured data. She is responsible in the IRIT (Toulouse Informatics Research Institute) of a team working on Information Systems and databases modelling and querying. She chairs the national research network about information, interaction, intelligence, GDR I3.

Denis Silveira is MSc in informatics from Federal University of Rio de Janeiro (IM/UFRJ) and PhD student in production engineering from Federal University of Rio de Janeiro (COPPE/UFRJ), developing a method and tool for the elaboration and validation of business process using OCL. His research interests include requirements engineering, precise software modeling and web accessible. He is assistant professor at the Computer Science Department, Catholic University of Rio de Janeiro. His professional activities also include software development consultancy for companies in Brazil.

Simeon Simoff is a professor of information technology and head of the School of Computing and Mathematics, University of Western Sydney. He is also an adjunct professor at the University of Technology, Sydney (UTS). Prior to this, he was a professor of information technology at the Faculty of Information Technology, UTS, where he established the e-Markets research program, currently running between UWS, UTS and UNSW (e-markets.org.au). He is also co-director of the Institute of Analytics

Professionals of Australia and Series Editor of the ACS Publication Series *"Conferences in Research and Practice in Information Technology"*. In 2000–2005 he was the associate editor (Australia) of the *ASCE International Journal of Computing in Civil Engineering*. He is founder and chair of the ACM SIGKDD Multimedia Data Mining workshop series MDM@KDD, the Australasian Data Mining Conference series AusDM, and the Visual Data Mining international workshop series at ECML/PKDD and ICDM events. His research interests include data mining and visual analytics, design computing, human-centred computing and normative virtual worlds.

Marcus Specht is professor for advanced learning technologies at the Open University of the Netherlands and is currently involved in several national and international research projects on competence based life long learning, personalized information support and contextualized learning. He received his Diploma in psychology in 1995 and a dissertation from the University of Trier in 1998 on adaptive information technology. From 1998 until 2001 he worked as senior researcher at the GMD research center on HCI and mobile information technology. From 2001 he headed the department "Mobile Knowledge" at the Fraunhofer Institute for Applied Information Technology (FIT). From 2005 he was associated professor at the Open University of the Netherlands and working on competence based education, learning content engineering and management, and personalization for learning. Currently he is working on mobile and contextualized learning technologies, learning network services, and social and immersive media for learning.

After years of experience in IT industry, **Yong Sun** received his Master's degree in multimedia from the University of Sydney. As a PhD student in the University of Sydney, he is participating enhanced PhD program jointly provided by National ICT Australia and the University of Sydney for a more practical research outcome. His dissertation research is focused on the development of a robust, flexible and portable multimodal input fusion technique that can adapt to other types of input modalities, to different types of applications and to multimodal constructions of different levels of complexity. His research interests are in designing applicable human-computer interaction technologies.

Gianluca Supino was born in Caserta, Italy, on January the 7th 1976. He graduated in electronic engineering at University of Naples Federico II in 2003, with a final dissertation about electromagnetic sensors for no destructive evaluations on conducting materials. In 2004 he received a Master's degree in software technologies. He currently works for Engineering.IT in Pozzuoli (Naples) and is employed in Research & Development department. He has been studying multimodality applications on mobile devices for the last two years, especially focusing on natural language processing.

Sladjana Tesanovic has obtained her Bachelor's degree at the Faculty of Electrical Engineering and Information Technologies, University "Ss. Cyril and Methodius" in Skopje, Macedonia. She is at the finishing phase of her Master studies at the same faculty. She works as a software developer in GISDATA. She develops applications related to geography information systems (GIS). Her favorite software environments and technologies are: VS.NET (Web, desktop and mobile), Oracle, SQL Server, ArcGIS Server. She has published several research papers and posters on International Conferences and International Journals. Her research interests are: distributed computer systems, ICT based collaboration systems, mobile services, artificial intelligence, image recognition.

Vladimir Trajkovik has obtained his degrees at the Faculty of Electrical Engineering and Information Technologies, University "Ss. Cyril and Methodius" in Skopje, Macedonia. From February 1995 to December 1997 he worked for Macedonian Telecommunications, His current position is as professor at the Faculty of Electrical Engineering and Information technologies. During the past 8 years he published more than 60 research papers presented on International Conferences or published in International Journals in Computer Science and Informatics. In the same, period he coordinated and participated in more then 10 bilateral and multilateral EU projects. His research interests include: information systems analyses and design, object oriented systems, distributed computer systems, distance educational systems, multi-agent systems, ICT based collaboration systems and mobile services.

Lode Vanacken obtained a Master's degree in computer science at the tUL in 2005. He is currently working as a PhD student at the Expertise Centre for Digital Media (EDM), a research facility at the Hasselt University in Belgium, and is a member of the HCI Research group. His research interests are human-computer interaction and more specifically multi-modal interaction in virtual environments with interests into interaction techniques and model-based design of virtual environments.

David C. Wilson is an assistant professor in the College of Computing and Informatics at the University of North Carolina at Charlotte. Dr. Wilson is an expert in intelligent software systems and a leading name in the field of case-based reasoning. Dr. Wilson's research centers on the development of intelligent software systems to bridge the gaps between human information needs and the computational resources available to meet them. It involves the coordination of intelligent systems techniques (artificial intelligence, machine learning, etc.) with geographic, multimedia, database, internet, and communications systems in order to elicit, enhance, apply, and present relevant task-based knowledge.

Norma Zanetti (1966) graduated in electronic engineering at Milan Polytechnic University in 1994. Since 1995 she is actively involved in international research projects co-funded by the European Commission, namely: Esprit, Tap, V VI and VII Framework Programme, eContentPlus. Since 2001, she has been involved, as NetXcalibur CTO, in research projects focusing on the implementation of mobile services in many application fields: intelligent transport systems (ITS), pervasive computing, eHealth, eGovernment and environment. Recently, she acted as project evaluator in the Ambient Assisted Living (AAL) sector and she was co-author of scientific papers on semantic-enabled technologies for esafety applications.

Index

Symbols

3D virtual counterpart mapping 206
(MultiModal Manipulation for 3D Interaction framework (M3I) 26

A

actual use (AU) 4
adapted multimodal end-user interfaces for XML-content 351
Adaptive Cruise Control (ACC) 233
Advanced Driver Assistance Systems (ADAS) 231, 232
AJAX (Asynchronous JavaScript and XML) 252
ALE LCMS 283
analytical modeling 450
ANDROME 158
annotation, a primitive operator 256
A-Posterior resolution methods,how integrate the interpretation methods 98
application definition 418
application prototype 157
architecture and communication standards 412
artificial intelligence-based fusion strategies 52
attributed relational graphs (AGRs) 91
AudioGPS 206
authoring-time content adaptation 352
autonomic Web processes 325

B

back-end architectural overview 323
BANCO (Browsing Adaptive Network for Changing user Operativity) 251
bayesian network theory. 48

behavioral profile, inducing the 126
behavioural intention (BI) 5
BGP-MS 124
BioAPI Consortium 410
biometric standards 418
Brazil 265
Brazilian Accessibility Model was designed (e-MAG) 267
browsing content 351
business logic 308

C

calibration distance 179
Call Control Markup Language (CCXML) 419
certification standards 411, 423
CHAT 293, 297
CoGenIVE (Code Generation for Interactive Virtual Environments) 155
Combinatory Categorial Grammar (CCG) 67
command buttons, use of for visually disabled 275
CoMPASS (Combining Mobile Personalised Applications with Spatial Services) 332
CoMPASS, multimodal interface 339
Computer-Aided Design (CAD) 246
computer input channels 36
computer output modalities 36
Computer Supported Cooperative Work (CSCW) 245
ConcurTaskTrees (CTT) 142, 155
Constraints Multiset Grammar (CMG) 47
content interchange formats (CIF) 285
content repository 311
content selection and structuring 113
contextual and semantic information 150